£2.00

Garden Ideas and Projects

A HANDBOOK FOR HOME GARDENERS

GARDEN IDEAS
AND PROJECTS

EDITED BY
RICHARD D. WHITTEMORE,
Former Director, American Garden Guild

AN AMERICAN GARDEN GUILD BOOK

Doubleday & Company, Inc.
Garden City, New York
1959

To W. S. W.

PREFACE

Under the imprint of the American Garden Guild have appeared more than twenty guide books to good gardening and many booklets on a variety of garden subjects—most of which took their inspiration from the *Home Garden Magazine,* now incorporated with *Flower Grower, The Home Garden Magazine.*

Garden Ideas and Projects, like its predecessors, started out in the pages of *Home Garden.* But unlike the books that have gone before, *Garden Ideas and Projects* shows the gardener how to perform small miracles with saw, hammer, and mason's trowel rather than with rake, hoe, and spray gun.

Within these pages are dozens of ideas on how to make gardens more attractive and livable with simple projects using wood or masonry. Here, too, are plans for special gardens and a valuable garden calendar for every part of the United States.

Among the booklets published by the American Garden Guild, two were outstanding in popularity—*The Self-Pronouncing Dictionary of Plant Names* and *500 Common Garden Mistakes Corrected.* Now long out of print, the material in both booklets has been revised and is included in *Garden Ideas and Projects.*

The editor acknowledges with thanks the contributions to this book by the following authors and illustrators:

— Ralph Bailey, for 16 how-to-do-it chapters and for *The Self-Pronouncing Dictionary of Plant Names*
— F. F. Rockwell, for *Lath Houses* and for *500 Common Garden Mistakes Corrected*
— Robert S. Lemmon, for *Make Nature Your Guide in Rock Garden Planning,* and for *A Garden To Attract Birds*
— Henry B. Raymore, for text and illustrations of *Tool House and Garden Workroom, Fences and Fence-Making, Gates and Entrances, Steps for Garden and Grounds,* and *Building Walks and Pavements*
— Henry B. Aul, for text and illustrations of *Building Formal Pools, Building Informal Pools,* and *Winter Sun-Catchers,* and for the illustration on page 191

— Carl T. Sigman and William J. Ward, for text and illustrations of *Concrete: How To Use It, Stone: How To Use It, How To Build a Garden Pool,* and for the illustrations on Pages 16, 18, 23, 26, 28, 40, 41, 44, 47, 49, 51, 61, 63, 97–99, 100–103, 104–110, 115–119, 158, 168, 194–198

— Montague Free, for *An Extra Pair of Hands* and *Permanent Edges for Walks*

— Julie Bedier, for *Three Handy Garden Gadgets*

— Arthur Fishell, for photographs, drawings, and text of *Gardens 'Round Your Windows*

— Douglas Elliott, for *Crazy Paving Makes Good Sense*

— John R. Griffith, for *Flags Without Stone*

— H. Stuart Ortloff, for *Terraces Double as Rock Gardens*

— David W. Bailey, for *How To Build and Plant a Dry Wall Garden*

— Harrie Wood, for the illustrations on pages 134–142

— Tabea Hoffman, for illustrations on pages 153–157, 159–167, 170–190

CONTENTS

Garden Ideas and Projects

TOOLS
AND EQUIPMENT

PIN-UP TOOL CHEST

How many times minor chores around the garden are neglected because there isn't time to sandwich them in between major occupations! If it didn't take so long to get the trowel from the garage. . . . If the plant labels were handy. . . . If you weren't dressed for the office. . . . If dinner weren't almost ready to go on the table. . . . That kind of thing. Well, here is a contrivance for eliminating some of those ifs. It houses, by the backdoor or on a post by the garden gate or in almost any convenient location, a few of the simple tools on which the performance of so many five-minute jobs depends. It is weatherproof, caterpillar proof, alibi proof. If you need a new washer or a different nozzle for the hose, here it is. If a shrub needs a bit of pruning, here is a pair of shears. When a flat of seedlings is ready for blocking, the sharp mason's trowel is ready on the hook. When you bring back a few cuttings from a neighbor's garden, here is the "rooting" hormone ready to apply on the way to the cold-frame. As the lawn mower squeaks past to begin its appointed rounds, here is the oil can.

In short, here is a devil's own invention to suggest bits and pieces of work for momentarily idle hands to do. In addition, of course, it serves larger operations; but essentially this pin-up dispenser is merely a penny-in-the-slot adjunct to the tool-shed proper.

The working drawings on the next page suggest, to anyone who would want to build it anyway, all the necessary procedures. Many of the details are, of course, optional—such as the caterpillar-proof screen mesh at the bottom and behind the ventilation holes above the door, or the "secret panel" latch for the door itself. (The only advantage of the latter is that since there is no handle showing, meddlers won't find it so easy to borrow your tools. They won't, presumably, know that a smart poke over the latch will make the door spring open.) It isn't necessary to hang up the pencil, but the loop illustrated immediately identifies it as belonging here and nowhere else. The cloth is for drying wet tools.

Plywood (the ½-inch weatherproof kind, which is available every-

PIN-UP
TOOL
CHEST

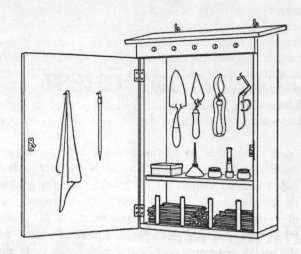

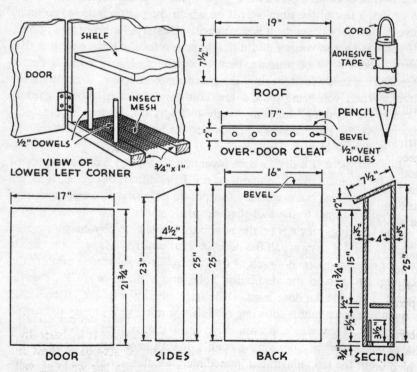

SHELF

DOOR

INSECT MESH

½" DOWELS

VIEW OF
LOWER LEFT CORNER

¾" x 1"

19"

7½"

ROOF

CORD

ADHESIVE TAPE

PENCIL

17"

2"

OVER-DOOR CLEAT

BEVEL

½" VENT HOLES

17"

21¾"

DOOR

4½"

23"

25"

SIDES

16"

BEVEL

25"

BACK

7½"

2"

½"

4"

½"

15"

21¾"

½"

5½"

3½"

¾"

25"

SECTION

where) or ordinary ¾-inch pine boards are good building materials. All screws and fittings should be brass. Tools required: saw, twist drill or brad-awl, brace and ½-inch bit, and a plane—plus tacks, hooks, eyes, hinges, and sandpaper. It should take two or three winter evenings at most to make. When it is finished and painted, hang it on hooks near the potting bench. Then when outdoor work begins, hang it on duplicate hooks where it will be handiest to the garden, the dinner table, the station bus—wherever it will be *most* handy *most* often.

RALPH BAILEY

HANDYMAN'S TOOL SHED

There probably never will be a tool house so handy to all parts of the garden, nor a gardener so conscientious, that every shovel, rake, and hoe will be under cover every night during the season. And just so long as objects in the open lose heat to the sky above them after sundown, there will be rust on many a tool come morning.

Since, however, man in general and gardeners in particular are ever striving to climb farther and farther out of the Primordial Ooze, aspiration need not die. We can all hope that someday, somehow, we shall find it both easy and pleasant to put our tools away in the proper places when we are finished with them. We can look to the time when cultivators need not rust and rake handles will not rise up to smite us in the back of the head as we make our way through the weeds.

With the blister-like tool shed illustrated by the drawings on the next page, the devil-and-the-deep-sea gardener, who has neither the ambition to put his tools in the cellar every night nor the space to put a real tool shed in his garden, stands a chance of conducting the tidy sort of operation he needn't be ashamed of.

This excrescence on the side of his suburban house is neither unduly obtrusive architecturally nor especially difficult to make. It is, basically, the special-purpose equivalent of the old-fashioned six-board chest in which your great grandmother stored everything from her wedding veil to her winding sheet. At least it has only six boards.

The working drawings and sketch on the next page will give to the

TOOL SHED

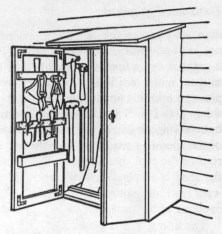

ROOF: SHEET COPPER OR ROLL ROOFING, STARTING AT TOP BEHIND SIDING

4"x 4" FLAT ANGLES

ONE OR MORE HORIZONTAL BATTENS LOCATED AS DESIRED

5'-6"

1" x 3"s

INSIDE VIEW OF DOOR

1"x 3" DOOR STOP

SIDES 1" x 12" STOCK

GRADE

CROSS SECTION

COVER MOLD

DOORS 5'-6"

LOCKER LATCH, WITH RODS FASTENING TOP AND BOTTOM INSIDE

DOORS: PRESSEDWOOD OR OUTDOOR PLYWOOD ON 1"x 3" FRAME

FRONT VIEW

LOCATION OF EQUIPMENT

ON DOORS: TROWELS, HAND TOOLS, MARKERS, BIN FOR PLANT LABELS, GLOVES, KNEELING PADS, SMALL DUSTER, SHEEP SHEARS, SICKLE, PRUNING SHEARS, ETC.

FACE OF HOUSE

11½"

4'-0"

PLAN VIEW

ON BACK WALL: (HANGING) RAKE, HOE, SCUFFLE HOE, EDGER, LONG SHOVEL, HOSE, LOPPING SHEARS, ETC.
(STANDING) SPADES, SHORT SHOVELS, RACK FOR HEAVY PLANTING STAKES, MATTOCK, CROWBAR, ETC.

ON SIDES: WRECKING BAR, HATCHET, HAMMER, SLEDGE, ETC.

man who knows the feel of a hammer and saw most of the hints, if not hard-and-fast instructions, he will need. In working out these plans a great many refinements and embellishments were ruled out as unessential. When and if you come to build it, you can have a good bit of pleasure thinking up and adding a batch of your own. The most important things are: 1 — Keep the construction simple. 2 — Fasten the two vertical battens (circular inset, opposite) securely to the house wall, and the sides of the shed to these. 3 — Flash or caulk carefully the joint between the roof of the tool shed and the wall of the house (or garage) from which the shed is suspended. If the shed is to be hung on a brick or masonry wall, rawl plugs must be used to hold the batten screws to it, and careful caulking of the roof joint would be in order instead of flashing.

The fitting of this garden catch-all is strictly up to you. But don't plan to store in it so much equipment that putting tools away and taking them out again will take all your working time. Science is wonderful, but it isn't everything.

RALPH BAILEY

TOOL HOUSE AND GARDEN WORKROOM

Every suburban or country place, however small, can be operated efficiently only with an adequate assortment of garden tools, and a proper place in which to keep them.

If possible, a small building devoted to nothing but garden tools, and equipped with a few shelves, drawers, hooks and bins, and a bench for potting, should be provided somewhere on the place. This can be so located that it is a definite part of the garden picture, and it can be good looking enough to add to the attractiveness of the scene, rather than detracting from it.

If a separate building is out of the question a wing can be thrown out from the garage, on axis, perhaps, with the flower or vegetable garden, so that it can become the terminal motif of the scheme.

The building for which working drawings are shown on the next two pages is plain and practical in the extreme, but it provides space for all

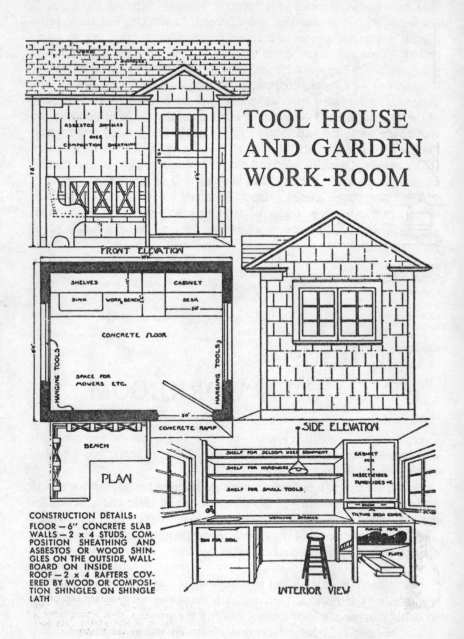

TOOL HOUSE AND GARDEN WORK-ROOM

FRONT ELEVATION

ASBESTOS SHINGLES OVER COMPOSITION SHEATHING

PLAN

SHELVES · CABINET

SINK · WORK BENCH · DESK

CONCRETE FLOOR

HANGING TOOLS

SPACE FOR MOWERS ETC.

HANGING TOOLS

CONCRETE RAMP

BENCH

SIDE ELEVATION

INTERIOR VIEW

SHELF FOR SELDOM USED EQUIPMENT
SHELF FOR HARDWARE
SHELF FOR SMALL TOOLS
CABINET FOR INSECTICIDES FUNGICIDES &c.
WORKING SURFACE
TILTING DESK COVER
BIN FOR SOIL
FLOWER POTS
FLATS

CONSTRUCTION DETAILS:
FLOOR — 6" CONCRETE SLAB
WALLS — 2 x 4 STUDS, COMPOSITION SHEATHING AND ASBESTOS OR WOOD SHINGLES ON THE OUTSIDE, WALLBOARD ON INSIDE
ROOF — 2 x 4 RAFTERS COVERED BY WOOD OR COMPOSITION SHINGLES ON SHINGLE LATH

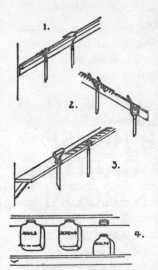

GARDEN TOOLS AND WORKSHOP EQIUPMENT

LAWN MOWER
(18" HAND MACHINE)
4-TINED DIGGING FORK
HOE
ROUND POINTED SHOVEL
4-TINED HAND CULTIVATOR
TROWEL *(WIDE)*
RAKE *(IRON)*
RAKE *(BAMBOO OR STEEL)*
WHEELBARROW
HOSE
(Above are minimum essentials. When you can, add)
HOSE REEL
SPRAY ATTACHMENTS
FOR HOSE
STAKES, WOOD, BAMBOO
POTS IN ASSORTED SIZES
RAFFIER AND BINDER TWINE
GARDEN LINE
SCISSORS
PRUNING SHEARS, SMALL
PRUNING SHEARS,
LONG HANDLED
PRUNING SHEARS, HEDGE
LARGE WATERING POT
SMALL DIGGING FORK
4-TINED MANURE FORK
EDGING TOOL
SQUARE EDGED SHOVEL
SCUFFLE HOE
TROWEL *(NARROW)*
SMALL WATERING POT,

LONG SPOUT
SPADE
LABELS, WOOD AND METAL
SPRAYER, KNAPSACK TYPE
DUSTER, SMALL HAND TYPE
SICKLE
SCYTHE
AX
HAMMER
NAILS, ETC., ASSORTED
PRUNING SAW
CROSS CUT SAW
PUTTY KNIVES
PLIERS
WIRE SNIPS
EDGING SHEARS
EDGING LAWN MOWER
GRASS CATCHERS FOR
MOWERS
SNOW SHOVEL
BROOM
BASKETS, BERRY AND
PICKING
SOIL SIEVE
TAMPER
CROWBAR
FLATS
SCREW DRIVERS
ASPARAGUS KNIFE
RIP SAW
POWER MOWER
WALKING CULTIVATOR
ROLLER

HOW TO HANG THINGS UP:
#1 — A SIMPLE HANGING RAIL FOR
HOES, CULTIVATORS, ETC.
#2 — PEGS OR HEAVY SPIKES DRIVEN
IN AT AN ANGLE WILL HOLD
RAKES, SHOVELS, FORKS
#3 — NOTCHES IN NARROW SHELF TO
RECEIVE HANDLES OR HEADS
OF TOOLS MAKE A SECURE
SUPPORT
#4 — OLD GLASS COFFEE JARS, WITH
LIDS FASTENED TO UNDER
SIDE OF A SHELF, ARE GOOD
FOR NAILS, ETC. TO USE, UN-
SCREW

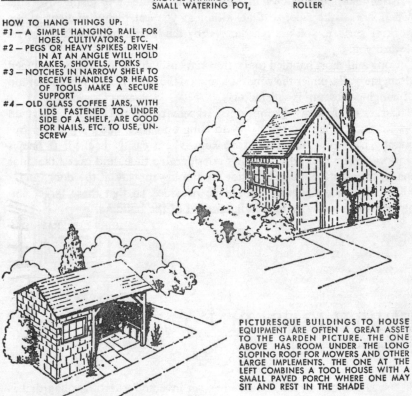

PICTURESQUE BUILDINGS TO HOUSE
EQUIPMENT ARE OFTEN A GREAT ASSET
TO THE GARDEN PICTURE. THE ONE
ABOVE HAS ROOM UNDER THE LONG
SLOPING ROOF FOR MOWERS AND OTHER
LARGE IMPLEMENTS. THE ONE AT THE
LEFT COMBINES A TOOL HOUSE WITH A
SMALL PAVED PORCH WHERE ONE MAY
SIT AND REST IN THE SHADE

the tools one is likely to need on the small place, and also a generous working space for potting and other indoor garden jobs. Running water is available from a faucet equipped to take a garden hose, and a short hose also should be available, equipped with a rose nozzle to use for spraying individual plants and washing pots.

A desk, whose lid closes to protect the contents from dust is a handy thing. Keep it equipped with paper, pencils, a selection of current (not last year's) catalogues, and your best garden books (which is to say the most practical ones). A drawer, lined with metal to make it damp and mouse proof, should be provided nearby for the storage of seeds. A tight cabinet with well fitting doors is handy to store spray materials and other things that should not be left around in the open. Open shelves above the work surface are an ideal place for small tools that do not hang up readily, boxes of small hardware items that are always in demand, and baskets, boxes and the like.

Note that the windows in this building, instead of being over the bench, are at the side, so that, although you get plenty of light at the working surface, you are not dazzled by the bright light coming directly toward you.

Long and short handled tools, that can easily hang up, can be arranged along the walls, under the windows, and on the rafters. Any secure method of hanging these up is satisfactory.

Larger implements, like mowers, wheelbarrows and rollers, can stand on the floor. They are too heavy to hang up easily, and they are so frequently used that they should be kept where easily reached. If one is working in the tool house for any considerable time, and needs the floor space, they can be parked outside. A sloping runway at the door, and a sufficiently wide doorway, should be provided so that these larger implements can easily be moved in and out of the building.

HENRY B. RAYMORE

FERTILIZER BIN

So far as can be learned, no one has yet invented a fertilizer bag that is able to hold up much longer than it takes to get it from the dealer's to the family garage. The old-fashioned cloth bags were reasonably durable, but they were porous to fertilizer from the inside and to air and moisture from the outside. The current paper affairs are hopeless, double-walled though they may be. With bone meal in them, they quickly rot. With complete fertilizer in them they will not stand the pounding that may be needed to obviate the effects of caking. With superphosphate inside they become so brittle that they will shatter at a touch.

Nor is it easy to provide other containers for fertilizers. Nitrogenous mixtures will corrode galvanized pails and cans in no time. Wooden boxes invariably leak. The answer would seem to be: stop improvising and make special plant food bins.

Here, on the next page, is the working story of the making of such a bin (or, if you are ambitious, a battery of bins). The "basic bin" was designed to meet several specifications: it will hold 100 pounds of the ordinary fertilizing materials most likely to be stored by the home gardener; it is strong enough to stand on its own legs, though it may be attached to a wall; its bottom is high enough so a bucket or small distributor may be placed below the delivery chute; its top is low enough so that any able-bodied male who can still carry his wife over a mud puddle may easily empty a full bag of fertilizer into the hopper; it will resist the chemical action of fertilizers and moisture.

Plywood, the weatherproof or outdoor kind, is the material to use for all bin panels, but hardboard, especially such a product as tempered "presdwood" or masonite will serve almost as well and will remain stable under conditions of considerable moisture.

The framework of the bin is simple but strong of itself. With the added reinforcement of what amounts to the "stressed-skin" construction of the side panels it should last many years. In fact the chief threats to its safety will be the garden wheelbarrow, the youngsters' bicycles, or the family car if—as is most likely—the bin is to grace the garage wall.

A study of the working drawings, over, will reveal to the initiated that the building of the bin (or bins) is simple enough provided all dimensions are carefully followed and all cutting done accurately. So always in such projects an hour of preliminary planning and preparation is worth four hours of fumbling improvisation. Once the details are understood, the actual building is as simple as walking across the street—it's just a matter of taking one step after another.

RALPH BAILEY

OPEN-AND-SHUT
FERTILIZER BIN

FRONT VIEW

HINGES AT BACK

¼" x 4" SLOT IN FRONT FOR SLIDE

A

SIDE VIEW

HINGES

¼"

21"

20"

18"

FRONT

BACK

PLAN "A-A"

C

B

B

¼"

10"

¼"

¼"

16"

¼"

C

NOTE—
WHEN MORE THAN
ONE UNIT IS TO
BE CONSTRUCTED,
2"x 2" CORNER POSTS
FOR ADJACENT
UNITS ARE MADE
COMMON TO
BOTH UNITS. SEE
PERSPECTIVE ABOVE

¼" x ½" TRACK

45°

6"

¼"x 4"
SLOT
FOR SLIDE

4"

3" HOLE
IN SLIDE AND
IN BOTTOM
OF BIN

¼" HARDBOARD SLIDE—
IN OPEN POSITION

SECTION "B-B"

2"x 2" CORNER POSTS

3" HOLE
IN SLIDE

¼" PLYWOOD

6"

6"

4"

6"

¾" x ¾"

3" HOLE

SECTION "C-C"

3" HOLE
IN SLIDE

2"

3" HOLE

¼"

¾"

SLIDE PULL

¾" x ¾"

PORTABLE POTTING BENCH

Just as the old fashioned lap-board enabled Grandmother to run up a dress for Mary Ann between supper and bedtime without messing up the dining table, so a potting bench can be set up for an hour's use without either wrecking the kitchen or scattering compost over the work bench. Primarily, the portable bench, illustrated on the next page, does two things—both of a useful nature. First, it keeps the soil all in one place, both in the mixing and the using. Second, it concentrates the actual work of potting, seed sowing, pricking off or whatever in one place, practically forcing on the most disorderly of gardeners at least a primitive kind of orderly procedure. Its use is just complicated enough to require some sensible plan of operation. It is also just simple enough to make it worth-while to set up if only for an hour's happy messing around.

In construction, the portable potting bench is no problem even for the carpenter who has advanced but little beyond the first saw-and-hammer stage of proficiency. But as with all gimmicks and what-you-may-call-'ems, honest workmanship is presupposed and careful working drawings are provided. The presence of earth, usually moist, calls for a work surface that will not roughen or warp easily. Also, since even a peck of earth is surprisingly heavy and the mixing of it a fairly stout operation, it calls for tight, well fastened side boards and clean design. For this reason the tool and label rack is behind the backboard and all cleats and stiffening members are *outside* the confines of the mixing and potting enclosure. The cleat under the front edge is, of course, not only a stiffener but a device to prevent the whole from slipping away from the

PORTABLE POTTING BENCH

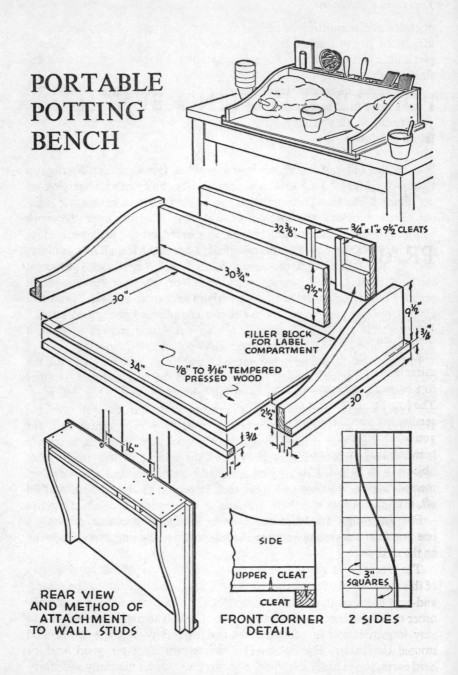

32 3/8"

3/4" x 1" x 9 1/2" CLEATS

30 3/4"

9 1/2"

30"

FILLER BLOCK
FOR LABEL
COMPARTMENT

9 1/2"

3/4"

34"

1/8" TO 3/16" TEMPERED
PRESSED WOOD

30"

2 1/2"

3/4"

16"

1"

REAR VIEW
AND METHOD OF
ATTACHMENT
TO WALL STUDS

SIDE

UPPER CLEAT

CLEAT

FRONT CORNER
DETAIL

3"
SQUARES

2 SIDES

operator and permitting dirt to get anywhere but on the floor. (You've no idea, until you've learned by bitter experience, of the abrasive qualities of just a little grit on a maple work bench or a porcelain table top or kitchen sink drainboard.)

You might, of course, leave this bench in place all winter if you have a work spot in a basement or garage corner. But if this will suffice for your needs at all you may, if you like, hang it up, leaving the tools and labels in place.

RALPH BAILEY

PRACTICAL GARDEN WAGON

The difficulties encountered in moving heavy or awkward loads around the garden by the ordinarily available means lies in lifting too much too high and then lowering it too far. The familiar garden wheelbarrow, miracle of applied leverage though it be, is still a long way off the ground to a bale of peatmoss and possesses no built-in sense of balance whatever. The low-slung "garden carts" or mobile dirt bins are fine for loads which readily assume the shape of what contains them but are of little use if you want to move a boulder or a Hemlock with an 18-inch root ball. The conventional baggage hand-truck is fine for rubbish barrels or large objects which will hold their shape with a minimum of supporting members. But they, like the wheelbarrow, must be balanced—fore and aft, even if not east and west.

For the gadget-minded but otherwise intelligent gardener, therefore, one practical answer may lie on the broad deck of the juggernaut pictured on the next page.

The worm's-eye view (and the worm had better keep his head down) of this movable platform presents no structural complexities to the butter-and-eggs home craftsman. Good hardware stores, the junk yard or a mail-order catalogue inventory the basic ingredients. The planks are subject to easy improvisation in arrangement and assembly—but the fewer and stouter the better. For relatively even terrain, and on good turf or hard earth, the vehicle, as shown, will carry any load a normally sedentary

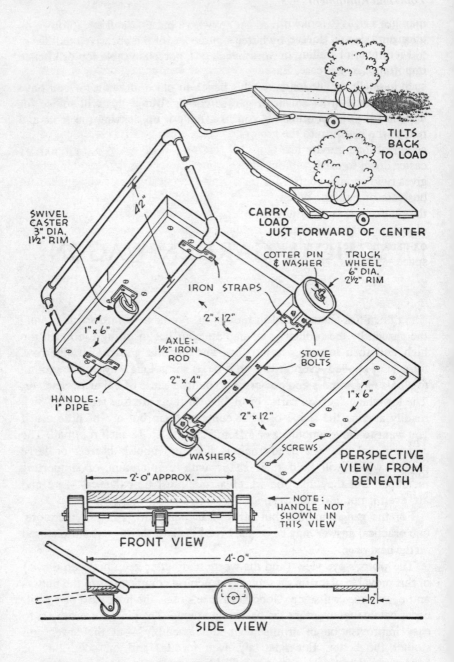

TILTS
BACK
TO LOAD

CARRY
LOAD
JUST FORWARD OF CENTER

SWIVEL
CASTER
3" DIA.
1½" RIM

42"

COTTER PIN
& WASHER

TRUCK
WHEEL
6" DIA.
2½" RIM

IRON STRAPS

2" x 12"

1" x 6"

AXLE:
½" IRON
ROD

STOVE
BOLTS

2" x 4"

1" x 6"

HANDLE:
1" PIPE

2" x 12"

SCREWS

WASHERS

PERSPECTIVE
VIEW FROM
BENEATH

2'-0" APPROX.

NOTE:
HANDLE NOT
SHOWN IN
THIS VIEW

FRONT VIEW

4'-0"

2"

SIDE VIEW

man has a right to fool with. For a better bearing surface over soft ground, a longer axle and double wheels are perfectly feasible.

Mere ease of pulling or speed of travel are not, however, of primary importance in this case. Ease of loading and unloading heavy weights, or such basically fragile loads as the root balls of shrubs and small trees, or such large and awkward shapes as bales and crates is given first thought. The balance of the vehicle is such that a light foot pressure will tilt the rear of the platform to the ground, making a ramp of it. Placement of the center of load gravity just ahead of the main wheels will bring the front caster down to earth without putting much weight on it. The pipe handle gives rigid enough control for jockeying and backing, as well as the main business of pulling. When the handle is dropped into loading position, the platform is entirely unobstructed on all sides, allowing the loading of objects far larger than the platform area. When not in use, this poor man's ox-cart may be stowed upright against a wall, using a minimum of floor space.

RALPH BAILEY

AN EXTRA PAIR OF HANDS

The old-time English garden laborer, with his trousers gartered with leather straps below the knees (to keep the bottoms out of the mud and to provide for free knee action) always included a pair of lifting boards in

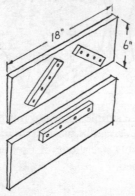

his equipment for picking up when engaged in sweeping walks and drives. These simple, inexpensive tools which anyone can make from odd pieces of lumber with a saw, hammer, and nails in less than 5 minutes, are used in any job which requires the transfer of debris from ground to wheelbarrow; or for picking up leaves, grass clippings, or any fluffy material which cannot conveniently be handled with a shovel.

Two pieces of beveled siding cut to a length of about 18 inches serve well as lifting boards. They should be reinforced by two cleats nailed on the back to form a broad V as indicated in the top sketch. The cleats, in addition to strengthening the boards, also afford good fingerholds. Any strong, light boards can be used, however, if siding is not available. Even if the boards are strong enough to do the work without reinforcement it is advisable to nail a cleat or cleats on each piece to indicate to searchers for an odd piece of board that it is a garden tool and not to be used to repair Junior's rabbit hutch. When intended primarily as a fingerhold, the cleat should be nailed parallel to the top edge of the board at a convenient distance to afford a good grip.

The way to pick up stones, twigs, broken glass and other debris is to hold the boards at an angle of about 45° on either side of the pile and push the lower edges together (see below). When gathering leaves and grass clippings, they are worked on somewhat the same principle as a clam-shell bucket and multiply the grasping power of the hands many times.

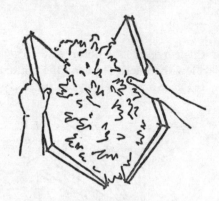

It is amazing that these simple tools are not more generally used. They are more efficient than a shovel in picking up loose debris and save hands from abrasion and possibly nasty cuts if used to gather the stones raked up when making a seed bed.

MONTAGUE FREE

THREE HANDY GARDEN GADGETS—from the distaff side

Any enthusiastic gardener loves garden gadgets, particularly if they really do a good job and fill a need. Like other members of the world-wide Green Thumb clan, I buy all the gadgets my budget will allow, and sometimes I make or contrive some for myself.

The home-made gadget I really purr over is my line-and-reel. It not only saved some money (to spend on other gadgets), but it is better than any I ever saw. Manufacturers take note. Patents *not* pending. It is very efficient, and besides, it is beautiful, at least to me.

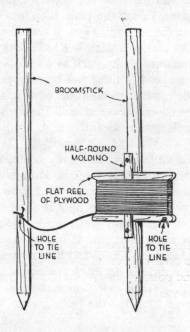

BROOMSTICK

HALF-ROUND
MOLDING

FLAT REEL
OF PLYWOOD

HOLE
TO TIE
LINE

HOLE
TO TIE
LINE

I took two discarded broomsticks and cut off the brooms. Then I sharpened the cut-off end of each, using a hatchet, a knife and a wood rasp until I got the right finish. Then, about 8 inches from the sharpened end of one stick I sawed and leveled off a strip on one side about ¼ inch deep and 6 inches long. Here I fastened my reel, cut from plywood with a jig saw into a sort of spool or reel shape. I screwed this reel firmly on to the flat surface where I had cut into the broomstick; then, to make it still more solid, I fastened a piece of half-round moulding over the plywood and up on the broomstick for a couple of inches on each side. All this was done carefully with small screws, not nails. The result was a light-weight reel and rod combination, perfectly firm and strong. I made my plywood reel to size, so that a string, passed once around it and over the broomstick, measured exactly one foot.

I bored a small hole in one corner of the plywood reel, and attached one end of a cord: not too heavy, but heavy enough to stand stress and strain. I wound 50 feet of the string on the reel. Since one complete turn is a foot, it is easy to measure. I bored a small hole through the other sharpened stick, about 8 inches from the sharp end, and fastened the other end of the cord in this hole. My reel was ready.

(I forgot to say that I had painted it in a handsome combination of white and scarlet enamel.)

I do love nice straight rows of flowers and "garden sass." When ready to dig or plant, I push the plain stick into the ground so the line just about rests on the surface. Then, taking loosely in both hands the stick on which the reel is fastened, I walk away to the other end of the row. The string unwinds by itself as I walk. I can count the number of revolutions it makes if I like, and know approximately the number of feet in the garden row. Arrived at the other end, I push the sharpened stick into the ground and leave it until the work is done. Then I can pick it up and walk toward the other end, winding as I go. Very neat.

Very good garden aprons, commercially made, are offered for sale in many places: real aprons, not the cute kind with pictures of watering pots printed on them. Sturdy aprons with big pockets, hooks for gloves and tools, and kneeling pad sewn right in front where the knees come. These are fine, but I think my home-made one is better. I made it of brown khaki, not too heavy, and it is long enough, but not very full or wide. I wanted to keep it cool and light in weight, for summer work, as far as possible. I did not do much sewing on it, but used leathercraft supplies and tools to some extent in making it, so it is very strong. I took an old luggage strap for the belt, leaving the buckle in place and

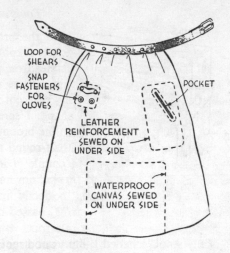

LOOP FOR SHEARS

SNAP FASTENERS FOR GLOVES

LEATHER REINFORCEMENT SEWED ON UNDER SIDE

POCKET

WATERPROOF CANVAS SEWED ON UNDER SIDE

punching holes in the other end so it buckles around me neatly. I riveted the apron to this sturdy leather belt, using about six of the small metal rivets used in leathercraft. A couple of small pleats take up what fullness there is at the waist line. I cut a slanting slit big enough to put my hand in comfortably, on the left side of the apron, bound it with strong tape, and then sewed a big patch pocket on the under side, making quite a neat and handy pocket for string, packets of seeds or whatever I may be using at the moment. On the right side I riveted a strong piece of leather on the under side of my apron, and used it as a base to attach the lower halves of two glove snap fasteners. The two upper halves of the fasteners I attached to two small leather tabs, and sewed the tabs to my garden gloves. I can snap the gloves to my apron and unsnap them instantly. They dangle outside, dry and uncrumpled—better off than in a pocket. When the gloves are worn out, I can remove the tabs and attach them to a new pair. I also riveted a small leather loop in this same reinforced area on the right-hand side. I can slip a pair of scissors or other small tool into it on occasion. On the underside of my apron, at knee length, I sewed a heavy waterproof plastic-coated canvas for kneeling.

I am "allergic to" bending over and stooping in the hot sun; indeed, a brief period spent weeding or planting in this position turns me purple and apoplectic. Therefore I devised a weeding stool, which is worth more than a dozen Rose bushes to me any hot day. It is rather rough, as I am no great shakes as a carpenter, but it is sturdy and just right for the job. I made it of empty crates, taking two strong reinforced

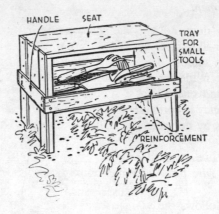

HANDLE SEAT TRAY FOR SMALL TOOLS REINFORCEMENT

ends for the "legs" of my stool. I nailed a light but strong board across the top for the seat. Half way down, I nailed strong pieces about 2 inches wide for reinforcements, and then nailed a thinner board across underneath these, reinforcing the stool still more and making a tray to hold a few small tools. I made handles on the sides, to pick it up by, and I can stick a tool into the handles when I need to, between thrusts of the trowel or weeder. I can place this little stool astride a row of vegetables or flowers (before they get too tall) and sit in comfort, weeding as far as I can reach: then move it and start again.

JULIE BEDIER

WITH TOOLS—IT'S THE UPKEEP

Two things the veteran gardener comes to realize if he has developed even a ham-and-eggs "feel" for tools in general. One is that a dirt-free piece of tool steel may deteriorate as rapidly as a mud-caked one. Another is that a tool with a blade that must make its way through soil—such as a spade or a hoe—must be smooth above all things.

But what about a sharp edge? I asked the boss of a crack transplanting crew at a famous nursery about that ten years or so ago. I'd watched him and his gang operate for an hour or two and marveled at the ease with which they dug and balled big trees and shrubs. I examined his sharp and mirror-like spade and asked him which was more important— a keen edge or a smooth blade. He scratched his head and then replied that a dull blade made for hard work—but that he wouldn't be caught dead with a pitted one. Once a spade blade becomes badly pitted, of course, its efficiency is permanently impaired. However, even a down-at-the-heel spade is by no means hopeless—especially if it is the only one you own.

Here are the five steps to *renewing* your old mistreated spade:

1. With a stiff *wire brush,* remove all rust from the back and front of the blade.
2. *Steel wool* follows the wire brush. But don't let it fool you. While it will polish the high spots and pull much corrosion out of pits and scratches, it will not really smooth the blade—which is the end to be sought. (Handle steel wool with gloves!)
3. An *old file* and *emery cloth* are the best "hand tools" for smoothing. The idea, of course, since you can't fill in the pock-marks, is to reduce the highspots. It thins the blade and is hard work, but essential.
4. A *squirt of oil,* spread by a rag, not only brings out any brightness you have produced, but shows up the deficiencies of your handwork. If you are conscientious, or if the spade is bad, you will use file and emery again.
5. A *keen edge* comes last. Clamp spade handle in a bench vise, face toward you, and with a *clean sharp file* ("mill-bastard" is the grade you'll want) work a true, even bevel at about 45° to the blade. Cut with a steady push stroke only.

For your hoe and similar tools, follow steps #1 through #4. In putting an edge on a hoe, however, file *against* the bevel, since it has less "spring" than a spade. File the sides of a hoe, too; you will work with the corner a great deal.

Right here let it be said that if a *new* spade is cleaned, dried and wiped with an oily rag *after each use,* it will never need anything but a renewed edge to keep it 100 per cent efficient. This is equally true of a garden hoe, scuffle hoe, axe, digging fork, mattock, scythe, sickle, pruning shears or any others which are either made of tempered steel, to hold an edge, or which present a large surface to the soil in the course of use. For bear in mind that a tempered tool is especially subject to rusting and pitting; that a rough surface is harder to push cleanly through the ground than a smooth one.

The advantages of modest electrical power equipment are many.

A second-hand quarter-horsepower motor, a three-dollar arbor, a six-by-one inch fine grit wheel, a wire brush, and a cloth buffer will do wonders. Catch a tool when it's new and the buffer, for polishing, and the grinder, for maintaining a cutting edge, are all you'll need in addition to the family oil can. For fine blades—knives, pruners, axes perhaps—a good oilstone is also essential.

For scythes and sickles, an old-fashioned natural scythe stone carried to the job in your hip pocket more than makes up for the slight bagginess about the jeans. You can perhaps pick up the soft English stones, and while they powder away at a tremendous rate, they will dress a curved edge like nothing else on earth. Apply the stone lightly but often if you would make the grass and weeds behave. A slicing cut is essential.

It is one of life's mysteries that a conscientious soul who would sit up half the night with a sick seedling won't clean a hoe once in a season. Yet nine out of ten of us are like that. We take pride in the well-being of our gardens. Yes, we even take pride in the quality of our tools, in the number of them we accumulate, in our ability to work with them hour after hour in the hot sun without wilting. Yet we won't take really good care of them. Perhaps it is the price we pay for regarding our gardens as a hobby instead of a way of earning three square meals a day.

A roll of steel wool, some emery cloth, and a bottle of oil, however, can prove a sound investment even for an uninhibited amateur.

RALPH BAILEY

AROUND-THE-GARDEN
PROJECTS With Wood

PLANT BOXES—BUILT-IN OR PORTABLE

Any container that will hold a reasonable volume of good soil with good provision for drainage will serve as a plant box. Properly proportioned and simply designed, it will serve almost any window, partner almost any architectural style, permit placement wherever seems good and fitting. On the next page are full, detailed plans for the basic construction of a "portable" window or porch box and its built-in counterpart. Small sketches in the upper corner suggest the finished products in use. All other drawings are simply the varied but vital details of "manufacture." In the portable box the secret of success is to keep the soil from coming in contact with the wood—hence the attention paid to a tightly soldered copper lining.

SENSIBLE IDEAS FOR TRELLISES

With a few notable exceptions, accounted for largely by frank modernists, the art of trellis design is still somewhere back in the General Grant era. Most trellises and arbors, whether of stock manufacture or custom made, are strictly "gingerbread"—cumbersome and fussy in appearance and structurally inadequate to the strains imposed upon them by a healthy vine. There seems to be a persistent belief, fostered by architects as well as millwrights, that the trellis is what people want to look at and that any vine that grows upon it, while inevitable, is some-

TWO KINDS OF PLANT BOXES

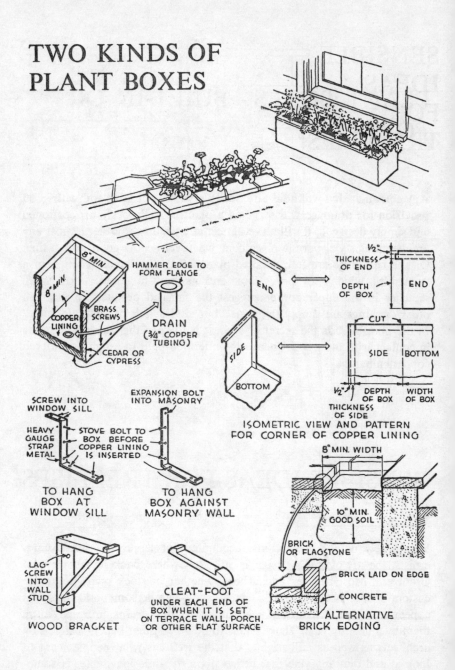

8" MIN

8" MIN

HAMMER EDGE TO FORM FLANGE

COPPER LINING

BRASS SCREWS

DRAIN (3/4" COPPER TUBING)

CEDAR OR CYPRESS

1/2"
THICKNESS OF END
DEPTH OF BOX
END

END

CUT
SIDE | BOTTOM
1/2"
DEPTH OF BOX | WIDTH OF BOX
THICKNESS OF SIDE

SIDE

BOTTOM

ISOMETRIC VIEW AND PATTERN FOR CORNER OF COPPER LINING

SCREW INTO WINDOW SILL

HEAVY GAUGE STRAP METAL

EXPANSION BOLT INTO MASONRY

STOVE BOLT TO BOX BEFORE COPPER LINING IS INSERTED

TO HANG BOX AT WINDOW SILL

TO HANG BOX AGAINST MASONRY WALL

LAG-SCREW INTO WALL STUD

WOOD BRACKET

CLEAT-FOOT
UNDER EACH END OF BOX WHEN IT IS SET ON TERRACE WALL, PORCH, OR OTHER FLAT SURFACE

8" MIN. WIDTH

10" MIN. GOOD SOIL

BRICK OR FLAGSTONE

BRICK LAID ON EDGE

CONCRETE

ALTERNATIVE BRICK EDGING

SENSIBLE IDEAS FOR TRELLISES

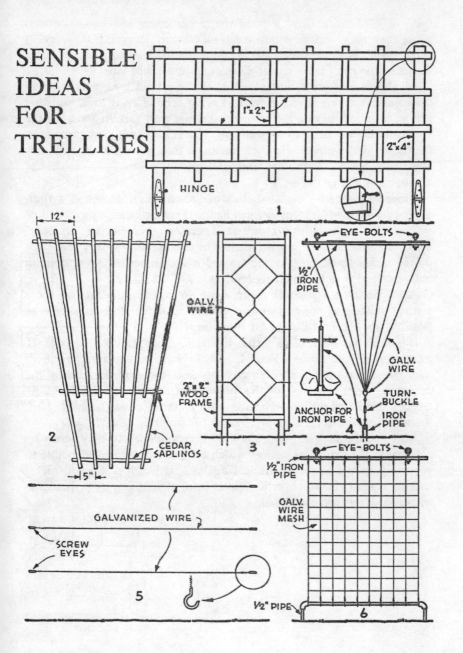

1'x 2"

2"x 4"

HINGE

1

12"

GALV. WIRE

2" x 2" WOOD FRAME

5"

CEDAR SAPLINGS

2

3

EYE-BOLTS

½" IRON PIPE

GALV. WIRE

ANCHOR FOR IRON PIPE

TURN-BUCKLE

IRON PIPE

4

GALVANIZED WIRE

SCREW EYES

5

½" PIPE

EYE-BOLTS

½" IRON PIPE

GALV. WIRE MESH

6

thing of a nuisance. And a good many gardeners and home owners, while they may gamble a bit, seem to concur. Doggedly they try to make their roses, their clematis conform to the garden ideas of some designer who can't tell a winter creeper from a fleece-vine.

All this sounds pretty ill-tempered, and it is. But it also leads up to the idea that a vine is either worth having around or it isn't, and that if it is, it's worth having for its own sake, not as a garnish for what the architects like to refer to as *treillage*. If trellises were that important, they'd be used without vines. (Sometimes they are so used, and very effectively, but that is another story and belongs primarily in the field of architecture, not gardening.)

Vines vary greatly in their habits of growth. Yet, except in a rudimentary way, they lack any *natural* habit. If not artificially supported or influenced, they usually just sprawl. Therefore they can be "trained," often very precisely, for a great variety of effects. And in very few cases do the means by which they are trained make an aesthetic contribution half so effective as the vines themselves.

All right, then doesn't it make sense to consider trellises as mere control devices, as convenient and efficient and therefore as simple as possible, for the best display of our vines?

It is from this point of view that the trellis ideas sketched on page 41 were worked out. Some (Nos. 1 and 2) have a structural value of their own against the shortcomings of some of the more formless of the deciduous vines. The rest of the suggestions are strictly the "control" devices mentioned earlier. Some suggest a pattern for vine training (Nos. 3 and 5); the others are simply frames for canes or tendrils.

All (and this may be important) are demountable, for easy access by painters to the structures against which they stand. All are adaptable to varying patterns. None, in the last analysis, is worth a plugged nickel without a good vine to cover it. Which is, of course, just as it should be where gardeners are concerned.

RALPH BAILEY

PICKET AND BATTEN GATE

One of the ground rules in a well-ordered garden is, of course, *don't swing on gates*. Usually it is small fry who are supposed to be the only violators. But one full-grown adult in a hurry can do more damage to a poorly constructed gate while he's fumbling in exasperation for the latch than any three youngsters who do their swinging slowly and methodically. It is, therefore, for slam-bang grown-ups that we propose this basic gate design.

The secret of a good home-made gate is two-fold: Its battens (the "Z") are properly placed and attached to the gate proper, and the posts are *deeply* set and firmly anchored against side-play. Latches give out only when they have to carry the weight of a sagging gate. And hinges let go only if they are too small—or fastened in the wrong place.

As far as design goes, your imagination and skill are the only limit. Dimensions, within reason, are largely optional. But whether your finished product is to be rustic or traditional, the underpinnings, the bracing, the fastenings must be secure. If you want to oil your hinges once in a while, there's no law against that.

This particular gate is patterned after one that has stood the test of time, children, adults, and the elements. It involves these basic raw materials: white pine posts (cedar, of course, if obtainable), pre-cut red cedar pickets, 1 × 4 inch (¾ × 3⅝ inch actually) white pine battens. The tools required are: a crosscut saw, hammer, twist drill (a bradawl would serve to start screw holes), and screw driver. A counter-sink makes a more finished job of the screw driving. The gate latch is a standard cast-iron, one-way affair, adaptable to either right or left-hand application on either side of the gate. (A similar device is available for a double-swing gate.) Any hardware store can supply latch, T-strap hinges, and spring closer. Use brass screws, except in galvanized hinges.

● The drawings tell you all you need to know about putting the gate together. But do all your figuring on paper before you start work. Check your grade and dimensions at the site. Then do your work on the cellar

PICKET-AND-BATTEN GATE

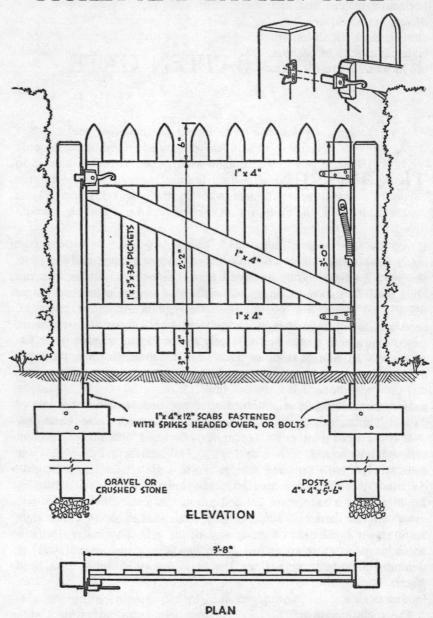

6"

1" x 4"

1" x 4"

2'-2"

3'-0"

1" x 3" x 36" PICKETS

1" x 4"

3" 4"

1" x 4" x 12" SCABS FASTENED
WITH SPIKES HEADED OVER, OR BOLTS

GRAVEL OR
CRUSHED STONE

POSTS
4" x 4" x 5'-6"

ELEVATION

3'-8"

PLAN

floor. You'll need elbow room. Lay the pieces out face down. Cut your horizontal battens first and fasten them to two end pickets with half-driven brads. Square up with a carpenter's square, and then, before cutting, mark the all-important diagonal batten with a straight edge after laying it exactly in position. Once the two end pickets and the battens are in place the rest is a cinch.

RALPH BAILEY

TEN-PASSENGER PICNIC TABLE

If you are so fortunate, or so wise, as to have a place where outdoor meals, however simple and informal, may be cooked and served of a summer's evening, you'll appreciate the necessity of a stable, spacious table hard by the fireplace. It may be very easy, conversationally, to whisk a table or two and eight or ten chairs down from the porch as need arises, but it takes more than a verbal arrangement to make al fresco dining both simple and pleasant. And if there are small fry to be reckoned with, tin table tops on wrought iron legs will not long be equal to the situation. Add to the complications an unpaved area of either turf or "forest floor," and outdoor dining becomes positively hazardous unless you and your guests are willing to sit cross-legged, like the pro-verbial Turks, with laps full of hamburgers, cole slaw, and ketchup.

It is for those who (a) like their picnic meals simple or (b) have rampaging youngsters to cope with that this design for a picnic table has been worked out. The original, of which measured drawings appear on page 47, was built some years ago for a family under both (a) and (b) headings. And it has served during off hours and off seasons as "jungle gym," aircraft carrier, heavy tank, alp, variety store, and ski jump. It is still steady as the bricks that support its four spreading legs. It has and needs no paint (just an annual swabbing with boiled linseed oil), it weathers beautifully, and it seats eight adults comfortably—ten in a pinch. Wiping with a damp cloth removes crumbs, and any stray footprints.

The tools needed to build this combination bench-table-bench are: saw, screwdriver, brace, bit and countersink, carpenter's square, rule, and a small chunk of soap to lubricate the heavy galvanized screws used in the assembly. The top and bench boards are yellow pine stair-tread stock, 12 inches wide, with rounded edges arranged as shown in the drawings. All other parts except cleats and braces are fir two-by-fours.

The actual construction is amazingly simple if you but draw the pattern of legs, horizontal top, and bench supports at actual size on the basement floor with a piece of chalk or heavy pencil. Draw a line first to represent the ground or base level, then erect a line perpendicular to it through the center of the parallel top line 30 inches away. All measurements may be made from these lines, the two-by-fours laid down and marked, and the two end assemblies joined, after cutting, flat on the pattern. The top is assembled separately, the braces fitted afterward. Drill all screw holes.

Oh yes—if you haven't an ample cellar exit, better work in the garage!

RALPH BAILEY

GARDEN BENCH

How it is with you I can't say, but in my garden a garden bench is used (a) as a place where small tools may be left out in the rain and (b) a vantage point for guest superintendents who might otherwise get lost in the weeds or fall into the silage cutter. There are the two subsidiary uses, of course, of providing rest for the perspiring or relaxing gardener and giving the garden a certain air of invitation.

There are, however, garden benches and garden benches. A regrettable majority of those available on the market are either costly misfits or plain junk. One answer, therefore, is to tailor your own benches to suit your own needs.

Unless you are a pretty expert mason or a blacksmith, your choice of construction material will be wood. And while some woods, such as Red Cedar, Redwood, Tidewater Cypress, and Teak, will last a long time without rotting, almost all others, even if kept painted, will give at the joints much sooner than you'd think. Therefore all joining and bracing—in fact, all points where wood comes against wood or against metal—should

TEN-PASSENGER
PICNIC TABLE

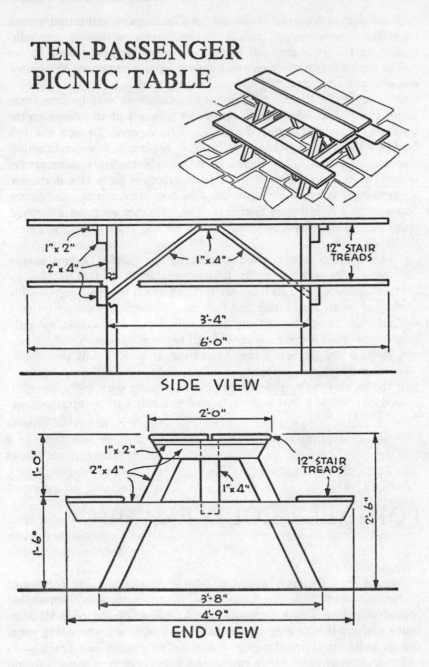

1" x 2"

2" x 4"

1" x 4"

12" STAIR
TREADS

3'-4"

6'-0"

SIDE VIEW

2'-0"

1" x 2"

2" x 4"

12" STAIR
TREADS

1" x 4"

1'-0"

2'-6"

1'-6"

3'-8"

4'-9"

END VIEW

be made tight and kept as simple as possible. Legs should be supported on bricks or stones or, if buried for sturdiness and stability, specially treated for rot resistance with linseed oil or asphalt compound.

The garden bench of which you see working drawings here has graced our garden for the past two seasons. And graced is a fair word to use. One reason is that there is not a single one-radius curve in its lines (that is, no curved line which could be drawn with a pair of compasses or could be the arc of a circle). This lends, I think, an air of lightness and fluidity which might otherwise be lacking. No board is wider than the standard 12 inches (11⅝ inches as it comes from the lumber yard). Greater width in profile is due to the arrangement of the back rest (which is surprisingly comfortable) and the fore edge of the seat. All lumber "dresses" to 1⅛ inches in thickness. The relatively unobstructed space below the seat front and between the legs permits grass to survive under the bench.

To anyone familiar with wood construction the dadoing of the seat into the bench sides will be readily understandable. It is a good idea to "butter" seat ends and dadoes—in fact, all wood-to-wood parts—with white lead before final fitting and fastening. Fastening is done with galvanized nails except for the top back rail, which was drawn up with brass screws after it had been shouldered between the bench ends. Note, too, the fact that the seat slopes from front to back slightly to prevent water from lodging in joints.

If the bench is to be painted (if it is not, better soak the joints with linseed oil), prime it first with plain lead and oil "cut" with turpentine.

RALPH BAILEY

PORTABLE COLD FRAME

It may be hard for cold frame veterans to understand, but there are probably many people who think a cold frame is too much trouble to bother with. But if such timorous citizens will build the *right* kind of frame and use it according to the dictates of common sense, they may change their tune. Here, on page 51 is one that's worth a trial.

For immediate reassurance be it said the two sashes shown are to be

GARDEN BENCH

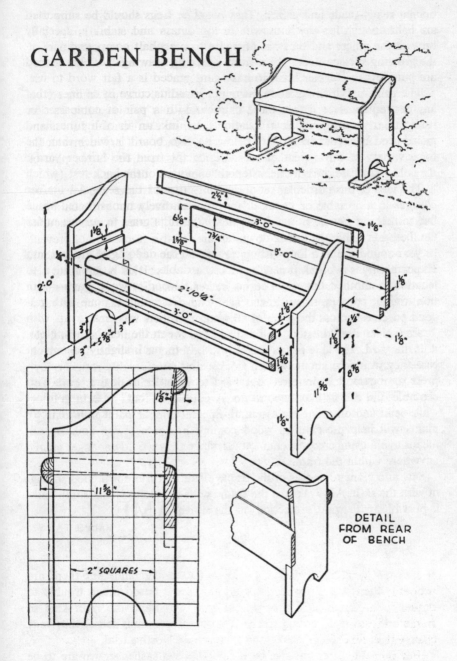

DETAIL
FROM REAR
OF BENCH

2" SQUARES

bought ready-made and glazed. They are 2 $\times$ 4 foot zephyr sashes that are light enough for any housewife to toss around while her husband is busy at the office, and they are of a size to permit reaching any part of the growing surface under them from either front or back. These sashes are puttyless—a further boon to busy gardeners.

The principal drawings show, at upper right, the finished frame set on any convenient 4 $\times$ 4 foot piece of ground—say the vegetable garden itself in early spring, a special location later, or even on the permanent raised seed bed (drawn directly below it), which will prove invaluable for a variety of warm-weather uses. Beside this seed bed is the plan of the cold frame. Below is a dimensioned "exploded" drawing.

The idea of this particular set of drawings is not to give you something *cheaper* in a portable or knock-down product than what you could buy but something *better*. Better in its adaptability. Better in construction. On the other hand, the knock-down features of this frame do not prevent its year-round use as a long-lasting, practical piece of garden equipment. Its portability is twofold. It may be picked up and carried bodily from one location to another; the use of corner stakes makes for sturdier construction, tighter corners, firmer anchorage. The galvanized lag screws get a good purchase across the grain of all wood members involved.

Sizes given are "dressed" or finished sizes for the lumber as you'll get it at the yard. The side pieces might also be bought undressed, in which case they would be about ¼ inch thicker and considerably rougher. Cypress or redwood is preferred but hard to get. White pine is quite acceptable and red fir may have to do. A couple of coats of light gray or white lead-and-oil paint are essential. Special copper paint non-toxic to plants will help preserve all wood coming in contact with soil. By all means avoid using creosote compounds, since they would endanger plants anywhere within the frame.

Saw and plane top edges of the frame clean and true for a good sliding fit with the sash. Always place the frame with the slope facing south and, if possible, with wind protection on the north.

RALPH BAILEY

PORTABLE
COLD
FRAME

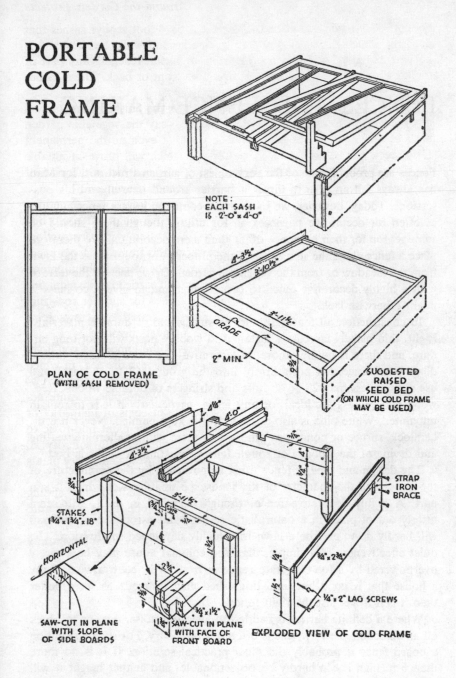

NOTE:
EACH SASH
IS 2'-0" x 4'-0"

PLAN OF COLD FRAME
(WITH SASH REMOVED)

4'-3½"

3'-10½"

3'-11½"

GRADE

2" MIN.

SUGGESTED
RAISED
SEED BED
(ON WHICH COLD FRAME
MAY BE USED)

4¼"

4'-0"

4'-3½"

3'-11½"

STRAP
IRON
BRACE

STAKES
1¾" x 1¾" x 18"

HORIZONTAL

¾" x 2¾"

¼" x 2" LAG SCREWS

SAW-CUT IN PLANE
WITH SLOPE
OF SIDE BOARDS

SAW-CUT IN PLANE
WITH FACE OF
FRONT BOARD

EXPLODED VIEW OF COLD FRAME

FENCES AND FENCE-MAKING

Fences are probably one of the very oldest of garden structures, for Man has always felt an urge to throw a barrier around himself and his possessions. Today, however, we in civilized communities use fences almost as often for decorative purposes as for utility, though there should be some reason for their existence other than mere decoration. We therefore place a fence along the street line of the property, or to separate the lawn from the meadow or from the vegetable garden. Or we enclose the terrace with a highly decorative fence to ornament it and to give a coziness it might otherwise lack.

In construction all fences should be sturdy and of durable materials. Light, thin pickets insecurely fastened to wobbly posts will not long endure, and there is nothing more undecorative—or more useless—than a dilapidated fence. Set posts firmly into the ground (3 ft. at least) and use nothing less than 2″ × 4″ rails and stringers of durable woods. Redwood and cypress are ideal for any fence, particularly if it is to remain unpainted. White pine is also durable if it is kept painted. Never use fir, hemlock, spruce or ponderosa pine where there will be alternate wetting and drying of the wood. For rough fences, chestnut or cedar is best.

The design and type of fence must be governed by the architecture of the house and the character of the landscape treatment of which it is a part. A highly decorative fence, though beautiful in itself, will seem utterly out of place in a naturalistic setting; and a rough post and rail will hardly do to enclose a lawn in a highly developed subdivision. The quiet effectiveness of a simple, dignified colonial house may be entirely overpowered by a too elaborate fence in front of it; contrariwise, many a house that is good but undistinguished may be made to seem better than it is if it has just the right fence.

Where a definite barrier is needed to keep out noise, dust or to block off an objectionable view, one is often in a quandary. For such a situation a board fence is probably the most practical solution. If it is no more than 6 ft. high it can hardly be objectionable, and at that height it will effectively block off traffic noise and dust, and may do much to shut out unpleasant sights. By increasing the spacing between the boards, by giving their tops an interesting shape, and by leaving the fence unpainted to weather a soft gray, it can be made to seem lighter.

Combining fences with masonry walls is often quite practical. A low wall of rough field stone may be appropriately topped by a simple white picket or slat fence. A more finished brick or stone wall of solid masonry needs something more elaborate. But be sure the fence is firmly attached to the wall by the iron rods built into the wall to hold the fence posts. Sections of fence may also be used in combination with hedges, or in places where space is too limited to permit the use of a hedge but where the barrier, nevertheless, must be provided.

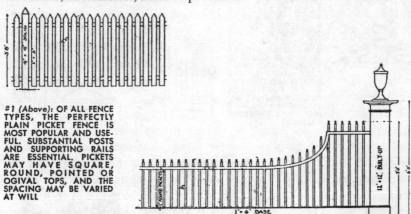

#1 (Above): OF ALL FENCE TYPES, THE PERFECTLY PLAIN PICKET FENCE IS MOST POPULAR AND USEFUL. SUBSTANTIAL POSTS AND SUPPORTING RAILS ARE ESSENTIAL. PICKETS MAY HAVE SQUARE, ROUND, POINTED OR OGIVAL TOPS, AND THE SPACING MAY BE VARIED AT WILL

#2 (Above): WHERE THE HOUSE IS FAIRLY LARGE AND ARCHITECTURALLY IMPORTANT, A STREET LINE FENCE USING TURNED PICKETS AND ACCENTED AT GATES AND CORNERS WITH HIGH, ORNAMENTAL POSTS MAY BE APPROPRIATE. SUCH A FENCE IS RELATIVELY COSTLY BOTH — ORIGINALLY AND IN UPKEEP, FOR IT MUST BE KEPT PAINTED. PICKETS MAY BE OF EVEN HEIGHT, OR BROUGHT UP TO A HIGHER LEVEL AT CORNERS OR POSTS, AS SHOWN. PICKETS ARE USUALLY DOWELLED THROUGH RAILS, BUT MAY BE APPLIED TO FACE OF RAIL AND THE NAILHEADS COVERED WITH A BEADED MOULDING WITHOUT DESTROYING THE EFFECT

#3 (Above): NOTHING IS BETTER THAN A BOARD FENCE TO SHUT OUT NOISE, DUST AND OBJECTIONABLE VIEWS. IF MADE OF CYRESS OR REDWOOD IT MAY BE LEFT UNPAINTED AND WILL WEATHER TO PLEASING INCONSPICUOUSNESS

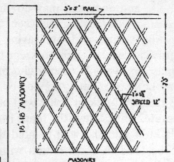

#4 (Left): WHEN A HIGH, SUBSTANTIAL, YET LIGHT-APPEARING FENCE IS NEEDED THIS COMBINATION OF MASONRY POSTS AND WOOD LATTICE IS SUITABLE. THE PATTERN MAY BE EITHER DIAGONAL OR HORIZONTAL-VERTICAL, AND SPACING MAY BE CLOSER FOR A DENSER BARRIER IF NEEDED. LATTICE SECTIONS ARE STRONGER IF THE STRIPS ARE CONTINUOUS AND LAP OVER EACH OTHER, BUT A MORTICED JOB WHERE THE STRIPS ARE ALL IN ONE PLANE IS MUCH MORE ELEGANT. A WIDE BASE-BOARD MAY BE SUBSTITUTED FOR THE LOW WALL, AND BUILT-UP WOOD POSTS FOR THE MASONRY PIERS

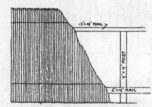

#5 (Right): THIS LIGHT, GRACEFUL, YET SUBSTANTIAL FENCE WOULD MAKE A HANDSOME ENCLOSURE FOR A TERRACE OR SMALL LAWN. THE DIAGONAL PIECES SHOULD BE MORTICED TOGETHER AND GREAT CARE GIVEN TO THE DESIGN AND TURNING OF THE FINIALS. FOR GREATER VARIETY ALTERNATING PANELS MAY BE OF DIFFERENT PATTERNS

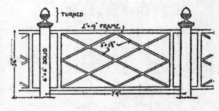

#6 (Below): OF ALL THE "UTILITY" TYPES OF FENCES SHOWN ON THIS PAGE, THE SPLIT CHESTNUT HURDLE IS PERHAPS THE MOST PRACTICAL BECAUSE IT IS PORTABLE. IT COMES IN 8' SECTIONS WHICH ARE SET IN THE GROUND BY DRIVING THE POSTS INTO HOLES ALREADY STARTED WITH A CROWBAR. THE SECTIONS ARE HELD TOGETHER NEAR THE TOP BY IRON PINS RUN THROUGH HOLES IN THE POSTS. MESH WIRE MAY BE FASTENED TO THE SECTIONS TO MAKE THE FENCE EFFECTIVE AGAINST POULTRY AND ANIMALS. NO PAINTING REQUIRED

#7 (Above): THE POPULAR SPLIT CHESTNUT "FRENCH" FENCE COMES IN SEVERAL STANDARD HEIGHTS AND EITHER CLOSE WOVEN OR SPACED ABOUT 1". IT MUST BE RIGIDLY FASTENED TO A SUPPORT OF 4" x 4" POSTS AND 2" x 4" RAILS SPACED 8' APART. TOPS OF THE STANDARD SECTIONS MAY BE RE-CUT TO ANY DESIRED LINE

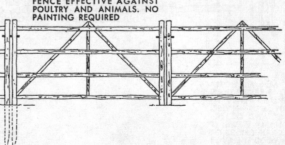

#8 (Below): THIS TYPE OF POST AND RAIL FENCE WITH DIAGONAL PANELS IS SUITABLE FOR ENCLOSING PADDOCKS, AND IN GENERAL AROUND FARM BUILDINGS. IT IS GENERALLY PAINTED OR WHITEWASHED AND MAKES A GOOD SUPPORT FOR CLIMBING ROSES OR OTHER VINES

#9 (Right): NOTHING IS MORE SERVICEABLE THAN THE WOVEN WIRE AND PIPE FENCE SHOWN HERE. IT SHOULD BE COVERED WITH SOME SORT OF VINE AS QUICKLY AS POSSIBLE

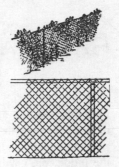

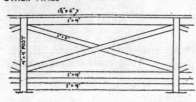

#10 (Below): OF ALL COUNTRY FENCES, THE OLD-FASHIONED POST AND RAIL, MADE OF HAND SPLIT CHESTNUT, IS PROBABLY THE MOST CHARMING. THREE-RAIL OR FOUR-RAIL TYPES ARE COMMONLY USED, AND RECENTLY A ONE-RAIL VARIATION USING VERY HEAVY POSTS HAS BECOME POPULAR OWING TO ITS FRE- **QUENT USE ON THE PARKWAYS NEAR NEW YORK. TWO TYPES OF POST ARE SHOWN; AT THE LEFT THE PIERCED POST WITH HOLES CHISELED INTO IT FOR THE RAILS, AND AT THE RIGHT, A DOUBLE POST WITH SLOTS FOR THE RAILS MADE WITH IRON PINS**

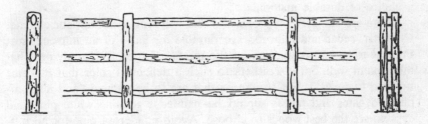

HENRY B. RAYMORE

GATES AND ENTRANCES

First impressions are always of the utmost importance. Hence a gate or entrance, whether it leads into the grounds as a whole, or into any particular garden, is of great concern to the landscape designer. It sets the mood, the keynote, for the whole composition.

On the following pages a selection of various types of gates and entrances is shown. They are typical, but by no means exhaustive. Throughout gardening history, designers have exercised their imaginations in this direction, and the variety of types and the infinite variation in detail is enormous.

Much of the work done by amateurs in this field is, unfortunately, flimsily constructed, and therefore soon loses its original attractiveness. Those examples which have endured from the past are the ones on which great pains were spent to make them substantial. Anything built of wood which stands out in all weathers has to be pretty carefully fitted together if moisture is not to penetrate the joints and soon cause the whole structure to fall to pieces. This is, then, a plea for careful workmanship and a choice of durable materials.

There are but a few sorts of wood that will long withstand our climate. Chestnut, cedar and redwood are durable for gates of an informal sort that are to be left to weather. Of the three, redwood is the only one that takes paint well, but it weathers to such a delightful color that it seems too bad to cover it. For structures that are to be painted (and all complicated gates and fences should be painted), genuine white pine and cypress are the best woods to choose. Avoid ponderosa pine for all outside work—and, of course, fir and hemlock are not at all durable in contact with moisture. Gray birch, which is so attractive for informal gates and barways, hardly lasts one season.

Use heavy, galvanized hardware for all hinges, latches and other metal parts. Posts should be of locust or chestnut, set at least 3 ft. into the ground, and the lower part should be treated with tar or other good wood preservative. Setting them in concrete often aids stability, especially where heavy gates are to be hung, but it does not seem to preserve the posts from rotting. When built-up posts are used, it is important to block tightly between the supporting post and the outer, decorative one, to prevent the structure from wobbling.

The placing of gateways is just as important as their construction They should always close an opening in a barrier of some sort, never stand alone in the open This seems too obvious to need stressing, but nevertheless one often sees gateways set up on the lawn, with no hedge or fence to prevent one from merely walking around them. They should separate areas used for different purposes, such as the street and the lawn, or the lawn and a flower garden. Where two areas are used for similar purposes, it is usually best to use an open archway rather than a gate, unless for some reason a definite barrier is needed. Furthermore, an archway needs to frame an important vista.

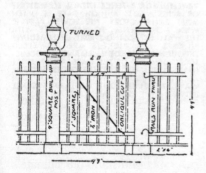

#2 (Left): OLD SALEM'S CHESTNUT STREET IS THE INSPIRATION OF THIS COLONIAL GATEWAY. USE IT AS A FRONT GATE OR IN A FENCE SEPARATING A SLOPING LAWN FROM A FEATURE SUCH AS A FLOWER GARDEN OR ORCHARD. THE LARGE, TURNED, SOLID URNS FORM THE ONLY DECORATION. THE GATE ITSELF IS MERELY A HINGED SECTION OF THE FENCE. IT OPENS INWARD ONLY, IS SUPPORTED BY STRAP HINGES AND FASTENED BY A SIMPLE HASP ON THE INSIDE. THE FENCE STRINGERS MUST RUN THROUGH THE HOLLOW, BUILT-UP POSTS TO PROVIDE ADEQUATE SUPPORT, AND MUST BE CUT ON AN OBLIQUE LINE WHERE THE GATE JOINS, SO THAT A STOP IS FORMED. THE IRON ROD RUN THROUGH THE GATE PREVENTS IT FROM SAGGING

#3 (Right): COLONIAL WILLIAMSBURG IS THE SOURCE OF THIS DOUBLE DRIVEWAY GATE. IT SUGGESTS A SIMPLE HOUSE SET IN SPACIOUS GROUNDS SOME DISTANCE BACK. IT IS EASY TO MAKE AND ANY LOCAL MILL CAN CUT OUT THE FINIALS ON THE SOLID POSTS WITH A BAND SAW. WHITEWASHED, OR PAINTED WHITE, IT WILL STAND OUT SHARPLY AGAINST THE GREEN OF SHRUBBERY OR EVERGREEN PLANTINGS

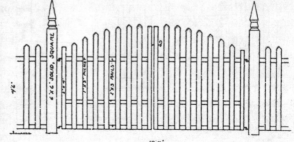

#4 (Below): A PLAIN PASTURE FENCE LIKE THIS NEEDS A SOMEWHAT MORE DECORATIVE GATE TO GIVE IT ACCENT. THIS CHIPPENDALE MOTIF IS SUFFICIENTLY INTERESTING AND ALSO STURDY ENOUGH TO BE PRACTICAL. THE JOINTS BETWEEN THE PARTS OF THE GATE SHOULD ALL BE MORTICED FOR STRENGTH, FABRICATED OF DURABLE WOOD, AND KEPT PAINTED.

#5 (Above): FOR AN OPENING IN A DRY STONE WALL, EITHER AS A FRONT GATE OR GARDEN ENTRANCE, THIS SIMPLE SLAT GATE HUNG ON UNOBTRUSIVE SOLID WOOD POSTS IS EMINENTLY SUITABLE. IT COULD BE PAINTED OR ALLOWED TO WEATHER

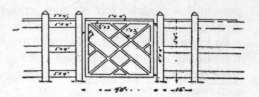

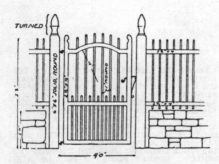

#6 (Left): FOR A FENCE ATOP A LOW STONE OR BRICK WALL, A HIGH GATE IS OFTEN MOST SATISFACTORY. THE LOWER PART IS MADE MORE DENSE, TO HARMONIZE WITH THE WALL, BY ADDING SHORT, INTERMEDIATE PICKETS. ALL PICKETS ARE DOWELLED THROUGH THE FENCE RAILS AND THE STRUCTURAL MEMBERS OF THE GATE. AN UNUSUAL HAND-WROUGHT IRON LATCH IS SHOWN. AS IN ALL GATES WHICH SWING BOTH WAYS, BE SURE TO LEAVE AMPLE SPACE BETWEEN THE GATE AND THE POSTS

#8 (Below): THIS "AMERICAN GOTHIC" GATE WOULD FORM A FITTING ENTRANCE FOR AN OLD-FASHIONED COTTAGE OR SIMPLE VILLAGE HOME. ALL PARTS OF THE GATE SHOULD BE MORTICED TOGETHER AND KEPT PAINTED

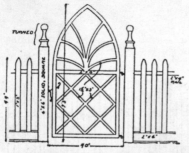

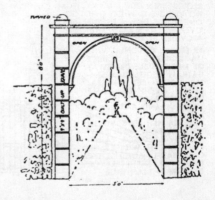

#9 (Right): THIS LARGE WOODEN ARCH NEEDS AN IMPORTANT VISTA BEYOND TO JUSTIFY IT, BUT IF THIS REQUIREMENT IS MET IT CAN "MAKE" A GARDEN. DO IT IN WEATHERED WOOD

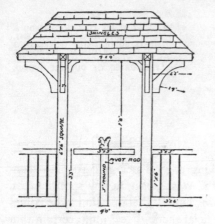

#10 (Left): LYCH GATES HAVE ALWAYS BEEN POPULAR WHERE A RUSTIC TYPE OF HOUSE SETS THE KEYNOTE OF THE SCHEME. A TURNSTILE, LIKE THE ONE SHOWN, WITH THE AMUSING FIGURE OF A SQUIRREL CRUDELY CARVED FROM A BLOCK OF WOOD, SERVES IN LIEU OF A GATE. A SOLID WOODEN GATE, LIKE THE ONE SHOWN IN THE SMALL SKETCH AT THE HEADING OF THIS ARTICLE, WOULD BE EQUALLY APPROPRIATE. SINCE A LYCH GATE IS QUITE A DOMINANT FEATURE IN THE LANDSCAPE: IT IS MOST SUITABLE AS THE STREET ENTRANCE TO THE PROPERTY

#11 (Right): FOR A PASTURE GATE, OR TO CLOSE OFF A WOOD ROAD, THIS RUGGED TIMBER GATE, OF ROUGH-HEWN CHESTNUT OR MAPLE LOGS, IS PRACTICAL AND DECORATIVE. THE USE OF A PIVOT ARRANGEMENT INSTEAD OF HINGES IS UNIQUE. BE SURE THE TOP BLOCK IS VERY STRONGLY BOLTED IN PLACE AND THAT THE SUPPORTING POST IS FIRMLY SET

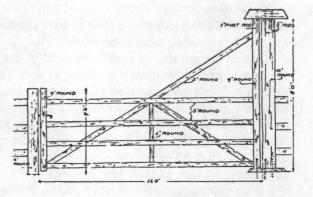

#12 (Below): FOR AN OPENING IN A HEDGE, LEADING FROM THE LAWN TO A FIELD WHERE ANIMALS ARE PASTURED, THIS OLD TIPPING STILE, FROM GREAT DIXTER, SUSSEX, ENGLAND, PROVIDES AN ODD BUT PRACTICAL SOLUTION. NO VEHICLE CAN GO THROUGH, OF COURSE. ONE HOLDS DOWN THE TOP BARS AND STEPS OVER. WHEN RELEASED THE COUNTER-WEIGHTS PROVIDED BY THE DIVIDED POST AT THE RIGHT BRING THE BARS BACK INTO PLACE. LIKE ANYTHING MADE OF WOOD WITH MANY MOVING PARTS, IT MUST BE ACCURATELY AND STURDILY BUILT. THE POSITION OF THE CENTER POST ON WHICH THE BARS PIVOT WILL VARY WITH THE LENGTH OF THE TWO ARMS AND THE WEIGHT OF THE WOOD USED. IT SHOULD BE ARRANGED SO THAT THE RAILS FALL EASILY INTO POSITION AND STAY THERE

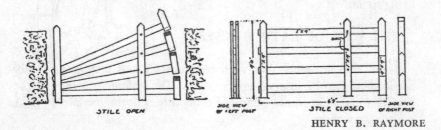

STILE OPEN

SIDE VIEW OF LEFT POST

STILE CLOSED

SIDE VIEW OF RIGHT POST

HENRY B. RAYMORE

LATH HOUSES

Have we in the East been overlooking a good bet in gardening techniques? I think that no one visiting the West Coast, at any spot between Point Loma and Seattle, can help asking himself that question as he comes across gardens that are grown in artificial shade. I feel quite certain that we might more profitably have borrowed from the Pacific seaboard the practice of utilizing lath houses than to have swallowed their B_1 vitamins and highly educated, fancy-bred earthworms.

Not that the growing of certain types of plants under lath structures has been any exclusive discovery of our western friends. The use of such shelters has long been common in Europe. Commercial growers in the East have employed them extensively in the growing of many types of plants—especially broad-leaved evergreens, such as Rhododendrons and Azaleas—during their babyhood. Nurserymen who have received their training in Holland—and there are none more skillful—seem to be particularly wedded to their lath houses.

But on private grounds one very seldom comes across a lath house, and where they are found, they usually exist for the express purpose of aiding in propagation, with no thought of utilizing them as an extension to the outdoor garden, in which a variety of plants that otherwise would encounter unfavorable environments may be grown satisfactorily if not to perfection. Contrast this with what one finds on the West Coast, where the shade garden is often an important part of the general layout—and frequently is almost a combination glassless greenhouse and outdoor living room.

THE WHY OF LATH HOUSES

Those who are unfamiliar with structures of lath may wonder what magic there can be in such contraptions. The definite advantages they provide for certain plants—and for many others during certain stages of growth—are three.

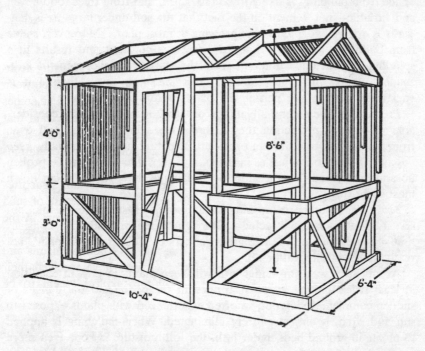

Here is a generalized construction drawing of a lath house roughly 10 by 6 feet in size. It is chiefly concerned with showing the framework necessary for a solid durable job. The roof slats might run in either direction, as desired. Walls below bench supports may be left open and door omitted, too. This 2 by 4 frame is strong enough to carry removable panels, glass, or snow fence.

Shade. First, there is controlled shade. Many plant species demand a certain amount of shade, and many more, while they will tolerate full sun, are far happier in partial shade.

On some places little or no shade is available, or if it does exist, it is not in a location so situated as to be convenient for the growing of plants. Shade from buildings is likely to be too dense, that from trees too uneven and variable—not to mention the fact that the soil under large trees generally is not well adapted to the growing of most plants. Moreover, shade from buildings, and often that from trees, is constant and results in a spindling growth quite different from the sturdier development of lath-shaded plants which get enough direct sunshine—even though it is constantly shifting—to permit the plant to function normally.

Protection. The second advantage of lath houses is the very considerable amount of protection they afford from winds, storms, and even from frosts. It is true that an open lath structure does not actually *keep out* any of these, but—just as in the case of sunshine—they are so broken up and moderated that the amount of damage they can do is cut down most surprisingly.

Moisture. Another astonishing thing about lath structures is the conservation of moisture effected—although, when you stop to consider that sun and wind are the two great robbers of moisture, perhaps it's not really so astonishing after all.

At any rate, watering under lath will keep plants in pots in condition at least twice as long as when applied in the open, and the danger of sudden complete drying out, so often experienced with plants exposed to sun and wind, is almost entirely eliminated. When mulching is applied to plants in ground beds under lath, the soil moisture is kept even more constant.

LITTLE SPACE, BIG RESULT

So much for the advantages of lath houses as far as the cultural side of growing plants is concerned. But there are other considerations equally important.

First among these is the possibility of utilizing a small space effectively for the growing of plants which you otherwise could not grow or could grow only less successfully. A space only a few feet square—say 8 × 12 —can be made a thrilling addition to the outdoor garden. Variety, both in the structure itself and of the plants to be grown in it, is—within climatic limitations—as wide as could be desired. Lath house gardening offers full scope to the gardener's imagination. Lath house construction may

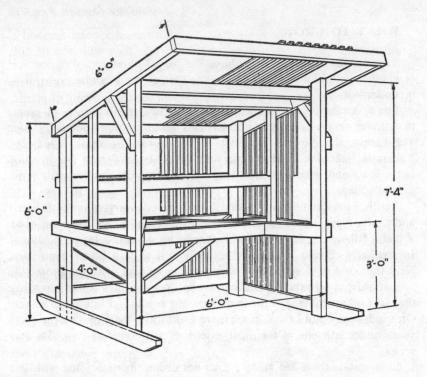

Here is the framework of a "portable" lean-to lath house. Its portability would really amount only to swinging its back toward sun or prevailing wind, since the 2 by 4 framing is heavy. Skids could be omitted for permanent setting on posts or cement blocks. Shelf and bench arrangement is wholly optional. Laths in 4-foot lengths may be accommodated as shown. One caution: Whatever size or type you build, avoid flimsy or haphazard construction.

be either very simple or very elaborate. The construction sketches here tell a carpenter or competent handyman all he needs to know about the basic principles.

Lath Living-rooms. As a matter of fact, the lath house, or some adaption of it, can be so handled as to make a most charming semi-outdoor living room. Unless there can be a considerable area under lath, living space must be at the expense of plant growing space, but usually a satisfactory combination can be worked out. In some instances part of the overhead structure is covered with glass or cello-glass (which is much cheaper but less permanent than glass), so that the "room" can be used even in rainy weather.

WHAT TO GROW

Anyone who thinks he might have use for a lath structure of one sort or another naturally wants to have some idea of what can be grown in— or under—it.

The first category to be considered is, of course, the group of plants that prefer semi-shaded conditions. This group is represented by such well-known shade-lovers as most of the Ferns, Fuchsias, Gloxinias, Tuberous Begonias, Peperomias, and Pick-a-back Plants (to mention but a few) and a host of semi-tropical and tropical species with ornamental foliage.

Another important group is the broad-leaved evergreens, both hardy and tender types, which require not only shade but protection from wind. Which of these can be grown will depend upon their relative hardiness. In southerly climates Camellias respond well to lath house conditions. Near the coast in Oregon Rhododendrons grow well, with the protection lath affords, in an exposed and windswept location that would seem like the most unfavorable spot for them that one could find in a day's search. On windswept Point Loma, in southern California, there existed for many years under lath one of the most extensive collections of Begonias ever seen.

I am certain there are many plants not ordinarily associated with lath house culture that would thrive under the conditions it can provide. Any number of our wildflowers, for instance, for which on many places it is almost impossible to find a congenial parking space, should do well under lath. The degree of shade and of protection can, of course, be controlled by the construction. In most houses the laths are placed their own width apart, giving a fifty-fifty division of shade and sunshine, but this can be altered to fit the conditions desired.

F. F. ROCKWELL

Pots on shelves create ever-changing pictures. You can grow the plants wherever you want to, and place them in position or take them off according to season and the amount of bloom. But they'll require careful watering and protection from wind.

GARDENS 'ROUND YOUR WINDOWS

There are more places to raise a beautiful garden than just in the ground. Window boxes are always good, but there are a few tricks that window boxes can't possibly perform. Here are four suggestions for the garden handyman, with easy-to-follow diagrams.

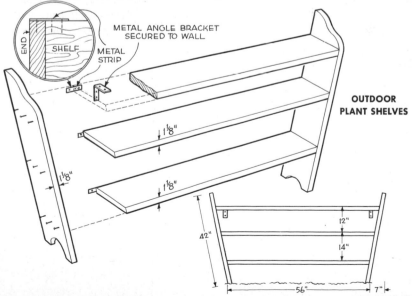

METAL ANGLE BRACKET
SECURED TO WALL

END

SHELF

METAL STRIP

OUTDOOR PLANT SHELVES

For a high window use plants that hang (right). Old-fashioned trailing plants, such as balcony type Petunia shown here, help pull window garden down to the ground. Or try Ivy-leaved Geraniums. For chunky boxes, chunky plants. Low windows, on the contrary, are best provided with upright plants, such as Geraniums, Begonias and Dwarf Petunias, which help to give privacy.

**ADAPTABLE
WINDOW BOX**

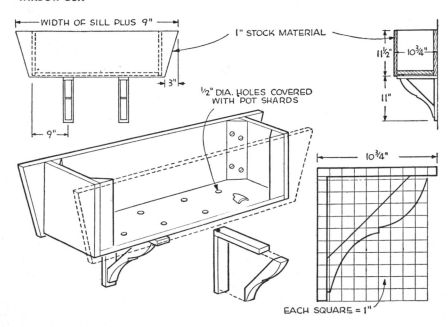

WIDTH OF SILL PLUS 9"

1" STOCK MATERIAL

3"

$11\frac{1}{2}$" $10\frac{3}{4}$"

11"

9"

½" DIA. HOLES COVERED WITH POT SHARDS

$10\frac{3}{4}$"

EACH SQUARE = 1"

Two-level shelf makes an interesting design. With an arrangement like this your pot garden can be varied to provide real distinction. Also, it has functional value in permitting easier opening and closing of shutters. Have pots in deep saucers.

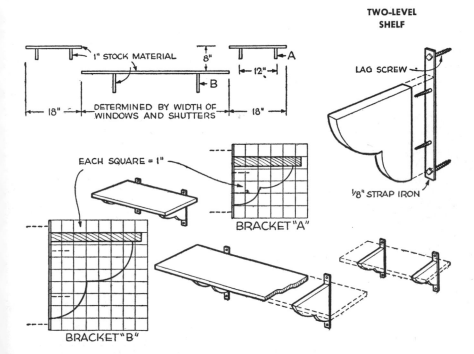

TWO-LEVEL
SHELF

1" STOCK MATERIAL

8"

A

12"

B

18"

DETERMINED BY WIDTH OF
WINDOWS AND SHUTTERS

18"

LAG SCREW

⅛" STRAP IRON

EACH SQUARE = 1"

BRACKET "A"

BRACKET "B"

Try cacti for a long low window. Here the problem is to relieve the bare, horizontal side wall. Lattice at ends and top provides support for quick-growing vines. Dwarf-growing Cacti and other succulents will thrive in blazing sunlight.

CORNER SHELF WITH LATTICE

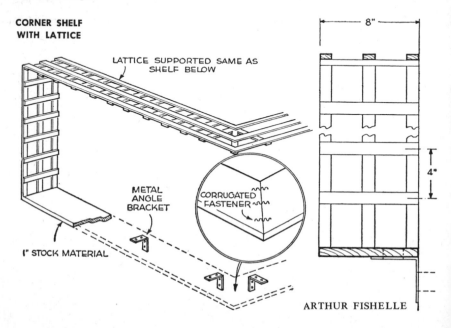

LATTICE SUPPORTED SAME AS SHELF BELOW

METAL ANGLE BRACKET

CORRUGATED FASTENER

1" STOCK MATERIAL

8"

4"

ARTHUR FISHELLE

AROUND-THE-GARDEN
PROJECTS With Masonry

CONCRETE: HOW TO USE IT

Concrete is a mass of fine and coarse materials, known as aggregates, which are surrounded and held together by hardened portland cement paste.

When the materials for concrete are first mixed together, the cement and water form a paste. The paste surrounds the particles of aggregate and holds them together to form concrete. This concrete is in a plastic condition. A chemical action then takes place between the cement and water causing the paste to harden.

The quality of the portland cement paste used determines how strong, how watertight, and how durable the hardened concrete will be. The quality of the paste is determined by the quantity of water mixed with the cement. For this reason the amount of water used is of great importance. If the paste is strong and the aggregate durable, the concrete is strong, durable, and watertight.

The constituents of concrete are water, portland cement, fine aggregate (sand), and coarse aggregate (pebbles).

Water used in mixing concrete should be clean, free from oil, alkali, and acid. In general, water that is fit to drink is suitable for use in concrete.

PORTLAND CEMENTS are hydraulic cements made by many different manufacturers, each with its trade name. They are available at all building supply yards in bags of one cubic foot.

SAND should be clean and hard, free from fine dust, loam and clay and vegetable matter. Such foreign materials prevent bond between the cement and sand and may result in a concrete too weak for its purpose. Sand should be well graded, containing particles not all fine nor all coarse, varying from fine up to those that will pass through a screen no coarser than ¼-inch.

PEBBLES or CRUSHED STONE should be free from foreign matter. Coarse aggregate includes all sizes ranging from ¼ inch up to 1½ or 2 inches. In thin walls or slabs the largest pieces of aggregate should never exceed one-third the thickness of the thinnest section.

THINGS TO REMEMBER ABOUT CONCRETE

Good quality concrete is the result of:

Using proper ingredients.

Correctly proportioning the ingredients.

Mixing them thoroughly.

Placing and spading the mixture into forms that are strong enough and placed to stay in position as long as needed.

Proper finishing.

Moist curing at favorable temperatures.

Sand may be dry, damp, or wet and the amount of water in the mix must vary accordingly.

Curing is a chemical action that must be accompanied by proper conditions of moisture and temperature.

Neither flagstones nor brick can be laid over a thin sheet of concrete. It should be no less than 4 inches thick.

PROPORTIONS

In any consideration of proper proportioning for concrete work, it is important to remember that the aggregates are held together by cement paste. Some jobs require better quality concrete than others. A Lily pool, for example, must be watertight and much stronger than a concrete footing under a garage. Because the cement paste in the concrete for the pool must be watertight, less water is used than in the case of the footing. So the type of job determines, in part, the amount of water to be used in the mix. Because dry sand is seldom available, the wetness of the sand is the other determining factor. Damp sand usually contains about ¼ gallon of water per cubic foot; wet sand contains about ½ gallon per cubic foot; and very wet sand contains about ¾ gallon. These varying combinations are condensed in the accompanying table.

It is desirable to get as much concrete as possible from each sack of cement: thus, the more aggregate mixed with the cement paste, the more

In areas where freezing temperatures occur, concrete walks, terraces, driveways, etc. must be laid over a bed of gravel or cinders at least 6 inches deep.

The depth of foundation footings must be below the frost line of the locality concerned.

Concrete sidewalks should be no less than 4 inches thick.

Concrete driveways should be no less than 6 inches thick.

A concrete retaining wall may need to be designed by an expert, but a rule of thumb is that the width of the base must be one-half the height and the wall 6 inches thick at the top.

If it has been necessary to leave a mix standing for a while, water must not be added to make it workable. Make a new batch.

Standing water must not be taken up by dusting on cement.

Wheelbarrows, shovels, trowels should be washed soon after using.

---

concrete will be produced. Also, the more aggregate used the stiffer the mix. But a too stiff mix will require an excessive amount of tamping and spading and, more important, may lead to porous or honeycombed con-

CORRECT PROPORTION OF MATERIALS FOR DIFFERENT PURPOSES

KIND OF WORK	GALLONS OF WATER FOR EACH I-SACK BATCH			TRIAL MIXTURE FOR FIRST BATCH			MAXIMUM AGGREGATE SIZE
	DAMP SAND AND PEBBLES	WET SAND AND PEBBLES	VERY WET SAND AND PEBBLES	CEMENT	SAND	PEBBLES	
GARDEN WALLS, RETAINING WALLS, NON-WATERTIGHT FOUNDATIONS, FOUNDATION FOOTINGS.	6¼	5½	4¾	SACKS 1	CU. FT. 2¾	CU. FT. 4	INCHES 1½
WATERTIGHT BASEMENT WALLS AND FLOORS, LAWN ROLLERS, COLD FRAMES, HOTBEDS, WELL PLATFORMS, SEPTIC TANKS, SIDEWALKS, FLAGSTONE WALKS, DRIVEWAYS, PLAY COURTS, BARBECUE BASE AND WALLS, PORCH FLOORS, GARDEN POOLS, STEPS, GATE POSTS.	5½	5	4¼	1	2¾	3	1½
FENCE POSTS, MAILBOX POSTS, FLOWER BOXES, BENCHES, BIRD BATHS, SUN DIALS.	4½	4	3¾	1	1¾	2	¾

Cement is spread on measured pile of sand

crete that will disintegrate under weather action. Experience shows that
for average jobs the proportion is in the neighborhood of 40% sand
and 60% coarse aggregate.

A trial batch may result in a mixture that is too wet or too stiff. This
is remedied by slightly increasing or decreasing, as the case may be, the
proportions of sand and pebbles, not the water.

MIXING

All materials should be accurately measured. A pail marked on the
inside at different heights to indicate quarts and gallons is handy for
measuring water. A pail may also be used for measuring cement, sand,
and pebbles. In mixing one-sack batches, it is not necessary to measure
cement, as one sack holds exactly one cubic foot. Sand and pebbles are
most conveniently measured in a homemade bottomless box 1 foot
square and deep.

Sand and cement mixed, pebbles ready in box

If laying a long driveway or some other big home job is contemplated,
the easy way out is to order ready-mixed concrete delivered to the site.
Another possibility is to rent a small machine mixer. Either way saves
a lot of hard work and makes for a good result.

A tight floor surface of some kind is necessary for a hand-mixing platform. The most satisfactory is a wooden platform made for the purpose (*see drawings*). It should be large enough to allow two men using shovels to work at the same time. Six or 7 feet wide by 10 or 12 feet long is a good size. Matched boards will make the joints tight. Cleats on the undersurface, spaced 2 feet apart, will hold the boards together, and a narrow strip around the outer edge on top will prevent mixing materials from being pushed off.

First, the measured quantity of sand is spread evenly on the platform, and on this the required amount of portland cement is distributed. The cement and sand are thoroughly turned with square-pointed shovels to produce a mass uniform in color. The proper amount of pebbles is then spread in a layer on top of it. Mixing continues until the pebbles are uniformly distributed throughout the mass, when a hollow or depression is formed in the middle of the pile to receive the correct amount of water. The finished mix must be a uniform combination of all materials.

Mix cement and aggregates to uniform mass

FORMS

Forms, the wooden molds into which the concrete mixture is placed, must be strong and well made, with no open cracks to allow water-cement paste to escape and change the character of the remaining mixture. One-inch-thick sheathing boards are good. Braces, stakes, etc., may be two-by-fours, and cross ties may be one-by-fours. Loops of heavy wire running across from form to form through holes in the forms and around free cleats against the outside surfaces are often necessary to prevent spreading. Wood spacers (1 × 2s) may be needed to hold opposite forms the correct distance apart. These are removed as pouring progresses.

Dry, untreated wood forms will absorb water from the concrete, often leaving the surface too dry for best results. For this reason and to prevent sticking of the concrete to the forms and to make removal easy, oil the inside faces with a light, clear lubricating oil cut with an equal amount of kerosene. An alternative is to wet the forms thoroughly with water.

In summer, wall forms generally can be removed after one or two days, and in colder weather after four to seven days. The test is whether the concrete is self-sustaining.

HANDLING

Concrete ought to be placed in forms within a half hour of mixing. It is deposited in level layers 6 to 9 inches deep, tamping and spading it the while, just enough to settle it thoroughly. It should be placed where it is to be used, not in piles and dragged, which causes segregation of the aggregates.

Push mixture into water basin made in center

If the work of placing must be interrupted, the top surface needs to be roughened just before it hardens to provide a good bonding surface for the next pouring. Upon resumption of placing, the preliminary treatment is thorough wetting of the surface.

Screeding is the operation used in making a non-skid walk, for example, of striking off the concrete to the proper level. It is done with a straightedge board several feet long, depending upon the job. Placed over the forms, this is moved back and forth with a sawing motion and at the same time advanced in a direction at right angles to the straightedge.

Floating is done to compact the surface and generally to smooth the result of screeding. It is done with a hand tool called a float and produces a "sidewalk" finish.

Troweling will polish the surface to a smooth finish and is done with a metal hand trowel. If it follows hand floating, wait for the former surface to become fairly hard.

What To Use For Coloring Concrete The Way You Want It

COLOR DESIRED	COMMERCIAL NAMES OF COLORS FOR USE WITH CEMENT	QUANTITIES REQUIRED (LBS. PER SACK OF CEMENT)	
		LIGHT SHADE	MEDIUM SHADE
GRAYS, BLUE-BLACK AND BLACK	GERMANTOWN LAMPBLACK OR CARBON BLACK OR BLACK OXIDE OF MANGANESE OR MINERAL BLACK	½ ½ 1	1 1 2 2
BLUE	ULTRAMARINE BLUE	5	9
BROWNISH RED TO DULL BRICK RED	RED OXIDE OF IRON	5	9
BRIGHT RED TO VERMILION	MINERAL TURKEY RED	5	9
RED SANDSTONE TO PURPLISH RED	INDIAN RED	5	9
BROWN TO REDDISH BROWN	METALLIC BROWN (OXIDE)	5	9
BUFF COLONIAL TINT AND YELLOW	YELLOW OCHRE OR YELLOW OXIDE	5 2	9 4
GREEN	CHROMIUM OXIDE OR GREENISH BLUE ULTRAMARINE	5 6	9

A successful concrete job is very strong in compression but for some uses requires strengthening in tension. This is done with metal reinforcing rods or wire mesh which must be free of rust or scale to avoid reducing the bond between the metal and the concrete. Reinforcement should be covered by a minimum of ¾ inch of concrete.

Concrete expands with a rise in temperature and contracts with a lowered temperature. It also expands with wetting and shrinks with drying. These characteristics make necessary the use of expansion joints, at a maximum of 30-foot intervals, in jobs such as sidewalks and driveways. The filler for such joints is often a bitumen-treated felt.

CURING

Concrete hardens because of a chemical reaction between portland cement and water. This vitally important process of curing continues so long as temperatures are favorable and moisture is present to hydrate the cement, and good conditions for it must be provided. The most favorable curing temperatures are from 70° to 80°. Freezing within the first twenty-four hours usually causes permanent injury to the concrete. By working with heated water and aggregates and keeping the concrete warm during the early stages of curing, a job may be done during freezing weather. *But an amateur without special equipment had best wait for higher temperatures.*

The desirable properties of concrete increase most rapidly during the first week of curing. This process continues markedly for three months and at an abating rate for many months. Once concrete has become thoroughly dry, no further gain in hardening takes place. Therefore, the rate of hardening is of special importance. Under many conditions (as large surface areas and warm weather), take precautions against too rapid evaporation which can cause weak, non-wear resistant, porous concrete. After the first day, frequent sprinkling of the surface or covering with a damp material will help. In the former case, drying out between sprinklings should be avoided. In the latter case the concrete may be covered with wet sand, burlap, straw, or canvas, kept wet for four to five days.

CARL T. SIGMAN
WILLIAM J. WARD, JR.

STONE: HOW TO USE IT

Flagstone paths, walks, and terraces lend naturalness and freedom to lawns and gardens and give a pleasant contrast to the harder, man-made lines of the house. There are many situations where grass walks are both preferable and practical, but when the wear of foot traffic is too great, a more durable surfacing is desirable. The use of flagstone introduces color and pattern, either formal or informal, into garden design to give character and contrast and artistry offered by no other element of design.

The commonly used materials are slate, bluestone, limestone, marble, and cast stone. All of these may be obtainable in a given area, but oftener than not, when cost and availability are factors, the best advice is to use the stratified natural stone of the vicinity. For most work it is necessary that one face of the stone have a level surface. This is important where furniture is to be used—as for a terrace—and the stone then should be laid on concrete.

Look over the accompanying drawings and decide which procedure you prefer and which is best for your purpose, your climate, and your soil condition. Good drainage is essential under any flagstone surface. The cinders—wetted and well compacted—are necessary for this purpose. Gravel, if it is more readily available or cheaper, will serve as well. But unless your soil is unusually porous or sandy, don't skimp this part of the job. If you use a concrete underslab, mix the concrete in the proportion of 1 part portland cement, 2¼ parts sand, and 3 parts gravel. The mortar joints and setting bed should be a richer and smoother mix: 1 part portland cement to 3 parts sand.

FLAGS WITH GRASS BETWEEN

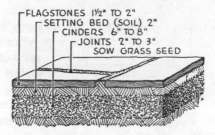

FLAGSTONES 1½" TO 2"
SETTING BED (SOIL) 2"
CINDERS 6" TO 8"
JOINTS 2" TO 3"
SOW GRASS SEED

Flagstones can be given a soil instead of sand setting bed over cinders. When handled in this way, they are suitable for walks but not for living or dining terraces, since they are subject to frost displacement. The random spacing within the general outline gives an informal, natural effect.

FLAGSTONES SET IN SAND

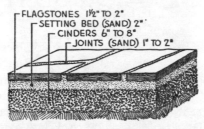

FLAGSTONES 1½" TO 2"
SETTING BED (SAND) 2"
CINDERS 6" TO 8"
JOINTS (SAND) 1" TO 2"

Flagstones of irregular shapes but regular outside edges provide an interesting pattern. Here they are given a sand setting bed over cinders. This makes them suitable for walks but not for living or dining terraces; they are subject to frost displacement.

MORTAR FOR MILD CLIMATES

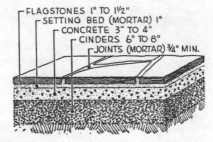

FLAGSTONES 1" TO 1½"
SETTING BED (MORTAR) 1"
CONCRETE 3" TO 4"
CINDERS 6" TO 8"
JOINTS (MORTAR) ¾" MIN.

Flagstones with mortar joints can be set on sand cushion over cinders in the paving of walks or terraces. Not as load-bearing as when a concrete slab is added, but the method does provide an even surface. Subject to frost displacement.

STONES, MORTAR, CONCRETE

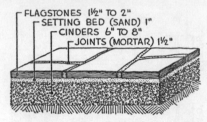

Flagstones in mortar on concrete slab over cinders make the best construction for walks or terraces. They are durable in low-temperature climates because undisturbed by alternate freezing and thawing. Good furniture surface and strong enough to stand up under gardening equipment traffic.

STEPS FOR CREVICE PLANTING

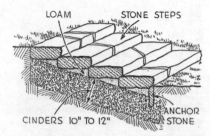

Informal cut stones bedded in loam over a substantial cinder base make a good appearance in natural surroundings. However, they are subject to frost displacement. Rock plants can be grown easily in the meeting joints of treads and risers, if desired.

PERMANENT MASONRY STEPS

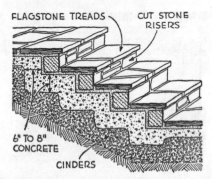

Flagstone steps and stone risers. Good for change of level in any flagstone job. One-inch board forms required against riser faces of concrete foundation. Concrete, flagstone, or brick a substitute for cut stone risers. Tread dimension 12" to 16" exclusive of nosing. Riser dimension 6½" to 5".

SIZE RELATED TO PURPOSE

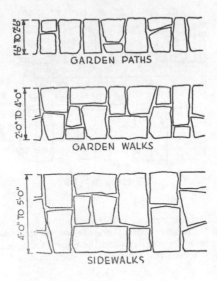

Width of paths and walks is dictated by use, amount of traffic, and design of garden or plot. Walks of medium importance for two people, not less than 4 feet. Stone patterning to suit conditions. Casualness of course and direction often desirable but not skirting of intentionally placed obstacles.

FOR A PERMANENT EDGING

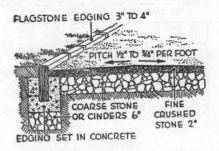

Flagstone edging set in concrete, used as a boundary for crushed stone or gravel walk surface over coarse stone or cinders. This arrangement is practical anywhere. The camber (pitch away from the center of the path) is important to provide for drainage and for inevitable settling from use.

SPACING OF STEPPING STONES

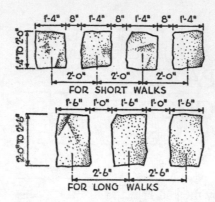

FOR SHORT WALKS

FOR LONG WALKS

Comfortable use of stepping stones calls for spacing that is variable with the length of the path. With faster gait—therefore longer strides—the spacing interval should be greater for longer walks than for short ones. Sod cut out to receive the flagstone is usually a satisfactory procedure.

FORMAL VERSUS INFORMAL

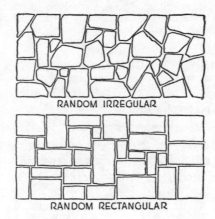

RANDOM IRREGULAR

RANDOM RECTANGULAR

Two of the almost numberless pattern possibilities in the use of random stones, purchasable from any supplier. Such stones are less expensive than those cut rectangular. The most formal effect is obtained from square and rectangular shapes fitted. Any really precise fitting, however, is difficult.

CARL T. SIGMAN
WILLIAM J. WARD, JR.

CRAZY PAVING
MAKES GOOD SENSE

They call it crazy paving. That may be because the man setting it in place feels crazy by the end of the day. Yet it's the sanest kind of thing for a path or terrace, because it's attractive, efficient, cheap, and can be successfully done by the home gardener with no previous experience at the job. I know because I've tried it.

For a long time, I used to look enviously at the pictures in gardening books and think how swell it would be if we could afford a paved area in our garden, but our budget just didn't run to professional landscaping. Then a friend who had done a bit of landscaping asked me why I didn't use concrete blocks. He said there were two ways of getting them. We could make them with a mixture of three parts sand to one part cement, shaping them in molds made with thin strips of board, or cutting them into the required shape after spreading the mixture out on a level space and allowing it to get half set before making the cuts with a trowel or knife. The other way was to go to a builder's yard and buy a load of old concrete chunks after a floor or path had been wrecked. Actually, we visited the local town yard, where we got a load of broken street paving. These slabs were especially good because they had uniform thickness and were level on both sides, making it much easier to set them in position, and also giving a flat final surface. There were two or three different colors and textures among them, which probably happened more by accident than by design, through the different sands used in different batches.

So that the paving would be flush with the lawn, we took out the soil to the depth of the blocks, levelled it and made it firm, and then set the blocks in position. We put ours on the plain soil; but if you like, you can make a base of gravel or clinker and set each block on little heaps of mortar placed at the corners. You then have to tap the block down to its right level, testing it with a straight-edge, which is just a strip of board that will reach across from side to side of the area you are paving. Putting the largest blocks at the edges, especially if a flower border runs along one side, makes for permanence: small blocks at the sides are likely to sink or work loose.

Let the spaces between blocks be about half an inch wide. We filled these spaces with mortar; but some people like to fill them in with a mixture of sand and soil so they can plant them with low-growing rock plants or grass.

The snag about filling in with mortar is that you need to be more fussy about drainage and will have to give the path a "crown" or raised center. A paved area will need to have enough slope to take the water off after a shower; and remember to make the slope go away from the house into a lawn or flower border. If after this you find there are still patches where the water collects, punch a hole through the mortar in the lowest part to let it drain.

A paved area is extra-good in the outdoor living room, as it is usable when grass would be too wet; and it is also better where there are chairs and tables, as the hard surface prevents their legs from sinking and making unsightly holes. It is also a handy way of dealing with a yard that is too shady and damp for grass to grow. A plant or two in a tub, or even a space where you can grow a small shrub, a conifer, or a few annuals, will break up the grayness and give a touch of color.

DOUGLAS ELLIOTT

FLAGS WITHOUT STONE

"A tiled terrace, no less!" wailed my friend the professor, scandalized that my humble cottage should sport such an extravagance. He didn't know, then, that the tiles in question cost me something less than 15 cents per square foot. They were precast cement paving stones. Furthermore they were home made and subtly colored.

The construction of these blocks is simple if you are used to handling cement. (See "Concrete: How to Use It," p. 71) "Floating in" the color, and pointing up for fine-grained texture, both require a little knowing how and can't be really put across by words alone.

To make anything out of cement you must first have forms to pour it in. The ones needed for cement tiles are so simple and crude that they aren't even carpentry. If you are making very random shape tiles, you don't even need square corners. Almost any lengths of wood will do for the forms, but it is easier to have it all the same thickness. Scrap two-by-threes are excellent. You can piece them together on a flat piece of ground to suit yourself. Nail them together lightly; there will be no great pressure from such small amounts of cement. If you don't hammer the nails in all the way, you can draw them out easily after the cement is dry. Then you can use the wood again to make more forms, if necessary.

You can mix the cement in any flat box that is big enough—say 2 ft. by 3 ft. or larger. You could knock together such a box or borrow a regular mortar bed. The cement mixture should be rich—two parts sand to one part cement. "Pointing up" or surfacing the tiles may be done with plain cement and color.

Tiles like these escape the monotonous look of the usual large sheet of commercial cement paving. The color, the texture, the lack of pattern, and, in short, nearly everything to do with those big areas is bad. Recently, colored cements and interesting finishes have been used to alleviate this ugliness. But even after employing a most skilled and most artistic cement mason to pour a single sheet terrace, you have a completely uniform area with no variety and no pattern. This linoleum effect is fine on a porch, but a bit dull for a terrace. I might add that any large cement area has to have excellent underdrainage and probably steel reinforcing incorporated with it, or it will crack.

There is a charm about little rock plants growing between paving stones. Twenty cents worth of portulaca seed scattered casually over the paving stones in May transforms even a well-trodden terrace into a colorful garden from August to October. Obviously nothing like this could happen if you threw the seed on a solid sheet of cement.

The first step in getting pleasant color is to use white cement. It is much easier to achieve clean pleasant colors with this than with the common dirty gray cement. Even gray tiles turn out a much pleasanter tone if made with white cement tinted with lamp black and blue. The reason is that gray cement is not clear gray at all, but a sort of greenish dirty tan.

Secondly, always tint with a little cement color. Even if you want white blocks, "point up" the surface with a sprinkling of neat cement and lime. The nicest tones of all in cement are grays which are made not only by adding pure carbon black but by adding a good deal of blue. Both these colors may be put right into the cement when you mix it. Most other colors are sprinkled on the surface and "trowelled in." Be sure to buy coloring matter especially made for cement; that is to say, lime-proof colors.

I think that in cement blocks it is wise to try for as fine grained a texture as possible. Use fine sand, and be careful about "pointing up" the surface. But fine-grained texture does not mean the block needs to be absolutely flat like a commercial tile. You can give it a crown, or stipple or brush the surface.

So if you are careful about texture and color, you can achieve effects about as good as the most expensive pavings. Not that cement tiles are ever copied imitations of other paving stones. Imitations are always phony. Cement has its own character. But you can make an almost un-limited variety of colors, textures, sizes, and shapes. You can pave your terrace with anything from tile-like, very smooth blocks of uniform size and color, to random size and shape stones reminiscent of a fieldstone courtyard, or even lay out a formal pattern.

JOHN R. GRIFFITH

STEPS FOR GARDEN AND GROUNDS

Gardens on various levels have a charm unknown to those all on a single flat plane. Differences in elevation, however, entail the use of steps or ramps to make the various parts of the garden accessible. These, in their own right, add much to the interest of the scheme.

In making steps, think not only of the need for a way to get up or down, but also of how the work is going to look and function. Narrow, steep flights of steps should be avoided, and long, unbroken flights of 15 or more steps are very tiring to traverse. Breadth is important. Make step flights as wide as possible, but proportioned to the other elements like walks, lawn areas, flower beds and borders.

A careful study of the chart on page 89 will be rewarding. Choose a ratio of run (tread measured without the nosing or overhang) to riser (step height) that fits the situation with which you have to deal, and follow it exactly. The ratios shown on the diagram have been selected

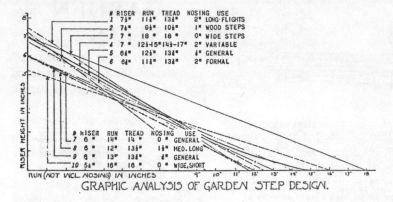

#	RISER	RUN	TREAD	NOSING	USE
1	7½"	11¼"	13¾"	2"	LONG·FLIGHTS
2	7¼"	9½"	10½"	1"	WOOD STEPS
3	7 "	18 "	18 "	0"	WIDE STEPS
4	7 "	12½-15"-14½-17"		2"	VARIABLE
5	6½"	12½"	13½"	½"	GENERAL
6	6½"	11½"	13½"	2"	FORMAL

#	RISER	RUN	TREAD	NOSING	USE
7	6 "	14"	14 "	0 "	GENERAL
8	6 "	12"	13½"	1½"	MED.LONG
9	6 "	13"	13½"	½"	GENERAL
10	5½"	16"	16 "	0 "	WIDE,SHORT

GRAPHIC ANALYSIS OF GARDEN STEP DESIGN.

from hundreds that have been measured and studied, and have proved themselves to be the most satisfactory.

Choice of materials depends, to a large degree, on the character of the situation. Brick, stone, concrete, logs, or sod are all suitable for certain places, but each has a definite character of its own, which it will impress on the scheme as a whole. Brick, or a combination of brick risers and walls with flagstone treads, seems most suitable for the rather formal Colonial, Georgian or Regency house or garden.

For the country farmhouse in a district where field stone abounds, dry stone walls and steps are probably the best choice. Cut, dressed stone walls and ramps with flagstone treads or steps made of heavy dressed stone slabs without supporting risers are good to use with a stone house or where the situation requires great dignity. Rougher stone goes well with the English or Normandy type house. For the ultra-modern house, concrete may well be the best material to choose. For a wooded situation there is nothing better than log steps.

Be sure that steps are well built: deep, substantial foundations; well fitted and neatly laid up stone, if you use that material. In all stone masonry a better appearance is achieved if the stones are laid with their long axis horizontal.

Stone side walls should never be less than 18" thick, and brick ones 12". Allowing the tread to hang over the riser to form a nosing often gives a shadow line that adds attractiveness. This overhang should be at least 1½". If wood is used for any steps, choose durable varieties like cypress or redwood. Fir or pine, or such hardwoods as oak and ash, are unsuitable, since they either lack durability or are likely to warp and split. Any wooden steps should be protected by linseed oil or Minwax, which can be colored.

GARDEN STEPS

#1 & 2 (Above and Right): STEPS SHOULD BE BROAD ENOUGH TO BE IN PROPORTION TO THEIR SURROUNDINGS. THE SECTION AT THE RIGHT SHOWS TYPICAL CONSTRUCTION ADAPTABLE TO STONE OR BRICK. CONCRETE FOUNDATIONS OR RUBBLE STONE MAY BE USED, AND, IF DESIRED, THE VISIBLE PORTIONS MAY BE LAID UP DRY. LARGE ENOUGH STONES MUST BE USED. HOWEVER, TO MAKE THE WORK STABLE, BRICK MUST ALWAYS BE MORTARED

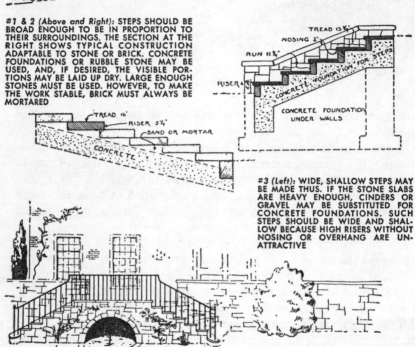

#3 (Left): WIDE, SHALLOW STEPS MAY BE MADE THUS. IF THE STONE SLABS ARE HEAVY ENOUGH, CINDERS OR GRAVEL MAY BE SUBSTITUTED FOR CONCRETE FOUNDATIONS. SUCH STEPS SHOULD BE WIDE AND SHALLOW BECAUSE HIGH RISERS WITHOUT NOSING OR OVERHANG ARE UNATTRACTIVE

#4 (Above): A PLAIN IRON RAIL DOES MUCH TO GIVE FINISH TO THIS DECORATIVE DOUBLE FLIGHT OF FLAGSTONE STEPS ON STONE RISERS. BUT THE BUILDING BEHIND SUCH AN ELABORATE APPROACH MUST BE WORTHY OF IT

#5 (Right): TO BUILD LOG STEPS, SET THE BOTTOM LOG FIRST, HOLD IT IN PLACE WITH TWO STOUT WOODEN OR STEEL PEGS DRIVEN 2' INTO THE GROUND AT EACH END. THEN FILL IN BEHIND THE LOG TO FORM THE NEXT HIGHER STEP, SET THE NEXT LOG AND SO ON. THE BANKS CAN BE HELD IN PLACE BY SMALL ROCKS, AND ATRACTIVELY PLANTED

#6 (Below): CURVED STEPS, THOUGH MORE EXPENSIVE ARE MUCH MORE INTERESTING THAN STRAIGHT ONES. THIS FIGHT LEADS TRAFFIC FROM ALL PARTS OF THE LAWN (upper level) TO THE MORE CONFINED PATTERN OF THE GARDEN BELOW. ALWAYS HAVE CURVED STONES CUT AT THE STONE YARD

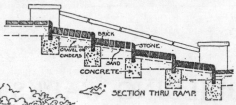

BRICK
GRAVEL OF CINDERS STONE
SAND
CONCRETE

SECTION THRU RAMP.

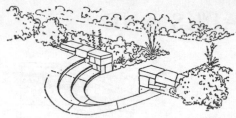

#7 (Above): SLOPES TOO FLAT TO ACCOMMODATE STEPS BUT TOO STEEP FOR EASY ASCENT MAY BE TREATED THIS WAY. BE SURE THE RISER STONES ARE FIRMLY HELD IN PLACE. THE SLOPING STEPS THEMSELVES CAN BE PAVED WITH BRICK OR STONE, OR COVERED WITH FINE GRAVEL OR TANBARK

#8 (Below): DIRECTION OF TRAVEL MAY BE INDICATED BY STEP TREATMENTS. HERE A RAMP ALONG ONE SIDE AND NONE ON THE OTHER SHOWS THAT TRAVEL FOLLOWS THE ARROWS

#4 (Above): WITH VARIABLE CURVED TREADS WIDER AT BOTTOM OF FLIGHT, IS THE IDEAL FOR FLIGHTS OF 7 OR MORE STEPS LEADING FROM HOUSE OR TERRACE

#9 (Below): IN THIS DOUBLE FLIGHT THE LOWER ONE HAS NO RAMP, INVITING ASCENT. UPPER FLIGHT HAS SLOPING RAMP TO GIVE A FEELING OF ADDED PROTECTION, DESIRABLE BECAUSE OF GREATER HEIGHT FROM THE GROUND

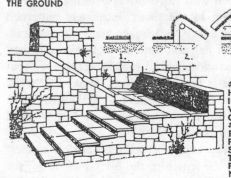

#10 (Above): THESE FOUR SKETCHES SHOW HOW TO MAKE SOD STEPS. #1: THE SUPPORTING PIPE WHICH SHOULD EXTEND ACROSS THE WHOLE WIDTH OF THE FLIGHT; SPACE CUT OUT TO RECEIVE THE FIRST PIECE OF SOD. #2: THIS SOD SET IN AND FOLDED OVER THE PIPE. #3: A TEMPORARY RISER SUPPORT IN PLACE, THE SOD FOLDED BACK OVER IT, AND SOIL TO FORM NEXT STEP FILLED IN AND TAMPED. #4: SOD FOLDED BACK TO ITS FINAL POSITION, TAMPED, CUT OFF TO RECEIVE THE NEXT PIECE; PIPE SUPPORT FOR THE NEXT STEP IN PLACE. REPEAT OPERATIONS FOR EACH STEP

HENRY B. RAYMORE

BUILDING WALKS AND PAVEMENTS

Landscape schemes are based on lines and areas on the ground. These form the structural basis for all plant compositions. The lines are either the center lines of areas (each of these lines is called "axis"), or lines of circulation, which often determine the shape of the various areas they traverse and which establish the coherence of the whole design by linking together its various sections. There should be no path, therefore, unless a basic line of circulation demands it, or unless it forms part of a geometric pattern.

The type of construction and the surface material of any path or paved area should be chosen both with a view to appearance and the use to which it is to be put. If it is just a utility path to get to the back door, or the garage, dryshod, there is no reason to make it elaborate. If, however, it is a featured area in the garden, then material, color, texture and scale are important.

Turf paths are most suitable in the simple garden, where the principal feature is the color in the flower beds. But they do not stand up under heavy traffic, and if they are to be used constantly, some more durable material is better. Brick blends well with surrounding planting and gives a feeling of quaintness and charm to the small, intricately patterned garden. Flag is useful for broader effects and larger areas like terraces, where furniture is to be used. Thin flag and slate are both useful if they are set in cement, but the pieces are too light to remain in place without this added holding material. Slate is the most colorful type of material obtainable, but it has the defect of flaking off under conditions of heavy frost. Heavy flag and brick, thoroughly tamped, can be laid in sand without trouble from loose bricks or stones.

To determine the width of a brick walk, between the edging courses, use a "module" which consists of the length of the brick plus ½ in. for the joint. Add to any multiple of this another ½ in. for the end joint,

#1 *(Below)*: **FLAGSTONE OR SLATE TERRACES ARE USUALLY RECTANGULAR, BUT ARE OFTEN MORE INTERESTING IF GIVEN SOME OTHER SHAPE AND PROVIDED WITH AN ADDED FEATURE LIKE THE RAISED FLAGSTONE POOL SHOWN IN THE ACCOMPANYING DRAWING. IF HEAVY FLAG IS USED IT MAY BE SET ON A SAND BED. SLATE OR LIGHT FLAG SHOULD BE SET IN CEMENT**

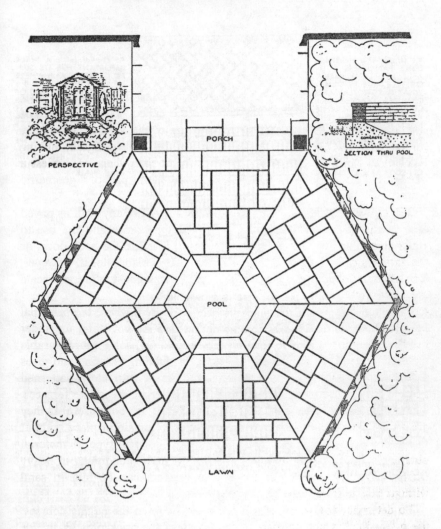

PERSPECTIVE

SECTION THRU POOL

PORCH

POOL

LAWN

#2 (Left): THE SIMPLEST AND MOST ECONOMICAL BRICK PATTERN IS THE ONE SHOWN. IT IS SUITABLE FOR A UTILITY WALK THAT IS NOT TO BE EMPHASIZED IN THE LANDSCAPE

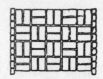

#3 (Right): A MORE INTERESTING PATTERN IS THE FAMILIAR "BASKET" DESIGN. HERE THE EDGING BRICKS HAVE BEEN SET ON END, GIVING GREATER DEPTH AND STABILITY

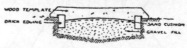

#4 (Upper rt.): HERRINGBONE PATTERN IS SUITABLE FOR EITHER BRICK OR TILE, BUT IS SOMEWHAT HARD TO LAY AND REQUIRES CONSIDERABLE CUTTING. IT MAY BE DONE AS SHOWN, WITH THE BRICK TRIANGLES ALONG THE EDGE, OR BY CUTTING OFF THE CORNERS OF THE OUTER ROW OF BRICK. THE EDGE, HERE, IS "SAW-TOOTH", BRICK SET ON EDGE AT A 45° ANGLE

#5 (Lower left): A WALK IMPORTANT FOR ITS SURFACE TEXTURE AND WHERE LENGTH IS TO BE STRESSED MAY BE LAID OF BRICK ON EDGE IN THIS SORT OF PATTERN. IT USES MANY MORE BRICK THAN THOSE WHERE BRICK IS LAID FLAT, BUT IS MORE SOLID. ONE WOULD VARY THIS PATTERN ACCORDING TO THE WIDTH OF ANY PARTICULAR WALK

=6 (Above): HERE IS SHOWN THE METHOD OF USING A TEMPLATE TO SMOOTH THE BED BEFORE LAYING THE FIELD BRICK. SET THE EDGINGS FIRST, THEN DRAW THE TEMPLATE ALONG, SMOOTHING OUT THE SAND FOUNDATION. CURVE THE BOTTOM OF THE TEMPLATE TO FORM THE CROWN (About ½" For A 4' Walk).

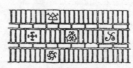

#7 (Above): THIS OLD SPANISH VARIATION OF THE BASKET PATTERN IS SUITABLE FOR TERRACES AND OTHER LARGE SPACES, OR AS AN INSERT IN WALKS OF OTHER PATTERNS OR MATERIALS

#9 (Above): IN THIS PATTERN 8" x 8" COLORED TILES HAVE BEEN INSERTED AT INTERVALS TO GIVE GREATER VARIETY TO A BRICK WALK

#8 (Above): IN THIS VARIATION OF THE BASKET PATTERN EIGHTH BRICKS OR QUARTER BRICKS SET ON END CAN BE USED FOR THE SMALL UNITS. IF UNEVENNESS IS NO DETRIMENT, SMALL, LONG STONES SET ON END WILL DO

#10 (Right): FOR A VERY WIDE WALK, FLAG AND BRICK COMBINE WELL. FOR NARROWER WALKS LEAVE OFF THE OUTER FLAG EDGINGS. THE SECTION ILLUSTRATES THE METHOD OF CONSTRUCTION, ON A GRAVEL FOUNDATION

#11 (Below): SKETCH AND PLAN. AROUND A SMALL DIPPING POOL A REGULAR FLAG PATTERN IS MORE EFFECTIVE THAN AN IRREGULAR ONE. NOTE THE PLANTING POCKETS WHERE AROMATIC PLANTS COULD SUITABLY BE USED

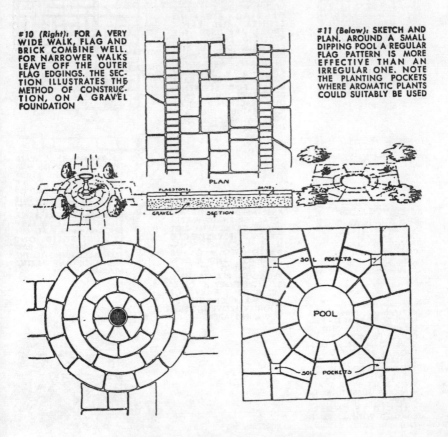

PLAN

FLAGSTONE   SAND

GRAVEL   SECTION

POOL

SOIL POCKETS

SOIL POCKETS

#12 (Above, Left): SKETCH AND PLAN. AROUND A BIRD BATH OR SUN DIAL SET AT THE CROSSING OF TWO WALKS, A FLAG PATTERN OF CONCENTRIC CIRCLES IS EFFECTIVE. IT REQUIRES EXPERT CUTTING, WHICH YOUR DEALER WILL HAVE DONE FOR YOU IF YOU FURNISH HIM WITH A DETAILED DRAWING AND DIMENSIONS. #13 (Left): OLD FLAT STONES FROM A STONE WALL MAKE A SERVICEABLE THOUGH UNEVEN PATH. #14 (Right): IN THE ORIGINAL OF THIS OLD FRENCH DESIGN, THE CENTER OF THE WALK WAS DEPRESSED AND SERVED AS A DRAIN ON WET DAYS

PLAN

GRITS   BRICK

GRAVEL BASE
TILE

SECTION

#15 (Left): GRAVEL WALKS MAY BE MADE EASIER TO WALK ON, AND TO KEEP WITHIN BOUNDS, IF BRICK OR FLAG STEPPING STONES, AND BRICK EDGES, ARE USED. THE SECTION SHOWS THE CONSTRUCTION. THE TILE DRAIN IS NEEDED ONLY IN HEAVY, WET SOILS.
#16 (Right): BELGIAN BLOCKS OR "SETS" ARE IDEAL FOR SLOPING DRIVEWAYS WHERE THEY GIVE TRACTION EVEN IN ICY WEATHER. THEY ARE MOST SATISFACTORY FOR ENTRANCE COURTS

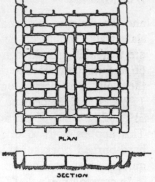

PLAN

SECTION

TURF   CURB

RICH LOAM   PLG

TILE

SECTION

#18 (Right): TAN BARK OR PINE NEEDLE TRAILS ARE IDEAL FOR SHADY PLACES WHERE GRASS WILL NOT GROW. THEY SHOULD HAVE A GRAVEL FOUNDATION TO PROVIDE DRAINAGE, AND A DURABLE EDGING, 2" x 8" REDWOOD PLANKS HELD BY PEGS EVERY 5' OR 6' ARE GOOD. THE LEVEL OF THE WALK SHOULD BE SLIGHTLY ABOVE THE SURROUNDING AREAS

TAN BARK   CURB

GRAVEL BASE

PLG

SECTION

#17 (Above): TURF WALKS NEED SOME SORT OF PERMANENT EDGE, AND A GOOD FOUNDATION OF RICH LOAM. STEEL EDGING, AT PRESENT UNOBTAINABLE, IS BEST, BUT THIN REDWOOD OR CYPRESS STRIPS HELD BY PEGS EVERY 5' OR 6' ARE A GOOD SUBSTITUTE. IN HEAVY SOIL TURF WALKS SHOULD BE UNDERDRAINED WITH 4" AGRITILE

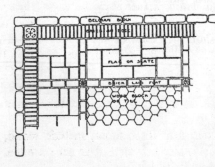

#19 (Above and at left): IN THESE DRAWINGS SEVERAL SORTS OF MATERIAL HAVE BEEN COMBINED IN A SINGLE ELABORATE PATTERN. ONLY WHERE VARIETY OF TEXTURES IS THE PRINCIPAL ELEMENT IN THE DESIGN, SUCH AS IN PATIOS, COURTS, AND THE LIKE, WOULD SUCH ELABORATENESS BE IN GOOD TASTE. USE DISCRETION. THE SKETCH SHOWS FLAG OR SLATE COMBINED WITH BRICK OR BELGIAN BLOCK IN A TERRACE. THE PLAN ALSO INCLUDES WOOD BLOCK AND TILE, BOTH OF WHICH ARE USEFUL AND BEAUTIFUL MATERIALS FOR SUCH A PURPOSE. WOOD BLOCK PARTICULARLY HAS MANY POSSIBILITIES FOR GARDEN USE THAT HAVE NOT BEEN DEVELOPED and the distance between edgings is arrived at. The width of flag and slate walks should be determined by the dimensions of the pieces that are available. Avoid cutting as much as possible, for it is difficult to do and wasteful of material. If you purchase an assortment of sizes, lay them out first, loosely, on the ground, to work out the pattern.

Walks laid in cement should have the joints at least slightly raked so that the lines of the individual units are not blurred or obliterated. This applies both to brick and flag. In ordering brick be sure to get hard-burned brick suitable for outdoor use. Soft brick will go to pieces quickly from frost action.

In constructing a walk, as shown in Figure 6, after you have smoothed the sand bed with the template, lay the field brick for quite a distance. Then fill the joints with sifted sand, wash it in, sweep off the surplus thoroughly and lay a heavy plank lengthwise of the walk against one curb. Pound the plank with a heavy tamper to set the brick or stone. Move the plank along, and thus cover the whole area. Then fill the joints again with sand, wash in, and brush off the surplus.

HENRY B. RAYMORE

PERMANENT EDGES FOR WALKS

An inanimate edge, as opposed to a living edge, is often the answer to the problem of providing a suitable line of demarcation between flower borders and walks or lawns and walks.

In the 15th Century, the shank bones of sheep were among the inanimate edges used. These were "stuck in the ground, the small end downwards, which will become white, and prettily grace out the ground". This suggests that our forefathers did not mind a charnel house atmosphere in their gardens, and that mutton was considerably cheaper than it is today.

Other inanimate edges, more practical in these times, include wood, metal strips (zinc, aluminum, or steel), stone or slate flags set on edge, uncut rocks, tile, terra cotta, or concrete curbing.

The character of the walks is related to the kind of edging used and each must be considered together. Often the edge of the walk itself may provide an effective and practical line of demarcation. This is especially true of concrete walks, the most utilitarian but not necessarily the most beautiful or pleasant to walk upon. However, that "concrete look" can be minimized by adding mineral pigments of the color desired (not more than 5 pounds per 100 pounds of cement, however), and by scoring the surface.

If there is a lawn area on one side, concrete walks should be laid so that they are level with the grade on the lawn side and an inch or two above soil level on the side nearest the flower border. This raised edge may be provided by means of a concrete curb or, preferably, when conditions permit, by grading the soil surface to just below the walk. The concrete itself should be 3 inches thick, laid on a cinder foundation or its equivalent about 9 inches deep. Walks of this nature permit plants to grow to the extreme limit of the front of the border because there is no danger of their being lopped off by lawn mowers or clippers. The planting can be either formal with a line of edging plants or informal with a variety of plants some of which deliberately are allowed to encroach on the walk.

Except for their usually better appearance, flagstone or brick walks have much the same qualities and edging potentialities as concrete walks. Flagstone walks may be of cut stones, square or rectangular, laid in either a regular or random pattern; or, the stones may be the irregular kind known as crazy paving. The last named demands a border of similar stones laid on edge to make a really effective edge, either flush with the grade or slightly raised according to circumstances. Flagstones may be set in concrete and grouted with cement, or laid on a dry foundation and the interstices filled with sand.

Brick walks, properly laid, are both pleasing and effective when suitably located. The edges may be bricks stood on end, or laid edgewise, either set flush with the walk or slightly raised. Like flagstone walks, they may be cemented or laid on a sand bed. Their lack of flexibility (it is difficult to lay a brick walk along a curved line) is their chief defect.

A foundation similar to that suggested for concrete walks is necessary, or at least desirable, for brick and flagstone walks. I have, however, known flagstones to be fairly successful when merely laid on the surface of sandy, well-drained soil.

Although I have seen and admired a garden in which there was no definite line of demarcation between the gravel walk and the flower border, with clumps of Nepeta, Ajuga, and Dianthus occasionally encroaching upon the walk, in general gravel, cinder (ugh!), or soil walks usually need something in the way of edging to prevent co-mingling of soil of the flower border with the material of the walk. There is a variety of material available.

A more formal edging to a border is achieved when flagstones are cut in squares or rectangles to make a permanent, winter-proof path.

An informal gravel path meanders between garden borders with nothing but a row of uncut stones to separate garden and walk. A few plants can spill over on the path.

One of the most pleasing edgings to a perennial border I have ever seen was of rather blocky rocks of various sizes set about 6 inches above the level of the walk and interplanted with easily grown rock plants such as Dianthus and Aubrieta. If a more formal setting is needed, the edging can be metal strips about 3 inches wide held in place by metal stakes, driven at least a foot in the ground, flush with the upper edge of the strip. Or, paving tiles can be used, set on edge with the major portion below ground.

Sometimes tiles are available made especially for edging purposes, with the top-edge ornamented. Usually, however, the less obtrusive the edging material the better is the general effect. Tiles, except perhaps in a frost-free region, will need to be reset periodically due to heaving as one of the effects of winter. This of course could be obviated by putting in a foundation and setting them in concrete. Before doing this, however, be very sure in your mind that you will never want to change the location of the walk or the flower border, an exhortation which applies also to builders of concrete, flagstone, or brick walks, if they are laid in cement.

An edging of brick is charming as well as useful. Notice how the path slopes slightly toward the lawn, with the edged bricks raised above the walk on the garden side, but flush with the grass.

A low retaining wall makes an attractive border edging, particularly when the garden is on a slope. Rock plants may be planted in the wall. Here the path at the base of the wall is gravel.

When flower borders have to be made across a slope, it is often desirable to make the lower edge in the form of a wall from 1 to 3 feet high. This may be of bricks or cemented masonry, or a dry rock wall may be constructed which offers a splendid opportunity to insert plants in the chinks. When edges of this nature are used, it is desirable to avoid grass walks because of mowing.

Walks of tan bark, like those of gravel, need a defining edge except when they are used in a woodland or wildflower garden. An appropriate edging to keep tan bark in place is wood strips about 3 inches wide and an inch thick held in place by wood or steel stakes. Such an edging can be fairly permanent if wood resistant to decay, such as Cypress, is used; or, other lumber treated with Cuprinol. Don't be tempted to use creosote as a preservative, which is toxic to plant life.

As a lawn edging, either in association with a gravel walk or a flower bed, probably the best of all is a metal strip set flush with the grade. Next best is a concrete or stone curb. Never, if you can avoid it, use rough stone or rock edging in conjunction with Grass—it is tough on the lawn mower and anathema to the user.

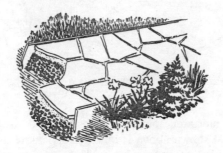

Flagstones laid on edge provide separation between walk and garden. To facilitate mowing, the edging should be flush with the lawn on that side. Flagstones can be laid on a sand or cinder bed.

MONTAGUE FREE

HAVE YOU TRIED CONCRETE BLOCKS?

Ugly ducklings though they may at first seem, concrete blocks are pretty useful members of the family of structural materials. While they will never turn out to be swans, they have, when properly handled, dignity and functional simplicity that can approach the handsome effects of far more expensive masonry.

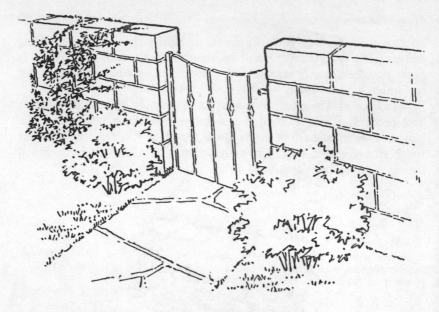

Laid up with mortared joints, perhaps painted with cement paints, such a wall as that shown above is quick, inexpensive and easy for even a ham-and-eggs kind of handyman to make. (Corner and cap blocks are used above where the familiar "holes" would otherwise show.) Used for such projects as are suggested on the following pages, their adaptability is obvious.

While some uses are "premeditated," calling for properly timed deliveries by the supply dealer's truck, others involve only a dozen or so blocks which are easy to keep "on inventory" around the place, just as you'd keep, say, old burlap bags, extra stakes, chicken wire, and spare bushel baskets. Every time you use them one way, you get a couple of other ideas.

Accompanying the drawings that follow are further notes on types and sizes of blocks generally available. Not all suppliers carry all kinds.

Two sizes of block—8x8x16 and 4x8x16 (back of seat) are used in decorative low wall above. Good footings, cement joints are required for permanence. Capping is of brick designs.

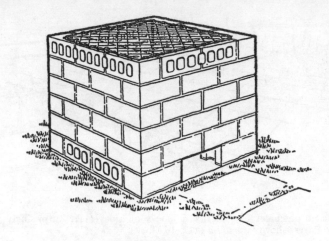

Set on sand or cinder base, improvised rubbish burner, needs no mortar joints; besides, what if they do need straightening each spring? Blocks on sides admit air for effective burning.

"Poor man's" version of terrace or low retaining wall is shown above. Holes may or may not split out with frost. Interlocking idea is primarily to vary the surface monotony, may add strength.

With sand or cinder bed, 4x18x16 blocks on sides make surprisingly good walks. Edgers shown are solid 3x12x16 blocks.

As temporary or permanent steps, standard blocks are good looking, durable, inexpensive, stand frost very well.

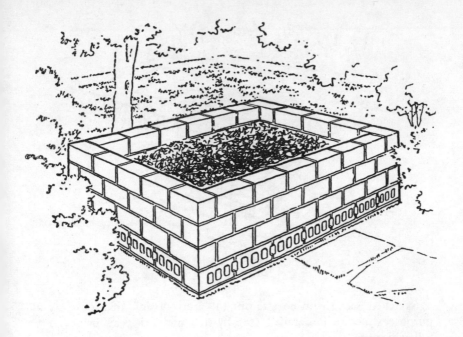

With or without cap and corner blocks or mortar, compost pits may be quickly set up; are as readily re-arranged or moved.

RALPH BAILEY

FOUR-WAY FIREPLACE

Most of you who make a point of living in your garden have experienced the smoke-filled lungs, burned fingers, bleary eyes and general frustration that can slay all the joys of outdoor cooking. The portable grills are either too flimsy or too costly to fill the bill. The simple little rustic hearths won't draw or won't cook. Fancy monuments with proper flues are for professionals.

Here is a careful attempt, based upon considerable experience, to provide a practical, adaptable, relatively simple apparatus for cooking a family spread in the back yard.

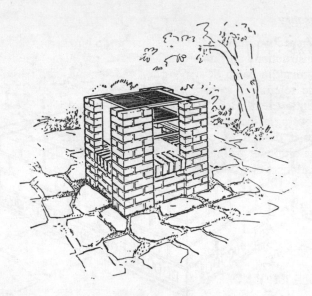

Sketched above with no attempt to "pretty it up", this four-way all-purpose structure is detailed step-by-step and brick by brick on the following pages.

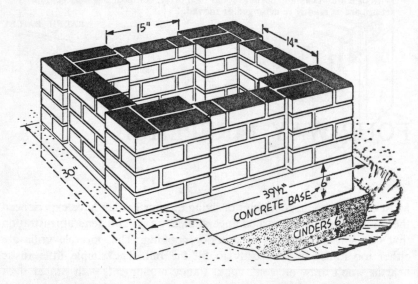

ABOVE: Step 1: Excavate foundation footing hole 12 inches deep by 30 by 39½ inches, allow space for wood forms if needed. Step 2: Tamp 6-inch cinder or sand layer. Step 3: Build forms if needed. Pour concrete base 6 inches thick. Allow to set thoroughly. Step 4: Lay bricks shown; allow mortar to set.

The perspective working drawings have been planned to make detailed written instructions all but unnecessary for any home handyman who has ever mixed a batch of cement and mortar and laid a brick.

Specific references to aspects of the construction are made in the supplementary text. Here are some general suggestions: Bear in mind when choosing a location that this "stove" can be worked at from all four sides if desired. Avoid placing it directly beneath tree branches. Improvise alternate grill recommendations if you wish, but be sure your improvisations will work. Count on charcoal or "briquets" for fuel.

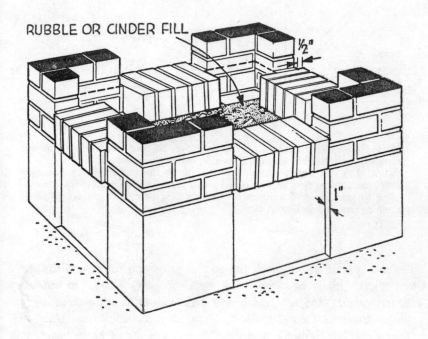

RUBBLE OR CINDER FILL

ABOVE: Step 5: Fill center with rubble or cinders and tamp. Step 6: Lay "soldiers" (bricks on edge) at low slope down toward outside between corners. Lay up L-shaped corner posts as detailed.

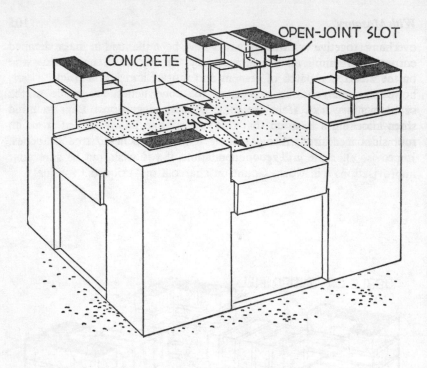

CONCRETE OPEN-JOINT SLOT

SLOPE

ABOVE: Step 7: Pour concrete ash floor over fill to dotted line on drawing above; troweling to higher point in center; match slope of "soldiers."
Step 8: Lay bricks shown with black tops. Study this and following drawings with great care, as slots here involved are of great importance. (If you are not going to purchase grill units mentioned on next pair of pages, do your re-planning now and with great care.)

The rest is plain sailing, with the special grills and frame and the sheet iron slides (made by your local metal worker) shown in cut-away fashion (*right*) and the frame and grill unit as manufactured by the Donley Brothers Co., Cleveland, Ohio. It is called Range Unit 20A (Catalogue, 8th Edition), and this one has a width of 18 inches, length of 29 inches, height of 14 inches. The door at one end must be sawed off. As adapted, it would weigh below 100 pounds. Grills are removable, may be used at three levels.

You will have noted from a study of all drawings that the mortar joints between bricks are slightly "raked" to give a shadow line and add pleasing texture to the whole. You will also have noted that the "soldier" overhang, together with the one-inch toe space let into the base between corners, will simplify cleaning out ashes and refuse. There is no paint on the metal work, which, since it is cast iron, is resistant to rust. It is, however, brittle, and if removed for winter storage should be placed out of harm's way. With the lower grills removed, incidentally, and the sheet metal sides adjusted for draft and wind direction, it makes a fine rubbish burner from which blazing paper cannot escape.

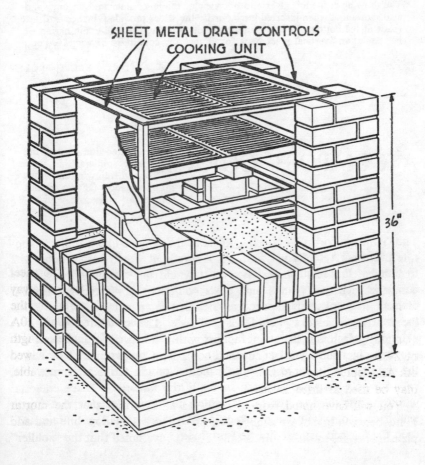

SHEET METAL DRAFT CONTROLS
COOKING UNIT

36"

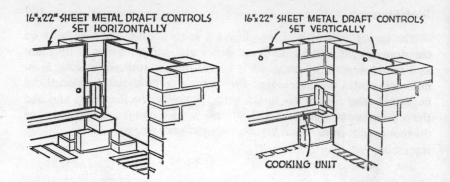

16"x22" SHEET METAL DRAFT CONTROLS
SET HORIZONTALLY

16"x22" SHEET METAL DRAFT CONTROLS
SET VERTICALLY

COOKING UNIT

When dropped into place vertically (right), the sheet metal draft controls will go clear to the floor of the fire pit. Thus one, two, or three sides may be shut off from prevailing winds or to hold heat in or to slow the fire. But in handling these when there is a fire going, remember that sheet iron gets hot; wear gloves. The drawing at the left gives another view of the inner slots and masonry and also shows that when inserted horizontally the slides provide 6 inches of draft space at the bottom. By experimenting you will find the best combination of horizontal and vertical placement for almost any conditions of wind, fire and use.

RALPH BAILEY

A COMPOST CORRAL

The "compost corral", opposite, looks at first glance like a pretty elabo-rate business. Actually it is not. As it stands, it would cost around $12 to build of first-hand materials, but it would last virtually forever. Its design is such that planks and posts could be substituted for cement blocks (the planks being spaced an inch or two apart for aeration, which the mortarless blocks would also allow). The compartmentation is planned to facilitate the manufacture within the cycle of a season ap-proximately a cubic yard of finished compost. Compartment No. 1 is at the right and is the largest. Compartment No. 2 is the next largest, and calls for no wire, since no fresh or really dry material is to be enclosed within it. The third compartment, which may be enclosed with a fourth wall if desired, is laid one block deep. It receives and may contain until used the finished or near-finished product.

The actual construction of the corral is clearly enough explained by the drawings. If one whole extra course or row of blocks can be laid as a foundation below grade, so much the better. But this is not strictly necessary, since on reasonably firm, level ground frost heaving will be negligible. The corner blocks are held in position by the iron rods, and the others may be quickly lined up if you are finicky. A little study of the diagrams will show how the two rows are arranged for something resembling an interlocking effect.

The operation of such a plant as this might be, basically, as follows: upon completion of construction (prior to setting up the wire fencing) remove 6 inches or so of the sod or soil in the floor of the largest, or "receiving," compartment. Then spread a layer of material to be composted to an approximated depth of 6 inches or so. Cover this with an inch or so of soil and, preferably, a good handful of ground limestone. Repeat the process until the material at hand has all been used, always finishing up with a layer of soil.

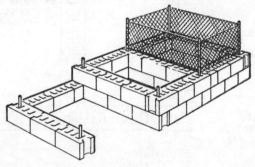

(See detail drawings on page 110)

As new waste material comes to hand, dump it in the compartment until there is sufficient to make another "deck."

Unless this filling is all done at once to the capacity of the fencing as well as the blocks, the fence will actually serve as part of the container only if a very loose, dry type of material, such as a row or two of cut Pea vines, is put in. For the most part the wire serves to keep light, dry material from blowing away and as a receptacle for leaves and cut-back plant tops in the fall. This sort of stuff can be left for the snows to pack down over winter. (Little effective decomposition—bacterial action, in other words—will take place during frigid weather, though frost action will help break up the contents of the bin.)

If you start the cycle, say, in August, layer and firm the raw material

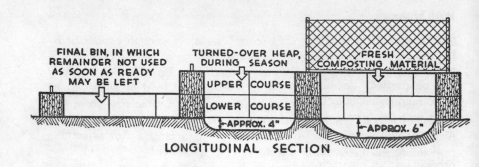

FINAL BIN, IN WHICH REMAINDER NOT USED AS SOON AS READY MAY BE LEFT

TURNED-OVER HEAP, DURING SEASON

FRESH COMPOSTING MATERIAL

UPPER COURSE

LOWER COURSE

APPROX. 4"

APPROX. 6"

LONGITUDINAL SECTION

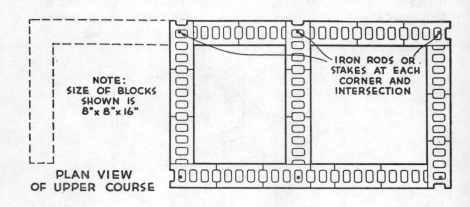

NOTE: SIZE OF BLOCKS SHOWN IS 8" x 8" x 16"

IRON RODS OR STAKES AT EACH CORNER AND INTERSECTION

PLAN VIEW OF UPPER COURSE

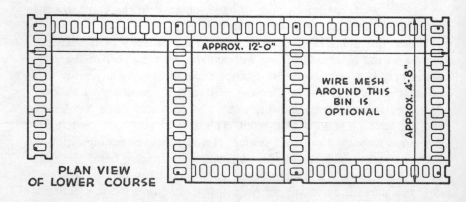

APPROX. 12'-0"

WIRE MESH AROUND THIS BIN IS OPTIONAL

APPROX. 4'-8"

PLAN VIEW OF LOWER COURSE

faithfully. Then when cool weather comes, fork over the contents of bin No. 1 into bin No. 2, repeating the excavating and earth-spreading process in much the same way as before. Now, however, the material will be partially decomposed and will not only mix, stack and settle more readily but take far less space. All fall clean-up (of a non-woody sort) and any leaves you can save may then be collected in bin No. 1, as mentioned before.

If the cycle is to begin in spring, then bin No. 2 should receive the product of bin No. 1 by mid-July, and bin No. 3 should receive this spring charge by early September. Before winter, usable compost will be yours.

This is one order of procedure, and a very general one. It calls for no applications of chemical fertilizer, for no proprietary "composting" compounds, for no manure. The use of any of these, or discreet combinations of complete fertilizer and manure (the latter alternating with or supplementing soil layers) will speed decomposition. All will require more attention to maintenance of moisture in the pile and will thus require the presence, usually by holes made with a crowbar or through cracks or gaps in the walls, of more air—lest either too much heat or rotting instead of orderly decomposition result.

RALPH BAILEY

SPECIAL
GARDENS

HOW TO BUILD
A GARDEN POOL

Many ingrained home gardeners have an inexorable urge to learn whether their green thumb can be a wet one too. Aquatic plants are not difficult to grow; they take only a minimum of know-how. A small garden pool is not hard to construct. But the perennial optimist is not always the experimenter.

He rides home from the office thinking of all the reasons why he should have a pool, picturing in what spot in the yard it should be built. The pages of his water plant catalogues are finger-marked from turning. Perhaps all his measuring of pros and cons leads him past every obstacle but one that remains a question: Would it be a safety hazard to children?

Some unprotected deep garden pools can be dangerous, and tragedies have happened. But without unusual precautions a shallow pool will

not be a menace. Because it is so shallow, here is such a pool, and it is one whose construction is not forbidding.

The accompanying drawings are intended to serve not as a specific design in themselves but rather to present the elements of a scheme. Pools, of course, can be formal or informal. In plan they can be round, half round, elliptical, square, rectangular, or combinations of these and other shapes. For naturalistic settings or for contrast, they can be unconventional and casual in form. The same construction elements apply.

Heavy sheet-steel pools of different designs and shapes are obtainable from handlers of water garden materials. A comparative newcomer on the market is the small pliable plastic pool. And from England comes word that a manufacturer there has an aluminum pool, shallow save for Lily pockets, available in this country. These all represent something of a shortcut to an end but do not lend themselves to individual designs for particular purposes. Concrete still remains a universal material that permits any design and, when properly handled, offers great permanence.

STEP-BY-STEP DETAILS FOR THE HOME HANDYMAN

The water gardener must first base his plan on a few fundamental rules. With these he may then settle on a course of procedure.

1. Full sunlight is necessary for best growth and formation of blossoms.

2. Allow 9 square feet of water area for each Lily or Lotus in small pools and more in larger pools.

3. Provide a minimum of 1 cubic foot of soil for each Lily or Lotus.

4. Plan for no less than 6 inches of water above the soil in a Lily tub.

5. Remember that Water-lily and Lotus roots are not deep growing. They require more width than depth—a minimum diameter of 18 inches.

6. Include oxygenating plants in containers by themselves: small boxes or 5-inch pots. Tops of pots should have fully 6 inches of water over them.

7. Provide 6 to 12 inches of soil depth for bog plants.

When size and shape are settled, planning for actual construction can start. Excavation is first, and this can commence when the proposed form of the pool has been marked out on the ground. The drawings show concrete 6 inches thick for the bottom and sides of the pool and bog, as well as for the floor and walls of the Lily pockets. This should not be skimped because a concrete failure in a pool means a leaking pool. In excavating, allowance must be made not only for the thickness of the concrete but

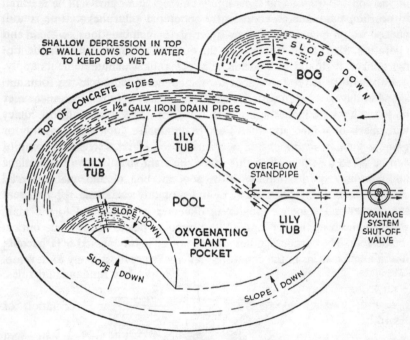

SHALLOW DEPRESSION IN TOP
OF WALL ALLOWS POOL WATER
TO KEEP BOG WET

SLOPE DOWN

BOG

TOP OF CONCRETE SIDES →

1½" GALV. IRON DRAIN PIPES

LILY TUB

LILY TUB

LILY TUB

OVERFLOW STANDPIPE

DRAINAGE SYSTEM SHUT-OFF VALVE

POOL

OXYGENATING PLANT POCKET

SLOPE DOWN

SLOPE DOWN

SLOPE DOWN

SLOPE DOWN

PLAN OF POOL AND BOG

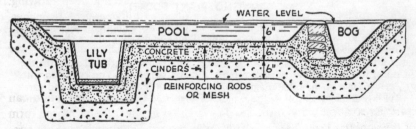

WATER LEVEL

POOL — 6"

BOG

LILY TUB

CONCRETE 6"

CINDERS 6"

REINFORCING RODS OR MESH

DIAGRAMMATIC SECTION THROUGH POOL AND BOG

One reason more people don't have garden pools is their danger to small children. Except for plant pockets, this is 6 inches deep. Actual size and shape is immaterial except for labor and materials also another 6 inches for gravel or cinders. This is an essential, particularly in climates with wide temperature ranges, to provide good drainage and thereby minimize the effects of freezing. Next the cinders are placed in position and wetted and thoroughly tamped. Some care will be required to position the cinders cylindrically about the Lily pockets into a well packed wall 6 inches thick. A cylinder of ½-inch wire mesh will aid this operation. Since this is to serve as the outer form for the concrete wall of the pocket, it should be done in a workmanlike manner.

Fabricating the reinforcement for the concrete is done to the form and shape of the excavation with the cinders in place. This reinforcement may be ¼-inch rods 6 inches apart each way, but it is less work to use heavy wire mesh of 4-inch squares. This is obtainable in widths possibly as great as the narrow dimension of a small pool. If not, two or more widths can be wired together. With this made the right size, laid on the cinders, and bent into conformation with the pool and bog, circular pieces can be cut out for the Lily pockets. A cylinder of the wire mesh the depth of the pocket and 4 inches greater in diameter is then wired to the main sheet of mesh at the top and to the circular piece, already cut out, at the bottom. The wiring together should not be lightly passed over because it is at angular turns in the concrete that cracks are most likely to develop.

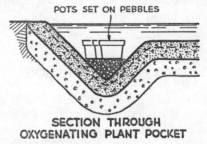

POTS SET ON PEBBLES

SECTION THROUGH
OXYGENATING PLANT POCKET

For a still-water pool, a few oxygenating plants are important, especially if fish are to be maintained in good condition. The drawing above shows how these plants may be accommodated.

If a long lasting, practical pool is desired (and what other kind is worth the effort it takes to build it?) the piping is vitally important. You could do with less—or more—than that diagramed opposite, but the workmanship and careful layout may well follow the principles suggested to control water level and drainage

Some further cutting and wiring may be necessary, perhaps for the oxygenating plant pocket or the bog, depending on shape and depth. In any case, with the job finished, the mesh can be left in position at the level of the cinders until concrete pouring starts.

One part portland cement, 2 parts sand, and 3 parts gravel make the best concrete for garden pools. The amount of water used per sack of cement is important. Four and one half to 5 gallons can be tried for the first batch to make a plastic mix, right to hold its shape but not crumbly. If too stiff, the next batch can be made with less sand and gravel, or if too wet, with more.

The entire pouring job should be done in one operation and should be completed in a half hour. This calls for good planning for the reason, among others, that the reinforcing mesh must be correctly located. It is done by raising the mesh into position during pouring. The correct position is 4 inches from the cinder side of the ultimate 6-inch thickness of concrete—or 2 inches from the finished surface. The raising operation is accomplished by pulling the mesh up at a number of strategic points with an improvised heavy wire hook after a couple of inches of concrete cover the bottom of the pool. This is repeated when the 4-inch thickness has been poured, and the mesh is then buried here with the final 2-inch thickness. A surer method of positioning the reinforcing, but one that takes more doing, is to suspend it at its finally desired location, before pouring starts, with wires from sufficiently rigid boards laid horizontally across the excavation.

To place the walls of the Lily pockets, the wooden tub, later to contain the plant, is used as the form. After the floor of the pocket is poured, the tub is set into the pocket and the walls are poured. Because the tub is in the form of an inverted truncated cone, if it was first thoroughly wet and is revolved slightly back and forth soon after pouring it can be removed when the walls have set. As an alternative a bottomless, collapsible, square wooden box of proper size can be used for a form instead of the tub. This can be homemade, but both round and square Cedar or Cypress tubs are available at water garden suppliers. A usable size for a commercially obtainable round tub is 21 inches in diameter and 11 inches in depth, and for the square tub, 18½ inches at the top and 10 inches deep.

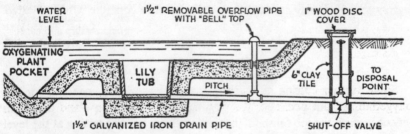

SCHEMATIC SECTION OF DRAINAGE SYSTEM

To place the concrete on the sloping sides a certain amount of hand troweling will be required, and the mix may need to be stiffer than for usual pouring.

When the concrete work is finished, it must not be allowed to dry out too quickly. To protect it from sun and drying wind for a week or ten days, it should be covered with straw, burlap, or canvas and sprinkled often. Another precaution is necessary to prevent injury to plants and fish from alkali. This can be accomplished by filling and emptying the pool several times during a period of at least two weeks. Then, to check the condition, pink litmus paper is placed in the water. If it turns blue, the water is still alkaline and unsafe.

A pool is bound to be an important element of any garden design and will, perhaps, take its place more fittingly in its surroundings if it is edged with a flagstone coping. In the case of the pool shown in the accompanying drawings, the stones may be set about the pool and across the top of the separation between pool and bog, allowing the bog plants to assume their natural forms to cover their concrete.

Now the only consideration omitted in the proper order of operations in most pool construction is water supply and drainage. A small pool is probably most easily filled with the garden hose. A Lily pool does not require fresh running water; in fact, all usual aquatic plants like water that remains at an even, warm temperature. Oxygenating plants and scavengers keep the water pure and clear. But those who wish to do so may run ¼-inch copper tubing to the pool under one of the edging stones. In cold areas provision might well be made for complete drainage.

The ability to drain the water out of a pool is not a requisite. By using the garden hose, water can be syphoned to lower terrain or to the basement drain or laundry tubs. But an easier way is simply to unscrew an overflow standpipe such as is indicated in the drawings. The drain disposal point may be lower ground, a sewer (if the local code permits), or a small dry well, which can be a hole 3 or 4 feet deep and filled with stones nearly to the top and covered with soil. Whatever the type, a drainage system obviously needs to be installed before concrete work is started.

CARL T. SIGMAN
WILLIAM J. WARD, JR.

BUILDING FORMAL POOLS

Formal pools, like formal gardens, need not be stiff, cold or uninviting. They are adapted readily to the regular proportions of the small garden on the average home grounds. The symmetry of their shape is particularly suitable to accent the ordered, balanced design of the distinctly man-made garden.

Whether the garden pool is built to provide a place for aquatic plants and fish, a cooling, decorative feature, a reservoir for dipping purposes, or a combination of these, the fact remains that it is one of the most popular of all the garden structures. Fall and up until freezing weather is the best time of year to build one. In the spring planting takes all the time, while summer heat is not conducive to deep digging and heavy mixing. Autumn is just right for pool and other garden construction.

EXCAVATION AND FORMS

Remember when excavating that the hole must be 1 ft. deeper than the finished depth of the pool. In solid soils, the clean-cut, vertical walls of the excavation may serve as outer forms; in crumbly soils and for pools above ground, both inner and outer forms will be required and the excavation must be at least 1 ft. greater than the finished length and width of the pool.

Forms are constructed of 1-in. boards nailed to braced 2 × 4's spaced 2 to 3 ft. apart. The inner form, suspended from 2 × 4's across the top of the excavation, is held 6 ins. above the drainage base of tamped cinders or gravel. Curved forms are made of 20-gauge galvanized iron.

Place all reinforcing and pipe and fittings before starting to mix and pour the concrete. Reinforcing bars are wired together where they cross or join. They should be held near the middle of the floor and walls.

THE CONCRETE MIXTURE

The standard waterproof concrete mixture consists of 1 part cement, 2 to 2¼ parts sand and 3 parts ½ in. to 1½ in. gravel or crushed stone. The 1 in. size mixes easily and, spaded into the forms, makes a dense concrete. Oil or wet the forms as the concrete is poured. To prevent leaks, material for the floor and walls is placed in one operation.

Forms are removed in 24 to 48 hours and the surfaces to be seen are polished with water and a hard brick or carborundum stone. Raw concrete should be sprinkled twice a day for ten days to make it cure thoroughly, dry out slowly. The twice-daily sprinkling will tend to wash off alkali apt to be present in the water of new concrete pools and harmful to fish and plants. Strong vinegar, added to the first filling at the rate of 1 pt. to 150 gal. of water and flushed out after two or three days, is another method of counteracting alkali.

Pool number 1, in the accompanying collection of formal pools (*opposite and on page 124*), might be built without drain and overflow. It could be emptied with a bucket or siphoned through the hose if a convenient low spot is available.

An ordinary hose nozzle would make a good fountain jet in pool No. 2. It could be adjusted to high or low jet or a narrow or broad spray. In the sketch, the circulating pump and pipes connected with it merely diagram such a system and are not meant to show the actual location of all valves, etc. The valve located next to the pump is closed to re-pack or do other work on the pump without draining the pool. It will be entirely practical to fashion this shallow pool of sheet lead or copper with soldered seams and held in bounds by the same brickwork.

In the strictly ornamental garden, dipping cistern No. 3 might have a decorative fountain head in place of the more practical fountain spout, threaded for hose connection. The niche could be painted a pleasing color or faced with colored tiles.

The heavy coping on pool No. 4 is a characteristic point of strength in the design of pools with walls and water raised well above the grade, particularly when they are located in the center of the patio, terrace or garden. These precast coping stones, the wall "tiles" and those shown on the patio floor are 4 ins. thick. The coarse aggregate, in the concrete mixture used in making them, should not be larger than ¾ in. Cove or a similar molding used in the forms for the fountain pier will give a finished shape around the fountain jet.

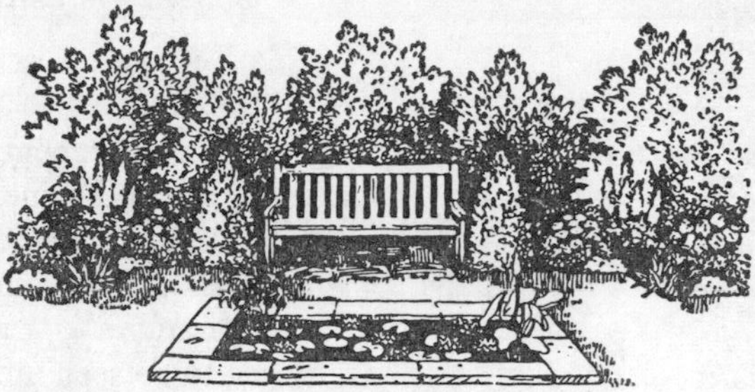

Pool #1 (Left): THIS STONE-COPED POOL, MEASURING 4'x7' INSIDE, IS LARGE ENOUGH TO GROW THREE WATERLILIES AND OTHER SHALLOW-WATER OR FLOATING PLANTS, BUT SHOULD NOT BE SO CROWDED THAT THE WATER SURFACE IS HIDDEN COMPLETELY. IT IS LOCATED TOWARDS THE END OF THE GARDEN AND, BEING ALMOST LEVEL WITH THE GRADE, SERVES AS A STRONG POINT OF INTEREST IN FRONT OF THE GARDEN BENCH TERMINATING THE VIEW. IT IS PLEASANT TO SIT NEAR A POOL, BUT THIS ONE COULD BE USED ALONE IN THE CENTER OF THE GARDEN

Pool #1 (Right): SECTION THROUGH THE POOL SHOWING THE CONSTRUCTION SUGGESTED TO SUPPORT THE 12" CUT FLAGSTONE COPING. THIS STONE, LAID ON A 3/8" BED OF CEMENT MORTAR, CONCEALS ALL ABOVE-WATER CONCRETE. THE POOL IS FILLED AND REFRESHED FROM THE GARDEN HOSE. IT IS EMPTIED BY UNSCREWING THE OVERFLOW PIPE FROM THE BRASS COUPLING SET IN THE BOTTOM OF THE POOL. WHEN IN PLACE, THIS PIPE, CAPPED WITH SCREEN TO PREVENT FISH OR DEBRIS FROM CLOGGING THE DRAIN, MAINTAINS THE WATER LEVEL AT THE TOP OF THE REINFORCED CONCRETE. THE DRAIN PIPE SHOULD LEAD TO DRY WELL OR STORM SEWER

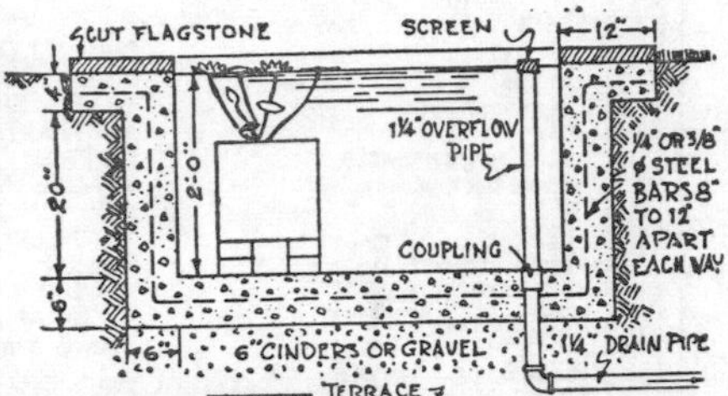
CUT FLAGSTONE
SCREEN
12"
1¼" OVERFLOW PIPE
2'-0"
20"
6"
¼" OR 3/8" ø STEEL BARS 8" TO 12" APART EACH WAY
COUPLING
6"
6" CINDERS OR GRAVEL
1¼" DRAIN PIPE

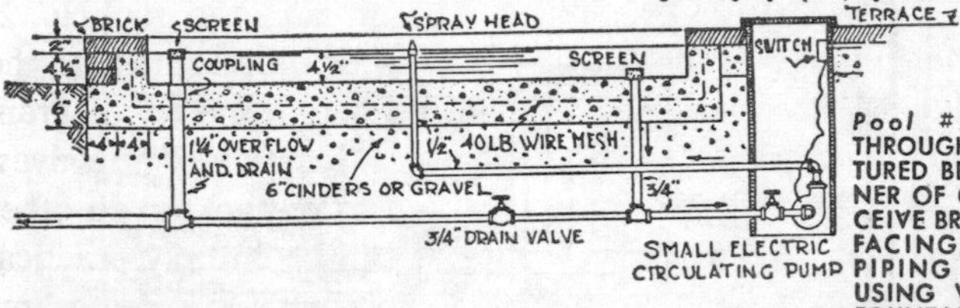
BRICK
SCREEN
SPRAY HEAD
TERRACE
2"
4½"
6"
COUPLING
4½"
SCREEN
SWITCH
4
4
1¼" OVERFLOW AND DRAIN
½"
40LB. WIRE MESH
6" CINDERS OR GRAVEL
3/4"
3/4" DRAIN VALVE
SMALL ELECTRIC CIRCULATING PUMP

Pool #2 (Left): SECTION THROUGH SHALLOW POOL PICTURED BELOW. NOTE THE MANNER OF CONSTRUCTION TO RECEIVE BRICK COPING AND WALL FACING; ALSO DIAGRAM OF PIPING AND PUMP FOR REUSING WATER IN THE SMALL FOUNTAIN JET. THE FIRST FILLING AND OCCASIONAL REPLENISHING ARE FROM THE GARDEN HOSE

Pool #2 (Right): POOLS ARE A PARTICULARLY COOLING FEATURE CLOSE TO THE HOUSE OR TERRACE. THIS ONE, MEASURING 2½' x 10½' WITH A 3½' SEMI-CIRCULAR RECESS INTO THE TERRACE FLOOR, HAS BEEN DESIGNED SPECIFICALLY AS A PLEASING, DECORATIVE FEATURE TO BE SEEN AND HEARD (FOUNTAIN JET) CLOSE AT HAND. WITH WALLS AND BOTTOM PAINTED BLACK, BLUE, GREEN OR ALUMINUM, THE 4½ INCHES OF WATER WILL CAST AS MANY PLEASING REFLECTIONS AS IF IT WERE 3 FEET DEEP. THE BRICK COPING AND WALLS MATCH THE BRICK OF THE TERRACE FLOOR AND WALKS. HERE IS A FEATURE TO CATCH AND HOLD THE INTEREST FROM SPRING TILL FALL. AS SHOWN IN THE ABOVE SECTION, POOL AND PUMPING SYSTEM COULD BE DRAINED TO A DRY WELL AT END OF SEASON

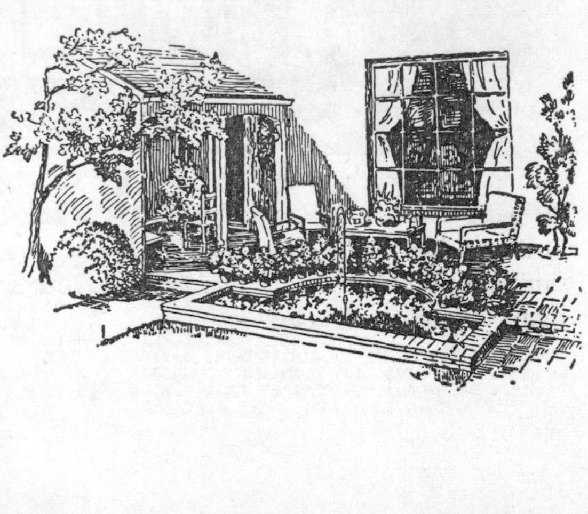

Pool #3 (Right): FLANKED BY BLUE-BERRY PLANTS, THIS ALL-CONCRETE DIPPING CISTERN, SUPPLIED THROUGH A FOUNTAIN SPOUT SET IN THE NICHE-PIERCED BACK WALL, TERMINATES THE MAIN PATH THROUGH THE VEGETABLE GARDEN. IT WILL MAKE AN EQUALLY ATTRACTIVE FEATURE AT THE END OR ONE SIDE OF THE FORMAL FLOWER GARDEN. THE FOUNTAIN SPOUT IS THREADED TO RECEIVE THE GARDEN HOSE FOR EXTENSIVE WATERING; OTHER TIMES THE WATERING POT IS DIPPED INTO THE CISTERN. FOR A COOLING, ORNAMENTAL EFFECT OPEN THE VALVE SLIGHTLY. POTTED PLANTS, MANY MORE THAN SHOWN, INVARIABLY ARE ARRANGED INTO CONVENIENT AND ATTRACTIVE GROUPS AROUND THE CISTERN

Pool #3 (Left): INSIDE OF CISTERN MEASURES 18" x 36" x 24". CONCRETE FOR PORTION OF STRUCTURE TO HOLD WATER SHOULD BE PLACED IN ONE OPERATION. SINCE ALL PARTS ARE CONNECTED WITH REINFORCING BARS, BOTTOM AND TOP OF BACK WALL MAY BE POURED BEFORE AND AFTER CISTERN RESPECTIVELY. AS FORMS ARE REMOVED, ALL SURFACES ARE RUBBED WITH A HARD BRICK OR A CARBORUNDUM STONE TO GIVE A SMOOTH, WORN FINISH. CORNERS AND EDGES ARE ROUNDED. WATER SUPPLY, LAID BELOW FROST, IS FITTED WITH STOP AND WASTE VALVE TO DRAIN END OF LINE AT SAME TIME CISTERN IS EMPTIED FOR WINTER

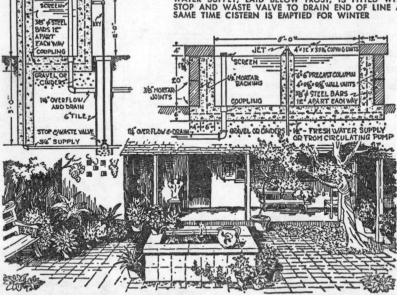

Pool #4 (Above): SECTION AND PATIO VIEW OF A 5' x 5' (INSIDE DIMENSIONS) CONCRETE TILE POOL. COPING AND WALL UNITS ARE FORMED AND FINISHED SEPARATELY. BY USING WHITE SAND, MARBLE CHIPS, GRANITE SCREENINGS OR OTHER COLORED ROCK MATERIALS IN PLACE OF THE USUAL AGGREGATE, MANY DESIRABLE COLORS AND TEXTURES ARE POSSIBLE. CEMENT FILM IS SCRUBBED FROM FACE OF TILE WITHIN 24 HOURS AFTER PLACING CONCRETE, AND SURFACE AND EDGES SMOOTHED WITH CARBORUNDUM STONE. TILE, ALSO, MAY BE COLORED WITH MINERAL PIGMENTS PLACED IN MIXTURE. THEY ARE LAID IN A MORTAR OF 1 PART CEMENT, 3 PARTS SAND AND 1/10 PART LIME. BROAD COPING OFFERS AN INVITATION TO PAUSE AND FEED GOLDFISH; ALSO A STAGE TO DISPLAY CHOICE POTTED PLANTS.

HENRY B. AUL

BUILDING INFORMAL POOLS

There are many degrees of informality in informal pools. One set back in the gracefully curving border of a small cottage garden may have nothing more than a slight irregularity in the broken flagstones coping its placid, lily-studded surface. Another, located in the rock garden and imitating a mountain stream, may have water splashing from left to right between and around boulders, large and small. They are both informal and delightful to the gardener who favors the occult or unsymmetrical rather than the symmetrical in gardens.

The informal pool is especially suited to the garden and home grounds of irregular shape or uneven grade, with existing trees and outcropping rocks to use as a basis and frame for additional work. It is a challenging form to follow, as is naturalistic gardening, on a flat, nearly treeless, corner lot. Yet one does discover charming, informal pools and plantings under just such conditions.

WHERE TO PUT IT

Informal pools, because they tend to imitate natural forms, are frequently located in the lowest spot of the garden. Because trees and shrubs and nearly all other plants need and thrive on moisture, it is not uncommon to find them, in the natural landscape, growing luxuriantly close to the water's edge. That is one reason the informal pool appears so natural with a background of planting—and so out-of-character without it. Remember, however, that sun must reach the pool to grow waterlilies successfully.

Except for the rushing, rock-strewn mountain stream, most natural pools and ponds have sweeping, graceful curves worn into their shore lines. Short, unnatural wiggles in the shape of an informal pool are not pleasing. Also, rocks do not stand on end in the meadow, woods or hillside, and neither should they do so when used to accent the shape of an informal pool. They should rest on their broad, flat bottoms as Nature intended them to, or, if they have been worn round by water, they should be placed in or close to the water.

SPECIFICATIONS

In general, specifications for building informal pools are the same as those for formal ones described previously. There are a few exceptions. So long as the slope of the sides is not steeper than a rise of 1 ft. in a 2 ft. run, no forms are required. If reinforcing bars are hard to find, a heavy-gauge wire fencing may be used to reinforce the dish-shaped pool. This is particularly true if water is to be kept in the pool, protected from hard freezing, through the winter.

Pool No. 1, in the accompanying illustrations of informal pools (*opposite and on page 128*), is located in a corner where trees, shrubs and flowers contribute the setting. The lawn in the foreground might be a sunny meadow in Nature, and (important) it leads right down to the water's edge in two places. Gardeners and garden visitors, alike, want a close look at the lilies and fish. The water is visible from the porch or terrace.

The meandering brook, No. 2, is suggested for the garden where space is not limited, and an unusual feature is needed. There is plenty of space here for waterside planting. If the water in this pool, because of its size and shape, develops a growth of blue-green algae, it may be controlled by evenly distributing copper sulfate at the rate of 1 oz. per 800 cubic feet of water. This treatment will not harm fish or plants, so may be used in all pools. Fish appreciate the algae as a food.

The series of pools, No. 3, is interesting in that no reinforcing is specified in the construction. The stone for this type work should be solid, without seams; bottom stones 10 to 12 ins. thick. Stones are well bedded in or held together with rammed joints of concrete-mortar. The coarse aggregate in this mixture should be no larger than ¼ inch. Note that all concrete is concealed by small stones.

If it is desirable to retain water in garden pools throughout the winter, cover the pool with boards and a burlap-filled mat of straw or leaves. If the pool is drained, keep the bottom drain open, fill the pool with leaves or straw and cover with boards or canvas. Hardy lilies may be kept in the winter-filled pool and, protected from hard freezing, the pool itself is less subject to heaving.

Pool #1 (Right): THIS INFORMAL POND OR POOL IS SET PART WAY BACK IN A CORNER OF THE FLOWER BORDER BACKED WITH SHRUBBERY AND TREES. HERE IT IS GIVEN A BACKGROUND AND ENFRAMEMENT PARTICULARLY IMPORTANT TO A FEATURE OF THIS KIND. IT IS LOCATED QUITE NATURALLY IN THE LOWEST CORNER OF THE GARDEN. BESIDES THE IRIS, MARSH MARIGOLD, ASTER AND OTHER FLOWERS CLOSE TO THE MARGIN, AN OCCASIONAL ROUNDED, WATER-WASHED BOULDER SERVES TO OUTLINE THE POOL'S SHAPE. ONE SPOT IS DEEP ENOUGH FOR A LILY; SHALLOW WATER PLANTS ARE GROUPED ELSEWHERE. THE LAWN REACHES TO THE WATER'S EDGE AT TWO PLACES

Pool #1 (Left): SECTION THROUGH GREATEST WIDTH. LENGTH 11' TO 12'; WIDTH 5' AT ONE END, 4' AT OTHER END AND 3' NEAR THE MIDDLE. SO LONG AS A SLOPE OF 1 TO 2 IS MAINTAINED, NO FORMS ARE NEEDED TO BUILD THIS POOL. LARGE AND SMALL STONES PLACED IN THE WET CONCRETE HELP TO HOLD IT IN PLACE AND FURNISH LEDGES ON WHICH TO SET AQUATIC PLANTS IN POTS. FILL WITH THE HOSE AND DRAIN TO DRY WELL OR SEWER BY REMOVING OVERFLOW PIPE

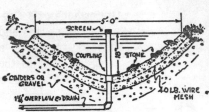

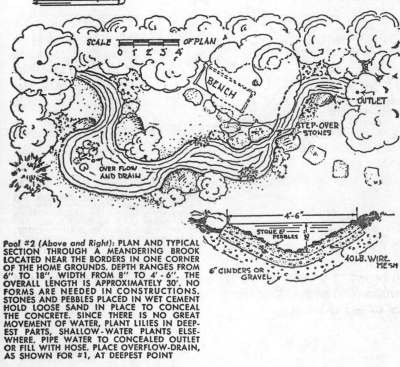

Pool #2 (Above and Right): PLAN AND TYPICAL SECTION THROUGH A MEANDERING BROOK LOCATED NEAR THE BORDERS IN ONE CORNER OF THE HOME GROUNDS. DEPTH RANGES FROM 6" TO 18", WIDTH FROM 8" TO 4'-6". THE OVERALL LENGTH IS APPROXIMATELY 30'. NO FORMS ARE NEEDED IN CONSTRUCTIONS. STONES AND PEBBLES PLACED IN WET CEMENT HOLD LOOSE SAND IN PLACE TO CONCEAL THE CONCRETE. SINCE THERE IS NO GREAT MOVEMENT OF WATER, PLANT LILIES IN DEEPEST PARTS, SHALLOW-WATER PLANTS ELSEWHERE. PIPE WATER TO CONCEALED OUTLET OR FILL WITH HOSE. PLACE OVERFLOW-DRAIN, AS SHOWN FOR #1, AT DEEPEST POINT

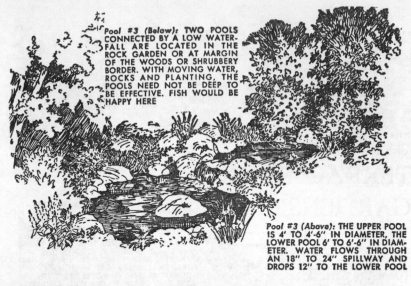

Pool #3 (Below): TWO POOLS CONNECTED BY A LOW WATER-FALL ARE LOCATED IN THE ROCK GARDEN OR AT MARGIN OF THE WOODS OR SHRUBBERY BORDER. WITH MOVING WATER, ROCKS AND PLANTING, THE POOLS NEED NOT BE DEEP TO BE EFFECTIVE. FISH WOULD BE HAPPY HERE

Pool #3 (Above): THE UPPER POOL IS 4' TO 4'-6" IN DIAMETER, THE LOWER POOL 6' TO 6'-6" IN DIAM-ETER. WATER FLOWS THROUGH AN 18" TO 24" SPILLWAY AND DROPS 12" TO THE LOWER POOL

Pool #3 (Below): LONGITUDINAL SECTION SHOWING SOLID ROCK WITH RAMMED CONCRETE MORTAR JOINTS ON TAMPED GRAVEL OR CINDER BASE TO FORM WATER-TIGHT POOLS AND WATERFALL

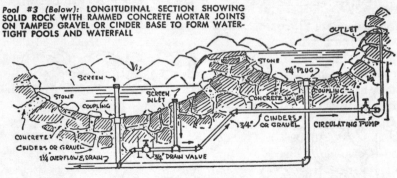

Pool #3 (Above and Left): SECTION AND PLAN SHOWING SYSTEM OF PIPES AND PUMP TO RE-USE WATER, ALSO OVERFLOW AND DRAIN LINES TO EMPTY POOLS AND DRAIN PUMP LINES. IN PLAN P = PUMP BOX, D = OVERFLOW AND DRAIN LINES, E = INLET TO PUMP, O = OUTLET FROM PUMP, V = DRAIN VALVE. THE POOLS ARE FILLED FIRST AND REPLENISHED OCCA-SIONALLY FROM THE HOSE. IN LATE FALL, ENTIRE SYSTEM IS DRAINED INTO DRY WELL

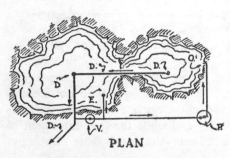

PLAN

HENRY B. AUL

TERRACES DOUBLE AS ROCK GARDENS

Too many terraces, many yards of path, are *in* the garden but not *of* it. Presumably their chief function of bearers of traffic makes them ineligible for consideration as planting areas. Occasionally they can be considered lawn, but if traffic is heavy, they really have no right to such a classification. The answer seems to be to flag them with stones—and then plant between the stones. That way they can be stepped on unreservedly and—if they have been properly set and interplanted—can become "of" the garden as well.

Grass, of course, is the common plant material to use between flags. But as a matter of fact, it is even harder to keep grass in good condition than to maintain honest-to-goodness plants, since grass must preserve an all-over neatness, like a carpet, to be right. Concrete suggests itself to the practical soul as the logical filler for paving of any kind. But practicality can be carried too far in a garden, especially where the area concerned is less architectural and more gardenesque in placing and use.

Bricks and heavy flagstones need not always be laid in cement, for they will stay in place quite well with a minimum of winter heaving if placed upon a well tamped bed of cinders or sand. Such a bed should be at least 6 inches in depth; 8 is probably better. The cracks between the brick or stone may be wider than when cement is used, and these can be filled with good soil and planted with grass, or one or more of the several good rock plants, such as Sedums and Thymes, which do not seem to object too strenuously to being trod upon. Such a treatment partakes more of the garden than of the house, and while the free movement of tables and chairs over it may not be as easy, the area is more pleasing to see and live with.

PICK YOUR SPOTS

Whereas the generous use of paved areas in the garden itself is possible and practicable it must be handled with care if the original garden scheme is not to be harmed. Pavements cannot be dropped haphazardly in any likely spot. They must be planned and so arranged that they become integral parts of the garden.

The site must be logical. Usually the central area of a small garden which has been developed as the focal point can be paved and, as a result, becomes a much stronger element in the garden design. So can the area about, or in front of, a terminal feature in a garden with a long axis. As a matter of fact any axis can, with good effect, be terminated with a paved area if it is kept in good proportion to the rest of the scheme.

Aside from size (scale), the shape of the area is also important. It should, in the main, conform to the shape of the surrounding garden pattern. Squares, oblongs or circles are all effective if they carry out the intent of the original garden design. The important requirement is always that *they fit into and become a part of the garden.*

The size and shape of the paving material are important, too, in creating a restful and harmonious effect. Brick can be laid in a variety of patterns, but the herringbone and basket-weave patterns are most commonly used, for they are not difficult to do and they are economical in the use of material. Slate for the most part, unfortunately, comes in random sizes and irregular-shaped pieces. This material, fairly thin and relatively small in size, should always be laid in cement mortar for a permanent job.

Flagstone offers a wider possibility, for it is generally obtainable in larger and heavier pieces. The random sized and shaped pieces should be avoided if possible in favor of the more regularly shaped pieces, squares or oblongs. These can be formed into more pleasing effects. Contrary to popular belief "crazy patterns" in paving do not necessarily add charm or quaintness to a garden scheme. More often they are not in too good taste and present a hazard to garden traffic. Good line and pattern are as important in paving as in other parts of garden design.

Flagstone, unless it is extremely thick and heavy sidewalk flag, can be cut with a stone hammer and chisel into proper sizes and shapes for many patterns.

When paved areas are large, as they have to be if they are to serve their purpose, it is advisable to introduce some planting to soften their harshness and to blend them into the surrounding landscape. Large terraces adjacent to the house often have generous planting areas next to the building where the traditional type of foundation planting, mostly low

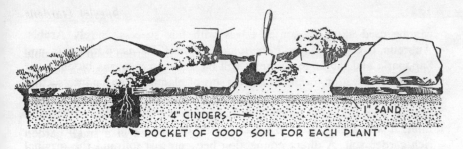

4" CINDERS →   1" SAND

← POCKET OF GOOD SOIL FOR EACH PLANT

A solid, well drained foundation is vital. So is a rich soil pocket for plants between flags.

flowering evergreens, can be utilized. In the wide terrace, planting spaces for small flowering trees such as Dogwood, Crab, or even fruiting Apples can be arranged. These trees, of course, should be high enough branched so as not to impede the use of the area below. In time they will provide delightful shade, as well as color when in bloom.

The expanse of large terraces or paved areas can also be broken up by the use of plants in pots or tubs. Small evergreens, or small flowering trees such as Oleanders in tubs, herbaceous material in urns or pots, and the like can be used effectively for they can always be moved out of the way if more space is desired for some special occasion. Frequently window boxes are used along the edges of the paved area for additional color, and demark the limits of the space. The European habit of using potted plants at the entrance, on the steps, or in corners often adds color and cheer.

When the paved area is well away from the house, and thus becomes a part of the garden, it is advisable to have the beds and borders come up to and enclose the area, at least on two or three sides. Often the space can be set apart and accented by enclosing it with a low hedge.

The planting of the paved area itself can be accomplished to a limited extent without hindering the free use of its surface. One of the objections to this type of planting can be overcome if low, prostrate plants are used. The taller ones create a bumpy effect that is not pleasing in appearance in spite of their gay color and variety, and they interfere with the free use of the area. For the most part all such planting should be restricted to the outer edges.

The only exceptions are the use of such plants as *Arenaria verna caespitosa,* a moss-like plant that prefers partial shade, a few of the smaller sedums, *Thymus serpyllum, Mazus pumilio, Veronica repens,* and possibly *Dianthus deltoides.* Practically all of the usual rock plants can be used along the outer edges with fair success. Surely Arabis, Aubretia, Creeping Phlox, *Polemonium reptans, Veronica rupestris,* and Saponaria and the larger sedums will be found in vigorous bloom.

The best location for plants of this sort of planting is at the intersection of three or four stones. Here a planting pocket can be devised by taking out the poor soil, sand or cinders that forms the bed for the paving and filling it with a prepared soil which should be part humus and part good, rich garden soil. A direct connection between this soil and the original soil below should be established so that enough soil moisture will get through to nourish the plant and help counteract the additional heat that is reflected from the stone paving. Rock plants, for the most part, prefer deep, cool, moist root channels.

Closely related to paved areas, though unplantable, are those which are covered with gravel. This material is frequently used in garden areas, or under trees. Usually whitewashed gravel is preferred, but colored gravel or even crushed bluestone can be used. The important thing to remember in the use of such a surface is that it must have a well tamped underbed of gravel, sand or cinders. The top dressing of gravel is usually one to two inches thick.

Gravelled areas are not too difficult to maintain. They need a deal of raking, wetting down and rolling to be in the best of condition, but if the gravel is held in place at the edges with metal curbs, or brick edges, they offer little difficulty.

H. STUART ORTLOFF

MAKE NATURE YOUR GUIDE
IN ROCK GARDEN PLANNING

The esthetic side of rock gardening, to use a somewhat indefinite term, has been a bone of contention for many years between those who feel that rocks have no place in any garden and the numerous others who claim that stones came before plants and therefore deserve first consideration. Viewed impartially, both sides are partly right and partly wrong. Which perhaps is only another way of saying that the visual success of a rock garden depends very largely upon the rocks that are chosen to go into it and how they are used. I'd even go so far as to say that good judgment in these matters can lead to a pleasing final success as surely as unsound thinking will produce a thoroughly unsatisfactory result nine times out of ten.

To start at the beginning, remember that a rock garden should be able to grow plants well and also look sane, settled and above all *natural,* if it is to prove truly pleasing in appearance. Nature herself demonstrates this latter principle countless times, as you will realize if you think back over the rocky scenes you have met and recall how the attractive ones featured aeons-old ledges, big out-crops and other basic formations, while the mere jumbles looked almost distasteful because of their confusion and restless air of disturbance.

Many people fail to recognize the fact that only indigenous, "deep-rooted" rocks can look settled and at peace with the world. Quite literally, a lot of us will collect all kinds and conditions of stones not too heavy to lift, pile them in a corner with a little interspersed soil to plant in, and call it a "rockery". Some even go so far as to make a point of constructing the heap with multihued stones from the seacoasts, mountains, petrified deserts, extinct volcanoes—the more gaudy and contrasting the better. As Liberty Hyde Bailey once remarked, if that's the kind of rock garden you want you should have taken up geology instead of horticulture.

This sort of hit-or-miss procedure is bound to lead to failure in

HARRIE WOOD

A GRANITE OUTCROP PROVES THE REPOSE
ARISING FROM UNIFORMLY SLANTED
LINES. If any one of these rocks were horizontal
or slanted in the opposite direction it would wreck
the whole composition. So, regardless of everything
else, determine your rock garden's angle and stick
to it. This principle holds with all sizes of stones
suitably shaped.

appearance and often in the well-being of the plants themselves. For it can be taken as an implicit rule that unless your rock garden looks restful and at ease, and its inhabitants well satisfied with their lot in life, it cannot live up to your expectations after the novelty of the thing has worn off.

I can think of no better preparation for a rock gardening venture than a preliminary, open-eyed study of how Nature manages such projects. Such a course will disclose, among other things, that many of the rock masses which please you owe a good share of their attractiveness to some underlying characteristic that runs through them, such as the direction of the stratification lines, uniformity of texture and color, the

LEDGES EMPHASIZE HORIZONTAL LINES. In many areas you will find that the predominating basic rocks are distinctly stratified in this way, sometimes with a downward pitch but always at a uniform angle. Such stone can be used handsomely if you retain its layer-like character. For best effects, leave substantial rock areas with little planting, to emphasize the lines.

sense of general unity that is apparent everywhere. Often there are but few plants, and these scattered, but they look as completely at home as if they had always lived there — the larger ones where there is the most soil space, the smaller ones in the little nooks and crevices. Even in cases where the growth is dense the pervading theme in the rocks which gives them their impression of stability and endurance is never hidden. Simple though these matters may seem, they are of fundamental importance and their reproduction in your own garden, with all the fidelity you can muster, will have a marked influence on your success.

FIVE ROCK TYPES:
Granite
Conglomerate
Ledge
Limestone outcrop
"Hard-heads" (useless)

As your observations of Nature's rock problems progress you will also learn what *not* to do. You may see, for example, the lack of harmony between radically different types of stones — granite and quartz, for instance—when in close proximity to each other. It will become apparent, too, that a stone lying wholly on the surface of the ground and another of the same type so deeply embedded that only its upper portion can be seen just don't harmonize as they should, chiefly because the former looks as though it were a newcomer. Similarly, a jagged point sticking up among low, rounded companions looks as out of place as a smokestack in a country village. And still another helpful lesson lies in the way the characteristics of a dominant mass, far too heavy for duplication in any man-made garden without the aid of a couple of motorized derricks, is often echoed on the slope below on a scale small enough for the construction facilities that you have at home.

Stone types and sizes vary tremendously from region to region, of course. You may find sandstone here, granite twenty miles away, limestone over in the next county, and so on. Not infrequently you will come upon areas which seem to have been a prehistoric dumping ground for millions of smooth, football-size stones of flinty hardness and exasperating monotony—the worst rock garden material imaginable, and rarely worth a second glance even in the surroundings where they have lain for thousands of years. A few widely distributed rock types that are excellent for your purposes are shown on these pages, and there are others that possess similar characteristics of stratification, contour of exposed surface, and uniformity of texture and color.

A rock garden should always look as if it had been made by Nature for the place it occupies. For this reason the native rocks of your region, assuming merely that they are physically suitable for the purpose, are far better than some foreign kind that can never look completely at home. Study the local natural formations until you really have the "feel" of them, and your problem of creating an idealized facsimile will be greatly lightened. Do not think for a moment that it will be necessary, or even

advisable, to try and duplicate some huge natural formation, size for size, for it's the principle that really counts. Almost invariably it is possible to scale down your structure to the space available for it, retaining all of Nature's good features and actually enhancing them by better planting.

To recapitulate in a practical way these sometimes elusive matters we have been considering, here is a set of specific pointers on the procedure of actual rock selection and installation: 1 — Use local material if possible, and have it uniform in color and texture. 2 — Decide on a natural-looking slant for the rocks, as shown in the illustrations, and *keep it uniform* throughout the structure. 3 — All rocks in contact with the soil should be set deeply — at least half of their bulk below the surface. 4 — Leave ample room for planting. 5 — Where plants are to go between superimposed rocks, as in a ledge effect, set them in place before installing the upper stones. 6 — If in doubt how a certain combination of rocks will look, set it up on a temporary trial basis before going through the labor of permanent installation. 7 — Use a variety of rock sizes, but have at least one relatively massive point as a background for the smaller compositions.

When it comes to a suitable location for such a garden, it is well to remember that unless there is some kind of background which gives

OUTCROPS OF LIMESTONE CAN BE PLEASANTLY PICTURESQUE. Normally their color is a soft gray, often nearly white, and very lovely in itself. Their handicap is that only plants which like or will endure a steady diet of lime can be grown on or near them.

HARRIE WOOD —

A rock garden should rise naturally from a low level to a higher one and appear to be a normal part of its surroundings. Very often a background planting of low shrubs and small trees will counteract any impression that the structure is artificial. Note the uniform pitch of the rocks and the interest provided by the contrast of angles, curves and textures of rock surfaces. Crevices in steps and paving are for plants.

you the impression that you are looking at a *natural* slope the whole affair is likely to look out of place. Thus, a rock garden set down in the middle of a flat, open lawn where you can stroll completely around it will never seem to be at home. Set it in a far corner, however, directly in front of evergreens or tall shrubs that overlap its top and prevent easy access from their side and it can be a complete success. After all a primary rule of the enterprise, with few exceptions, is that it is to be seen from one side only, which enables you to develop that chosen side with maximum effectiveness.

The first important step in successful rock garden planting is to forget many of the time-honored rules that you follow when selecting, arranging and growing plants in a border, bed, or other conventional form of designed gardening.

To be fully satisfying a rock garden must catch the spirit of one of nature's most highly specialized environments, and one which in invariably characterized by restraint in the size and habits of the plants involved. To overload it so badly that you can't see the rocks for the flowers would be as serious an error as to give the rocks such prominence that the flowers look lost among them. A balance must be struck between these two main elements which will produce an impression of pleasant naturalness throughout the composition — a much easier thing to say than to accomplish!

One of the concepts to forget is that the soil should be reasonably "rich" in the usual gardening meaning of that term. Such soil, in a rock garden, would promote unnatural size and rankness of growth in some of the plants, and death by overeating in the case of others. A satisfactory basic mixture consists of 3 parts average garden loam, 2 parts crushed stone ($\frac{1}{8}$th to $\frac{1}{4}$th inch diameter), 1 part coarse sand, and 2 parts humus (leafmold or finely crumbled peatmoss), thoroughly mixed before using. If these ingredients produce a strongly acid mixture, add ground limestone until an approximately neutral condition is attained. Avoid all fertilizers and special plant stimulants, but be prepared to vary the proportions of sand, gravel and humus, as well as the degree of acidity, in some parts of the garden where you intend to use plants with special requirements.

Excellent drainage is of primary importance, not only in the upper few inches of soil, but at the lower levels as well. Dank, stagnant conditions underground or at the surface are anathema to rock plants, very many of which are alpine in origin. Thus, before any of your prepared soil is applied, the underlying grade of the whole area should slope freely from top to bottom without any interruptions by deeper pockets which might serve as subterranean reservoirs.

One excellent building procedure is to locate your most dominant rock mass first, bedding it in the basic slope and allowing for a fill-in of prepared soil at least a foot or 15 inches deep. This amount of fill-in should be planned for the whole area, even though it may necessitate removal of much of the existing soil. In such a case, better do the necessary cutting down right at the start.

This dominant rock will be literally the keystone around which the rest of the composition will be developed, so take plenty of time to make it right. Next, mark out the general course of the proposed access path, if any, and move a few of the secondary-size rocks into rough position, always remembering to allow for that foot or more of soil fill still to go.

Step back, now, and appraise the general impression of these various base features, thinking of them as well as you can in the light of additional rocks and fill that would tie them together and provide more coherence. Probably you will decide that some shifting here or there will improve the prospects; if so, make the changes now, for to do so later on would entail extra labor. Step back for another appraisal, and continue the process until you are pretty well satisfied that these fundamentals are as they should be. By that time the chances are that you will have a surprisingly clear mental picture of what your finished rock garden is going to look like — believe it or not!

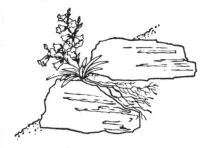

Place your plants according to their growth habits; some are upright, others squatty, still others love to fill in the crevices. Rock chips of about half-inch size make a neat and permanent plant-saving mulch.

A downward slope of the upper rock surfaces will help to carry rainwater back into the slope instead of losing it by run-off. Plant roots will develop splendidly under such conditions, though the soil surface area may be very small.

Garden loam, coarse sand, humus and rock chips, thoroughly mixed together and used to a depth of a foot or more, are a mixture that will have much to do with the success of your plants. Under no circumstances give them a stimulating "rich" garden soil.

Now, with some of the key points and their levels established as guides, and an idea of where some of the "basic" plants (background shrubs, permanent accents like dwarf evergreens, etc.) are to go, the real building job begins.

Start at the lowest point of the slope, place the most important rocks in position, and fill in all around them with prepared soil, tamping it at strategic points to give them a firm setting. A good general rule to follow, from the standpoint of appearance as well as permanent steadiness, is to have two-thirds of each rock underground and one-third visible above the surface when the job is done. Give each rock a similar tilt backward and downward into the slope, as shown in the large drawing. This will be of great help in attaining the desired unity in the general composition besides having a tendency to direct rainfall back into the slope where it should go.

Leave plenty of irregular shaped planting areas among the rocks, but don't make them so small that the garden will look pock-marked. Keep the soil grades gentle, to minimize washing out by heavy rain; some pockets can be nearly level, supported by a rock along the lower side. In many cases it is advisable to have narrow, irregular soil lines between adjoining rocks to connect some of the major pockets; plants will eventually fill these in, making for a pleasing continuity of effect.

Broadly speaking, finish the lowest level before moving into the higher level behind it. Let the rocks themselves carry the main burden of building up the slope, but carefully avoid any impression of a series of distinct tiers. The whole operation should be calculated so that, when you finally reach the top, you will have a reasonably uniform but not monotonous-looking slope.

Yes, I know that all this sounds a bit vague, but I can assure you that in actual practice it won't prove at all difficult except in the actual physical labor involved. Just remember to back off frequently and appraise the developing job. This, plus a certain amount of tentative trial and error experimenting, will give you the results you're after. And don't forget to study the drawing on page 139 until its principles have really soaked in, for that will prove immensely helpful.

Many perennial nursery catalogs contain good basic lists of plants suitable for rock gardens, and of course you can raise many kinds from seed if you have the time. Assuming that you decide to buy young plants, get them pot-grown if possible, for greater ease and success in planting.

Dwarf shrubs, whether evergreen or deciduous, should have their roots balled and burlapped, for the same reason. Learn the general growth habit of each before putting it in the ground, as this frequently determines whether it should go close to the base of a rock which will serve as a background, or just above one down whose face it can cascade, or in a narrow crevice between two or three. Always, however, be sure to place your plants where they will have plenty of opportunity to send their roots far back among and under the rocks as they develop. And don't crowd them!

With strong, well grown plants, early fall is a good planting time, assuming merely that you can finish the job at least six weeks before the first freezing weather. A permanent mulch of ½-inch stone chips is excellent rock garden plant insurance, and a light covering of Pine or Hemlock branches, or excelsior held in place with wire netting, will lessen casualties among the plants during the first winter.

WHAT TO GROW IN YOUR ROCK GARDEN

Defining the characteristics of a good rock garden plant is rather like ordering a suit of clothes by mail, sight unseen. The fit may or may not be good, depending on the character, build, and preferences of the person (or garden) that is to wear the article. It is entirely feasible, though, to set down certain generalities which apply to virtually all rock gardening projects, to serve as a sort of basic guide in your personal selection problems.

Since a rock garden is essentially a more or less accurate imitation of a rock-strewn, elevated bit of natural land, the plants for it should be of low stature, since that is the kind that normally grows in such places, as contrasted with the tall lush herbage of deep rich bottom-lands. A 6-foot clump of Delphinium growing among the rocks would look as incongruous as a 6-inch Crested Iris in the middle of a big perennial border.

Rock plants should have rugged constitutions, too, and be reasonably long-lived, because frequent replacements would be more fussy and time-consuming than in the unhampered spaces of an open garden. This means that, as a general rule, perennials are desirable and annuals pretty much taboo. Furthermore, each plant, *as an individual,* should be of unusually acceptable appearance, since the very nature of a rock garden focusses attention on the details of its occupants.

Good growth manners are important, because the planting areas, while numerous, are too small to permit the use of invasive characters that like to spread all over the lot. You shouldn't tolerate kinds that would crowd out everything else for yards around, any more than you would others that might bury the rocks from sight.

It would be just grand if we could select a good list of plants that have all these desired characteristics, and at the same time would furnish a succession of bloom right through the outdoor season, but — well, nature just doesn't make them. With very few exceptions, you have to accept the fact that a rock garden's blossom season is restricted to a big burst in spring and early summer, and a smaller show from late summer until fall, leaving the midsummer weeks well-nigh flowerless. It by no means follows, however, that the garden need be uninteresting during the dog-days, for many rock garden plants have varied and extremely attractive leaves from frost to frost, which some retain even through the winter. Hence, in making your selections, you will do well to pay far more attention to their foliage than you would in average regular flower gardening.

Whereas the mainstay of your plantings will consist of herbaceous flowering plants — that is, kinds which die down to the ground, or nearly so, with the onset of winter — you should also include a few miniature shrubs which will retain their above-ground forms throughout the year. Some of these will be literally evergreen, while others may drop their leaves for the cold months and grow no new ones until spring. But regardless of whether or not they present a year-round semblance of active life, they will all contribute a sense of permanence and harmonious contrast whose value can be realized only when it lies there before your eyes.

Contrary to a rather widespread belief, it is *not* necessary, or even desirable, that all rock gardening plants shall hail from the high mountains. Actually, many low-landers are completely worthy of inclusion, and often they are more amenable to moderate and even sea-level altitudes than are the true alpines. I raise this point without any thought of disparaging those numerous rock-garden purists who stress the high-altitude origin of their plantings, for theirs is an absorbing and often strikingly effective hobby. But real success along that specialized line is seldom achieved without long experience, for it involves much knowledge of varied soil mixtures, exposures, drainage conditions, and other vital details. If you are one of these envied experts, then these lines are hardly for you. But remember that even a top-level rock gardener was once a beginner, and came up the hard way after starting with just the sort of fundamentals that we have been discussing here.

No amount of theorizing can be wholly helpful without its complement of specific details. So, to clinch the story, we give you now, on the following pages, a basic rock-plant list which, though it obviously cannot cover the entire field of material, will provide a good start in that direction. From it, as your enthusiasm and experience grow, you may move on into whatever degree of specialization your fancy and opportunity suggest.

PERENNIALS

Name	Effectiveness
Aethionema armenum	Blue-gray leaf mat, pink-mauve flower stalks in late spring.
Alyssum saxatile citrinum	Dainty, prostrate, gray-leaved, many pale yellow flowers in mid-spring. 10 inches.
Androsace sarmentosa Chumbyi	Silvery rosettes, rosy flowers in early summer. 5 inches tall.
Anemone pulsatilla	Large purple or white flowers in April, before finely cut leaves develop. 1 foot.
Aquilegia flabellata nana	Lovely little Columbine. Sturdy white flowers on 8-inch stems in early summer.
Arenaria montana	Dark green mat covered in late spring with large white flowers.
Armeria caespitosa (Thrift)	Wee mound of tiny rosettes, starred with pink blossoms in early spring.
Aster alpinus	Substantial tufts with violet and gold flowers on 6-inch stems in May and June.
Campanula carpatica	Leafy tufts with white, light blue, or violet bell flowers all summer. 10 inches high.
Dianthus arenarius (Pink)	Generous low mat-former. Fragrant pink or white flowers in late spring.
Geum montanum	Low and tufted. Many short-stemmed golden blossoms in spring.
Gypsophila repens (Babys-breath)	Sheet or low mound of dainty foliage, and tiny white or rosy flowers. 6 inches high.
Iberis sempervirens	Spreading, handsome evergreen to 1 foot tall. Flat white flower heads in spring.
Iris tectorum (Roof Iris)	Showy blue or white flowers on 15-inch stalks. Typical Iris foliage. Late spring.
Iris cristata (Crested Iris)	Mat-forming, numerous light blue flowers on short stems in mid-spring. 8-inch leaves.
Linum alpinum (Flax)	Graceful, airy, and blue-flowered. To 1 foot tall.
Phlox subulata	Trailing, tiny-leaved mat with countless showy spring flowers.
Saxifraga aizoon	Low, thick-leaved rosettes, pink or creamy sprays on 20-inch stems. Late spring.

Remarks

Perfectly hardy and easy to grow in full sun where the soil is deep, perfectly drained, and alkaline rather than acid.

Likes a sunny, well-drained spot large enough for it to grow 1 foot or so across. Easily raised from seed.

A compact but spreading mat, best used on flat or sloping area with perfect drainage and hot sun.

One of the best rock plants to serve as an eye-catching mound, concluding its display with plumy seed pods. Deep, well drained soil and ample sunlight.

Easily grown and delightful, though less graceful than most Columbines. Deep soil, at least half sun. Good as small individual accent plant.

Outstanding in deep, gritty soil where it can spill down over a sunny rock. Easily grown from seed.

Unexcelled in a sunny, perfectly drained crevice or stony slope where no surface moisture ever collects in winter. Not hard to grow from seed.

An easy and effective early-blooming Aster for sunny, well drained spots. In addition to this type, there are white-flowered forms and a few pinks.

Indispensable in the larger areas, where its strong, showy growth can develop freely. Easily grown from seed. Sun or light shade.

Easily grown almost anywhere, even in partly shaded spots. Prefers a neutral or slightly alkaline soil.

An easy and excellent tufted carpeter, asking for little more than plenty of sun and a fair amount of space to spread across.

Like a miniature edition of the border Babys-breath in general effect. Full sun and a deep soil that is alkaline rather than acid.

A plant with plenty of "weight", growing strongly and requiring sun and considerable space. Cut back moderately after blooming to maintain density.

Fine for accent use here and there. Not particular as to soil, but prefers plenty of sun and good drainage.

Easy to grow in any well drained, sunny or lightly shaded soil. Forms sizable mats, so should be given space if possible.

Very desirable to provide spray-like effect in a sunny, dryish location. Like a miniature ordinary garden Flax.

Valuable for good-sized sheet in any sunny, well drained place. Superior forms are: Apple Blossom, pale pink; Alba, pure white; Vivid, salmon pink.

Excellent to furnish tall and showy grace as a foil for lower flowers. Fair amount of sun, but by no means a baking location.

Name	Effectiveness
Saxifraga Macnabiana	Purple-spotted white flower sprays on 1-foot stalks.
Sedum Ewersi	Trailing stems, gray and roundish leaves, crimson flowers in late summer. 1 foot.
Sedum dasyphyllum	Minute grayish leaves, pinkish gray star flowers in early summer. 2 inches high.
Sempervivum arachnoideum (Cobweb Houseleek)	Slowly increasing low mound of green rosettes covered with white "cobwebs".
Thymus serpyllum albus (Thyme)	Gray-green creeping mat covered with white blossoms in summer.
Tunica saxifraga	Tufted and spreading to 1 foot or more. Clouds of little pink blossoms all summer.
Veronica rupestris	Prostrate trailer, spreads compactly. Short spires of blue flowers in early summer.

BULBS

Crocus Tomasinianus	Very early spring flowers, pale silvery lilac outside, darker inside.
Leucojum aestivum (Snowflake)	Drooping white blossoms on 8-inch stems in mid-spring.
Narcissus (February Gold)	Orange trumpet and yellow perianth, very early. 1 foot.
Muscari armeniacum (Grape-hyacinth)	Deep cobalt blue, white rimmed flowers on 8-inch stems; fragrant. Mid-spring.
Scilla siberica (Var. Spring Beauty)	Deep, rich blue starry flowers in early spring. 6 inches or so.
Tulipa dasystemon (Tulip species)	White flowers with yellow eyes, in spring. 6 inches tall.
Tulipa Kaufmanniana (Waterlily Tulip)	Large, waterlily-like white flowers striped red on outside. Very dwarf.

SHRUBS

Chamaecyparis obtusa nana (Dwarf Hinoki Cypress)	Dense miniature evergreen tree, to 3 feet high eventually.
Juniperus horizontalis procumbens (Creeping Juniper)	Dense evergreen trailer only a few inches high.
Leiophyllum buxifolium (Sandmyrtle)	Tiny rounded evergreen shrub, little white flowers in late spring. To 18 inches.
Picea glauca albertiana (Alberta Spruce)	Dwarf, conical Spruce, growing slowly to about 4 feet.
Taxus cuspidata densa (Japanese Yew)	Low, compact but irregular, dark evergreen, bush-like in character. Very hardy.

Remarks

A desirable medium-height sort that has many rock garden uses where a "change of pace" is desirable.

Worthwhile largely because it flowers so late in the season. Likes sun but is not particular about soil.

A neat little carpeter, evergreen like so many other Sedums. Well drained position and full sun exposure.

Evergreen, and does well in shallow soil and full sun. Bright red flowers on fat 4-inch stalks from old rosettes.

Spreads rapidly over low rocks and shallow soil in full sun. Forms a dense but delicate blanket, as leaves are very small.

A delicate, unobtrusive but charming plant useful in many rock garden spots and companionships. Full sun advisable.

Invaluable, but in time must be watched lest it overrun small neighbors. Perfectly hardy and very free-flowering if given sun and good drainage.

Typical large Crocus-type blooms. Plants increase rapidly by offsets and self-sowing seeds. Welcome in any sunny part of the rock garden.

Sun or part shade, regular soil. Plant 4 inches deep in groups of at least three. Variety Gravetye Giant is one of the best.

A delightful bicolor hybrid that flowers for several weeks. Valuable anywhere that the soil is deep, in sun or summer shade.

Stronger than most Grape-hyacinths, with larger flower heads of typical form. Best in small groups. Sun or part shade.

Taller than most sibericas, and more showy. Best used in small groups, sun or part shade. Plant 3 inches deep, in early autumn.

Truly dwarf, often with several flowers on a stem. Best in groups of 3 or 4. Dry, sunny location.

Small groups in full sun and well-drained soil. Gaiety is one of the best varieties — really outstanding.

An excellent year-round accent-point where moderate height is needed. Deep soil and full sun for best development.

Spreads delightfully over rocks or soil. Needs deep root pocket and full sun. There are other similar but taller forms.

Choicest of the choice for sandy, acid soil, full sun or part shade. Variety *prostratum* is similar, but all branches hug the ground.

An exceptionally dense and symmetrical little pointed evergreen of formal appearance. Deep soil and full sun advisable.

Valuable in fair-sized rock gardens to add year-round "weight" to the rear areas. Sun or part shade, deep soil.

ROBERT S. LEMMON

HOW TO BUILD AND PLANT A DRY WALL GARDEN

Yes, a dry wall garden is a rock garden—of a sort. In fact, it's the only sort of rock garden which seems really to belong among the boulder-strewn uplands of southern New England. Perhaps this indigenous quality is what pleases us most about our dry wall garden.

Yet it has plenty of other good reasons to recommend it to the attention of home gardeners. Carefully laid, the dry wall itself forms a permanent and functional part of the garden scheme. It may retain a banking, provide needed air drainage for an upper terrace, enclose a sunken Herb or Rose garden, form a transitional feature between two different ground levels, or terminate a garden vista at the property line. Ingeniously planted, this same dry wall becomes a thing of striking beauty, a part of the garden most rewarding to the gardener's efforts and a center of attraction for garden guests.

Of course, it is not as easy to build and plant a rock wall as it is to spade and sow a Bean patch. Once do the job right, however, and you'll never have to do it over. You will find no lack of colorful plants ready to set up permanent housekeeping in the crevices of your wall. Plenty of them will stand hard freezing weather; most of them will bear long hours of blazing sunlight. By selecting your planting subjects wisely, you can manage to have a long blooming season. And as for weeds, the few that find a foothold in the rock wall may be disposed of with hardly the bother of stooping—as easy as picking Pole Beans.

Good drainage is essential to the dry wall; a rock plant wouldn't be a rock plant if it liked muddy feet. More important still, especially if the wall is to be a high one, is the problem of preventing heaving by frost action. From one to two feet of loose grouting in a trench at the foot of the wall will insure against serious damage.

The stones that went into my particular rock wall were granite. I found them scattered on the slope below our old farmhouse, the debris of an orchard wall thrown up by the first settlers. But gardeners less happily situated than I can use a variety of other material with equal success. Weathered limestone, rough slabs of slate, bluestone—these are available elsewhere, and since they are naturally stratified in form, may be laid up with even greater ease by the amateur wall builder.

It is well to find room for the heaviest stones at the bottom of the wall. They should rest solidly on the grouting. Any that show a tendency to "diddle" must be securely chocked with wedge-shaped fragments. Irregular field stones will not lay up in even courses, but it is sound practice to build your wall in horizontal layers. Always use battens and a mason's line; never trust your eye alone to keep straight a long stretch of wall. And always remember that stone must rest securely on stone—never on earth—or else the first spring thaw will cause your rocks to shift.

Unless your local climate is unusually moist, you will do well to "rake" the face of your rock wall sharply. That is, set each succeeding course of rockwork a little behind the course below. A good rule calls for a setback of one foot for every five feet of height. This setback will mean that rain falling at the top of the wall will trickle back between the stones all the way down to the base without washing out the soil which is packed in all the pockets and the crevices of the wall.

Filling in the soil around a dry wall is tricky. If many air pockets are left, it will be impossible for the roots of your wall plants to secure a sufficient supply of moisture. Wherever possible, "break" your joints. This means that a vertical crevice between stones should never extend through more than one course, otherwise washouts will be certain to result.

The time to plant a rock wall is while it is in process of building. Select a crevice so shaped as naturally to catch and retain its share of rain water. The opening in the face of the wall may be small, but make sure that there is room at the back for a generous root growth. Lay your plant material in position, fan the roots out downward and backward; tamp in plenty of rich loam with added leafmold and compost. Sprinkle ground limestone and a little bone meal into the fill that goes behind the wall. Water well, fill in with more loam any holes which wash open, and you are ready to lay the next course.

Don't make the mistake of spacing your plants too close together; most of them are rampant growers. Choose subjects with an eye to (1) their blooming season, (2) their color, both of blossom and of foliage, (3) their predilections as to sunshine or shade, and (4) their habits of growth.

And what to plant? There are a number of sure-fire choices for the sunny wall. Arabis, white and pink, Aubrietia, and *Cerastium tomen-*

tosum (Snow-in-Summer) thrive in all weathers, especially the last named, which is notable for its luxuriant gray-green foliage. *Iberis sempervirens* is never happier than when digging itself into a vertical wall. *Alyssum citrinum* combines a clear soft color with interesting leafage. *Campanula garganica* and *C. muralis,* the Sedums, Edelweiss, Santolina, *Aethionema cordifolium,* and *Gypsophila repens* are all to be recommended. The judicious gardener will avoid the overshowy rock Phlox but will not omit the delightful *P. divaricata.*

If your wall is in partial shade, you will find that the Sempervivums flourish, and the Saxifrages and the Primulas. The delicate flowers of *Linaria alpina* will do well here. *Campanula carpatica* and *Arenaria montana* and *A. balearica* are exceedingly graceful. You will discover many more.

DAVID W. BAILEY

A GARDEN
TO ATTRACT BIRDS

FIRST PRINCIPLES

It would be perfectly possible, no doubt, to enjoy lovely home grounds and a thoroughly successful garden without the presence of a single bird —possible, but completely undesirable. Without getting sentimental about it, I've never met a gardener to whom the early spring warble of a bluebird, the flash of a hummingbird's ruby-red throat in the June sunlight, or the sight of a robin splattering in the bird bath on a baking August afternoon, fell short of being a major highlight in the day's puttering around among plants. Birds go with gardening as naturally as ducks do with water, and most of us feel that the more of them there are

around the better. It is with the ways and means of achieving such a
final objective that this section is concerned.

Our desirable native birds—the robins, chickadees, cardinals, hummingbirds, song sparrows and all the rest without whose presence we
would feel cheated of one of the solid pleasures of suburban or country
living—decide to visit your garden and grounds, and perhaps make
their home there for a time at least, for pretty much the same reasons that
would influence you. Chiefly, they want congenial surroundings—peace
and quiet, reasonable safety from their enemies, plenty of food and water,
a comfortable spot to spend the night, perhaps an ideal nook to set up
housekeeping and raise a family. Most of them are conservatives in the
sense that they are suspicious of anything that looks odd or strange according to their lights. And they are complete realists in their refusal to
be taken in by any fancy fixings that do not satisfy these fundamental
desires.

Providing successfully attractive conditions for birds is by no means
difficult even on small properties, once the principles are understood, for
birds are confirmed wanderers and explorers and surprisingly quick to
take advantage of any good opportunities they come across. I know a
50 by 100 foot place in the outskirts of a big city, which, besides the
owner's family of three, is the more or less regular home of nine different
kinds of desirable wild birds and the casual stopping place of at least
twenty more. This may sound surprising, but actually it is a situation
which can be matched by anyone similarly situated who sets out to "plan
it that way". The tangible assets are mainly shrubs chosen for their production of berries that birds like as well as density of growth that provides
safe nesting sites and hiding places, a couple of fair-sized evergreen trees
for winter shelter, a few properly designed and well-located nest-boxes,

two feeding stations that are never without plentiful seeds and other favorite foods from November to April, and a warm-weather bathing and drinking pool in which the water is kept constantly clean and fresh. And finally, a quiet sort of human family that never scares the wits out of its bird guests by shooting off firecrackers or running the radio full blast with all the windows open.

Before you turn to the practical, how-to suggestions in the pages which follow, let me stress the importance of an attitude toward birds which, however much it may be stimulated by sympathy, is always implemented by common sense. The dominating instinct of all birds is to remain alive, if possible, in a world which, to them, holds a never-ending series of perils that would drive us insane if we had to face them so directly in our own affairs. The success of your bird-attracting efforts will

be in direct ratio to your realization of this hard fact and the extent to which you capitalize on that understanding. The objective is well defined, good fun, and thoroughly worthwhile. And you don't need to turn your place or your other interests upside down to attain it.

HOMES AND SHELTERS

A well balanced bird-attracting program can well begin with providing nest-building facilities for certain species which can be expected to utilize them, and non-nesting shelter for the more numerous kinds which are likely to drop in for a visit even though, for one reason or another, they have no intention of setting up housekeeping. Not infrequently these two classes of enticement overlap in their effectiveness, so let's straighten out the confusion a bit. First, the housing problem:

For present purposes there are two general classes of birds: (1) those which habitually nest in "natural" places, such as the branches of trees, in bushes, and on or near the ground; and (2) those which will patronize the various kinds of bird houses and nesting shelves made by man. The former group is definitely in the majority, and includes such old favorites as catbirds, the various sparrows, cardinals, vireos, hummingbirds, towhees (chewinks), blue jays, warblers, thrushes, orioles, brown thrashers, and so on. The latter group is pretty much limited to those which, in their normal wild state, nest either in holes in trees (the woodpeckers, nuthatches, chickadees, crested flycatcher, wrens, bluebird, tree swallow and purple martin), or on more or less flat surfaces such as a rock crevice (in the case of the phoebe) or a tree crotch (like the robin). A hole-nester would no more think of going out on a limb to raise her family than a branch addict would choose a bird house for that or any other purpose, so the obvious thing to do is to provide for *both* classes. Incidentally, lest you think I have forgotten something important, these pages will purposely avoid saying a good word, in any connection, for the imported English sparrow and the equally obnoxious starling, both of which are hole-loving immigrants and inexcusable bullies in the opinion of people who believe in giving our native birds a fair break.

For the "natural-site" species the ideal combination is thick shrubbery; a few good-sized deciduous trees like Oak, Maple, Elm and Apple; a Pine or two if there's room; several small, dense evergreens, preferably Junipers; and a bit of more or less "wild" land in which long grass, small trees and bushes grow uncut and undisturbed. The ordinary red-berried Barberry, especially if allowed to grow in its rather graceful natural form, has a particular homemaking appeal to catbirds and song sparrows, both of which seem to like the protection of its twigginess and countless spines through which they manage to slip without the slightest difficulty. Oaks and Pines are favorites of blue jays and perhaps mourning doves, if there are any around. Maples seem to be especially designed for robins, a big Elm is the Baltimore oriole's idea of heaven, and a sizable apple tree is likely to attract almost anything from a humming-bird up, including the incomparable kingbird.

If you have one or more of the dense, upright-growing Junipers you can be quite sure that any lady chipping sparrow in the neighborhood will rent it for the nesting season, and a well filled mixed shrub border containing such kinds of Spiraea, Viburnum, Forsythia, Weigela and the Bush Dogwoods is likely to attract any one or more of a half-dozen bird species. In case you happen to be one of those gardeners who let their climbing Roses grow into a bit of a tangle the chances are that when the leaves drop in the fall you'll see where at least one pair of birds— maybe brown thrashers, catbirds, song sparrows, cardinals, or even wood thrushes—took advantage of its secluded interior to build a nest and raise their youngsters.

I fully realize that on many small home properties a "wild" section such as was mentioned would look out of place and be virtually impossible for one reason or another. If you can manage one, though, by all means do so, even though it may be only a few square yards in extent. The more tangled and overgrown it is the better, for it is here that you will have your best chance to attract the more shy kinds of birds such as yellow warblers, vireos, towhees and least flycatchers. Others among the species formerly mentioned will patronize such a spot, too, so you can't very well lose, whatever happens. But for really top results remember that a "wild" section should be really as *wild and undisturbed* as possible. If it contains an old dead tree stub or two, so much the better, for woodpeckers may chip out a nesting hole in it, and chickadees and nuthatches, too, love to pick around such a relic.

The popularity of your place will be definitely increased if, in addition to such natural nesting places as we have been talking about, you provide a few man-made bird houses to accommodate the several species that insist upon building in holes. For most of us, depending somewhat upon the part of the country in which we live and also upon the fact that certain of the hole-builders are really forest birds by nature, the list of such tenants is very brief although high in quality—hardly more than wrens and bluebirds, together with purple martins in some regions where this striking species is found. Only on rather large, secluded places are you likely to have much luck with the nuthatches, chickadees and woodpeckers, and then only if the houses quite closely resemble the dead tree stubs or heavy branches in which their nesting cavities are usually found.

The simpler and less showy a bird house is the greater the likelihood of its attracting a pair of tenants. It should always be strictly a one-door, one-compartment, one-family affair, except for the sociable purple martins which definitely prefer multiple-family homes. Windows, chimneys, front porches and fancy paint are wholly out of order, for they are more likely to repel birds than attract them.

Robins rarely, if ever, nest in bird houses of the conventional type, but they will often utilize a shelter like this one, the construction plans of which are on the following page. They always seem to prefer some substantial support for their mud-and-grass nests—tree crotches, the junction of a good-sized limb with one of its side branches, the top of an exposed beam or similar shelf-like space, a dense mass of honeysuckle vine. A single pair will build from one to three nests in the course of a season, each one in a different site. The eggs, usually four to a nest, are unspotted and, as you might guess, "robin's egg blue" in color. The mud used in construction is carried in the birds' bills from some nearby wet spot and skillfully combined with rather fine grasses and similar material to form a mass which, when it dries, has considerable strength and durability. (Construction details, page 158.)

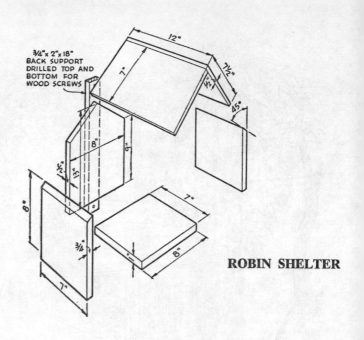

3/4" x 2" x 18"
BACK SUPPORT
DRILLED TOP AND
BOTTOM FOR
WOOD SCREWS

12"

7"

7½"

½"

45°

8"

9"

13"

½"

8"

7"

8"

3/4"

7"

ROBIN SHELTER

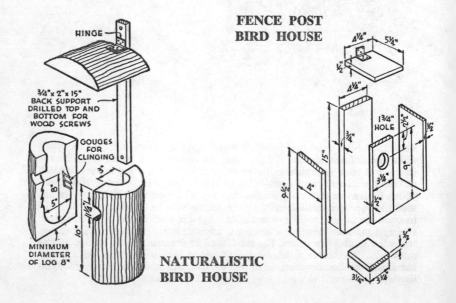

HINGE

**FENCE POST
BIRD HOUSE**

3/4" x 2" x 15"
BACK SUPPORT
DRILLED TOP AND
BOTTOM FOR
WOOD SCREWS

GOUGES
FOR
CLINGING

3"

8"

5"

1¼"

10"

MINIMUM
DIAMETER
OF LOG 8"

**NATURALISTIC
BIRD HOUSE**

4¼"

5¼"

½"

4¼"

3/4"

1¾"
HOLE

2½"

1½"

9½"

4"

9"

3/4"

½"

½"

3¼"

3¼"

Cavity-nesting species like a definitely open approach to their nest boxes—just why is hard to explain. Midday shade from above, however, is advisable to keep the interior from overheating on hot days, to the detriment of old and young birds alike. A few ¼-inch holes bored through the walls just below the roof are a good ventilation provision, in any event. The top of a tall fence post in open country is a good bluebird site, if the danger from prowling red squirrels and cats is negligible. A hinged roof facilitates removal of the old nest when the birds leave it, and a good cleaning of the interior—always a wise preparation for the next tenant. A dull, neutral-colored paint applied to the outside of the house will make it less conspicuous and considerably longer-lived.

Anyone with a little spare time and a moderate handiness with saw, hammer, wood drill and screwdriver can build bird houses that will be

Bird	Floor Area	Back Depth	Front Depth	Floor to Entrance	Entrance Diameter	Height Above Ground
Bluebird	5″ × 5″	9″	8″	6″	1½″	5′-10′
Chickadee*	4″ × 4″	9″	9″	6″	1⅛″	6′-15′
Flycatcher,						
Crested	6″ × 6″	9″	8″	6″	2″	8′-20′
Nuthatch*	4″ × 4″	9″	9″	7″	1¼″	12′-20′
Purple						
Martin**	6″ × 6″	6″	6″	1″	2½″	15′-20′
Swallow,						
Tree	5″ × 5″	7″	6″	1″-4″	1½″	10′-15′
Woodpeckers						
Downy*	4″ × 4″	9″	9″	7″	1¼″	6′-20′
Flicker	7″ × 7″	17″	16″	13″	2½″	6′-20′
Hairy*	6″ × 6″	14″	14″	10″	1½″	10′-20′
Redhead	6″ × 6″	14″	13″	10″	1½″	10′-20′
Wrens						
Bewick's	4″ × 4″	8″	7″	1″-5″	1⅛″	6′-10′
House	4″ × 4″	8″	7″	1″-5″	1⅛″	6′-10′

*By far the best box is a naturalistic one made from a section of tree trunk or heavy limb, sawed in half lengthwise, hollowed out as shown in diagram page 158, and the two halves put together again with long brass screws. It is quite a job to make, but will last for years. It is most likely to be used if attached to the top of a natural, bark-covered post or fastened to a tree trunk with nails driven through a strip of wood screwed to its back and extending a few inches beyond top and bottom. Also a possible night shelter in winter.

**Dimensions given are for each of the multiple compartments.

just as well patronized and last fully as long as any that can be bought ready-made. Essentially, all you need is a simple box of first-grade white pine ⅞″ thick, somewhat higher than it is wide, with a hinged top slanted forward enough to carry off the rain and projecting perhaps ½″ beyond the front and side walls. The type illustrated on pages 159 and 162 is perfectly satisfactory for the cavity-nesting species likely to visit your place, with the probable exception of nuthatches, chickadees and woodpeckers, whose special requirements will be considered later. The table above shows the dimensions for the various species.

Such a box, painted dark green, brown or gray and put together with screws, will last for years. It is inconspicuous and the thickness of its wood will provide sufficient insulation against overheating in summer unless it is placed in a really sunny place, in which case a half-dozen ¼″ holes drilled through the side and front walls just below the top will provide needed cooling ventilation. The hinged top, which normally is held in place with small galvanized screen hooks and eyes, simplifies removal of the old nest and thorough interior cleaning as soon as the family has departed—a sanitary courtesy which the next pair of home hunters is sure to appreciate, since none of these birds likes to build a new nest on top of an old one.

Elm trees are attractive to many kinds of birds, chiefly for the insect food they find there but, in the case of the Baltimore oriole, for nest-building as well. This tuneful, black-orange-and-white fellow very definitely prefers the tip of a high, drooping elm branch as the spot to weave the skillfully fastened, pouch-like nest so characteristic of his race. There it will swing and toss in the wind sometimes for several years before the last bits of it give way and fall; very rarely does one of them break loose during the first (and only) year it is used, so firmly is it lashed to the supporting twigs. Incidentally, it is the sober-colored lady of the house (the lower one of this pair) that does all the building; her mate just sports around and whistles cheerfully.

The tree-section type of bird house (plans on page 158) is quite a chore to make, but it is so natural in appearance that it will be utilized by the more particular kinds of cavity-nesters as well as the less choosy species. Since the former are the chief reason for making it, their preferences in the way of a site should be considered, also. The best location is on a more or less vertical tree trunk or heavy limb—the sort of place where the birds might hollow out a cavity themselves by chipping away at the dead wood. Attachment is by a vertical strip of wood screwed to the back of the house. Hinged top permits cleaning.

Actually, almost any kind of dark, hollow receptacle may gain tenants among the cavity-builders. Hollowed, well cured gourds are often used by wrens, and sections of rot-hollowed limbs such as are sometimes found in old, neglected orchards, can be utilized to advantage. The chief fault of most of these devices is that they do not last as long as a well-built, regular house; also, they are likely to develop rain leaks at any time.

Excellent shop-made bird houses, of course, are available for people who do not have the opportunity, skill or inclination to build their own. Most garden supply stores carry a considerable variety of designs, well built and reasonable in price. Among these my personal preference is for those made chiefly or entirely of cedar wood, with the bark on the outside; they are unobtrusive and naturalistic in appearance, and birds use them freely.

The multi-room martin house is an exception to that remark about naturalistic wood; it is too complicated in construction to warrant the use of anything except first-class dressed lumber. Incidentally, martins don't object at all to its looking artificial; on the contrary, the regularity with which a colony of them returns, year after year, once they have nested in it, seems to be proof that they thoroughly approve of both the appearance and the facilities provided.

The same stores that sell actual bird *houses* also carry, as a rule, the roofed-over shelves which robins, and sometimes phoebes, like as nesting places. A couple of these will be worth getting unless your property is already provided with natural nesting sites such as these birds prefer.

The observance of a few general principles will have a lot to do with the success of your bird-housing plans. Besides the various heights above the ground given in the specifications table, remember that these birds like a definitely open approach to their home sites; consequently, it is a mistake to place a house where it will be half buried in foliage. Actually, the best location is one which directly faces a wide-open space fifty or more feet across. It is a good idea, though, to choose a location that is shaded during the middle of the day, as the interior of even the best-designed bird house can get unconscionably hot if the sun beats down on it for hours at a time. For some reason, however, this does not seem to bother the purple martins; apparently it is a part of martin nature to like the sunniest, most exposed spot to be found.

The trunks and large limbs of trees are satisfactory anchorages for bird houses; their chief fault is their accessibility to marauding red squirrels and sometimes cats. The ideal support is probably the top of a post or a section of galvanized pipe into which a wooden plug has

Purple martins are sociable birds and customarily nest in colonies where inter-family conversations (and squabbles) are convenient and unending. A house for them, consequently, should be a multiple dwelling with a separate room for each pair. Building one at home is quite a construction operation, so most people prefer to buy one ready-made. It should contain not less than four rooms, and a dozen is not too many since the colony is likely to grow from season to season. Location is important—the top of a tall, heavy post in a fully exposed spot. Martins look like glorified swallows and are primarily insect-eaters.

been fitted to permit attachment of the box by a screw through the bottom or back. The pipe will be both cat- and squirrel-proof if at least 6 feet high and beyond jumping distance from the nearest tree, wall or other take-off point. A wooden post should be fitted with a flaring metal collar, described in the section on feeding stations, if you have reason to anticipate either cat or squirrel trouble.

And don't put up too many houses, lest their tenants spend a large part of their time trying to chase each other away. Two or three to an acre is usually enough—except in the case of wrens, whose boxes can be as close together as 75 feet without leading to too many civil wars.

Well, so much for nesting places. Now for non-housekeeping shelters of one kind and another.

The birds that are potential visitors to your place like natural protective cover for three purposes: (1) a safe place of retreat from their habitual enemies, chiefly cats and a few kinds of hawks; (2) shelter from storms (especially in winter); and (3) places to roost at night. To only a very limited extent will any of them put man-made devices to such uses, perhaps because their motives for seeking shelter are purely instinctive and therefore are served only by completely natural means.

The safety-from-enemies motive is best met by very thick-growing woody plant masses of one kind or another—a catbrier tangle, a Barberry hedge, large Forsythias, a jungle of Honeysuckle vines, for example. For storm shelter there is nothing quite equal to the various kinds of evergreen trees, especially Pines, Cedars and Yews. These, too, are favorite night-time retreats, though hardly more so than very dense deciduous shrubbery, vines, and those kinds of Oaks which hold their leaves far into the winter.

The great majority of shelter purposes can perfectly well be served by plants of definite ornamental value, so there's no need to make your place look like a piece of rundown wilderness just for the sake of the birds. If you keep in mind the general principles noted above you will find that, in whatever part of the country you live, there are plenty of available plants that will be welcomed by the birds and at the same time fit acceptably into your home planting plans.

FOODS AND FEEDING

You might not expect to find a similarity between birds and healthy children, but there is one: both are always hungry and so, if opportunity arises, always eating. Which goes a long way to explain why one of the surest ways to make your place popular among the neighborhood birds is to provide plenty of the kinds of food they like.

It is sometimes said that if you put out food for the birds you will spoil them, because easy living will turn them into sissies and make them indifferent to their normal job of consuming weed seeds, gobbling insects and their larvae, and otherwise doing their bit to maintain Nature's balance and help alleviate some of your gardening headaches. In theory this sounds plausible, but on the facts it just doesn't hold water, as you will discover if you watch some particular individual and check the amount of time he spends at the feeding station against that devoted to scrabbling around in search of his usual supply of nourishment. In the final analysis it is probable that the presence of a well-stocked feeder will actually increase the customary number of insects and seed pests destroyed by birds on your place, simply because there will be more birds around to hunt them out.

It is in winter, of course, that bird-feeding efforts will win the greatest response, chiefly because that is when the supply of natural foods is at a minimum, and also because the colder the weather the more provender the birds will need to keep them warm and strong. Indeed, I am almost tempted to say that from the time the trees leaf out in spring until their greenery starts to change color in the fall it is hardly worth while to keep the feeding program going even on a part-time basis, except as it involves various summer and early fall fruiting plants suggested later. This is the breeding and general activity season for all kinds of insects and hence the time of such abundant food supply that most kinds of birds will be quite indifferent to your efforts to give them a nutritional lift. Conversely, water for bathing and drinking takes on increased attraction value during the warm months.

With an eye to the period from late autumn to early spring, then, here are some practical suggestions, introduced by a few broad, clarifying principles:

Except in the warmest parts of the United States, the number of bird species likely to visit your place in winter is smaller than in spring and summer, because a lot of the warm-weather kinds will have migrated to the south where the weather is warmer. A few will be year-rounders (permanent residents, to use the ornithologists' term), such as the song sparrow, chickadee, downy woodpecker and white-breasted nuthatch, to cite some familiar examples. These will be supplemented by certain other species—tree sparrows, juncos, white-throated sparrows, perhaps crossbills and redpolls, for instance—whose breeding grounds are considerably farther north than your locality; they move down to spend the winter in what to them must seem a mild climate. When spring

Probably the best all-around winter bird-feeding unit, especially for the finches and other seed-eaters, is the so-called "weathercock" feeder which swings with the wind like a weathervane and thereby maintains a practically storm-proof interior. Its design can vary considerably so long as this pivoting feature is maintained, but the one pictured here and detailed on the following page is a standard type. The two side windows are important, since birds will enter more willingly if they can see out in several directions. Preferably it should be located in an open space, within easy flying distance of shrubs or trees but far enough from the latter to keep squirrels from jumping onto it. If the bottom of the feeder is about 5 feet from the ground, it will be safe from cats and still low enough to allow easy replenishment of the food supply. Such a station, put into operation in November and kept going until spring, will be a magnet for many birds and an endless source of pleasure and amusement.

WEATHER-PROOF
BIRD FEEDER

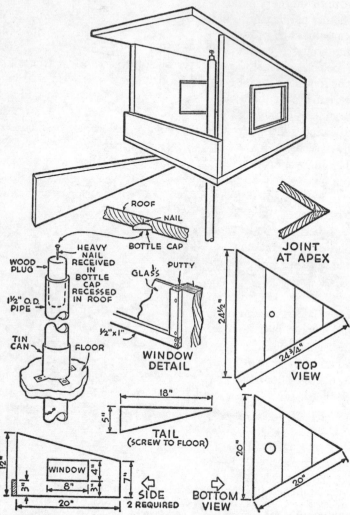

ROOF

NAIL

BOTTLE CAP

JOINT
AT APEX

WOOD
PLUG

HEAVY
NAIL
RECEIVED
IN
BOTTLE
CAP
RECESSED
IN ROOF

GLASS

PUTTY

1½" O.D.
PIPE

½"x1"

TIN
CAN

FLOOR

WINDOW
DETAIL

24½"

24¾"

TOP
VIEW

18"

5"

TAIL
(SCREW TO FLOOR)

20"

12"

WINDOW

4"

3"

8"

3"

7"

20"

SIDE
2 REQUIRED

20"

20"

BOTTOM
VIEW

Three-quarter-inch dressed lumber of good quality is the best material for the main parts of the weathercock feeder, except for the "tail" which can be of ½-inch stuff. Screws are used instead of nails when putting it together and careful construction is important both for weather-tightness and in order to insure the perfect balance which is necessary to its proper pivoting operation. As the plan shows, the whole device really hangs from the pivot point in the roof, which must be at the exact center of the assembled weight so that the supporting galvanized pipe will clear the sides of the floor hole through which it passes; it may take some experimenting to determine the precise position of this pivotal point. Heavy grease in the bottle-cap prevents rusting.

returns these winter visitors will head north and you won't see them again until the next autumn.

Whether permanent residents or merely winter visitants, the birds that you can attract by providing a food supply can be divided into two fairly definite groups: "vegetarians" and "non-vegetarians". I say "fairly definite" because, actually, neither group invariably restricts itself to the kind of food it is supposed to eat. I have seen a slate-colored junco—a vegetarian if ever there was one—dart out from a shrub and snatch a small miller in mid-air as deftly as any flycatcher could. The first group includes the sparrows and finches, whose winter food consists primarily of seeds. In the second group are the insect-eating chickadees, nuthatches and woodpeckers, all of which will feed eagerly on suet. Members of both groups may on occasion feed on the berries and fruits of certain trees and shrubs, or on special items that might surprise you; thus, blue jays, nuthatches and chickadees all go for sunflower seeds in a big way, and another favorite of theirs is peanut butter, probably because of the amount of oil it contains.

Bearing these various facts in mind, suppose we look now at a wintertime food list which is planned to provide a practically complete menu with the exception of those items produced by growing plants which are discussed later. First, meals chiefly for the "vegetarians":

The favorite basic diet for the several winter sparrow species, purple finches, goldfinches and other seed eaters consists of seeds, obviously. Millet and hemp are especially popular, cracked corn much less so. I am not too keen about the "bird-feeding mixtures" commonly offered for sale; the several different ones I have tried proved expensive and contained such a high percentage of seldom-touched seeds that the waste was considerable. Chick scratch-feed, obtainable at any poultry supply store, is fairly satisfactory. Personally, I prefer to buy the two or three special favorites separately, along with sunflower seeds for the particular edification of the jays, chickadees, nuthatches and purple finches. A home-made mixture of these, in about equal proportions, is hard to beat.

Some of the experts frown on the use of stale bread crumbs as a winter food, I suppose because they contain less concentrated nourishment. Birds like them pretty well, though, and they do help out in case the real seed supply runs temporarily low. They will be doubly welcomed by chickadees and jays, especially, if they are stirred around in a little hot bacon grease or some other animal fat before being distributed outdoors.

Actually, almost any kind of cracker or stale cake crumbs is worth putting before the winter birds. Even doughnuts that have become too

The outside of a window ledge, on the sheltered side of the house, is a first-class location for a feeding station; winter birds will soon discover it and quickly become accustomed to eating their meals within a few feet of people inside the room. The best type has glass ends, an open front and a hinged glass back next to the window to enable one to replenish the food without going outdoors.

hard for human consumption will do a lot more good on the feeding shelf than in the garbage can.

As has already been said, animal fats are standard food for the non-vegetarian species. Good beef suet is the best, but fat trimmings from any of the meats bought for your own table will do very well indeed. These foods need no cooking or special preparation; they are at their best when completely raw. Their appeal is widened to cover some of the seed-eaters, however, if you melt them and then stir in about an equal quantity, by bulk, of hemp and millet seeds. This mess can be applied hot to pine cones, or stuffed into the holes of a feeding stick when partly cooled.

Much depends upon the way the various foods are made available to the birds. Since snow obviously conceals and makes them more or less unattainable temporarily, and exposure to rain will turn the grains soggy and perhaps sour, some sort of shelter from the elements is important. A plain wooden shelf at least a foot square, with a tight overhanging roof of some sort, will serve fairly well. The food will be better protected from driving storms, however, if the shelf has three walls as well as the roof, with the fourth side open for the birds to go in and out. The device will be much more successful if a pane of glass is set into each wall, as birds like to be able to see out when they are feeding. The open side, of course, should face in the direction from which the winter storms are least likely to come. This point is automatically taken care of by the "weathercock" feeder whose projecting tail causes it to pivot like a weathervane and always face the wind. Whatever the design of the tray, a light wooden coping an inch or so high will prevent a good deal of the grain being scratched out by the feeding birds. White is a standard color for feeding trays, perhaps because it is the least conspicuous when the ground is covered with snow.

While a feeding shelf is designed primarily for the seed-eaters, a little extra attention will draw most of the suet-feeders, also. Leaving the suet lying loose on the floor is likely to prove wasteful, for any blue jay that arrives is sure to fly away with large chunks and lose most of them. To avoid such difficulties, a wire or string mesh pocket can be nailed on the inside of one wall to hold the suet so that it will be pecked out bit by bit instead of bolted wholesale. A still better plan is to install a feeding stick, which is merely a short section of some soft-wooded branch three or four inches thick in which a number of one-inch holes have been bored and filled with suet, or the suet-seed mixture previously mentioned. The stick can be held upright by driving into the floor of the tray a headless nail which will fit into a small hole drilled in the center of one end of the stick. Thus, the gadget can be removed easily for refilling when empty. A somewhat longer feeding stick, wired to a tree trunk or heavy branch, will prove highly attractive, too. Or one of these devices can be hung from a strong branch by means of a wire attached to one end; several kinds of birds will feed at it even though it is swinging free in the air. Fully open pine cones, dipped in heated fat and, after cooling, hung by strings from the branches, will also prove popular.

A stationary feeding shelf can be placed in a variety of locations. A windowsill is excellent, for there the birds will be in full and close view from the room, especially if the side next to the window consists chiefly of glass. Another good location, which can be made cat- and squirrel-proof with a circular metal collar two feet wide, flaring out and slightly downward from the support, is on top of a firmly set wooden or metal post standing five or six feet above the ground. For a third idea, suspend it by a heavy wire from a stout tree limb; this may or may not protect it from raids by squirrels, but there is little chance that cats will get at it provided you hang it at least five feet from the ground.

Besides their installation on a feeding shelf, suet holders will be in steady winter demand by chickadees, brown creepers, nuthatches and woodpeckers if you fasten them to tree trunks at such heights as make them readily accessible for refilling. Quarter-inch or ½-inch mesh wire is the material generally used for making the holders; squares of it about 6″ × 6″ will serve if attached by several wire nails driven into the wood and slightly bent, but a box-like affair not more than a couple of inches from front to back and equipped with a hinged lid for easy re-filling is more workmanlike. Some people believe that the use of wire mesh of any sort is undesirable, on the theory that a bird's eye coming in contact with the metal as he picks at the suet through the openings in very cold weather may freeze fast to it. I have never been able to run down an authenticated case of such a mishap. Its occurrence seems highly unlikely, since birds are no more prone than we to go around rubbing their eyeballs on foreign substances, of wire or anything else, whether the weather's cold or hot. If you have misgivings, though, simply substitute a container made of string mesh, or even narrow strips of wood with openings be-tween them. Or lacking all of these, tie sizable chunks of suet to the trunk or limb with several laps of cord.

A person who is fairly handy with tools can easily make his own feed-ing devices, for they need not conform to any special size, pattern or pro-portions. Perfectly good and serviceable ones can be bought ready-made, too; you will find them advertised in various magazines and newspaper garden columns, as well as on display in garden supply stores and many suburban hardware centers.

One final bit of advice before we go on to the next section and look at "natural" food: once you start feeding the winter birds, don't give it up until spring has really come. Actually, birds are more likely to need your help late in the winter when their normal sources of supply begin to run short than they do earlier. In addition to that, it's hardly fair to get a lot of them thoroughly accustomed to coming around several times a day for a much-needed handout, and then cut them adrift without anything.

PLANTS THAT FURNISH NATURAL FOOD

I have never seen a complete tabulation of the number of bird species that, at one time or another, subsist in large measure on either or both of the two general classes of plant-produced food: seeds and small, berry-like fruits. Undoubtedly the grand total is impressive, for well-authenticated reports state that as many as 118 different kinds of birds will eat the blackish little berries of our common wild elder, and that each of at least a half-dozen other berry-bearing native plants is patronized by fifty or more species. Very few indeed of the trees, shrubs and vines that bear fruit the size of grapes or smaller are entirely ignored by birds, and I suppose that virtually every kind of plant in the enormous group that forms what we commonly call seeds contributes its share of provender to sustain the feathered population.

It is evident, therefore, that well chosen living plants can play a leading part in enhancing your home grounds' attractiveness to birds. They cannot, to be sure, take over the job accomplished in winter by the program discussed earlier, unless you plant on a scale and at a cost that are all but prohibitive. But they are a first-class supplement to your own direct efforts, and some of them have the added advantage of being far more effective during the warmer months than any other bird-attracting schemes you can evolve. The number of birds that flock to a Cherry tree when the fruit is ripe, or patronize a Blueberry or Raspberry planting, or a patch of buckwheat, under similar circumstances, is impressive albeit sometimes a little irritating!

In view of all this it would seem to be simple enough to turn your home grounds into a sort of avian Delmonico's simply by planting them with all kinds of food-bearing things. From a realistic standpoint, though, this would be neither wise nor as alluring to the birds as you might think. In the first place, that kind of planting would be pretty sure to look confused and uninteresting from the landscaping standpoint, and therefore unsuited to the kind of home properties most of us have and the kinds of life we live. And secondly, such a miscellaneous collection would probably contain a good many plants of varied appearance but duplicating attractiveness to birds, so that they would serve no purpose which could not be matched by a smaller, more thoughtfully selected list.

Since you want to please yourself as well as the birds with the plants around your home, I suggest that you choose as food producers only those which have at least a fair share of landscaping merit. There are such—plenty of them—that you can buy from the better nurseries in various parts of the country. In the main, that is the sort selected for the lists which follow. Even a few of them, interspersed among the more usual home-grounds plantings which you may already have, will increase the number and variety of your bird visitors materially.

Let me especially recommend that you select kinds which will provide a succession of foods over a long period—from June until mid-winter, if you have the space. After the latter date all of the natural food plants will have exhausted the bulk of their supplies, and the bird-feeding project will have to rely on the foods which you yourself provide.

And now for the plants and some of the more important bird species which patronize them, grouped according to their fitness for certain broad sections of the country.

These Look Well and Birds Like Them

Based on U. S. Department of Agriculture Data

NORTHEAST, MIDDLE ATLANTIC AND MIDWEST STATES

Trees

Kind	Chief Value	Birds Especially Attracted
Apple	Nesting	Many kinds, especially bluebird, flicker, hummingbird, kingbird
Birch, Gray *Betula populifolia*	Food—winter seeds, aphids in summer	Goldfinch, siskin, titmouse, warblers, vireos, etc.
Cedar, Red *Juniperus virginiana*	Fruit, shelter, some nesting	Bluebird, cardinal, cedar waxwing, chipping sparrow, mockingbird, robin and others
Dogwood, Flowering *Cornus florida*	Fruit, some nesting	Brown thrasher, purple finch, robin, towhee, vireos and many others
Elm, American *Ulmus americana*	Nesting, food	Baltimore oriole (nesting), brown creeper, chickadee, nuthatches, purple finch, scarlet tanager, warblers, woodpeckers, etc. (insects and larvae)
Hawthorns *Crataegus coccinia, C. cordata, C. crusgalli*	Fruit, some nesting	Hermit thrush, purple finch, robin, various others
Holly, American *Ilex opaca*	Fruit, protection, some nesting	Cedar waxwing, flicker, hermit thrush, robin and others
Juneberry *Amelanchier* species	Fruit	Blue jay, cardinal, catbird, flicker, thrushes, vireos and numerous others
Mountain Ash *Sorbus americana* and *Sorbus aucuparia*	Fruit	Baltimore oriole, brown thrasher, catbird, cedar waxwing, red-headed woodpecker, robin, etc.

Pepperidge, Sour Gum *Nyssa sylvatica*	Fruit, some nesting	Catbird, cedar waxwing, flicker, mockingbird, robin, thrushes, many others
Pine, Austrian and White *Pinus nigra and P. strobus*	Shelter, some nesting	Blue jay, various finches, hermit thrush, mourning dove and others
Sassafras *Sassafras variifolium*	Fruit	Catbird, flicker, robin, towhee, vireos, many others

Shrubs

Kind	*Chief Value*	*Birds Especially Attracted*
Barberry, Japanese *Berberis thunbergi*	Protection, nesting, fruit (slight)	Catbird, chipping sparrow, hermit thrush, junco, song sparrow, tree sparrow
Bayberry *Myrica carolininsis*	Fruit, some nesting	Bluebird, catbird, flicker, hermit thrush, myrtle warbler, tree swallow and many more
Blueberry *Vaccinium corymbosum*	Fruit	Bluebird, brown thrasher, catbird, thrushes, towhee and many more
Chokeberry *Aronia arbutifolia* and *A. melanocarpa*	Fruit	Brown thrasher, catbird, meadow lark and others
Dogwood, Shrub *Cornus alternifolia* and *C. amomum*	Fruit	Bluebird, brown thrasher, cardinal, catbird, flicker, purple finch, robin, thrushes, towhee, etc.
Elder *Sambucus canadensis* and *C. racemosa*	Fruit	Bluebird, catbird, flicker, mockingbird, robin, thrushes, towhee, vireos, etc.
Euonymus, Winged *Euonymus alatus*	Fruit, protection, nesting	Catbird, brown thrasher, cardinal, finches, towhee
Honeysuckle *Lonicera morrowi* and *L. tatarica*	Fruit, nesting	Catbird, brown thrasher, robin, thrushes, towhee and others
Snowberry *Symphoricarpos albus*	Fruit	Cedar waxwing, robin, pine grosbeak, etc.

Spicebush *Benzoin aestivale*	Fruit	Veery, vireos, wood thrush, etc.
Sumac *Rhus canadensis*	Fruit	Bluebird, various finches, robin and others
Viburnum *Viburnum aceri- folium, V. denta- tum, V. lentago*	Fruit, some shelter and nesting	Bluebird, cedar waxwing, flicker, purple finch, robin, thrushes and many others
Winterberry *Ilex verticillata*	Fruit	Bluebird, brown thrasher, cedar waxwing, hermit thrush, purple finch and others

Vines

Honeysuckle *Lonicera japon- ica halliana*	Fruit, nesting, shelter	Bluebird, chipping sparrow, goldfinch, pine grosbeak, pur- ple finch, robin, many others
Virginia Creeper *Parthenocissus quinquefolia*	Fruit, shelter	Flicker, mockingbird, purple finch, robin, many others

Hummingbird Special

Abelia	Cypress Vine	Hollyhock	Petunia
Albizzia	Daylily	Honeysuckle	Phlox
Althea	Delphinium	Hosta	Scabiosa
Azalea hinodegiri	Four-o'clock	Iris	Scarlet Runner Bean
Beautybush	Fuchsia	Lantana	Scarlet Sage, Salvia
Kolkwitzia	Geranium	Larkspur	Snapdragon
Beebalm, Bergamot	(*Pelargonium*)	Lilies	Spider Plant
Buddleia	Gilia	Mertensia	Tritoma
Campanula	Gladiolus	Mimosa	Trumpet-vine
Cardinal Climber	Great Solomon's	Morning-glory	Weigela
Columbine	Seal	Nasturtium	
Coral-bells	Hibiscus	Penstemon	

SOUTHEASTERN STATES

Trees

Kind	*Chief Value*	*Birds Especially Attracted*
Cedar, Red *Juniperus virgini- ana*	Fruit, nesting, shelter	Bluebird, cardinal, cedar wax- wing, chipping sparrow, mockingbird, robin, etc.

Dogwood, Flowering *Cornus florida*	Fruit, some nesting	Bluebird, brown thrasher, cardinal, flicker, robin, thrushes, vireos and others
Hackberry, Sugarberry *Celtis laevigata*	Fruit, nesting	Bluebird, brown thrasher, cardinal, flicker, mockingbird, robin, thrushes, etc.
Holly, American *Ilex opaca*	Fruit, shelter, some nesting	Brown thrasher, hermit thrush, mockingbird, robin and others
Juneberry *Amelanchier canadensis*	Fruit, some nesting	Bluebird, cardinal, catbird, flicker, scarlet tanager, thrushes, etc.
Sweet Bay *Magnolia virginiana*	Fruit	Robin, sapsucker, vireos, etc.
Pepperidge, Sour Gum *Nyssa sylvatica*	Fruit, some nesting	Bluebird, brown thrasher, flicker, robin, thrushes, etc.
Sassafras *Sassafras variifolium*	Fruit	Bluebird, brown thrasher, flicker, mockingbird, robin, thrushes and others

Shrubs

Bayberry, Wax Myrtle *Myrica cariniensis, M. pumila, M. cerifera*	Fruit, some nesting and shelter	Brown thrasher, downy woodpecker, catbird, flicker, mockingbird, myrtle warbler, towhee, tree swallow, vireos, etc.
Beautyberry *Callicarpa americana*	Fruit, some nesting	Brown thrasher, cardinal, catbird, mockingbird, towhee and others
Blueberries, Huckleberries, (*Vaccinium*)	Fruit, some nesting	Bluebird, blue jay, brown thrasher, catbird, robin, towhee and many others
Elder *Sambucus canadensis*	Fruit	Bluebird, catbird, flicker, mockingbird, robin, thrushes and many others
Inkberry *Ilex glabra*	Fruit	Bluebird, catbird, mockingbird, thrushes, towhee, etc.
Spicebush *Benzoin aestivale*	Fruit	Cardinal, catbird, robin, vireos, etc.

Coralbead *Cocculus carolinus*	Fruit	Brown thrasher, mockingbird, robin, thrushes, etc.

Cedar waxwing and pepperidge berries

Vines

Kind	*Chief Value*	*Birds Especially Attracted*
Grapes, various wild	Fruit	Blue jay, cardinal, catbird, cedar waxwing, flicker, robin, summer tanager, etc.
Honeysuckle, Trumpet *Lonicera sempervirens*	Fruit, some nesting and shelter	Catbird, mockingbird, robin, vireos and others
Virginia Creeper *Parthenocissus quinquefolia*	Fruit	Bluebird, catbird, flicker, etc.

SOUTHWESTERN STATES

Trees

Cedar, Red *Juniperus virginiana*	Fruit, shelter, nesting	Bluebird, cardinal, cedar waxwing, flicker, mockingbird, robin, etc.

Dogwood, Flowering *Cornus florida*	Fruit, nesting	Bluebird, brown thrasher, cardinal, catbird, cedar waxwing, red-bellied woodpecker, many others
Holly, American *Ilex opaca*	Fruit, shelter, nesting	Bluebird, brown thrasher, catbird, hermit thrush, mockingbird, robin, etc.
Pepperidge, Sour Gum *Nyssa sylvatica*	Fruit, nesting	Brown thrasher, catbird, cedar waxwing, flicker, mockingbird, robin and others
Sassafras *Sassafras variifolium*	Fruit, some nesting	Bluebird, catbird, kingbird, red-eyed vireo, etc.

Shrubs

Beautyberry *Callicarpa americana*	Fruit, some nesting	Brown thrasher, cardinal, catbird, mockingbird, thrushes, towhee and others
Black Haw, Southern *Viburnum rufidulum*	Fruit, some nesting	Brown thrasher, cedar waxwing, robin, etc.
Blueberries and Huckleberries, various *Vaccinium*	Fruit, some nesting	Bluebird, blue jay, brown thrasher, cardinal, catbird, kingbird, mockingbird, orchard oriole, titmouse, towhee and others
Dogwood *Cornus amomum, C. asperifolia, C. femina*	Fruit, some nesting	Bluebird, brown thrasher, cardinal, catbird, cedar waxwing, flicker, robin, thrushes, vireos, etc.
Elder *Sambucus canadensis*	Fruit	Bluebird, brown thrasher, flicker, mockingbird, many others
Spicebush *Benzoin aestivale*	Fruit, some nesting	Cardinal, catbird, red-eyed vireo, thrushes, etc.
Sumac *Rhus copalina, R. canadensis, R. typhina*	Fruit	Bluebird, brown thrasher, flicker, hermit thrush, mockingbird and others

Vines

Grapes, various wild	Fruit	Blue jay, cardinal, catbird, cedar waxwing, flicker, mourning dove, red-headed woodpecker, thrushes, etc.
Honeysuckle, Trumpet *Lonicera semper-virens*	Fruit, shelter, some nesting	Catbird, hermit thrush, purple finch, robin and others
Virginia Creeper *Parthenocissus quinquefolia, P. heptaphylla*	Fruit	Bluebird, brown thrasher, mockingbird, red-bellied woodpecker, robin, thrushes, etc.

NORTHERN PLAINS AND ROCKY MOUNTAIN STATES

Trees

Cedar, Red *Juniperus virginiana*	Fruit, shelter, nesting	Bluebird, cedar waxwing, olive-backed thrush, robin, etc.
Mountain Ash *Sorbus decora*	Fruit, some nesting	Catbird, cedar waxwing, evening grosbeak, robin, etc.
Serviceberry *Amelanchier canadensis*	Fruit, nesting	Catbird, cedar waxwing, flicker, robin and others

Shrubs

Blueberries and Huckleberries, various *Vaccinium*	Fruit, some nesting	Bluebird, brown thrasher, cedar waxwing, flicker, robin, thrushes, and others.
Dogwoods, Bush *Cornus racemosa, C. stolonifera, C. amomum,* etc.	Fruit, some nesting	Bluebird, catbird, cedar waxwing, evening grosbeak, flicker, olive-backed thrush, robin and others
Elder *Sambucus canadensis*	Fruit	Bluebird, brown thrasher, catbird, flicker, thrushes, towhee, many others

Honeysuckles, Bush *Lonicera dioica, L. birsuta,* etc.	Fruit, some nesting	Bluebird, catbird, robin, thrushes and others
Junipers *Juniperus communis, J. horizontalis, J. utahensis*	Fruit, shelter, some nesting	Evening grosbeak, robin, thrushes, etc.
Nannyberry *Viburnum lentago*	Fruit, some nesting	Bluebird, catbird, flicker, hermit thrush, robin, etc.
Silverberry *Elaeagnus argentea*	Fruit, nesting	Bluebird, brown thrasher, robin, thrushes, towhee and others
Sumac *Rhus copallina, R. glabra*	Fruit	Bluebird, flicker, hermit thrush, red-headed woodpecker, robin, etc.

Vines

Grapes, Wild *Vitis vulpina, V. cinerea*	Fruit	Brown thrasher, catbird, flicker, kingbird, robin, etc.
Virginia Creeper *Parthenocissus quinquefolia*	Fruit	Bluebird, catbird, flicker, robin, vireos, many others

CALIFORNIA

Trees

Cherry, Bitter *Prunus emarginata*	Fruit, some nesting	Brewer's blackbird, Bullock's oriole, California jay, cedar waxwing, grosbeak (black-headed), russet-backed thrush, western tanager, etc.
Dogwood, Pacific *Cornus nuttalli*	Fruit, some nesting	Bluebird (western), California thrasher, flicker, kingbird, thrushes and many others
Juniper, Sierra *Juniperus occidentalis*	Fruit, shelter, nesting	Cedar waxwing, flicker, grosbeak (evening), robin, solitaire, thrushes, etc.

Mountain Ash, Western	Fruit, some nesting	California thrasher, cedar
Sorbus americana sitchensis		waxwing, grosbeak (evening), robin, thrushes and others

Shrubs

Elder, various *Sambucus*	Fruit	Bluebird, California thrasher, California towhee, flicker, kingbird, thrushes, etc.
Honeysuckle *Lonicera hispidula, L. interrupta*	Fruit, some nesting	California thrasher, robin, solitaire, thrushes, towhee (spotted), wren-tit, etc.
Juniper, California *Juniperus californica*	Fruit, shelter, nesting	Cedar waxwing, flicker, grosbeak (evening), solitaire, thrushes and others
Serviceberry *Amelanchier alnifolia*	Fruit	Bluebird (western), cedar waxwing, flicker, grosbeak (evening), thrushes, etc.
Sumac, various *Rhus*	Fruit	Bluebird (western), flicker, grosbeak, (evening), robin, thrasher (California) and others.

NORTHWEST COAST STATES

Trees

Dogwood *Cornus nuttalli*	Fruit, nesting	Bluebird, cedar waxwing, flicker, grosbeaks (evening and pine), purple finch, robin, many others
Madrona *Arbutus menziesi*	Fruit, shelter, nesting	Bohemian waxwing, cedar waxwing, flicker, robin, solitaire, etc.
Mountain Ash, Western *Sorbus americana sitchensis*	Fruit, some nesting	Bluebird, grosbeaks (evening and pine), robin, thrushes, etc.
Pine, Western White *Pinus monticola*	Shelter, nesting	Bluebird, jay (western), robin, siskin, etc.

Robin and towhee are among the species that like dogwood berries

Shrubs

Elder
   *Sambucus calli-
   carpa*
	Fruit	Bluebird, grosbeaks, robin, russet-backed thrush and others

Blueberries and Huckleberries, various *Vaccinium*	Fruit, nesting	Bluebird, cedar waxwing, flicker, robin, thrushes, etc.

Serviceberry
   *Amelanchier
   florida*
	Fruit, some nesting	Bluebird, grosbeaks, robin, solitaire, thrushes and others

Sumac *Rhus triloba*	Fruit	Bluebird, evening grosbeak, flicker, robin, etc.

WATER TO DRINK AND BATHE IN

If birds ever thought about such things, I suspect that a never-failing supply of fresh, cool water would be a star feature in their conception of summer in the Happy Hunting Grounds. Here on earth it is so vital—and obviously enjoyable—a factor in their warm-weather life that they wouldn't give it up in the Hereafter. Certainly we, planning as we are to make our home grounds especially attractive to birds, would be missing one of our very best opportunities if we failed to give water a major spot in the whole spring-to-autumn program.

Under normal circumstances it is probable that a bird's need for liquid refreshment, so to speak, is satisfied from a number of sources. Streams, swamps and ponds, of course, constitute a primary supply, unless severe drought dries them up. A part is played, too, by the juices of berries and other small fruits, and it may well be that a certain amount of the necessary supply comes from dew and from the raindrops that remain on the foliage after a shower. In any given locality, though, some or all of these opportunities for a drink (and in the raindrop case, a bath as well) may become scarce or even vanish entirely, and that's not so good. At such times, especially, a well-planned and well-tended bird pool is as popular a rendezvous as any oasis that the Sahara ever knew.

On the face of it, any kind of container that would hold water and be accessible to birds might seem to fill the bill, but actually it probably won't. Birds are choosy and have their own definite likes and dislikes. One of their notions is that the best way to get a drink—and the only way to take a bath—is to find a supply of water so shallow at the edge that they can wade right into it without getting wet above their feet unless they want to. Also, they thoroughly dislike a slippery surface—I suppose they don't enjoy falling any more than we do. Certainly they have an instinctive fear of drowning, and so you will never see one of them venture into water too deep to stand in safely, even though he may duck

his head completely under during the process of taking his favorite type of splatter-bath.

Out of these various considerations the specifications of a first-class bird pool begin to emerge rather clearly. For one thing, the depth of water from rim to center should increase evenly and very gradually (a slope of 1 inch in 7 is enough), starting at zero. Also, be sure to avoid material that is or may become slippery, such as glazed earthenware or painted metal. Slightly roughened cement and stone are both ideal. Sometimes a sprinkling of clean, coarse sand or fine gravel can be used to cure undue smoothness.

More or less circular or oval shapes are perhaps the most useful, since

A depression—natural or man-made—on top of a large rock outcrop can be developed into a perfect bird bath that will last just about forever. This drawing of one that actually exists suggests several popular features worth noting. First, full exposure and consequently safe, easy arrival and departure. Second, shallow margins with very gradual slope to the deeper center. Third, plenty of nearby spots to sit in the sun, preen feathers, and generally enjoy summer life. Fourth, enough ornamental planting to look well to human eyes. And finally, freedom from nearby shrubs or other concealment for sneak attacks by cats.

they can be entered with equal ease at all points. Since the purpose is to provide facilities for bathing as well as drinking, and since more than one bird may be using it at the same time, the water area should not be less than a foot across—preferably two or more, if you can arrange for that much.

Types and forms of baths can vary almost indefinitely provided they conform to the foregoing simple principles. Suppose we look at some of the possibilities from which you can choose according to your particular conditions and preference.

At the same stores that sell bird houses you are likely to find at least a fair assortment of baths, usually made of terra cotta, cement or sometimes concrete. Most of these look best in somewhat formal, well-tailored situations, but are perfectly all right almost anywhere. Other things being equal, birds will patronize them freely. Whether the bath is designed to go on top of a pedestal or be placed directly on the ground is neither here not there; both types are equally good.

If your grounds are on the formal side, and you don't mind the extra cost, one of the baths fitted with a simple, central jet fountain to be connected with the house water supply system may be well worth considering, as birds are particularly attracted by the sprinkle of falling water drops on hot days. (Incidentally, if you use a lawn sprinkler to any extent, it is more than likely that some of the birds will learn to love flying through its shower.)

The great majority of baths offered for sale are intended to be filled and emptied for cleaning by hand and have no provision for piping. This helps keep the cost down and from the practical standpoint is fully satisfactory. Just one word of warning: be sure and empty any terra cotta or other cement-like bird bath and store it under cover before winter shuts down; otherwise it may split or chip badly from frost action working inside the damp cement.

If you like to fuss around with such things, there are all kinds of opportunities in the way of home-devised bird baths. To note some of the best:

A dependable natural stream, no matter how small, can be made doubly popular by constructing a shallow, sand-bottom bay in a sunny spot somewhere along its course, or perhaps merely moving a few rocks so as to provide the graduated depth already described. Since birds seem to prefer an easy approach to the water, whether for bathing or merely to get a drink, the land immediately surrounding the pool should be cleared of all brush, large weeds and similar obstacles for three feet or so back from the edge.

A small brook that keeps going all summer is a star bird attractor, especially if enhanced by an open, shallow bay for complacent drinking and bathing. Many species will patronize such a spot, and often its margins will prove a popular place for robins to collect the mud which they use in nest building. Such a stream also may offer opportunity for broadening a pool below a natural waterfall so it will be improved for the birds' use. In all such work an important factor is very shallow margins.

If there is a large outcropping of ledge rock on your property it may well be the clue to a first-class bird bath. Not infrequently there is a natural depression near the top of such an outcrop which, if it is not already deep enough, can be made so by some earnest work with a stone mason's chisel and heavy hammer. The more irregular the outline of such a basin the more naturalistic it will look, and in size it can be as large as circumstances and your energy may determine. I have such a place that is roughly 5 feet long by three in width, and on a hot summer day it is the center of a sort of three-ring flying circus. It holds about ten gallons of water, which are replenished by hand unless a rainstorm is obliging enough to save us that trouble. The basin never leaks or cracks in winter, and when it needs cleaning the whole business is simply sprinkled with sand to act as a slime cutter and then swept out with an old kitchen broom and some water.

Lacking a suitable rock outcrop, an excellent simulated one can be made from a good-sized rough slab of any non-stratified rock, hollowed out by a stone mason and sunk flush with the ground. Such an installation really has all the merits of one that "grew there"; the only criticisms are the effort and expense of making it.

A good in-the-ground bath can also be made by scooping out a properly graduated depression in the soil and lining it with a 2-inch layer of reinforced concrete applied directly on the soil. If the location is naturally well drained, and heavy-gauge poultry netting is used for the reinforcement, frost damage to the concrete is unlikely to be so serious that a little fresh cementing in the spring won't repair it. The best lining of all, of course, is sheet lead, for it lasts just about forever.

There are no hard-and-fast rules governing a successful location for a bird pool, but it is worth while to consider certain factors which, in the long run, can mean better patronage than you would otherwise get.

Some cats are inveterate stalkers and killers of birds, and since there is no telling when a feline of this type is going to show up in your neighborhood, you will do well to arrange matters so that there is no low shrubbery or other concealment within 12 or 15 feet of the bath which pussies can use as cover for sneak attacks. Birds are constantly alert to danger and will take off with astonishing speed if they catch sight of a cat in the open. But if said cat can crawl up unseen until she (he or it) is close enough for one lightning spring, it won't be so good for the

Conventional manufactured bird baths of this general type are fully satisfactory if they are kept clean and refilled with fresh water every day or two during hot weather. Perhaps they look best in rather formal surroundings, but that is a minor consideration. In the matter of care, the inside of the basin part can be quickly cleaned, when necessary, by scouring with sand and a wad of burlap. Both basin and pedestal should be stored in a dry place for the winter to prevent frost damage to the exposed cement when it is wet.

bathers or drinkers. You need have no reservations about the birds' willingness to patronize a fully exposed pool, once they get accustomed to it. On the contrary, I sometimes think that the more open the immediate location the better they like it, especially if there is shrubbery, a small tree or other protective cover within a few yards into which they can dart if they think danger threatens and also use as a final survey point before coming in for water.

Sunny days are the most popular for bird splattering, presumably because the subsequent drying out process is quicker and more enjoyable under such conditions. Furthermore, post-bath fluttering, preening and basking in broad sunlight are no less popular with birds than with people, as you will soon discover if there is a sun-drenched rock, fence top or other accommodating spot within flitting distance of the pool. Those that come merely for a drink may not bother with such a luxury, but the bathers often will, and their obvious pleasure in the process is one of the events in any bird-watcher's day.

In very many ways the overwhelming majority of the native bird species you will come in contact with are fastidious to the *nth* degree. It is not surprising, then, that they prefer fresh water to stale and clean containers to scummy ones. In practical terms this means that the water in a bathing and drinking pool should be completely changed no less frequently than every two days in average spring and summer weather, and every day when things are really hot and dry. On especially baking days,

A lawn sprinkler on a hot day may prove thoroughly delightful to the neighborhood birds once they get the idea of flying through its drops for an open-air shower bath. The readiness with which they take to this particular kind of refreshment clearly points to the part which natural raindrops play in their natural lives, not only as a substitute for a bath, but perhaps also as an emergency method of getting a drink. Birds, after all, are complete realists!

WINTER DRINKING FOUNTAIN

HANGING SEED-
FEEDER, SUET-CAKE
HOLDER ON TRUNK

WINDOW-SILL FEEDER

BOX ON FENCE, VINES AND SUET STICK ON TRELLIS

Some final suggestions you may want to try

too, a refilling with cold water in early afternoon will bring a surprisingly quick response, particularly if the pool is in full sun. As for the containers themselves, cement and terra cotta pools are easily scoured with coarse sand, a good-sized wad of burlap and a little water, then flushed and emptied; this is a weekly chore, or more often if conditions indicate the need. Lest these attentions sound over-fussy, just watch the results!

If you are so fortunate as to possess a natural pond of fair size, cherish it with all care for it is one of the most effective magnets for our native birds that one could name. Not only will the water expanse itself lure species which otherwise probably would not come around, such as the several kinds of swallows which habitually drink while on the wing by skimming low and scooping up the water in their bills like a fast locomotive filling its tank from a trough between the rails. Of equal importance, I think, is the attractiveness of the surroundings—marshland, bushes, tall grasses—which will draw still other kinds unlikely to pay much attention to drier, more sophisticated places. Ten minutes' watching on a summer morning will demonstrate very clearly indeed what a center of interest to the neighborhood birds such a body of water usually is.

Circumstances vary, of course, but if the idea is at all feasible let me urge that you utilize at least a part of the immediate surroundings of such a pond for the "wild spot" mentioned in the first part of this chapter. It may call for some additional planting, but many times you need do no more than let Nature take her course in building up the kind of cover that many birds prefer above all others. Guard against fire, hunters and cats, and what on its face is no more than a simple body of water can become in time the center of a virtual bird sanctuary.

And speaking of water for birds, what about its being a breeding place for millions of mosquitoes—whether it be in the form of a natural pond or brook, or merely a little artificial basin on a pedestal at the end of the garden path? Well, there is no doubt at all that mosquitoes do lay their eggs in water, and that the larvae that hatch from those eggs rather speedily turn into insects with all the unpleasant characteristics of their ancestors. But primarily it is stale, stagnant water rather than the fresh, flowing kind that provides the conditions for pestiferous mosquito breeding. Hence, so far as the usual types of bird bathing places are concerned, you merely clean them out and refill at frequent intervals, thus checkmating the mosquito peril before it can really get going. A pond or stream, quite candidly, *can* be something else again, but maybe you can manage to keep away from it a bit on hot, insecty evenings!

And so, here endeth the last chapter of this short course in happy days for busy birds. The suggestions you have read are intentionally brief, for their purpose is to point the general direction of the path rather than to label every detail of its turns and hills and valleys, which inevitably vary from home grounds to home grounds and from region to region. But they are fundamental and provide, I hope, enough definite information to set you right on any matters that are likely to arise. If they do this, and thereby pave the way for three birds to dwell about your place where one dwelt before, then I know you will feel that they are worth while.

ROBERT S. LEMMON

A GARDEN FOR GAMES

A garden is usually a one-man dog, so to speak, looking for proprietary attention to some one member of the family above all others. But a well-bred dog should be a joy and comfort to the entire household, even if only one master shoots over him, feeds him, and combs the burrs out of his coat. Which is a wordy way of saying that the whole family should enjoy the garden, even though only one member may be boss.

Simply looking at beautiful plants is not, of course, the whole idea. Nine gardens out of ten are mounted in a setting of turf, and good turf is best enjoyed in the using of it. Hence the following story on six lawn or yard games and how to accommodate them. This is not to suggest that every lawn should become an athletic field. It is rather to suggest that good lawns actually seem to thrive with moderate exercise, as do people. It is further to suggest that gardeners should not be hogs.

The one continuing requisite of a turf game area is, of course, turf. Without going into details about maintenance of lawn surface for continuous use, it should be said that grass to be played on, whether for croquet or badminton, should be well supplied with humus in its soil, kept closely planted with vigorously growing grass, and maintained at a height considerably greater than purely decorative spreads. As a sort of rule-of-thumb ideal, let's say that good games grass should grow *faster* than plain lawn areas, should be cut *oftener,* but should *never* be cut so short.

Beyond that, in the average home grounds of modest size capable of supporting one or two games layouts, ordinary good lawn procedures will be sufficient: feed in *early* spring and again about Labor Day; roll after spring frost has gone; keep a springy surface by deep watering in dry times; do any supplementary seeding in early September. Where possible, shift court lines slightly during each season to avoid excessively worn spots.

Further hints are offered in the detailed discussions that follow.

COMPROMISE CROQUET COURT FOR FAMILY USE

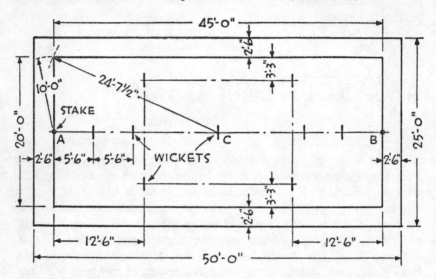

An official croquet layout is 70 feet long between stakes and 28 feet wide between centers of the wing wickets. The boundaries would add considerably to those dimensions. If you have that much space, well and good. If you have not, or if you are a stickler for tournament play, an area 35 feet by 20 will offer plenty of fun. The arrangement above is a compromise on several counts, but it is adequate for six- or eight-ball play and ample for a standard four-ball match. Naturally, the grass in the area should be even and in good condition. Except at the stake wickets, wear is not likely to be excessive, so ordinary turf will stand the gaff. Any of the above dimensions may be altered, though certain relationships, obviously, should be maintained. What kind of a set you buy is your business, as are the rules you follow. But I offer this suggestion for what it is worth: Buy or make wicket pegs (pointed, 6 inches long, bored to receive wicket uprights) and set flush with the ground. Then wickets may be lifted at mowing time without making it necessary to re-locate the wickets each time the grass is cut. Allow plenty of surrounding space,

especially if teen-agers are going to belt their opponents' balls to king-
dom come at every opportunity, and make any vulnerable plants or
garden beds in the danger zone severely out of bounds.

The court layout on opposite page (and similarly three of those that
follow) includes on the line, AB, a midpoint, C, from which a radius is indicated to the upper left corner (in this case 24'-7½"). From point
A a 10'-0" radius is shown. Intersection of arcs (dotted lines) as pro-
jected with measuring tape or garden line, marks corner of court. Repeating the process defines the area to which other dimensions relate.

DECK TENNIS ON GRASS IS EASIER ON THE FEET

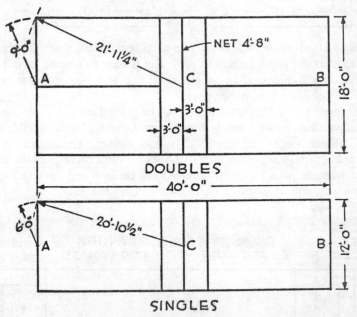

The layouts above are of official deck tennis size for both doubles and
singles, and call for a heavy net 4'-8" from the ground. The method for
laying out the areas quickly and easily, by fixing the corners from the
midpoint (C) of the center line (AB) is similar to that used for croquet
on the preceding page. Actually, of course, these dimensions may be
varied considerably without spoiling the fun. And dirt (even concrete if
your feet are tough) will do.

One condition though: don't hem in your deck tennis court with choice
plants. The havoc that may be wrought by the wayward rubber ring is
terrific.

BADMINTON DESERVES A WELL-LAID COURT

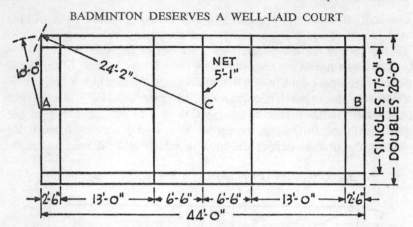

Actually you can enjoy badminton in a stubbly meadow, since the "bird" never touches the ground while in play. But it may be a game of infinite precision and complexity, in which footwork is of great importance. Therefore better surface, better play.

Badminton and volley ball might both be played on one area, simply by dusting new lines or using badminton lines for deck tennis. But the badminton net is higher (5'-1") and lighter. The court layout above is of official size and includes all lines for both singles and doubles. It is advisable to place the court where it will be level and sheltered from strong winds, with reasonable space surrounding the lines.

HORSESHOES ARE HARD ON TURF — EASY ON SPACE

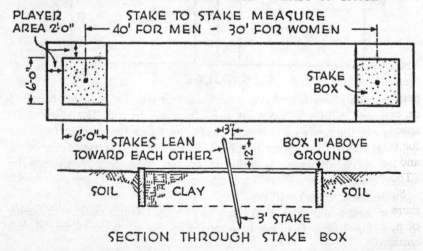

SECTION THROUGH STAKE BOX

Two lengths of iron rod and two pairs of old horseshoes (real ones) have led to many a joyful ringer. But some attention to layout and "official" shoes make for better sport. Whether you want to go all out for the championship set-up shown and described on page 196 is up to you. In any event, it's just as easy to lay out a few lines as not while the stakes are being set (either in pipe sockets, for easy removal, or on a permanent basis). There is no doubt that the clay boxes make for better play and, more important, for less risk of wild deflections of the shoes into any luckless spectators and plants near by.

VOLLEY BALL IS A BALL, A NET, AND A GANG

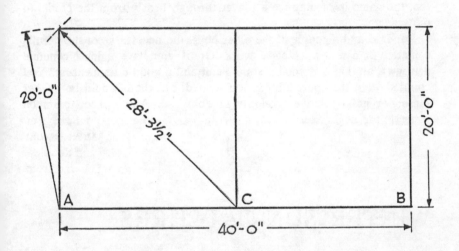

The official dimensions of a volley ball court are twice the accepted "junior" lengths shown above. But volley ball is strenuous, and any but perfectly conditioned players can run their tongues out to their knees on even this abbreviated field. Besides 80 by 40 plus surrounding free space is too much for any but large places to accommodate. So settle for these measurements if you can, alter them as circumstances dictate, and you'll still offer plenty of fun for up to a dozen afficionados at a time. (The noise is sure to be terrific.)

Since volley ball and deck tennis are largely young people's games, there will be a great deal of jumping and scuffing just for the sheer hell of it, and the grass is bound to take a beating, so govern yourself accordingly.

SHUFFLEBOARD IS NOT A LAWN GAME AT ALL

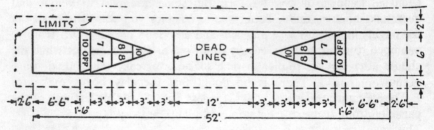

You can't very well play shuffleboard on grass, but once you have built a concrete playing surface, it will last a lifetime. Appropriately, too, the game itself may see a player through nearly from the cradle to the grave.

For Dad and a couple of the older boys, the necessary construction is a matter of a few week-ends' work. Or, if you have a level concrete driveway, all that is needed is some paint and a good tape measure. You could shorten the court a bit if you wished, but there would be neither sense nor great relative economy in doing so. And upkeep costs on concrete are negligible.

RALPH BAILEY

WINTER SUN-CATCHERS

You can add more than half a year to the out-of-door enjoyment of the home grounds, watch the changing season at first hand, and retain a healthy tan by establishing and using a warm corner, wall or planting to catch and hold the radiant heat of the winter sun. Fortified with a steamer rug or lap robe, you may spend many enjoyable hours in these sun-catchers from late fall, through winter into early spring.

The main requirements for such a spot are that it face the southern sun (slightly west of south being the ideal), and that it be sheltered from the cold winds and storms that come out of the North in the winter-time. In the summer, prevailing breezes from the southwest bring cooling temperatures to the area. It should be floored to make conditions always dry underfoot and furnished with at least one permanent bench.

A wall of the attached or detached garage, facing in the right direction, may be the basis for a fine sun trap. Provide additional shelter with a wall, tall hedge or fence and pave the corner with stone, brick or wooden chunks, as shown on page 201 (top). If recent storms have provided quantities of tree limbs, saw them into 4 to 6 inch lengths, soak thoroughly in creosote and they are ready to set on end, close together, on a tamped cinder drainage base. Sand is swept into the spaces between the chunks after they are in place. They make a warm, dry floor easily swept of snow.

The permanent Dutch bench placed against the wall is sheltered partially from storm by the low extension of the main garage roof. This small roof not only contributes a spot of shade around the bench in summer-time, but improves the year-'round appearance of the garage as do the small-leaved Holly, upright Yew and dwarf spreading Yew.

Gardens or grounds with deep border plantings of evergreen and deciduous materials may have a spot properly oriented that, with minor shifting of plants, will provide an area to develop as an all-year lounge. The one illustrated (page 201, center) is approximately 10 ft. deep and 12 ft. across.

The paving, of large and small broken stone, should be laid on a 6 to 8 in. drainage base of cinder or gravel. Pavings to be used in early spring when thawing takes place need good drainage.

The rustic bench and boulder fireplace are other important permanent fixtures of this scheme. The fireplace may be used as a warming unit only or may be fitted with a 12 by 20-in. plate for cooking purposes. When this is in place, smoke draws out the chimney notch. For a warming fire the plate is rested against the back of the fire box to act as a heat reflector. Pine and cedar, sprawling juniper, andromeda and laurel are among the evergreens found in mixed borders to give winter color and shelter to such a spot.

You may have a fence-corner facing in the right direction, or, as illustrated (page 201, bottom), a fence to which a section or two may be added to form a warm corner. Floor the area with creosote-treated, 2-in. plank spiked to timber sills, bedded into a drainage base of cinders or gravel. There should be an air space between the soil level and the floor plank.

Using the fence posts as back support, build in a permanent corner-bench using an open type construction for quick drainage of water and free circulation of air. Thoroughly prime all bench members as they are assembled.

Plants around the corner and in the border will consist of evergreen trees and shrubs for winter color with accenting deciduous materials for fall foliage, berries or spring blossoms.

A deep planting of deciduous shrubs and trees at one end or in a corner of the lawn or garden may be the perfect location for a circular paving, inclosed on the cold side with a semi-circular wall or sapling fence, ideal to catch and hold a maximum of sun and heat. The wall illustrated (page 202, top) is brick, 4 inches thick. It could be made of stucco-covered cinder block, stone or concrete.

The paving 14 ft. in diameter may be of brick or stone on a cinder or concrete base, or poured concrete marked off in squares or concentric rings leading up to the central camp fire site. Fire bricks are used to curb a space 3 ft. in diameter to accommodate a warming fire or fitted with removable spider-type grill for minor outdoor cooking. A drain in the fire circle is piped to a dry well.

The base of the permanent bench extending around the wall is constructed of the same material used in the wall. This is topped with a seat surface made of planks or heavy boards built in sections to fit the curve. Back-rest pads, too, are in four sections. They are fashioned of canvas or awning cloth filled with cotton tufted securely to hold their shape. Large eyelets along the top of the pad are attached to matching hooks around the wall to hold them in place. They are taken in after use.

It is practical to equip this unit with temporary arbor rafters, as shown in the isometric sketch, to furnish summer shade to the lounge. A 3-by-8, notched to receive them, serves as the front support for 2-by-4 rafters. The ends on the wall fit down over short rods set in the top of the wall.

Where the garden side of the house faces a warm quarter it is possible to create a spot sunny and warm enough for adults and infants. Many terraces may be transformed by using a thick, clipped hedge to fend the cold winter winds blowing in from one side or the other. Juniper, upright yew or arborvitae, set close in fertile soil and sheared every year before growth starts, will quickly form a solid windbreak.

Where no terrace exists, build one of regular solid masonry to harmonize with other masonry details about the house. Try to connect the paving with the porch or door leading to the garden. Such an arrangement has the advantage of being extremely convenient. A high-headed shade tree to the south, southeast or southwest of the terrace will cast only a tracery of its branches over the area in the winter; in the summer it will form comfortable shade. (See illustration, page 202)

Those who overlook a view or garden towards the north normally are driven indoors early by cold fall and winter blasts. They need a windbreak of glass. The sheltered overlook, illustrated at bottom of page 202, modern in its use of fixed sash in 6 in. concrete walls, stone or concrete floor, wooden benches and roof, contrast refreshingly with the natural surroundings. The roof makes the shelter useful in summer. A similar plan could be of hewn timbers and cedar shakes.

WINTER SUN-CATCHERS
for THE HOME GARDEN
DESIGNED & DRAWN BY H.B.AUL, LA

AGAINST THE DETACHED GARAGE

FIRE BRICK LINING

HEARTH

COOKING PLATE

CHIMNEY NOTCH

PLAN OF FIREPLACE

FIREPLACE AND PAVED AREA IN
SHRUBBERY BORDER

FENCE-CORNER IN THE GARDEN

SUGGESTED BENCH AND
FENCE CONSTRUCTION

SUMMER LOUNGE

WINTER SUN-CATCHER

HEDGE AND HOUSE-
SHELTERED TERRACE

WARM OVER-LOOK

HENRY B. AUL

500 COMMON GARDEN MISTAKES CORRECTED

MISTAKES TO AVOID
IN GROWING ANNUALS

Sowing seed too deeply

Fine seeds should be scattered on seed-bed and pressed in by tamper; cover larger seeds with depth of soil equal to their diameter when sowing indoors, 3 or 4 times their diameter when sowing outdoors.

Waiting until spring to plant all annuals

Hardy annuals can be planted in autumn for an early start in spring. These include Alyssum, Calif. Poppy, Calliopsis, Calendula, Centaurea, Cosmos, Gypsophila, Larkspur, Nigella, annual Pinks, Snapdragon, Snow-on-the-Mountain and Sweet Peas.

Starting Scabiosa, Begonia, Verbena, Petunia, Lobelia, Cobaea Scandens, China Asters and Snapdragons too late

These need a long season of growth. Start the seeds indoors in March.

Planting Ageratum, Cape-marigold, Ipomoea, Mignonette, or Nasturtiums too early out-of-doors

These are tender annuals. Plant seed indoors in March (except Nasturtiums which dislike transplanting) or outdoors when all danger of frost is past and the ground has warmed up.

Using infected soil for sowing seed in flats

Sterilize the soil; or use sterile sand watered with nutrient solution; or sow on sphagnum moss as described in Leaflet No. 243 U. S.

Dept. of Agriculture, obtainable for 5 cents from Supt. of Documents, Washington 25, D.C.

Using old seed
Before planting old seed, test its germination by placing a few seeds on moist blotting paper or old sheeting covered with soup plate to keep in moisture. The percentage of germination can then be calculated.

Planting seeds of annuals too thickly
If seedlings come up very thickly it invites attack by damping-off fungi, and it is almost impossible to thin them. Very fine seed should be mixed with sand to aid in distributing it evenly.

Planting annuals seeds in poorly prepared soil
See that the seed-bed is well worked, raked smooth, the surface soil pulverized, before planting.

Growing annual herbs in rich soil
For best fragrance and flavor, most herbs must be grown in a sweet, sandy soil, in sun and not too well fertilized.

Trying to grow most annuals in acid soil
Do not try to grow annuals (except Calliopsis, Marigold, Nicotiana and Verbena which tolerate acidity) in soil below pH6.5. To sweeten soil add lime at the rate of 15 to 25 lbs. per 500 square feet.

Planting annuals without due regard to their heights
A "wild" garden is pretty, but every bloom is better seen and enjoyed if flowers are carefully stepped back according to height, with procumbent or dwarf edgers in front and tall growers in the rear.

Planting annuals in shade
Very few annuals do well in shade. At least morning sun should be available. Although a few annuals, like Balsam, Lobelia and Browallia, will grow fairly well in the shade, they will not be so satisfactory as those which receive ample sunshine.

Planting Nasturtiums in too rich soil
This results in vigorous vine growth but few or no flowers. They bloom best on a lean diet. Surplus nitrogen especially is to be avoided.

Transplanting annuals in dry, sunny weather
Choose a cloudy day, when soil is moist, if possible. Then the operation of watering is eliminated and newly set plants will not be
wilted by strong sun.

Planting Cosmos without protection from strong winds
The slender stems and branches of Cosmos are easily blown about
even when staked. Plant against a fence or shrubbery border to give
protection, or provide support *before* plants are full grown.

Transplanting (or pricking off) Lobelia seedlings singly
Lobelias of the "bedding" types should always be transplanted into
flats in little bunches of five or six plants each.

Transplanting Salpiglossis
This lovely annual resents transplanting. Prepare bed with great
care and plant seeds where they are to grow.

**Transplanting California Poppies, Mignonette, Gypsophila, Godetia,
Nasturtiums and Portulaca**
These resent transplanting and seldom do well if so treated. Sow
them where they are to grow.

Getting in a rut when ordering annuals
Try a few flowers new to you each year. Some of these may suit
your soil and climate to a T. Torenia or Wishbone Flower is excellent for late summer and fall. Seeds are difficult to germinate but
once established they self-seed, coming up freely very late in spring
Moss Verbena, also self-seeds well. It is a "natural" for walls, walks
and rough spots. Color: deep orchid.

Failure to select disease resistant varieties
Especially with Snapdragons and Asters, disease-resistant types will
help to avoid disappointing losses.

Permitting seedlings started indoors to grow "leggy" and weak
If annual seedlings started indoors begin to look weak and gangling
before it is time to set them out, try to rig up a cold frame or window greenhouse to give them sunshine and clean air.

Neglecting to thin annual seedlings
Thin to the distance at which they should grow, *before* they begin

to crowd each other. Unless they are *very* small, a cloudy day is preferable for this work.

Failure to provide early support for annual vines

Ipomoea, Cobaea Scandens, Sweet Peas and other annual vines will not grow as they should unless string or other tall support is provided as soon as the plants are set out.

Letting weeds get a start among the annuals

If plants are set 6 to 12 ins. apart, ground must be kept free of weeds by cultivation or mulch. Planting close is not usually good practice but it does prevent weeds from starting if time is not available for frequent cultivation of soil.

Expecting one planting of Calliopsis, Centaurea, Gypsophila, Nigella or Phlox Drummondi to give a full season of bloom

These have short blooming periods. Succession planting or substitutions are necessary to give continuous color throughout the season.

Depending too much on annuals

Use annuals to fill in and help through the succession of bloom. They need the help of bulbs, perennials and flowering shrubs.

Planting the same thing in the same place year after year

Rotate annuals like vegetables for variety in landscaping effects and better culture without using large quantities of fertilizer and soil conditioners.

Failure to eradicate undesired self-seeded annuals before they become weeds

Pull these up as soon as they are recognizable.

Failure to plan color schemes for beds before purchasing annual seeds

Plan first, then buy seeds in species and varieties to give the needed colors and heights.

Failure to try out new improved varieties of annuals, especially Petunias and Marigolds

It is not necessary to grow purplish Petunias which sprawl all over the bed. New varieties, dwarf or bushlike, are available in salmons, soft shades of rose, peach-red, burgundy and deep violet blue. Improved Marigolds range from edgers to tall shrublike plants. Flowers range from pale yellow to deep red and from singles to chrysanthemum and dahlia-flowered types of great size.

Neglecting the regular cultivation of annual beds

Do not let the soil cake. Keep cultivated between the plants. Mulching is also desirable, in which case, cultivation will be unnecessary after mulch is applied.

Trying to grow Sweet Peas in sections where hot nights and hot dry days come in early summer

If Sweet Peas are tried under these conditions, sow seed *at earliest possible moment* in spring, or in the fall. Water deeply once a week and select spring-flowering type, which is heat resistant.

Pinching back annuals which produce spikes of bloom

Stocks, Larkspur, Celosia, etc. should not be pinched back.

"Sprinkling" bed of annuals instead of giving a thorough watering

If annuals are suffering from drought, give the bed a deep, thorough watering which will last a week or ten days. Shove end of hose in among plants and let water run slowly for a long time. Wetting tops may encourage fungus troubles.

Neglecting to pinch Ageratum, Browallia, Calendula, Phlox, Salpiglossis, Schizanthus, Verbena and Zinnia.

These will branch better and form sturdier plants if pinched, though bloom will be somewhat later.

Permitting Snapdragon, Verbena and Stocks to bloom themselves to death

After a heavy period of bloom, cut back and give a light dose of fertilizer. They will then give a later period of healthy bloom.

Failure to remove seed pods

This results in reduction of flowering.

Crowding plants

Most annuals should be planted six to twelve inches apart to allow for full development.

Thinking that "French" and "African" Marigolds came originally from these countries

They are native to Mexico, and so are Ageratum and Cosmos.

Failure to stake tall growing annuals in time to prevent them from being permanently misshapen

Branching annuals can often be "brushed" with light inconspicuous twigs or small branches instead of staked, thus producing a more natural effect. Plants which produce single spikes should be staked with bamboo or other stout sticks.

MISTAKES TO AVOID
IN GROWING BULBS

Using animal manure to fertilize Lilies

This may encourage basal rot. Preferably use bone meal or a complete fertilizer high in potash such as 5-10-10.

Failure to distinguish between base rooting Lilies and stem rooting Lilies

The base rooting types should be placed with the tips of the bulbs 2 or 3 inches below the surface. The stem rooting types should be planted 6 or 8 inches deep.

Using manure as a winter mulch for Tulips

This is likely to cause trouble as manure sometimes harbors Botrytis blight. Use clean straw, or salt meadow hay, and apply after a hard freeze.

Transplanting Narcissus too shallowly

In light soil they should be set with their bases 6 to 8 inches deep. In heavy soils, 5 to 7 inches deep.

Planting bulbs upside down

It puts them to the trouble of reversing themselves. Usually the pointed end should be up. When in doubt, consult someone who knows.

Forcing bulbs that are planted in pots before they have developed good root systems

Pot grown bulbs such as Tulips, Hyacinths and Daffodils must have good root systems developed before subjecting them to forcing temperatures. After the bulbs are potted in the fall, bury them out of doors under six inches of sand or ashes for 6 or 8 weeks before bringing them inside.

Keeping bulbs of Tulips, Daffodils or Hyacinths past the fall season to plant in spring

They will not flower. These need a long term of prior rooting before they will bloom. Therefore, they must be planted in fall in order to develop bloom for the following spring.

Failing to recognize the value of the "lesser" bulbs

Chionodoxa, the wild Crocuses and diminutive Narcissi are, because of their small size, particularly valuable in the intimate garden and the rock garden.

Planting hardy bulbs in poorly drained soil

Will shorten the life of the bulbs. New bulbs will be poorly developed and flowers will be inferior. Development ceases after a time or the bulbs will rot off.

Planting old bulbs of Montbretias (Tritonia) for flowers

Old bulbs mostly produce foliage but no flowers. Use young bulbs for flowering. The old bulbs can be planted to mother new bulbs.

Replanting Tulips over and over again in the same beds without resting or changing the soil

Repeated plantings of Tulips in the same soil invites diseases such as fire blight. Three years is the limit of time that a Tulip bed should be used. Then the location should be changed, or the soil replaced. Tulip beds should be rested at least two years, and well limed in the interim.

Mulching bulb beds before the ground is frozen

Bulbs require a low soil temperature to insure root and bud development. Too early mulching causes a premature leaf growth to the detriment of the bulb. The main purpose in mulching is to keep the frost in the ground. Late mulching accomplishes just that.

Removing mulches from bulb beds too early

Mulches serve the springtime purpose of keeping the frost in the ground, and protecting the buds from low temperatures. New plantings of Tulips and Daffodils benefit most from mulching, older beds in climates similar to New York really do not require it.

Failure to remove faded flowers from Tulip and Daffodil plants

Tulips and Daffodils begin forming seed as soon as the flower folds. The process of seed making robs the plant of most of its vitality, and will reduce the future blooming and propagating quality of the plant.

Cutting and removing Tulip and Daffodil foliage too soon after flowering

Foliage should never be removed until at least half of the leaf surface has browned off. This indicates that the bulb has completed its growth for the following year. If the bed is required for a follow-up planting, remove the bulbs with roots and foliage intact, and heel them in, until the maturing process is completed.

The practice of manuring a new bulb bed by mixing the manure into the soil

Bulbs coming into contact with decayed manure or any organic matter are prone to rot. Manure or similar material should be buried beneath the bulbs, with at least two inches of soil as separation.

Failure to mulch Bulbous Irises in fall

Mulch Bulbous Irises by covering lightly with evergreen boughs or other material that will not mat down to protect the bulbs and fall-grown foliage through the winter.

Failure to water bulbs potted for forcing

Bulbs intended for forcing, must be thoroughly saturated immediately after potting and placement in the pit or cellar. Satisfactory bloom requires early rooting before low temperatures have set in, and early rooting can be encouraged only by the constant presence of moisture. If stored in cold cellars, this moisture must be maintained constantly by watering weekly during the storage period.

Failing to plant Tulips to proper depth with consideration for size of bulb and texture of soil

In light sandy soils, bulbs 12 ctm and over should be planted 10–12″ deep for best results; 11–12 ctm size 8–10″; 10–11 ctm size 6–8″ deep and smaller bulbs no less than 5 inches. In heavy clay soils deduct 2″ from these depths. Proper depth is insurance against the bulb splitting up, protection in severe climates and the means of assuring a longer and more satisfactory blooming period if the spring is hot and dry.

Storing Callas, Ismenes and Caladiums too cool

Store at 45 to 50 degrees. They will not stand 38 to 40 degrees which is satisfactory for Tigridias, Gladiolus, Montbretias, etc.

Treating Daffodils and Narcissi as formal bedding plants

The beauty and charm of these lovely spring flowering bulbs lies in their informality. Planting them in orderly rows deprives them of much charm and effectiveness. If you must plant them in formal fashion, use only large trumpet varieties such as King Alfred, Lord Wellington, Mrs. E. H. Krelage, Aerolite, Emperor, etc.

Moving spring-flowering bulbs, that are established, too late in the fall

Established bulbs of Daffodils and Narcissi should never be transplanted or moved after August 15; Tulips after Sept. 1st; and early bulbs such as Crocus, etc., never later than July 30. Root action on these bulbs starts after the above dates and moving them after the root growth starts interferes with blooming and is very often fatal. Newly purchased bulbs may be planted as late as December in most sections because they are kept in a dormant condition until they are delivered.

Failure to plant several different types of Daffodils

By a careful selection of types (as well as varieties) six weeks of bloom can be had from Daffodils with a color range from white, through cream to yellow and orange. Heights too, vary from a few inches to 3 feet or more and size of flower from an inch to 4 or more inches in diameter.

Failure to make a ground plan record of bulb beds

In extensive bulb plantings, a ground plan record is invaluable. Tags and labels are often lost or destroyed. A ground plan gives the location of each variety even when the plants are dormant.

Neglecting yearly feeding of established Daffodil plantings

A fall dressing of bone meal and an early spring dose of complete fertilizer keep the bulbs blooming well until they become over-crowded. At that time, take up and replant.

Planting Daffodil and Tulip bulbs without thorough preparation of soil

"Naturalizing" Daffodils does not mean digging little holes and sticking in the bulbs. The ground in which they are to be set must be thoroughly worked, fertilized and provided with first-class drain-age if the plants are to grow vigorously and bloom freely. This is true of all spring-flowering bulbs.

Overpotting Amaryllis, Veltheimia and Crinums

These bulbs dislike over-potting and disturbance of their root sys-tems. Repot only when absolutely necessary and then to a pot only one size larger.

Planting Amaryllis, Veltheimia, Callas and Crinums too deep

The upper third of these tender bulbs should be exposed above the soil.

Trying to force the same bulbs two years in succession

Hardy bulbs forced for early flowering should be set out in the garden to mature their foliage and grow on for a year or two. Tender bulbs such as paper white, Soliel d'or etc., which are grown in pebbles or fiber are best discarded by the amateur after their flowering period. Amaryllis, Veltheimia and allied types which have a summer rest period and are grown on in soil, bloom each year with proper care.

Storing Ismene bulbs right side up

This practice causes rot in the embryo flower within the bulb.

Leave dried foliage on the bulbs and hang them from the ceiling of the storage cellar, stems down. Temp. 45 to 50 degrees.

MISTAKES TO AVOID IN GROWING EVERGREENS

Cultivating ground under broadleaf evergreens
By disturbing surface roots this does more harm than good. Mulching is preferable to cultivation.

Keeping evergreens too dry
Evergreens require an abundance of water, except for certain Pines and Junipers which thrive in dry soil.

Failure to water evergreens late in the fall
This often results in desiccation and death. Evergreen foliage loses water even in winter. A supply should be stored in the soil by late fall watering and conserved by an application of a mulch.

Failing to keep a close watch on Junipers and Spruces for spider-mites (red spiders)
It is important to apply remedial measures—rotenone sprays, syringing with plain water, sulphur dust—before the pests make headway or irreparable damage may result.

Planting evergreens too close together
Evergreens are beautiful specimens in themselves. Crowding destroys the effect.

Using Arborvitae, Spruce and similar evergreens in city plantings
For lasting effect, Yews are preferred.

Waiting to kill bag worms until after the bags have been formed
Spraying with arsenate of lead, tartar emetic or rotenone sprays should be done early in the season.

Neglecting to prune evergreens
Tipping back young branches in the spring before growth starts will help shape the plants.

Cutting back evergreens to hard wood
Usually no new growth will be formed and the tree will remain misshapen.

Planting too deeply
Evergreens should not be planted any deeper than the depth at which they grew in the nursery.

Removing burlap and breaking ball at planting
It is safer to leave the ball intact. Untie burlap after tree is placed and tuck in bottom of hole. Pack soil firmly above burlap.

Removing winter evergreen protection too soon
March winds often do more damage to evergreens than the low temperatures of the winter. Therefore, even though spring days make the urge almost undeniable, think well before removing protection too soon.

Planting coniferous evergreens in the shade; (Fir, Spruce, Cedar, etc.)
These plants need full sunshine and will not thrive in shady locations. Hemlock and Yew, however, will endure partial shade.

Planting conifers in poorly-drained soils
Although some evergreens grow wild in swamps or wet places those preferred for garden use demand moist, but well-drained soil.

Planting those "cute little" Pines, Spruces and other forest-type trees along the house foundation line
They look nice when the nurseryman sells them to you, but they're only baby trees and will grow into giants taller than the house itself—and there's no way of stopping them except chopping off their tops and ruining their appearance. The remedy is to buy *only true dwarf* types that will never grow more than 6 ft. tall, at most.

MISTAKES TO AVOID
IN GROWING FRUIT

Planting Currants near Pines

Currants, especially black Currants, are the alternate host for the disease known as white pine blister rust. Successful raising of currants demands the elimination of white pine as the easiest preventive measure.

Picking fruit from newly planted Raspberries, Blackberries, Currants, etc.

Inasmuch as the size and quality of the succeeding crop depends on the new canes that are being formed, all of the plant's strength should be directed to the making of as many strong new canes as possible. This can best be accomplished by removing all flowers the first season thereby diverting the plant's strength to new cane growth.

Leaving Raspberry canes which have fruited in place until the following spring

These should be cut out as soon as the fruit has been gathered to make room for young canes which will bear fruit the following year.

Not pruning Raspberries

Fruiting canes are cut to the ground after bearing. The new growth is pruned half the length of the canes, when leaf buds begin to appear on the stalks in the spring. This prevents too much top growth and encourages fruit.

Constant heavy pruning of young fruit trees

Will force considerable vegetative growth and delay the beginning of the bearing stage. In the pear, there is the added danger of fire blight disease. Prune very little after the head is formed until bearing begins.

Planting fruit trees in a low lying site or pocket for protection

There is no protection. Cold air flows down and collects in such places making it colder than higher ground. Late frosts will cause injury where higher places escape. With poor air circulation, disease is always present.

Planting dwarf fruit trees too deeply

If planted so that the grafted part is buried, roots will form above the graft and a tall tree will result. The dwarfing quality is in the grafted root-stock. Keep the union (point of graft) above the soil level.

Growing Peaches by planting pits

Will not produce the same peach variety and is likely to be inferior. Peaches are grown by budding or grafting the named variety, mostly, on the seedling peach.

Setting fruit plants in a shady situation

Fruit will not be produced. All fruit plants need full sunshine to develop fruit tissue and ripen the fruit. Plants are weakened in shade.

Allowing fallen fruit of any kind to lie around under the tree, bush, or vine and rot

Insects or disease may be harbored and perpetuated unless you gather up the fallen fruit and bury it deeply underground, or take other complete disposal steps.

Planting Strawberries in soil that grew sod or was unused for a number of years

Roots will be eaten by white grubs which are always present here. Put soil in shape by planting a crop that needs cultivation; Corn, Cabbage, Tomatoes, etc., for one or two years prior to planting Strawberries.

Failing to protect fruit trees from rabbits

Rabbits are likely to severely injure and often kill young fruit trees by girdling the bark at base of trunk during winter when food is scarce. Cylinders of tarpaper tied around trunks (leaving an air space between paper and bark) will prevent injury, but paper should reach at least 15 ins. above level of snow when ground is covered.

Planting Blueberries on alkaline soil

They require a soil constantly kept acid. Treatment of alkaline soil before planting is not sufficient. Acidity must be maintained by annual applications of acidifying mulch, such as sawdust.

Planting pot-grown Strawberry plants too late in fall, and expecting crop of berries the following June

They should be set out early enough to have 2 to 3 months of growth before ground freezes, and thus establish fairly substantial crowns.

Planting single specimens of Pears, some varieties of Apples and Peaches, and other non self-pollinating tree fruits

In planting such, make certain that a suitable cross-pollinating variety is provided. This information can be obtained from your nurseryman or your state experiment station.

Planting Strawberries too deep or too shallow

If plants are set too deep, crowns may easily be covered with soil, causing new leaves to rot at the crown and possibly destroying the crown. If too shallow, roots are left exposed, or plants may be heaved out of ground during first winter after planting.

Assuming that several different kinds or varieties of fruits can be sprayed or dusted at one time for control of insects or diseases

Effectiveness of control measures depends largely upon proper "timing" to catch certain stages of bud, flower, or fruit development. Hence, any spray calendar for homegrown fruits is quite complicated.

Using poison sprays (such as arsenate of lead) on fruits nearing maturity

Spraying at this stage should be avoided or material (such as pyrethrum) that is readily washed off, employed.

Letting Grapevines go unpruned

Unpruned Grapes will grow vigorously and produce well for several seasons but are difficult to again bring under control. For satisfactory fruit production they are best, *and easiest,* pruned every fall or winter.

Failure to protect from birds

These "feathered friends" are pretty certain to harvest, or spoil, a large part of any crop of such homegrown fruits as Strawberries, Raspberries, Blueberries and Cherries. Mechanical protection by covering with heavy cheesecloth or with plant-protecting cloth (sold by most seed houses) is surest—and in the end—easiest protection.

Picking and handling fruits carelessly, resulting in slight bruising, or tearing from stems

All tree fruits, even when quite "firm" should be handled at every stage of harvesting with greatest care. Avoid also tearing stems from branches, as this may injure fruiting spurs.

Letting Pears get too ripe before picking

Many varieties ripen from the core out, and if left with soft spots on the surface may be decayed inside. Some varieties are best picked while still hard, wrapped in papers, and stored in a dark, fairly cool place.

Storing imperfect fruits

"One rotten apple may spoil the barrel"—and one tiny spot or bruise is pretty sure to spoil the whole fruit. Examine carefully every specimen selected for storing. Those not perfect can be set aside for early use, or canned.

MISTAKES TO AVOID
IN GROWING HOUSE PLANTS

Using ordinary garden soil for house plants
No matter how good the garden soil is for vegetables, flowers, etc., it usually needs the addition of leaf-mold or humus and sharp sand (and ofttimes some fertilizer) to make it suitable for plants that are to be grown in pots.

Overpotting plants
One mark of a good cultivator is to grow plants that are large in proportion to the pots they occupy. A specimen that is all pot and little plant is not good. This does not mean that repotting or potting on into bigger receptacles should not be promptly attended to when required. It is just a caution to use judgment as to the size the specimen is likely to attain within a reasonable time.

Potting Christmas Begonias too firmly
Christmas Begonias of the Melior and Glory of Cincinnati types thrive in a light, humusy soil that is pushed loosely into place about the old ball at potting time rather than being packed firmly.

Potting Cacti in a heavy, rich soil
The plants will grow too fast; they will be too soft and will not bloom. Use a very sandy, gritty soil and good drainage.

Overwatering pot plants
Inexperienced indoor gardeners usually overwater. Give just enough to thoroughly moisten the soil in the pot when the surface feels dry. Blooming plants usually need more water than foliage plants or bloomers which are not in flower.

Overwatering Terrariums

Give moisture to Terrariums only if the soil feels dry when the finger is pressed into it. If water collects on the glass sufficiently to "run," remove cover for a day or two.

Watering house plants by the calendar

Plants should be watered whenever they need it, which is generally when the surface soil begins to dry out. They should then be given a thorough soaking and water withheld until the soil again begins to get dry.

Failing to give forced potted Hydrangeas and Azaleas enough water while in bloom

These plants are pot-bound. Soak pots in bucket of water once a week and water daily but do not permit water to stand in saucer after soil is soaked.

Keeping Pot-grown Cactuses too dry

When grown in pots Cacti need reasonable amounts of water—occasional soakings. These soakings will be less frequently needed than is the case with most other plants, but still they are necessary to wet the soil through. Be sure that the soil is porous and the drainage perfect.

Standing house plants in a watertight jardiniere

There is danger that water will collect in the bottom of the container, partially submerge the pots and make the roots unhealthy.

Standing house plants outside during cold rains

While there can be no objection to standing many kinds of house plants out of doors on warm, rainy days, it is definitely harmful to follow this practice when the outdoor temperature is below that to which the plants have been accustomed indoors.

Failure to fertilize plants during their best growing periods—spring, summer and early fall

Use fertilizer tablets or liquid fertilizer once a month. Do not fertilize during the dark days of winter.

Using castor oil or tea leaves as fertilizers for house plants

Both are valueless.

Failing to understand that all plants which live more than one year must have a "resting period" when they can consolidate their gains, so to speak, and prepare for future efforts

Don't expect them to keep growing and flowering forever.

Failing to keep the surface of the soil in house plant pots lightly cultivated so that the roots can get some air

Watering tends to pack it hard, and it must be broken up. On smallish pots, an old kitchen fork isn't a bad cultivating gadget.

Neglecting to increase stock of house plants

Most house plants can be readily increased by slips, bulblets or division. Start young plants of favorite house plants each year. Then you will have a good young plant ready to replace the old one that should be discarded. Any surplus young plants make excellent gifts, or can be "swapped."

Keeping ungainly specimens from year to year

When house plants outgrow the space you have to spare, root cuttings from the parent plants and discard the parents. Most house plant cuttings root readily. Don't be crowded out of your own living room by a Monstera for instance. Cut off the top to the size you wish. Pot it up and it will live and thrive. Discard the root and lower stem.

Keeping gift plants too warm

Most flowering gift plants thrive better in a cool sun porch than in an overheated room. Among these are Cyclamen, Christmas Cherry, Azalea, Hydrangea, Geraniums, Primulas and Cinerarias. Poinsettias need 70 degrees and sunlight.

Buying diseased or pest infected house plants

When buying plants from a greenhouse or florist, inspect them carefully for mealy bug, white fly, aphids, etc. Buy only clean plants.

Permitting a pest-infested house plant to contaminate its neighbors

Segregate any pest-ridden plant until clean. If you are unable to eliminate the bug or disease in a reasonable time, destroy the plant.

Neglecting regular pest control

A weekly inspection for pests and diseases on house plants is essential. As soon as pests appear, follow an intensive spraying program until they are under control.

Leaving Azaleas to take care of themselves after blooming

Tender Azaleas used for indoor bloom need water and sunlight *after* flowering and a place in the summer garden in broken sunlight where they will get plenty of moisture at all times.

Expecting Geraniums and Heliotrope to bloom indoors in winter and go on flowering outdoors in summer

Geraniums and Heliotrope grown as young budding plants for winter bloom indoors cannot be expected to bloom in the garden in summer. When set out in their pots for their "vacation," cut them back and let them rest without too much water. If they are to bloom the following winter, remove any summer buds which appear.

Expecting hot-house Azaleas to make good house plants for years

Such plants are forced in a greenhouse where the atmosphere is moist. In the drier atmosphere of the home they will not bloom as well and may drop their leaves. In the North greenhouse Azaleas will not live out of doors over winter. In the South they will, if properly cared for.

Washing the foliage of fuzzy or hairy-leaved plants

African violets, *Pelargonium tomentosum,* Gloxinia and other hairy-leaved plants should be dusted with a soft brush if necessary, but never washed.

Neglecting to wash shiny-leaved plants

A weekly foliage bath is a fine general conditioner for shiny-leaved house plants. It removes dust and grime, gives moisture directly to stems and leaves, improves appearance and discourages insects.

Oiling leaves to make them shine

This clogs the stomata (breathing pores) and is especially injurious if the oil is applied to the underside of the leaf where most of the breathing pores are situated.

Failure to shade house plants for a week or two when they are first put out of doors for the summer

The sudden exposure to burning sun after the subdued light of a room is likely to cause burning of the foliage.

Subjecting foliage plants to direct sunlight

Most foliage plants such as Philodendron, Ivy, Ferns, Peperomis, etc., do better in indirect light.

Giving blooming Fuchsias too little light indoors

Fuchsias, although they enjoy some shade in the garden, flower best in a sunny window indoors.

Growing African violets in homes where artificial gas is used

Usually in such homes the small amount of ethylene in the gas will prevent flowering.

MISTAKES TO AVOID IN USING INSECTICIDES AND FUNGICIDES

Spraying without making sure that the spray is adapted to the purpose

It is of little or no use to apply an insecticide to cure a fungus or bacterial disease or vice versa. No spray will cure virus diseases or conditions that are brought about by poor environment. Be sure the diagnosis is correct before the remedy is applied.

Guessing at dilutions of spray materials

The amounts safe to use on various plants have been worked out. The margin of safety between the killing of the pest and tolerance of the plant is narrow, hence directions should always be followed, otherwise both the pest and the plant may be killed.

Using nicotine solutions for chewing insects

Nicotine kills by contact such pests as aphids and thrips, which suck juices out of plants.

Using a stomach poison insecticide against sucking insects

Such insecticides are designed to kill insects which actually eat parts of the plant. Except for a few which kill by contact and also by poisoning the insect's food, they are useless against insects which stick their beaks into the plant tissue and suck the sap.

Using a fungicide such as Bordeaux mixture when an insecticide is needed

Although Bordeaux mixture is effective against flea beetles and to some extent is a deterrent against leaf hoppers, as a usual thing it is of no value as an insecticide.

Using sulphur sprays or dust on plants outside when the temperature exceeds 85 degrees

Burning is bound to follow. Wait until the evening or early morning.

Using insecticide and fungicide dusts when the foliage is moist or wet in the mistaken belief that it "holds" better

Dusts should always be applied when the foliage is dry.

Failing to use seed disinfectants to prevent "damping-off" of seedlings, rootings, etc.

Semesan and red copper oxide or spergon are great aids in preventing damage from fungus disease, such as "damping-off" of seedlings, rotting of seeds in the soil, and other seed-born diseases and molds which might kill the plant without these protectants.

Using cure-alls

There are no insecticides which kill all the different pests. Specific materials should be used.

Spraying during extreme heat of the day

Many spray materials are either ineffective or cause damage when the temperature is above 85° F.

Using stomach poisons on leafy vegetables

Such materials as arsenicals, tartar emetic, should not be used on parts to be eaten.

Failing to consult spraying charts for apples

Certain pests on apples do their damage at specific times. It is a waste of time and of spraying material to spray apples without taking into account just when the damage will be done.

Waiting until insects have done a great deal of damage before starting to fight them

Timing is of the utmost importance in insect control. It is easier to kill 500 insects than 5 million and in the case of insects such as canker worms they are easier to kill when they are young; and it is sensible to do so before trees are defoliated.

Using old Bordeaux mixture spray that has been left over for some time

This will destroy foliage. Discard any left over after spraying and only use the freshly made mixture.

Mixing cryolite with lime as a dust or spray

The foliage of plants on which it is used will be injured. Mix instead with flour or talc 3 parts to 1 of cryolite.

Using a dormant oil spray on evergreens on a dull cold day

Dormant oil sprays are best used on a bright clear day when the temperature is well above 45° F.

Fumigating soil with chloropicrin (tear gas) to kill insects while plants are growing there

The fumes will kill the plants if less than 5 feet distant.

Fumigating a greenhouse with cyanide gas when the foliage of plants is wet

This will cause severe burning. No watering should be done for several hours before fumigation. The foliage must be completely dry.

Planting seeds in soil less than 24 hours after it has been treated with formaldehyde

The germinating power of the seeds will be impaired. Allow this duration at least, then open up the soil by turning it over before sowing seed.

Mixing incompatible insecticides

Sulfur with oil sprays, soap with arsenicals will cause "burning" of foliage.

Using too much dust when dusting seeds to prevent disease organisms

The seeds may not germinate or the seedlings may be stunted or killed as they emerge from the seeds. Study the manufacturer's directions closely and treat only the seeds he lists.

MISTAKES TO AVOID IN GROWING LAWNS

Failure to feed lawns

One of the commonest of garden errors is to take the nutrition of a lawn for granted. Lawn grasses can rapidly deplete a soil of mineral fertility. Proper and regular spring and late summer feeding will insure a strong stand of lawn grass that is the best insurance against the encroachment of Crab Grass and other weeds.

Application of slowly acting organic fertilizers in the spring

These may become available just about time for germination and growth of Crab Grass, thus accentuating the trouble.

Feeding a lawn in the heat of midsummer

This will cause burning of the grass and further stimulate weeds. Feed in early spring and again in early fall when the soil holds plenty of moisture.

Top dressing a fall-made lawn with fresh manure over winter

An infestation of weeds is sure to follow. No top dressing is necessary if grass has made good growth. If growth is not adequate and there is danger of washing, cover in early winter with a light mulch of salt hay or small twiggy branches.

Watering the lawn by merely sprinkling the surface

Watering is likely to do more harm than good if it is not thorough enough to soak the ground to the roots.

Using a heavy roller when soil is still wet in spring

Except on a very light sandy soil, this will result in so compacting the surface soil that growth of grass plants will be retarded.

Using a solid roller on a lawn

It will tear up the grass and leave a depression when the roller is turned. Young grass especially will be injured. Use a sectional roller. The sections revolve as the roller is turned. If a solid roller is in use, make a wide turn or turn on a path instead of the lawn.

Attempting to level a lawn by rolling it

This should be done by grading. The purpose of rolling is to press the grass back into the soil if it has been upheaved by the effects of winter and to flatten minor surface inequalities.

Sowing grass seed (for a lawn) in late spring

Early fall is the best time to sow grass seed, or very, very early spring. Late sown grass seed usually dies out or is crowded out by weeds during the summer.

Letting newly seeded surfaces dry out during germination period

This is the most critical time in starting a new lawn. Unless rain or cloudy weather follows seeding, it is advisable to water every day, to keep surface constantly moist.

Planting the lawn with bent grass unless you can provide great care

Bent Grass demands cutting twice a week. It is also subject to brown patch and dollar spot during the muggy days of July and August.

Using oats or rye as nurse grass in a lawn mixture

They grow too fast for the slower grasses. The latter are either shaded out completely or may be severely scorched when the nurse grass is cut and they are suddenly exposed to the full sun. Rye Grass or Red Top are best as nurse grasses, in a lawn mixture.

Mowing grass too close

Setting the mower closer than 1½ inches is undesirable for most lawns. This is particularly important with blue grass lawns and during the extreme heat of the summer.

Removing grass clippings

Clippings are very useful as additions of organic matter and should not be removed unless the grass has been allowed to grow too tall.

Leaving heavy grass clippings on the lawn in the early season when the weather is moist

This will cause damping off disease. Rake off the clippings and use for a garden mulch. Light mowings can be left on the lawn.

Mowing young grass in a new lawn with a poor mower

It is likely to pull the grass out by the roots. Roll first with a light roller then mow with a sharp, evenly set lawn mower.

Sodding in shady spots

The usual sod is largely Blue Grass which does not grow well under shade. Use ground covers instead.

Sowing grass seed in very shady spots

Usually a waste of time. Shade loving ground covers, like Vinca minor, euonymus, or pachysandra would be more suitable.

Failure to prepare soil properly for a new lawn

The soil preparation should be thorough with inclusion of humus and fertilizers. Good drainage is essential.

Allowing weeds to spread in the lawn

Prompt eradication as they appear will prevent the weeds from getting out of control.

Buying cheap grass seed

The cheaper grades usually contain too high a percentage of timothy or Perennial Rye Grass which do not produce satisfactory lawns.

Raking lawns in spring
If done, should be very light, otherwise humus is removed and roots damaged.

Applying lime in spring
Rarely necessary in average soils. Most grasses do best in slightly acid soils. Liming promotes growth of weeds.

Using lime too frequently on the lawn without making sure that it is needed
Lime is not a universal corrective. Even moss in the lawn does not always indicate the need for lime. Before applying lime to the lawn have the soil tested.

Allowing grass to grow long at end of season
Lawn grasses do not need a mat of dead foliage for winter protection; and too heavy a growth may smother out some areas. It also makes ideal wintering quarters for rodents and other lawn pests.

Using weed killer in excessive amounts on a lawn
This will kill the grass as well as the weeds and poison the soil against any further planting for some time.

Permitting a truck or other heavy machine to drive over frozen turf
Injury will be caused, necessitating digging up the tracks the following spring. Keep all traffic off permanent turf when it is frozen.

Bringing subsoil to the surface when making a new lawn
Only the best soil should be used for the surface seed-bed.

Seeding a bank or terrace without protection from washing out
Firm the surface when the seed is sown, then cover with a very thin burlap or sprinkle with a light layer of salt hay until the grass shows. Remove the hay gradually. The burlap can be left to disintegrate.

MISTAKES TO AVOID
IN GROWING PERENNIALS

Planting Peonies too deep
The crown should be one to two inches below the surface. Planting at greater depth is likely to prevent blooming.

Transplanting Peonies in the spring
Early fall is the proper time.

Splitting up Peonies and Poppies in the spring
Flowering will be prevented for that year at least. These perennials bloom early from buds that grew the previous summer but developed in spring. Splitting up in spring stops development. Poppies best divided in August. Peonies in September.

Failing to pinch back Chrysanthemums
Most Chrysanthemums grow too tall and their bloom will suffer unless the tips of the growing stems are nipped off at least twice; once when the stems are 6 or 8 inches tall and again about 4 weeks later.

Pinching back Delphinium plants
The shoots from the base of the Delphinium produce terminal flower spikes and pinching back, as is done with many other plants, interferes with the blooming.

Allowing Chrysanthemums to grow in one spot without division for several years
The best results with Chrysanthemums are accomplished by divid-

ing and transplanting them every 2 or 3 years, using the vigorous outside sections of the clump and discarding the old center clump.

Attempting to carry Chrysanthemums over the winter in cold sections without protection

Most of the hardy Chrysanthemums are not hardy enough for that. The best practice is to transplant them to a cold frame for the winter. If this is not possible, they should be protected with a blanket of evergreen branches.

Mulching Chrysanthemums with heavy covering

Hardy 'Mums make dense crowns that are easily smothered out by too much moisture. The most essential requirement is perfect drainage. Any mulching material should be light and dry, admitting air freely.

Cutting back Chrysanthemums when tall to make them branch

Only a few laterals will be forced out a few inches below the cut but not over the lower parts of the stems. The lower stems will be bare making plants top-heavy. To induce branching at the base, the plants must be pinched when about 6 inches tall. About four weeks later, give a second pinching.

Dividing Dahlia clumps without regard to buds

Each division should include a portion of the old stem attached to the neck of a tuber and a growing bud or eye.

Storing Dahlia roots over winter in a temperature too high or too low

40° to 55° is the best. Freezing will ruin the roots. Too high a temperature will dry them out or cause them to sprout too soon.

Putting on a winter mulch too early

If the mulch is for the protection of plants that are not hardy, it should be placed before hard freezing, but truly hardy plants should not be mulched until after the ground freezes. In this latter case, the mulch is not to protect the plants from the cold, but to prevent alternate freezing and thawing which is injurious.

Failure to divide perennials such as Shasta Daisies, Asters and others at regular intervals

Usually large clumps are best divided in the fall. This enables the gardener to renovate his soil and eliminate crowding.

Planting in poorly drained soil

Not only will the resulting growth be poor, but death will occur during winter because of heaving.

Spraying the "blacks" on Delphiniums with a fungicide for disease control

These are caused by mites and are best controlled by sprays containing rotenone or nicotine or dusting with fine sulphur.

Planting sun-loving perennials in the shade

Most perennials grow best in full sunlight. A partial list of those for shade is: Aconitum, Ajuga, Aquilegia, Aruncus, Convallaria, Dicentra, Helleborus, Hosta, Mertensia, Myosotis, Primula, Trillium, Viola.

Placing low perennials at the rear of the border

In planting the border always keep in mind the mature heights of the plants so that the small ones will be in front and not hidden by the tall ones.

Failing to remove promptly the dying flower trusses of garden Phloxes, Asters and hardy Chrysanthemums

If left unpicked the flower trusses often produce viable seeds which fall down among the parent plants, in due time germinate, and grow into vigorous specimens that usually choke out the choicer parent varieties. The seedlings are almost invariably very much inferior to the parents.

Failure to cut off and burn old dead parts of diseased or insect infested plants.

These harbor insect and disease pests for the next year and should be burned

Planting small perennials singly throughout the border in order to make them "go further"

Perennials, except for massive types such as Peonies and Daylilies, show off to the best advantage when each variety is planted in groups and not singly, each group having three or more plants.

Depending on fall-planted Pansies for summer bloom

The Pansy plants of the spring markets are at their maturity when purchased in March and run out in early summer. Pansy seeds planted early in the spring will provide plants for summer and fall blooms.

Failing to separate Coral Bells every two years

In order to produce copius bloom on Coral Bells, these plants should be divided or separated into several small divisions and re-planted every two years. In this way, Coral Bells make one of the loveliest border plants, blooming from May throughout the summer, and providing evergreen leaves throughout the winter.

Transplanting all kinds of perennials in the fall

Such late summer bloomers as Chrysanthemums, Japanese Anemones, Helianthus, and hardy Asters should be planted in the early spring. Iris should be planted in July or August, Peonies in August or September, Oriental Poppies in August.

Failure to sow Aquilegia seed early enough to guarantee the following season's bloom

Aquilegia seed should be sown from February to early July. Sowing after the latter date will usually produce a plant that will not bloom the following year.

Shortening the period of Pansy bloom by failure to remove the fading flowers

As with any other long blooming flowering plant, allowing it to dissipate its strength through seed making, will shorten its blooming period. Remove blooms as soon as they begin to fade.

Overemphasis of one plant in the perennial border

Dominant perennials such as Phlox, Oriental Poppies, Hemerocallis, Anthemis, etc., will soon take over a border if they are not curbed. These varieties and others, while desirable, should be divided every three years at least discarding the excess if necessary. The successful perennial border depends upon diversification and constant bloom.

Planting Bearded Iris in the shade

It is quite a common sight to see large groups of Iris foliage without bloom, in shady areas. While it is true that Iris will grow and even multiply in shade, the blooming tendencies are seriously impaired, and a location with a minimum of four hours of full sunlight should be chosen.

Overfertilizing Bearded Iris

After summer separation, bearded Iris can stand very moderate amounts of commercial fertilizer and slightly more bone meal. Fairly good soil is all that Iris need. Overfertilizing will cause soft growth that renders the plant subject to many degenerative diseases.

Placing the rhizome too deep when planting Bearded Iris

In light, sandy soil the rhizome should be covered only about one inch. In heavy soil it should be planted so that the top of the rhizome is exposed.

Planting Irises too shallow

While the rhizomes of Bearded Iris should not be planted deep, it is equally a mistake to "float" them on the surface of the soil, as sometimes advised. Cover sufficiently to prevent washing out by rains, with just the tops of the rhizomes showing.

Failure to lift and transplant Bearded Iris frequently enough

They should be dug and replanted every three years or so in order to prevent overcrowding and the spread of disease. If they are to be replanted in the same place, the bed should be re-dug and fertilized. If disease is present, it should also be sterilized.

Cutting back the green foliage of Iris in summer or fall

Leaves turning brown should always be removed promptly, but the cutting of green foliage is likely to affect adversely the following year's bloom. An exception to this rule, however, is the necessity for cutting back the leaves half-way when Irises are being divided and transplanted.

Fertilizing Bearded Iris with animal manure

This is likely to induce root rot. It is safer to use bone meal, wood ashes and commercial fertilizer low in nitrogen which should be thoroughly mixed with the soil before planting.

Planting tropical Water-lilies in early spring in outdoor pools in deep water

This will result in stunting, if not in killing the plants which are raised in greenhouses. Planting is best done when the water has warmed up and only enough water put into the pool to just cover the crowns. Water depth is increased as growth develops.

Planting hardy Water-lilies in running water or in shade

Water-lilies reach their best development in still water and in full sunshine. The temperature of running water is usually lower than still water and the growth of the roots is slowed up.

Trying to winter over old tubers of tropical Water-lilies

The old tubers usually decay. Young plants grown throughout the summer in four-inch pots produce tubers that may be kept perfectly through the winter.

Taking up Gladiolus corms before the leaves start to turn brown

Browning of leaves indicates that the new corm has fully developed.

Working, or cultivating the perennial bed too early in the spring

Many perennials show no sign of growth until after weeds start, and too early hoeing or other work among them is likely to injure brittle shoots about to push up through the surface.

Cultivating soil too deeply in the perennial border

Many species form roots near the surface and working soil more than an inch or two deep may result in serious injury. Shallow cultivation *plus mulching* is the answer.

Planting tall, or very bushy species in the middle or foreground of the border

Either type casts considerable shade, and is likely to injure growth of lower sorts, as well as detracting from the general appearance of the border.

Gathering wide open blooms for cut flowers

Flowers for indoor decoration should, with few exceptions, be cut in the full-bud or half-open stage; spikes (such as Gladioli or Delphiniums) when the first florets open.

Waiting until pests get really bad before applying control measures

Many plant pests (and diseases also) spread with almost incredible rapidity. Applying remedies *at the first sign of trouble* not only saves time, trouble and materials, but results in more effective control.

Failing to have new plants ready to "fill in" when there are fatalities in the border

In the best managed flower beds there are sure to be some failures or deaths during the season. Have extra plants on hand, in a frame or the vegetable garden, to make replacements. Even annuals will fill the bill temporarily.

Failing to provide supports (for species requiring them) while plants are still fairly small

Full grown plants cannot be properly tied or held up. Put stakes, brush or other support in place when they are about half grown.

Providing an unbalanced diet

Most perennials make a rather slow steady growth and "forcing" them with plant foods high in available nitrogen is poor practice. Use, rather, a complete plant food providing phosphorus and potash. Wood ashes and bone meal are excellent additions.

Failure to make soil firm about roots when transplanting

If loosely planted in the fall, roots are more likely to be heaved out by freezing of soil; in the spring, loose soil allows moisture to escape too freely so that root dies from dryness.

Failing to cut off leaf stalks of Peonies just below soil line in the fall

The resting spores of botrytis, one of the most troublesome of Peony diseases, are formed on the bases of infected stalks. Removal of these reduces the possibility of infection the following year.

MISTAKES TO AVOID IN GROWING ROSES

Pruning rambler Roses at the same time as Hybrid Teas
Ramblers should be pruned immediately after flowering, the canes which have flowered being cut back to the ground.

Pruning large-flowered climbing Roses in the same way as ramblers
The large-flowered climbers do not produce new canes as freely as the ramblers. Pruning them is a matter of removing the old flower clusters and cutting out enough old canes to make room for the new ones that develop.

Failing to Prune Hybrid Tea Roses properly in early spring
Proper pruning helps to combat disease and insect pests and maintains the quality of plant and flowers. Weak growth should be cut out and strong canes cut back one-third to two-thirds.

Failing to prune away sucker growths from budded Roses
Most Roses are budded or grafted. Only the tops represent the kind of rose from which flowers are wanted. The roots are of a different and (from the point of view of floral display) inferior kind. Shoots that arise directly from the root, and which are of a distinctly different appearance from the stem shoots should be cut away.

Failure to prune hard at planting
Pruning to 4–5 buds from the base in Hybrid Teas and 5–7 buds in Hybrid Perpetuals will result in heavier canes and better growth.

Pruning Roses in late spring after growth has begun
This results in delayed bloom and inferior flowers which are produced in hot weather. Early growth produces best Roses.

Watering Roses with a spray that wets the foliage
This is objectionable because it helps to spread the "black-spot"
disease. A better way is to use a porous hose which is placed on the
ground and from which the water seeps out.

Planting too deep or too shallow
The union between bud and understock should be about one inch
below surface. This reduces suckering and develops heavy stems
from the base.

Assuming that Roses need heavy clay soil
On the contrary, soils high in organic matter, loamy in texture,
well granulated, are best. If clay soil is used, mix two inches of fine
cinders and two inches of rotted manure with it.

Planting without paying attention to drainage
Drainage is the key to success in growing Roses and must be
assured.

Liming Roses
Roses need no lime unless the soil is extremely acid.

Applying bone meal to the surface of the soil
Bone meal is only useful when worked into the soil. Its penetration
is very slow so most of it is wasted if applied to the top.

Assuming that a manure application is sufficient fertilization
In addition, a "complete" fertilizer (5–10–5) should be applied in
the spring, and again in June, using it at the rate of 2 pounds to
100 sq. ft.

Forcing growth with quick-acting fertilizers
High-nitrogen fertilizer applied to Roses at any season is likely to
result in soft growth, a ready prey for the many diseases that attack
this queen of flowers.

Fertilizing too late in summer
Late fertilizing of Roses (after mid-August in the northern states)

is likely to result in vigorous vegetative growth that will not "ripen" properly before freezing weather and is, therefore, especially subject to winter injury.

Cutting Roses with long stems too freely

Loss of much foliage devitalizes bush, and there is some evidence that it makes it more susceptible to disease.

Failure to mulch the beds

A mulch of peat, ground corncobs, spent hops or well rotted manure is desirable soon after growth starts. Better moisture conditions are maintained and weeds reduced.

Waiting until a heavy dose of mildew develops before using control measures

Dust with fine sulphur at the very first sign of mildew. Keep a dust of sulphur on foliage during spring and early fall.

Allowing black spot to spread

At the first sign of black spot dust with dusting sulphur, or use Fermate as a spray. Gathering and burning of fallen infested leaves is advisable.

Planting late in the spring

Late planting fails to get plants established before hot weather. Poor growth or death may result. Fall planting is satisfactory if bushes are hilled up with earth and mulched for the winter.

Buying waxed Roses without careful inspection

The stems of these may be shriveled and thus will not grow.

Allowing Roses to lie around before planting

Upon receipt, place in a bucket of water and after soaking for at least thirty minutes, plant at once. If storage is necessary before a planting, place in a cool, dark spot and keep stems and roots moist. Heeling in the ground and covering tops is satisfactory.

Jamming roots in a small hole

Make hole large enough and deep enough to contain all roots. Spread roots, pack good soil about them, and water. Leave a depression about the plant, water again and mulch.

Planting Roses in the shade

Roses do poorly under such conditions. Partial shade is acceptable provided morning sun is available.

Planting Roses too close to shrubs or trees

They are likely to suffer from lack of moisture.

Planting Roses in the summer

Only Roses which are established in pots should be planted in summer. The best planting time for Roses is late fall or very early spring.

Planting Climbers without providing supports in advance

Posts, stakes, arbors or trellises should be in place before plants are set out. Canes should be supported *as they grow,* or they will always look "tied up." Roots will be injured too, in providing supports after plants have made considerable growth.

Planting too closely

While some of the weaker growing Hybrid Teas may be set as close as 5 to 15 inches apart (as often advocated), this does not provide enough room for vigorous growing sorts, especially in rich soil. These will require 20 to 24 inches—very strong growers considerably more.

Planting "bush" Roses in with Hybrid Teas

Hybrid Rugosas, Hybrid Perpetuals and other hybrids sometimes classed as "bush" type Roses, will overrun weaker growing varieties and should be given a place, or places to themselves.

Trying to grow Hybrid Roses without adequate winter protection

In sections where winter temperatures go to zero or lower, a mound of soil should be raised around the plant to a height of 6 or 8 inches.

"Hilling up" in fall with soil dug from between plants

This practice may result in injury to roots, and leaves them with little covering against winter's cold. Whenever possible, bring in soil for hilling, and supplement it with thorough mulching.

MISTAKES TO AVOID IN GROWING SHRUBS

Mutilation of flowering shrubs and trees by improper cutting of flowers

Flowering branches should never be cut back further than a strong growing shoot that will provide the succeeding year's bloom. Tall, spindly Lilacs are the result of improper cutting. Proper cutting requires the removal of branches from all portions of the plant equally. Tip end cutting on most shrubs is permissible, long stems should only be taken when the shrub is heavily overgrown, and the stem should be cut back as far as possible to insure graceful shaping.

Failure to remove suckers from understocks of grafted plants

If this job is neglected the suckers may grow and ultimately crowd out the desired grafted portion.

Failure to cut out Lilac suckers

The young suckers coming up from the base of the Lilac drain the plant of nourishment. At least 80 per cent of them should be cut out as soon as they appear. The remainder are left to replace old diseased or dying branches which may later have to be cut out.

Pruning shrubs in fall before plants become dormant

This will stimulate summer formed buds into growth that will be killed by first frost. Wait until a hard frost has ended growth activity.

Pruning over-large shrubs by cutting off the ends of their branches

This causes what remains of the pruned wood to send out many side branches, thereby making the shrub look dense and "stubby" and spoiling its normal shape. A much better plan is to achieve the desired reduction in size by cutting off the largest shoots *at the ground level;* this will not alter the plant's natural grace.

Pruning out the new growth at the base

This should be left and the older wood removed yearly, a few stems at a time.

Pruning Buddleia alternifolia hard in the spring

Unlike the common Butterfly Bush (Buddleia Davidi), *Buddleia alternifolia* bears its flowers on the growth produced during the previous season; if these are cut away in spring, the amount of bloom produced later is proportionately reduced.

Planting shrubs after foliage develops

This usually results in partial or complete loss. Late fall or early spring planting is advisable.

Pruning Forsythia, Lilacs and other spring blooming shrubs before they flower

As far as pruning is concerned, all shrubs are divided into two general groups: those which should be pruned after they flower in the spring, (Forsythia, Lilacs, etc.) and those which should be pruned in the very early spring before the leaves appear. This second group includes Hydrangeas (of the P.G. type—*not* "French" Hydrangeas), Rose of Sharon, etc., and flowers are produced on shoots grown the *current season,* hence an early spring pruning will not hinder their flowering properly.

Pruning without intelligent consideration of the purpose to be accomplished and the probable result of the cuts made

Pruning demands a "common sense" approach. Consideration must be given to the desired effect whether flowers (and fruits) are produced on old wood, or new wood, whether extension of growth is desired and many other factors. Often a judicious "thinning out" is preferred to hacking back branches. In many cases (for example, Magnolias and Rhododendrons) little or no pruning is required.

Failure to cut off branches at transplanting time

It is usually advisable to cut off approximately one-third of the branches of a shrub or tree at the time of transplanting, unless it is being moved with a ball of earth about the roots.

Failure to cut hedge plants severely as soon as planted

Hedge plants should be dense and bushy and so should branch from the base. Many species do best, when, after planting is completed, they are cut down to within 6 inches of the ground and so forced to sprout from the base.

Trimming a hedge so that it is wider at the top than at the bottom

This makes the hedge more susceptible to breakage from snow and by shutting off light results in loss of leaves and branches in the lower part of the hedge so that it is not well clothed from top to bottom.

Shearing shrubs in formal shapes

This is usually inappropriate for informal plantings. Besides, no renewal of the plant can be accomplished in this manner.

Jamming the roots into a hole too small

Shrubs should not be planted in a hole so small that the roots are crowded. Prepare a wide, deep hole in which the roots may be spread out in the same position they had previously been in.

Planting when the soil is too wet

If the soil is worked and stamped on when wet and muddy it will dry out in brick-like consistency. Never work or dig in it unless it is loose and friable, breaking up easily in the hand. If it sticks together in a gummy mass it is too wet.

Spreading commercial fertilizer on the roots of the shrub in a half filled hole

Such a practice will usually burn or even kill the roots. A small amount of fertilizer can be placed in the bottom of the hole, covered with a few inches of soil and the plant placed on top of that.

Pulling a shrub or tree up in the woods and expecting it to live in the garden

A plant growing undisturbed in the woods is often the most difficult to transplant. Dig it carefully with all its roots intact for sometimes there are only a few very long roots. Better still, root prune it a year before removing it from the woods.

Carrying a shrub or tree with bare roots on the side of a car without adequate covering

A frequent mistake in transporting plants. The rush of air quickly dries out the roots unless they are thoroughly wrapped.

Planting shrubs too near the house or garden walk

Whenever planting shrubs or trees, consideration should be given to spacing them so that when they are fully grown they will have plenty of room. If space is not available, use varieties that remain small when mature. Many a specimen is marred by continuous shearing merely because there isn't room for it to grow naturally.

Selecting shrubs that all bloom at one time

Weigelas, Mock oranges and the Virginia Rose bloom together and might make an interesting group in the garden but too many should not be used. Rather select plants which bloom at different periods in order that there will be interest in the shrubbery for as long a period as possible.

Planting tender kinds of azaleas that have been purchased as Easter plants in the outdoor garden after they have finished blooming

If you want to plant your Easter Azalea outdoors after blooming, make sure that you obtain a variety that will prove hardy in your locality. Florists force both hardy and tender kinds into bloom for Easter.

Using Maple leaves year after year on Rhododendrons

This mulch tends to be alkaline and also tends to pack down and almost form a cake or crust. It is better to use oak leaves and pine needles.

Cutting "French" Hydrangeas down to the ground-line in spring

This is a common cause of failure to bloom, because in most varieties the shoots which bear the flowers are produced only from near the tips of the canes. Canes which have flowered can be cut back immediately the blossoms fade. Spring pruning should be restricted to the removal of spindling canes and tips injured by winter.

Spraying Boxwood for miner after the pests have flown

Boxwood should be examined carefully from the middle of April. As the Boxwood miner matures, the orange-colored larvae become active underneath the blister on the underside of the leaf. The spray will not do its work until these larvae mature, break through this leaf blister, and take wings in flight. Spraying any time before this or after is useless. It is in flight that they deposit the eggs for next year's crop of pests. This is what you wish to prevent.

Failing to spray for mildew on Lilacs in the spring

Little can be done to counteract unsightly mildew on Lilacs when it appears in mid-summer. The control for this disease should begin before it appears on the plant. Sometimes, depending upon the weather, preventatives can be started in July, but better begin dusting with sulphur in May or June.

Planting shrubs or young trees in hardpan (hard subsoil)

Such soil area is waterlogged in wet weather and throughout the winter causing root rot. It is hard and dry in summer and roots become embedded as in concrete; poor root growth and a stunted top results. Break up the subsoil before planting and mix in ashes or other grit.

Planting hedge by setting young plants close together for quick effect

Young plants, especially evergreens, should be spaced so that the roots and tops will develop unrestricted. Too close together, there is root competition at once. Later, plants are starved. Better buy larger and fewer plants.

Planting Daphne cneorum in poorly drained places

This unpredictable Daphne abhors wet feet. Always make sure that drainage is good.

Forking, digging and cultivating near Rhododendrons, Azaleas and other ericaceous plants

Plants belonging to the Erica family all have a vast network of feeding roots near the soil surface. Don't break them by cultivating the soil; instead protect them with a suitable mulch.

Planting Rhododendrons that are intended to bloom in too dense shade

While it is true that Rhododendrons will live and grow in quite heavy shade, they bloom much more profusely if given considerable light. A "dappled" shade suits them well or the north side of a building or hill where they get good light but not the direct hot rays of midday.

Failing to remove promptly the dead flowers of Rhododendrons, Azaleas and Lilacs

If not removed they produce seed. Seed production is a weakening process and the plants are apt to bloom more sparsely the following year because of this.

Cutting back Rhododendrons, Mountain Laurel, Azaleas to shape them

These do not repond with new shoots as well as the regular deciduous shrubs. Pruning results in loss of flowers and needed foliage. Only in cases of disease or insect injury, or when plants are exceeding their allotted space is cutting back done.

Failure to keep the plant watered after transplanting

Never let it completely dry out, nor give it too much water, but see that it has enough the first year, then it will become well established.

Allowing roots to become dry when transplanting

When a tree or shrub is dug the roots should be kept moist *at all times* until it is replanted. Moist burlap, kept around them is good. Even allowing the roots to dry out 10 or 15 minutes in the sun while the hole is being dug may result in serious injury as this kills the fine feeding roots.

Planting out shrubs that were dried out in transit

This may result in complete loss. The roots cannot take enough moisture from the soil until tissue is again soft. Cut ends off roots and ⅓ or more of tops and immerse whole plant for 24 hours or more in water.

Bringing Azaleas, Laurel, Rhododendron, Blueberries into the garden without establishing acid soil conditions

These plants all grow best in an acid soil (pH 4.5–5.5). While an alkaline soil may be acidified with aluminum sulphate, the use of organic materials with an acid reaction is preferred—Oak and Pine leafmold, acid peatmoss, etc.

MISTAKES TO AVOID IN HANDLING SOILS AND FERTILIZERS

Using lime on Potato land

This will create a favorable condition for the spread of the Potato scab disease which exists in an alkaline soil and is increased by liming. Potato soil must be neutral or slightly acid.

Using bone meal or nitrate of soda on Potatoes

Being alkaline these will create conditions for the growth of the Potato scab disease which is controlled by keeping soil slightly acid. Use sulphate of ammonia or cottonseed-meal instead.

Walking over the soil without thought of the harm that may be done

This is particularly harmful on heavy, clayey soils if they are at all wet. Avoid tramping, wheeling and trucking over these as much as possible. When planting do not tramp around on the soil more than is absolutely necessary.

Using fresh chicken or rabbit manure in soils for immediate planting

High ammonium content may cause damage to roots.

Spreading bone meal on surface of soils

Phosphorus penetrates soil very slowly. Bone meal should be mixed with soil when it is prepared.

Thinking that lime is good for everything that ails a garden

It may be desirable to add lime to correct an over-acid condition of soil, but if put on when it is not needed, may do harm. It is of very little avail against soil pests but may sometimes be of value as a deterrent against leaf-eating insects and quadrupeds if dusted on the foliage.

Liming soils which show excessive growth of moss

Usually it is not lime that is needed but complete fertilizers and soil aeration.

Planting Cabbage, Broccoli, Cauliflower or Brussels Sprouts without liming soil

Lime is necessary with these crops to prevent the slime mold that causes large swellings to form on the roots. Use agricultural lime 40 lbs. per 1000 sq. feet.

Mixing slaked (builders) lime with animal manures

This will cause loss of the ammonia or nitrogen, the most important food element. The manure is best dug under and agricultural lime spread on the dug surface, 40 lbs. per 1000 sq. feet.

Mixing lime with acid phosphate

This will render the phosphates useless to the plant. The phosphate is best dug into the soil with manure. The agricultural lime should be spread on the surface of the dug soil.

Using the same quantity of slaked (builders) lime as ground limestone (agricultural lime)

This may cause over-liming and injury to plants and soil. Only 75 lbs. of slaked lime should be used for 100 lbs. of ground limestone.

Killing grubs by using quicklime (burnt lime) in the garden or on the lawn

Quicklime will burn up the humus in the soil and also any plants that come in contact with it. The action is short and may not touch the grubs at all. It is best to use arsenate of lead.

Putting lime on acid soil plants, Rhododendrons, Azaleas, Mountain Laurel, Blueberries

Very often fatal to acid soil plants. Lime sometimes leaks out of house foundations into soil containing these plants and also from lawns nearby that have been heavily limed. Keep soil well supplied with acid peat moss or Oak leafmold.

Using bone meal or nitrate of soda on acid soil plants like Rhododendrons, Azaleas, Mountain Laurel, Blueberries

These fertilizers are alkaline. If soil is inclined to alkalinity or is neutral, acid soil plants will be injured. These need an acid fertilizer, such as sulphate of ammonia or cottonseed meal.

Assuming that "woods dirt" is good soil

It does contain a high percentage of humus, but usually has poor fertilizing value. Mixed with loam, it is satisfactory.

Failure to provide adequate underdrainage in water-logged soils

Most plants grown in gardens need well-drained soil, provided by the installation of underground tile drains when necessary.

Assuming that Oak or Walnut leaves strongly acidify soils

This may happen during the process of decomposition but it soon wears off. However, one should not assume that the practice of mulching Rhododendrons with Oak leaves is not useful in maintaining soil acidity—the annual addition of fresh leaves maintains the flow of acidity.

Burning leaves in the fall

They make excellent composts and should not be wasted.

Using diseased plants and foliage in composts

Frequently the fungus spores are not killed by fermentation and will make trouble.

Walking on garden or working with the soil when it is sopping wet

This is likely to compact the soil too much, drive out air and make the soil unhealthy for the roots of plants.

Thinking that if 5 lbs. of commercial fertilizer per 100 sq. ft. is good, 10 lbs. will be twice as good

The nutrients in many commercial fertilizers are highly concentrated and immediately available, and an overdose may do a great deal of damage. Follow the directions of the manufacturer or experiment stations and other authorities.

Failure to break lumps below the surface when spading or forking the garden
> These, if not broken down, may leave undesirable air spaces.

Constant heavy applications of fertilizers to young fruit trees
> Much shoot and leaf growth will result and early bearing prevented by holding up the development of fruit buds. Promote root development by digging in organic matter when planting the trees. Light, annual fertilizing is best done when bearing begins.

Applying fertilizer early in fall
> This will stimulate a soft growth that will not harden before winter and will result in winter injury. Outdoor fertilizing after September is questionable in cold regions.

Using fertilizer to force, or stimulate, dormant or badly checked plants into growth
> This will cause further injury. Plants can only use active fertilizer when roots and tops are in full growth and in a growing temperature.

Putting large amounts of the standard chemical fertilizer mixtures in the soil in which seeds are about to be sown or plants set
> If these "raw" materials come in direct contact with small roots they are almost sure to "burn" them—that is, cause serious injury if not actual death; it's only when dissolved in water that plants can absorb them safely. The right procedure is to make sure that such dissolving takes place before the roots make contact with the valuable chemical foods in the mixture. Hence, the practice of placing the fertilizer *beside* the plant, where the rain or watering will gradually carry its nourishment down to the root area.

Raking the surface of the whole garden to a fine "seed-bed" condition immediately after digging or plowing
> This is a mistake. The surface should be left roughly levelled until the time for sowing or planting arrives. Then an area sufficient for immediate needs should be raked and the remainder left until actually needed.

Spading without taking out a trench first
> When digging is to be done a "trench" or "ditch" should always

be formed first and should be maintained between the newly dug and the undisturbed areas as the digging proceeds. Digging is easier this way and weeds, manure and debris are more easily buried.

Using fertilizer carelessly when setting out plants

Fertilizer must be well worked into the soil and not allowed to touch the young transplants. It will burn leaves and roots by contact or if washed into centers of flat-growing plants like Lettuce, Pansies, Petunias, etc., will cause rotting.

Side dressings of fertilizer on a dry soil

A concentration of fertilizer in a dry soil close to the active growing roots will draw the moisture out of the plant roots resulting in "burning." Soil must contain plenty of moisture before fertilizer is applied.

Putting active fertilizer on young seedlings

This will force soft spindly growth or burn the tender roots. Seedlings are not able to assimilate active chemical fertilizer except as a weak solution (1 teaspoonful in gal. water). Slower acting organics are better, such as steamed bone meal or dried manures.

MISTAKES TO AVOID IN GROWING TREES

Planting in holes too small for roots

The hole should be large and deep enough to contain all the roots without pruning except for broken tips.

Planting too close to drives

This results in barking of trees and development of cavities.

Planting in narrow parking strips

If these are bounded by sidewalks and pavement, the space allotted is not adequate and trees will not grow satisfactorily. Planting on the lawn side of the walk is better.

Planting too close

Depending on the kind, adequate space should be allowed for specimen development unless a grove is desired. Street trees should be planted 40–75 feet apart.

Planting too deeply

Aeration is reduced and quick development of new roots is impeded. Plant no deeper than in original growing conditions.

Failure to mulch trees after planting

A mulch of peat, straw, or any litter will help retain moisture.

Failure to wrap trunk after planting

Wrapping of the trunk with burlap is desirable to reduce borer attacks and as a prevention against sun scald.

Failure to provide catchwater basins or saucers for transplanted plants, trees and shrubs

Inasmuch as the main requirement of a newly transplanted subject is sufficient water, it is important that a saucer should be built up around the base of each plant, to catch and retain water, particularly rain water. The practice of hilling the soil around the base of the plant should be done only in the fall, when the purpose is to drain off excess water.

Failure to provide adequate drainage

With the exception of such trees as Willows, adequate drainage is extremely important. For large trees where natural drainage does not exist, tiling is needed.

Whitewashing tree trunks to prevent insect attack

This is practically valueless for the purpose intended.

Using any soil available on the place

Trees are planted for permanency and the soil used about the roots, unless naturally rich, should be a good compost with such a complete fertilizer as 10–6–4 mixed at the rate of about two pounds to a wheelbarrow of soil.

Failing to work fine, loose soil thoroughly around and among all the roots when planting a tree

To do a good job you need (1) your own fingers, (2) a blunt stick to poke with, and (3) a pail or more of water to flood the soil and settle everything in place. Leaving vacant air spaces among roots may kill some of them.

Failure to guy and stake trees after planting

Injury to newly forming roots by wind movement may be prevented by using three guy wires attached to the tree by running through rubber garden hose put around the trunk or main branches. These should remain attached for two years.

Tying wire tightly around a young tree or branch to hold it steady

This will cause constriction. The part above the wire may die or be seriously injured by having the sap flow cut off. Use insulated wire, or run the wire through a piece of rubber hose, and allow room for development when tying.

Failure to paint a tree wound

All tree or shrub wounds over 2 inches in diameter should be painted with white lead paint, shellac or better still, one of the commercial asphaltum paints manufactured for the purpose.

Using indiscriminate wound dressing

Cheap paints and home-made preparations may do more harm than good. Special paints are available.

Using creosote as a disinfectant on tree wounds without protecting the cambium layer (the thin tissue just under the bark)

This will cause the latter to kill back and prevent healing. The cambium must first be covered with a coating of shellac and the creosote confined to the center of the wound or cavity.

Filling cavities in tree trunks with concrete, without removing all infected wood

The concrete does not help strengthen the trunk and the organisms causing decay may continue to flourish behind the concrete which masks their destructive work.

Nailing into trees, wrapping wire around stem

Such practices will eventually result in disfigurement and disease.

Failure to make undercut when removing large branches

The weight of the branch is likely to cause a break resulting in a jagged tear which may extend a considerable distance down the trunk. An undercut should first be made a few inches from the point where the final cut is to be. The second cut from above should be an inch or two beyond the first one. This leaves a stub which can be steadied with one hand while the final cut with the saw is being made.

Leaving stubs when cutting branches from trees and shrubs

The cut should be made close to and parallel with the parent trunk of branch. If a shoot is being shortened, the cut should be made about ¼ in. above a bud. Stubs invariably die back and may afford an opportunity for the entrance of organisms causing disease.

Breaking off a branch and leaving ragged wound

All stubs should be cut off flush with the trunk and all wounds or scars on the trunk of trees should be smooth and not ragged. Sometimes it is well to cut off ragged edges of bark with a knife so that the bark around a wound is clean, alive and held firmly to the tree in a solid line.

Allowing two leaders to form in a single trunk tree

Certain trees like Paper Birch, Pin Oak, Lindens, Ash, Tupelo and most of the Firs, Spruce, Pines and Hemlocks grow best when they have a single trunk. When a second leader appears it should be cut back or cut out entirely.

Trying to "break out" evergreen branches held firmly to the ground by snow and ice

Such branches should not be touched. As the ice and snow melts they will gradually be released with a minimum amount of injury whereas they are easily broken if one tries to pry them loose before the snow and ice melt.

Transplanting an evergreen in June or July

These are the worst months of the entire year for transplanting evergreens. Late August and early September are best, although some can be moved in early spring.

Planting Cedar trees near Apple trees, including the ornamental Crab Apples

Cedar-apple rust which develops in the cedars in March sends out spores from the gelatinous orange "apples" formed on the cedar trees, which are carried by the wind to members of the apple family to complete the life cycle of this disease. The elimination of cedars in the vicinity of apples is the easiest preventive measure.

Cutting the leading shoot of young shade trees at planting time

This will cause dangerous crotches to form and spoil the shape. Retain the leader and cut back the laterals (side growths).

Pruning Maples or Birch in early spring or late winter

This results in bleeding which cannot be stopped by painting the wound. Pruning is best done in early autumn—September, October.

Transplanting native Cedars from rough, rocky ground and expecting them to live

Unless they're very, very small, it's just about impossible to get them out with enough roots to enable them to survive for more than a few weeks or months.

Planting only one yew

These plants may not fruit, since the sexes are separate, unless two plants are near each other, one male and one female. These can be identified at flowering time by the nurseryman.

Transplanting an evergreen without a ball of earth about the roots

All evergreens, both narrow leaved and broad leaved, are best transplanted with a ball of earth about the roots.

Planting only one Holly tree if you expect berries

Holly trees are dioecious; that is, there are male and female plants and plants of each sex are necessary in order to produce berries on the female tree. In selecting trees at the nursery, be sure that you have at least one male to insure pollination of the female trees.

Planting an evergreen which normally grows to tree size in front of a window

Remember that although some evergreens like Hemlocks, some Arborvitae, and some Chamaecyparis look well as small plants, they soon shoot up into tree size and have no place in front of windows.

Expecting plants to grow under Norway Maples
Frequently the Norway Maple is in a prominent position in the lawn and shrubs or flowers are desired underneath. The feeding roots of this tree are so near the surface that often *nothing* will grow satisfactorily under it. Better surface the soil with slates or pebbles if bare soil is not satisfactory.

Planting shallow rooted trees like Maples in lawns
Under such conditions good lawns cannot be expected.

Failure to cut off suckers from the understock of grafted plants
Peaches, Apples, Oriental Cherries and Crab Apples are all grafted and shoots from understock, yielding inferior plants should *always* be cut off.

Neglecting to cut out dead or diseased branches
These should always be cut out as soon as noted to prevent spreading of diseases.

Neglecting to prune espalier Apples and Pear trees severely enough
It is necessary during the dormant season to prune all previous season's growths that are not needed for extension of the main stems back to one or two eyes. If this is not done the spurs soon become too long and assume the character of sizable lateral branches.

Keeping seeds of certain plants dry and warm during the winter preparatory to sowing them in the spring
Many tree seeds—Nuts, Oaks, etc.—lose their viability unless they are mixed with moist sand or peatmoss and kept in a cold place over the winter.

Failure to water evergreens in late fall after a dry spell
This is the time when they need water most. Water thoroughly before the ground freezes.

Neglecting to prune trees and shrubs when they are transplanted
When trees are dug up almost invariably a considerable portion of the root system is left behind. It is necessary to remove some of the top growth to bring about a better balance between shoot and root.

Failing to provide abundant late summer and autumn water for trees and shrubs (especially evergreens) planted less than two years

It is vitally important that such plants enter their dormant season with a good supply of internal moisture, which calls for an extra amount of water in the soil until such time as their root systems are fully established in the new locations.

Failure to provide adequate means of watering trees
Surface applications usually do not penetrate deeply enough. Upright 3 or 4 inch tiles set flush with the surface of the soil will help. Water should be poured in these frequently.

Taking the advice of unreliable tree-service men
They may advocate injections, soil treatment, and sprays which may do no good and may cause a lot of damage through subsequent neglect or because of toxic substances employed. Consult a reliable arborist.

Spraying Peaches with arsenate of lead at usual strength and frequently
Arsenical sprays are injurious to Peaches. No more than one application per season, when all petals have fallen used at the rate of 2 tablespoonfuls lead arsenate, 1 tablespoon lime to 1 gallon water. This is used to control curculio.

MISTAKES TO AVOID IN GROWING VEGETABLES

Planting Corn in a single row
Corn should be planted in two or more rows to aid pollination. Single row planting is likely to result in many undeveloped kernels.

Allowing Corn to grow too thickly

Crowding will reduce yield. In rows 30 in. apart, thin to 1 ft. between plants. In hills 36 in. apart, each way, thin to 3 stalks to the hill.

Cutting Asparagus prematurely

Cutting should be deferred until the second year after planting to allow development of a strong root system.

Walking up and down the rows of planted seeds (to see if they are up) when the soil is wet and muddy

This is unwise because it tends to force all the air out of the soil and pack it together so that it dries out to a brick-like consistency. In such soil, it is difficult if not impossible for roots to grow.

Failure to thin seedlings of vegetables while they are still young

If too closely crowded none of the seedlings are able to give a good performance because of intense competition.

Thinning out Lettuce, Carrots, Beets, Radishes and Turnips to full recommended distance at time of first thinning

Half grown specimens of all of these are good for kitchen use. Lettuce, for instance, can be thinned to four inches, and every other plant used in immature state, leaving 8-inch spaces for heads to mature.

Planting vegetable seeds too thickly in the rows

Kinds having small seeds such as Carrots, Spinach, Kohlrabi, should be planted about 3 to 5 times as thickly as the final spacing.

Trying to grow Beets on an acid soil

Beets need an *alkaline* soil; hence, add lime.

Expecting good vegetables from a poor soil

Some soils are so poor that nothing will do well in them. If you have this kind of soil, admit it and take steps to improve it *before* planting. Don't blame poor growth on the plants!

Sowing Peas too thinly

It takes many Peas to provide a row that will give good picking. Seeds set approximately 2 in. apart over the entire bottom of a shallow six-inch-wide drill (or two 3" wide drills closely paralleling each other) will not prove too many.

Sowing Lettuce much too thickly

A respectable Lettuce plant certainly covers a circular area having a diameter of from eight to nine inches or more. Therefore, theoretically four to five seeds per yard of row would be sufficient. In practice we increase this by three or four times, but it certainly isn't desirable to sow Lettuce seeds as thickly as those of lawn grass!

Thinking that warmth and moisture alone are sufficient for raising seedlings in the house

Those who attempt to raise seedlings on top of the cellar furnace are sadly disappointed in the results. Abundant light and adequate ventilation are also necessary for stocky, healthy seedlings.

Neglecting to use a garden line as a guide when making drills or furrows in the vegetable garden

It is argued that more plants can be grown in a crooked row, but it complicates the problem of caring for the crop and makes a sloppy looking garden.

Cutting the leaves from Tomato plants to allow sunshine to reach the fruit to ripen it

The color is produced in Tomatoes independently of light conditions. Reduction of foliage may make the plants more susceptible to diseases causing defoliation.

Cutting the leaves of Carrots, Beets, etc., to make them produce larger roots

The leaves manufacture food for the nourishment of the roots. If foliage is luxuriant and normal roots are not produced, it probably means an insufficient supply of phosphorus and potash in the soil.

Sowing seeds too deep

While there are few who go to the extremes of the lady gardener who planted her Carrot seeds 8 ins. deep because she wished the resulting Carrots to be 8 ins. long—(This is an authentic case!)—there are many who habitually plant their seeds too deep and then blame the seedsman for their failure to germinate. A good general rule in outdoor planting is to cover the seeds with soil equal in depth to 3 or 4 times the diameter of the seed.

Planting Peas too late in the spring

Peas should be planted as early as possible in the spring in order to have maturity in June. Peas are cool weather crops and need the cool nights and bright days of early spring, both for germination and yield. Peas are hardy and will withstand considerable frost. Plant around the middle of March.

Using the same spray for Beans that is used for tougher vegetables such as Cabbages

Beans are a tender crop and can be burned up with too strong sprays and dusts, just as they are more easily damaged by frost. Follow the directions carefully while spraying beans, and never use Bordeaux mixture.

Planting Pepper seeds too late

Pepper plants should be ready to transplant to the garden as soon as all danger of frost is over. Peppers require from 65 to 80 days from seed to maturity and since they are a tender crop, often they are nipped by the frost just as they are coming into maturity because seeds are planted too late in the season. Seeds of Peppers should be planted indoors, and the plants set out when settled, warm weather is reasonably sure.

Using too much nitrogen in fertilizer during the flowering and fruiting season

Nitrogen encourages leaf growth and should be withheld as plants near the flowering and fruiting period. It is a mistake to keep forcing plant growth with too much nitrogen when we desire flowers and fruit (such as Tomatoes).

Failing to use inoculant on Peas and Beans and other legumes when growth is not satisfactory

Experiment is now sufficient to show that growth of legumes is definitely stimulated by inoculant. The inoculant contains legume bacteria (which encourage the forming of nodules on the root), thus aiding the plant in taking and using nitrogen from the air. The inoculant is dusted on the seed before planting and a 10c packet will inoculate ten pounds of seeds.

Planting Potatoes without using semesan for disease control

This simple treatment of Potatoes aids greatly in the control of scab and rhizoctonia. Even certified seed potatoes are benefited from this kind of disease preventive.

Not burning Corn stalks in the fall

Burning the Corn stalks is the easiest form of control of the European Corn borer. The larvae of this pest winter over in the old stalks. The stalks should be burned to reduce infestation the following year.

Storing vegetables that are better left in the ground

Parsnips, Salsify, Jerusalem Artichokes should be left in the ground where they have been grown. Jerusalem Artichokes, especially, mold and wither if dug before time for use.

Picking vegetables too late for best flavor and texture

Vegetables left too long before picking become tough and less sweet; especially those vegetables of which we eat the seed or pod as Peas, Beans, or Corn. Without regard for our taste, nature continues to develop the seed, to store up fat and starch and toughen the seed coatings for safe preservation of the life within. The best flavor and texture combination is usually at the turning point between maximum growth and storage of energy in the seed.

Picking root vegetables too soon

It is very often stated that very young Carrots are a choice vegetable. They are tender, it is true, but not sweet unless they are at least of finger size. Root vegetables do not start storing sugar until toward maturity and Carrots, Parsnips, Turnips and all other root crops reach maximum flavor when Nature's storage process is complete. Sometimes a compromise must be made between tenderness and sweetness.

Planting Carrots in too heavy soil

To obtain long, straight Carrots, the ground should be deeply prepared and light in texture, so that the roots can go down without too much opposition. Adding sand to the soil provides a good medium for the growth of Carrots.

Planting Spinach for a summer crop

Spinach should be planted very early in the spring, as soon as frost is out of the ground, or in August for a late fall crop, or in September, to be left in the ground all winter and harvested in March and

April. For summer greens to take the place of Spinach, the New Zealand variety of Spinach may be used.

Planting Head Lettuce for a summer crop

The leaf varieties and romaine Lettuce (cos) are more satisfactory for summer Lettuce. The head varieties tend to bolt to seed during the long days of July and August and are better planted for early spring or late fall, when the days are shorter.

Storing Onions immediately after digging

After harvesting, Onions should be dried off for several days (until the stem is thoroughly dry) before storing for winter. Onions may then be put in mesh bags and safely stored in a cool, dry, dark place.

Letting vegetables stand too long after picking

Sugar content of vegetables is rapidly turned into starch after picking. This is a natural process and though it can be delayed by cooling quickly, the flavor is always affected adversely. The old adage, "Have the water boiling before you go to pick the corn" is just as true for Peas, Beans, Asparagus and many other vegetables.

Too early planting of Potatoes for winter storage

Unless a cool storage room is available, the Potatoes are better in the ground than in too warm storage, but if left in the ground after maturity, they become susceptible to disease and to rodents and white grubs which may do great damage before the Potatoes are dug. Therefore, plant them as late as possible so that the digging time may coincide with best conditions for storage. Consult the number of days necessary for maturity. Count back from frost to decide the proper planting date for your special variety.

Neglecting to grow a late crop of Chinese Cabbage

Chinese Cabbage is one of the most easily stored vegetables providing crisp greens throughout the winter and as late as May. Lift the Cabbage before a hard frost, stand upright in a cool, dark cellar in a shallow box of moist sand. The outside leaves may deteriorate if the storage room is too warm, but the inside may even continue to grow during the winter months.

Sowing seeds of Peas and Spinach in summer

Seeds will not germinate or plants will not develop. These are cool season crops. They will only grow in early spring or fall.

Saving seeds for next year's planting from any of the cucurbit vegetables (Melons, Squashes, Cucumbers) where two or more different varieties are grown in the same garden

Melons do not cross with Squashes or Cucumbers, but if two or more varieties of either of these is planted they are likely to be cross-pollinated by insects so that seeds saved from them are pretty sure to produce "mongrels."

Picking Beans when the foliage is wet

Rust and anthracnose are nearly always present on Beans. Picking when the foliage is wet is the best way to distribute the rust disease over the entire planting. Pick only when the foliage is dry.

Working among Celery plants when the foliage is wet

Celery leaf blight is thereby spread. Where it is prevalent, keep the trenches wide apart and when watering let the water flow into the trench instead of spraying it over the plants.

Locating a vegetable garden near trees

Tree roots spread rapidly in soil dug and fertilized for vegetables robbing them of both plant food and moisture. Shade from nearby trees, if dense, is fatal to practically all vegetables. Even partial shade will reduce crops decidedly.

Failure to practice crop rotation in the home-vegetable garden

Many failures due to disease particularly in the brassica family which includes all the Cabbages, Turnips, and Radishes, can be attributed to the fact that they are planted year after year in the same ground and same location. Two years should intervene before any of these crops are planted in the same soil. This does not affect Peas, or Beans, any leafy green crop, Corn or Tomatoes, and they should be rotated with the brassicas.

Neglecting to plant winter cover-crops on sloping ground

The easiest and most effective way to prevent winter erosion is to sow rye or Rye Grass, any time up to hard freezing—the earlier the better. Valuable humus is added when crop is dug under in spring.

Planting vegetables on soil when green manure crop has just been turned under, without supplying extra nitrogen

In decaying, the "green-manure" crop draws heavily on nitrogen supply in the soil, thus temporarily robbing plants of this element. This "borrowed" nitrogen is returned later, but in the meantime, nitrogen (in the form of nitrate of soda or its equivalent) should be supplied.

Planting tall growing vegetables on east or south side of low growing ones

Corn, staked Tomatoes, Pole-Beans, and the like, cast sufficient shade to seriously hinder growth of such low growers as Bush Beans and root crops.

Failing to hill up small plantings of Corn

Corn in fairly large patches—like trees in a forest—to a large degree protects itself from wind and storms. Substantial hilling, where only a few rows are planted at a time, will aid greatly in preventing such damage.

Letting plant-pests get a head start before employing control measures

A 24 or 48 hour interval between the time a pest appears and dusting or spraying to control it may make all the difference between success and failure. Where possible, the garden should be examined daily for first signs of any new pest.

Storing Squash, Pumpkins and Sweet Potatoes with root crops

These vegetables require a hot (50° to 60°) dry temperature, just the other extreme for root crops.

Planting Onions on new soil

More than any other vegetables, Onions demand well worked, finely pulverized, fertile soil.

Neglecting to make late plantings of Carrots, Beets, Turnips, and Spinach

These are among the most satisfactory of fall vegetables; moreover young roots, just reaching maturity are of better quality *and keep better* than overgrown old ones from earlier plantings.

Neglecting to hill up Celery as it grows

Celery plants tend to spread unless the soil is kept worked up to the stalks as they develop, holding the leaves in an upright position and thus facilitating moderate blanching as the crop nears maturity.

Failure to tie up Cauliflower heads
Unless the leaves are tied together at the tips when the heads begin to form (2 or 3 inches in diameter) they will turn brown and be of inferior flavor when fully grown.

Planting Cabbage or other crucifers in infected soil
If club-root has attacked the crop, plants should be set out the following season at some distance away.

MISTAKES TO AVOID
IN GROWING WILD FLOWERS

Collecting Fringed Gentian plants in the wild
The Fringed Gentian is a biennial and this year's flowering plant will have disappeared next year. Grow your own plants from seed or procure first-year plants from suppliers.

Failure to apply a winter mulch to plants with long-lasting foliage,
such as: Trailing Arbutus, Oconee Bells, Foam Flower, Pipsissewa, etc.
These are natives of the woods and are accustomed to a natural leaf mulch. Exposure to the elements, especially the wind, during winter is frequently fatal. The best mulches are Pine needles or Oak leaves.

Transplanting Pipsissewa (Chimaphila maculata or C. umbellata)
from the woods
The long, wiry roots are difficult to move without fatal injury. It is better to propagate plants by rooting cuttings made in July.

Collecting wild plants of Trailing Arbutus
Collected plants are rarely transplanted successfully. It is better to grow them from seed or to secure small pot-grown specimens from dealers.

Using a heavy winter mulch composed of Maple leaves, hay or other material that forms a wet, heavy blanket impervious to the air

This is likely to cause the plants to rot or to seriously handicap the early spring growth. Use such materials as Oak leaves, Pine needles, evergreen branches or salt hay.

Planting wild flowers in a location directly exposed to the wind

Many of the delicate natives of the woods are more seriously harmed by exposure to the wind than by any other factor. Give them the protection of a stone wall or some natural windbreak.

Keeping hardy wild flowers in pots in the house the year 'round

Plants which in nature go through a freezing winter season, require this freezing period for proper growth. If such plants are grown in pots for indoor bloom, they should be plunged into the ground outdoors for the winter with a protective mulch.

Handling carelessly the roots of spring flowering plants such as Trilliums, Bloodroot, Lady's Slippers, Trout-lilies, Solomon's seal, etc.

In many of the spring flowering plants, the growing bud for the following year is well developed in the fall which is the proper time for planting. Carelessness in handling or planting the roots can easily break off or damage the fragile new shoot.

Buying spring-flowering plants from suppliers for spring planting

Despite the fact that native plants are widely advertised for sale in the spring, the early flowering sorts should be purchased and planted only in the fall. Plants delivered in the spring are usually kept over the winter in storage and will almost certainly be in poor condition. If they are dug in the spring and shipped with bare roots, they will suffer severe and probably fatal shock. They can be shipped safely and in good condition during the dormant season, in late summer and fall.

Planting Ferns too deeply

The crown should never be covered. In transplanting ferns, from the wild, observe carefully the position of the clump before taking it up and replant it in the same way.

Planting the wild garden on a slope without taking measures to prevent washing away of the soil

Winter thaws and rains are likely to wash the plants out of the earth or to bury them deeply in silt, unless the erosion is prevented by some means, such as the judicious and naturalistic placing of rocks and logs.

Transplanting from the wild during the period of active growth without an adequate ball of earth around the roots

Many natives may safely be transplanted in the spring even in bud or flower, but only if a sufficiently large ball of earth is taken, so that disturbance of the root is completely avoided.

Cutting down the foliage of Trilliums, Bloodroot, Solomon's seal, etc. when it starts to look bedraggled

The foliage should be allowed to die off in its own good time. Cutting it before it has died down interferes with the proper development of the root for next season's growth.

Failure to weed the wild garden

Coarse growing plants such as wild Mint, Goldenrod, Clover, etc., are likely to invade the artificial wild garden and give the natives of the woods heavier competition than they are used to. These undesirables should be kept weeded out, even after the spring flowering season is over.

Planting the natives of the woods in heavy clay soil

Practically all of these plants require a light, humusy soil. In preparing the ground for them, sufficient leaf mold or peatmoss should be mixed thoroughly into the soil to approximate the texture of the soil in their native habitat.

Permitting bog plants to dry out during the summer

The natives of wet woods, bogs and swampy meadows such as the Lady's Slippers, the fringed Orchids, the Cardinal-Flower, the Marsh Marigold, etc., require continual moisture throughout the year. If necessary, the spot where they are planted should be watered frequently enough to prevent drying out.

Planting Lady's Slippers too deep

The new growing bud which will be very conspicuous at planting time in the fall should be placed not more than one inch under the surface. The long wiry roots should be spread out fan-wise and slanting downward.

Digging wild Blue Lupine and Butterfly weed

These plants have long tender tap-roots and transplanting from the wild is unsatisfactory. They may be raised much more easily from seed.

Bringing wild flowers from the woods without first studying their growing conditions

Good conservation practice demands that wild flowers should be brought to the home garden from the woods only if they are growing in abundance in their native stand and only if you can establish conditions in your garden in which these plants will thrive; that is, similar to the conditions from which they have been taken.

Transplanting lime-loving plants to acid soil

Walking Fern and Maidenhair spleenwort, growing in lime rocks in Oak woods, will not become established in the garden unless these conditions can be fulfilled. They are much better left to grace the rocks of their native home.

A VARIETY OF MISTAKES TO AVOID IN GARDENING

Moving seedling plants from house or hot-bed into the open without a period of "hardening off"

The sudden change in light, temperature and wind exposure will injure the plants unless they are given an intermediate period in a coldframe where they are gradually given greater exposure to outdoor conditions.

Failure to properly ventilate coldframes and hot-beds

In the early spring months when the sun is beginning to have considerable power, plants in coldframes may suffer damage from overheating if the sash is tightly closed all day. A watch should be kept on weather conditions and the frame ventilated by tilting the sash on the side opposite from the direction of the wind.

Failure to match the cambium layers of understock and scion when grafted

It is in these areas only that union takes place.

Allowing Tuberous Begonias to stay in the ground until heavy frosts

They should be lifted before killing frost and ripened off for winter storage in dry sand or soil.

Failing to thin out seedlings early enough

Plants need light and air to develop sturdily. If they crowd each other too long in infancy they become spindly and weak. Pull out the surplus before the plants are of such size that the leaves of any individual seriously shade those of its neighbors.

Sowing seeds too deeply

Seeds should not be covered with soil to more than from once to thrice their own shortest diameter. The heavier covering is advocated with sandy, light soils and for summer sowings; the lighter covering for heavy, clayey soils and for early spring sowing.

Sowing too thickly

Seeds of plants that are to mature where sown without transplanting should be sown not more than four or five times as thickly as the plants will finally stand. Seeds of kinds that are to be transplanted should be spaced so that four or five times their own mean diameter separates them.

Using rich soil in seed flats

The seed is a unit in itself and needs no nutrient for sprouting. All the seed needs is light soil and moisture. Fertilizer in the seed flats often burns the tender sprouts of the seedling. It is better to add gentle applications of fertilizer after the roots have taken hold.

Thinning seedlings after growth has advanced

Vegetables, especially the root crops, are badly affected if thinning is delayed because the roots are likely to have become entwined. It is not possible to thin without disturbing the roots of all the plants. Thinning is first done when the seedlings are small. The second thinning gives the right spacing.

Placing too much reliance on fertilizers, seed-treating chemicals, root-inducing substances and so forth

These and many other purchasable supplies are aids, and often very important aids to good gardening. But alone, they will not do the trick. Day by day care in providing an *environment* as ideal as possible for the particular plants being grown is basic.

Failing to "steal" as big a start as possible on the spring season

Great advantage results from getting as much spading and plowing done in the fall as is practicable; from getting tools in condition and repair, from having flats, stakes and other supplies on hand well before they are actually required.

Failing to attack weeds early enough

Weeds are much easier to hoe down when they are small than when they are big and they grow mighty fast. Therefore, keep the hoe going on every favorable occasion through the growing season.

Neglecting to keep a note-book record

Memory is fallible. Keep a record of sowing dates, planting distances, results and other pertinent data relating to your garden. It will prove invaluable in future planning and will considerably supplement what you read or learn at lectures. After all, these data and observations refer to *your* garden.

Cultivating too deeply

Surface cultivation is important, but never disturb the soil so deeply that the roots of growing plants are damaged. An inch or an inch and a half deep is usually the maximum near plants. Plants of the Erica and Vaccinium families root so closely to the surface that no cultivating should be done near to them.

Breaking the "balls" of pot-grown plants and spreading out the roots when planting them in the garden

This should never be done. All the advantages of growing in pots are lost if the roots are severely disturbed at planting time.

Destroying the praying mantis

This strange looking creature should be recognized and treated with respect, for he has great capacity to destroy many insect enemies.

Failing to stake and tie early enough

Plants that need or may need support during the growing season should be given this attention early. It is much simpler to do it this way and tie as may be needed during the growing season than to wait until a summer storm lays the plants low and then attempt to retrieve them.

Overcrowding outdoor plants. (One of the commonest of errors)

Foundation plantings, herbaceous borders, shrub borders, etc., are almost invariably too thickly planted. Annuals and vegetables are set too closely together. Trees are given insufficient room to develop. It takes courage to plant sparsely so that specimens have room to grow, but along that road lies ultimate success. Interplanting with a variety that is later to be removed will sometimes bridge the gap successfully.

Failing to clean tools when they are put away (or worse still, failing to put them away)

If tools are cleaned and the metal parts wiped with a slightly oily rag, when they are put away each day, they will be in good condition to use again. Dirty, rusty tools add greatly to the effort expended in doing a piece of work.

Buying poor quality tools

Garden tools are called upon to do surprisingly heavy work. Cheap "ten-cent" store tools are expensive in the long run. Expect to pay a fair price and get quality tools of a size and character adapted to the strength of the user.

Straining pruning shears by cutting over-large branches with them and damaging their cutting edge by using them on wire or other noncuttable substances

The gardener should respect his tools and handle them with care. A "strained" pruning shear will never be the same again no matter what is done to straighten it out.

Neglecting to make the first outdoor sowings of hardy seeds early enough in the spring

Peas, Spinach, Larkspurs, Cornflowers and lawn grass are a few examples of many crops that thrive best when sown early. The first sowings should be made on the first occasion when the ground is workable. Many amateurs miss this opportunity. Rains follow, sowings are delayed two or three weeks or longer and crops are less satisfactory.

Saving seeds of hybrids

Neither flowers nor vegetables which are hybrids will produce true to the parent but will produce offspring with characteristics of both parents inferior to the hybridized product. Hybrid Corn, Cucumbers, Tomatoes (from crossing in-bred strains) offered by seedsmen belong in a different category.

Planting any but disease-resistant varieties, if disease-resistant varieties are available

Although the specific disease may not be present in the vicinity, disease resistance also means in plants a higher resistance to unfavorable growing conditions. The last long drought proved that disease resistant varieties came through better than others.

Using methods suitable in spring for seed germination during the hot months of July and August

The hot days of July and August bake the soil and the hard crust may prevent seed germination, unless special precautions are taken. Plant the seeds in shallow drills watering with a starter solution (one cup of 5–10–5 to 4 gallons of water using one cupful per foot). Cover with light soil mixed with sand and cover all with a light mulch. Push the mulch aside when the seedlings appear. Pine needles are good for this purpose.

Arranging cut flowers in too little water

Flowers should be immersed in water up to the bloom for at least an hour before arranging in vases. Better to leave them over night. Flowers take water through the length of the stem and keep from wilting when transferred to a vase. See that a good portion of stem is supplied with water for a longer lasting arrangement.

Failing to label the garden

Even the best of gardeners forget varieties and dates of planting, valuable information for next year's plants and for the friends who visit the garden.

Chasing toads out of the garden

The toad in the garden is one of our best friends in the control of insects. He is better than a spray in that he never ceases his vigilance, nor is he washed away by rain.

Deep planting of young plants that grow from a low crown, Pansies, Delphiniums, Petunias, Lettuce, Strawberries

Covering the young crown (growing point) when planting will result in rotting at the growing point. The first leaves (those above root) should barely rest on the soil surface. Do not leave a depression around such plants to hold water.

Setting out plants with bare roots without cutting back the top

Loss of roots must be balanced by removing part of the top. Through losing roots the plant cannot furnish enough moisture to the unrestricted top. The plant may die back entirely. Cutting part of the top (about ⅓) assures a moisture supply for the buds or leaves and restores balance.

Grouping plants that have different requirements

It is a mistake to combine Rhododendrons, Mountain Laurel, etc., requiring acid soil with Lilacs that need alkalinity; primulas that need boggy conditions with dianthus that needs perfect drainage; Tuberous Begonias that need shade with Roses or other plants that need sun. Plants with specific demands should be kept separate.

Pruning plants infected with disease and failing to disinfect the tool after each operation

This just spreads the infection. After each cut, disinfect the tool with formaldehyde or alcohol.

Leaving plant roots exposed to air while setting out other plants

Drying the roots checks the plant. Roots must always be kept moist. Plunge roots in water, or cover with wet burlap while planting is going on.

Slacking up on the September weeding with the excuse that it's too late in the season to bother

Unless you keep them under control, the weeds will ripen thousands of seeds for next year's garden.

Planting anything in a hole just big enough to accommodate its roots, especially in hard ground

Such procedure seriously interferes with future growth because the roots can't spread freely in their search for food and moisture. The correct procedure is to loosen the soil thoroughly with a spading fork over an area at least twice as wide and deep as the present roots will occupy, and then dig the actual planting hole.

Putting off until spring the many gardening tasks that can better be done in the fall

Tasks such as spading up new beds, putting compost on the vegetable plot, planting Roses and sowing grass seed—the spring season is so short and hectic—and the weather so uncertain—that many headaches are saved by getting a good fall start.

Cultivating too deeply around growing plants

Most vegetable and flowering plants have a fine network of roots near the surface that is disturbed by deep cultivation. This practice can cause stunted growth in the plants, and in some cases, leads to their destruction.

Digging up beds and borders at random throughout the garden whenever a few plants are on hand to stick in the ground

The effect is hodge-podge. It's a much better practice to plan everything on paper before planting is done, and in the event that plants arrive unexpectedly, heel them in a special nursery bed or coldframe until you know just where you want to put them for the best effect.

Purchasing oversize vegetable and annual flowering plants

Tomato plants in six inch pots have been eagerly sought after by many who fail to realize that too early flowers on these plants very often fail to set fruit, and that the small plant bears fruit almost as soon. Pot-bound plants of Celery, Broccoli, Parsley, etc., often bolt to seed. Potted annuals in full bloom at planting time are usually greenhouse grown and potbound, so that after the first flush of bloom is over the plant takes time out to form a new set of roots and flower buds, allowing the young seedling to catch up.

Failure to unpack plants promptly

Too often plant buyers will receive a package of plants early in the week and allow it to remain unpacked until the week-end. Plants can remain out of the ground safely a full week or more, if they are unpacked and watered when necessary, but often become useless if compressed and dried out in a carton or box.

Failing to water transplanted plants and seedlings properly or suffi- ciently

Many failures with plants are due to insufficient watering. This elementary procedure is too often neglected. Every plant should be watered individually immediately after planting regardless of the time of day or weather conditions. Saturate the ground around each plant making provisions to keep the water from running off.

Purchasing overage and so called fruiting and flowering size trees, bushes and herbaceous perennials

Inasmuch as older plants resent and react unfavorably to transplant- ing in proportion to their age, any gain that may be anticipated is usually lost by the length of time required for the older plant to get over the shock. A young plant in competent hands can be shaped and endowed with a better constitution in its permanent lo- cation than an older plant. Avoid the purchase of fruiting size fruit bushes and vines, Asparagus roots over two years old, fruit trees over three years old and hedge plants over 18″ in height.

Planting a twining vine like Bittersweet at the base of a young tree

Such a vine will quickly twine around the trunk and branches and choke the tree to death. It is better not to plant any vine to climb on a tree.

Watering by the "little and often" method rather than soaking the soil thoroughly and then leaving it until it is nearly dry before watering again

Nightly sprinklings do not usually provide a satisfactory method of watering. In special cases such sprinklings may beneficially supple- ment more thorough soakings, but always watering should be done in such a manner that the soil to a considerable depth is saturated.

Planting a clinging vine, like Boston Ivy or English Ivy on a wooden house

Better erect a wire or two and plant a twining vine like Bittersweet or Honeysuckle. When the house is to be painted the vines are easily laid on the ground and then put up again.

Planting a twining vine like Bittersweet or Wisteria without providing support

Such vines will not cling to wood or stone unaided, but must have a trellis, wire or other support around which to twine.

Planting too thickly when starting seeds in pots or flats

This results in serious overcrowding which encourages damping-off and weak leggy growth.

Neglecting to summer-prune non-flowering wisterias

Winter pruning alone frequently encourages vigorous vegetative growth. Try shortening back the long current season's growths of wisterias from midsummer on, cutting them back to six or seven eyes. In winter cut the same growths back to about two eyes.

Watering the garden at high noon of a sunny, very hot summer day

Wait until late afternoon or evening, when less water is lost by immediate evaporation.

Training vines against painted walls

Many sprays discolor painted surfaces; repainting necessitates "taking down" the plants usually with resulting injury to them in the process.

Using weed killer to kill weeds before planting a crop

The soil will be poisoned and the crop plants retarded or killed. Weed killer will kill *all* plant growth.

Tying any kind of plant to a stake or other support so closely that the stem lacks ample room for future growth in diameter

This often results in pinching it so tightly that the sap flow is cut off and the plant dies. Labels fastened with wire around a branch, and guy wires (even though cushioned) encircling the trunks of newly planted trees, should be similarly watched. In all tying, fasten the material tightly to the support and loosely around the plant.

Using a two-edged saw for pruning

The saw with horse teeth along one edge of the blade, and fine ones along the other, is a delusion and a snare. Whichever set you use, the other is very likely to cut into perfectly innocent nearby branches and injure them badly.

Setting herbaceous plants below grade

This may or may not be harmful in the growing season as a result of washed-in soil forming too deep a covering. In winter it becomes a real hazard, as water will collect in the depression, freeze solid and possibly kill the plant.

Failure to put drainage material in flower pot

Several pieces of broken pottery or coarse, irregular gravel in the bottom of the pot will prevent soil from clogging the hole and blocking the escape of excess water.

F. F. ROCKWELL

YOUR GARDEN AROUND THE YEAR

A Practical Calendar for Home Gardeners

JANUARY

West Coast

GENERAL:

Last moment for catching up on neglected chores. Time, too, for dormant sprays on deciduous shrubs and trees. Do not get these sprays on evergreens; and, especially in California, be certain plants are really dormant.

There are probably new Christmas plants from the florist in your house. Californians can very often carry these on in a sheltered patio, by bringing the very tender ones indoors overnight. Northerners frequently find a slightly heated sunroom a solution. Problems can be individually solved if a few well-known plant preferences are considered.

House plants should be kept away from gas fumes—another reason for having a patio when possible. Northerners often cook with electricity, but the oil fumes from a furnace burner that needs cleaning are deadly. Northerners will also find their house plants (especially African violets) do better with fluorescent light to help out on dark days.

NORTHWEST:

Seize those days that often come in January with a false promise of spring to finish off all the neglected chores. The Polyanthus, English and Julia Primroses with all their progeny, that bloom here through the winter, will welcome a mixture of leafmold with all-purpose fertilizer worked in around them.

Get sodden leaves off the rock garden and keep them off. Stick a few conifer branches among tender plants toward the side most exposed to cold; and in borders also. Field mice are deadly at this season, using mole runs. Watch Tulips, Lilies and Crocus especially, and look for burrows under Rhododendrons and Heaths. Follow directions on poison baits offered locally. Look for mice in the rock garden, too. They will be much worse in the country than in the city, but they need watching everywhere.

January is not a good month to sow seeds here, even under glass, except those that germinate very slowly, as some alpines (which take several months). However, greenhouse or hothouse facilities alter this if fluorescent lighting is installed to bolster daylight after germination.

Garden chores this month can rightly include a blazing fireplace, a comfortable chair, and daydreams that rise from nursery catalogues. Consider space at hand, growing conditions, neighboring plants. One unusual plant well placed gives more zest than six mediocre ones.

Clean garden paths; repair trellises, gates, tools, frames; get seed flats ready, soil sterilized or treated, winter weeds out. Prune deciduous hedges such as Hawthorn and Beech, also Privet and Laurel. Do not prune top growth on Lilacs, though suckers and dead wood may be removed.

When using strong clean-up sprays on deciduous material, protect evergreens with some type of covering.

Feed any shrubs or trees overlooked earlier, but preferably with a slow acting fertilizer unless in active growth. Primroses need generous supplies for immediate use, as many have been in sporadic bloom for some time, and are due for their heaviest very soon.

Lawn Moss through the winter is usually the result of phosphorous lack in our soils. Rock phosphates cannot go in for a month or two yet; but superphosphates and bone meal should be applied at once.

Be ready with light covering or extra branches for borderline plants during possible cold snaps this month. Check stored Begonias, Gladiolus, and other tender bulbs. Watch for mice both here and among the hardy garden ones.

It's too early to sow vegetables outdoors, but if late summer and fall planting was done, Endive, Savoy Cabbage, Winter Spinach, Parsnips, Swiss Chard, Leeks, Kale, possibly Brussels Sprouts, and Salsify may be harvested as needed.

CALIFORNIA:
Prune Chilean-jasmine (Mandevilla) to force new summer-flowering shoots. To encourage Wisteria flowers cut all new long shoots back to not more than six buds. Prune Oleanders; but take only dead wood from Magnolia, Catalpa, Daphne, Locust and Golden Chain. Cut back Creeping Fig, Ivy, and Honeysuckle, the last to the ground if badly out of bounds. Watch hardier Trumpet Vines. Prune fruit trees and Roses, except ramblers and climbers that bloom only once.

Take Fuchsia cuttings from the green tips the latter half of this month along the Coastal areas.

Plant Violet runners 12 inches apart, either in shade or with only morning sun. Be sure pots, flats, and plants in the shade house are not dripped upon. Stretch a wide strip of burlap around the lower walls of the lath house to protect tender plants from cold.

Remember that Cacti need charcoal in the soil. Though year-around outdoor plants in semi-tropical parts of California, many make splendid window or porch plants through winter; others need patio shelter.

FOG BELT:
January is a planting month, though prevailing weather of a particular year moves the calendar forward or back. Roses, fruit trees, evergreens are set out; border plants divided or purchased; and a sizable list of less hardy bulbs planted, even Tuberous Begonias started if thoroughly rested material is obtainable. Among others are Nerine, Gloxinia, Ismene, Caladium, Amaryllis, Gladiolus, Calla, and Tigridia. Calla does much better with acid soil and some manure from time to time.

Occasional heavy rainstorms make seed sowing somewhat hazardous in the open; but transplantable annuals and nearly all perennials are safe in flats or pots under shelter. Sow Pea, Beet, Endive, Lettuce, Turnip, and Rutabaga seeds in the Bay area and down the Peninsula. Set out Broccoli, Cabbage, Brussels Sprout, and Cauliflower. Plant Rhubarb.

The last week is usually timely for Fibrous Begonia and Chrysanthemum cuttings.

Keep the garden cleaned up, stir lightly any packed surface soil from heavy rains, taking care not to damage surface roots. Use a general-purpose spray. Watch Roses for black spot and mildew. Evergreens tolerate only a summer spray.

This is the usually accepted month for Rose planting here, and for Rose pruning. Get in an early spray afterwards to scotch any insects, mildew, black spot or rust.

Plant or move evergreen shrubs and trees; also fruit trees. Border plants such as Phlox and Penstemon may be divided. Watch for a chance to spade both for planting and for sowing, although sowing in open ground cannot be done until February. Nearly all perennials, and such annuals as will be transplanted (Arctotis, giant Petunias, etc.) may be sown under glass. Note that Snapdragons should be kept in rapid growth, so wait with these unless your facilities allow growth without check. Advanced gardeners with greenhouse facilities may sow seeds of Gloxinias, Tuberous Begonias, African violets and Streptocarpus. Keep temperatures above 55° at night, below 75° during the day.

Prune Fuchsias from the fifteenth on through next month. Start old plants into growth, and take cuttings for later plants. Hydrangeas should also be pruned back to force new bloom.

SOUTHERN CALIFORNIA:
This is a busy time, as much plant material is dormant only this month, or only a part of it. Trim and shape evergreens and deciduous material before growth starts. Go after the heavy-growing vines before they make dense thickets, cutting out dead, ill-formed, and weaker wood. Prune Roses.

Plant Roses now. Azaleas, Rhododendrons and Camellias may still be planted. A number are in bloom now; this will help you choose. Plant fruit trees.

The Amazon-lily (Eucharis grandiflora) carries winter bloom in outdoor shade, but only if left undisturbed: so use care in planting or digging near it. A coarse, fibrous but richly fertile soil, and much water, are to its liking. Tigridias, Gladiolus and Calla lilies may be planted.

When disturbing beds for planting, dig in a little compost, rotted manure or commercial fertilizer where plants are ready to start into growth. Never put manure on Delphiniums, but use a balanced commercial fertilizer around clumps when new shoots show.

Do all possible planting of shrubs, trees, and large perennial plants. Look for new things in the nurseries. Fremontia needs full sun, and is good for dry gardens, but resents root disturbance. *Plumbago capensis* covers large sandy banks, feeds heavily, and needs very little water. Light blue flowers last all summer. Plant the much used Achimenes from January 15th on: Gloxinia, Gladiolus, Calla, Canna and Tigridia plant as convenient.

Start perennial seeds in flats or frames. Have good Stocks, Snapdragons, Petunias, and others coming on for early spring, which should burst into bloom before winter flowers finish. Cinerarias may be sown in flats.

Try planting a Chayote seed (the entire fruit!) for something unusual in a mildly flavored vegetable to eat hot or in salads. Set the large end down, the small or stem end just above the surface. The vine will cover several yards of fence or trellis.

South

When making a landscape plan for the home grounds, budget the yearly expenditures and the work to be done each year. The cost of maintaining any new project in landscaping should be carefully considered as well as its initial expense, for careful grooming is as important to the appearance of the garden as it is to the individual.

Winter injury to plants, especially in the Upper South, is often caused partly by lack of moisture in the soil. Dormant plants, notably evergreens, need water in the winter. This applies to mixed shrub beds, as well as to other plantings, in winter when the soil is dry.

Walks, drives, terraces, outdoor furniture, bird baths and pools often need minor repairs or reconditioning. Why not do this work while gardening is not as urgent as it will be later? It is a good idea, also, to check and replenish your garden tools. Sandpaper the rough spots off those tool handles. Oil the metal parts and paint all tools that need it.

A striking floral effect can be part of the annual parade of flowers in the garden if six or more Paul's Scarlet or Blaze climbing Roses are planted on a fence, trellis, gateway or terrace. Space the plants 6 to 8 feet apart for best results. Other climbing Roses that have attained great popularity in the South because of their beauty and reliability there are: Mermaid, pale yellow; Silver Moon, white; Mary Wallace, pink; Marechal Neil, yellow; and Dr. W. Van Fleet, pink.

Many plant diseases pass the winter on diseased parts of plants. This is one reason for cleaning up and burning all plant residues that might harbor them. Roses are especially benefited by such attention.

The Japanese Cherries, Japanese Crab apples and Flowering Peach trees are not usually dependable in the Central and Lower South. Great care is required in spraying for insect and disease control, and even then results are often disappointing. The most reliable small flowering trees for the South are: Dogwood, pink and white; Magnolia, all types; Redbud, Mimosa, White Fringe tree and Crape myrtle (when it's mature).

It is suggested that more of these broad-leaved evergreen shrubs be used in home landscape plantings: Chinese Holly (*Ilex cornuta Burfordi*), Japanese Holly (*Ilex crenata* varieties), Nandina, American Holly (*Ilex opaca*), Camellia (*C. japonica* and *Sasanqua*), Azalea, Abelia, Euonymus, Jasmine and Boxwood. The life of these plants is usually long and the landscape effect they create, when blended with deciduous flowering shrubs, is excellent.

In the Central and Lower South these annual seeds of popular summer flowers can be planted in such protected locations as seed box, hotbed, or sheltered bed in flower border: Ageratum, Periwinkle, Verbena, Salvia and Petunia. There are usually a few good days for planting seeds and plants this month in the vegetable garden if the soil has been prepared for planting beforehand. Therefore, at the first opportunity clean up, fertilize and plow the garden.

Here are some interesting facts that might help in ordering seed for your next vegetable garden: A quart of Onion sets contains 125 to 150 average-size bulbs, and will plant 25 to 30 feet of row. An average trade package of Beet seed will plant 30 to 35 feet of row, Carrots 30 feet, Lettuce 25 feet, Okra 25 feet, Radishes 30 to 35 feet, Spinach 25 feet, Mustard 20 to 25 feet, and Turnips 30 feet of row. A peck of Potato seed tubers will plant 60 to 75 feet of row and yield 10 to 12 pecks of Potatoes.

A small index-card file of your gardening work will prove helpful and very interesting if kept from year to year. Records on plants you acquire might include: name and variety of plant or seeds; date ordered and from whom. Other valuable data could cover the number of plants or packages of seed, cost, date received, date planted, and dates of bloom.

Use the following vines to add interesting variety to the landscape planting: Autumn and Jackman Clematis, Woodbine Honeysuckle, Trumpet-creeper and Wisteria.

Ranch-type houses are very easily overplanted. Low plants with horizontal lines are excellent for these homes because they blend well with the lines of the house. Examples are Pfitzer Juniper, Japanese Yew, and Japanese Holly. English Ivy, trailing from low porch or window boxes are also attractive embellishments for the ranch home.

Precautions for cold weather include: mulching bulbs and perennials with leafmold, peat or clean hay; mounding soil around Roses to a height of 10 to 12 inches; delaying pruning of Roses until late February; keeping evergreens watered; sprinkling frozen foliage of semi-hardy evergreens early on cold mornings before sun thaws tissue.

Improper pruning tools are most frequently the cause of poor pruning practices among amateur gardeners. Long-handled orchard pruners are ideal for such shrubs as: Rose of Sharon, Crape myrtle, Vitex, Butterfly bush, Abelia, Weigela and Kerria. Also have a pair of good hand pruners.

Even if it is raining while shrubs and trees are being planted, water all newly transplanted material thoroughly immediately after planting.

Planning the flower or vegetable garden on paper can be as fascinating as planting the seed, bulbs or plants later on. In drawing to a certain scale you will find cross-section (graph) paper most helpful.

A bird bath is more than an ornament for the garden. Keep it filled with water and suet and grain available close by.

Anyone can afford attractive floral arrangements to brighten the home in mid-winter by using forced sprays of Golden Bell (Forsythia), Pussy Willow, Winter Jasmine, Winter Honeysuckle or Flowering Quince.

When locating the outdoor barbecue oven remember to have it convenient to the kitchen, private, and simple.

Small flowering trees have an important role to play in every home garden. Consider these: Japanese Cherry, Japanese Crab apple, Flowering Peach, Dogwoods, and Japanese Magnolias.

The best growing temperature for pot plants is 55 to 70 degrees. Give them morning sun. Feed plants in 4- to 6-inch pots every three to four weeks with ½ cup per plant of a solution of commercial fertilizer made by dissolving 1 tablespoon fertilizer in 1 quart of water. Water pot plants when soil crumbles between fingers.

In the flower garden plant early-flowering Sweet Pea seed, Pansy and Day lily plants, bulbs of Hyacinth, Narcissus, Dutch Iris, Regal Lily, Tiger Lily and Philippine Lily.

In seed flats start Petunia, Salvia, Snapdragon, Ageratum, Periwinkle and Verbena.

In the garden, enclosure is as important as a frame to a picture. These shrubs are excellent flowering-border plants: Abelia, Flowering Pomegranate, Butterfly bush, Azalea, Crape myrtle, Althea, Virginal Mock orange and Winter Honeysuckle. Using one variety, substitute these beautiful plants for the overplanted Privet hedge.

Great masses of color, in exquisite shades, are produced by several varieties of climbing Roses. These are especially desirable where ground space is limited. Great favorites are: Paul Scarlet, Blaze, Mermaid, Silver Moon, Mary Wallace, Dr. Van Fleet and Marechal Neil.

LOWER SOUTH:

Select one plant from this group and plant a hedge of it, if you desire a beautiful border planting: Crape myrtle, Chinese Hibiscus, Lantana, Oleander, Plumbago, Bottlebrush, Azalea, *Camellia sasanqua* or Louis Phillipe Rose.

Plant a Fig tree or two for fruit in abundance. The variety Celeste or Little Sugar Fig is the most popular kind. Prune the tips of branches of mature Fig trees and keep inner branches and sucker growth from ground cut away.

Plant these bulbs: Gladiolus, Cannas, Caladium, Calla lilies, and Amaryllis.

Sow seed or set plants of these varieties of flowers in open garden: Sweet Alyssum, Arctotis, Calendula, Coreopsis, Daisy, Forget-me-not, Four-o'clock, Hollyhock, Petunia, Phlox, Pinks, Snapdragons, Stock, Sweet William and Verbena.

For shade trees plant Water Oak, Live Oak, Pecan, or Pine.

There is a select assortment of hardy vines for the gardener to consider: Clematis, Fig Vine, Yellow Jasmine, Rose-of-Montana, Bougainvillea and hybrid Trumpet-creeper.

Fragrant foliage adds spice to the garden atmosphere. Plants of outstanding merit for this purpose are Lavender, Rosemary, Santolina, Lemon-verbena, Rose Geranium, Sage, Tansy and Camphor tree.

Work to do in the home vegetable garden includes: planting seed of Carrots, Lettuce, Mustard, Garden Peas, Spinach and Turnips; setting plants of Cabbage, Cauliflower, Broccoli, Onions; and planting seed Potatoes.

Try the double row planting—two rows, 10 inches apart, for all vegetable seed sowing done now. A side dressing of 1 pound nitrate of soda to each 100-foot row of growing vegetables will prove very profitable.

North

All late-flowering deciduous shrubs can be pruned on mild days now. But don't prune spring bloomers until they have finished blossoming from buds that were formed last season.

Plants "breathe" through their leaves by means of microscopic openings somewhat like pores, and anything that clogs these holes will obviously lead to trouble. Such a condition is particularly likely to develop on smooth-leaved "foliage" plants indoors during the winter, where there is no chance for rain to wash off dust and oily deposits from smoke. A weekly sponging with slightly soapy water helps a lot.

If a thaw clears the snow from the ground, you will do well to look over all the winter mulches for signs of their having been blown out of place. For best results, a mulch should be of uniform depth.

Mid-winter is the perfect time to mull over those changes in their plantings that most gardeners consider making every year. Too often, unhappily, the mulling fails to lead to conclusions on specific action. If that has often been your situation, you'll find a pencil, eraser and some sheets of paper for rough plan drawing will help a lot.

The realization that a few rotting apples can spoil a whole barrelful during the storage season is ample justification for picking over your crop now and discarding any that are not in perfect condition.

Knowing the probable ultimate size of every young tree or shrub you buy is essential to the fullest long-range satisfaction, especially if you are selecting material for specific places and purposes. To disregard this fact is to court disappointment a few years hence.

The advice to try out at least one unfamiliar type or variety of plant every year is a sure way to keep your garden interest keen. Besides this, it will broaden your plant knowledge and opportunites for enjoying fresh beauties out-of-doors.

It is the nature of plants to grow in the direction of the strongest light, a trait that is seldom noticed in the outdoor garden unless a shrub or tree is situated where one side receives considerably more light than another. Indoors during the winter, the habit is quickly evidenced by the way plants kept near a window bend outward toward the sunlight, often in only a few days. You can't change their nature, but you can offset its effect by turning the pots half way around every few days to prevent lop-sidedness.

Nearly all kinds of trees and shrubs can be planted as successfully in spring as in autumn, and some actually prefer the former season. But the job must be done early, preferably when the leaf buds first show signs of swelling, and replanting should take place immediately.

FEBRUARY

West Coast

GENERAL:
California is safe for open ground sowing except for seeds of Cyclamen and a few subtropicals. In the North, start main crops of half-hardy annuals in flats, pots, or (preferably) individual plant bands in a con-

tainer that self-waters from below. Set outside on warm sunny days, but bring indoors nights. Try shaking a pinch of Rootone in a packet of seeds before sowing.

Blooming bulbs in active growth need potash and phosphorus for next year's flowers. Well-rotted manure makes a good mulch, while wood ashes supply potash, and bone meal or superphosphate gives phosphorus. Or use a complete chemical fertilizer, but do not let any directly contact foliage or bulb. Annuals and perennials need food; rock gardens and lawns a good top-dressing.

Give Roses a good feeding—rotted manure, special Rose food, or good compost. Roses set out on this Coast in March start into full growth immediately, before roots take hold. Give solution of Transplantone when planting, to start strong root-hair growth, continuing every ten days until roots take firm hold. It's a good idea to puddle the roots in a pail of thin mud overnight, unless they are balled and burlapped. Use a combination fungicide-insecticide on Roses every two weeks in the South; in the North, begin spraying as soon as the leaves are out. Do not wet foliage when watering.

Bait for slugs, snails, earwigs and sowbugs. Hand-pick slugs at night, using a flashlight to spot them. Examine particularly Lily shoots poking above ground for if they are eaten off, the bulb may die.

Planting goes on all along the Coast; but in Washington and Oregon consists mainly of larger material—shrubs, trees, established hardy perennials and rock plants, not tender bulbs or seedlings.

Change from dormant sprays on deciduous shrubs and trees as soon as new growth or budding shows. Use summer sprays on evergreens; all-purpose on Roses. Spray soil also when spraying for weevils for which Lindane seems effective. Slug eggs resemble small masses of cooked tapioca. Turn over dead leaves, composts, stones, and stir the soil to find and destroy them. Spread slug bait.

When making garden plans in limited space, note some attractive vegetables such as Globe Artichokes for tall border; Eggplant and Peppers; and for edging, Parsley or Strawberries. The last may also be planted in barrels or pyramids. Stepped-up boxes on the edge of the drying yard or even the patio will grow many, though Lettuce and other salad greens probably yield most in satisfaction for the space.

Repot any Fuchsias, pruning both tops and roots. When new growth is visible on dormant potted Gloxinias, repot in fresh compost, but carry on the dry side until roots are really active.

NORTHWEST:

The care of rock, vegetable, and Rose gardens is of prime importance this month. Go over the rock garden, marking any lack of color. Be certain of summer and early fall bloom by planting dwarf Campanulas in numerous species, Violas and late Gentians. Rock gardens and rock walls are gay with color this month. It is worth driving through residential districts of Seattle and other Northern cities just to view these and make plans. Visit the Daffodil and other early bulb fields in Washington and Oregon to choose varieties for fall planting. Watch too for the new Flowering Quinces in a wide color range.

Raspberry mosaic, which makes fruit dry, crumbly, flavorless; and leaves small or distorted, can be severe here. Dig out and burn diseased plants and start a new bed 100 feet away. Use more resistant varieties— Washington, Lloyd George, Newburg, or Marcy.

Plant yellow Onion sets. Divide Chives. Corn does not tolerate our cold spring nights, so sow Laxton's Progress dwarf Peas in rows 3 feet apart. They will protect the vulnerable Corn seedlings (to be sown in early May between the then 18-inch high Pea rows) from hot sun and high winds. Sow the main crop of Tomatoes and early Cucumbers indoors, to be set out in mid-April under hotkaps.

Start Tuberous Begonias on a flat of slightly moist peatmoss indoors to plant outside in early May. At the end of the month pot up Mexican Tuberoses to set out in May.

Early in the month, use the last strong clean-up spray on deciduous shrubs and trees, provided they are not in leaf or flower bud.

Spring may be later if fall was unusually dry and warm, so use discretion in starting spring work. If Polyanthus, English, and Julia Primroses are blooming staunchly, go ahead with such outdoor sowing as is suggested. Indoor seedlings after germination will need fluorescent lighting through heavily clouded weather. A pinch of Root-grow shaken in the packet gives added strength. Tender plants outdoors will need extra protection. Use Fir or similar branchlets early in the month.

Patio, terrace, and window plant boxes are attractive now with a backbone painting of very dwarf compact conifers, and several winter-blooming *Erica carnea* in variety for color. St. Brigid Anemone will bloom in a somewhat sheltered placing: or use an interplanting of hardy bulbs from the very smallest and earliest to later Tulips. Some planter boxes are large enough for low-growing evergreen Rhododendrons like Bow Bells, or *Azalea hinodegiri* with bulbs between. When grown in large pots, they can, if so desired, be plunged pot and all in the garden later to make way for bright summer annuals.

Sow indoors Petunia, Aster, Lobelia, Balsam, Drummond Phlox, and Salvia. Most rock garden plants may be sown in flats or coldframe. Established rock shrubs and alpines can be set out. Sow Sweet Peas the last week.

Sow Cabbage, Cauliflower, Celery, and Lettuce indoors: Nobel Spinach, Broad Windsor Beans, and a smooth-seeded Pea, such as Laxton's Superb, outdoors. Wrinkled seeded ones tend to rot in cold wet soil and take later sowing. Windsor Beans withstand wet cold, mature when other types are being sown.

Prune bush Roses, also summer- and fall-blooming shrubs. Prune Blueberries before the sap starts, cutting back to leave three to five fruit buds to each branch. These are round and about three times the size of slim leaf buds that are carried nearer the branch base.

CALIFORNIA:

Plant Roses, divide Gerberias anytime from now into April. Sow Lily seeds outdoors. Prune back Fuchsias from one to as much as two-thirds, mulching well with shredded manure if obtainable, or compost, leaf mold, and fertilizer.

Start Tuberous Begonias in flats on peatmoss or suitable material, merely pressing the tubers down, not covering. Water sparingly until 2-inch sprouts with leaves are formed. Use care not to rub the tubers when planting. Advanced gardeners may sow under glass seed of both Begonias and Gloxinias during the first week of February. Leaf cuttings of mature Gloxinia leaves are started in moist sand around Valentine's Day. Keep a bit of leaf stem.

Plant Asparagus crowns. Set out Cabbages, Onions, Leeks, Garlic.

Set Broccoli in the Bay Area and on down the Coast; also in Sonoma and similar valleys. Sow Beets, Carrots, Salsify, Chard, Rutabagas, and Turnips throughout; Lettuce, Peas, and Kale except in the Imperial and similar valleys, where Celery is now being harvested as a winter crop, but is being sown under glass in all but the warmest parts of California.

As growth starts, feed plants well, especially Roses, flowering shrubs, and vines. Spray Peaches and Nectarines against curly leaf in late February just as the buds begin to swell.

FOG BELT:

Besides the chores under both General and California, intensive placing of established plants for three periods of flowering, early and late spring and summer is done. Among them are Delphinium, Columbine, Penstemon, Phlox, Carnations, Pelargoniums, Verbenas, African and Transvaal Daisies, Cup-and-saucer Bellflowers, and Fibrous Begonias. Plant late spring and summer bulbs—Tigridias, Dahlias, Gladiolus, Calla, Spider-lilies, and most of the true lily family among exotics. Of annuals, Nasturtium and Sweet Pea seeds are large enough to withstand most rain; but finer seeds generally need protection from washing out or beating down. Set out Cauliflower plants.

Deciduous flowering shrubs, trees, and flowering fruit trees may still be planted: Fuchsias the last week unless spring is late. *Francoa ramosa* is a good companion.

Finish getting new beds made and planted, and old ones conditioned. This is a good time to plant Hibiscus and Bougainvillea. Also Gloxinias, Begonias, Agapanthus, and Fuchsias. Try cream Russel Lupines around scarlet or orange Oriental Poppies, which so often clash with other border colors.

Phlox, Delphinium, and similar perennials may still be divided. Take Chrysanthemum cuttings when the shoots reach 4 inches. Watch for slugs on these new shoots, especially on Delphinium.

Sow annuals not yet in, and succession vegetables; though wait until it is warm enough for Tomatoes and Zinnias to grow without check. There is still time for another crop of Head Lettuce before warm weather forces one to turn to loose-leaf types.

SOUTHERN CALIFORNIA:

Many subtropical bulbs, plants, trees, and shrubs may go in now (Caladiums and Tuberoses with a bit of shelter). Shell-flower, *Alpinia speciosa,* is a very fragrant, large and striking plant for a warm garden with ample water. It grows as high as 12 feet, from a rhizome. Even the 2-foot leaves are spicily fragrant. Drooping racemes of waxy white flowers with yellow lips carry Orchid markings of red or brown and last for many months. Humid air and rich, moist garden soil are its requirements.

Shade houses take Begonias of all types, Gloxinias and Ferns. Polyanthus will linger on among the Ferns, and can be lifted in full bloom from a winter border. Give them cottonseed meal to encourage more flowers. The green-fingered will want an Orchid or so in a hanging bark basket. Trailing basket Fuchsias are for those who prefer an easier plant.

Cut back such plants as Geraniums and Fuchsias to produce bushy growth. Chrysanthemum clumps can be divided, or take 4-inch cuttings from new shoots and start in moist sand.

Spring sprays and pest control get into full swing in February; but most plants are too active for dormant sprays. Use an all-purpose on Roses every ten days as soon as they leaf out.

Practically everything in the garden needs well-balanced fertilizer, though cater to those plants such as the acid lovers that need their particular type. Lawns will profit if food is given them in time for rains to wash it well in.

This is a real planting month both for seeds and plants, with annuals heading the list. Only the very tender, or those extremely fine, will need under-glass or special sowing; but evolve some device to prevent washing away should a late heavy rain occur.

Add Sprekelia to your bulbs if you have not already. Alstromeria grows well with the Spider-lily in rich loamy soil. There are two varieties of the latter, *Hymenocallis macrostephana* in bloom now, and *H. calathina* that will not flower until June and July.

Plant Caladium, Glory-lily, Gladiolus, Montbretia among others. Shade house owners will find an increasing number of suitable Orchids among the dealers.

Sow Corn, Tomatoes, and Beans in the Imperial and similar valleys; also set out Tomato plants.

South

LOWER SOUTH:

Annual flowers that often reseed themselves successfully are: Ageratum, Arctotis, Argemone, Balsam, Coreopsis, Four-o'clock, Gypsophila, Gaillardia, Larkspur, Oenothera, Petunia, Phlox, Torenia and Vinca. These seedlings should be located and preserved when cleaning flower beds for replanting.

Commercial fertilizer should be thoroughly mixed with the top 6 to 8 inches of soil in flower beds at least ten days before flower seeds are to be sown. This will prevent burning of tender seedling roots by contact with fertilizer.

Excellent background material for the annual or perennial borders are these: Hibiscus, Lantana, Jasminum, Duranta, Plumbago, Azalea, Viburnum, Nandina, and Malvanicus.

Perennials suited to this area are somewhat limited. Plants of the following set in clumps in front of a shrub border are effective additions to the garden: Achillea, Angelonia, Asclepias, Shasta Daisy, Dianthus, Gaillardia, *Salvia azurea, Salvia farinacea,* Stokesia and Baleriana.

In planting Water-lily pools remember that one third of pool surface should be open water. Cypress boxes 2 feet by 2 feet by 1 foot deep are recommended. Fill with fertile loamy soil and top with one inch of sand. Have them ready to plant in early March.

If you have frequent occasion to use garden stakes and could use a screen planting, too, why not combine both needs and solve them by planting one of these varieties of bamboo: *Phyllostachys bambusoides, Phyllostachus aurea* or *Arundinaria japonica.*

Beautiful, graceful planting effects can be made by planting one or more of these grasses: *Cortaderia argentea* (Pampas-grass) from Argentina; *Arundo donax* (The Giant Reed); *Cymbopogon citratus* (Lemongrass); or *Erianthus ravennae* (Plume-grass).

If you like a blue theme in your annual flower bed, try sowing seed of Centaurea (Ragged Robin) in assorted shades of blue with Didiscus and Nemophila. The yellow of Linaria will form a good contrast with the blue if you prefer a complementary color combination.

Bulbs are so easy to grow and so little trouble. The current planting calendar includes: Achimenes, Alpina or Shell-flower, Crinum, Hedychium or Butterfly-lily, Hymenocallis, *Liriope muscari* or Lily-turf, Tigridia or Mexican Shell-flower, Zephyranthes or Rain-lily.

CENTRAL SOUTH:
Hydrangeas need attention this month: pruning out old wood, applying fertilizer and root pruning, if plants are old and not flowering satisfactorily.

Using a sharp spade cut a circle having a 20-inch radius around the plant to a depth of the spade blade.

Spray plants infested with scale insects with winter strength oil emulsion. Examine these plants for scale infestation: English Ivy, Flowering Quince, Japanese Magnolia, Pyracantha, Flowering Peach.

Ferns need repotting when they become severely pot bound. Shift to larger container using well-rotted leafmold, if possible. Rotted cow manure is a fine source of food for Ferns. Native Ferns should be moved to the garden as early as possible for best results.

Lawns can be planted if young plants are used in establishing the grass. There are five main lawn grasses for this area: Bermuda, St. Augustine, Carpet, Centipede, and Zoysia. Prepare soil as carefully as you would for sowing flower seed, adding 6 pounds complete fertilizer per 100 square feet of area.

Favorite varieties of dwarf Azaleas based upon numbers sold are: Coral Bells (shell pink), Christmas Cheer (red), and Hinodigiri (red).

Prune Rose bushes just before new growth begins, cutting a vigorous bush back to 18 to 20 inches and leaving five to eight stems. Cut weak growing varieties back to 8 to 10 inches leaving three to five stems.

UPPER SOUTH:

Sow these flower seeds in hot bed or seed boxes: Ageratum, China Aster, Cosmos, Marigold, Petunia, Periwinkle, Salvia and Verbena.

Ground cover plants make a permanent cover for areas around and under trees, shrubs and areas on steep slopes. These evergreens are recommended: *Pachysandra terminalis, Vinca minor, Vinca alpina, Nepeta Mussini* and *Iberis sempervirens*.

Hardwood cuttings of these shrubs will produce an abundance of plants for future expansion of border planting: Crape myrtle, Althea, Mock orange, Spirea, Butterfly bush, Hydrangea, Jasmine, Deutzia and Weigela.

Garden briefs: Sow Sweet Peas, prune trees, keep Rye Grass lawns clipped close, water evergreens during dry spells, feed birds, turn pot plants to prevent "leaning" towards light. Don't get impatient and work garden soil when it is too wet.

North

No better time than right now for pruning fruit trees, Grapes, and small fruits in general. Let Apple and Pear prunings lie where they fall: rabbits will go after these before attempting to gnaw bark from upright trunks. On a warm day, too, dormant spraying may be done.

More than likely you can get a running start with your lawn this month. Anytime the ground is bare, apply a complete plant food—such as a 5–10–5 formula, at the rate of about 4 lbs. per 100 square feet. Spring thaws and rains will carry it down to the roots. If there are patches which need reseeding, they may be sown as soon as soil cracks, caused by thawing, appear.

And while you have the lawn in mind, *get that mower sharpened now*. Recall how long you had to wait last spring, when dozens of other gardeners all wanted the same job done at the same time?

Some of your favorite house plants getting leggy? Cut them back now, or next month—unless they are just coming into bloom—to produce compact stocky new growth. This is especially important for those which are to be set out of doors in spring to provide summer bloom.

If your place is in need of new planting or rejuvenating, you can solve your landscaping problem by calling in a local landscape architect to make a plan for you to carry out (this will cost only a nominal sum). You may be able to locate a landscape gardener to do the entire job (be sure to get a competent person) or, by studying books of plans and planting and putting the whole thing down on paper, you can do it yourself.

Pale, slightly cobwebby leaves on any of the greenhouse or indoor plants indicate red spider mites. Get busy immediately with sulphur dust followed in 24 hrs. with strong cold water spray.

Outdoor spraying of all kinds requires a minimum air temperature of 40°, and 50° is better. . . . "Mummified" fruits clinging to the twigs of apples or other twigs are frequently disease laden, so pick them off and burn.

Burn old rubbish in garden. Many pests will be eliminated.

In planning for perennial plantings, figure on putting not less than three plants of one kind in any particular spot. If they're worth having, they're worth a group display. . . . Also, don't forget that an occasional "promontory" of some medium-height kind edging into the low front of the border gives pleasing variety.

Any winter pruning of shrubs that flower in spring will take away buds that should begin to open in a month or two; for example, Forsythia,

Lilacs, Winter Jasmine, Mock orange, Spirea and flowering Quince. Leave these alone and prune only dead wood or broken branches.

Clean dead wood from all trees.

Most fruits, including Pears, Plums, Apples and bush fruits such as Gooseberries and Currants should be pruned on any except a very cold day. Prune Grapes now if the work has not already been done.

Assemble flats, soil and tools for early sowing. Deep flats are desirable for seedlings that grow slowly. Heavy crates from the grocery store about 5 inches deep are ideal. The soil mixture may consist of 2 parts garden loam, 1 part sand and 1 part leafmold, peatmoss or humus. . . . A little hand seed-sower which you can get at the seed store is a good gadget for indoor planting. . . . Salpiglossis, Snapdragons, Stocks, Delphiniums, and Mignonette may be started later on in the month.

Seed of slow growing plants are sown now if not before. . . . Start annual Canterbury Bells, too, and perennial seeds.

MARCH

West Coast

GENERAL:

Pests are growing as rapidly as the plants this month, also fungus diseases. Map out a spray program. The rare pests that attack succulents should be hand picked or carefully washed off with water. Use a combination spray on Roses for aphids, mildew, and rust every ten days.

Spread slug bait thoroughly and often. Fine meshed wire screening around new shoots of choice plants is added insurance.

March is an important lawn month. Reseed bare spots; top-dress and feed old ones—spent mushroom soil, peat, compost, chemical lawn fertilizers, or trade mixtures of barnyard manure. Sow Blue Grass seed over a thin lawn after reconditioning soil. New lawns are also made in March. Mixtures for local conditions are usually best; but if enough water is obtainable, straight Blue Grass is fine for hot valleys of California. Once seeded, lawns should be kept continually moist.

Plant Gladiolus, Tigridia, and Montbretia. Group a dozen or so Galtonia together in a close clump for best effects.

This is the last month for Rose planting. Bare-root ones are best puddled; also give Transplantone to induce quick growth of root hairs.

NORTHWEST:
Sow hardy annuals in the open; but half-hardy and tender ones need the indoors or coldframe. Annual Poppy seeds scattered between Iris clumps give later color. Sow Sweet Alyssum, Blue Anagallis, Candytuft, and Virginia Stock in rock gardens for later color.

Once established in this region, the beautiful blue *Meconopsis Baileyi* grows as easily here as any other Poppy. Set plants out only when very small; or scatter seeds where to grow for next year's bloom. Humus and dappled summer shade suit it. Avoid lime and commercial fertilizers.

In this generally acid region, most gardeners should give a little additional lime every year or so to Lilacs, Clematis, Wisteria, Tamarisk, Brooms, and Delphinium.

Make Strawberry beds in well cultivated sandy loam, or plant in pyramids or barrels, remembering the center irrigation in these last two. Give Currants and Gooseberries one ounce per bush of magnesium sulphate. They also need potash and iron. Most of their later troubles arise from a deficiency of these three chemicals and can be prevented if you take the proper measures now.

CALIFORNIA:
Top-dress Azaleas, Camellias, Rhododendrons, and other acid-soil

shrubs with 6 inches of peatmoss and leafmold. Give an acid fertilizer four to six weeks after bloom is over.

Cut back Fuchsias, Marguerites, Geraniums, and similar plants heavily for bushiness. Start cuttings.

Sow biennial and perennial seed for next year. Such plants as the Transvaal Daisy that resent frost are handled more easily in movable seed flats.

Plant Canna, Dahlia, Gloxinia, Begonia, and Agapanthus. Give Carnations sun on the Coast, but partial shade in interior valleys. Spade bone meal and rotted manure into the soil a couple of weeks before planting. Divide Chrysanthemum clumps. Start cuttings as soon as new shoots are 4 to 6 inches high.

Spray Citrus trees for scale, aphids, and red spider. Great care is required if DDT is mixed with the Rotenone.

Prune Jasmine when flowering stops. Note that Chilean-jasmine is a Mandevillea, and is not pruned for several months yet.

FOG BELT:
Set out earlier started seedlings and new plants to bloom shortly. Prepare soil for those that will flower in late spring, summer, and fall from annual seed sown now as well as mature perennial and biennial plants. Try several massed groups of Salpiglossis in a border. Don't overlook summer bulbs. Set out Fuchsias and flowering shrubs.

Finish dividing or planting such perennials as need it, particularly Fibrous Begonias and Transvaal Daisies.

Plant Potatoes, Artichokes, Rhubarb, and Asparagus. Practically all leafy vegetables may be sown where to grow; also Peas, Beets, Carrots, and Onions; but use flats and some protection for Eggplants, Tomatoes, and Peppers.

SOUTHERN CALIFORNIA:
Subtropicals become more and more widely used. This is the time to plant tubers of *Alpina speciosa* or to divide old clumps. Bird of Paradise (*Strelitzia reginae*) needs much humus, and prefers growing by itself. *Philodendron selloum,* with exceptionally exotic foliage, grows happily in the open. Named Hibiscus shrubs in newer varieties bring

wide color range, also vary in size from the compact sulphur-yellow Paradise Moon to the vigorous Bride. A newer use is found for Bougainvillea in clothing banks.

Consider fruit trees even in patios for both shade and harvest; but get them in at once. Two Plums are needed—red Satsuma and amber-fleshed Santa Rosa are well flavored and the former makes good jam. Yellow Apples thrive better here, Winter Banana and Yellow Delicious among others. Use Royal and Blenheim Apricots on the Coast, Tilton in interior valleys. Walnuts and Pecans are pleasing summer shade trees.

Sow Bush Beans, Celery, Corn, Lettuce, Onions, summer Spinach; and as the ground warms, Cucumbers, Tomatoes, Okra, Eggplant, Melons, and Squash. Plants of Tomatoes, Eggplant, and Peppers may also be set out along the Coast and in the Imperial Valley.

Top-dress Peruvian-lily (Alstromeria) when spring growth appears, using well rotted manure if possible.

Dichondra is offered in a shaker package with White Clover. The latter acts as a nurse plant besides giving nitrogen until the Dichondra crowds it out in about eight months. Dichondra stays green the year round here.

South

GENERAL:

Overgrown evergreens, both broad-leaved and narrow-leaved, are most often the reason Southern homes are made less attractive by the foundation planting instead of more attractive, as originally planned. Recommendation: remove these monsters or try pruning.

When pruning evergreens try to maintain the natural appearance of each plant. Use hand pruners or orchard pruners for this job—not hedge shears. Study shrub outline before pruning and reproduce in miniature.

Evergreen shrubs such as *Abelia grandiflora,* that produce many stems at the crown, respond favorably to complete rejuvenation—that is, simply cutting everything back to ground level. This is often the surest way to get a vigorous, entirely new shrub from an old plant. This system does not work with single-stemmed shrubs.

Evergreen trees, shrubs and vines can all be planted if a ball of earth is moved with the roots of these plants.

The Chinese Holly (*Ilex cornuta Burfordi*) is reported by many nurserymen to respond most favorably to late spring planting. This is also true for Dogwood—try moving while in bloom.

Shade trees transplanted this past fall, winter and spring have a far better chance of survival if a protective wrap of burlap or waterproof paper is placed around the stem from ground to first branches. This is very important.

Are you struggling to establish a shrub planting in a shaded location? Consider these—Boxwood, Japanese Holly, Mahonia, Nandina, Euonymus, Azalea, Winter Honeysuckle, Pearl Bush, Anthony Waterer Spirea, Forsythia, Sweet Shrub, Snowball, Hydrangea, and Mock orange.

Vermiculite is used widely in seed boxes and seed beds. It is also used as a mulch on shrub and flower beds. This material is not a fertilizer. It consists of mica exploded at high temperatures.

Spray Azaleas just after flowering, using this mixture: one gallon water, three level tablespoons white oil emulsion, two level tablespoons powdered derris and one teaspoon Black Leaf 40. This spray controls lacebugs, thrips and mites when applied directly to infested parts of plants. To control scale insects and mites on Camellias, use this spray mixture: one gallon water and six level tablespoons white oil emulsion.

Cannas are among the most colorful of the summer-flowering plants. Plant Canna roots 3 inches deep and 12 to 18 inches apart in rich soil in a sunny location. Water regularly for best results.

A good plan for a city garden 20 feet by 50 feet in the South would include most of these vegetables (varied slightly to conform with the family food habits): Tomatoes, 60 feet (rows 1, 2, 3); Pole Snap Beans, 60 feet (rows 4, 5, 6); Squash, 20 feet (row 7); Okra, 20 feet (row 8); Eggplant, 10 feet, Pepper, 10 feet (row 9); Bush Snap Beans, 20 feet (row 10); Radishes, 10 feet, Parsley, 10 feet (row 11); Onions, 20 feet (row 12); Lettuce, 20 feet (row 13); Turnips, 20 feet (row 14); Mustard, 20 feet (row 15); Carrots, 10 feet, Corn, 10 feet (row 16); Corn, 20 feet (row 17); Beets, 20 feet (row 18). Rows 10 through 18 should be replanted with Pole Snap Beans, Butter Beans or Tomatoes in June or July as early crops mature.

All plants growing near trees need more frequent watering than plants in open areas. Root competition from trees will do great damage to all plants near them if water is not generously applied.

Cottonseed meal is a safe and effective fertilizer for Azaleas. Scatter it lightly on the top of the ground around the plants, and allow it to wash into the soil. Do not cultivate Azaleas, as they are shallow-rooted. The Kurume (dwarf) varieties are best adapted to the Central and Upper South gardens. The Indica Azalea varieties are best adapted to the gardens of the Lower South. Balled plants of either can be set now.

Bulb plantings for your consideration include: Gladiolus, Ixia, Tuberose, Caladium, Montbretia, Dahlia and Rain-lilies. Try to avoid growing Gladiolus in the same soil used last year for this flower: rotation will help control the rots that attack the corms.

Tomato plants can be protected from cut-worms by wrapping a paper collar around the stem, inserting the collar in the soil, and holding the top together with a paper clip.

LOWER SOUTH:
Japanese Yew (*Podocarpus macrophylla*) is a multi-purpose plant, found highly effective as an accent in tall narrow screen effects, background plantings and clipped hedges. Its dark green evergreen foliage is rich, dense and distinctive.

The many varieties of Chinese Hibiscus will add beautiful color effects to the landscape planting about the home.

Azaleas should be sprayed immediately after flowering to control lace bug, mites and thrips. The spray mixture to use contains: one-half pint white oil emulsion, one and one-half ounces powdered derris and 6 teaspoons of Black Leaf 40 in 6 gallons of water.

Camellias infested with scale and mites need spraying immediately after flowering with a mixture made of one pint white oil emulsion in 6 gallons of water. By the way, there is great pleasure in grafting Camellias.

With spring "busting out" all over, the urge to plant is only excelled by the great variety of things available for planting. After the middle of the month it is usually safe to "shoot the works" on annual flowers, all vegetables and tender bulbs as Tuberoses, Dahlias and Caladium.

CENTRAL SOUTH:
When soil is sufficiently dry to work, the following bulbs can be planted: Caladium, Cannas, Tuberoses, Gladiolus, Dahlias and Oxalis.

Transplant seedlings of Eggplant, Pepper and Tomato from seed flats or hot bed to coldframe or plant bands. This is usually done immediately after second pair of leaves form. Plant these vegetable seeds: Beets, Collards, Carrots, Kohlrabi, Leaf Lettuce, Mustard, Onions, Parsley, Peas, Chinese Cabbage, Radish, Turnips and Spinach. If plants are available place these in garden: Head Lettuce, Cabbage, Cauliflower, Brussels Sprouts, Bermuda Onions and Celery.

Last call this planting season for Roses, shade trees, deciduous shrubs, woody vines, unless moved in cans or with ball of soil.

Keep Rose plants and beds free of dead or diseased leaves and spray every two weeks with a good fungicide such as Bordeaux mixture, wettable sulphur or fermate.

Prune Butterfly bush back to the ground—treating as a herbaceous perennial each year. Also prune *Spirea Thumbergi* and Winter Honeysuckle immediately after flowering, removing only old branches.

UPPER SOUTH:
Use plants of perennial flowers, rather than seed at this time of year. There are many kinds available; examples are: Candytuft, Chrysanthemums, Columbine, Canterbury Bells, Gaillardia, Hollyhocks, Shasta Daisies, *Phlox divaricata* and *Phlox subulata*.

Kentucky Blue Grass seed, and other lawn grass seeds usually mixed with it, sprout and begin growth most successfully when the weather is cool and soil moist. These conditions usually exist this month.

Remember that Kentucky Blue Grass requires a neutral or slightly alkaline (sweet) soil. The surest method of providing the correct soil conditions is having a soil analysis made by the experiment station of your State Agricultural College.

Deep (10–12 inches) seed bed preparation is essential for fine lawns. Mix humus with top 6 inches of soil. Humus is available as clean, well rotted manure, leafmold and peat. Also apply lime (100 pounds agricultural lime per 1000 square feet is usual application) and commercial fertilizer (40 to 50 pounds of 5–10–5 per 1000 square feet). Pulverize all clods to leave surface smooth. Sow 5 pounds Kentucky Blue Grass lawn seed or lawn mixture per 1000 square feet. Sow when air is still. Divide seed into two equal parts, sowing half when walking east and west and sowing other half walking north and south.

Plant these roots and tubers in vegetable garden: Asparagus (seed or crowns), Horseradish, Rhubarb, Artichoke (Jerusalem or Globe) and Irish Potatoes.

Although late fall and early winter planting of Cornflower, annual Phlox, California Poppies, Shirley Poppies and Larkspur produce best results, these hardy annuals can still be planted, if you will hurry.

North

Early March is just about the last chance you'll have to prune Grapes. Soon sap will be rising and any cuts may bleed excessively.

Rolling a lawn when it's wet in spring can do about as much harm as good, especially if the soil is heavy. Some soils, if packed down when wet, just won't loosen up enough as they dry to admit the amount of air that grass roots need.

Annual Poppies (Shirley, Opium, etc.) must get an early start. It's not too soon to plant seeds in the open ground if you want these beauties to reach early summer perfection.

Wrens and bluebirds will be house hunting any day now. Remember, the plainer and less conspicuous the birdhouse, the better your chances of renting it.

Strawberries and bush fruits will benefit from a surface application of a complete fertilizer. Prune dead canes from all bush fruits.

This is the time to enjoy the intrepid Crocus and Snowdrop. Do not cut off their foliage until it has turned brown.

If you are not growing Strawberries because you don't have space enough for an old-fashioned bed or plot, go modern with a Strawberry pyramid. It will take up little garden space—and you will be eating strawberries!

If March winds prove too much, warm up by turning the compost pile. You will stay even warmer if you start digging this material into the vegetable garden.

After all there are few cut flowers which can match Sweet Peas! This is the last call for planting seeds.

If you have any extra space in a coldframe, try forcing a few clumps of choice Chrysanthemum varieties dug from the open ground for cuttings and divisions.

Use temporary guards around Lilies to protect them from mad March hares.

Perennials, Roses, shrubs, trees will all be starting into active growth as the frost comes out. This is the season when they are especially in need of quickly available plant food, so apply fertilizers without delay.

Available nitrogen is particularly needed, as nitrogen in the soil may be in such form as to be locked up for several weeks yet.

Jump the gun on spring by cutting sprays of early-flowering shrubs such as Forsythia, Japanese Quince, early varieties of Spirea, and Barberry; also fruits such as Peach, Cherry and Plum. Select small, gracefully curved branches, and submerge in tepid water for a few days; then crush the stems and place in deep water. Syringe frequently to keep stems moist.

The lawn—and the gardener as well—benefit when it is given early attention.

Sharpen the pruning shears and take advantage of fleeting periods of good weather to finish any remaining dormant pruning. Put Grapes first on the list, and don't be afraid to cut them back hard. Go over fruit trees—even the ornamental ones are the better for being kept fairly open. Delay on Roses until after danger of really hard freezes; but then get busy before they start leafing out.

Don't be in too great a hurry to remove mulching material. If the ground is frozen beneath it, it will help delay the emergence of new growth, and with most plants, this is desirable. Do remove it, however, once growth starts.

Planting—of seeds and dormant shrubs and trees—can well be done with many species long before the average amateur thinks of undertaking it. With really hardy subjects, the earlier the better. *Cautions:* be sure the soil is dry enough to crumble readily; see that fine soil, or, better, a prepared compost, is packed close around the roots; and mound soil up about the stems of shrubs and Roses to protect the lower buds.

APRIL

West Coast

GENERAL:

Peonies do best if given two cups of non-acid liquid fertilizer as the buds form; Stocks, one tablespoon balanced fertilizer. Hungry Cannas need food at two-week periods. Spring bulbs are brighter if fed liquid commercial fertilizer as buds show color. Christmas Cactus needs this when new growth starts, in addition to bone meal and charcoal in the compost. Keep it well watered, but not sodden; give ample light without direct sun.

Sow Beets and Lettuce everywhere though not in the Sacramento, San Joaquin, or Imperial Valleys or mountain areas. Carrots and Chard except for the Imperial Valley and Mountain areas; Turnips and Ruta-bagas except for interior California valleys. Plant Potatoes and set Cabbage plants except in the Citrus belt and Imperial Valley. Set Cauliflower north and in the Bay Area.

Chrysanthemums like sun, but not wet foliage. Keep them fastened off the ground. Spray from the base upward often, but mildly to prevent burn. Hunt cutworms and slugs with a flashlight besides bait. Shade divisions and cuttings until rooted.

Plant Dahlia; *Iris Kaempferi, I. sibirica, I. laevigata;* summer-flowering Oxalis; Day lily: Tritonia, Tigridia, Canna; Hardy Water-lilies; continue to plant Gladiolus at two-week intervals.

Cool to cold nights, prevalent on this coast, are a check to normal development, particularly in seedlings and young plants, even though frosts are over in many sections. As one goes north from California, numerous devices must be employed to protect such plants as Snapdragons and Tomatoes, that resent check in steady growth. Coldframes, hotkaps and movable night covers can be employed. Californians should note that Purdue University advises spraying Tomatoes with PCA and BNOA plant hormones where cold nights prevail to increase yield. Further north, where the nights are even colder, Tomatoes should be kept under hotkaps or glass at night.

Do not cut Asparagus or Rhubarb the first year after planting.

Botano de luxe is a good fungicide for Primroses; but mix it with equal parts of unscented talcum powder when dusting young seedlings. Specialists advise not to use any pre-emergent fungicide when sowing Primrose seeds.

Irrigate the ground heavily around Roses the day before spraying, so the leaves will be filled with moisture and will not absorb the spray material into them: it is needed on the surface.

Little and often is the rule for fertilizing; but give Fuchsias a heavy application in mid-April. Feed Azaleas early with cottonseed meal or other acid fertilizer. Sweet Peas in California alkaline soils need one ounce of ammonium sulphate dissolved in two gallons of water at two-week intervals. Most hedges need two cups of balanced fertilizer to each 15 inches of row, when spring growth starts.

Rhododendron chlorosis (foliage yellowing, often stunting) is usually caused by too much lime. At times, only part of the plant is affected, especially if it is near stucco or concrete walls or walks. Lack of magnesium or of available iron may also cause it; treat with aluminum sulphate and Epsom salts.

Prune any frost-injured branches as soon as frosts are over. Also prune early-flowering shrubs and trees in regions where they have finished blooming.

NORTHWEST:
Keep spent flowers in the rock garden picked or sheared if plants

are to continue to bloom. Shear Heaths hard as soon as the flowers die so the new growth will be compact.

Divide Chrysanthemum clumps; take cuttings or rooted shoots from them as soon as the shoots are 4 or 5 inches high.

Burn Holly leaves showing Holly miners. And do not let Holly hedges shoot tall leaders, even if several prunings are required.

Sow Parsley where it is to grow, the first week of April; Escarole the middle of the month, and the first sowing of Beans at the end: but apply lime or gypsum in advance for these last. Leeks do well in this region. Sow Onions, fall Cabbage and Brussels Sprouts in the open. Set out Cabbage and Cauliflower plants where they are to grow. The last half of the month, set out Tomatoes under hotkaps.

English Primroses, Polyanthus, and the Julia clan bloom for months in rock gardens, border, woodland, poolside, or as ground covers. Other species stretch bloom over eleven months. When they become crowded, lift and divide after flowering.

Prune Fuchsias in late April or May here, setting these as well as new plants outdoors. Few varieties are winter hardy in most gardens north of California. The so-called Cape-fuchsia, *Phygelius capensis,* a 3-foot hardy shrubby plant here, bears intense scarlet flowers from July through September.

Wait until after the 15th to sow Marigold seed. All need sun; and the African types much more food and moisture than the French. Tall Nasturtiums make good screens, and both kinds cover banks well, being especially valuable in poor clay soils. For sandier soils use the brilliant ground-creeping hardy *Verbena Venosa* Flame that blooms all season until heavy frost. Stocks, Pansies, and Snapdragons are all valuable in border or patio here.

April is pest month; but wait until the last week to spray Holly, as the pest must be caught just as it emerges. Spray with DDT, repeating about May 10th and again twelve days later. Drench the ground early in the month with this or Lindane for cutworms wherever possible. Use fungicides and all-purpose sprays regularly; bait heavily and often for slugs.

Prune Holly hedges. Don't let any hedge reach ultimate height rapidly, or the lower part will be spindly. Prune hybrid Tea Roses; evergreens lightly.

Spray Currants and Gooseberries with Lindane-based spray the 15th, repeating ten days later, also apply a fungicide around the base. Onion sets are the rule here as the Onion fly disdains them, but bothers seedling Onions. Spinach and Lettuce need lime in our usually acid soils. Sow Kale and Peas early; but not Bush Beans until the last week, and no Pole Beans this month. Limas are not satisfactory here. Plant Globe Artichokes, either side suckers or young plants, fertilizing heavily.

MOUNTAINOUS REGIONS:
As fast as soil is workable, prepare it for planting. Also start indoors seeds needing a long growing season. Peas and Kale may both be sown in the open as soon as ground is workable. Set out Broccoli.

Such flowering shrubs as Lilacs are more satisfactory in mountain regions than in lowland California gardens. Mock orange, Spirea, Forsythia are others. Flowering Cherries and Crab apples stand out against native conifers. Practically all Firs, Spruce and Junipers are good; and among broad-leaved ones are Kalmia, Abelia, Pyracantha, native Rhododendron, and up to 5000 feet the hardier Cotoneasters. Brownell and Floribunda Roses come through nicely.

CALIFORNIA:
Get shade houses in shape for summer.

Note Primroses are happier here than in the open. Tuberous and Rex Begonias, Fuchsias, Gloxinias, Strelitzia, woodland Lilies, and Streptocarpus are suitable. Hanging baskets use Achimenes and trailing Fuchsias. *Begonia glaucophylla* in variety make good basket plants, though tending to scant bloom. Cymbidium Orchids are fine for shade houses; while more hardy types suit the less ambitious.

Beans, Squash, and Corn may be sown everywhere except in the mountains and the Imperial Valley or similar; Muskmelons except in mountain and Bay areas; but Watermelons are only for the warm interior valleys in April. Set out Pepper and Tomato plants except in mountain districts. Plant Onion sets through Central and Southern California.

Take greenwood cuttings of Sun-roses for potting up in six weeks. This is good ground cover for slopes.

Late-blooming crimson Kaffir-lily is best used only well south. Plant rose-pink Mrs. Hegarty farther north. Plant Caladium, Zephranthes, Freesia, and Tuberous Begonias.

Watch for drying out, particularly among seedlings and newly-set plants. Water heavily to encourage deep penetration of roots; then stir the topsoil to destroy weeds and form a moisture-retaining mulch.

Feed Gardenias one ounce of iron sulphate dissolved in two gallons of water, repeating in several weeks.

If your garden is very small, why not make in addition a quick-change potted garden for constant color and variety. Local dealers have good offerings. A small propagating box can provide other plants coming on from cuttings.

FOG BELT:
Soil preparation, sowing and planting, weeding, pest control, staking, and tying up new growth keep the April gardener busy. Feed established lawns, and watch that new ones do not dry out and crack between rains. Start ground covers.

Treat Roses to balanced fertilizer and a good mulch. Water deeply, but keep foliage dry. Give a multi-purpose spray every ten days. Spray evergreen Oaks the second week in April.

Be patient with Tree Peonies. Strong bloom is not due until the third season as they need two for establishing root growth.

Fuchsias are fine with Rhododendrons, Azaleas, Hydrangeas, and Woodwardia Ferns. Watch for new varieties. The Fog Belt is their ideal home. Pinch new shoots back for bushy growth, and keep continually moist until October.

SOUTHERN CALIFORNIA:
It is not too late to plant balled and burlapped shrubs or those in containers; also Olive, Citrus, and Avocado trees; Grapes and Berries. Plant Camellias, Azaleas, and Ceanothus. This is a month to plant most subtropicals.

Vine seeds and annuals may be sown in the open; but best results are had in flats with Aster, Didiscus, Stock, Lobelia, Salvia, and annual Carnation. This is also true of perennial Delphinium, Gerberia, and Primula. Sow sky-blue Oxypetalum this month for its low star-like sprays. April-sown *Calceolaria mexicana* blooms in June, the yellow pouches brightening a shady place. This is more of a small ground cover than the much larger flowered usual type.

Plant Poinsettia cuttings. Also plant Tuberoses in addition to other bulbs mentioned. Finish any plant division necessary. Prune hedges. Water as needed, especially Roses, newly planted material, and seed beds. Set gopher traps, and slug poisons. Spray especially for thrips and mildew.

South

GENERAL:

Mix 1 pound of complete commercial fertilizer with 5 gallons of water and use this solution to water newly transplanted flower and vegetable plants. This is called a starter solution.

Plant seeds of these flowers: China Aster, Calliopsis, Coreopsis, Cosmos, Morning-glory, Moonvine, Marigold, Portulaca, Petunia, and Zinnia.

Layerage is a simple, easy form of plant propagation. A lower branch is notched at the point of contact with the earth, buried while still attached to the parent plant and left in this position until the branch roots. These plants can be started by layering: Hydrangea, Weigela, Japanese Magnolia, Pyracantha and Azalea.

Black spot is a mortal enemy of the Rose. It can be recognized by the irregular jagged spots on the Rose leaves. Regular spraying and sanitation are the only controls. An excellent spray is made by dissolving 2 level tablespoons of Fermate in one gallon of water. Use this once a week, covering the entire plant.

Here is a rule of thumb for fertilizing lawns: Use 1 pound of nitrogen to each 1000 square feet of lawn area. In mixed fertilizers, such as 5–10–5, there are 5 pounds of nitrogen to each 100 pounds of the fertilizer, 10 pounds of phosphorus and 5 pounds of potash. Therefore a standard application of this mixture would be 20 pounds of 5–10–5 mixture per 1000 square feet of lawn, since it takes 20 pounds to make one pound of nitrogen.

The number of fertilizer applications to place upon a lawn per year will vary according to conditions. In general, give Bermuda Grass six applications per year (1 pound nitrogen per 1000 square feet), St. Augustine Grass, four applications, Zoysia grass, four, Kentucky Blue Grass, three, Centipede Grass, two, and Carpet Grass, two.

Fertilize Roses using 4 pounds of complete commercial fertilizer per 100 square feet of bed space. Another excellent Rose fertilizer is to be had in cottonseed meal, using ½ pound per plant.

Empty spaces and skips in the plantings can be filled by setting potted Roses, flowering shrubs, perennials and vines from your nurseryman.

Remember that frequent picking of flowers will prolong the flowering season of Pansy, English Daisy, Sweet Pea, Calendula and Violet.

The new soil conditioner Krilium is expensive but effective in developing better textures in heavy clay soils. It is not recommended for soils in good physical condition and has little or no value in sandy soils.

Lawn pests, such as ants, can be controlled by using chlordane (50%), mixing 6 tablespoonsful in 3 gallons of water, and sprinkling this amount over 100 square feet of area.

Dust or spray Rose bushes with an effective fungicide every ten days to two weeks during this period. Apply a complete commercial fertilizer, such as 4–12–4, to Rose plantings, at the rate of three pounds per 100 square feet, and water it into the soil. Cottonseed meal is also a very good

Rose fertilizer. Use about two handfuls of cottonseed meal per bush; scratch into the soil.

Prune out enough old wood in early-flowering shrubs, such as Forsythia, to keep new shoots coming from the ground level. Pinch out the growing tips of these early-flowering shrubs so new shoots branch.

These seeds should be sown in the flower garden: China Aster, Calliopsis, Coreopsis, Cosmos, Morning-glory, Marigold, Portulaca, Petunia, Salvia and Zinnia. Plant Cannas throughout the South. Divide and plant Tuberoses. Make additional plantings of Gladiolus. Oxalis bulbs can be planted in flower beds as an edging.

It is extremely important to keep these flowers picked to prolong their flowering season: Pansies, English Daisies, Sweet Peas, Calendulas, Violas and Violets.

Plants can be moved more easily if the hotbed or plant box is watered thoroughly a few hours before transplanting from it is done. And there is a definite advantage in transplanting seedlings on a cloudy day or in the late afternoon. Newly transplanted plants should be watered immediately and shaded the first two or three days.

Keep winter lawn grass closely mowed to prevent the formation of seed, and to let light into Bermuda Grass. An application of ammonium sulphate or nitrate of soda, using two pounds per 100 square feet, will burn out coarse grasses but will not injure Bermuda Grass. This chemical should be applied when the grass is dry. Water and wash it into the soil after the coarse grasses have died. Established Bermuda lawns having thin or bare spots can be repaired by loosening the soil in the thin areas, then sowing Bermuda Grass seed or setting sprigs of the Grass 12 inches apart. Roll and water immediately. Southern lawns are greatly benefited if they can receive a thin top-dressing of good soil every year. A good yardstick to use is a 2-inch layer of fertile, loamy soil added every five years.

The vegetable garden plantings should include everything that the family will eat. The tender vegetables, such as Beans, Cantaloupes, Tomatoes, Okra, Peppers, Eggplant, Squash and Watermelon can be planted throughout the South. Make second plantings of Sweet Corn, if there is room in the garden for this delicious vegetable. The hybrid varieties such as Golden Cross Bantam and Aristogold III are excellent for southern gardens. Plantings may still be made of Carrots, Leaf Lettuce, Radish, Mustard, Turnips, Beets and Swiss Chard.

Keep vegetable plants thinned for highest quality and quantity production. Do not let vegetable plants grow like hair on a dog's back! Thin with a heavy hand. Year in and year out, Tomatoes that are pruned and staked give best results. Use 5-foot stakes, driven 1 foot into the ground. Prune the Tomatoes to two stems, and tie every 12 inches.

The French gardener often uses a hoe with a 3-foot handle: it keeps him nearer the ground when cultivating the garden. There is no substitute for hand weeding close to the plants. Pull those small weeds before they get large. This is a simple but important rule of gardening.

A wildflower section in your garden will bring great pleasure to all. Try these easily transplanted kinds that can be found at this time of the year while they are in flower: Birds-foot Violet (*Viola pedata*), Pinkroot (*Spigelia marilandica*), Blue Phlox (*Phlox divaricata*), Smooth Phlox (*Phlox glaberrima*), Downy Phlox (*Phlox pilosa*), Penstemon, and Blue Flag (*Iris versicolor*).

UPPER SOUTH:
An excellent lawn grass mixture: 14 pounds Kentucky Blue Grass, 6 pounds English Rye Grass, 6 pounds Redtop and 2 pounds White Clover. Use 2 pounds mixture to 1000 square feet on good seed bed.

Work in the flower garden includes planting Gladiolus, Cannas, Oxalis and Dahlias. Set stakes as the Dahlia tubers are planted. Dig and divide Chrysanthemum plants, resetting single plants and pinching tips to promote branching.

In the vegetable garden plant Beets, Collards, Carrots, Kohlrabi, Leaf Lettuce, Mustard, Onions, Parsley, Peas, Chinese Cabbage, Radish, Turnip and Spinach.

Very interesting landscape effects can be obtained in limited areas by developing and training these plants on a wall or fence in an espaliered effect: *Euonymus patens, E. seiboldi, E. fortuni,* Cotoneaster species or Elaeagnus species.

CENTRAL SOUTH:

Bermuda Grass lawns can be established either by sprigging with plants or by seeding. Zoysia grass is usually established by sprigging rather than seed.

Make another planting of Gladiolus. If Dahlias have not been planted they need to be set at once.

Try an espaliered effect using these plants: Pyracantha species, Chinese Holly, *Photinia galabra, Camellia japonica* or *Camellia sasanqua.*

In the vegetable garden plant all kinds of Beans, Corn, Cucumbers, New Zealand Spinach, Squash and Okra. Set plants of Eggplant, Pepper, Tomato and Sweet Potato. Also make a second planting of the cool-weather vegetables if needed.

Lawns planted now will establish themselves very rapidly. Set plants of Carpet, Centipede, St. Augustine or Zoysia Grass. These can be mixed on large areas where growing conditions vary greatly.

Plant bulbs of Tuberoses and Ixia. Set plants of Gerberia and Caladium.

Divide Bearded Iris immediately after flowering and reset very shallow. Let the foliage of Dutch Iris and other spring-flowering bulbs mature before digging or removing the tops.

Cut back the tops of early-planted Dahlias to make them branch.

Paint tips of cut Rose stems immediately after gathering flowers, using a good pruning paint or orange shellac, especially where the stems are larger than a lead pencil. This has been found effective in controlling stem canker.

Use one teaspoonful copperas (iron sulphate) to 3 gallons of water and apply to 50 square feet of space for the control of chlorosis—the yellowing of foliage of Roses, Azaleas, etc.

North

If Peony blight has been a problem in past seasons, start spraying young shoots now with Bordeaux mixture, drenching the surrounding soil at the same time. Two or three applications a week apart may be necessary.

So you think Dahlias are ugly? Have you tried the winsome Pink Lassie? Considered a miniature Peony type, it has soft pink, open-centered flowers with twisted petals. Its height is about 2½ feet, ideal for the perennial border. Order tubers now.

If you're just itching to plant seeds in the open ground, go ahead, sowing such cool weather lovers as California Poppy, all annual Poppies and Larkspur.

As soon as Delphinium clumps break into growth, start spraying with Di-Mite to stop the pernicious Cyclamen mites dead in their tracks. Repeat every five days or so—or until the pests seem to be under control.

While tramping around the country keep your eyes peeled for wild edible greens. For instance, Dandelion greens are at their best now as are the tasty young shoots of Water-cress. Be sure you gather the latter from unpolluted water.

April weather is proverbially erratic. Dig and prepare soil as early as possible for both vegetables and flowers—then you can take advantage of warm dry days, as they come along, for planting. Hardy species of both vegetables and flowers can be planted while nights are still frosty. Peas and Sweet Peas especially should be gotten in early—every day's delay lessens the chance of success with them.

Make cuttings or single stem-divisions of Chrysanthemums as soon as new growths are 2 or 3 inches long. Started in sandy compost and then repotted, they will make full size flowering plants by autumn.

Portulaca or Rose-moss makes a colorful, weed-smothering ground cover for beds or dry banks. Mix the tiny hard seeds with fine sand and sow thinly on raked surface.

Asparagus is readily grown from seed. Sow now, spacing seed 1 inch apart, cover 1 inch deep. Thin to about 4 inches, and have strong roots ready for transplanting in fall.

To protect Cabbage, Broccoli and Cauliflower from root maggots, surround each stem, when setting out plants, with a tar-paper square slit to the center, and pressed close to the ground.

When pruning Roses, remove and burn not only the clippings but also any old leaves, twigs, dead weeds, etc., from the soil surface.

To get the longest season of bloom from Tuberous Begonias and Gloxinias, start tubers now in peatmoss compost, and then transplant to pots. Both plants are excellent for a shady porch or for window boxes in semi-shade.

Use care in spring clean-up in the rock garden: many species are just starting growth, and tender shoots are easily injured. Now is the time to restrain over-ambitious colonies by removing surplus plants.

Top-dress tulips with dried blood or feed with liquid manure. . . . *Don't* cut off the leaves of bulbs that have finished blooming until they turn brown.

As soon as room is available, plant Melon and Cucumber seeds in the hotbed for an early crop.

Harden off, in the coldframe, seedlings that were started in the hotbed.

Watch seed pots that have wintered in a coldframe. Many alpine plants and Primroses sown last year will, in the frame, probably be sprouting now, and will soon collapse if allowed to get dry or if exposed to full sunshine. Their arch enemy is the pill bug or wood louse. Control with brown sugar mixed with enough Paris Green to color it. . . . Scatter it around, but not among, seedlings.

Don't split up or move hardy Asters after growth has been well advanced.

Set Gladiolus corms 4 to 5 inches deep and 6 inches apart in rich, well-dug soil. Allow 2 feet between the rows. Keep planting them at 2-week intervals, so that you will have a succession display all summer. Many gardeners prefer the cautionary practice of disinfecting the corms before planting with a solution of 1 oz. of bichloride of mercury to 7½ gals. of water.

About the middle of the month (after ground warms up) plant Dahlia tubers. Dig holes 8 inches deep, set tubers with sprouts upward and cover with 3 inches of soil. As plants grow, gradually fill in hollow with soil. Place stout stakes alongside the tubers when you plant them so that the roots are not disturbed later on.

A few easily grown herb seeds planted now will reward you with plenty of seasoning for summer meals. Try Basil, Sweet Marjoram, Summer Savory, Borage and, of course, Parsley and Chives.

Hydrangeas must be frequently watered, often twice daily if the air is very dry.

Rake the lawn and apply a dressing of commercial fertilizer. Then roll it thoroughly. Dig out weeds as soon as they start growing.

While removing mulches, cultivating or doing other work in the perennial border be especially careful not to break the new growth which is appearing. It's as brittle as it is important.

As soon as the position and shape of established plants is clearly marked by the young shoots, bone meal and pulverized manure mixed in equal parts can be applied as a light top-dressing around them and slightly scratched into the soil.

Lift and divide any plants that are too large or too cramped in their present location. It is a good time to divide and replant Chrysanthemums.

When dividing and transplanting, be generous with the room you give them. . . . Remove all covering from tender plants.

Finish pruning Roses. . . . Prune Forsythias and other early-blooming shrubs when the flowers have faded. . . . From most summer and autumn flowering shrubs remove ⅓ to ⅕ of top growth and a few of the oldest canes from the ground line. . . . From Butterfly Bushes, Hydrangeas and Golden Hypericum remove only winterkilled wood. *Don't* prune Buddleia alternifolia. It flowers on last year's wood.

Winter-protection earth mounds can now be removed—but do it gradually.

April is the time to replace on their supports all Climbers that were bundled and laid down for the winter.

MAY

West Coast

GENERAL:

Watch that lawns, borders, Rose gardens, and evergreens do not dry out. Greatest danger is in California valleys, but even the North Pacific can have dry spells.

Apply multi-purpose sprays regularly; fungicides, where needed in the soil; set slug and earwig baits. Take care that weed killers do not get on garden material.

Sow Beans, Carrots, Corn, Squash except in such climates as Imperial Valley, and protect from frost in highest mountains. Set out Eggplants, Tomatoes, and Peppers likewise. Sow Beets, Chard, and Lettuce except in hot interior valleys; Muskmelons except in the Bay area. Peas are sown only north and in cooler mountain regions; Watermelons only in warmer gardens, notably California valleys. Broccoli, Cabbage, and Cauliflower may be set out north and in the mountains; Rutabagas and Turnips may be sown.

Keep all seedlings and young plants moist after setting out, Petunias in particular. Petunias respond to well-rotted manure in soil, and quick, balanced fertilizer as bloom begins. Watch closely for slugs; and prevent seeding if you want long-continued bloom.

Plant Naegelia, Tuberoses, Dahlias, Water-lilies, and *Acidanthera murielliae*.

Feeding, pest control, summer mulches where needed, watering, and tender and succession planting are the big chores this month. All plants in active growth, including ripening bulbs, need food, with Chrysanthemums, Roses and Peonies among the heavier feeders. In general, a balanced all-purpose fertilizer every two to four weeks will do; but note plant tastes for more or less of one ingredient or another.

Use multi-purpose spray every ten days, getting it under the leaves. Read labels carefully: some of the newer sprays are too toxic for amateur handling. Continue baiting for slugs. Some gardens need soil fumigation for wireworms, millipedes, and webworm moth eggs. When watering, soak the ground, not the plant: Fuchsias and Celery like wet tops, but many plants mildew, especially Delphiniums, Sweet Peas and Roses. Continue to prune spring-flowering shrubs and vines as they finish blooming.

For fragrance, and requiring little trouble on this coast, where it is generally hardy, is the sweet-scented Gladiolus, *G. Murieliae* (*Acidanthera Murieliae* in many catalogues), with white blossoms centrally splotched with clear purple.

NORTHWEST:

Tulip fields in the Puget Sound region, and also down into Oregon are worth seeing. The Rhododendron tour on the Olympic Peninsula comes late in May where seeing them in natural habitat is inspiring. Do not plan to dig or pick—they are rightly under rigid protection! For garden varieties see the Seattle Arboretum.

Top-dress Azaleas and Rhododendrons with peat. Apply acid fertilizer, watering thoroughly the day before as well as after. Remove fading flowers so side shoots just below will develop for next year's bloom.

Cut faded Lilacs and Laburnum. Prune whip-like Wisteria growths back to 8 inches of leafy stems. Shear rock garden carpeters such as Aubrietia, Sedum and Phlox before they seed. Keep cutting fading flowers from intermittent bloomers.

Crab Grass is not rampant here; others commonly mistaken for it are not killed by Crab Grass sprays. Spray Holly around the 10th and again the 22nd against leaf miners.

Finish planting Water-lily pools. The tropicals can go in now. Remember all need sun, and pools should have some oxygenating plants.

May means planting tender bulbs such as Tuberoses, sowing seeds, setting out seedlings previously started indoors or in frames. Water earlier-started Tuberous Begonias well the day before planting out shallowly in peat, leafmold, and compost among house plants summered outdoors, Ferns, in porch and window boxes, hanging baskets, and more or less shaded borders.

Sow Zinnias and Marigolds where they are to grow. Set out Petunias, Lobelias, Heliotrope, and Snapdragons among others. Get Chrysanthemums started if not already done.

May is hectic living for Northwest gardeners, with flower and vegetable seedlings to be set out, half-hardy seeds such as Zinnia to sow in the open, the herb garden to start, tender summer bulbs to plant, such rock plants as Aubrietia to shear, spent flower heads to cut from early shrubs, and Forsythia to prune to within 4 inches of the old wood. With all this, keep close watch for plants just under the surface.

Last-moment perennials can still be set in vacant rock garden or border spaces. Do it as early in the month as possible.

Clean garden pools if this is not already done. Stock them with both fish and aerating plants. Set out Water-lilies: hardy types are usually preferred here.

The big Asiatic bog Primulas that bloom heavily in May need much water to keep them flowering through the next two months. Keep an all-purpose bait beneath all Primrose leaves to catch root weevils in their adult beetle stage, and also slugs and earwigs.

Set out all vegetables that were sown indoors or in frames before the end of May. Keep Squash, Cucumbers, Peppers and Tomatoes under hotkaps if possible until the 15th, both for pest protection and cold nights. By that time, you will have early beetles under control. Make two sowings of Bush or Pole Beans early and late in May for succession. Sow New Zealand Spinach in late May, and also Oakleaf Lettuce. Set out Celery plants any time, preferably in a double-row trench.

Melons, Cantaloupes and Corn are not easily grown in this region, as there is not enough hot growing weather, and nights are cool. If you do try, this is the month to start.

Set out herbs in late May, in the sun; except Mint, which needs light shade and moisture. Herbs can usually be had in small pots at a few cents from local markets in the larger cities: a good way to acquire a wide assortment of just one or a few of a kind.

CALIFORNIA:

Fogs return this month along the Central Coast, to last until October, while back from the ocean the interior valleys become really hot, so that deep mulches are imperative—especially around Gardenias, Rhododendrons, Clematis, Peonies and Phlox. Well-rotted manure is good. Peat-moss must be watched or it will draw water *from* the soil, unless a slowly running hose is used where the water can penetrate. There have been some good reports of Tree Peonies from these valleys. Petunias and Zinnias are a real standby: sow early.

Lath houses can use another sowing of their annuals for continuous bloom. Look for unusual basket plants in local nurseries, particularly in the Southwest, where specialists offer rare species of Ferns, Begonias, Orchids and other plants for tropical effects.

Eggplant and Peppers will not grow until the soil is warm. Okra and

Melons are also hot weather crops. All can be started in May, early or late according to local conditions. Give Eggplant one tablespoon of super-phosphate per plant; Peppers and Melons two of complete fertilizer. Manures sometimes flavor Melons. Moisture is imperative: but too much sends Peppers to leafage and turns Eggplant leaves yellow; too little stops growth. Melons do not form the sugar necessary for flavor in cool or cloudy weather. Okra germinates poorly, so sow it thickly. Pick the pods before the seeds develop to keep them bearing.

Valley gardeners, note that Tree Peonies demand protection from drying out, and high winds. A mulch is helpful.

Remember that big vines must have much water and fertilizer; watch out for supporting wires when they are heated by the blazing sun. Touch one and you'll see why vines are harmed.

Tuberous Begonias are best grown in sun through foggier parts of the fog belt such as San Francisco, even Santa Cruz. Elsewhere and south grow them under trees that let in early and late sun, or in lath houses. All day shade is required in hot valleys, much peat in soil and as top dressing. Water early, for night wet causes bud drop, stem mold, eventual bulb death.

Get a soil fumigant into lawns before webworm moths lay eggs. Watch for brown patch.

FOG BELT:
May is still time to plant subtropicals, shrubs, trees, and other material just able to come through the region's winters when once established, also very tender bulbs. A moisture basin helps shrubs and trees through the first summer. Among vines to plant are Cardinal Climber, Canary-birdvine, Bougainvillea, Morning-glory, and the shrubby evergreen Streptosolen, hardy from San Francisco south if sheltered in northern limits.

Plant Fuchsias and Heliotrope. Get annuals like Tithonia, Zinnias, Marigolds settled in. Salpiglossis, Phlox, Venidium, Cosmos, and Pen-stemon are suggestions among a long list. Plant Amaryllis, Morea, and Bearded Iris. Place Dahlias in full sun.

Spring-flowering vines and shrubs, hedges, evergreens may all be pruned, shaped, or thinned as desirable. Fasten up climbing Roses, but prune only Belle of Portugal, taking out older canes.

Prevent earwig propagation the last week in May by setting poison bait.

Dahlias like the fog belt, but require full sun. Feed them sparingly at first to encourage slower growth and more flowers.

SOUTHERN CALIFORNIA:

Plant early fall borders: bulbs, late annuals and perennials. The Gloriosa-lily may be left to establish itself in the sheltered open in the Southwest, where it will bloom in late summer.

Sweet Potatoes are a long-season hot weather crop, good in poor sandy soil. Organic matter and nitrogen produce too much vine. Use a 2–8–10 fertilizer before planting, and again in four or five weeks.

After the first year, Epiphyllums need a balanced fertilizer. This Cactus group also needs charcoal mixed with its compost of coarse sand, leafmold and loam. Star Cactus (Astrophytum), Echinocactus, and the Mammillaria groups need good ground watering from time to time through spring and summer.

Plantings now are mainly for fall bloom, or the late summer annuals. Sow all perennial seed for fall transplanting. Petunias, if sheared back later, can be treated as perennials, or sow a flat now for more in the fall. Most annual seeds go into open ground; but Petunias, Asters, Dianthus, Nicotiana, Salvia, and Gomphrena are usually started in flats. Plant Casaba, Gourds, Okra.

Plant "balled and burlapped" or container Avocado, Olive, and Citrus trees, subtropicals, evergreen shrubs that go in shade; but keep all thoroughly watered, and shade at first.

Pinch back Chrysanthemums, and water well to discourage red spider. Be sure sprays are keeping aphids and thrips off Roses. Prevent mildew by not wetting foliage of Sweet Peas, Delphinium and Roses, especially late in the day. Mealy bugs, thrips, scale, red spider, and ants are particular pests this month.

Bearded Iris is ready to divide this month; new stock may be planted. Take Poinsettia cuttings for Christmas-blooming plants.

Water-lilies may still be planted. Strangely, the tropicals bloom latest into the fall, though resenting cold spring nights far more than do the hardy. Also most tropicals can get along with fewer hours of direct sun, blooming fairly well with only four, an asset in patio pools overly shaded.

South

Climbing Roses need the old wood—older than two or three years—removed by pruning after flowering. Train vigorous new growth. Horizontal branches on a fence usually produce more blooms than vertical stems on a trellis.

A pinch in time saves nine where summer pruning of shrubs is involved. Remove the rapid growing tips of such shrubs as Forsythia, Weigela, Abelia, Pyracantha, Spirea, Lonicera and Ligustrum to force branching and keep plants within bounds.

Do not water established flowers until absolutely necessary. Frequent shallow watering is definitely harmful. If wilted plants do not straighten up over night, water beds with a 1-inch soaking.

The main requirement of Gladiolus is water during the growing season. This ideal cut flower is well adapted to southern climate if abundant water is available.

Transplant seedlings of annuals such as Zinnia, Marigold, Verbena and Petunia where seedling stands are too thick. Water and shade immediately after transplanting.

Remove old flowers from Snapdragon, Stock, Petunias, Verbena, Larkspur, Ragged Robins, and Phlox to encourage new flower production.

Violets need to be dug, divided and reset in enriched soil every few years. Flowering will be greatly accelerated if this job is done right now.

Vegetables with ornamental possibilities are hot Pepper and Eggplant. The former makes a colorful border plant; the latter has coarse foliage for contrast and intriguing fruit displays.

Shrub plantings should be distinctly separated from lawn areas by a neat, trim shrub bed outline cut into the turf. Pulverize the soil in shrub beds 6 to 8 inches deep, removing all grass and weeds. Fertilize shrub and lawn areas with twenty-five pounds of complete fertilizer (such as 4–12–4 mixture) to each 1000 square feet, and water into the soil.

During dry spells, special attention should be given shrubs and trees that were planted this year, and to newly established lawns. Soak the ground when watering—do not sprinkle lightly.

Deep placement of fertilizer around trees, and heavy applications of fertilizer (thirty to thirty-five pounds per 1000 square feet) on shaded areas of lawn, will partly offset shade-tree competition with lawn grasses. In shaded areas first try shade-tolerant grasses such as St. Augustine, Zoysia or Kentucky Blue Grass, plus heavy fertilization. If they fail, then try Vinca or English Ivy for a ground cover.

Earthworms in the lawn can be controlled by using twenty pounds of arsenate of lead to 1000 square feet of area. This is a poison, so use with caution. Ants, moles and crickets in the lawn can be held in check with chlordane used as prescribed by the manufacturer. Keep weeds pulled or dug out of lawns to prevent seeding and further spread.

The list of flower seeds to plant is extensive, but the more valuable ones to consider are: Ageratum, Sweet Alyssum, Balsam, Cockscomb, Coral Vine, Cosmos, Four-o'clock, Ice-plant, Marigold, Ornamental Pepper, Periwinkle, Petunia, Portulaca, Sunflower, Torenia and Zinnia. Alternanthera is a bedding plant that makes an excellent border for flower beds or walks. It is available in assorted foliage colors, growing only a few inches tall, thriving in heat and strong sunlight. This plant is propagated by cuttings. An interesting and attractive flowering border results when *Hibiscus rosa-sinensis* (Chinese Hibiscus) is under-planted with Portulaca.

Formal garden areas should be relatively level for best results. They should be enclosed, and all garden lines clearly defined. Be modern— light your garden this summer for more enjoyment from your gardening efforts. A well-placed floodlight or two will prove that the southern garden is most beautiful and pleasant at night.

Shrub pruning should be continued during the growing season to control the shape and height of the plants. Frequent light pruning and pinching now is better than heavy pruning all at one time.

Thousands of dollars are spent unwisely each year for poor quality barnyard manure to be used as fertilizer for shrub and flower beds throughout the south. Much of this manure has been exposed to the weather and all fertility value has been leached out by the rain. Serious and troublesome infestations of weeds are carried in seed form in this manure. Much better buys are available through the purchase of commercial manure for plant nutrients, and peatmoss, humus, leafmold or even good garden loam for the soil-conditioning elements.

Zoysia Grass (Zoysia matrella) is an excellent lawn grass for the South. It was introduced from the Orient several years ago by the United States Department of Agriculture. It has a fine leaf, is very dense and dark green, making a thick turf in sun or shade. This grass does not produce seed, so must be started by setting the plants. Several nurseries are in a position to supply this excellent lawn grass. Would-be miracle-seekers have spread the rumor that no lawn mowing is necessary with this grass; but a more attractive turf is developed when regular mowing is done.

UPPER SOUTH:
Annual seeds to plant include: Amaranthus, China-aster, Balsam, Cardinal Climber, Celosia, Cleome, Cosmos, Cypress-vine, Euphorbia, Crotalaria, Globe Amaranth, Portulaca, Salvia, Scabiosa, Statice, Sunflowers, Vinca, Verbena, and Zinnia. Plants of these can also be set out now as can plants of bedding Begonias, Geraniums, and Alternanthera.

Wait until tops die down on spring-flowering bulbs before removing them. When leaves are ⅓ dead, appearance of bulb beds can be improved by tying loose knot in foliage.

Sweet Peas will flower over a much longer period if a 2-to-4-inch mulch of clean straw is placed around the plants.

If you particularly like brilliant colors in the garden, plant Clarkia and Godetia.

Apply 3 to 5 pounds complete commercial fertilizer (6–8–4) to bearing Peach, Plum and Apple trees. Summer prune or train young fruit trees. Remove all low branches, and thin upper branches when new growth is 4 to 6 inches long. On Peaches and Plums, leave three to five branches spaced 6 to 8 inches apart with the lowest 18 inches from the ground. When scaffold limbs (those left) are 20 inches long, pinch out growing tip. With Apples leave five to seven branches with lowest 24 inches above ground.

CENTRAL SOUTH:

Bulbs to plant for current season bloom include Gladiolus, Tuberoses, Dahlias, and Caladium.

All annual flower seed listed under Upper South can be planted in this area plus Ice-plant and Torenia. Set plants of Alternanthera, Blood-leaf, Coleus, Copper-leaf, Croton, Elephants-ear, Hibiscus and Lantana.

Prune and stake early Tomatoes, using 5-foot stakes driven 1 foot into the ground. Allow two to three stems to develop and remove all others. Tie at 12-inch intervals with soft cord.

Beware! Watch all narrow-leaved evergreens for bagworms. When observed, spray immediately with mixture of 12 teaspoons of arsenate of lead in each gallon of water. Handle this material with caution.

LOWER SOUTH:

Gardenia is a shrub with prolific flowering characteristics when correctly grown. White fly is its greatest enemy, enabling a dark smutty fungus to develop on the foliage. Dust every ten days with 5% DDT for control.

Aphids or plant lice attack Roses and succulent growth of other plants with devastating results. Control by using nicotine sulphate in soapy water. Again, cautious reference is made to that powerful insecticide, Parathion.

Azaleas and Camellias are now producing new wood that will produce flowers next year. You can help these plants by providing a 3-to-4-inch mulch of clean straw, pine straw or other good material.

St. Augustine Grass is an excellent lawn grass for sunny or shady locations. It has good salt tolerance, so is fine for the seaside. It has poor wear resistance qualities, so should not be used where much walking is to be done. The "blue" variety is of questionable value because so few pure strains are now available.

Flower seeds to plant include: Ageratum, Sweet Alyssum, Balsam, Cockscomb, Coral-vine, Cosmos, Cypress-vine, Four-o'clocks, Globe Amaranth, Gourds, Marigold, Moonflower, Periwinkle, Petunia, Portulaca, Sunflower, Torenia and Zinnia.

This is an excellent time to plant palms.

Door-yard citrus plantings need fertilizer application of complete commercial fertilizer (4–6–8) using 1 pound fertilizer per year of age up to 10 years and ½ pound for each additional year of age.

North

This is the gardener's busiest month. Fortunately the days are getting longer, and before train time in the morning or at dusk in the evening, it is possible at least to make notes of the things that will most need attention over the week end—and that's a good thing to do!

Strawberries, the home gardener's favorite fruit, are hungry plants. For big luscious berries, that will quickly fill a basket, give them an extra feeding now. Go through the patch first to get out all weeds—especially those in or near the crowns—and then apply a general-purpose plant food, 3 to 4 pounds to 100 feet of row. Water in thoroughly, immediately after, to remove any that may adhere to foliage and carry the fertilizer down to the roots. Repeat watering if weather is dry while fruits are forming.

Lawn areas should be making rapid growth. Cut frequently, but not too short—1½ inches is better than close trimming. Unless fertilizer has already been applied, give a generous feeding now. Also watch for first signs of Crab Grass—broad coarse leaves of a different color. Seedling plants come out with a pinch, but once they are firmly rooted you'll have a real battle on your hands—and knees.

As flowers begin to fade on spring bulbs, snap off old blooms. This is especially important with Tulips as fallen petals may help spread the dreaded "fire" disease. Do not cut Tulips with long stems and leaves if you want to have good flowers again next year.

Many early-flowering trees and shrubs can be transplanted while in full bloom. These include Dogwood, Redbud, and such broad-leaved evergreens as Azaleas, Andromeda (Pieris) and Mountain Laurel.

Don't overlook your opportunity to get dramatic summer highlights from tender bulbs that can be planted now to bloom from July on.

Plant Gladiolus corms at 2 to 3 week intervals to insure succession of bloom.

Be sure to leave the foliage of Daffodils and Crocuses to ripen before cutting. Now is the time to give them a dressing of plant food to aid in storing up next years' food. . . . Set out tuberous-rooted Begonias started in the house. Or plant the tubers outside in a partially shaded spot with the concave side just below the soil level.

If rabbits are plentiful, better fence in the hardy Lilies with wire netting of some sort. The little beggars love to nibble the tips of the new stalks when they're only a few inches high.

When *warm* settled weather comes, house plants are repotted as necessary and set on a sheltered porch or plunged in the garden.

Geranium cuttings are taken late this month or early next for winter-flowering plants.

The Cyclamen continues its rest, but outside now, laid on its side under an arbor or beside a house wall.

Poinsettias are pruned to 6 ins., repotted, watered and returned to sun and heat. As new shoots appear, cuttings are taken.

Cut back Hydrangeas and repot; use 1 tsp. alum for blues, a sprinkling of lime for pinks. Plunge in lightly shaded garden spot.

Young African violets, Rubber plants and Wax plants, Crassulas, Begonias, Passion vine and Pandanus are better on porch than in garden for summer.

Learn to keep an eye out for plant insect enemies and diseases whenever you're around the garden; discovering and combating them at the earliest possible stage in their career of crime is vitally important.

If you haven't already secured your spray and dust materials for the season, better get them at once. When these things are needed, they're needed fast!

If you want extra-large and perfect Peony flowers, disbud them by taking off the side buds when they attain the size of small peas. This leaves only the terminal bud which will develop into a large flower because all the strength of that shoot is thrown into the one bud.

This is the best month to plant or divide Christmas Roses (*Helleborus niger*). They like lime, lots of rotted leafmold, some well decayed manure, and plenty of moisture now, though a dry September often means a heavy flower crop.

Divide English Polyanthus and similar types of Primroses after they have finished blooming.

Supports for the Peonies, Baby's-breath and other bushy-growing plants that are likely to lop over as they approach full growth should be put in place while the stalks are still less than 1 ft. tall. Three or four stakes equally spaced around each plant and connected at the top with strong, soft string are a good support. Spreading plants, such as Baby's-breath and Gaillardias, are often better supported with brushwood.

Keep Pansies constantly picked, and cut back all leggy growth.

Watch Irises in case the Iris borer is present: the signs are an oozing of watery matter on the leaves and a softening of the rhizomes. Cut out infected parts and burn.

Chrysanthemum cuttings will root readily now and provide plants for this fall. Start them in the coldframe or a special bed.

Seeds of Marigolds, Zinnias (all types), China asters, Ageratum, Cosmos, Nicotiana—in fact, just about all kinds of summer-blooming garden annuals—should be sown outdoors during May. If you delay until next month, the flowering season will be unduly short.

Continue successive sowings of annuals for late bloom: African daisy (*Arctotis*), Mignonette, Larkspur, Bachelor's buttons and Baby's-breath. In unexpected and important gaps, fill in with florist's in-bloom annual plants, especially fringed single or double Petunias.

May is a first-class month to sow perennial seeds in a finely prepared outdoor bed provided with a cheesecloth screen to ward off too hot sun and prevent severe damage by heavy rain. Started at this time, many kinds of seedlings will be big enough for permanent planting by September 1st.

JUNE

West Coast

GENERAL:

Top-dress lawns, feed Roses and perennials, give acid fertilizer to Rhododendrons, Camellias and Azaleas not recently fed. Water soil both before and after fertilizing. In cutting off faded flowers, watch out for new buds forming at their bases. Cut off the dead flowers of bulbs, but never the foliage until it is completely browned. Divide such Daffodils as need it, burning any bulbs having soft rot or containing grayish-white grubs of Narcissus fly. Curing them is not necessary if healthy bulbs are reset at once; but do not replant them in soil where diseased bulbs were found.

Shorten Wisteria side shoots. Only such rambler and climbing Roses as bloom once are pruned after flowering. Watch for unwanted suckers on Snowberry, Flowering Quinces, and Lilacs, especially.

Sow perennials everywhere, though particularly in the Northwest. Gardeners in Southern California and interior valleys should prepare to shade seedlings with lath, screen sash, or other devices.

Such Iris as are through blooming may be divided or planted.

Coast gardens should be back to normal after the bad winter and late spring. Watering is the heaviest June chore, though less important in the Fog Belt. Soak deep and early. Wet foliage in late afternoon causes Begonia bud drop, mildew and other troubles on many plants. Mulches help retain soil moisture.

June continues the long coastal growing season. Colder mountain areas use their short one to the utmost; interior California valleys struggle with water trenches, deep mulches, windbreaks to conserve all possible moisture.

When watering trees, shrubs, borders, rock plants, and lawns, soak deeply. Keep water off most foliage but get it under the mulches.

Continue multi-purpose sprays and dusts, fungicides, DDT for thrips; bait for slugs, earwigs, and sowbugs.

Sow Beans, Corn, and Squash except in the Imperial and similar valleys; Lettuce and Chard likewise, though not in Sacramento and San Joaquin Valleys. Set out Eggplant and Peppers except in the Imperial Valley; set Tomato plants except in valley regions; plant Potatoes north and along the coast.

Pinch or prune young fruit trees to shape; and if necessary, Apple, Pear, Plum, Quince, Peach, and Apricot trees set out this spring may be topped.

When bloom is over prune and cut out old canes of the climbing and rambler Roses that flower only once.

Keep Chrysanthemums pinched or cut back until mid-summer. Iris through blooming may be planted or divided as needed. Perennial and biennial seeds may be sown throughout. Sow slopes more thickly at the top, as seeds work down.

NORTHWEST:

A two- or three-month period with no wetting rain is likely. A hose is useless sprayed against the face of a rock wall, but is fine if laid along the top so the water percolates down behind the wall, where the real roots are. This is also true of steep rock gardens. Lesser slopes are aided with upended drain tile sunk a few inches in the ground, at strategic points, and kept filled with water. Screen the protruding ends with larger plants or small shrubs.

When sowing biennial and perennial seeds, remember that Lilies make a fine hobby in this region. Start with the quick-flowering group that includes Regal and Centifolium varieties.

Sow Savoy Cabbage in rich, moist soil for the winter; also Broccoli, and if desired, Kale and Batavian Endive. Continue to watch Strawberries and Primroses for weevils.

Sow last of late summer annuals at once. Zinnias and Marigolds mature faster at this time if sowed where they are to grow. Plant Tuberoses and any summer bulbs not yet in, also more succession Gladiolus. June is best here for sowings of perennials and biennials for next summer's bloom. New shades in Wallflowers make them valuable among Tulips.

Take cuttings of deciduous shrubs.

Try soil sulphur around Heaths in hard or heavy soils, digging in every year or two. Large-flowered Clematis needs lime in this generally acid region. Watch for weevil grub among Primroses. Keep big Bog Primroses wet, cutting faded flowers unless desired for seed.

Sow Savoy Cabbage, Kale, Kohlrabi here and in mountain regions into California. Also set plants of Broccoli, Cabbage, and Cauliflower. Blueberries must have water all summer, preferably underground. Peat or humus is necessary to produce right conditions for micro-organisms needed by their roots. Give acid fertilizer.

CALIFORNIA:

It is fog time in the Bay region, stretching to Santa Barbara; but val-

leys in from the ocean are really hot. Drying winds are as much of a
menace as parched ground in Santa Clara as well as the interior. Even
Geraniums need some shade and water to bloom all summer. Annuals
must not dry out. Young plants and seedlings need cheesecloth or lath
protection. Older ones need deep mulching, sometimes water trenches.
Lath houses protect from drying wind and heat in interior valleys, especially if plants like Fuchsias that enjoy fine misty spraying are used.
Helxine and Lobelia can furnish carpet. Try a jungle Orchid, possibly
Epidendrum Obrienianum if sun filters in well. Begonias, Gloxinias, and
Streptocarpus dislike interior heat, but are good shade house subjects if
in situations where they escape the last late afternoon wetting down
given Fuchsias. Under drier and *not* acid conditions, Heath-like Boronia
is very fragrant.

See that Chrysanthemums do not burn or dry out. Cultivate Roses
and newly planted material in particular. Compost and mulch.

Gerberias will not grow in cold or hard ground; crowns must be at soil
level. In hot valleys give some shade and mulch with peat; but small
gravel and all-day sun in the fog belt.

Keep Delphinium on slow steady growth. Bone meal is good, no acids.
Cut flower stalks before they seed to get later bloom.

Sow Muskmelons in central valleys, Citrus belt, and southern coastal;
also make successive Watermelon sowings in interior valleys.

FOG BELT:
Now that the fogs are in, this region has more in common with the
North Pacific than with the rest of California. Use summer plants that
like fogs and cool nights; Gloxinias, Fuchsias, Begonias, and Geraniums
in wide variety; Streptocarpus for the advanced gardener. Pansies thrive
as edgings or ground covers. Plant Zephyranthes now after a rain or a
watering for quick bloom. Try Nerines. Dahlias may still be planted; also
Gladiolus for later bloom.

Sow succession annuals. Pinch back buds of recently set out ones to
produce heavier later bloom. Also sow vegetables for succession. Fogs,
humidity, cool nights, but enough sun to permit maturing, allow a wide
choice of plant material.
Pelargonium, Geraniums, Fuchsias, Hydrangeas, and Tuberous Begonias are sturdy fog belt plants, the last replacing winter Cinerarias.

Hydrangeas need much food and water as they come into bloom. Lady Washington Pelargoniums drop their lower leaves if roots become too dry. Ivy Geraniums can cover banks, fences, walls, trail from window and porch boxes, or garden urns. Use short-jointed wood for all Geranium cuttings.

Give Amaryllis liquid manure or commercial fertilizer as buds form. Sulphate of potash and bone meal to Dahlias; acid plant food to Camellias, Rhododendrons, and Azaleas. Take half-ripened cuttings of these last three, also Daphne. Marguerite cuttings strike quickly in June.

Bait for ants, grasshoppers, earwigs, slugs; set gopher traps.

INTERIOR VALLEYS:
Fine gardens are possible here with deep mulching up to 3 or 4 inches or more, trench watering, wiser choice of plant material—often especially bred to withstand heat as some new Fuchsias—and protection from drying winds with lath house, Tamarix, or other means. Fuchsias need shade and mist-spray in early morning and again at 5 P.M. Keep their roots moist. Consult your local nursery for Carnations to bloom all summer.

Dig deep trenches in the Rose beds, filling twice a week with water, then covering, or raking mulch in when water is absorbed to prevent evaporation. Here and elsewhere mulching also prevents soil hardening. Gazanias, Dimorphothecas and Arctotis are all easily grown, spreading ground covers.

SOUTHERN CALIFORNIA:
Nearly all South African succulents are dormant from May to September, and should not be fed. Water them only once a month unless they are planted in small containers. Most Cacti rest in the winter and are active all summer. However, there are numerous exceptions in both groups. Complete liquid fertilizers are proving exceptionally good for Cacti when they are in active growth. Use running water and a soft toothbrush, rather than insecticides, to remove any pests. Gasterias and Haworthias need light shade.

Complete liquid fertilizer is also good for Gloxinias and Streptocarpus, whether grown in shade house or elsewhere. Feed Citrus trees: ammonium phosphate, up to four pounds for a large tree, is an old standby.

Gardenias, Camellias and Azaleas need water and mulches. Spray Fuchsias with a fine mist.

Plant Sprekelia, Nerine, and Lycoris. Try a small colony of mixed Sparaxis and Streptanthera for the interesting crosses they make. Carnations that have been blooming since late winter should be pruned, then rested for a month.

Sow flower seeds in June as in May. Young plants need shading, much care in watering.

Watch particularly that Gardenias do not dry out; and be generous with mist sprays as well as ground water on Fuchsias. Roses, Azaleas, Camellias, Rhododendrons, and lawns need deep soaking. Give Roses a heavy mulch, and spray against mildew at two-week intervals.

Continue to plant Dahlias, divide or plant Iris. Plant Tuberous Begonia seedlings, also mature bulbs, Amaryllis, Lycoris, and Nerine. Set out Tithonia, Asters, Zinnias, Cosmos, Portulaca, and Marigolds.

South

GENERAL:
Successful summer care of Boxwood is complicated by these facts: The plant is very shallow rooted and quick to resent dry soil conditions; red spider is its mortal enemy; and hot weather intensifies both problems. Suggestions: Keep soil moist by frequent watering and use of mulch; do not cultivate around these plants; and apply controls for red spider.

The Pfitzer Juniper, a low spreading evergreen, is used extensively throughout the South. This plant often spreads beyond desired size unless given regular corrective pruning. Prune several times a year, cutting longest branches back so the cut is concealed by foliage on the shorter branches. This should keep it within bounds.

Spray Azaleas to control mealybugs, lacebugs, thrips, mites and Peony scale, using this mixture: ½ pint white oil emulsion, one and one-half ounces powdered derris and six teaspoons Black Leaf 40, in six gallons of water. This spray will also control lacebug on Pyracantha, and white fly on Gardenia.

It is late in the season now to make bulb plantings. However, if you hurry, these can be planted successfully: Dahlia, Amazon-lily (Eucharis), Louisiana Iris and Water-lily. Hardy Water-lilies produce the most blooms when the water depth of the planting area does not exceed 2 feet. Press the roots into the mud, at a slant, so that the growing tip is level with the surface.

Bagworm is one of the most destructive pests among the insects that attack narrow-leaved evergreens. Watch these plants closely, and spray with twelve teaspoonsful of arsenate of lead to each gallon of water at the first sign of infestation.

Apply dusting sulphur to plants such as Roses, Phlox, and Zinnias at the first sign of powdery mildew. Wettable sulphur spray can also be used, or any Rose spray containing a fungicide.

Soak soil during dry spells to a depth of 6 or 8 inches, in late afternoon. A 4-inch mulch of loose material, such as hay, grass clippings, leaves, straw or peatmoss, will conserve moisture, keep down weeds, and keep the soil cool. Try it.

Stake and tie Dahlias: they need support. Be careful not to damage the tubers when placing the stakes. Keep suckers removed to develop the main stem.

Annual flower seeds to plant include: Ageratum, Sweet Alyssum, Balsam, Cockscomb, Cosmos, Four-o'clock, Marigold, Periwinkle, Torenia, and Zinnia. For quicker results, set out plants, if available. Other flowering plants to consider are: Alternanthera, Chrysanthemum, Fancy-leaved Caladium, Coleus, Croton, Elephant-ear, Plumbago, Salvia, and Sweet Sultan.

Cut flowers regularly from Nasturtium, Cosmos, Petunia, Marigold and Zinnia to encourage flowering. Remove old flower heads from these plants to keep them from going to seed: Ageratum, Cockscomb, Cornflower, Gaillardia, Scabiosa, Verbena.

Nasturtiums that are mostly foliage and producing few flowers are growing in soil that is too rich in nitrogen. Stop adding nitrogen-carrying fertilizer to their soil.

Keep weeds out of garden and flower beds. They steal plant food, use precious moisture, harbor insects and diseases and look—to put it mildly—out of place.

Plant these in the vegetable garden: Pole Snap Beans, Pole Lima Beans, Corn, Crowder Peas, Field Peas and Tomato plants. Tomato plants are often staked and tied to good advantage. The ties should be placed every 12 inches. Another vegetable that is helped by staking is Eggplant. Keep vegetables harvested at the season when each variety is at the peak of quality.

Continue to practice summer pruning and pinching with your shrub plantings to promote branching, to produce additional flowering wood, and to control the shape and height of the plant. The best time to shape a plant is when it is growing—not after it has stopped. Remove the old flower heads from Crape myrtle, Lavender-bush (Vitex) and Butterfly bush to encourage the formation of new growth.

Most of the spring-flowering bulbs, such as Narcissus, Jonquil, Crocus, Squill, Roman Hyacinth and Snowdrop should be left in the ground from year to year. If the bulbs become extremely crowded and small, dig when the foliage is brown, divide, and replant in newly prepared and fertilized soil immediately.

It is important to keep lawn grasses cut at the specific heights required by the growth habits of each kind of grass. The grasses that creep or spread by means of stolons (underground stems), such as Bermuda Grass, Bent, Centipede, St. Augustine and Zoysia, can be clipped quite close: as short as ½ to 1 inch. Those grasses that do not produce stolons, such as Kentucky Blue Grass and Fescue, should be left taller, cut at a height of 1½ to 2 inches.

UPPER AND CENTRAL SOUTH:
The vegetable garden planting list includes: bush and pole Snap Beans,

bush and pole Lima Beans, Cantaloupe, Chard, Citron, Corn, Crowder Peas, Cucumbers, Eggplant (plants), Gherkins, Herbs, Mustard, Okra, Pepper (plants), Pumpkin, Radish, Tomato (plants), and Watermelon.

Hurry with those late plantings of Gladiolus, Cannas, Caladium, Dahlias and Tuberoses—this is the last call. Existing plantings of these flowers require abundant water for best results. Soak soil thoroughly when water is needed.

Both tender and hardy Water-lilies can be planted in the garden pool. Rule of thumb: plant one Lily for every 10 square feet of area in small pools, or one Lily for every 16 square feet in large pool.

Tulips are increasing greatly in popularity throughout the South since deep planting has been used with the accompanying success of this method in flower production. Plan a Tulip bed for your garden and order bulbs for fall planting this year.

The old flower heads of Butterfly bush, Crape myrtle, Azaleas and Lilacs should be removed to encourage formation of new growth and new flower buds.

CENTRAL AND LOWER SOUTH:
Azaleas and Camellias receive their second and last feeding for the year.

Carpet Grass and St. Augustine Grass need abundant moisture at all times. Bermuda, Zoysia and Centipede Grass will tolerate dry soil without serious damage.

The best protection against weeds in the lawn is a vigorous turf produced by good lawn management of heavy fertilization, thorough watering and regular even mowing.

Dallis Grass (Paspalum)—lawn weed extraordinary—can be eradicated by a 10-day shading of infested area, using black building paper. This treatment will not hurt Bermuda Grass.

The foliage of spring-flowering bulbs can usually be removed as the new bulbs have been formed and the leaves have completed their work.

Dutch, English and Spanish Iris plantings can remain undisturbed for 4 to 5 years if growing in fertile well-drained locations. These bulbs should be dug, divided and replanted every 4 to 5 years.

Pinch out growing tips of Poinsettia stems if these plants have grown too tall for location in the past years. Tips of stems can be rooted in clean sand to produce additional plants.

North

Weeds in the cotyledon stage look quite innocent; but that is the time to get them. The moment your back is turned they'll be growing like Jack's Bean stalk. You can kill more of them, while they are in the baby stage, with a rake or a scuffle hoe in five minutes than you can in five hours with a hoe later on. Mulch everything you can to keep weeds down. Where you can't mulch, keep the ground stirred to prevent their getting a start.

With the advent of a few really hot days you'll find the insect pests making a sudden appearance. Check now to see that your supply of dusts and sprays is adequate and the sprayer or duster in good working order.

As soon as the foliage on spring bulbs turns yellow and falls, you can cut it off at ground level—*but not before*. Cutting too soon results in injury to the new bulbs forming underground, and that in turn will mean fewer and poorer flowers next spring.

If you plan to add to your collection of garden Roses, this is the month to check up on new varieties. Best way to do this is to visit a nearby nursery or a public Rose garden, and see for yourself which ones appeal most to you.

With most of the planting done, the garden jobs to concentrate on now are weeding, feeding and watering. No matter how often the advice is repeated, most beginners will not learn, except through bitter experience, that one hundred *small* weeds can be destroyed in half the time it takes to get rid of one that has grown up.

A supplementary feeding will benefit most half-grown plants. Give them lunch now, as well as breakfast at planting time. One to two pounds of a complete plant food per 100 square feet of bed area will be sufficient.

Plants can't grow normally without adequate soil moisture. This is especially true during their early stages of development, whether from seeds or from roots remaining permanently in the ground. Begin watering before the soil dries out to any considerable depth. Conserve moisture by mulching early.

Pinch back garden Chrysanthemums to encourage development of side shoots. This will give compact, self-supporting plants and more flower sprays.

In the vegetable garden sow now seeds of Cabbage, Broccoli and Brussels Sprouts to supply strong transplants to set out in mid-July for fall crops.

When cultivating soil in which young annual seedlings have been set, place a small inverted pot over each plant in the area. This permits fast, safe work.

Older Geranium plants are pruned back 5 or 6 ins. and repotted if there will be room for them in next year's window garden. Otherwise they are discarded.

White callas are gradually dried off and given a 3-month rest.

Watering of pot plants outdoors is a regular chore since restricted root systems cannot forage for moisture, and rainfall is inadequate while evaporation is high.

Dahlias may be planted up until about mid-June.

Feed liquid manure to Amaryllis bulbs to encourage next year's flower buds. Bee-like flies hovering around the plants may spell destructive larvae, so net them.

Still time to sow Delphinium seeds in a coldframe or other sheltered bed. Transplant to another bed in September. Some may even bloom a little before frost.

Arabis, Iberis, Alyssum, dwarf Phlox and many other low growers benefit by shearing after they've bloomed. And the young growths you remove make grand cuttings for rooting in a closed, shaded frame.

When cutting Peonies, always leave at least two-thirds of the foliage which the plant normally carries. This is necessary to continued well-being.

Tie tall plants (like Delphiniums and Lilies) to their supports *as they grow*. Once they flop over or break it is difficult to get them straight again.

Light surface cultivating is just as important a weed control measure in the flower garden as it is among the vegetables.

Columbine borers generally start in the upper growth and work toward the roots. Wilted branches signal their presence.

Irises can be divided and replanted as soon as they have fully finished flowering. New below-ground growth begins at that time.

Finish up the perennial seed sowing early in the month, if any remains to be done. The young plants should have time to gain considerable size before cold weather.

The yellow or broad mites which cause delphinium blacks and dried-up English primrose leaves are persistent June pests. Counterattack with sulphur dust, preferably combined with nicotine or rotenone.

Watch for evidence of 4-lined leaf bugs as shown by yellowish dots on various perennial leaves. Catch 'em young (they're red, then) and treat 'em rough with any good contact spray.

Keep up the spray or dust program to ward off mildew and black spot.

Rose flowers should be cut with some discretion. Cut the stems no longer than will be used. Removing too much growth weakens the plant.

Remove flower heads from Lilacs and Rhododendrons for tidiness and to conserve the plants' energies.

Early June is positively the last call for pruning spring-flowering shrubs, if you want to avoid sacrificing next year's bloom.

All trees and shrubs planted during the past 12 months should be watered generously in dry weather. Also, check guy wires to make sure their loops are big enough to leave ample room for the wood to grow.

Wilted main shoot tips on Pines indicate borers. Cut off below lowest point reached by the pest in his downward progress through the center of the shoot.

The soft, short new growths that start from around the flowering tips of hardy Azaleas will root readily in a sand-peatmoss mixture.

Sheared deciduous hedges should be trimmed before the new growth hardens sufficiently to make it difficult to cut.

JULY

West Coast

GENERAL:

Watering is the great July chore; but sparingly with Daphnes as this is their needed rest period. Fuchsias and ferns need much. Young seedlings must not dry out and need considerable shading—screens, lath, muslin, or cheesecloth.

July is a good time for layering Carnations, also for cuttings of many woody plants. Use half-ripened Ceanothus wood; but non-flowering side shoots of Cistus, and keep these close under shaded glass.

If buds show on Chrysanthemums, feed with commercial fertilizer; likewise Tuberous Begonias after a first teaspoon of cottonseed meal per plant. Fertilize Camellias early in July, and Fuchsias late. Continue to feed Roses.

Prune Brooms as soon as they finish flowering, also any late Jasmine.

Sow garden-saved Delphinium seed at once.

Sow Beans, French Endive, Corn throughout; Beets and Carrots the length of the Coast and such valleys as the Santa Clara; Lettuce, Turnips, and Rutabagas in the mountains. Plant Potatoes everywhere except mountains and Sacramento Valley. Set out Celery only in cooler districts.

Garden work in July is important: pest control, maintenance, watering, starting seeds and plants for fall and winter bloom, sowing perennials (including alpines) for next year. Despite all this, chores do lessen enough to let us enjoy our own gardens, visit others, and on vacation trips call in at some of the fine big public plantings up and down the Coast.

Keep weeds out; cut spent flowers promptly; continue to bait for slugs and earwigs, and to use a good all-purpose spray regularly over the entire garden. With the exception of a few plants like Fuchsias and Celery that ask for a frequent, fine mist on their foliage, soak the ground deeply once or twice a week. Lay hose without a nozzle on a shingle to prevent the soil from washing out. Lawns can take sprinklers: but soak the soil.

Apply sufficient fertilizer to keep plants in robust growth. Give Fuchsias special feedings in late July; also Camellias if not fed in June. Roses and Chrysanthemums are hungry plants. Fertilizers in liquid form are good mid-summer pickups in borders.

Autumn Crocus may be planted late in July.

NORTHWEST:
Rock gardens need attention. Slugs are particularly fond of Campanulas, Gentians and Violas. An interplanting of *Sedum brevifolium* will usually attract their attention first, where they are easily seen. The Sedum can hold its own.

Keep dead flower heads sheared, especially on Heaths, Thymes, Dianthus, *Hypericum coris,* and the small rock garden Brooms. And water the ground, not the plant tops! Primroses, especially the Candelabra and Florindae bog groups, will self-sow and flourish right in a soil-bottomed pool or small rill when growing along the edges.

Rhubarb and Asparagus are best not cut after the first week in July. Sow Saint Valentine Broccoli and Savoy Cabbage, the former for eating in February and March, the latter for winter. Make another sowing of Bush Beans. Lettuce is crisper when cut early, with the dew still on it.

Watering is the most imperative July chore in this region, regular use of insecticides a close second. Combat lace-bug nymphs on Azaleas and Rhododendrons with summer oil spray. Use rotenone on vegetables too near maturity for deadlier treatment; poison bait for earwigs, slugs, and weevils.

Keep borders weeded and spent flowers cut, burning faded Iris blooms, a favorite housing for earwigs. Spread compost if possible, or peat, especially over Lilies. Cut back new Wisteria growth to three eyes.

Set out seedlings started last month before they crowd in flats. Perennials for next year may still be sown if all were not managed in June, also alpines.

Sow Chinese and Savoy Cabbage, Kale, Lettuce, and St. Valentine Broccoli besides those mentioned under general. Set out Celery, Broccoli, and Cabbage plants. Do not cut Asparagus or pull Rhubarb after the first week in July. Tomatoes are helped with 1 ounce per plant of sodium nitrate watered in when the first fruits set. Continue regular balanced fertilizer. Do not feed Blueberries after harvesting. Cut out and burn old Currant canes after picking.

Plant Autumn Crocus, Cyclamen, and Christmas-rose. Mountain Avens (*Dryas octopetala*) makes a pleasing ground cover in a sunny open place, forming a low shrubby mat of semi-evergreen Oak-like leaves, overlaid with yellow-stamened white blooms in summer, and later, silvery seed heads. Propagate from cuttings of mature wood now. Seeds are possible, though slower.

CALIFORNIA:

Here, too, water is all-important. Use care to get enough on lawns, particularly Bent. Cut this short in the fog belt, longer to protect roots from drying winds elsewhere. Catch Bent cuttings—they are fine on compost piles, but not for use while green. Dichondra is killed by 2–4–D and similar weed controls: slugs devour it; hand-pick and bait.

Water Citrus trees deeply every two or three weeks, and feed—superphosphate, commercial fertilizer, blood meal, or Chilean nitrate according to soil. Like Rhododendrons, mulch instead of hoeing, as feeder roots are near the surface. Spray Oranges and Lemons before flowers open wide, or after fruits are Cherry size. Watch for and trap gophers.

Keep Cinerarias well shaded, spraying twice daily with water if they droop. Tuberous and Fibrous Begonias, Cyclamen, ferns, Fuchsias prosper in lath houses; while Camellias, Hydrangeas, and Azaleas need this cooler going if back from ocean moisture.

Cut back Artichokes that have ceased bearing. Mulch with manure and compost. Set Broccoli in the Sacramento Valley; Tomatoes from the Bay area south except in the Imperial Valley.

Set out, or divide after four years, the winter-blooming *Iris unguicularis* in sandy soil in the sun. A little bone meal and water at planting, but more prolific bloom comes with poor fare.

– FOG BELT:

Fogs make good sowing weather; but also force much care to keep pests under control. Slugs, caterpillars and earwigs are deadly among seedlings and young plants, especially at night.

Seed sown now of Early Cosmos, Mimulus, Nasturtium, Calendula, Nemesia, annual Phlox and Candytuft will bloom in the fall. Usually sown in flats are the perennials and biennials for next spring's color; but also satisfactory is a prepared seedbed in an out-of-the-way corner. Use wire mesh screens to shade the young seedlings and keep off pests. Set poison containers nearby to control ants. Pansies, Cup-and-saucer Campanulas, Gerveria, Snapdragons, Pyrethrum, Salpiglossis, Delphinium, Calceolaria and Penstemon are among those to start.

The fog belt dovetails warm valleys such as Santa Clara so closely, gardeners must draw their own distinction. Even the Berkeley hills alter climate in just the Bay area. Valley winds are hot and drying; in San Francisco and similar regions, cool and humid. Valley gardeners have a hectic watering problem; fog-land ones, merely a reasonable one.

July is the month to sow biennials and perennials for next year; hardy annuals for wintering over, after the 15th.

Topdress lawns. Feed with well-watered-in ammonium sulfate at ten-day intervals to crowd out weeds by strong grass growth.

Pinch back Chrysanthemums, or disbud those needing it. Cut Shasta Daisies back within 2 inches of the base after flowering, for another later crop. Watch Transvaal Daisies for crown rot—water ground deeply, keeping it off tops. July is the best time to bud Roses.

SOUTHERN CALIFORNIA:

Water, cultivate, spray, mulch, and feed. Southwest gardeners must consider alkalinity when choosing plant food. Avoid any sodium content such as sodium nitrate. Use ammonium phosphate or ammonium sulfate for a quick pep-up; and a balanced commercial fertilizer and blood or cottonseed meals for more lasting effects. Sulphur aids slow release of acids into the soil. Pile the peat or leafmold mulches deep around Fuchsias, Camellias, Rhododendrons, and Azaleas.

Sow Calceolaria, Verbena, Cineraria, Stock, Pansies, Violas, and Snapdragons in flats; Winter Sweet Peas in the usual trench; broadcast Salpiglossis and Cornflower. Also for open ground are Nasturtium, Calendula, Marigold, Early Cosmos, and annual Phlox.

Cut down Asparagus foliage when it dries. Use early Bean varieties when sowing. Practically any desired vegetable is a good bet for sowing along the South Coast. Try budding a poor bearing Avocado with buds from a more prolific tree. Those bothered by light frosts might investigate the Zutano variety.

Deep watering is imperative, and also good feeding to keep up with fast growth. Heavy mulches are well worth the labor of pushing them back for watering, if necessary, as they hold moisture and keep down weeds. Or a canvas hose can be easily inserted under them. Thoroughly rotted manure, when procurable, feeds as well as mulches. Any potted or tubbed plants will need even closer watching. Remember the hungry, thirsty vegetables. Peach and Nectarine fruit split is due to insufficient water in the ground. Soak lawns well in the morning where possible.

Ants are a particular nuisance in this region. Their control lessens the spread of aphids, mealybugs and scale. Wash ants out of Globe Artichokes with a strong force from the hose. Use care about ant poison containers near vegetables.

South

GENERAL:

Dig, divide and reset spring-flowering bulbs. Soak soil thoroughly a day or two before digging. Have new beds, where bulbs are to be reset, well fertilized and prepared. Narcissus, Hyacinths, and Tulips should be dug and divided every three to four years.

Control grubworms by using 5 to 10% chlordane dust placed in upper 3 inches of soil near plants.

Roses will continue to flower all summer if properly watered, cultivated and sprayed for disease control.

Gladiolus thrips is a small but very injurious insect. It is only $^1/_{25}$ inch long. Heavy infestations will completely ruin a flower crop. Symptom: whitish streaks on flower petals. Control: dusting foliage regularly with 5% DDT.

Order Pansy and English Daisy seed now if you wish to grow your own plants.

It is extremely important to apply ½ to 1 inch of water at each watering for flowers, shrubs or vegetables. If you are in doubt as to the amount your sprinkler applies per hour, place a pan with vertical sides in area being watered. When water in pan is 1 inch deep, move sprinkler.

Do not apply fertilizer to flower beds, shrub beds or lawn grass when soil is dry because severe burning will usually result. Soak soil thoroughly before any fertilizer applications are made.

Fall garden site for flowers or vegetables should be prepared three weeks before seeds are sown, if possible.

Throughout the South cuttings of Azaleas, 4 to 6 inches in length, placed in a mixture of ½ sand and ½ peatmoss, watered thoroughly, surrounded by humid atmosphere and partially shaded, will root in six to eight weeks.

Azaleas will thrive under such deep-rooted trees as Pine and Oak, but will wither and die under Elm and Maple because the roots of these trees are near the surface of the ground.

Azaleas are sun-loving plants in their native habitat, but eastern and northern exposures around the house provide more satisfactory growing conditions for Azaleas than southern or western exposures. Blistered withering leaves on Azaleas tell a graphic story. Study your shrub plantings so that needed changes can be made this fall and winter.

The second and last application of fertilizer for this season should be applied to Azalea plantings through the South. An excellent mixture to use is one made of 2 pounds of cottonseed meal and 1 pound of ammonium sulphate, used at the rate of 1 to 2 pounds per 100 square feet. Water the soil generously immediately after the fertilizer is applied.

Azaleas must have abundant moisture in the soil at all times, especially now while forming the flower buds for next season's flowers. Use a soil mulch of pine straw, peat, leafmold and water as often as needed. Garden plants—both vegetable and flower—need one inch of rain every week or ten days. If you use a sprinkler to water your garden and do not know how long it takes that sprinkler to deliver a one-inch rain, place a straight-sided pan in the area being watered and record the length of time it takes the sprinkler to put one inch of water in the pan. Never water an area less than this determined length of time.

Lawn grasses can be literally cut to death during the hot dry periods of summer. The blade of the mower should be raised to cut at a height of at least 1½ to 2 inches.

Spring-flowering bulbs can be dug, divided and replanted if they need to be separated. Dig and replant the same day, if possible. Do not let them dry out.

Deep-planted Tulips—those set 10 to 12 inches deep—can be left undisturbed after first season's flowering. They will usually produce good flowers the second year, although they may be somewhat smaller than the first season's bloom. After the second season's bloom Tulips should be dug, separated, stored and replanted in the fall.

A few new plants of your favorite shrub can be propagated by layerage. Simply notch the bark of lower branches, leaving attached to the plant. Then bury the notched portion in a shallow trench, holding limb with brick or stone. Water during dry periods. After roots form, cut limb from parent plant and set new plant where it is to grow.

The leaves of African violets will scorch if exposed to direct sunlight in the South from mid-morning to mid-afternoon. Partially shaded east or north windows will provide excellent light conditions for this great pot plant favorite.

LOWER SOUTH:
Lawns can still be planted, using Bermuda or Carpet Grass seed, or St. Augustine, Zoysia or Centipede Grass cuttings.

Gardeners in Florida and along the Gulf Coast should keep Poinsettias disbudded (or growing tips pinched back) until next month. This keeps the plants from growing too tall and gives more blossoms.

Plant Gladiolus now, knowing you can expect excellent results if water can be applied as needed. Throughout the South the flowers of Gladiolus can be protected from extreme heat by frequent sprinkling.

Gardens in this region are often most colorful in late fall and early winter when planned and planted in the summer months. Sow these seed: Sweet Alyssum, Cosmos, Marigold, Periwinkle, Petunia, Portulaca, and Zinnias. Sow where the plants are to grow as they resent transplanting in hot weather.

In the vegetable garden, plant Parsley, Pumpkin, Squash and Tomatoes, Cauliflower, Celery, Eggplant, Pepper and Broccoli.

Bulbs to plant now include *Nerine sarniensis* and *Lycoris aurea.*

Apply commercial oil emulsion spray, summer strength, to Citrus plantings to control scale.

Another very colorful and unusual ornamental is Golden Dewdrop

(*Duranta repens*) which has blue flowers and yellow fruit, and is grown from seed or cuttings.

CENTRAL AND UPPER SOUTH:

There's still time to plant the seed of Zinnias, Marigolds, Portulaca and Petunias in the flower garden and Lima Beans, Field Peas, Rutabagas and Tomato plants in the vegetable garden.

Order these perennial seed for sowing next month: Anchusa, Aquilegia, Candytuft, Canterbury Bells, Coreopsis, Clove Pinks, Foxglove, Gaillardia, Gypsophila, Hollyhock, Lupine, Platycodon, Blue Salvia, and Sweet William.

It is not too late to pinch out the tip buds of Chrysanthemums. This will keep the plants from getting tall and leggy and make them produce many more flowers. If large specimen flowers are desired, do not pinch, but disbud later.

Madonna Lily bulbs are dormant and ready for planting or division and replanting. Top of bulbs should not be more than 2 inches below surface of ground.

The Japanese Magnolia (*Magnolia Soulangeana*) has been an especially fine early-flowering ornamental tree this past spring. If more plants are desired from one you have, they can be produced by layerage done now. Notch lower branches, bend and pin to ground, cover with soil. Detach from mother plant when rooted.

Fall is the time to set plants in the perennial border. Sow these seeds: Anthemis, Cerastium, Echinops, Gerberia, Geum, Heliopsis, Linum, Lychnis, Penstemon, Physalis, Platycodon, Pyrethrum, Silene, Stokesia, Veronica.

CENTRAL AND LOWER SOUTH:

Fall flower gardens produce most vivid colors of the year. Fill the empty spaces in border by sowing seed of Balsam, Celosia, Calliopsis, Four-o'clocks, Marigold, Portulaca, Tithonia, Torenia and Zinnia.

Withhold water from Hollyhocks after they flower since excess moisture often damages roots.

When watering Roses, keep water off foliage as much as possible to prevent spread of disease. Canvas hose that permits slow soaking of soil, without wetting foliage, is highly recommended.

Zinnias are very susceptible to mildew, so water as for Roses.

Remove old flower heads from Crape myrtle plants as soon as blossoms fade because seed pod development takes great amount of nutrients from the plants.

Plant these vegetables: Pole Snap Beans, Bush and Pole Lima Beans, Carrots, Crowder and Field Peas, Rutabagas and plants of Tomatoes and Sweet Potatoes.

Texas' state flower—the Bluebonnet—grows beautifully in this area. Sow seed in good seed bed, covering seed lightly.

North

This is the month to mulch—flower beds, shrubs and trees, Roses and the vegetable plot. Even such heat lovers as Corn can benefit. Use any material that won't mat down into tight layer; coarse, half decomposed material from the compost heap is fine.

Later on this month you can expect the foliage of Oriental Poppies to start dying down, a good sign that it's time for transplanting. New leaves will form by the end of August and September.

If you cut off the upper portions of Delphinium flower stalks when the bloom has gone by, you will better the prospects of a second blossom display in September.

Don't neglect climbing Roses after the June burst of bloom. Unlike rambler types, these should *not* have the old growth cut back to the ground. Some of the oldest wood should be cut out to make room for vigorous new shoots. Framework canes can be left for years.

Toughest season for the lawn lies ahead. Help it with a top dressing, preferably of both compost and fertilizer. Use a spike-toothed tamper roller if turf is tight. Then water thoroughly.

This is the month when three of garden's worst enemies combine to work havoc with flowers and vegetables. They are bugs, drought and weeds. The one big secret in controlling pests is to *spot them early*. A few minutes spent daily on an inspection trip will work wonders in keeping your garden clean. Applying mulches wherever you can will aid greatly in the battle against drought and weeds.

Do you want big Dahlias—the kind that win blue ribbons at shows? If so, you must not only feed them well, but keep pinching out side shoots and secondary buds.

If you like flowers indoors in winter, sow seeds or make cuttings now. Among the former are many of the low-growing annuals, such as Ageratum, Sweet Alyssum, English Daisies, Dwarf Marigolds, Cupid Zinnias, Begonias and Calendulas. Make cuttings of Geraniums, Lantana, Periwinkle and Heliotrope.

When Lilies are through blooming remove the tops of stalks, to prevent formation of seed, unless it is wanted for planting. The few species and varieties that form bulblets along the stem can readily be propagated by planting these in a bed a few inches deep.

If all the Daffodil leaves have not yellowed, indicating that ripening of the bulbs is complete and that the foliage can be cut off, comparative neatness can be gained merely by bending them over at the ground line and letting them lie flat on the surface.

Lily staking should begin while the plants are still less than 18 ins. tall. This is especially important in windy locations.

Do *not* prune newly planted Apple, Plum, Cherry or Peach trees. They need all their available leaf surface.

Currants to be used for jelly are best picked when slightly underripe, fully ripe if used for jams.

If leaf spot is present on Cherry trees, spray after picking the fruit with

2 qts. lime sulphur in 24 gals. water. . . . If overloaded Peaches have not yet been thinned, remove surplus for large, healthier fruit.

If Primrose, Hollyhock and Phlox show signs of yellowing and drying up, red spiders may be at work. Syringe frequently and spray with rotenone. If it is damp, Aconitum and Delphinium need sulphur treatment for mildew.

You can still plant Gladiolus corms up until mid-July. This is a little late, but it is possible to get by with it in sections which do not have early frosts.

Cut out old Delphinium stems. They will bloom again in the fall on new growth from the crown.

Snipping off all flower heads before they form and mature seeds will help a lot in keeping volunteer seedlings from messing up your careful color schemes.

Give weekly applications of liquid manure to Roses. . . . Keep up the spraying or dusting program for disease control, but *don't* dust or spray when temperature is above 100. . . . It may not be necessary to fight disease so constantly during dry weather, but plants should be protected during every rainy period.

Take cuttings from flowering shoots of Climbers and bedding Roses. They should be about 4 in. long with the basal cut made just below a node. Remove the lower leaves. Root under shaded glass jars in sharp clean sand. Keep constantly moist.

Shear hedges of Yew, Hemlock, Arborvitae and Cypress now.

Syringe newly planted evergreens in the evening during hot, dry weather. They can absorb a great deal of water through their leaves in this manner. Spraying should be done only during the evening, giving the plant plenty of time during the night to absorb the moisture.

You will have more Rhododendron flowers next year if you remove dead flower clusters before the seed forms. Buds for next year are formed at this time, and you will want the plant's energy to go into bud rather than seed formation. . . . If Rhododendron leaves droop and curl inward, they want water. . . . Mulch broad-leaved evergreens heavily with peatmoss or dead oak leaves. Water thoroughly.

A material that permits fairly free passage to rainfall, such as coarse, dead tree leaves, loose straw or excelsior, is excellent hot-weather mulch for trees and shrubs. Peatmoss must not be permitted to dry out, as it then practically prevents rainwater from reaching the soil.

Soak all trees and shrubs that were planted this year. Abundant water is essential throughout their first summer.

Noticeable signs of leaf injury by caterpillars should not be neglected. Sulphur dust will help control mildew on Lilac and some Rose leaves.

AUGUST

West Coast

GENERAL:

The usual pest control programs continue, with use of multi-purpose sprays, fungicides, poison bait and summer oil applied to trees and shrubs prone to black scale.

Budding, layering, and cuttings of half-ripened wood are important in August. Difficult large-leaved Rhododendrons strike more easily now. Stand the pot of sand in water to slip cuttings in without damage and to make close soil contact.

Use care in pruning, know correct times and whether to cut out all old flowering wood, or merely to shape it. All Ceanothus need summer checking to prevent legginess. Prune Daisy bush (*Olearia Haasti*) immediately after flowering. Do *not* prune Rhododendrons. Prune conifers while active; but except for Chinese Fir (Cunninghamia) and Yews, leave some needles on all cut branches unless you want to eliminate entirely. When imperative, remove complete large limbs in August.

Dahlias respond to potash and phosphorus, but work it in 6 inches out from the stem. Plant Iris and Madonna Lilies.

Intelligent watering and continued use of an all-purpose spray are the big chores, with correct plant feeding, starting of cuttings, care of seedlings not far behind. California is looking forward to its warmest weather, while the North Pacific is already cooling.

Continue slug and earwig baits and watch for moles, gophers, and field mice. Apply summer oil spray to trees and shrubs prone to black scale, and hose conifers often for red spider.

Sow Beans every two weeks, but only Bush types in the North Pacific, Limas only in Southern California coastal regions; Lettuce everywhere except southern interiors. Set Broccoli plants except extreme south coast and interior.

NORTH PACIFIC:
Begin withholding water from shrubs and trees by mid-August, even earlier for hardiness borderliners like Laurestinus, shrubby Veronicas, Grecian (Bay) Laurel, and Ceanothus.

Pacific Hybrid Delphiniums and Russel Lupines will continue to bloom if flowering stalks are cut back. Cut leggy Pansies back to crown leaves and feed, water, and mulch well for fall bloom. Cut stalks of Romneya back to the ground leaves before they seed to conserve plant strength though it will not bloom here again this year.

Set out Savoy Cabbage for fall, and sow Copenhagen Market for spring, also Parsley. Cut back a Basil plant or so for a second crop through fall. Sow succession Spinach every two weeks.

Prune dead blooms from Heaths promptly. The twisted Heath needs heavy cutting as it is best kept under 18 inches. Topdress with sand and peat or leafmold. Continue to shape Wisteria. Prune summer-flowering shrubs as bloom ceases. Give Holly hedges their second semi-annual pruning. Prune deciduous trees to preserve open form. Cuts on Walnuts, Birches, and Cherries heal better this month, though they resent interference with large limbs at all times.

Fertilize Roses for the last time in late August; also Camellias, Rhododendrons, and Azaleas.

Watch for diseased leaves on Hollyhocks and Phlox, burning at once, spraying plants with a copper fungicide. Look for thrips on Iris, Delphinium, and Hollyhocks.

Divide and replant Iris, order new. Plant Autumn Crocus, Winteraconite: and in late August, Roman Hyacinths and China Lilies may be started. Our native broad-leaved evergreens move best at this time.

Start cuttings of Fuchsia, and Pelargoniums or Geraniums if they can have indoor winter growth. Even hardy shrub cuttings are best carried in a frame their first winter. Use rather soft growth for hybrid Brooms.

Cut out rogue berries and old canes. In mid-August snap off unfruited Grape side branches exactly where they join the main vine. Cut away side leaves of Brussels Sprouts. Keep Tomatoes staked. Slip a shingle under any Squash or Cucumbers resting on the ground. Sow Parsley for next spring, Onions, and Copenhagen Market Cabbage. Sow Spinach every two weeks, remembering that it and Lettuce need a limed soil. Sow Beets, Endive, and one more planting each of Bush Beans and Carrots. Set out Savoy Cabbage and Broccoli.

CALIFORNIA:

Lightly prune all Rose stems, that have bloomed, to within two or three buds of the main branch. Give deep watering, multi-purpose spray, and generous balanced fertilizer to obtain continuous fall Roses, possible through most of California.

Increase depth of mulches around Azaleas, Rhododendrons, Camellias, and Daphnes, but do not overwater the last, as it needs a resting period.

Give Fuchsias a fine mist spray on foliage wherever fogs do not supply it. August cuttings root best; also Ceanothus in variety native to different types of California climate.

Mexican Tulip-poppy (Hunnemannia) is native, and a fine bushy border plant 2 feet high. Sow where to grow this month, or transplant when only a few inches high. Sow Cape-marigold (Dimorphotheca) for winter bloom; also Stocks and Snapdragons in mild sections but do not allow seeds to dry out—cover with wet burlap until they germinate unless you garden in heavy fog areas. Then use screens with laths spaced ½-inch apart, or in less bright regions, cheesecloth. Once a seed is moistened, it must not dry out.

Keep the garden cleaned and pest free. Heavy watering continues, with the hottest part of the summer ahead in most regions. Many seeds are sown to take advantage of warm soils and less cold nights; but except in foggiest parts these will need much shading. Hot drying winds, especially in interior valleys, must be blocked off. Garage, shade house, lath, screens, or shaded loggia are usable. Until seeds germinate, keep them covered with wet burlap in all warmer parts. Planting is heavy for fall, winter, and spring gardens. Wallflowers do well in the valleys, and Iceland Poppies continue blooming even with winter-frosted stems. Begin sowing Sweet Peas in late August. Sow Dimorphotheca, Pansies, Stocks, and Snapdragons for winter and early spring bloom. Gerberia, Calceolaria, Cineraria, Mexican Tulip-poppy, Penstemon, Horned Poppy, Agathea, and Calendulas are others to remember.

Take cuttings from new growth of Petunias, and carry on as for Geraniums, which in all their forms, including Pelargoniums, are well taken this month. The last, even when mature, are not frost hardy, and need somewhat sheltered placing. Let Pelargonium cuttings form a callus before inserting. Make Fuchsia cuttings, also Ceanothus.

Prune out weak Rose growth. Cut back stems through flowering to two buds from the main stem. Feed and water well for good later bloom.

Prune Fremontia to keep the center open; Abelia, Pyracantha, Japanese Quinces lightly; deciduous trees before they shed.

Stop cutting back Chrysanthemums, increase water. Feed Azaleas, Camellias, Rhododendrons.

Sow Lettuce and Chard everywhere except interior southern valleys; Bush Beans everywhere; Cabbages, Carrots, and Beets along the coast and northern valleys.

FOG BELT:

Finish July seed sowing. Set out all seedlings as soon as they leaf. Gerberia, Penstemon, Godetias, and Pansies brighten borders, but almost anything may be sown at this time. Do not sow Tomatoes and similar slower growers that need warm weather.

Globe Artichokes bear here from November to June. Cut old parts back about 4 inches below the surface; then begin feeding heavily about ten days or so later to make strong new growth. Water and keep free of ants.

For under-tree planting use Hosta, Lobelia, Freesia, Primroses, Cineraria, Begonias, and Ferns. Ivy Geraniums are a good holding cover for sloping banks. Prune the Lady Washington Pelargoniums, cutting out old browning wood to encourage new for next year's flowers.

Plant steep banks in August. Ivy Geraniums are among ground covers, and this is the best month to make cuttings. Use them also in boxes and hanging baskets.

Practically all types of seeds may be sown, even Amaryllis, Agapanthus, Iris, Galtonia, and others by those who like to experiment. Window, porch, and roof boxes need fresh supplies to replace tired plants. *Francoa ramosa* groups well with Fuchsias in moist shade. Among biennials that can be sown at this time are Evening-primroses, *Echium wildpreti, Glaucium flavum;* and among annuals, Viola, Cornflower, Clarkia, Godetia, Candytuft, and Larkspur.

Besides other bulbs mentioned, Ixia, Cyclamen, Tritonia, and Moraea may be planted.

Prune Lady Washington Pelargoniums, removing browned and hardened wood. Make cuttings from firm green side shoots, removing stipules and lower leaves. Also, this is a good time to take cuttings of Marguerites, and generally speaking, of anything with half-ripened wood.

Besides vegetables mentioned elsewhere, set out Broccoli and Cabbages. Parsley, Mint, Sweet Marjoram, and Winter Savory are handy herbs. Water berries heavily, cut all canes that have finished bearing to the ground, and spray new canes with summer oil.

When continuing pest schedules, watch particularly for diabrotica.

SOUTHERN CALIFORNIA:
Watering is the big chore, check into the ground often, and dig small irrigation trenches if water is not getting down. Deepen all mulches, especially back from the Coast. Give Globe Artichokes, Fuchsias, Gardenias, and similar plants frequent mist watering from overhead.

Have some movable screens of burlap, muslin, palm fronds, etc., for shading handy to set up quickly where young plants, or those less heat resistant are getting an overdose of hot sun or drying wind. These are useful on the Coast and imperative in the Interior Valleys.

Get the ground ready and keep it moist for fall seedlings and bedding-out plants. August is a difficult month for seed sowing; but with facilities and time to keep them cool, moist, and shaded, they get a long season of growth to become well established before November's cold nights arrive.

This is the last month to set out Tomatoes for open harvest. Plant Calla, Anemone, Freesia, Nerine, and Ranunculus, among others. Take cuttings of any Penstemon you particularly like.

In general, no let-up in watering with the hottest season just ahead, and resting periods for most plants not due for some months. Desert Cacti and most succulents are the exception. Shrubs and trees need deep watering: young seedlings require constant watching.

Gardens that get Colorado River water may need an extra treatment for excess alkalinity brought on by heavy summer watering. Use gypsum or calcium sulphate (1 pound to 100 square feet at this time) if your city treats the water supply to soften it; use soil sulphur for untreated water.

Plant bulbs of Anemone, Calla, Oxalis, Ornithogalum, Ranunculus, and Nerine.

All vegetables may still be quite generally sown with the exception of Melons and Tomatoes, though plants of the last may be set. Endive will do better than Lettuce. Lima Beans should be sown the first week, and only along the coastal strip. Give Artichokes an overhead watering; they miss summer fogs in southern California. Citrus trees may be planted.

South

GENERAL:

Ideas for electrifying the garden: use 200- to 300-watt spot or floodlight on garden features; mercury-vapor floodlight to highlight green colors; border light near ground and shaded from eye using 10- or 15-watt bulbs; under-water lighting in pools using waterproof sockets.

Wood used by gardeners for stakes, poles, fences and frames should be treated before using to prolong life of this material. Use copper napthenate as a preservative.

Do you know the purpose of a pre-emergence herbicide? It kills germinating weed seed. There is one now that has possibilities for the home gardener, recommended for cautious use in controlling weeds in Strawberry and Asparagus beds. It is called Crag Herbicide-1 or SES. It can also be used to control weeds around well-established perennials and shrubs.

Spare the pruning shears and spoil the shrub planting. Use orchard- or hand-pruning shears and keep shrubs under control by regular formative pruning as the shrubs grow.

Gladiolus corms can be dug as soon as the tops turn brown. Dry these corms and store in trays in cool, well-ventilated place.

LOWER SOUTH:

Seed to sow in the flower garden: Balsam, Celosia, Cosmos (late), Marigold, Mignonette, Morning Glory, Portulaca, Texas Blue Bonnet, Tithonia, Torenia and Zinnia.

Rhizomes, tubers and bulbs to plant in the flowering borders: *Ama-*

ryllis belladonna, Colchicum, Cooperia, Day lily, Hosta, Iris, Liriope, Lycoris, Sparaxis, Sprekelia, Sternbergia, and Zephyranthes.

Plants for transplanting to flower beds include these varieties: Acalypha, Ageratum, Alternanthera, Anchusa, Balsam, Begonia, Celosia, Coleus, Cosmos, Croton, Geranium, Lantana, Marigold, Petunia, Phlox, Sweet Sultan, Tithonia, Verbena, Vinca and Zinnia.

Vegetable seeds to sow in garden: Bush Snap Beans, Broccoli, Brussels Sprouts, Cabbage, Cauliflower, Carrots, Collards, Kale, Radish, Squash, Swiss Chard, Tendergreens, Tomato and Turnip.

Sow Calendula and Stock seed for winter flowering. These seeds should be sown in seed boxes, transplanted to flats and then to the beds where they are to flower.

Poinsettia plants can still be cut back, if they are too tall. The Poinsettia flowers will be produced upon the side branches that will be formed.

Remove old flower heads and seed pods from Crape myrtle to prolong the flowering season of this great favorite.

Water St. Augustine Grass lawns regularly and thoroughly. Apply 2 to 4 pounds of complete commercial fertilizer per 100 square feet of lawn area every 6 to 8 weeks to maintain a rich green turf.

Prune leggy Hibiscus plants heavily to force new growth to develop low on the plant and to stimulate flower production.

Cuttings of Azaleas, Camellias and other flowering shrubs are usually successfully rooted when wood is mature but not yet hard. Make tip cuttings, place in clean moist sand, shade and keep watered. Transplant to shaded area when well rooted.

CENTRAL SOUTH:

Plant these in the vegetable garden early this month: Irish Potatoes, Rutabagas, Pole Snap Beans and Tomato plants. These late in month: Bush Snap Beans, Beets, Carrots, Lettuce, Parsley, Mustard, Cabbage, Kale, Chinese Cabbage, Swiss Chard, Turnips and Tendergreens.

Soak Beet and Swiss Chard seeds overnight before planting. Moisten seed drill before sowing these soaked seeds.

Place the fall vegetable garden on a spot that was free of weeds in July, if possible. Break or spade the soil to a depth of 8 inches. Add one inch of well-rotted manure or 4 pounds of complete commercial fertilizer per 100 square feet. Disc, harrow or rake to pulverize.

Insure a satisfactory stand of plants by opening the seed drills twice the depth used for spring planting; run drills full of water, sow seed in wet soil, cover with dry soil and firm. Do not water again until seedlings are up.

Mulch fall crops with 4 inches of grass clippings, clean hay, oat straw or pine straw to conserve moisture.

Plant Gladiolus corms if irrigation can be supplied. Dig mature Gladiolus corms after tops die back, dry them thoroughly and cure in a cool, moist-free place.

Plant seed of Ageratum, Sweet Alyssum, Balsam, late Cosmos, Four-o'clocks, Marigold and Zinnias.

Web worms make unsightly tents on Pecan trees. This pest can be controlled by spraying the Pecan trees with one pound calcium arsenate to fifty gallons of water or Bordeaux mixture. On a few trees these webs can be carefully cut out or burned.

CENTRAL AND UPPER SOUTH:
The stately, beautiful Madonna Lily is well named. To enjoy its beauty next spring, plant bulbs in mid-summer.

Sow these perennial seeds in protected, well-prepared seed bed: Anthemis, Aquilegia, Cerastium, Crotalaria, Cynoglossum, Daisy, Hollyhock, Linum, Penstemon, Physalis, Platycodon, Pyrethrum, Stokesia, Tagetes, Veronica and Viola.

Lawn grass pests, such as army worms, can be controlled by using 1½ pounds DDT dust to 1000 square feet of lawn area.

Home orchard jobs: destroy weeds and grass around trees, remove and destroy all rotten and wormy fruit. Prune out and burn dead or badly damaged branches. Remove all suckers at base of trees. Continue spraying late Apples with Bordeaux.

New Youngberry and Boysenberry plants can be produced by layering (burying) tips of canes 3 to 4 inches deep. Tips root and can be cut and transplanted later.

These flowers will mature before frost: Ageratum, Sweet Alyssum, Balsam, Late Cosmos, Four-o'clocks, Marigold, and Zinnias.

Plant seeds of these perennials to produce strong plants for next spring: Anthemis, Cerastium, Crotalaria, Cynoglossum, Delphinium, Flax, Hollyhock, Penstemon, Pyrethrum, Stokesia and Veronica.

Sow Pansy seeds in partly shaded locations and water carefully the first few weeks. Transplant to seedling flats or coldframes when plants have developed four sturdy leaves.

Plant Madonna Lily bulbs in well-drained, medium-heavy soil that is full of humus. Set the bulbs on clean sand, tipped slightly on side, with top of bulb 2 to 3 inches below the surface of the ground. Plant in full sun for best results.

Order Narcissus, Hyacinth, Crocus, Tulip, Lily, Snowdrop and Scilla bulbs for fall planting.

Thin out French Hydrangeas to reduce the size of the plants and increase the size of the flowers next summer. Add lime to the soil for pink flowers and sulphur or aluminum sulphate to the soil to make Hydrangea flowers blue. Stems removed from Hydrangeas in thinning can be rooted if treated as cuttings. Other shrubs that can be propagated by cuttings are: Azalea, Abelia, Forsythia, Weigela, and Pfitzer Juniper.

Allow Roses to rest by withholding water and fertilizer. Remove all dead and diseased leaves from both the plants and the ground. Dust with any good fungicide such as dusting sulphur (9 parts) and fermate (1 part) for black spot control.

Cut back Coleus, Geranium, Sultana, and Begonia to make stocky well-shaped pot plants for the months ahead when they are moved into the house.

Cut back Dahlias leaving about one-half of top of plants for the production of the spectacular crop of flowers that will be produced in the late fall.

North

While August in northern states, in the mid-west and the east, is more or less an in-between period, there is plenty to keep the gardener busy during week-ends and cool evenings.

Thin out biennials—Pansies, Violas, English Daisies, Foxglove and others—already started to provide plants for setting out this fall or next spring. If left crowded in the seed bed they will never amount to much.

Start a new compost heap. There's much raw material available at this season—grass clippings, weeds, vegetable tops, cornstalks, etc. A little stable manure, if available, or coarse semi-decomposed screenings from an old compost heap, will help greatly in "kindling the fire" to get the new heap decomposing quickly. In dry weather water frequently enough to keep the pile moist, but never soaking wet.

Provide against injury from sudden August and September wind-storms by staking tall plants—Gladiolus, late Lilies, Delphiniums, hardy Asters and the like.

Never let Phlox go to seed if you wish to keep your colors true.

Gardens suffer from late summer doldrums these days. Most folks are away on vacations; some, just back, find other matters pressing for attention. But it's unwise to throw in the green-thumb gloves completely. That only means more work, with proportionately less reward, later on.

Last call for starting biennial and perennial seeds! These include Pansies, Violas, English Daisies, Campanulas, Siberian Wallflower (Cheiranthus), Dianthus, Hollyhocks, Gypsophila, and Iceland Poppies. Started now they will be large enough to transplant in fall (4 to 6 inches apart each way) and become well established before hard freezing. If mulched, they can all spend the winter in the open. Given a frame, however, they will get an earlier start next spring and do a better flowering job.

Cover crops for soil improvement (to be dug under next spring) can go in any time now—the earlier the better. Winter Rye, Rye Grass, Winter Vetch and Crimson Clover are excellent for this purpose.

Sudden windstorms are to be expected this month and next. Tie up Asters, Helenium, tall-growing Chrysanthemums, Delphiniums (even second growth) and others likely to be blown down.

SEPTEMBER

West Coast

GENERAL:
Summer is over along the North Coast, and usually winter rains set in well before the month is out. Mountain gardeners through southern Oregon and northern California must do in this one month whatever fall work their winters permit, as killing frosts are due by the last week. California's Fog Belt is getting its best growing weather of the year with warm ground, moderate nights, and sufficient fog to break late summer daytime heat. Seedlings and young plants thrive in it. Farther south and in hot interior valleys, the great chore is still maintenance, with intelligent watering and mulching at the head of the list.

Plant Iris of all types; or lift and divide such clumps as need it. Do not cut foliage of strong-growing Bearded divisions; but trim poorer ones back to 4 or 6 inches.

Divide Peonies if imperative. Get bulb orders in early, and have beds prepared. Consider the many new Day lilies, both evergreen and deciduous, tall and dwarf. They do well the length of the coast and supply good color over long periods with minimum effort.

Continue all-purpose spray programs, fungicides, slug baits. Feed Dahlias and Chrysanthemums, and keep well staked.

Gardeners along the Coast, and most others, especially from Santa Barbara north through Oregon and Washington, will be going in strongly for soil conditioning and cleanup, though for differing reasons—those in the far South getting fall- and winter-flowering plants in as rapidly as summer ones make way; and those in the Fog Belt enjoying some of its best sowing and seedling setting weather of the year. In mountain gardens of Northern California and Southern Oregon, hurry to sow and plant whatever can live through the cold winter before the first killing frost, due around Grant's Pass, Oregon, the last week in September. On the North Coast the cleanup and spading is being rushed before fall rains so saturate the ground that it will be impossible to do it for the heavy shrub, Rose, and other planting of the next two months, as well as the earliest next spring planting. Natural drainage in steep hillside gardens removes this need to hurry.

Continue a good spray program, watching Roses for mildew wherever rains come, and using a 2-percent oil emulsion or all-purpose spray on shrubs and trees prone to scale and red spider. Where possible, treat soil with a soil fungicide. Watch for and bait for slugs. Immediately burn all diseased plants and leaves, put others on the compost heap and keep well wet down, adding a sprinkling of fertilizer from time to time as the pile builds up.

NORTH PACIFIC:
Get the garden cleaned up, places conditioned and ready for fall planting. September and October are the big bulb planting months, beginning with the small hardy bulbs and Narcissi, Lilies as early as available. Divide Lily-of-the-valley and Montbretia. Remember small native bulbs for any woodsy garden corners: Trillium, Erythronium, Cypripedium, Dodecatheon, and for careful gardeners, *Iris Douglasiana* and *I. Gormani*.

Many broad-leaved evergreens move best as the rains begin, particularly the natives. Conifers may be planted at the same time. *Abelia grandiflora* needs sun here, but not reflected heat. *Magnolia grandiflora* thrives if given good drainage and ample space to develop. Bloom comes from June to October; but use a smaller Magnolia for any but spacious gardens.

Get fall pruning done by mid-month. Cut back new growth ends heavily on Japanese Quince to get bloom all the way to the branch ends next spring. Keep late-flowering shrubs pruned as soon as bloom ceases.

Take side branch cuttings of Poinsettia. Old plants do not usually bloom here again. Repot any summer-resting Gloxinias and Cyclamen, and prepare to carry on in a cool room indoors. Also pot up and plunge outdoors any bulbs for indoor winter forcing. Begin potting tender Fuchsias, Geraniums, and similar material that must be wintered indoors, but set outside until frost is imminent.

September is the big lawn planting month here.

Begin planting hardy bulbs as soon as they are obtainable from local growers. The Chinese Sacred Lily, Paper White, and Soleil d'Or Narcissus will flower indoors in December if started this month in fiber or pebbles and water. Plant St. Brigid Anemone in a sheltered leafmoldy corner for outdoor bloom from late February on. Compost and bone meal are good additions to most bulb beds.

Rock gardens need overhauling, with cleaning up and pruning first, followed by applications of bone meal generally. Use cottonseed meal or other acid fertilizers on acid lovers such as Heaths that flower through fall and winter. Plant division, also new planting, can begin as soon as the rains have soaked the ground thoroughly. If summer bloom was scarce, consider *Lithospermum diffusum* blooming in acid soil from June to October. *Viola gracilia* and *V. cornuta,* with all their named varieties and hybrids, also have a long blooming season. Dwarf Campanulas, the Maiden Pink, dwarf shrubby native Penstemon, in wide variety, give two or three months of summer bloom. For something very small in a peaty pocket is the 4-inch mossy Nana form of the Fox Heather (Calluna).

Tie big Dahlia blooms. Watch Chrysanthemum staking; and if some shelter from rain can be devised, better and longer bloom is possible. Begin potting off such tender material as must be wintered indoors, also a few tender annuals that began blooming too late for a good outdoor show. Place on a porch until well established.

Harvest any kelp obtainable, chopping up and digging into soil, or putting on compost. It seems especially to benefit our soil, Asparagus and Roses in particular liking it.

Continue to sow Spinach every two weeks using Winter Spinach for the last sowing. Sow Copenhagen Market Cabbage. Set out plants of St. Valentine Broccoli, and Savoy Cabbage for winter eating. Use a sharp knife to harvest Squash with 1 inch stem.

Condition fall and winter frames. Start another compost pile. If kelp is available, use it.

Divide and set out perennials as soon as rains start.

Set out Savoy Cabbage and St. Valentine Broccoli. Sow Copenhagen Market Cabbage, and continue Spinach sowings at two-week intervals. Devise rain shelter for Tomato fruits if possible.

Rock gardens need a good clean-up, refurbishing with leaf soil, stone chips, or small gravel around sensitive collars, some bone meal late in the month, and preparation for putting in new plants. For late winter bloom consider the earliest Primroses and Polyanthus, Saxifrages, Soldanella, Snowdrops, Scilla, Crocus species; then other small bulbs like the Waterlily Tulip, miniature Narcissi. Various Gentians of the Acaulis group are breathtaking. Plant some of the many newer small hybrid winter-blooming Ericas. Local specialists carry these, and also splendid dwarf Rhododendrons perfectly proportioned and small enough for even the curtailed rock garden. Sow dwarf Wallflowers in a difficult wall—they earned their common name! Larger walls can take the big ones.

MOUNTAINOUS REGIONS:
Mountain regions extend the length of the coast, with altitude governing more closely than latitude. Lower foothills, and some more southern coast ranges partake of milder, more general conditions than are referred to as mountainous under this heading. Most mountain planting is left for spring, though ground should be conditioned for it so that the short

growing season can be utilized next year. Dig holes for trees and shrubs, filling with straw or other protective material. Keep good compost safe from hard freezing to get new plants and seedlings started in the spring.

Divide perennials that need it. Sweet William, Lupines, Shasta Daisies, Coreopsis, Scabiosa, Gaillardia, and Anchusa may be planted now to winter over. Plant the really hardy bulbs and Day lilies. A continuous blanket of snow offsets many degrees of low temperature.

Grade and condition ground for lawns; but do not sow until spring. A low shrubby ground cover may work out better than a lawn, especially if summer water is short.

Mountain gardeners will do all their fall work this month. Among annuals that will winter over are Pansies, Scabiosa, Lupines, and generally below 3000 feet, Snapdragons. Gaillardia, Anchusa, Coreopsis, and Sweet William are planted now; Shasta Daisies and Russell Lupines also; but most other perennials including trees and shrubs wait for spring. Divide such Delphinium, Campanulas, and similar plants as need it. Plant Daffodils, Grape-hyacinths, Scilla, Tulips, Day lilies, and Iris. Do not sow lawns until spring, but prepare ground now with a heavy mulch of manure if possible, and spade under at sowing time.

The fine native Rhododendrons cover many acres through parts of this region, gaining compactness without flower sacrifice at higher altitudes. The rock garden is another natural for these mountains, where a number of the most prized alpine plants are native. All alpines are accustomed to a short summer season, winter snows and winds.

CALIFORNIA:

If plants are not doing well, get a good soil test. Sulphur, free or in several of its combinations, overcomes too much alkali. Humus is the great cure for most other California soil troubles from sand dunes through red or yellow clay to straight adobe; but it must be applied generously and dug in deep. Watch for an opportunity to do this as summer annuals are pulled.

Sow Godetias—they like to be crowded! Pinch Stocks at 6 inches for bushiness, but remove side shoots if you want large blooms. Sow Calendulas, winter Sweet Peas, Nasturtium. Plant Hibiscus, Carnations, Calceolaria, Hollyhock, and Passion-flower.

Sow Beets and Carrots; Lettuce except in the southern interior where Peas can be sown. Sow Celery in warm regions. Set Cabbage, Cauliflower, and Broccoli from the Sacramento Valley on down through the Bay area and southern coastal. Sow Endive, Leek, Radish, Parsley, and Spinach in the Fog Belt.

Plant Calla lilies, Alstroemeria, *Anemone coronaria,* Ranunculus, Tritonia, Sparaxis, and Iris.

Coastal gardeners, especially in the Fog Belt, must race to get seeds sown and the many seedlings set in place for fall gardens. In much of the Fog Belt it is possible also to plant some vines, shrubs, and trees. Many Interior Valley and desert gardeners are still struggling with water and shade problems, eagerly setting out seedlings in any cool spell, and shading carefully. Keep mulches on wherever gardens remain hot especially on Rhododendrons, Camellias, Azaleas, and Roses. Continue to feed the last in all but coldest regions of California as fall is a heavy blooming period for them here.

FOG BELT:

Prepare now for three seasons to come. Sow as many seeds as can be given good care. Remember Godetia, Clarkia, Lupine, Coreopsis, Larkspur, Snapdragon, Gaillardia are California natives even though you choose the hybrid descendants. Pansies, Stock, and Calendulas can brighten the shorter days ahead.

Get started on bulb planting, though so-called Dutch bulbs usually wait for October and November. Plant Cyclamen, Clivia, Calla, winter-blooming Oxalis, Freesia, Watsonia, Ixia, Tritonia, St. Brigid Anemone, Ranunculus, and Mariposa-tulips.

Watering continues, especially for conifers and evergreens, Fuchsias and other moisture lovers. Give less to plants entering a rest period, also the very tender ones. Finish by four o'clock because of mildew danger.

Give last feeding of the season to Camellias, Rhododendrons, or Azaleas that were overlooked in late August. Feed Roses with commercial fertilizer for their fall blooms.

Cut back perennials as they finish blooming; divide and reset those that flower early in spring. Geraniums and Fuchsias are allowed to grow without pruning now until after winter frosts, though cuttings may be taken. No more hedge pruning this year.

Sow Beets, Carrots, and Lettuce. Set Broccoli, Cabbage, and Cauliflower plants, also in the Big Valley. Artichokes do particularly well in the Fog Belt, and bear from November to June. Plant in early fall in rich soil with crowns just above surface. Water well and continue giving commercial fertilizer.

SOUTHERN CALIFORNIA:
Watering, mulching, seedling shading are still the big chores. Hot interior valleys may need trench irrigation for Roses, borders, and less drought-resistant plants. Basins around shrubs and trees conserve moisture, especially if mulched. Most sub-tropicals take moderate watering, and succulents but little.

Pests are thriving. Besides the usual all-purpose spray, get around with a summer oil emulsion.

Prune hedges, and give Roses a light shaping.

Roses and winter-flowering shrubs need good feeding, Gardenias an acid fertilizer with peat and moisture.

Get fall and winter annuals and other plants in wherever summer ones leave space. Bulbs mentioned for the Fog Belt may be planted, also Peruvian-lilies. The Dwarf Pomegranate makes a striking edging up to 1 foot in height with showy orange-red flowers all summer and conspicuous fruits. Or use singly in patio, rock garden or border. *Poinciana Gilliesi* (Bird-of-Paradise), Cockspur Coralbean, and *Stephanotis floribunda* (madagascar-jasmine) are handsome sub-tropicals.

Practically all hardy vegetables may be planted along the southern coastal strip, and another crop of Snap Beans. Peas may be sown both here and in the interior valleys; also Celery seed except in colder elevations.

South

GENERAL:
Continue to dust Roses with an effective fungicide such as fermate-sulphur mixture. Severe die-back is often caused by a weakening of plants due to black spot.

Fertilize Chrysanthemum plants with nutrient solution made by dissolving 1 pound of complete commercial fertilizer in 5 gallons of water. Soak soil before applying (1 pint of solution per plant).

Dutch Iris are very satisfactory cut flowers or perennial border highlights. Plant these bulbs in cutting garden and cultivate like a garden crop for easiest culture. Plant in groups for best garden effects.

Free flowering of both perennial Phlox and Verbena is greatly stimulated by removing old flower heads and feeding with liquid fertilizer.

Check with your local weather bureau to get average killing frost date in your vicinity. Any up-to-date seed catalogue gives number of days various vegetables require to mature from time seeds are sown. You will be surprised how many vegetables can be planted in the fall garden.

A mulch of 3 to 4 inches of straw, clean hay or leaves conserves moisture and keeps down weeds in the fall garden.

Sow these now for bloom next spring: Coreopsis, Larkspur, Ragged Robin, Texas Bluebonnet and Poppy.

Iris, including Bearded, Japanese and Siberian varieties, need to be divided and replanted every few years for most satisfactory growth and flowering.

If you have an aquarium or goldfish bowl which is not being used for fish, make it into a miniature greenhouse for growing ferns, Lycopodium and Selaginella. A shallow layer of moss, clean sand or pea gravel is the growing medium. A cover of glass holds moisture and provides good growing conditions.

Saintpaulias often develop ring spot when cold water strikes the leaves. Careful watering will protect these favorites from discoloration.

Chrysanthemums and Geraniums are both susceptible to bacterial leaf spot causing lower leaves to turn yellow and drop. Control with spray of 1 tablespoon of fermate mixed with one gallon of water.

UPPER SOUTH:
Plant Peonies, covering the tips or buds only 1¼ to 1½ inches deep after first preparing the soil thoroughly to a depth of at least 12 inches.

Dutch Iris are very satisfactory bulbs for southern gardens. They follow Narcissus in the spring floral parade and provide excellent flowers for garden color and cut flower purposes.

Kill undesirable weeds and help the lawn grasses by applying a mixture of one pound sodium salt form of 2,4-D and 100 pounds of complete commercial fertilizer (mixing thoroughly), using 10 pounds per 1000 square feet of area.

Give Chrysanthemums a feeding of liquid fertilizer made by dissolving one pound of complete commercial fertilizer in 5 gallons of water. Soak the soil with hose, then apply one quart of solution around each clump or plant. Roses will also respond favorably to a similar feeding.

Dig, separate and replant single plants of Violets, Shasta Daisies, Thrift, Japanese, Siberian and Bearded Iris, Rudbeckia, Physostegia and perennial Phlox. If these plants are not in your garden, secure and plant them now.

Kentucky Blue Grass is the best foundation lawn grass for the Upper South. It needs well-drained soil having high fertility and does best in full sun, but will tolerate shade. It must have abundant moisture. In need of protection when young, it is usually not sown alone. This seed mixture is excellent for lawn development: 14 pounds of Kentucky Blue Grass, 6 pounds of English Rye Grass, 2 pounds White Clover, 6 pounds Red Top. Sow mixture at the rate of 4 pounds per 1000 square feet on well-prepared seed bed.

Sow these vegetable seeds: Mustard, Radish, Spinach, Turnip, Kale and Leaf Lettuce. Also plant Onion sets.

CENTRAL SOUTH:

Sow Italian or English Rye Grass at the rate of 5 to 10 pounds of seed per 1000 square feet for a winter lawn. These seeds can be planted in thick Bermuda Grass turf with excellent results. They can also be planted on bare areas for soil conservation and to make a temporary lawn during the winter months.

Sow these annual flower seeds in fertile, well-prepared soil, where plants are to flower next spring: Bluebonnet, Calliopsis, Coreopsis, English Daisy, Larkspur, Drummond Phlox, California Poppy, Sweet William, and Cornflower.

Feed Roses and Chrysanthemums. Dig and divide perennials such as Violets, Shasta Daisies, Iris and Day lilies.

Layer (bury) tips of Youngberry and Boysenberry plants to produce new, young, vigorous plants to be used in making additional planting of these delicious fruits. The new plants will be ready for planting next spring.

LOWER SOUTH:

Hardy annuals that can be seeded for winter flowering are: Calendula, Stock, Snapdragon, and Petunia.

The large-flowering, Ten-Week Stock is especially recommended. This strain flowers early and is available in pink, yellow, blue, red, white and lavender.

Snapdragon plants that have lived through the summer can be carried through the winter for a magnificent display of early blooms next spring. Cut back the plants to 12 inches, water and mulch with clean straw. This practice often proves satisfactory in the Central South too.

Set plants of these Grasses in well-prepared, fertilized soil to establish a new lawn: St. Augustine, Centipede, Zoysia or Carpet.

Bulbs to plant in sunny locations are: Spuria Iris (*Iris spuria*), Cape Cowslip (*Lachenalia*), Snowflake (*Leucojum aestivium*), Grape-hyacinth (Muscari) and Oxalis. Bulbs to plant in partially shaded locations are: Camassia, Freesia, Ranunculus and Squill.

Plant these vegetable seeds in the home garden: Beets, Carrots, Chinese Cabbage, Swiss Chard, Head and Leaf Lettuce, Mustard, Radishes, Turnip. Also plant Onion sets or plants.

North

Start lifting Gladiolus as soon as the leaves begin to brown. Don't forget that all-important dusting with 5 percent DDT of each corm before final storage.

If you are planning new gardens for planting next spring, now is a good time for the spade work. For those who really need convincing, remember how many days of rain we get in the spring!

Most perennials (with the exception of those which normally flower at this season, such as hardy Asters and Chrysanthemums) can be divided now. The earlier in the fall this is done, the better established the plants will be for the winter months.

Continue to fight black spot on Rose foliage. Pick off any infected leaves and destroy any leaves on the ground under the plants. Spraying or dusting for black spot must continue right up to the arrival of winter which generally means the end of October.

Pansies and other biennials and perennials grown from seed early in the season can be transplanted now. They can be planted in their permanent garden positions or lined out in nursery rows.

Now's the time to sow the new lawn and also any bare spots in the old. Go easy on the watering. Gently and constantly should be the watchword.

In the excitement of choosing Tulips and Daffodils, don't forget the dainty Scillas, Crocuses, Snowdrops and Grape-hyacinths. They can be planted now. Mix bone meal in well with the soil before setting the bulbs.

Seeds of perennials planted early this month will have about six weeks of growing weather. Delphiniums should be shaded lightly and kept moist. Allow the seedlings to remain untouched over winter and transplant in the spring.

Give Rhododendrons a dressing of peatmoss or leafmold, to be left in place permanently. Plant Lilacs in well-prepared soil that has been limed.

When watering the flower bed, don't forget the shrubs nearby. They're likely to be thirsty at this time of the year.

Bring house plants indoors. Repot those that have outgrown their containers and feed with commercial fertilizer. Verbena, Heliotrope, and Ageratum, if taken up and potted, will flower indoors for a month or two. Take up young plants of Zinnias, Marigolds, and Petunia and pot in rich, light loam. Keep well watered and in a sunny location. Pinch back to prevent them from getting leggy.

Watch those weeds! If they go to seed now your troubles will be tenfold next year. Besides they'll look better on the compost pile!

When the Asparagus stalks have turned yellow, cut them down to the ground and apply a mulch of well-rotted manure to the bed. Radishes, Spinach, Lettuce, Carrots, Chives and Onion sets can be sown in the coldframe for early winter use.

Bring in Squash before they get nipped by frost. Collards, Kale, and Brussels Sprouts can be left until after the first frost.

Set out pot plants or well-developed runners of Strawberries after the soil has been prepared and manure applied. Try the recently introduced variety, Red Star, which has been making Strawberry headlines.

Stake Chrysanthemums to prevent damage from wind and storms.

When setting out perennial plants, be sure to label them so you'll know what's coming up next spring. Before planting the perennial bed, make a plan keeping in mind height, coloring and flowering time. Indicate on your plan where each plant is to be set and allow for new additions.

Day lilies which have grown too lustily can be divided now, which will give their roots time to take hold before winter.

Strawberries: Manure and prepare soil. Set out pot plants or well developed runners. Use more than one variety to insure fruiting.

Daffodils can be planted this month, about 4 ins. deep to top of bulb. Take care in preparing the soil for them or you won't get the results you should. Mix bone meal in well with the soil before setting the bulbs. Don't select just one or two varieties; Daffies come in so many lovely forms that a collection, even if small, will be a source of interest and pleasure.

Lift Cannas, Dahlias, Tigridias and Tuberoses after the first white frost. "Cure" in an airy room for a few days and store in a cool place.

Snowdrops, Crocuses, Grape Hyacinths and Scillas go in late this month, about 2 to 3 ins. deep.

Pot Freesias and Lachenalias and keep in a coldframe until hard frost threatens. They do not have to be kept in the dark. Give all light possible.

At end of month pot Korean 'Mums. Bring indoors just before frost.

Apples, Pears and Grapes may be ordered now for delivery after the leaves fall. Or, you can order these, along with Peaches and Plums, for delivery in time for spring planting.

If you want dwarf Apple trees order early as the supply of this stock is often limited.

All fruits to be stored should be picked before they are dead-ripe. Never attempt to keep any damaged fruit. Pick with stems attached. Avoid injuring fruit spurs formed for next year's crop.

Grapes: Pick only when ripe and only when bunches are dry. Too much handling destroys berry's protective bloom. Make jelly before grapes are dead ripe, juice just before grapes burst. Mash (no water), simmer, strain through bag, sweeten to taste, boil, store in hot sterile jars. (No need for pressure cooking or water bath, government advice to the contrary.)

Take in all house plants that have been out for the summer. Re-pot those that have grown considerably and feed with commercial fertilizer.

Take cuttings of English Ivy to be grown in colorful jars filled with water.

Young, sturdy plants of Zinnia, Marigold, Ageratum, Verbena, Petunia, Lantana and Coleus taken up, set in rich, light loam in pots, will make good house plants. Keep them well watered, set them in a sunny location and pinch back to prevent their getting leggy.

Take cuttings of Rosemary, Sage, Lavender, Lantana and Heliotrope. Winter these indoors or in greenhouse.

Plant perennials *early* this month to give them 6 weeks of growing weather.

Early September is not too late to sow Delphiniums. Shade lightly and keep moist. Allow the seedlings to remain untouched over winter and transplant in the spring.

Move the double-hoop Peony supports to the Chrysanthemums or stake the more rampant growers by placing 3 inconspicuous stakes at regular intervals on the outside of the plants and drawing a cord looped around them. . . . Hardy 'Mums in reserve planting can be lifted after watering and set in the garden. Choose dull weather.

Cut seed pods off Phlox.

Take cuttings of rock garden plants after rains have softened growth. Need coldframe or cool greenhouse for winter. . . . Take cuttings of Heliotrope, Fuchsia, Lantana for stock plants or training into standards.

Keep crowns of Pansy seedlings above soil when transplanting.

Keep 'Mums well staked as they grow. Feed with manure water.

Bleedinghearts should be dug and divided if plants have become crowded. . . . Now is the time to start lifting, dividing and replanting perennials in the border if this task is necessary.

Before you do any renovating, make a plan on paper and indicate where each plant is to be reset and where new additions will go in, keeping height, color and flowering time in mind.

Cease all feeding, watering, cultivating.

Increase vigilance against black spot. . . . Removal of all decayed blooms will lessen infection from mildew. . . . Keep infected leaves destroyed.

All the Coast is busy planting: the North rushing to get things in for next spring, and Californians giving first consideration to late fall and winter bloom. Bulb planting is a big chore—bulbous Iris, Lilies, "Dutch" bulbs, Lily-of-the-valley, and all the hosts of small bulbs. Even among the large Tulips, a dozen of a single color grouped are more effective than varied or scattered plantings.

Plant Day lilies, Peonies, perennials, rock plants: also most succulents where hardy, using glaucous ones, not hairy, in foggy or rainy regions. Remember the ground covers over bulbs, shallow-rooted low mats to prevent mud splashings: some interplanting of taller to provide support to large-flowered slender-stemmed ones.

Prune out weak or rampant growth, even removing some plants where over-crowding is bad. Shape up others, and avoid top-heavy hedges causing scrawny lower parts.

OCTOBER

West Coast

NORTHWEST:

October work is extemely important for next year's garden in this region. It is the main transplanting month for most evergreens of all types; and toward the end, for some deciduous types. Move vines when leafless. Plant Roses. Divide perennials. Set biennial and perennial seedlings, including rock plants, into permanent places.

Fill spent planter boxes with fresh soil. Space miniature evergreen shrubs in them with hardy small bulbs between, such as winter-flowering species of Crocuses and Snowdrops. In a sheltered box plan late winter bloom from St. Brigid Anemones; or plant the box with small winter-blooming hybrid Ericas. Polyanthus Primroses flower through much of winter here; early Tulips and Hyacinths bloom outside almost as soon as indoors.

Rake out lawn moss, brown Wire Grass, and Clover after mowing. Mow again, using a grass catcher, then rake in a top dressing. October brings a fungus, the one with tiny orange cups, sooty lumps, and stringy white strands. Sift coarse sand over, then apply a copper fungicide heavily.

Lift, cure, and store Tuberous Begonias as soon as the tops fall over. If frost is due before this occurs, move plants into shelter to finish ripening.

Take deciduous shrub cuttings from ripened shoots; also before frost, Fuchsias, Geraniums, and Heliotrope to carry on indoors or in a warm or well-protected frame. Choice plants can be carried on under glass or in a cold room. Sow hardy annuals such as Cornflower, Myosotis, Calendula, and Clarkia. Sow Pansies in the coldframe.

October is the bulb planting month. Plant Narcissi of all types, followed by Tulips, then Hyacinths. Continue to plant Iris, also small bulbs like Scilla, Muscari, Snowdrops. Plant Crocus, Camassia, and Anemone. Do plant Lilies; they like the region and will reward you amply.

Sow Winter Spinach for all-winter use. Move seedlings of Copenhagen Market Cabbage to garden rows. Heavy root growth goes on all winter, with heads forming in earliest spring. Clean up as crops are harvested; condition soil for spring if not too wet.

Flowers of *Camellia sasanqua* in variety are beautiful here in October. Fall foliage lacks the brilliance it has in most regions; but our native Vine Maple (*Acer circinatum*), a small tree to 25 feet, turns a striking red. Native Dogwood (*Cornus Nuttalli*) turns a softer rose, and is considered by those who know it the finest of all Dogwoods. Sourwood (*Oxydendron arboreum*) turns scarlet here, and is useful among the acid-desiring Rhododendrons, Heaths, and others we use so freely. *Enkianthus perulatur*, a slender 5-foot shrub, colors brilliantly for us.

For bloom, consider fragrant Japanese Apricot (*Prunus mume*) that does unusually well in this region if given a warm place, often flowering from January to April. It comes in variety, from white to red, single or double. Or try one of the several Osmanthus shrubs for fragrant late fall, winter, and spring bloom.

Rock gardens, walls, perennial and shrub borders are all refurbished this month. It is the big month for planting Tulips, Hyacinths, Lilies; but put the Daffodils in first. Field mice seem to avoid the other bulbs as well if they are heavily interplanted with Narcissus. Mass the small bulbs—Scilla, Muscari, Crocus, Snowflakes, Chionodoxa—in borders or rock garden, also around trees. This region is exceptionally favorable to all these hardy bulbs. Bone meal seems best for soils here, and if dug under at planting time, will be acting later when the new roots need it.

October is the big Rose planting month in Northern Oregon and Washington. They are hardy here without winter protection, like our soils and climate, respond to good tilth, ample food, careful spraying, and at least half sun.

Plant spring-flowering shrubs and trees; but be prepared to protect young Camellias and others of borderline hardihood through possible severe cold spells in mid-winter.

Lavender is hardy here; Heliotrope and nearly all Fuchsias are not. Geraniums sometimes live for several years in sheltered positions, but are not reliable. All may be rooted from cuttings under glass at this time.

One of the greatest rock garden charms is that spice of something new. Drop in at a specialist's nursery for something unusual if you have not made a list of things seen through the year. Watch that elfin types are not placed next to the rampant. *Anemone vernalis* is pleasing with an acaulis type of Gentian. Angel's Tears and *Iris reticulata,* protected from mud splashing with a carpet of *Sedum acre,* are another. Be generous with bone meal in all but acid pockets for plants of that type. Look to the stone chip mulches around Androsaces and others that cannot take wet crowns.

Use frost-dropped green Tomatoes for pickling. Those picked green will ripen faster if placed in a closed box or drawer with several Apples. For slow ripening, pull plants, remove leaves, hang upside down in a dark room around 65 degrees.

Maple and other large leaves are fine for compost piles, but deadly when matted down by winter rains over plants.

CALIFORNIA:
October is a month to start new lawns and condition old ones.

Continue general-purpose sprays and slug bait. Watch Chrysanthemums for diabrotica. Remove suckers and last year's old flowering wood from deciduous shrubs. Water young, tender, or newly set plants earlier now that nights are chilly.

In colder regions pot or tub such subtropicals as may need later patio or glass protection during frosty periods.

Sow cool-weather vegetables generally; Lettuce, Peas, Turnips, Rutabagas, Kale, Kohlrabi throughout California; Carrots in the big valleys
and southern coastal; Beets from the Bay Area down the Coast and
through the Citrus belt to Arizona. Endive grows faster in cold wet
weather than does Lettuce. Set out Cauliflower and Cabbage plants;
Broccoli through the Citrus belt and along the Coast.

If Stocks do not make strong root growth before cold weather, they
will stunt with little or no bloom.

When planting bulbs, the tomato-red *Tritonia crocata* is hardier than
Freesia. Interplant Godetia with Dutch Iris. Plant St. Brigid Anemone
and winter-blooming Oxalis all along the Coast. The Kafir Lily is hardy
from Central California on South, needs shade, and will bloom from
December to March. Calla lilies will even make a hedge.

Remember both shrub and bulb natives when planning new material,
planting the former just before rains set in. Of bulbs, *Brodiaea californica, B. capitata, B. ixioides* are for sandy leafsoils; *B. lacta, B. coronaria,* and *B. Laxa* for heavy wet ones. Mariposa-tulips must bake and
dry out in summer.

Babianas, like Freesias, need rich sandy loam, and are useful for
edgings or rock gardens. Continue to plant Clivia on through December
in shaded rich moist ground where they can be left undisturbed,
but they are tender where it is colder than in the Bay Area. Plant
Ranunculus, Anemone, Peacock-iris (Moraea).

Cut water on Tuberous Begonias to encourage their rest period.
October is the best month to plant or to move Tree Peonies.

Set Cauliflower and Cabbage throughout. Sow Peas, Turnips, Rutabagas, Kohlrabi, and Lettuce as desired. Bear in mind that Endive
does better than Lettuce in the rainy season. Sow Carrots in the Big
Valley and along the South Coast; Beets in the Bay Area, Coastal,
and Citrus Belt.

To obtain Carnations by Christmas, pinch back each stem to force
flower-bearing new succulent growth.

FOG BELT:
Set annuals into permanent places for winter bloom. Stocks need

good root growth now to avoid winter stunting. Seeds may still be broadcast of Virginia Stock, Shirley Poppies, Godetia, Larkspur, Clarkia, Bachelor's Buttons, Linaria, and Sweet Alyssum. Sow Sweet Peas; and plant Snapdragons, Pansies, and Cineraria, but protect the last from possible frost and cold winds.

Some tender plants will need mulching or frost protection soon. Watch Hibiscus, Gardenia, Ginger; some choicer Fuchsias and Pelargoniums; Bougainvillea, Lantana, and young Citrus trees.

Watch Chrysanthemums closely for diabrotica (use arsenic-based spray). Scale on evergreens are at a stage to be quickly killed now with oil spray.

Green-wood Rose cuttings, 7 inches long, inserted to half their length in partial shade may be ready to set out by spring.

Plant Penstemon, Verbena, Gaillardia, Scabiosa, and Gypsophila. Plant Azaleas, Rhododendrons, and Camellias. If Roses suitably prepared for moving are obtainable, they can gain several months' root growth.

Lifting fogs along this belt make good growing weather in still warm soil for setting out both perennial and annual seedlings. Even in frost belts back from the Coast where bloom will wait for spring, a good October start will speed flowering. Stocks, Snapdragons, Calendulas, Pansies, Violas, and the Fairy Primrose are all hardy in the Fog Belt. Plant Sweet Peas.

Some of the more tender borderline plants grown in this region are best with a root mulch and other plants or a wall for shelter against possible later frosts. Among them are Hibiscus, Gardenia, Lady Washington Pelargoniums, Cineraria, very tender types of Fuchsia, some Bougainvillea.

Carnation cuttings are still possible this month, also green wood Rose cuttings. Carnations may also be layered. Begin giving Tuberous Begonias very little water to encourage rest. Do not lift until the stem falls with a light touch, for if cut the bulb does not seal properly.

Broadcast seed of Larkspur, Shirley Poppies, Godetia, Clarkia, Virginia Stock, and Sweet Alyssum.

Plant Globe Artichokes along the Fog-belt Coast 6 feet apart with crowns just above the surface. Asparagus likes river delta lands along the Coast. Plant now.

Plant tree Peonies in the sun in the Fog Belt, and do not let other plants close enough to brush or drip on them.

Plant a summer-flowering tree this month or next. As suggestions, the blue-flowered Jacaranda; light pink *Lagunaria pattersoni;* red Flame Tree (*Sterculia acerifolia*)*;* if your soil is dry, creamy-clustered Japanese Pagoda Tree.

SOUTHERN CALIFORNIA:
Feed Roses lightly. Water and continue careful spraying. Give liquid fertilizer to Chrysanthemums for long season bloom. Pinch off Dahlia side buds to keep them blooming.

For easier division, soak Agapanthus root stocks in water several hours first.

Chionodoxas, Siberian Scilla, and English Iris are not very satisfactory in warm winter climates. The possible tender or subtropical more than make up for them—Climbing Peruvian-lily (*Bomarea caldasiana*) for half shade, Peacock Iris (*Moraea glaucopis*), Calla lily, Watsonia, Glory-lily, Tritonia, Ixia, Canna.

Work on next year's garden now, as well as that of the remaining year. Continue planting shrubs and trees as for September. Fertilize all winter-blooming ones well. Keep Roses watered. Give peat to Azaleas, Rhododendrons, Camellias, and similar shrubs. Order new ones for fall planting.

Sow new lawns; refurbish old. Plant Dichondra.

Sow practically all annuals in open ground this month and next, including winter Sweet Peas, also wildflowers. Bartonia is a useful native. Sow Carnations, Pansies, Stocks, Petunias, Phlox, and Verbenas in flats; also Snapdragons, Canterbury Bells, Gerberia, Penstemon, Hollyhocks, and Violas. Continue to plant cool-weather vegetables in variety.

Bulb planting is important; but Tulips and Lily-of-the-valley are best first stored in the refrigerator for several weeks unless your nurseryman makes this part of his service for this region. Plant Easter Lilies, Calla, Amaryllis, Ixia, Sparaxis, Watsonia, Billbergia in addition to those mentioned for California.

South

GENERAL:

When seeds are sown in the fall, it is very necessary that soil and seeds be in close contact with each other because moisture is very limited. Firm soil over seed by rolling a wheelbarrow or the wheel of a garden plow down the planted row.

Spinach requires a sweet soil. If soil has an acid reaction, add lime and work into soil before planting seeds.

One of the easiest, surest, quickest pot plants to grow is the Paperwhite Narcissus. Place five or more large bulbs in a shallow bowl of pebbles, water and place in dark closet for two weeks. Then place in sunny window, turning daily to keep stems straight. New plantings every week will keep the beauty and fragrance of this flower in the house for four and five months.

The Bald Cypress tree (*Taxodium distichum*), although commonly associated with water and swamps, will also make a beautiful long-lived lawn tree away from water.

Spring-flowering bulbs, like many industries, are moving south because they are finding conditions favorable for growth, with the Central and Upper South more favorable for Tulips, large-flowered Narcissus, Hyacinth and Crocus.

Plant Tulips in well-prepared soil, slightly raised beds, 8 to 12 inches deep in sandy loam soil, 6 to 8 inches deep in clay soil and 6 to 12 inches apart.

Crocus bulbs are tiny but tough—once established they continue to return as one of the earliest spring arrivals each year. They are very effective tucked in here and there among shrub plantings. Set 2 to 4 inches deep and 6 to 8 inches apart.

Divide Violets. Set Viola, Pansy and English Daisy plants. Transplant seedling perennials. Set Peony plants.

The beauty of a Rye Grass winter lawn depends upon this grass getting thoroughly established before the cold weather slows down its growth. Sow seed—10 pounds per 1000 square feet—as soon as possible and water well.

Native plants having colorful autumn foliage are: Brook Euonymus, Common Sassafras, Flowering Dogwood, Rough-leaved Dogwood, Sumac, Virginia Creeper, and Virginia Sweetspire. Perhaps there is a spot in your landscape planting for some of this brilliant color.

Mature Flowering Dogwood trees often produce great masses of brilliant red berries in the fall. Many know the flowers, few know the fruit.

It takes a lot of leaves to make a little leafmold, so save them all in a secure pen. Add a sprinkling of superphosphate to the leaf pile as leaves are added to hasten the process of decay. Keep leaves damp and turn pile occasionally to keep leaves from over-heating.

LOWER SOUTH:
Plant Beets, Carrots, Mustard, Head and Leaf Lettuce, Radish, Spinach, and Onions. Sow Cabbage, Cauliflower, Brussels Sprouts, and Broccoli for late transplanting.

Calendulas and Stock are grown from seed sown in seed boxes or in the open garden. Good seed of the better varieties give best results. Massed bed plantings make most attractive garden pictures.

Winter-flowering Sweet Peas produce more abundantly if a trench

12 inches deep is dug, partly refilled with 4 inches of well-rotted manure mixed with 4 inches of topsoil, then seeds sown 4 to 6 inches deep. Pull soil to plants as they grow until soil is level.

Plant, rebuild and enrich Calla lily beds. In making new plantings of Calla lilies, make beds 3 to 4 feet wide, turning entire area to a depth of at least 12 inches. Mix 2 to 3 inches of well-rotted manure with soil as it is turned. Water and let soil settle several days. Set roots, either clumps or single plants, 12 inches apart and cover 3 to 4 inches deep. After planting, mulch with a layer of oak leaves.

Camellia japonica daikagura is in flower now, and has been on the garden stage for several weeks. It has medium to large variegated blooms. If you plan to add this charming and unusual shrub to your garden, select a shady location to protect its early flowers from the burning autumn sun.

Flower seed to be sown in open beds, where they are to flower: Anchusa, Bluebonnet, Calliopsis, Candytuft, Cornflower, Didiscus, Feverfew, Helichrysum, Larkspur, Nemophila, Nierembergia, Annual Phlox, Shirley Poppy, and Sweet Pea.

Flowering plants to set for winter bloom: Ageratum, Alyssum, Calendula, English Daisy, Pansy, and Stocks.

Bulbs to plant are too numerous to permit a complete listing, but here are a few important ones: Alstroemeria, Amaryllis, Anemone, Cooperia, Crinum, Gladiolus, Freesia, Hyacinth, Ismene, Kniphofia, Lilies, Liriope, Morea, Narcissus, Oxalis, Ranunculus, Scilla, Sparaxis, Watsonia, and Zephranthes.

Vegetable plants produce edibles in a very short time, so try these, if the plants are available in your area: Broccoli, Cabbage, Cauliflower, Celery, and Head Lettuce.

Vegetable seed to plant include these frost-resistant kinds: Beets, Carrots, Chard, Collards, Chinese Cabbage, Endive, Lettuce, Mustard, Onion sets, Radish, Spinach, and Turnips. Bush Snap Beans are worth a chance.

Don't forget to plant a few Strawberry plants as they will repay you abundantly next spring with delicious fruit.

CENTRAL SOUTH:

Flower seed to sow in open beds include: Calliopsis, Coreopsis, Corn-flower, Larkspur, Phlox Drummondi, Shirley Poppy and Sweet Peas. Sow the seed broadcast, on well-prepared beds, where plants are to flower.

Plant Lilies in groups, wherever possible, rather than singly. Set the bulbs about 12 inches apart in soil thoroughly conditioned with compost, well-rotted manure and bone meal. Do not use fresh manure or heavy applications of commercial fertilizer on Lilies. Worthwhile varieties are: Regal, Siberian, Henry, Hanson, showy Japanese, Tiger, American, Turk's Cap, Goldband, Phillipinense, and Creole.

Properly planted, Italian or English Rye Grass will not injure established Bermuda or Carpet Grass lawns when seeded upon them. Clip the Bermuda or Carpet Grass to a height of 1½ inches. Apply evenly 4 pounds of complete commercial fertilizer per 100 square feet of area, and water thoroughly. Sow Rye Grass seed uniformly over the area at the rate of 5 to 6 pounds per 1000 square feet and work into sod with the back of a rake. Then water again. Keep Rye Grass clipped to a height of 2 inches.

Zoysia Grass is one of the earliest lawn grasses to begin growth in the spring and one of the last to turn grey in the fall. It produces a dense sod and crowds out weed Grasses. It grows slowly and does not require frequent mowing. This is one of the most favorable times of the year to set Zoysia plants—it does not make seed. The plants should be set in well-prepared, enriched soil, 12 inches apart. This Grass is also excellent for the Lower South.

The Iris family offers great variety and beauty of flower at a very moderate cost. Dutch Iris bulbs are easily grown. The Bearded Iris is extremely well adapted to the Southern garden—add at least 5 new varieties each year to your collection.

Vegetable seed to plant are: Radish, Spinach and Turnips. Also plant Onion sets, Chive, Sage and other herbs. Asparagus plants can be ordered and planted.

Gather green Tomatoes just before frost, handle gently and place a drop of paraffin on the stem scar before storing in a cool place. Remove the paraffin a few days before the Tomato is to be used. The air entering the stem scar permits the Tomato to ripen.

Care should be taken not to allow fallen leaves to mass in a few places on the lawn and smother the grass. This is especially true with Kentucky Blue Grass lawns.

Observe and make notes on hardy Chrysanthemums flowering in your area. Add new varieties to your collection next spring from a list that is made from personal preference and choice.

Clean up the flower and vegetable garden, removing all dead tops of plants, weeds, unoccupied stakes and litter. Insects pass up the clean garden, but they certainly homestead the neglected garden for winter quarters.

Plant Spinach, Rape, Kale and Leaf Lettuce.

The landscape uses of *Camellia sasanqua* are many. It is especially desirable as a hardy prolific fall-flowering evergreen. It makes a fine formal or free-growing hedge. Or use as specimen plantings or corner plantings around the house. Select your varieties from plants in flower at your local nursery.

Broadcast sowing of Larkspur, Cornflower, Poppy, Drummond Phlox, Calliopsis, Texas Bluebonnet, and Coreopsis is recommended.

UPPER SOUTH:
Plant Spinach, Rape, and Kale. Order Asparagus, Rhubarb and herb plants for garden.

Keep newly planted Kentucky Blue Grass lawns thoroughly watered at all times. New lawns of this grass can still be sown.

Treated bulbs of Amaryllis are available for forcing as pot plants. They will bloom fifty to sixty days from planting, and are easily grown.

North

An old scheme for extending the Tomato season (but still a good one) is to pull up Tomato plants before frost and hang by the roots from cellar rafters. Tomatoes on these plants will ripen at least until Thanksgiving.

If you have a sunny indoor window, lift a plant or so of Parsley for use during the winter.

If rainfall has been skimpy, newly transplanted trees and shrubs, especially evergreens, will need additional soakings.

Remember, if your perennial border did not please this past season, fall is the time to take drastic action. Divide Phlox and Day lilies and other over-crowded clumps. Don't waste good garden space on magenta Phlox seedlings. There are too many new Phlox varieties in clear, luscious colors to permit such folly.

Gardeners interested in propagating their own plants from cuttings can get busy this month. Cuttings can be taken of such tender bedding plants as Geranium and Heliotrope. Take root cuttings of Phlox, Japanese Anemones, and hard wood cuttings of shrubs.

House plant enthusiasts will want to be looking ahead to potting and repotting operations necessary during the winter months. Start putting soil under cover now. When out in the country, fill a bushel basket with leafmold, so ideal in soil mixtures for African violets and Begonias.

It is not too late to plant such cover crops as Winter Rye. This is only practical, of course, in the vegetable garden or areas where annuals, Dahlias, etc., are grown for cutting.

Flower arrangers will be thinking of winter bouquets and material to be used in Christmas decorations. Collect seed pods along roadsides and in fields. All sorts of meadow grasses will be conspicuous now as well as the old standbys, Bayberry, Sumac, and Cattails.

Mulch Strawberries, Raspberries and other cane and bush fruits, using strawy manure. Do not cover crowns of Strawberry plants.

Take a walk on a clear October day and notice the trees that are trying so hard to attract your attention with their bright fall colors. If there are any you can't recognize, bring back leaves for identification.

Gather nuts while on this same trip.

The seed pods of many plants provide excellent material for winter arrangements. Milkweed, Sumac, Cattails and Meadow Grasses are all useful for this purpose.

Start planting hardy spring-flowering bulbs as soon as they are available.

Get Narcissus, Muscari, Snowdrops, Scillas, Crocus and other small bulbs in without delay.

Plant such bulbs about 4 ins. deep. Hyacinths, Tulips and Dutch Irises are best planted late in month but let tulips wait until next month.

Lift Gladiolus corms and Dahlia roots now. Let them dry off for a day, then store where it is cool and fairly dry—but *don't let them dry out enough to shrivel.*

Pot up Daffodils, Tulips and Crocuses for forcing indoors. Plant them in rich, loose soil in bulb-pans and set them in a protected coldframe until they have made strong roots. In about 6 to 8 weeks they will be ready to bring into the house to start into growth.

Fumigate Peach trees for borers by placing paradichlorobenzene crystals in a ring around the tree, 2 ins. from the bark. Mound up soil over the crystals. The fumes will catch the young worms just after they hatch.

Apply tree tanglefoot bands to trees that are troubled with canker-worms or inchworms. The bands will catch the moths as they start their climb up the trunks.

In rural areas, wrap young orchard fruit trees in bands of tar paper 3 ft. in height to protect against rabbits.

Before freeze, bring in soil for potting and seed starting during indoor months.

For window and greenhouse, pot Hyacinths, Daffodils and Tulips.

See that labels of choice subjects are in place and will remain through the winter so there will not be any mix-ups and weeding out of plants in spring.

Clean up perennial beds, removing and burning old stalks as soon as they've ripened. This prevents spread of diseases.

Plant Pansies where they are to flower. Giant flowers with good stems are impossible from spring planting. In most sections, Pansies will winter outdoors if beds are free from flooding and plants are lightly covered with hay or litter to protect them from wind and sunshine while frozen. Cover *after* first hard frost.

Many perennials can still be planted. Exceptions are Pyrethrum, Heuchera and Delphinium.

All young perennials need protection.

Take cuttings of doubtfully hardy perennials. Winter Chrysanthemum and other hardier cuttings in frame; others in greenhouse or sun porch. Penstemon, Dianthus, Salvia Farinacaea and others root readily from cuttings but are often winter-killed in garden.

Spray Lilacs, Euonymus and Bittersweet for the inevitable scale.

Aphids may do damage now. Spray with Black Leaf 40.

Remove seed pods of Hybrid Tea and other bedding types since the developing seeds compete for food that should be stored to increase cold resistance during winter.

In cold climates where Climbers are likely to be injured, remove the canes from their supports and pin to the ground.

Hill up soil to at least 6 ins. around Hybrid Teas, just before hard freeze.

NOVEMBER

West Coast

GENERAL:
Planting continues up and down the West Coast. An intensive clean-up and spray program is needed to prevent as many pests as possible from wintering over. Fungicides are important in all regions where rains, fogs, or dews are heavy. In dry regions and where rains are delayed water Camellias and Azaleas in particular, as spring bud-drop among them is usually traceable to dry roots in fall. Plant Rhododendrons at their exact former depth.

Deciduous shrubs and trees may be lightly pruned, removing only old or weak branches, shaping where necessary; but note Flowering Quince blooms on the same wood for several years.

Continue stacking compost; but burn all diseased or woody material, also any weeds full of seeds. Turn the pile every couple of months or so.

NORTHWEST:
Finish planting as early as possible. It is sodden, not frozen soil that

holds up late fall and winter work. Plant any Roses, Rhododendrons, and bulbs not done in October, also all but the most tender shrubs and trees. Crocuses do well here, being cheerily bright at the right time in border, rock garden and woodland.

Spray for leaf miner, particularly on Rhododendrons, Azaleas, Lilacs, Viburnum, and sometimes, Boxwood. Sodden crowns of Delphinium encourage rot—work a fungicide in soil around them, cover crowns with sand or ashes. Soils in some regions usually need liming for these perennials.

Give lawns balanced fertilizer; but most other plants except the very few normal winter-bloomers here need their rest period encouraged. Bone meal will not injure them as it is not immediately active.

Sow seeds of very hardy annuals where they are to bloom—Clarkia, Candytuft, Forget-me-not, Larkspur, Linaria, Shirley Poppies. Save the Snapdragon plants, which here are usually better the second summer, but need to be cut down before frost blackens them.

Just as long as the ground is workable, condition and ready it for earliest spring planting, which the climate makes possible long before a spade can be touched to soil. Use new chemical conditioners on hardpan and clay, but never on sand. Dig bone meal in generously. It works well here when applied around three months before desired effect.

November is the time to tuck in the garden. Give lawns balanced fertilizer; but in general apply only slow-acting bone meal. Barn-yard manure or partially decomposed compost may be dug in and left rough when preparing for earliest spring flowers and vegetables. Get all possible humus in and spading done, for the ground will be too wet to condition at a time when these might otherwise be planted.

Burn diseased material; clean out hiding places where pests might be wintering over. Compost leaves as our winters are too wet and lacking in deep freezes for them to be used as mulches; but partially decomposed compost is suitable, and also does much to prevent mud spattering and soil washing.

For very small gardens, a large garbage can with bottom knocked out is a handy compost-pile container; it can be tipped on its side to remove compost from the bottom as it becomes ready.

Fungicides are extremely important in this damp region. Crown rot, not freezing, is the greatest danger in border and rock garden. Spray for leaf miner. If scale or aphids bother conifers, spray with an oil emulsion.

Continue planting bulbs, especially Lilies. This is a splendid bulb region. Not only Daffodils, but Lilies naturalized in country gardens are breath-taking; but slug baiting is imperative. Plant Tulips, Hyacinths, and all the small hardy bulbs.

Continue to plant Roses. Choose for fragrance, habit, foliage, bud, flower, and color. Ruth Alexander, a fairly old Climber disappointing in most regions, does remarkably well here.

This is a fine region for Flowering Cherries. Plant Subhirtella varieties at once, particularly autumnalis. This blooms usually in October, then again in March and April; but at times carries a few flowers right through winter.

Except in unusually cold years, *Arbutus unedo* is decorative all winter with clusters of creamy bells against the pleasing foliage, and also red fruits of late summer still holding. This is an acid lover, a smaller southern European and Irish kin to our native Madrona tree. Two plants are needed for fruiting.

Plant Rhubarb and Asparagus. Sow Laxton's Superb Peas in rich sandy soil for earliest spring, protecting lightly with a little supporting brush. Sow very hardy annuals for early spring flowers. Sow Sweet Peas in a well-drained trench.

As buds start on Christmas Cactus, increase water. A hot dry room will cause bud drop; counteract with a fine mist spray if necessary. Temperatures from 60° to 65° are best. Give ample light, but not direct sun. This is a jungle, not a desert, Cactus.

CALIFORNIA:

Tulips demand cool soil for planting, and are best held into late November or December. If not nursery chilled, give them several weeks in the refrigerator before planting in regions warmer than the Bay Area. Species of Tulips from the dry rocky regions of Asia Minor are fine for rock gardens and slopes in much of California's similar climate. Protect all bulbs from gophers. Though these usually bypass

Narcissi and Muscari, they are very keen for the Dutch Hyacinths, which should not be planted before the last week in November. They need partial shade in California. Avoid the Barri group of Daffodils in hot interior valleys.

Give Rex Begonias an Oak-leaf mulch. Get Tuberous ones dried off and lifted. Finish shade house watering before noon. Plan drip protection against heavy rains.

Keep Camellias deeply watered until rains come. Spring bud drop usually comes from root drying in fall, also to some extent among Azaleas and Rhododendrons. Plant new ones this month; but note that only in very foggy regions will they tolerate full sun.

Keep Roses watered, but decrease gradually. Do not prune heavily until they finish flowering. Many growers now plan their real rest period through the hot summer, taking bloom through much of the winter, in which case, encourage growth now.

Trench-irrigate Sweet Peas, being careful that they do not dry out. Chemical fertilizer applied every two or three weeks as soon as color shows should be applied. Keep oil sprays away—they weaken vines and discolor bloom.

Sow Peas in all but the mountains; and Lettuce likewise except in Bay Area; set out Cauliflower plants; sow Turnips and Rutabagas in the Big Valley, Bay Area, and Southern California. Plant Asparagus, or topdress old beds with manure.

Plants in active growth, and those whose normal bloom is still ahead, also hardy shrubs and trees, lawns too, will need watering if rains are late. Withdraw it from those entering dormancy, and in general, apply somewhat sparingly to subtropicals. Continue to feed such plants as late Chrysanthemums that still have a considerable period of bloom ahead; also flowers that bloom normally late fall to mid-winter.

Except for the Fog Belt, Azaleas do not tolerate mid-day sun in California. Plant anytime through November to March except in cold sections; Camellias after the 15th into February. Remember the acid soil and leafmold mulch. Spread and water roots well.

Plant Anemones point down; Ranunculus prongs down. Soak both in water for 2 hours only, just before planting. Protect Lilies, Tulips, and Hyacinths from gophers by planting in deep wire baskets or perforated cans with an inch of rim protruding above ground. Gophers are too wise to eat Daffodils, as bulbs are said to contain strychnine. Gophers also avoid Muscari.

Sow Peas in all but mountain regions; Lettuce except in the same and the Big Valley. Sow Carrots, Beets, Turnips, and Rutabagas in Southern California, the last two also in the Bay Area and the Big Valley. Set out Cauliflower in Southern California; Onion sets from now until April here and in Central regions. Topdress Asparagus beds.

FOG BELT:
Get mulches on and staking done before any beating rains can do damage. Newly set plants will particularly need mulches or compost. Among other things, this lessens erosion.

Spray Roses with an all-purpose spray. Best to begin encouraging a rest period toward the end of the month; but cuttings may be rooted.

Treat any lawn weeds before it gets too cool or wet for weed killers. Feed grass with balanced fertilizer.

Plant Dutch Iris 5 to 9 inches deep; and Lily-of-the-valley with the roots straight down, except with large clumps where the outer ones may be spread out. Plant Crocus, Camassia, Tritonia, and Watsonia; Sweet Peas, Snapdragons; Conifers and Heaths.

With fogs over, but short hard rains soon due, first chore is to get gardens in condition to take them. Such taller plants as late Dahlias, Chrysanthemums, and others that may be beaten down should be staked. Low-growing mat-forming ground covers prevent unsightly mud splashing. Steep banks, even lesser slopes, need good cover to prevent erosion. Make shallow basins to hold individual plants in setting these, and choose according to exposure, moisture, and soil at hand whether using ground-hugging plants, dwarf-spreading shrubs, or those of full size

Prepare to shelter border-line sub-tropicals, though frosts in most cases are not due this month. Often strategic placing of a nearby hardier shrub is sufficient. Such patio plants as may need short or occasional indoor winter shelter should be in proper containers to move inside quickly at sudden change.

Should November prove dry, trees and shrubs, as well as smaller plants, will need watering, but keep tender ones and sub-tropicals on the dry side.

Poinsettias and other normal winter bloomers need food.

Use weed killer where needed on lawns before weather becomes too cold or wet for best results. Feed old ones with balanced food.

Plant Camassia, Watsonia, Tritonia, Lily-of-the-valley, Dutch Iris, and Clivia besides bulbs mentioned under California. Among shrubs are Bouvardia, Rhododendron, Azaleas, Daphnes and Erica. Artichokes may still be planted this month and next.

Continue good spray programs including fungicides. Bait for snails and slugs.

BIG VALLEY AND INTERIOR:
Watch offerings of California growers when buying bulbs and plants. They have been breeding for your conditions, getting Daffodils for hot dry climates; others to stand up to hard rains at their bloom period in late winter. In general, avoid the Barri group in the hot interior.

Chinese Delphinium, though splendid along the Coast, is rarely satisfactory inland; but the Blue Lace-flower and annual Candytuft are fine inland when sown in the fall. Calendulas and Stocks may still be planted in southern interiors; Pansies now and through winter.

SOUTHERN CALIFORNIA:
Planting continues on a large scale; but most gardeners prefer January for Roses. In buying plants, use care to get the right ones for the locality. In hot gardens substitute glossy-foliaged *Bignonia violacea* for the large-flowered Clematis varieties. It will climb or root along the ground, and also does well in desert interiors. Pink Powder-puff Bush and *Wigandia carcasana* are also good in warm inland valleys not below 27°.

Consult the local nursery for the best Avocado for your district. Claims along the South Coast favor Hermosa, Ventura, and Bonita

Peaches as doing well without so much winter cold as needed by most.

Rake out Bermuda grass. Fertilize and re-seed old lawns. Plant new ones.

Most perennials are ready for division. Crinums will bloom better next spring if divided now. Many perennials can be sown in flats, including Gerberia, Penstemon, Delphinium; also Carnations, Snapdragons, Verbenas, and Pansies. Continue open sowing of annuals as in October.

Feed Camellias, mulch with leafmold. When planting these, also Azaleas and Rhododendrons in alkaline soils, use more peat than soil.

Besides other bulbs mentioned elsewhere, plant Ixia, Amaryllis, Easter Lilies, Sparaxis, Oxalis, Watsonia, Anemones, Ranunculus, Ismene, Alstromeria, Billbergia, and Calla. Older plantings of Calla can be divided.

As perennials enter their dormant period, divide and replant. Encourage tuberous Begonias and others that should be resting to do so. All plants need some rest although many attempt to carry on in this climate. Winter-flowering plants grow strongly this month, and they need both food and water—Poinsettias, Christmas Cactus, Aloes, winter-flowering Pansies, Violas, Stocks, Oxalis, and Cinerarias among others. It is normal for late Chrysanthemums to continue through early winter here.

Delay heavy Rose pruning until bloom is over, which may not happen for a month or two in some cases. Roses can be planted in November; but late winter and earliest spring are usually preferred. Make future Rose beds before winter rains so they will be ready for later planting.

Tulips and particularly Hyacinths need cool planting. Best not plant the latter before the last week of November. Place Parrot Tulips in sun, others in partial shade. Plant Amaryllis, Babiana, Freesia, and Amarcrinum. Sow Swan River Daisies or Sweet Alyssum for a ground cover. Pansies and Violas will make a blooming winter ground cover, then continue on under tall Tulips or bulbs of similar height later. Sow also Schizanthus, Dimorphotheca, Calendula, and Gilia.

Begin watching the young sub-tropicals. It is possible some will need burlap or other protection from unusual frost or sun scald.

Get any watering necessary in the shade house finished by noon. Also make plans to protect plants from flooding raindrip during spells of heavy rain.

South

GENERAL:
Violets respond to heavy application of well-rotted fertilizer, producing a more abundant crop of blossoms in early spring.

Remove old flowers from perennials as soon as they fade.

The Southern Magnolia can be espaliered with interesting results. Young plants can be forced to produce several branches by cutting the plant close to the ground. These branches can be pruned and trained to grow on a trellis or close to a wall.

Redbud and Dogwood trees are well adapted to planting in almost every southern home grounds development. They combine readily with other flowering trees or shrubs and can be used as a specimen tree. Plant at least 20 feet apart.

Crape myrtle flowers gradually become smaller as the plant grows older unless severe pruning is practiced to reproduce vigorous new growth. This pruning may be done any time after the leaves drop. Fertilization should accompany the pruning.

Plant Sweet Peas using the trench method with 4 to 6 inches of well-rotted manure under the seed bed.

Add deciduous flowering shrubs to the shrub border planting, giving careful consideration to these: Althea, Pearl bush, Deutzia, Mock orange, Flowering Quince and Hydrangea.

Broad-leaf evergreens that top the list of favorites as ornamental shrubs are: Japanese Holly, Nandina, Japanese Barberry, Chinese Holly, *Camellia sasanqua,* Kurume Azalea, Euonymus and Firethorn.

The most important watering given any plant is the first one after transplanting. Apply water generously when the hole around the plant is only two-thirds full of soil.

Make hard-wood cuttings of flowering shrubs needed in greater numbers. Mature branches, the size of a lead pencil cut into sections 10 inches long, can be inserted into the ground 8 inches deep in a cool shady spot. They will root in a few months.

Set plants of Stokes' Aster, Michaelmas Daisy, Fountain-grass, and Gaillardia. They are all perennials adapted to southern conditions.

Examine Flowering Quince, Flowering Peach, Flowering Crab, Japanese Magnolia and Firethorn for scale. If infested, spray with white oil emulsion.

Transplant perennial plants such as Shasta Daisies, Violets, Asters, Day lilies, Coreopsis and Hollyhocks.

LOWER SOUTH:
Young Calendula, Stock, Snapdragon and Wallflower plants should have their growing tips snipped out to produce a bushy plant.

Apples are not generally successful in this area. Pecan varieties for the home grounds are Stuart, Lewis and Desirable.

Camellia japonica responds to bud pruning, especially those varieties that produce an abundance of flower buds. Remove all but one to two flower buds in each cluster.

Good flowering bulbs are Ranunculus, Yellow Calla lily, Hymenocallis, Watsonia, Zephyranthes and Freesia.

Sow these flower seed in beds in open garden: Alyssum (sweet),

Baby's-breath, Blanket-flower, Texas Bluebell, Bluebonnet, Candytuft, Chinese Forget-me-not, Coreopsis, Cornflower, English Daisy, Shasta Daisy, Four-o'clock, Hollyhock, Liatris (Gayfeather), Blue Laceflower, Larkspur, Drummond Phlox, Pinks, California Poppy, Iceland Poppy, blue Salvia, Scabiosa, Sweet Pea, Sweet William and Verbena.

Sow these flower seed in flats or boxes, to be transplanted to open garden when large enough to move: Calendula, Lobelia, Pansy, Petunia, Snapdragon, Stock, Viola and Wallflower.

Calendula, Stock and Snapdragons planted earlier in fall should have tops pinched out to encourage the formation of several branches and delay flowering.

Plant spring-flowering bulbs until bed space or money is exhausted. There is a thrill and satisfaction produced by Tulips, Hyacinths, Narcissus, Dutch Iris, Crocus and Squills in full flower that has no equal.

Plant Beets, Carrots, Radish, Chard, Lettuce, Mustard, Onions, Parsley, Turnips and Spinach in open garden. Thin planting of these vegetables made earlier. Apply one pound nitrate soda as side-dressing to each 100 feet of row to establish vegetables. Do not let this material touch plants.

CENTRAL SOUTH:
English and Italian Rye Grass can still be planted as a temporary lawn on new areas or as a winter lawn grass on established Bermuda sod.

The double Flowering Peach tree is more successful in this area than the Japanese Flowering Cherry tree. There are different colors to suit your wishes—white, light pink and rose. They occasionally produce fruit that is edible but quite small.

Varieties of Apples for this area are: Early Harvest, Lodi, Williams Early Red, Golden Delicious and Stayman Winesap.

Pecan varieties for the home landscape planting: Stuart, Success, Schley and Desirable.

There is still opportunity to plant Leaf Lettuce, Spinach and Onion sets or plants.

UPPER SOUTH:

Chinese Holly (*Ilex cornuta Burfordi*) has grown steadily in popularity for several years and is now high on the shrub hit parade. It is a broad-leafed evergreen having dark glossy foliage with one to three spines to each leaf. It grows to a height of 12 to 15 feet with a spread of 6 to 8 feet, but can be pruned to any height or shape. The branches that are removed make beautiful holiday decorations as the large red berries are very bright and showy.

The flowering deciduous (those that drop leaves in winter) shrubs will provide a long season of bloom if careful planning is employed in the selection of varieties to be added to your planting. First to flower are Winter Jasmine (*Jasminum nudiflorum*), Winter Honeysuckle (*Lonicera fragrantissima*) and Flowering Quince (*Chaenomeles*). These are followed by the summer-flowering shrubs with a long season of bloom such as Althea, Crape myrtle, Vitex, Flowering Pomegranate, Spirea Anthony Waterer, and Hydrangeas.

Nandina domestica, an oriental plant used widely in the South, often produces many seedlings under old established plantings. These seedlings can be readily transplanted to make beautiful low hedges, borders and additional foundation plantings in either sunny or shady locations.

Prepare flower beds and vegetable garden for spring planting. Turn soil when dry enough to work, mixing leaves, weed-free manure and commercial fertilizer into soil to a depth of 8 to 10 inches. Leave surface of soil rough.

Centaurea, Cornflower, Bachelor's Button are all names of the same hardy annual. Seed sown in well-prepared soil where they are to flower will produce an abundance of blue, pink, red, maroon or white flowers next May to July. Best results will be secured if these seed are sown in sunny borders.

Larkspur is quite well adapted to gardens of the South as a bedding plant for sunny exposures. The new giant double varieties are very beautiful. The seed will germinate better if placed in freezing unit of refrigerator for 4 or 5 days before planting.

Transplant seedlings of Anchusa, Armeria, Candytuft, Sweet Sultan and Viola.

Camellia sasanqua has many uses in the landscape plan. The fall-flowering evergreen is able to stand below-freezing weather more successfully than its relative, *Camellia japonica*. It makes a fine informal hedge, border planting, background planting for Roses, perennials, or annuals and can be used in corner plantings around the house.

Plant Spinach, Asparagus crowns, herbs and Kale in open vegetable garden. Plant Lettuce, Radish, Mustard and Onions in coldframe. Set Strawberry plants in garden.

Persian Lilac is the only species of this fine shrub that has proven successful in this area of the South. The winters are not long enough or cold enough to cause the flower buds to form on the lovely French hybrid Lilacs.

North

Clean up and burn all frost-killed plants.

Packets of half-used seed from last spring's sowings should be carefully fastened and put in a tight tin container in a cool room or attic to keep until next year.

Lily bulbs are often rotted by water gathering among their scales in winter unless surrounded by an inch or so of coarse sand.

It isn't the moles that eat Tulip bulbs, but the mice that follow the moles' burrows. Plant Tulips early this month. Remember that they must be in a well-drained spot. Set them 6 ins. deep in finely dug beds or borders and give them a mulch of straw or leaves.

If not already done, put wire mesh, heavy building paper or light roofing paper collars around fruit trees to protect them from damage by mice, rabbits and deer.

Grape vines may be pruned now, though many people favor very early spring for this work. Trim back to short spurs with 2 or 3 buds, or to several one-year old canes, leaving a dozen buds on each.

After the ground freezes, apply a mulch of salt hay to Strawberries.

Bring in a box of good garden soil and another of compost, for use throughout the winter for potting up house plants, and for starting early seeds indoors.

Watch Ferns for scale—little brown or whitish specks that appear on the plant. Spray frequently with water, and if infestation becomes severe use Volck or lemon oil.

Cacti make interesting subjects for indoor gardens and they are a lot easier to care for than many other pampered plants.

The Wax-plant and many Cacti require a cool spot and only one weekly watering through the winter.

Don't keep potted plants standing in saucers of water; they can be killed by drowning as well as by thirst.

If any dead perennial stalks remain, cut them off 2 ins. above the ground; their stubs will help to catch and hold snow.

Wait until the ground is frozen at least 2 ins. deep before applying winter mulches, and then use materials like straw, salt hay or stiff leaves which will not mat down.

Young perennials from summer-sown seed are best carried through the winter in a shaded frame and set out in spring; if already in the garden, be sure to mulch them.

Set in the coldframe any plants that are not absolutely hardy so that your winter losses will be as light as possible. These include Wallflowers, Sweet Williams, Tritomas, Penstemons, Thymes, Heucheras, Campanulas, some Chrysanthemums, Dianthus, *Salvia larinacaea*.

Roses are planted now, in deeply prepared soil to which compost, rotted manure and bone meal have been added.

Put no winter coverings on Roses until all their leaves have dropped and the wood has been thoroughly ripened by frosty weather.

Then (after hard freezing) apply straw jackets, leaving top open for circulation of air, in Zones 2, 3 and 4.

If not already done, lay Climbers on ground, peg down and bundle with straw, in Zones 2, 3, 4, and 5.

All prunings and other debris should be raked up and burned lest it harbor over-winter diseases and insects.

Until hard freezing weather continue deep soaking of evergreens, both narrow-leaved or "needle" sorts, and broad-leaves like Rhododendrons. In many sections the summer's drought will result in spring losses because the plants have gone into the winter without a water reserve.

Most kinds of woody plants that shed their leaves in autumn can be planted until real winter weather.

Put wire guards around trunks of young Apples to prevent bark gnawing by rodents.

For newly set Rhododendrons, and those in exposed locations, it is safe procedure to erect a windbreak of burlap or storm fencing.

Prune back any unwieldy shrub growth and take out dead branches.

Give the compost heap a final thorough forking and watering to speed winter disintegration.

If there's any doubt about your outdoor storage place being perfectly drained, correct it now before the ground freezes.

DECEMBER

West Coast

GENERAL:

Do any necessary pruning before winter spraying, cutting out diseased or damaged wood to the ground if necessary Christmas cutting will give evergreens all the mild trimming required if carefully done, also most berried shrubs.

More care is needed with oil sprays on this Coast, particularly in California, as dormant periods are shortened for some plants and, for others, nonexistent. Use summer strength for these, and avoid rainy, windy, or hot days. Dormant oils cannot be used on evergreens, or at full strength in lath or greenhouses. Spray deciduous fruits with winter oil emulsion when dormant. Use only summer strength on Wisteria, Clematis, and Roses. Spray with a copper based fungicide several days before applying oil.

Pacific Coast gardens are rich in Christmas gifts. Even gardenless friends appreciate dish and pot material for indoor decoration, often for window, roof, or porch boxes. Dwarf evergreens that were started from cuttings, a potted flowering plant, or even a small fern can glorify a pottery dish. There are abundant northern mosses for background in fish-bowl terrariums. Californians make dish gardens with small offsets of the more attractive Echeverias, Kalanchoes, Aloes, Haworthia and Gasteria, with rugged long-lasting Crassulas and Mexican Sedums for backbone. Even under adverse conditions these should outlast the winter.

NORTHWEST:

In normal years November work may be continued into December, especially planting, though it is better not to disturb fleshy rooted plants such as Delphinium. Plant fruit trees. If you have an electrically heated coldframe for bottom heat, you can start many cuttings, notedly a single Camellia leaf with basal bud attached. Use half-ripened wood for broad-leaved evergreens.

Keep garden cleaned, paths raked, country gardens cut and brush burned. Use winter clean-up spray on dormant plants; but only summer strength on broad-leaved evergreens. Get bait under things where slugs winter. Those masses that look like fish eggs are slug eggs. Check stored bulbs for mice and dampness; protect them from possible frost. Witch Hazel takes winter pruning, but only enough to bring out its pleasing tracery. Use care around Helleborus as creeping stems are close to the surface.

Planter boxes and tubs can be shifted to more sheltered places if contents are tender. Glass houses or heated frames used for most active material need fluorescent lighting these darkest months. Watch coldframes for fungus rot. Rockroses and Escallonias come through here, but need shelter from the occasional north and northeast winds. Note any standing water in the garden and drain. Sometimes it indicates a strategic place for later construction of a Water-lily pool.

For a light shade tree, consider a Birch. White bark of Paper Birch contrasts with our many conifers and broad-leaved evergreens; and the European White Birch is an unusually safe winter tree. Birches are more attractive when grouped.

Though English Holly is a big standby here, not all gardeners realize it comes in a number of varieties, or that many fine species are possible. Belgian Holly has smooth Daphne-like leaves, and lacks the sharp spines that make the English our best protective hedge, but then trimming is less hazardous for the Belgian kind, and it is less uncomfortable at close quarters. Besides the red-berried, there are among the three hundred or so species some with yellow, pink, orange, scarlet, even ice-white and cream berries. Some are tropical, and there is not more than a sampling on the market; but watch local dealers. Self-sown seedlings make fine hedges, though growth is slow the first two years. Bone meal and compost are good; but avoid strong commercial fertilizers and standing water.

Lawn moss outgrows grass in winter unless good applications of rock phosphate now, superphosphate later, are made. Lime tends to release phosphate and potash in the soil for grass root use—grass can fight moss if it has enough available phosphate.

When planting, use great care with rock-garden conifers which are truly dwarf in scale. Such admirable backgrounds as Mugo Pine soon become too large among average rock plants. Local specialists carry truly dwarf conifers. Don't put spreading Junipers near small plants. Their big value is to clothe and hold steep banks, to keep trespassers from cutting a lawn corner, or to soften precipitous walls of large granite boulders.

"Oregon Mist," a day-after-day fine drizzle with low-hanging clouds through periods between, makes up most of the North Coast rainy season. Conifers, Heaths, broad-leaved evergreens thrive lustily. A few upright coniferous branchlets will protect plants of borderline hardihood. Leaf-mold mulching helps if thoroughly dessicated; but sodden leaves are anathema.

Overlooked perennials may still be divided or purchased with the exception of those tending to crown rot. This is also true of changes in the rock garden. In the main it is better to confine planting to hardy shrubs and trees. This is the time to plant fruit trees.

Gardens here should be green and pleasing through the winter with the numerous evergreens both native and nursery grown we use: English Holly, Cotoneasters, and other berried shrubs; winter-flowering Ericas, and lushly green lawns. Place good hybrids of Darley and Spring Heaths under windows. Gain further color with potted Christmas or house plants indoors as foreground to the outer greenery. Helleborus, the Christmas-rose, needs an evergreen ground cover to prevent mud splashings. A pane of glass protects petals.

Parsnips and Salsify keep best if left in the garden over winter here, but Carrots freeze. Brussels Sprouts are usually safe. Don't discard Parsley plants, as they live two or three years in this climate.

CALIFORNIA:
Sprinkle plants caught in a night frost with water before the morning sun touches them, as injury is lessened by slow thawing.

Use a summer oil spray around the bases of Fremontia, Lantana, and Ceanothus, also the crowns of Transvaal Daisies; and a good fungicide on Nectarines, Peaches, and Apricots.

Plant perennial borders through this month and next as opportunity offers. Spade under annuals as they finish, and recondition soil. Sprays of taller plants still in bloom such as Salvias, Rudbeckia, and Michaelmas Daisies may be pegged down over bare places; or buy a flat of Pansies or Dimorphotheca if you failed to sow seed earlier.

Look for bushy plants when purchasing Azaleas and Gardenias, and in growing the latter, permit only one bud to a leaf axil. *Daphne odora* may be planted even in full bloom if moved with a good root ball. For an outdoor living Christmas tree, Nordmann, Spanish, and the mountain form of the White Fir are good. Plant during the rainy season.

Feed plants that bloom normally in California winters like Poinsettias, winter Primroses, Pansies, and Stocks. Withhold it from such as Fuchsias and Roses to force them into the rest period.

Prune Roses as soon as they become dormant between now and February.

California rains are mostly short, but very hard, with much strong sun between. Even so, some succulents need rain shelter, particularly the hairy types and those from Southwest deserts and Mexico. Christmas Cactus and the Queen of Night are jungle plants. South African ones grow through long drought with a rainy season similar to California.

Garden clean-up and planting continue. Mulch any ground not in immediate use with several inches of compost, then top-dress with manure for the rains to wash in. Rabbit or sheep manure is better mixed with two parts of leafmold.

Spray for both pests and fungi. Winter-strength sprays are in general too strong, as most material is not yet sufficiently dormant. Never use oil sprays on succulents; but give the winter ones fertilizer, and protect hairy types from rains. Bait for snails and slugs.

December is a good time to plant perennial borders. Get seed orders in for early annuals. Buy deciduous plants in winter both for lower price and for better results in planting. Evergreens are also better moved with winter rains. When setting grafted trees, face scar union to east or north, away from strong sun. Use powdered charcoal on any cut or bruised Begonia tubers. Store cool in open, well-ventilated flats.

Cold soil is anathema to Gardenias. In cooler gardens tub-grown plants can be shifted to suitable temperatures. Cape-jasmine is a bit more tolerant than the larger flowered Mystery Gardenia, a large shrub to 6 feet that demands even more heat, water, and heavy feeding for its winter and spring bloom. Both take half shade in warmer interior belts, but need sun on the coast. For containers the late-winter-blooming Veitch Gardenia is half as large as Cape-jasmine, and usually evergreen. Even smaller is the foot-high *G. radicans* with 1-inch flowers and very small leaves, happily far less demanding. One part bone meal to two parts each blood and cottonseed meal is a recommended monthly feeding. Acid is imperative, and if soil needs it in December, use iron sulfate.

FOG BELT:

Make, repair, or paint seed flats, trellises, planter boxes, containers, and similar garden furnishings. Clean and oil tools. Speed lagging blooms on Christmas pot plants with liquid chemical fertilizer.

Prepare to shift or plant new shrubs and other material. Roses may be planted or pruned from now on. Consider one at least of the newer Camellias. Azaleas and Magnolias also go in now. Sow Clarkias, Alyssum, Larkspur, Godetia, and Candytuft. Continue bulb planting. Dutch Iris and Crinum may still go in, also Amaryllis, Anemone, Ranunculus, and Lilies.

Protect young trees from rabbits and rodents. Feed plants nearing winter bloom; mulch acid lovers with peat. Though peat or compost may suffice the larger garden conifers, small potted ones with curtailed root run need manure mixed with this. Leafmold or peat mulches protect borders from beating rains.

Prune Ericas and allied plants as they finish blooming; summer-flowering shrubs like Veronica and Hydrangea should be pruned early enough to allow new growth that carries next season's bloom.

Dilute outdoor sprays for shade house or under glass. Use only summer-strength oil on Wisteria, Roses, Clematis, and Trumpet Vine.

Now is the time to plant Onion sets.

Most gardens need some protection from hard packing soil, or from erosion during recurring hard winter rains. Mulching, particularly with well rotted manure, prevents packing provided ridging is applied wherever necessary to keep it from washing away. Careful original grading, deep rooting plants, and ground covers lessen erosion.

Prune Hydrangeas at once if not done already, as later flowers are produced on wood formed after bloom is over. Prune more severely in sun than in shade.

Prepare Rose beds when soil is workable. Roses may be planted from now through late February.

Prune only broken or too old wood on Azaleas, Rhododendron, Camellia, Magnolia. Prune Ericas as soon as they finish flowering, cutting off dead blooms and scraggly branches. Soil sulphur is recommended for Heaths in alkali soils, and the usual peat or leafmold mulch.

Keep Oak leaves and Acorns raked off lawns. Combined with Magnolia and Loquat leaves they are slow to compost, so separate piles may be advisable.

Plant Amaryllis, Lilies, Anemone, Gladiolus, Day lilies, spreading the roots of the last horizontally.

SOUTHERN CALIFORNIA:

Clean up, plant, and pursue pests. Especially spray Roses, and prune unless they are blooming. Plant Camellias, Azaleas, Hollies, and Ericas, Yew, Cypress, Redwood, and Pines. When growing citrus trees in a small garden, choose companion plants of similar tastes—Lavender, Broadleaf Correa, Lantana, Rockroses, Day lilies, Gaillardia, Marguerites, Dianthus, and Sedum are a varied few.

Plant ferns among flowers in lath house and shady borders, also Narcissi, Callas, and woodland Lilies. Use florists' Cyclamen on the coast and in warmer interior belts; but spray for Cyclamen mite. Plant Polyanthus and Baby Primroses in front of ferns. Winter Pansies are California classics, but do best with sun.

Continue to plant bulbs. Mulch Tulips with humus and keep ground moist for long stems. Natal-lily (*Moraea iridioides*), to 2 feet high, is a good hot-garden substitute for Iris.

December is not a big sowing month; but some annuals such as Poppies, Bartonia, Calendula, Sweet Peas, and Clarkia can be sown. Use flats if Pansies, Snapdragons, Larkspur, and Phlox are started.

Avocados may be planted in warmer regions; but protect from frost. Plant Rhubarb, Potatoes, Onion sets, Cauliflower, and Cabbage. Sow cool-weather vegetables including Brussels Sprouts, Peas, Beets, Winter Spinach, Leeks, Lettuce, Endive, and Cress.

Most plants may be set out this month with the exception of tender sub-tropicals. Fruit trees now, but more usually January. Plant conifers and flowering shrubs. Set out Carnation, Cineraria, Stock, Larkspur, and Viola plants; but wait to sow seeds of annuals. Gladiolus, Lily-of-the-valley, and Amaryllis can be planted. The large Cyclamen is an outdoor plant in much of Southern California, though often grown in shade house or patio to protect from rain. Watch for Cyclamen mite on this. Rotenone or nicotine sprays are effective.

Spring borders must be planned while fall flowers still linger, and an entire garden of winter bloom is just coming into flower—*Magnolia soulangeana, Acacia baileyana,* Azalea, Camellia, Amazon and Kafir Lilies, September-set Petunias, Pansies, and Stocks, to mention a few. Brilliant Poinsettias are in full bloom as are Roses and Chrysanthemums.

Watch vines and as soon as dormant, prune from ⅓ to ½ of old wood, also thinning undergrowth of the more rampant.

South

GENERAL:

Shrubs should be planted in thoroughly prepared planting beds where sod has been removed, fertilizer added and entire bed spaded to a depth of at least 10 inches. Do not plant shrubs in pocket holes dug in sod.

To prepare a planting bed for shrubs first locate positions of plants with small stakes. Then outline bed with garden hose or rope, enclosing groups of planting stakes. Place a line of stakes along inside of hose, remove sod within this area, add fertilizer, spade and rake.

The amount of fertilizer to add to shrub beds will vary with conditions, but a general rule to follow is to use 1 pound complete commercial fertilizer for each 20 square feet of bed space and 2 inches of well rotted manure, both well mixed with soil.

Edge the newly prepared shrub bed by throwing the soil toward the middle of bed, away from clean-cut edge of sod. It may be necessary to remove some soil from beds to prevent excessive mounding of center.

Phosphate is an important element in plant food, stimulating flower and fruit production. It can be secured as superphosphate (acid phosphate), basic slag, and mixed fertilizers. It must be mixed with the soil at the time the soil is prepared for planting as it does not dissolve and travel through the soil. It is a mistake to believe that all plant food needed by plants can be added after plants are established, without reworking the soil.

Potash is a general plant conditioner that intensifies flower color and stimulates fruit production. If your flowers lack brilliance or your berry-producing plants are disappointing, add potash to soil (surface application is satisfactory). Sources of potash are: muriate of potash, wood ashes and mixed fertilizers.

Examine shrub beds carefully to locate any volunteer shrub or tree seedlings that should be removed. Hackberry and Elm seedlings often become troublesome weeds. Nandina, Wax-leaf Privet and other choice volunteer seedlings can be transplanted to nursery rows to be grown on for future use.

Practically all plants are dormant; the soil is in fine condition to work; the weather is cool, but not too cold for comfort—so this is ideal planting time for trees, shrubs, vines, Roses and perennials.

Using special equipment, you can transplant large trees, but trees 6 to 8 feet tall are usually the best size to move under ordinary conditions.

When transplanting any plant, dig the hole deeper and wider than the root system of the plant. Place fertile topsoil in bottom of hole, mixing a small quantity of complete commercial fertilizer with soil, and covering this mixture with a thin layer of topsoil. Set plants slightly deeper than they were growing in nursery row.

Water is a clean, convenient medium for growing many plants such as Coleus, English Ivy, Wandering Jew, Vinca, Devils-ivy, Hyacinth and Narcissus. A Sweet Potato makes an interesting plant in water medium. A few crystals of epsom salts added to the water stimulate the plants.

After transplanting trees, water thoroughly and set stakes or support trees with guy wires. Three wires, carefully attached to a tree 4 to 5 feet from ground will suffice for 6- to 8-foot trees. Short sections of garden hose with guy wires run through them will protect tree bark from injury.

After shrubs are planted, spade entire shrub bed area to a depth of at least 6 inches, removing all grass and weeds. Level with rake and trim edges of bed for neat, attractive finish.

Winter injury to shrubs can often be prevented by maintaining adequate moisture in soil during the winter. Soak the shrub beds thoroughly if rains have not provided sufficient moisture.

All dead and diseased wood should be removed from trees, shrubs, vines and Roses by careful pruning. Large cuts, to remove limbs 2 or more inches in diameter, should be painted with waterproof paint.

Flower beds for spring planting will be greatly improved if they are cleaned, fertilized and spaded now. Leave surfaces of soil rough so weather can break down soil particles. Use four pounds of complete commercial fertilizer to each 100 square feet of bed space.

Lilies provide beautiful color accent in shrub borders when planted in groups. Widely used and admired are: Regal Lily, Tiger Lily, Speciosum Lily and Formosa Lily.

The several varieties of Dutch Iris, with their rich brilliant colors, rate star billing in the bulb garden. The flowers are lovely in the garden or in floral arrangements, having a rather long life in either category.

Mature wood, the size and length of a lead pencil, of several flowering shrubs will root easily. Notable examples of easily propagated shrubs are: Winter Honeysuckle, Weigela, Beauty-bush, Butterfly bush, Abelia, Althea, Forsythia and Spirea.

Exotic, unusual shrubs that have to be petted are all right for the plant collector's garden, but in the foundation planting around the house use the most rugged and reliable plants.

Prune shrub plantings to remove dead wood, excess growth and straggling branches. If the pruning of broadleaf and narrowleaf evergreens is done near Christmas time, excellent holiday decorating material is made readily available.

A wire coat hanger bent into a circle makes an excellent frame for a Christmas wreath, with the hook for hanging already attached.

CENTRAL AND LOWER SOUTH:
Camellia plants growing in dense shade, or in very fertile soil, tend to produce fewer flowers than those growing in sun and in soils of average fertility.

Camellias growing in full sun are more likely to be injured by cold weather than plants growing in partial shade because rapid thawing of frozen tissue in this plant often kills it. Temporary shade protection on mornings when the temperature is below freezing will help plants growing on locations that receive full morning sun.

These shrubs will add lovely fragrance as well as color to your garden: Abelia, Butterfly bush, Daphne, Escallonia, Honeysuckle, Cape-jasmine, Night-blooming Jasmine and Sweet Olive.

Dig and store Dahlia tubers and Tuberose bulbs in a cool dry place. They should be allowed to dry thoroughly for twenty-four hours before being placed in storage. Leave the tubers and bulbs in clusters, storing them in inverted positions in peatmoss or sand.

Flower seeds to plant include: Alyssum, Baby's-breath (single), African Daisy, California Poppy, Calendula, Chinese Forget-me-not, Coreopsis, Candytuft, annual Carnation, Gaillardia, Godetia, Hollyhock, Hunnemannia, Larkspur, Scabiosa, Snapdragon, Sweet peas, Stocks and Verbena. The plants of most of the flowers can also be set in open beds now.

Bulbs to plant are: Amaryllis, Crinum, Eucharis, Dutch Iris and Tulips from cold storage.

Vegetable seeds to plant are: Beets, Brussels Sprouts, Broccoli, Carrots, Collards, Lettuce, Onions, Radish, Garden Peas, and Turnips.

Plant hardy annual seed, such as: Arctotis, Coreopsis, Candytuft, Cornflower, Strawflower, Larkspur, California Poppy, Shirley Poppy and Drummond Phlox.

Pansies and English Daisies (plants) must be planted now if a long season of bloom is desired.

Bulbs that can still be planted include Japanese Lilies, Dutch Iris, Ranunculus, Tulips, Hyacinth, Daffodils.

UPPER SOUTH:

Evergreens frequently need two or three liberal waterings during winter. Cold injury is much more severe when the soil is dry.

Two or three strands of heavy cord tied around evergreens such as Greek Juniper, Swedish Juniper, and Irish Juniper will prevent serious damage from snow and ice during winter. These should be removed in spring.

Plant Asparagus, Globe Artichoke, and Horseradish in the vegetable garden. Plant Radish and Lettuce seed in the coldframe and flavoring herbs in the herb garden.

A dark, inconspicuous strand of small wire, placed around upright Junipers and Arbor-vitae plants may save them from severe damage by ice.

Mulch perennial and Rose beds with 4 to 6 inches of leaves, straw or grass. It is usually a wise practice to pull soil up around Rose plants to a height of 8 to 10 inches. Place mulch over these soil mounds.

These bulbs can still be planted: Anemone, Ranunculus, Tulip, Narcissus, Hyacinth, Squill, Snowdrop, Crocus and Grape-hyacinth.

Cut flowering stems of Chrysanthemums and other perennials back to the ground as they finish flowering.

North

A thorough clean-up and burning of garden rubbish will destroy many wintering-over insect eggs, larvae and disease germs. Lime sulphur and miscible-oil sprays are the standard controls for scale insects on trees, shrubs and vines.

Climbing Rose canes can be badly injured if whipped around by winter winds, so tie them to the trellis unless they have been bundled and laid on the ground. Make notes on any Rose plants you see with colorful hips or seed fruits, as a guide to future ordering.

After its fall rest, the Christmas Cactus now requires plenty of sun, watering about every third day and plant food according to the brand directions.

Keep all house plants free of dead leaves or dying branches. Stir top soil frequently with a fork. Feed only those in active state of growth.

Set out bird feeders and keep filled with wild bird seed, crumbs and suet. Equally important for them is water, which birds often cannot obtain during freezing spells. Put it in a cement or wooden container rather than metal.

Take cuttings of Begonias and Geraniums for extra plants next summer. Cut pieces of healthy, firm branches 3 or 4 ins. long just below a joint. Remove lower leaves and insert slip in clean sand, or a 50-50 mixture of sand and peatmoss. After small roots have formed, pot up in light soil and keep repotting to larger containers as the plants grow.

Pot up some more Daffodil bulbs for bloom indoors in late winter. Set them in the coldframe until roots have formed, then bring in to a cool room for gradual forcing.

Plants in full growth should have an application of plant food now. Use a prepared tablet or powder dissolved in water, or else the liquid kind from your seed store; follow directions carefully.

The Christmas Cactus after a fall rest now requires plenty of sun, watering about every third day and plant food according to the brand directions.

If Crassula or Jade plant leaves are yellowing or falling, omit water entirely for 1 or 2 weeks and thereafter water only about once or twice weekly; examine joints for presence of mealy bugs.

Let Begonias dry out a little between drinks.

Watch the heavy foliaged Rubber plants, etc., for scale on underside of leaves.

Place a "keep off" sign on the lawn for the winter, or better still, place some sort of barrier across "short cuts" likely to be used. Serious injury is caused by tramping sod during alternate freezings and thawings.

Even though the ground may be still frost-free, any proposed transplanting of perennials had better wait until spring. The plants would not have time to re-establish themselves before really cold weather, and winter damage might be considerable.

Mulches go on this month, as soon as the ground is frozen solid. Leaves, salt hay, evergreen branches and straw are good materials; for acid loving plants, use peatmoss, Pine needles and Oak leaves.

Don't make that winter mulch too thick, lest the plants be smothered and perhaps rotted. Two or three inches of light material is usually enough.

Store up clean wood ashes from the fireplace this winter, to spade into the ground in early spring. Wood ashes are a good source of potash.

Newly set trees should have firm support supplied either by 3 guy wires, securely anchored, or by a stout stake driven into the ground. Old hose or coarse burlap will protect the bark of the tree against injury from the support holding it.

Pruning should receive attention now. Cut back old growth, crossed limbs, branches growing inward to the trunk. If the autumn storms did most of your pruning for you, ragged branches and broken limbs will still have to be taken off. Saw close to the trunk of the main limb so as to leave no "knobs" sticking out. Paint large cuts over with prepared tree paint.

If good sized trees are to be moved, dig, permit root ball to freeze, then transplant.

Check labels attached to branches, as well as all guy wires, to make sure they are not cutting into the bark. . . . Wisteria and other woody vines grown on supports should be inspected for weak ties or other attachments. . . . A permanent, year-round mulch of Oak leaves under Rhododendrons, Azaleas and Mountain Laurel helps maintain soil acidity and stabilize moisture.

THE HOME GARDENER'S SELF-PRONOUNCING DICTIONARY OF PLANT NAMES

FOREWORD

The purpose of this "dictionary" is to make it easier for home gardeners to pronounce and understand the true names of plants.

There is an almost frightening disagreement among authoritative reference works as to the spelling of botanical names of plants, as to their derivations and meanings and, above all, as to their pronunciation. In the realm of "common" names, there is sheer chaos. Throughout, it has been our effort to follow, in all instances, what seemed the soundest authority and, if necessary, to set up our own. To that end, many source books, several of them available to gardeners generally, were consulted. For the spelling of the botanical names, the chief authority has been *Hortus Second,* compiled by L. H. Bailey and Ethel Zoë Bailey. For the derivation or detailed significance of the generic names, as well as for their pronunciation, the chief authority has been *Webster's New International Dictionary, Second Edition.* For the names of species, L. H. Bailey's *Standard Cyclopedia of Horticulture* and *Hortus Second* have been referred to about equally as guides.

The phonetic spellings throughout are our own and are designed solely as keys to the sounds it is necessary to make in order to transfer the written words into intelligible speech. In every aspect of the preparation of this pronouncing guide we have endeavored to interpret in a common-sense way the prevailing weight of horticultural acceptance. Where we have deviated from the sources just mentioned, and many others as well, we have done so to achieve directness and to avoid confusion. In general, we follow here the approach to the handling of plant names which was evolved for THE HOME GARDEN.

RALPH BAILEY

GENERIC PLANT NAMES
Genus: singular — Genera: plural

The generic name, or genus, serves a plant as the surname serves a person. The specific name, or species, serves a plant as a given name serves a person. Specific names are considered beginning on page 483. Below begins the listing, in alphabetical sequence, of over 2000 plant genera which are or have been under cultivation in this country (most agricultural and non-horticultural plants being omitted).

After each generic entry, which is printed in **bold face,** a derivation, meaning, or interpretation follows *(italicized, in parentheses),* if such exists or is generally significant. This interpretation may be a person's name; a literal translation of the plant name or its component parts, whatever the language of their origin; or a significant translation with or without its application to the plant genus concerned.

In every case a phonetic—foh-*net*-ik—pronunciation is provided, according to sounds and without regard to any known rules for syllable division or grammar. The stressed sound is printed in *italic* type. The other sounds are in ordinary type, strung-together-with-hyphens. When pronounced in sequence, at normal speed, they should give an accurate pronunciation of the whole word.

Next follow, under each entry, the common name of the genus, if any; or the common name of a species if it is the only species known or commonly in cultivation; or the common name of one or more important species, together with their specific names. Other notes of interest are occasionally included.

A

Abelia (*for Dr. Clarke Abel*) — Ab-*beel*-ee-uh: Glossy Abelia

Abies — *Ay*-bih-eez: Fir.

Abronia (*delicate*) — Ab-*roh*-nee-uh: Sand-verbena.

Abrus (*delicate*) — *Ay*-brus.

Abutilon — Ab-*yew*-til-on: Flowering-maple.

Acacia (*point, thorn*) — Ak-*kay*-see-uh, Ak-*kay*-shuh.

Acaena (*thorn*) — Ass-*see*-nuh: New Zealand Bur.

Acalypha — Ak-al-*lye*-fuh: Copper Leaf, Three-seeded Mercury.

Acanthocereus (*thorny-Cereus*) — Ak-anth-oh-*seer*-ee-us.

Acantholimon (*thorny-Sea-Lavender*)—Ak-anth-oh-*lye*-mon: Prickly Thrift.

Acanthopanax (*thorny-Panax*) — Ak-anth-oh-*pay*-nax.

Acanthus (*thorn*) — Ak-*kanth*-us: Bears-breech.

Acer — *Ay*-ser: Maple.

Achillea — Ak-il-*lee*-uh: Yarrow.

Achimines (*suffering-from-cold*) — Ak-*kim*-in-eez.

Acidanthera (*sharp-anther*) — Ass-id-*anth*-er-uh.

Acineta (*immovable*) — Ass-in-*nee*-tuh.

Aconitum—Ak-oh-*nye*-tum: Monks-hood, Aconite.

Actaea — Ak-*tee*-uh: Actea, Baneberry, Cohosh.

Actinidia (*for ray-like styles*) — Ak-tin-*nid*-ee-uh.

Actinophloeus — Ak-tin-oh-*flee*-us: Cluster Palm.

Adansonia (*for French botanist Michael Adanson*) — Ad-an-*soh*-nee-uh: Baobab-tree.

Adenanthera (*for glandular anthers*) — Ad-en-*anth*-er-uh: Bead Tree.

Adenocarpus (*for glandular fruit*) — Ad-en-oh-*karp*-us.

Adenophora (*for glandular nectary*) — Ad-en-oh-*foh*-ruh: Ladybell.

Adiantum (*unwetted*) — Ad-ee-*an*-tum: Maidenhair Fern.

Adlumia (*for American gardener John Adlum*) — Ad-*loo*-mee-uh: Climbing Fumitory, Mountain Fringe, Alleghany Vine.

Adonis (*for mythical Adonis*) — Ad-*doh*-niss, Ad-*don*-niss: Pheasants-eye.

Adoxa (*without-glory*) — Ad-*dox*-uh: Musk-root.

Aechmea (*for pointed calyx*) — *Eek*-mee-uh.

Aegopodium (*goat-foot*) — Ee-go-*poh*-dee-um: Goutweed.

Aërides (*air-plant*) — Ay-*ehr*-id-eez.

Aesculus — *Ess*-kew-lus: Horse-chestnut, Buckeye.

Aethionema — Eeth-ee-oh-*nee*-muh: Stone-cress.

Agapanthus (*love-flower*) — Ag-ap-*panth*-us: Lily-of-the-Nile.

Agathis (*ball of thread: for clustered flowers*) — *Ag*-ath-iss: Dammar-pine.

Agave (*admirable*) — Ag-*gay*-vee.

Ageratum (*not-growing-old*) — Aj-er-*ray*-tum.

Aglaonema (*bright-thread*) — Ag-lay-oh-*nee*-muh.

Agrimonia — Ag-rim-*moh*-nee-uh: Agrimony.

Agrostemma (*field-garland*) — Ag-ros-*stem*-uh: (See Lychnis)

Agrostis (*field, as to habitat*) — Ag-*ross*-tiss: Bent-grass.

Ailanthus — Ay-*lanth*-us: Tree of Heaven.

Ajuga (*not-yoked, as to calyx*) — Aj-*yew*-guh: Bugleweed.

Akebia — Ak-*kee*-bee-uh.

Albizzia (*for an Italian family, the Albizzi*) — Al-*biz*-ee-uh.

Alchemilla—Al-kem-*mill*-uh: Ladys-mantle.

Aletris — *Al*-et-riss: Star-grass.

Alisma — Al-*liz*-muh: Water-plantain.

Allamanda (*for Swiss scientist, J. N.*

S. *Allamand*) — Al-lam-*mand*-uh.
Allium — *Al*-lee-um.
Allionia — Al-lee-*oh*-nee-uh: Umbrella-wort.
Alnus (*the classical name*) — *Al*-nus: Alder.
Alocasia — Al-oh-*kay*-zee-uh.
Aloe — Al-*loh*-ee.
Alonsoa (*for Spaniard Alonzo Zanoni*) — Al-*lon*-zoh-uh.
Alopecurus (*fox-tail*) — Al-oh-pee-*kew*-rus: Meadow-foxtail.
Alpinia (*for Italian botanist Prosper Alpinus*) — Al-*pin*-ee-uh.
Alsophila (*grove-loving*) — Al-*soff*-il-uh: Tree-fern.
Alstroemeria (*for Baron Alstroemer*) — Al-strem-*meer*-ee-uh: Alstremeria.
Alternanthera (*alternate-flowers*) — Al-ter-*nanth*-er-uh.
Alyssum — Al-*liss*-um: Alyssum, Madwort.
Amaranthus (*unfading*) — Am-ar-*ranth*-us: Amaranth.
Amarcrinum (*for Amaryllis and Crinum*) — Am-ar-*krye*-num.
Amaryllis — Am-ar-*rill*-iss.
Amelanchier — Am-el-*lank*-ee-uh: Shadbush.
Amellus (*for river Mella*) — Am-*mell*-us.
Amianthium — Am-ee-*anth*-ee-um.
Ammobium (*living-in-sand*) — Am-*moh*-bee-um: Winged Everlasting.
Amomum — Am-*moh*-mum.
Amorpha (*formless*) — Am-*morf*-uh: False-indigo.
Amorphophallus (*irregularly-phallus-formed*) — Am-mor-foh-*fal*-lus.
Ampelopsis (*vine-like*) — Am-pel-*lop*-siss.
Amphicome (*for hairy seeds*) — Am-*fik*-om-ee.

Amsonia (*for physician Charles Amson*) — Am-*soh*-nee-uh.
Anacampseros — An-ak-*kamp*-ser-oss.
Anacardium (*for heart-shaped nut*) — An-ak-*kard*-ee-um: Cashew.
Anacyclus — An-ass-*sye*-klus.
Anagallis (*delighting*) — An-ag-*gal*-liss: Pimpernel.
Ananas — An-*nan*-ass: Pineapple.
Anaphalis — An-*naff*-al-iss.
Anchusa (*for a skin paint*) — An-*kew*-suh: Alkanet.
Andira — An-*dye*-ruh: Angelin-tree.
Andromeda (*for mythical Andromeda*) — An-*drom*-ed-uh: Bog-rosemary.
Androsace — An-*dross*-ass-ee: Rock-jasmine.
Anemone (*wind*) — An-*nem*-on-ee: Anemone, Windflower.
Anemonella (*little-Anemone*) — An-em-on-*nell*-uh: Rue-anemone.
Anemopsis (*Anemone-like*) — An-em-*mop*-siss: Yerba Mansa.
Anethum — An-*neeth*-um: Dill.
Angelica (*lovely*) — An-*jell*-ik-uh.
Angelonia — An-jel-*loh*-nee-uh.
Angraecum — An-*greek*-um.
Anguloa (*for Spanish Don Francisco de Angulo*) — An-gew-*loh*-uh.
Anigozanthos (*expanded-flower*) — An-ig-oh-*zanth*-os.
Annona — An-*non*-nuh.
Anoda — An-*noh*-duh.
Antennaria (*antennae-like, as to some parts*) — An-ten-*nay*-ree-uh: Everlasting.
Anthemis — *Anth*-em-iss: Chamonile.
Anthericum (*flower-hedge*) — Anth-*ehr*-ik-um.
Anthriscus — An-*thrisk*-us.
Anthurium (*tail-flower, as to appearance*) — An-*thew*-ree-um.

Anthyllis (*downy-flowers*) — An-*thill*-iss.

Antiaris — An-tee-*ay*-riss: Upas-tree.

Antidesma — An-tid-*dess*-muh: Big-nay.

Antigonon (*opposite-angle, as to drooping flowers*) — An-*tig*-oh-non.

Antirrhinum (*snout-flower*) — An-tihr-*rye*-num: Snapdragon.

Aphelandra — Af-fel-*land*-ruh.

Apios (*for Pear-shaped tuber*)—*Ap*-pee-os: Ground-nut.

Apium — *Ay*-pee-um: Celery.

Aplectrum (*without-spur*) — Ap-*plek*-trum: Putty-root, Adam-and-Eve.

Apocynum — Ap-oh-*sye*-num: Dog-bane.

Aponogeton (*for its aquatic habit*) — Ap-poh-noh-*jeet*-on.

Aporocactus (*impenetrable-Cactus*) — Ap-or-oh-*kak*-tus.

Aptenia — Ap-*teen*-ee-uh.

Aquilegia (*water-drawer; possibly, by an earlier name, for an eagle*) — Ak-wil-*leej*-ee-uh: Columbine.

Arabis — *Ar*-ab-iss: Rock-cress.

Arachis — *Ar*-ak-iss: Peanut.

Aralia — Ar-*ray*-lee-uh.

Araucaria — Ar-raw-*kay*-ree-uh.

Araujia — Ar-*raw*-jee-uh.

Arbutus — Arb-*yew*-tus.

Archontophoenix (*majestic-Phoenix*) — Ark-on-toh-*fee*-nix: King Palm.

Arctostaphylos (*bear-grape*) — Ark-toh-*staff*-il-os: Bearberry, Manzanita.

Arctotis (*bear's-ear*) — Ark-*toh*-tiss.

Ardisia (*pointed, as to stamens*) — Ard-*diz*-ee-uh.

Areca — Ar-*reek*-uh

Arecastrum—Ar-ek-*kast*-rum· Queen Palm

Aregelia (*for botanist C. von Regel*) — Ar-rej-*eel*-ee-uh.

Arenaria (*for sand*) — Ar-ren-*nay*-ree-uh: Sandwort.

Arethusa (*for mythical nymph*) — Ar-eth-*thew*-suh.

Argemone (*for an eye disease for which this may have been remedial*) — Ar-*jem*-on-ee: Prickly-poppy.

Argyreia (*silvery, as to under-leaves*) — Ar-jih-*ree*-uh.

Aridaria — Ar-rid-*day*-ree-uh.

Ariocarpus — Ar-ree-oh-*karp*-us.

Arisaema—Ar-riss-*seem*-uh.

Aristea (*stiff, as to leaf points*) — Ar-riss-*tee*-uh.

Aristolochia — Ar-rist-oh-*loh*-kee-uh: Birthwort.

Aristotelia (*for Aristotle*) — Ar-rist-oh-*teel*-ee-uh.

Armeria — Arm-*meer*-ee-uh: Thrift, Sea-pink.

Arnebia — Arn-*nee*-bee-uh.

Arnica — *Arn*-ik-uh.

Aronia — Ar-*roh*-nee-uh: Choke-berry.

Artabotrys (*suspended-grapes*) — Art-*tab*-ot-riss: Tail-grape.

Artemisia (*for wife of Mausolus*) — Art-em-*miz*-ee-uh: Wormwood.

Arthropodium (*jointed-foot*) — Arth-roh-*poh*-dee-um.

Artocarpus (*bread-fruit*) — Art-oh-*karp*-us: Bread-fruit.

Arum — *Ay*-rum.

Aruncus (*the classical name*) — Ar-*runk*-us: Goats-beard.

Arundinaria — Ar-run-din-*nay*-ree-uh.

Asarum — *Ass*-uh-um: Wild Ginger.

Asclepias — Ass-*kleep*-ee-ass: Milk-weed.

Ascyrum — Ass-*sye*-rum.

Asimina — Ass-*sim*-in-uh.

Asparagus — Ass-*par*-ag-us.
Asperula (*roughish, as to leaves*) —
Ass-*pehr*-yew-luh: Woodruff.
Asphodeline — Ass-foh-del-*lye*-nee:
Jacob's rod.
Asphodelus — Ass-*fod*-el-us: Asphodel.
Aspidistra (*small-round-shield, for
shape of stigma*) — Ass-pid-*dist*-ruh.
Asplenium (*not-the-spleen, as to medicinal use*) — Ass-*pleen*-ee-um:
Spleenwort.
Aster (*star*) — *Ass*-ter.
Astilbe (*not-shining*) — Ass-*till*-bee.
Astragalus — Ass-*trag*-al-us: Milk
Vetch.

Astrantia (*star-like, as to umbels*) —
Ass-*trant*-ee-uh: Masterwort.
Astrophytum (*Star-plant*) — Ass-*troff*-it-um: Star Cactus.
Athyrium — Ath-*theer*-ee-um: see
Asplenium.
Atraphaxis — At-ruh-*fax*-iss.
Atriplex — *At*-rip-plex: Saltbush.
Aubrietia (*for French painter Claude
Aubriet*) — Aw-*bree*-she-uh.
Aucuba — Aw-*kew*-buh.
Aureolaria — Aw-ree-ol-*lay*-ree-uh.
Averrhoa (*for Arabian philosopher
Averrhoes*) — Av-er-*roh*-uh.
Azalea — Az-*zay*-lee-uh: see Rhododendron.
Azara (*for Spanish naturalist Azara*)
— Az-*zar*-uh.

B

Babiana — Bab-ee-*ay*-nuh.
Baccharis — Bak-*kar*-iss.
Bactris (*cane*) — *Bak*-triss.
Baeria (*for Estonian naturalist Karl
von Baer*) — *Behr*-ee-uh: Goldfields.
Balsamorhiza — Bol-sam-or-*rye*-zuh:
Balsam-root.
Bambusa — Bam-*bew*-suh: Bamboo.
Banksia (*for English naturalist Sir Joseph Banks*) — *Banks*-ee-uh.
Baptisia (*a-dipping, as for color dyeing*) — Bap-*tiz*-ee-uh: False or
Wild Indigo.
Barbarea (*for Saint Barbara*) —
Barb-uh-*ree*-uh: Winter-cress, Upland-cress.
Barklya (*for Australian Sir Henry
Barkly*) — *Bark*-lee-uh.
Barleria (*for botanist J. Barrelier*) —
Bar-*leer*-ee-uh.
Barosma (*heavy-smell*) — Bar-*roz*-muh.
Barringtonia (*for English judge and

naturalist Daines Barrington) —
Bar-ring-*toh*-nee-uh.
Bauera (*for Francis and Ferdinand
Bauer, botanical painters*) —
Bahw-er-uh.
Bauhinia (*for Swiss botanists Jean
and Gaspard Bauhin*) — Boh-*hin*-ee-uh.
Beaucarnea — Boh-*karn*-ee-uh.
Befaria — Bef-*fay*-ree-uh: Tar-flower.
Begonia (*for Michel Bégon*) — Beg-*goh*-nee-uh.
Belamcanda — Bel-am-*kan*-duh.
Bellis (*pretty*) — *Bell*-iss.
Bellium (*for its likeness to Bellis*) —
Bel-lee-um.
Beloperone (*for arrow-shaped anthers*) — Bel-op-er-*oh*-nee.
Benzoin (*perfume, as to resin*) —
Ben-zoin: see preferred Lindera.
Berberidopsis (*Berberis-like*) — Berber-id-*dop*-siss.
Berberis — *Ber*-ber-iss: Barberry.

Berchemia — Ber-*kee*-mee-uh.

Bergenia (*for German botanist K. A. von Bergen*) — Ber-*jee*-nee-uh.

Berteroa — Ber-ter-*roh*-uh.

Bertolonia (*for Italian botanist Antonio Bertoloni*) — Ber-toh-*loh*-nee-uh.

Beta — *Bee*-tuh: Beet.

Betula — *Bet*-yew-luh: Birch.

Bidens (*two-teeth, as for its awns or bristles*) — *Bye*-denz: Bur-marigold, Tickseed.

Bifrenaria (*twice-strapped, as to pollen*) — Bye-fren-*nay*-ree-uh.

Bignonia (*for French Abbé Jean Paul Bignon*) — Big-*noh*-nee-uh: Trumpet-flower: see also Campsis.

Billardiera (*for botanist J. J. Labillardière*) — Bil-lard-*deer*-uh.

Billbergia (*for Swiss botanist J. G. Billberg*) — Bil-*burr*-jee-uh.

Biscutella — Bye-skew-*tell*-uh.

Bixa — *Bix*-uh: Annatto.

Blandfordia (*for the Marquis of Blandford*) — Bland-*ford*-ee-uh.

Blechnum — *Blek*-num.

Bletia (*for Spanish pharmacist Luis Blet*) — *Blee*-tee-uh: see Bletilla.

Bletilla (*diminutive of Bletia*) — Blet-*till*-uh.

Blighia (*for Wm. Bligh, British mariner*) — *Blye*-gee-uh: Akee.

Bloomeria (*for American botanist H. G. Bloomer*) — Bloo-*meer*-ee-uh: Golden-stars.

Blumenbachia (*for Dr. J. F. Blumenbach*) — Bloo-men-*bahk*-ee-uh.

Boehmeria (*for German botanist G. R. Boehmer*) — Boh-*meer*-ee-uh.

Boltonia (*for English botanist James Bolton*) — Bolt-*toh*-nee-uh.

Bomarea (*for French naturalist J. C. V. de Bomare*) — Boh-*may*-ree-uh.

Borago — Boh-*ray*-go.

Boronia (*for Francesco Borone*) — Boh-*roh*-nee-uh.

Botrychium (*for grape-like parts*) — Boh-*trik*-ee-um: Grape-fern, Moonwort.

Bougainvillea (*for French navigator L. A. de Bougainville*) — Boog-in-*vill*-ee-uh.

Boussingaultia (*for French chemist J. B. J. D. Boussingault*) — Boo-sin-*gol*-tee-uh: Madeira- or Mignonette-vine.

Bouvardia (*for French physician Chas. Bouvard*) — Boo-*vard*-ee-uh.

Boykinia (*for one Dr. Boykin*) — Boy-*kin*-ee-uh.

Brachichyton (*for overlapping hairs and scales*) — Brak-ik-*kye*-ton: Bottle-tree.

Brachycome (*short-hair, as to tufts*) — Brak-*kik*-oh-me: Swan River Daisy.

Brachipodium (*short-foot*) — Bak-ip-*poh*-dee-um.

Brachysema (*short-standard, as to flower*) — Brak-iss-*seem*-uh.

Brassavola (*for Venetian botanist A. M. Brassavola*) — Brass-av-*voh*-luh.

Brassia (*for American botanist William Brass*) — Brass-ee-uh.

Brassica (*Latin for Cabbage*) — *Brass*-ik-uh: The Cole crops and Mustards.

Brevoortia (*for naturalist J. C. Breevoort*) — Brev-*voor*-tee-uh: Floral Fire-cracker.

Brickellia (*for one Dr. John Brickel*) — Brik-*kell*-ee-uh.

Brodiaea (*for Scottish botanist J. J. Brodie*) — Broh-dih-*ee*-uh: Brodiea.

Bromelia (*for Swedish botanist Olaf Bromel*) — Broh-*mee*-lee-uh.

Bromus (*classical name for Oats*) — Broh-mus: Brome-grass.

Broussonetia (*for French naturalist Pierre Broussonet*) — Broo-soh-*nee*-she-uh: Paper-mulberry.

Browallia (*for Swedish botanist J. Browall*) — Broh-*wal*-lee-uh.

Brownea (*for one Patrick Brown*) — Brown-ee-uh.

Bruckenthalia (*for an Austrian, von Bruckenthal*) — Brook-en-*thay*-lee-uh: Spike-heath.

Brunella — Broo-*nell*-uh: see Prunella.

Brunfelsia (*for German botanist Otto Brunfels*) — Brunn-*fel*-zee-uh.

Brunnera — Brunn-er-uh.

Brunsvigia (*for the Duke of Brunswick*) — Brunz-*vij*-ee-uh.

Bryonia (*to sprout, as of annual growth of tuber*) — Brye-*oh*-nee-uh: Briony.

Bryophyllum (*sprouting-leaf*) — Brye-oh-*fill*-um: see Kalanchoe.

Buckleya (*for American botanist S. B. Buckley*) — Buck-lee-uh.

Buddleia (*for English botanist Adam Buddle*) — Bud-*lee*-uh: Butterfly-bush.

Bulbine (*classical word for bulb*) — Bulb-*bye*-nee.

Bulbinella (*diminutive of Bulbine*) — Bulb-in-*nell*-uh.

Bulbocodium (*woolly bulb*) — Bulb-oh-*koh*-dee-um.

Bulbophyllum (*bulb-leaf*) — Bulb-oh-*fill*-um.

Bumelia — Bew-*mee*-lee-uh: Chittamwood, False-buckthorn.

Buphthalmum (*ox-eye*) — Bewf-*thal*-mum: Ox-eye.

Bupleurum — Bew-*ploor*-um: Thorough-wax.

Butomus (*ox-cut, as too sharp for forage*) — *Bew*-toh-mus: Flowering-rush.

Buxus — *Bux*-us: Box.

Byrnesia (*for E. M. Byrnes*) — Burn-*zee*-uh: see Graptopetalum.

C

Caesalpinia (*for Italian botanist Andreas Caesalpinus*) — Sez-al-*pin*-ee-uh.

Caiophora — Kay-*off*-or-uh.

Cajanus — Kaj-*ay*-nus: Pigeon-pea.

Caladium — Kal-*lay*-dee-um.

Calandrinia (*for Swiss botanist Jean Calandrini*) — Kal-an-*drin*-ee-uh.

Calanthe (*beautiful-flower*) — Kal-*lanth*-ee.

Calathea (*basket, as to shape of flower*) — Kal-ath-*ee*-uh.

Calceolaria (*little-shoe, as to shape of flower*) — Kal-see-oh-*lay*-ree-uh: Slipperwort.

Calendula (*for the calends, the first of the month when plant was supposed to bloom*) — Kal-*lend*-yew-luh.

Calimeris (*beautiful-parts*) — Kal-*lim*-er-iss.

Calla — *Kal*-luh: Water-arum, Wild Calla.

Calliandra (*beautiful-stamens*) — Kal-lee-*and*-ruh.

Callicarpa (*beautiful-fruit*) — Kal-lik-*karp*-uh: Beauty-berry.

Calliopsis — Kal-lee-*op*-siss: see Coreopsis.

Callirhoe (*beautiful-flow*) — Kal-*lihr*-oh-ee: Poppy-mallow.

Callistemon (*beautiful-thread, as to*

color of stamens) —Kal-liss-*steem*-on: Bottle-brush.

Callistephus (*beautiful-crown*) — Kal-*liss*-tef-us: China Aster.

Callitris (*beauty*) — Kal-*lye*-triss: Cypress-Pine.

Calluna (*to sweep clean, to beautify*) — Kal-*lew*-nuh: Heather.

Calocephalus (*beautiful-head, as to flower*) — Kal-oh-*seff*-al-us.

Calochortus (*beautiful-grass, as to foliage*) — Kal-oh-*kort*-us: Mariposa-lily, Globe-tulip.

Calodendrum (*beautiful-tree*) —Kal-oh-*den*-drum: Cape Chestnut.

Calonyction (*beautiful-at-night*) — Kal-oh-*nik*-tee-on: Moonflower.

Calophaca (*beautiful-Lentil*) — Kal-*off*-ak-uh.

Calopogon (*beautiful-beard, as to fringed flower lip*) — Kal-oh-*poh*-gon.

Calothamnus (*beautiful-bush*) —Kal-oh-*tham*-nus.

Caltha (*the classical name*) — *Kalth*-uh: (includes Marsh Marigold).

Calycanthus (*for flower with conspicuous calyx*) — Kal-ik-*kanth*-us: Sweet-shrub.

Calypso (*for mythical goddess*) — Kal-*lips*-oh.

Camassia — Kam-*mass*-ee-uh: Camass.

Camellia (*after Georg Kamel or Camelli*) — Kam-*mell*-ee-uh.

Camoensia (*for Portugese poet Louis Camoens*) — Kam-oh-*en*-see-uh.

Campanula (*little bell*) — Kam-*pan*-yew-luh: Bellflower.

Campsidium (*Campsis-like: see below*) Kamp-*sid*-ee-um.

Campsis (*curved, as to stamens*) — *Kamp*-siss: Trumpet-creeper.

Camptosorus (*for bent or irregular parts*) —Kamp-toh-*sohr*-us: Walking-fern.

Campylotropis (*for its curved parts*) — Kam-pye-*lot*-roh-piss.

Cananga — Kan-*nan*-guh.

Canarina (*for Canary Islands*) — Kan-ar-*rye*-nuh.

Candollea (*for Swiss botanist A. P. de Candolle*) — Kan-*dol*-lee-uh.

Canella (*little-reed*) — Kan-*nell*-uh: Wild Cinnamon.

Canistrum (*reed-basket*) —Kan-*nist*-rum.

Canna (*the classical name*) — *Kan*-nuh.

Cantua — *Kan*-tew-uh.

Capparis (*the classical name*) — *Kap*-par-iss: Caper-bush.

Capsicum (*box or chest, as to fruit form*)—*Kap*-sik-um: Red-pepper.

Caragana — Kar-ag-*gay*-nuh: Pea-tree, Pea-shrub.

Cardamine — Kard-*dam*-in-ee: Bitter-cress.

Cardiospermum (*heart-seed*)—Kard-ee-oh-*sperm*-um: Heart-seed.

Carduus (*classical name of Thistle*) —*Kard*-yew-us: Plumeless Thistle.

Carex — *Kay*-rex: Sedge.

Carica — *Kay*-rik-uh: Papaya.

Carissa — Kar-*riss*-uh.

Carlina — Kar-*lye*-nuh.

Carludovica (*for Spanish Carlos IV and Maria Luisa*) — Kar-lew-doh-*vye*-kuh.

Carmichaelia (*for Scottish botanist Dougald Carmichael*) — Kar-mye-*keel*-ee-uh.

Carpanthea — Kar-*panth*-ee-uh.

Carpenteria (*for Dr. William Carpenter*) — Kar-pen-*teer*-ee-uh.

Carpinus — Kar-*pye*-nus: Hornbeam.

Carpobrotus — Kar-poh-*broh*-tus.

Carthamus — *Karth*-am-us.

Carum (*classical name to Caraway*) — *Kay*-rum.

Carya (*classical name for Walnut tree*) *Kay*-ree-uh: Hickory.

Caryopteris (*nut-wing, as to fruit calyx*) — Kay-ree-*op*-ter-iss: Blue-beard.

Caryota (*nut, as to fruit*) — Kay-ree-*oh*-tuh: Fish-tail Palm.

Cassia — *Kass*-ee-uh: Senna.

Cassinia — Kass-*sin*-ee-uh.

Cassiope (*for mythical Cassiopeia*) — Kass-*sye*-oh-pee.

Castanea (*the classical name*) — Kast-*tay*-nee-uh: Chestnut.

Castanopsis (*Chestnut-like*) — Kast-an-*nop*-siss.

Castilleja (*for Spanish botanist Castillejo*) — Kast-il-*lee*-yuh: Painted-cup.

Casuarina (*for supposed resemblance of its twigs to cassowary feathers*) — Kass-yew-uh-*rye*-nuh: Beef-wood, She-oak, Australian-pine.

Catalpa — Kat-*tal*-puh.

Catananche — Kat-an-*nan*-kee: Cupids-dart.

Catasetum (*downward-bristle*) — Kat-ass-*see*-tum.

Catesbaea (*for English naturalist Mark Catesby*) — Kayts-*bee*-uh: Lily-thorn.

Catha — *Kayth*-uh.

Cattleya (*for English botanist William Cattley*) — *Kat*-lee-uh.

Caulophyllum (*stem-leaf*) — Kaw-loh-*fill*-um: Blue Cohosh.

Ceanothus (*classical name for a Thistle*) — See-an-*nohth*-us.

Cecropia — Sek-*kroh*-pee-uh.

Cedrela (*from Cedrus, the Cedar, whose wood it resembles*) — Seed-*ree*-luh.

Cedronella (*diminutive of Cedrus, the Cedar, which it resembles as to odor*) — Seed-ron-*nell*-uh: Canary-balm.

Cedrus — *Seed*-rus: Cedar.

Celastrus — Sel-*last*-rus.

Celmisia — Sel-*miz*-ee-uh.

Celosia (*burning, as to fiery color; or dry, as to lasting flowers*) — Sel-*loh*-shee-uh: Coxcomb.

Celsia (*for Swedish botanist Olaf Celsius*) — *Sell*-see-uh.

Celtis — *Sell*-tiss: Hackberry.

Centaurea — Sen-taw-*ree*-uh: (This large genus includes the Basket-flower, Dusty-miller, and Corn-flower or Bachelor's-button, and Knapweed.)

Centaurium—Sen-*taw*-ree-um: Centaury.

Centradenia (*spur-gland, as of anthers*)—Sen-trad-*dee*-nee-uh.

Centranthus (*spur-flower*) — Sen-*tranth*-us.

Centropogon (*spur-beard, as to fringed stigma*) — Sen-troh-*poh*-gon.

Cephalanthus (*spur-head, hence flowers in heads*) — Sef-al-*lanth*-us: Button-bush.

Cephalaria (*head, as to flower clusters*) — Sef-al-*lay*-ree-uh.

Cephalocereus (*head-Cereus, for woolly top*) — Sef-al-oh-*seer*-ee-us.

Cephalotaxus (*for Taxus- or Yew-like appearance and flowers in heads*) — Sef-al-oh-*tax*-us: Plum-yew.

Cerastium (*horned, as to shape of pod*) — Ser-*rass*-tee-um: Mouse-ear Chick-weed.

Ceraptopteris (*horned-Fern*) — Ser-at-*top*-ter-iss: Water Fern, Floating Fern.

Ceratostigma (*horned-stigma*) — Ser-at-oh-*stig*-muh.

Ceratozamia (*horned, as to scales; see Zamia*) — Ser-at-oh-*zay*-mee-uh.

Cercidiphyllum (*Cercis-like leaf*) — Ser-sid-if-*fill*-um: Katsura-tree.

Cercidium — Ser-*sid*-ee-um.

Cercis — *Ser*-siss: Redbud, Judas-tree.

Cercocarpus (*for its long-tailed fruit*) — Ser-koh-*karp*-us: Mountain Mahogany.

Cereus — *Seer*-ee-us.

Cerinthe (*beeswax, as in the flower*) — Ser-*rinth*-ee: Honeywort.

Ceropegia (*wax-fountain, as to flower appearance*) — Ser-oh-*peej*-ee-uh.

Cestrum — *Sest*-rum.

Chaenomeles (*split-apple*) — Kee-*nom*-el-eez: Flowering Quince.

Chaenostoma (*gaping-mouth, as to coralla*) — Kee-*noss*-tom-uh.

Chaerophyllum (*scented-leaf*) — Kee-roh-*fill*-um: Chervil (one of two kinds).

Chamaecyparis (*dwarf-Cypress, as to resemblance*) — Kam-ee-*sip*-ar-iss: False-cypress.

Chamaedaphne (*ground-Laurel, for its habit and evergreen leaves*) — Kam-ee-*daf*-nee: Leather-leaf.

Chamaedorea (*dwarf-gift*) — Kam-ee-*doh*-ree-uh.

Chamaelirum (*dwarf-Lily*) — Kam-ee-*lihr*-ee-um: Blazing Star, Fairy-wand.

Chamaerops (*dwarf-shrub*) — Kam-*mee*-rops.

Charieis (*elegant*) — *Kay*-ree-is.

Cheilanthes (*lip-flower*) — Kye-*lanth*-eez: Lip-fern.

Cheiranthus (*hand-flower*) — Kye-*ranth*-us: Wallflower (*C. cheiri*).

Chelidonium (*for Swallow, at whose spring arrival time it flowers*) — Kel-id-*doh*-nee-um: Celandine.

Chelone (*tortoise*) — Kee-*loh*-nee: Turtle-head.

Chenopodium (*goose-foot*) — Kee-noh-*poh*-dee-um: Goosefoot, Pig-weed.

Chimaphila (*winter-loving*) — Kye-*maf*-fil-uh: Pipsissewa.

Chimonanthus (*winter-flower*) — Kye-moh-*nanth*-us.

Chiococca (*snow-berry*) — Kye-oh-*kok*-uh: Snowberry.

Chiogenes (*snow-products*) — Kye-*oj*-en-eez: Creeping Snowberry.

Chionanthus (*snow-flower*) — Kye-oh-*nanth*-us: Fringe-tree.

Chionodoxa (*snow-glory*) — Kye-oh-nod-*dox*-uh: Glory-of-the-snow.

Chionophila (*snow-loving*) — Kye-oh-*noff*-il-uh.

Chironia (*for mythical Chiron, a centaur*) — Kye-*roh*-nee-uh.

Chlorogalum (*green-milk, for its juices*) Kloh-*rog*-al-um.

Chlorophytum (*green plant*) — Kloh-*roff*-it-um.

Choisya (*for Swiss botanist, J. D. Choisy*) — *Koy*-see-uh or *Shwah*-zee-uh: Mexican-orange.

Chorizema — Koh-*riz*-em-uh.

Chrysalidocarpus (*chrysalis-fruit, as to shape*) —Kriss-al-id-oh-*karp*-us.

Chrysanthemum (*gold-flower*) — Kriss-*anth*-em-um.

Chrysogonum (*for its golden flowers*) — Kriss-*og*-on-um: Golden-star.

Chrysopsis (*for yellow flower-heads*) — Kriss-*op*-siss.

Chrysosplenium (*golden-band*) — Kriss-oh-*spleen*-ee-um: Golden Saxifrage.

Cibotium — Sib-*boh*-tee-um.

Cicer — *Sye*-ser: Chick-Pea.

Cichorium — Sik-*koh*-ree-um: Chicory (*C. intybus*), Endive (*C. endivia*).

Cicuta — Sik-*kew*-tuh: Water-hemlock.

Cimicifuga (*bug-repelling*) — Sim-iss-*siff*-yew-guh: Bugbane.

Cineraria (*for ash-colored down on leaves*) — Sin-er-*ray*-ree-uh.

Cinnamomum — Sin-am-*moh*-mum.

Circaea (*for mythical Circe*) — Ser-*see*-uh.

Cirsium — *Ser*-shee-um: Plumed Thistle.

Cissus (*classical name for Ivy*) — *Siss*-us.

Cistus (*rock-Rose*) — *Siss*-tus: Rockrose.

Citharexylum (*zither-wood*) — Sith-uh-*rex*-il-um.

Citrullus (*little-Citron*) — Sit-*rull*-us: Watermelon (*C. vulgaris*).

Citrus — *Sit*-rus: Orange, Lemon, Grapefruit, Tangerine and Bergamot are included in this genus.

Cladanthus (*branch-flower*) — Klad-*anth*-us.

Cladrastis (*branch-brittle*) — Klad-*rast*-iss: Yellow-wood.

Clarkia (*for American explorer William Clark, of Lewis and Clark fame*) — *Klark*-ee-uh.

Claytonia (*for early American botanist John Clayton*) — Klay-*toh*-nee-uh: Spring Beauty.

Cleistocactus (*closed-Cactus*) — Klye-stoh-*kak*-tus.

Clematis (*brushwood, as to woody, twiggy effect*) — *Klem*-at-iss: Clematis, Virgins-bower.

Cleome — Klee-*oh*-mee.

Clerodendron — Kleer-oh-*den*-dron: See preferred form below.

Clerodendrum — Kleer-oh-*den*-drum: Glory-bower.

Clethra (*ancient name for Alder*) — *Kleth*-ruh: White-alder.

Clianthus (*glory-flower*) — Klye-*anth*-us.

Clintonia (*for N. Y. Governor DeWitt Clinton*) — Klin-*toh*-nee-uh.

Clitoria (*closed-up*) — Klye-*toh*-ree-uh: Butterfly-pea.

Clivia (*for the Duchess of Northumberland, of the Clive family*) — *Klye*-vee-uh: Kafir-lily.

Clystostoma (*beautiful-mouth*) — Klye-*tost*-om-uh.

Cnicus — *Nye*-kus: Blessed Thistle.

Cobaea (*for Spanish botanist B. Cobo*) — Koh-*bee*-uh.

Coccolobis (*seed-pod*) — Kok-*kol*-oh-biss.

Cocculus (*little-seed*) — *Kok*-yew-lus: Snail-seed.

Cocos (*stone or berry, as to fruit form*) — *Koh*-koss: Coconut.

Codiaeum — Koh-dih-*ee*-um: Croton.

Codonopsis (*bell-like, as to flower shape*) — Koh-don-*nop*-siss.

Coelogyne (*hollow-pistil*) — See-*loj*-in-ee.

Coffea — *Koff*-ee-uh: Coffee.

Coix — *Koh*-ix.

Colchicum (*for ancient Colchis*) — *Kol*-chik-um: Autumn-crocus.

Coleus (*sheath, for manner in which stamens are joined*) — *Koh*-lee-us.

Colletia (*for French botanist Philibert Collet*) — Kol-*lee*-shee-uh.

Collinsia (*for American botanist Zaccheus Collins*) — Kol-*lin*-zee-uh.

Collinsonia (*for English naturalist Peter Collinson*) — Kol-in-*soh*-nee-uh: Horse-balm, Citronella.

Collomia (*glue, as to sticky character of seeds*) — Kol-*loh*-mee-uh.

Colocasia — Kol-oh-*kay*-see-uh: Elephants-ear.

Columnea (*for Italian nature-writer*

Columna or Colluna) — Kol-*lum*-nee-uh.

Colutea (*a pod-bearing tree*) — Kol-*lew*-tee-uh: Bladder-senna.

Combretum (*a rush*) — Kom-*breet*-um.

Commelina (*for Dutch botanist Kaspar Commelin*) — Kom-el-*lye*-nuh: Dayflower.

Comptonia (*for English prelate Henry Compton*) — Komp-*toh*-nee-uh: Sweet-fern.

Conandron (*for cone-shaped anthers*) — Kon-*and*-ron.

Conicosia — Kon-ik-*koh*-see-uh.

Coniogramme — Koh-nee-oh-*gram*-ee.

Conium (*from ancient name for Hemlock*) — Koh-*nye*-um: Poison-hemlock.

Conophytum (*cone-plant*) — Koh-*noff*-it-um: Cone-plant.

Convallaria (*valley*) — Kon-val-*lay*-ree-uh: Lily-of-the-valley.

Convolvulus (*rolling-around*) — Kon-*volv*-yew-lus: Bindweed.

Cooperia (*for English gardener Joseph Cooper*) — Koo-*peer*-ee-uh: Rain-lily, Prairie-lily.

Copernicia (*for the astronomer Copernicus*) — Koh-per-*nish*-ee-uh.

Coprosma (*dung-odor*) — Kop-*ross*-muh.

Coptis (*cut, as to divided leaves*) — *Kop*-tiss: Gold-thread.

Corchorus (*named for a bitter-tasting wild plant*) — *Kork*-oh-rus.

Cordia (*for German botanists E. and V. Cordus*) — *Kord*-ee-uh.

Cordyline (*club-like, as to roots*) — Kor-dil-*lye*-nee: Dracena.

Corema (*for broom, as to its bushy aspect*) — Koh-*reem*-uh.

Coreopsis (*bug-like, as to its fruit*) — Koh-ree-*op*-siss: Tickseed.

Coriandrum — Koh-ree-*and*-rum: Coriander (*C. sativum*).

Coriaria (*for leather, as to use of its leaves in tanning*) — Koh-ree-*ay*-ree-uh.

Cornus — *Korn*-us: Dogwood.

Corokia — Kor-*roh*-kee-uh.

Coronilla (*little-crown, as to flowers*) — Kor-oh-*nil*-luh.

Coronopus — Koh-*ron*-oh-puss: Wart-Cress.

Correa (*for Portuguese botanist Correa de Serra*) — *Kor*-ree-uh.

Cortusa (*for Cortusus, botanist of Padua, Italy*) — Kor-*too*-suh.

Corydalis (*named for crested-lark, or the lark's spur that is suggested by the flower*) — Koh-*rid*-al-iss.

Corylopsis (*Hazel-like*) — Kor-il-*lop*-siss: Winter-hazel.

Corylus — *Kor*-il-us: Hazelnut, Filbert.

Coryphantha (*top-flower*) — Kor-if-*anth*-uh.

Corytholoma (*for helmet shape of flowers*) — Koh-rith-oh-*loh*-muh.

Cosmos (*harmony*) — *Koz*-moss.

Costus — *Kost*-us: Spiral Flag.

Cotinus — *Kot*-in-us.

Cotoneaster — Kot-toh-nee-*ass*-ter.

Cotyledon (*cup-shaped hollow*) — Kot-il-*leed*-on.

Crambe — *Kram*-bee.

Crassula (*little-thick, as to thickish leaves*) — *Krass*-yew-luh.

Crataegus (*flowering-thorn*) — Krat-*teeg*-us: Hawthorn, Thorn-apple.

Crepis — *Kreep*-iss: Hawks-beard.

Crinodendron (*Lily-tree*) — Krye-noh-*den*-dron.

Crinodonna (*hybrid name for a hybrid plant, a cross between a*

Crinum and Amaryllis belladonna) — Krye-noh-*don*-nuh.

Crinum (*the Greek word for Lily*) — *Krye*-num.

Crithmum — *Krith*-mum: Samphire.

Crocosmia (*Saffron-odor*) — Kroh-*koz*-mee-uh: Coppertip.

Crocus (*Saffron*) — *Kroh*-kus.

Crossandra (*fringe-anther*) — Kros-*sand*-ruh.

Crotalaria (*for rattle, as to seeds in the pod*) — Krot-al-*lay*-ree-uh: Rattlebox.

Crucianella (*little-cross, as to leaf arrangement*) — Kroo-shee-an-*nell*-uh: Crosswort.

Cryophytum (*frigid-plant*) — Krye-*off*-it-um: Ice-plant.

Cryptanthus (*hidden-flower*) — Krip-*tanth*-us.

Cryptogramma (*hidden-line, for the spore-cases under the fronds*) — Krip-toh-*gram*-muh: Rock-brake.

Cryptomeria (*hidden-part, probably as to cone-seeds within bracts*) — Krip-toh-*meer*-ee-uh.

Cryptostegia (*hidden-roof, as to concealed crown in the corolla tube*) — Krip-toh-*steej*-ee-uh: Rubber-vine.

Cryptostemma (*hidden-crown*) — Krip-toh-*stem*-muh.

Cucumis — *Kew*-kew-miss: Muskmelon (*C. melo*), Cucumber (*C. sativus*).

Cucurbita — Kew-*kerb*-it-uh: (This genus includes several species of Gourd, Pumpkin and Squash.

Cuminum — *Kew*-min-um: Cumin.

Cunila — Kew-*nye*-luh: Maryland Dittany, Stone-mint.

Cunninghamia (*after R. Cunningham, English physician and plant collector*) — Kun-ning-*ham*-ee-uh: China-fir.

Cuphea (*hump, as to a protuberance on calyx-tube*) — Kew-fee-uh.

Cupressus — Kew-*press*-us: Cypress.

Curculigo (*for curculio, a snout beetle or weevil, as to form of ovary*) — Kur-*kew*-lig-oh.

Cyanotis (*blue, as to petals*) — Sye-an-*noh*-tiss.

Cyathea (*cup, for shape of fronds*) — Sye-*ath*-ee-uh: Tree-fern.

Cycas (*inaccurately derived from the old Greek name for Doom Palm*) — *Sye*-kass: (A genus of a family of plants called Cycads.)

Cyclamen — *Sik*-lam-en.

Cyclanthera (*circle-anther*) — Sik-*lanth*-er-uh.

Cyclophorus (*circle-bearer, perhaps alluding to round spore-cases*) — Sye-*kloff*-or-us: Felt-fern.

Cycnoches (*Swan-neck, as to shape of column*) — Sik-*noh*-keez: Swan Orchid.

Cydonia — Sye-*doh*-nee-uh: Quince. (For the Flowering or Japanese Quince, often listed under Cydonia, see Chaenomeles.)

Cymbalaria — Sim-bal-*lay*-ree-uh.

Cymbidium (*small-cup, as to shape of lip*) — Sim-*bid*-ee-um.

Cymbopogon (*boat-beard, as to boat-shaped bracts*) — Sim-boh-*poh*-gon.

Cynanchum (*dog collar*) — *Sin*-nan-kum.

Cynara (*Artichoke*) — *Sin*-er-uh.

Cynoglossum (*dog-tongue*) — Sin-oh-*gloss*-um: Hounds-tongue.

Cypella — Sye-*pel*-luh.

Cyperus — Sye-*peer*-us: Galingale, Umbrella-plant (*C. alternifolius*).

Cyphomandra (*lump-male, for its hump-shaped anthers*) — Sye-foh-*mand*-ruh.

Cypripedium (*Venus-slipper*) — Sip-rip-*peed*-ee-um: Lady-slipper.

Cyrilla (*for Italian physician Domenico Cirillo or Cyrillo*) — Sihr-*ril*-luh: Southern Leatherwood.

Cyrtanthus (*curved-flower*) — Ser-*tanth*-us.

Cyrtomium (*curved, as to leaflets*) — Ser-*toh*-mee-um.

Cyrtopodium (*curved-foot, as to shape of lip*) — Ser-toh-*poh*-dee-um.

Cystopteris (*bladder-feather*) — Siss-*top*-ter-iss: Bladder-fern.

Cytisus — *Sit*-iss-us.

D

Daboëcia (*Irish name, for St. Dabeoc's Heath*) — Dab-oh-*eesh*-ee-uh: Irish-heath.

Dacrydium (*little tear, as to gummy exudation*) — Dak-*rid*-ee-um.

Dahlia (*for Swedish botanist Andreas Dahl*) — *Dahl*-yuh.

Dais — *Day*-iss.

Dalbergia (*for Swedish naturalist Nils Dalberg*) — Dal-*burr*-jee-uh.

Dalibarda (*for French botanist Thomas Dalibard*) — Dal-ib-*bard*-uh.

Danae (*for mythical mother of Perseus*) — *Day*-nuh-ee: Alexandrian-laurel.

Daphne (*for mythical nymph who escaped from Apollo by being turned into a Laurel tree*) — *Daff*-nee.

Daphniphyllum (*Laurel-leaf: see above*) Daf-nif-*fill*-um.

Darlingtonia (*after botanical writer William Darling*) — Dar-ling-*toh*-nee-uh: California Pitcher-Plant (*D. californicus*).

Dasylirion (*thick-Lily, as to trunk*) — Dass-il-*lihr*-ee-on: Sotol.

Datura — Dat-*tew*-ruh.

Daucus — *Daw*-kus: Carrot.

Davallia (*for Swiss botanist E. Davall*) — Dav-*val*-lee-uh.

Davidia (*for French missionary-botanist Armand David*) — Dav-*vid*-ee-uh: Dove-tree.

Decaisnia (*for French botanist Joseph Decaisne*) — Dek-*kay*-nee-uh.

Decodon (*ten-tooth*) — *Dek*-oh-don: Water Willow, Swamp Loosestrife.

Decumaria (*for its ten-part flowers*) — Dek-yew-*may*-ree-uh.

Delonix — Del-*lon*-ix: Royal Poinciana (*D. regia*).

Delosperma (*visible-seed*) — Dee-loh-*sperm*-uh.

Delphinium (*dolphin, referring to shape of nectary*) — Del-*fin*-ee-um: Larkspur.

Dendrobium (*tree-life, for its growth without soil, as in trees*) — Den-*droh*-bee-um.

Dendrochilum (*tree-lip, for its epiphytic growth, as in trees, and the lip-like parts of the flowers*) — Den-droh-*kye*-lum.

Dendromecon (*tree-Poppy*) — Den-droh-*mee*-kon: Bush-poppy, Tree-poppy.

Dennstaedtia (*for German botanist A. W. Dennstaedt*) — Den-*stet*-ee-uh: Cup-fern.

Dentaria (*pertaining-to-the-teeth, for root form*) — Den-*tay*-ree-uh: Toothwort.

Desmanthus (*bundle-flower*) — Des-*manth*-us.

Desmodium (*chain-like, for its joint-*

ed pods) — Des-*moh*-dee-um: Tick Trefoil, Tick Clover.

Deutzia (*for Dutchman Johann van der Deutz*) — *Dewt*-see-uh.

Dianella (*diminutive of Diana, mythical goddess*) — Dye-an-*nell*-uh.

Dianthus (*Zeus-flower*) — Dye-*anth*-us: Pink.

Diapensia — Dye-ap-*pen*-see-uh.

Diascia (*to adorn*) — Dye-*ass*-see-uh.

Dicentra (*two-spur, as to flowers*) — Dye-*sent*-ruh: Bleeding-heart (*D. spectabilis*).

Dichorisandra (*combination word referring to its two groups or series of anthers*) — Dye-kor-iss-*and*-ruh.

Dicksonia (*for English botanist James Dickson*) — Dik-*soh*-nee-uh.

Dicranostigma (*two-headed-stigma*) — Dye-kray-noh-*stig*-muh.

Dictamnus — Dik-*tam*-nus: Dittany, Fraxinella, Gas-plant, Burning-bush.

Dictyosperma (*netted-seed*) — Dik-tee-oh-*sperm*-uh: Princess Palm.

Dieffenbachia (*for German naturalist E. Dieffenbach*) — Deef-en-*bak*-ee-uh.

Dierama (*funnel, as to shape of flower*) — Dye-er-*ray*-muh.

Diervilla (*for French surgeon Dierville*) — Dye-er-*vil*-luh: Bush-honeysuckle.

Digitalis (*finger-like, as to flower shape*) — Dij-it-*tay*-liss: Foxglove.

Dimorphotheca (*for its two-formed seed-cases*) — Dye-mor-foh-*theek*-uh: Cape-Marigold.

Dionaea (*for mythical Venus*) — Dye-oh-*nee*-uh: Venus Fly-trap.

Dioscorea (*for Greek herbalist Dioscorides*) — Dye-os-*koh*-ree-uh: Yam.

Diosma (*divine-odor*) — Dye-*oz*-muh.

Diospyros (*Zeus-grain, for its edible fruit*) — Dye-*oss*-pihr-os: Persimmon.

Diotis (*two-ear, for two ears at base of corolla*) — Dye-*oh*-tiss: Cottonweed.

Dipelta (*two-shield, for two shield-like flower bracts*) — Dye-*pelt*-uh.

Diphylleia (*two-leaf, for its two unusual leaf forms*) — Dif-*fil*-lee-uh: Umbrella-leaf (*D. cymosa*).

Dipladenia (*double-gland, as to nectaries*) — Dip-lad-*deen*-ee-uh.

Diplazium (*twofold*) — Dip-*lay*-zee-um.

Diplotaxis (*double arrangement, presumably of some parts*) — Dip-loh-*tax*-iss: Rocket.

Dipsacus — Dip-suh-kus: Teasel.

Dipteronia (*double-winged, as to fruits*) Dip-ter-*roh*-nee-uh.

Dirca (*named for a fountain near ancient Thebes*) — Dirk-uh: Leatherwood.

Disa — Dye-suh.

Discocactus (*disk-Cactus*) — Disk-oh-*kak*-tus.

Disocactus (*two-formed-Cactus*) — Dye-soh-*kak*-tus.

Disphyma (*two-nodule, as to tubercles of fruit cells*) — Dis-*fye*-muh.

Disporum (*double-seed, as to two-ovuled cells*) — Dis-*poh*-rum: Fairy Bells.

Dizygotheca (*for its doubled anther cells*) — Dye-zye-goh-*theek*-uh: False-aralia.

Dodecatheon — Doh-dek-*kayth*-ee-on: Shooting-star, American Cowslip.

Dodonaea (*for Dutch botanist Rembert Dodoens*) — Doh-doh-*nee*-uh.

Dolichos — *Dol*-ik-oss: Hyacinth-bean.

Doodia (*for English botanist Samuel Doody*) — *Doo-dee*-uh.

Doronicum — Doh-*ron*-ik-um: Leopards-bane.

Dorotheanthus (*gift-of-the-gods-flower*) — Dor-oth-ee-*anth*-us.

Doryanthes (*spear-flower*) — Dor-ee-*anth*-eez: Spear-lily.

Dorycnium — Dor-*rik*-nee-um.

Douglasia (*for Scottish botanist David Douglas*) — Dug-*lass*-ee-uh.

Dovyalis — Doh-vee-*ay*-liss.

Downingia (*for American horticulturist A. J. Downing*) — Down-*inj*-ee-uh.

Doxantha (*glory-flower*) — Dox-*anth*-uh.

Draba — *Dray*-buh.

Dracaena (*she-dragon*) — Dras-*seen*-uh: Dracena.

Dracocephalum (*dragon-head*) — Dray-koh-*sef*-al-um: Dragonhead.

Dracunculus (*little dragon*) — Dray-*kunk*-yew-lus.

Drimys (*acrid, as to flavor of bark*) — *Drye*-miss.

Drosanthemum (*dew-flower*) — Dros-*anth*-em-um.

Drosera (*dewy*)—*Dross*-er-uh: Sundew.

Dryas (*mythology: dryad, wood-nymph*) — *Drye*-ass.

Dryopteris (*Oak-feather, hence Fern*) — Drye-*opp*-ter-iss: Woodfern.

Duchesnea (*for French botanist A. N. Duchesne*) — Dew-*kess*-nee-uh: Indian-strawberry, Mock-strawberry.

Duranta (*for Roman herbalist C. Durante*) — Dew-*rant*-uh.

Dyckia (*for German botanist Salm-Dyck*) — *Dik*-ee-uh.

E

Ecballium (*a throwing out*) — Ek-*bal*-lee-um: Squirting-cucumber.

Eccremocarpus (*pendant-fruit*) — Ek-rem-oh-*karp*-us: Glory-flower.

Echeveria (*for botanical illustrator Echeveri*) — Ek-ev-*veer*-ee-uh.

Echidnopsis (*viper-like, as to serpentine stems*) — Ek-id-*nop*-siss.

Echinacea (*sea-urchin-like, spiny as to bracts*) — Ek-in-*nay*-shee-uh: Cone-flower.

Echinocactus (*spiny-Cactus*) — Ek-in-oh-*kak*-tus.

Echinocereus (*spiny-Cereus*) — Ek-in-oh-*seer*-ee-us.

Echinocystis (*spiny-bladder, for its prickly fruit*) — Ek-in-oh-*sist*-iss.

Echinomastus (*spiny-breast, for its spiny tubercles*) — Ek-in-oh-*mast*-us.

Echinopanax (*spiny-Panax*) — Ek-in-oh-*pay*-nax: See preferred Oplopanax.

Echinops (*sea-urchin-like, spiny as to scaly parts*) — *Ek*-in-ops: Globe Thistle.

Echinopsis (*sea-urchin-like, spiny*) — Ek-in-*nop*-siss: Sea Urchin Cactus.

Echium (*from word for viper*) — *Ek*-ee-um: Vipers-Bugloss.

Edgeworthia (*for English botanist Edgeworth*) — Ej-*worth*-ee-uh.

Edraianthus (*for its stalkless flowers*) — Ed-rye-*anth*-us.

Eichhornia (*for Prussian official J.*

A. F. Eichhorn) —Ike-*horn*-ee-uh.

Elaeagnus — El-ee-*ag*-nus.

Elaeocarpus (*oil-fruit*) — El-ee-oh-*karp*-us.

Elaeodendron (*oil-tree*) — El-ee-oh-*den*-dron.

Elaphoglossum (*stag-tongue, as to fronds*) — El-af-oh-*gloss*-um.

Elettaria — El-et-*tay*-ree-uh: Cardamon.

Eleusine (*for mythical Ceres, goddess of the harvest*) — El-yew-*sye*-nee.

Elisena — El-iss-*seen*-uh.

Elsholtzia (*for German physician and botanist J. S. Elsholtz*) — El-*sholt*-see-uh.

Emilia — Em-*mill*-ee-uh.

Emmenanthe (*month-long-flower, for long-lasting corolla*) — Em-men-*anth*-ee.

Empetrum (*in-rock, for its adaptability to rocky locations*) — Em-pet-rum: Crowberry.

Encelia (*little-eel, for form of seeds*) — En-*seel*-ee-uh.

Encephalartos (*within-the-head-bread, for texture of interior of trunk*) — En-sef-al-*lart*-oss.

Enkianthus (*pregnant-flower, for appearance of flowers within the flowers*) — En-kee-*anth*-us.

Eomecon (*dawn-Poppy*) — Ee-oh-*meek*-on: Snow-poppy.

Epacris (*pointed-at-end, as to leaves*) — *Ep*-uh-kriss.

Ephedra — Ef-*feed*-ruh: Mexican Tea, Joint-fir.

Epidendrum (*on-trees, as to epiphytic, non-terrestrial habit*) — Ep-id-*den*-drum.

Epigaea (*on the earth, for its trailing habit*) — Ep-ij-*ee*-uh: Trailing Arbutus, Mayflower (*E. repens*).

Epilobium (*on-the-pod, as to flower structure*) — Ep-il-*loh*-bee-um: Willow-herb.

Epimedium — Ep-im-*meed*-ee-um.

Epiphyllum (*on-the-leaf, as to the leaf-like flower branches*) — Ep-if-*fill*-um.

Episcia (*shady, as to its habitat*) — Ep-*piss*-see-uh.

Epithelantha (*like-a-nipple-flower*) — Ep-ith-el-*lanth*-uh: Button Cactus.

Eragrostis (*love-grass*) — Ehr-ag-*gros*-tiss.

Eranthemum (*spring-flower*) — Eer-*anth*-em-um.

Eranthis (*spring-flower*) — Eer-*anth*-iss: Winter Aconite.

Ercilla — Er-*sill*-uh.

Eremochloa (*desert-grass*) — Ehr-em-*mok*-loh-uh: Centipede-grass.

Eremurus (*solitary-tail, as to single flower spike; perhaps desert-tail, for habitat in desert or lonely places*) — Ehr-em-*mew*-rus: Desert-candle.

Erepsia (*taken-away, perhaps for separation of this genus from genus Mesembryanthemum*) — Ee-*rep*-see-uh.

Eria (*wool, as to downy leaves of some species*) — *Ehr*-ee-uh.

Erianthus (*wool-flower*) — Ehr-ee-*anth*-us: Plume-grass.

Erica — *Ehr*-ik-uh: Heath.

Ericameria (*Heath-like*) — Ehr-ik-am-*meer*-ee-uh: Mock-heather.

Erigenia (*early-born, for its spring flowering*) — Ehr-ij-*een*-ee-uh: Harbinger-of-spring.

Erigeron (*early-old, for the hoary effect of some of its species*) — Ehr-*rij*-er-on: Fleabane.

Erinus — Ee-*rye*-nus.

Eriobotrya (*woolly-cluster*) — Ee-ree-oh-*bot*-ree-uh: Loquat.

Eriogonum (*woolly-knee, for woolly*

stems and leaf bases of some species) — Ee-ree-*og*-on-um.

Eriophorum (*wool-bearing, as to flower perianth*) — Ee-ree-*off*-or-um: Cotton-grass.

Eriophyllum (*wool-leaf*) — Ehr-ee-oh-*fill*-um.

Eriostemon (*woolly-stamen*) — Ehr-ee-oh-*steem*-on.

Eritrichium (*very-hairy, as to woolly tufts of some species*) — Ehr-it-*trik*-ee-um.

Erlangea (*for the University of Erlangen, Germany*) — Er-*lang*-ee-uh.

Erodium (*heron, suggested by its long-beaked fruit*) — Ee-*roh*-dee-um: Herons-bill.

Eruca — Ee-*roo*-kuh: Rocket-salad, Roquette.

Ervatamia — Er-vat-*tay*-mee-uh: Crape-jasmine.

Eryngium — Ee-*rin*-jee-um: Eryngo.

Erysimum (*hedge-Mustard*) — Ee-*riss*-im-um: Blister-cress.

Erythrina (*red, for its flowers*) — Ehr-ith-*rye*-nuh: Coral-tree.

Erythronium (*red, as to certain species*) — Ehr-ith-*roh*-nee-um: Adders-tongue, Trout-lily.

Erythroxilon (*red-wood, as to certain species*) — Ehr-ith-*rox*-il-on: Coca, Cocaine-plant.

Escallonia (*for Escallon, Spanish traveler in South America*) — Ess-kal-*loh*-nee-uh.

Eschscholzia (*for German botanist J. F. von Eschscholz*) — Esh-*sholt*-see-uh: California-poppy (*E. californica*).

Escobaria (*broom, spiny tufts*) — Ess-koh-*bay*-ree-uh.

Escontria (*for Mexican Don Blas Escontria*) — Ess-*kont*-ree-uh.

Eucalyptus (*well-covered, as to buds*) — Yew-kal-*lip*-tus: Gum-tree.

Eucharidium (*agreeable*) — Yew-kar-*rid*-ee-um: See Clarkia, under which genus this is now included.

Eucharis (*agreeable, graceful*) — *Yew*-kar-iss: Amazon-lily.

Eucomis (*having-fair-foliage*) — *Yew*-kom-iss.

Eucryphia (*well-concealed, as to corolla hidden by calyx*) — Yew-*kriff*-ee-uh.

Eugenia (*for Prince Eugene of Savoy*) — Yew-*jeen*-ee-uh.

Euonymus (*of-good-name*) — Yew-*on*-im-us: Spindle-tree.

Eupatorium (*for King Eupator of ancient Pontus*) — Yew-pat-*toh*-ree-um: Thoroughwort, Boneset.

Euphorbia — Yew-*forb*-ee-uh: Spurge.

Euphoria (*well-bearing, perhaps, for the way it carries its fruits; perhaps well-being, for after-effects of eating them*) — Yew-*for*-ee-uh: Longan.

Euploca — *Yew*-plok-uh.

Eupritchardia (*the attributive generic name, Pritchardia, has now been superseded*) — Yew-pritch-*ard*-ee-uh: Pritchardia.

Euptelea (*handsome-Ptelea, hence handsome Elm, as suggested by its fruit*) — Yew-*teel*-ee-uh.

Eurya — *Yew*-ree-uh.

Euryale (*for one of the mythical Gorgons*) — Yew-*rye*-al-ee.

Eustoma (*good-mouth, as to corolla*) — *Yew*-stom-uh.

Evodia (*fragrance, as to leaves*) — Ee-*voh*-dee-uh.

Evolvulus (*rolled-out, hence not twining as is Convolvulus, for example*) — Ee-*vol*-vew-lus.

Evonymus — Ee-*von*-im-us: See Eu-onymus, the preferable spelling.

Exacum — *Ex*-ak-um.

Exochorda (*external-cord, as to a characteristic of the ovary*) — Ex-oh-*kord*-uh: Pearl-bush.

F

Fabiana (*for Spanish botanist Francisco Fabiano*) — Fay-bee-*ay*-nuh.

Fagus (*the classical name*) — *Fay*-gus: Beech.

Fatsia — *Fat*-see-uh.

Faucaria — Faw-*kay*-ree-uh.

Fedia — *Feed*-ee-uh: *African*-valerian.

Feijoa (*for Spaniard J. de Silva Feijo*) — Fay-*joh*-uh.

Felicia (*happiness*) — Fel-*lish*-ee-uh.

Fenestraria (*with-a-window, as to translucent area on leaf*) — Fen-ess-*tray*-ree-uh.

Ferocactus (*wild-, fierce-Cactus*) — Fee-roh-*kak*-tus.

Ferula (*perhaps derived from word for rod, for stout stems*) — *Fehr*-yew-luh: Giant Fennel (*F. communis*).

Ficus — *Fye*-kus: Fig.

Filipendula (*thread-hanging*) — Fil-ip-*pen*-dew-luh: Meadowsweet.

Fittonia (*for English botanists Elizabeth and Sarah Fitton*) — Fit-*toh*-nee-uh.

Fitzroya (*after English admiral Robert Fitzroy*) — Fitz-*roy*-uh.

Flacourtia (*for French administrator Etienne de Flacourt*) — Flak-*koor*-tee-uh.

Flemingia (*for John Fleming, authority on Indian medicinal plants*) — Flem-*min*-jee-uh.

Foeniculum — Fee-*nik*-yew-lum: Fennel.

Fontanesia (*for French botanist René Desfontaines*) — Fon-tan-*neez*-ee-uh.

Forestiera (*for French physician Charles La Forestier*) — For-est-*yeer*-uh.

Forsythia (*for English horticulturist William Forsyth, who brought it from China*) — For-*sith*-ee-uh: Golden-bells.

Fortunella (*for Robert Fortune, Scottish botanist and explorer*) — For-tew-*nell*-uh: Kumquat.

Fothergilla (*for English physician John Fothergill*) — Foth-er-*gill*-uh.

Fragaria — Frag-*gay*-ree-uh: Strawberry.

Francoa (*for a Spanish botanical patron Franco*) — Fran-*koh*-uh.

Frasera (*for English botanist John Fraser*) — *Fray*-zer-uh: Columbo.

Fraxinus — *Frax*-in-us: Ash.

Freesia (*for Swedish botanist Elias Fries*) — *Free*-zhee-uh.

Fremontia (*for American general J. C. Fremont*) — Free-*mont*-eeuh: Flannel-bush (*F. californica*).

Fritillaria (*dice-box, for markings on petals*) — Frit-il-*lay*-ree-uh: Frittillary.

Fuchsia (*for German botanist Leonhard Fuchs*) — *Few*-shuh.

Fumaria (*smoky*) — Few-*may*-ree-uh: Fumitory.

Furcraea (*for French chemist Antoine de Fourcroy*) — Fur-*kree*-uh.

G

Gagea (*for botanist Sir Thomas Gage*) — Gay-jee-uh.

Gaillardia (*for French botanist Gaillard de Marentonneau*) — Gay-lard-ee-uh.

Galanthus (*milk-flower*) — Gal-*anth*-us: Snowdrop.

Galax (*milky, as to white flowers*) — Gay-lax.

Galega (*milk, as to a probable old medicinal use*) — Gal-*lee*-guh: Goats-rue (*G. officinalis*).

Galium (*bedstraw*) — Gay-lee-um: Bedstraw.

Galtonia (*for anthropologist Sir Francis Galton*) — Gol-*toh*-nee-uh: Giant Summer-hyacinth (*G. candicans*).

Gamolepis (*joined-scales, as to bract formation*) — Gam-*mol*-ep-iss.

Garcinia (*for French botanist Laurent Garcin*) — Gar-*sin*-ee-uh: Mango-steen.

Gardenia (*for American botanist Alexander Garden*) — Gar-*deen*-ee-uh.

Garrya (*for Michael Garry of the Hudson's Bay Co.*) — Gar-ee-uh: Silk-tassel Bush.

Gasteria (*like a stomach, as to swollen flower base*) — Gas-*teer*-ee-uh.

Gaultheria (*for Canadian botanist and physician M. Gaulthier*) — Gol-*theer*-ee-uh: One of several species, *G. procumbens*, is called Wintergreen, Checkerberry or Tea-berry.

Gaya (*for botanical writer Jacques Gay*) — Gay-uh: Lacebark.

Gaylussacia (*for French chemist J. L. Gay-Lussac*) — Gay-lus-*say*-shee-uh: Huckleberry.

Gazania (*for Theodorus of Gaza, medieval Greek scholar*) — Gaz-*zay*-ne-uh.

Geitonoplesium — Gye-ton-oh-*plee*-see-um.

Gelsemium — Jel-*seem*-ee-um: Carolina Yellow Jessamine.

Genipa — *Jen*-ip-uh: Genip.

Genista (*broom*) — Jen-*nist*-uh: Broom.

Gentiana (*for Gentius, an Illyrian king, said to have discovered its tonic qualities*) — Jen-shee-*ay*-nuh: Gentian.

Geranium (*crane, for resemblance of fruit to a crane's bill*) — Jer-*ray*-nee-um: Cranesbill.

Gerbera — Jer-*beer*-uh: See below.

Gerberia (*for German naturalist Traugott Gerber or Gerberus*) — Jer-*beer*-ee-uh: Transvaal Daisy or Barberton Daisy (*B. Jamesoni*).

Geum — *Jee*-um: Avens.

Gilia (*for Spanish botanist Philip Gil*) — *Jill*-ee-uh.

Gillenia (*for German botanist Arnold Gill*) — Jil-*leen*-ee-uh.

Ginkgo — *Gink*-goh: Maidenhair-tree.

Gladiolus (*little sword, as to leaves*) — Glad-ee-*oh*-lus: (Same in both singular and plural).

Glaucidium (*denoting a rather bluish green*) — Glaw-*sid*-ee-um.

Gleditsia (*for German botanist J. D. Gleditsch*) — Gled-*dit*-see-uh: Honey Locust.

Globularia (*for globular flower-heads*) — Glob-yew-*lay*-ree-uh.

Gloriosa (*glorious*) — Gloh-ree-*oh*-suh: Glory-lily.

Glottiphyllum (*tongue-like-leaf*) — Glot-if-*fill*-um.

Glycine (*sweet, as to taste of root*) — *Gliss*-in-ee: Soybean (*G. Max*).

Glycyrrhiza (*sweet-root*) — Gliss-ihr-*rye*-zuh. Licorice.

Glyptostrobus (*marked-cone, as to seed cones*) — Glip-toh-*stroh*-bus.

Gmelina (*for German botanist S.G. Gmelin*) — *Mell*-in-uh.

Gnaphalium (*wool-of-the-Teasel, for woolly leaves*) — Naf-*fay*-lee-um.

Godetia (*for Swiss botanist Charles H. Godet*) — Goh-*dee*-shee-uh.

Gomphrenia (*from a classical name for a kind of Amaranth*) — Gom-*free*-nuh.

Gongora (*for Cordovan bishop Antonio Caballero y Gongora*) — Gon-*goh*-ruh.

Goodia (*after Peter Good, its discoverer*) — *Good*-ee-uh.

Goodyera (*for English botanist John Goodyer*) — Good-*yeer*-uh.

Gordonia (*for English nurseryman James Gordon*) — Gor-*doh*-nee-uh.

Grammatophyllum (*letter-leaf, as to spotted flowers*) — Gram-at-oh-*fill*-um.

Graptopetalum (*engraved-petal, as to color-dotting*) — Grap-toh-*pet*-al-um.

Graptophyllum (*written-leaf, as to colored foilage*) — Grap-toh-*fill*-um.

Grevillea (*for botanical patron Charles F. Greville*) — Grev-*vill*-ee-uh.

Grewia (*for English plant anatomist Nehemiah Grew*) — *Grew*-ee-uh.

Greyia (*for administrator Sir George Grey*) — *Gray*-ee-uh.

Griselinia (*for Venetian botanist Griselini*) — Griz-el-*lin*-ee-uh.

Guaiacum — *Gwye*-ak-um: Lignumvitae.

Gunnera (*for Norwegian naturalist J. E. Gunnerus*) — *Gunn*-er-uh.

Guzmania (*for Spanish naturalist A. Guzman*) — Guz-*man*-ee-uh.

Gymnocalycium (*naked-calyx, as to ovarian scales*) — Jim-noh-kal-*liss*-ee-um.

Gymnocladus (*naked-branch*) — Jim-*nok*-lad-us: Kentucky Coffeetree.

Gynura (*ovary-tailed, as to shape of stigma*) — Jye-*new*-ruh.

Gypophila (*gypsum-loving, as to limey soil preference*) — Jip-*soff*-il-uh: Baby's-breath (*G. paniculata*).

H

Habenaria (*rein or strap, as to shape of flower parts*) — Hab-en-*nay*-ree-uh: Fringed Orchis, Rein Orchis.

Hacquetia (*for B. Hacquet, writer on Alpine plants*) — Hak-*kwee*-shee-uh.

Haemanthus (*blood-flower*) — Hee-*manth*-us: Blood-lily.

Hakea (*for German baron von Hake*) — *Hah*-kee-uh.

Halesia (*for English botanist Stephen Hales*) — Hay-*lee*-zee-uh: Silverbell.

Halimodendron (*salt-tree, as to habitat on salt plains*) — Hal-im-oh-*den*-dron: Salt-tree.

Hamamelis (*at-the-same-time-fruit, for the presence of flowers at fruit-*

ing time in some species) — Ham-am-*meel*-iss: Witch-hazel.

Hamatocactus (*hooked-Cactus, for nature of spines in some Cactus genera*) — Ham-at-oh-*kak*-tus.

Hamelia (*for French botanist H. L. Duhamel-Dumonceau*) — Ham-*mee*-lee-uh.

Hardenbergia (*for German Countess Hardenberg*) — Har-den-*berj*-ee-uh.

Harpephyllum (*sickle-leaf, as to pointed form*) — Harp-ef-*fill*-um: Kafir-plum.

Harrisia (*for Jamaican botanist William Harris*) — Har-*riss*-ee-uh.

Hatiora — Hat-ee-*ohr*-uh.

Haworthia (*for English botanist J. H. Haworth*) — Haw-*worth*-ee-uh.

Hebe (*for mythical goddess of youth*) — *Hee*-bee.

Hebenstretia (*for German physician J. E. Hebenstreit*) — Heb-en-*stree*-shee-uh.

Hedeoma (*sweet-odor, presumably; for fragrant flowers*) — Hee-dee-*oh*-muh.

Hedera (*classic name for Ivy*) — *Hed*-er-uh: Ivy.

Hedychium (*sweet-snow, for color and fragrance of flowers in some species*) — Hee-*dik*-ee-um: Ginger-lily, and (*H. coronarium*) Garland-flower.

Hedysarum (*sweet-spice, as to flower scent*) — Hee-*diss*-er-um.

Helenium — Hel-*leen*-ee-um: Sneezeweed.

Helianthella (*little-sun-flower*) — Hee-lee-anth-*ell*-uh.

Helianthemum (*sun-flower*) — Hee-lee-*anth*-em-um: Sun-rose.

Helianthus (*sun-flower*) — Hee-lee-*anth*-us: Sunflower.

Helichrysum (*sun-gold, as to flower heads*) — Hel-ik-*krye*-sum: Everlasting.

Helicodiceros (*spirally-two-horned: application vague*) — Hel-ik-koh-*diss*-er-os: Twist-arum.

Heliconia (*for Helikon, seat of the mythical muses*) — Hel-ik-*koh*-nee-uh.

Heliocereus (*sun-Cereus*) — Hee-lee-oh-*seer*-ee-us.

Heliopsis (*sun-like, as to flowers*) — Hee-lee-*opp*-siss.

Heliotropium (*sun-turning, originally applied to flowers that always faced toward the sun*) — Hee-lee-oh-*troh*-pee-um: Heliotrope.

Helipterum (*sun-wing, as to tropism of certain parts*) — Hee-*lip*-ter-um: Everlasting.

Helonias (*marsh*) — Hee-*loh*-nee-ass: Swamp-pink.

Helleborus — Hel-leb-*boh*-rus: Hellebore, and (*H. niger*) Christmas-rose.

Helxine — Hel-*zye*-nee: Babys-tears.

Hemerocallis (*day-beauty, for its flowers, which fail to last overnight*) — Hem-er-oh-*kal*-liss: Day-lily.

Hemigraphis — Hem-ig-*graff*-iss.

Hemionitis (*mule, for those of its fronds which are sterile*) — Hem-ee-oh-*nye*-tiss: Strawberry-fern.

Hemiptelea (*half-Elm*) — Hem-it-*teel*-ee-uh.

Hepatica (*liver-like, as to leaf shape*) — Hep-*pat*-ik-uh: Liverleaf.

Heracleum (*for mythical Hercules*) — Hehr-ak-*klee*-um. Cow-parsnip.

Herniaria (*from same root as word hernia, perhaps for swollen joints*) — Her-nee-*ay*-ree-uh: Herniary, Rupture-wort, Burst-wort.

Hesperaloe (*western-Aloe*) — Hess-per-*al*-oh.

Hesperethusa (*for one of the mythical Hesperides*) — Hess-per-eth-*thew*-suh.

Hesperis (*evening*) — Hess-per-iss: Rocket.

Hesperoyucca (*western-Yucca*) — Hess-per-oh-*yukk*-uh.

Heterocentron (*unlike-spurs, as to anthers*) — Het-er-oh-*sent*-ron.

Heteromeles (*differing-fruit*) — Het-er-oh-*mee*-leez: Toyon, Christmas-berry.

Heterospathe (*differing-spathe*) — Het-er-oh-*spayth*-ee.

Heterospermum (*differing-seed*) — Het-er-oh-*sperm*-um.

Heuchera (*for German botanist Johann Heucher*) — Hew-ker-uh: Alum-root, and (*H. sanguinea*) Coral-bells.

Hevea — *Hee*-vee-uh.

Hibbertia (*for English botanist George Hibbert*) — Hib-*bert*-ee-uh.

Hibiscus (*classic name for Marsh Mallow*) — Hye-*bisk*-us: Rose-mallow.

Hidalgoa — Hye-dal-*goh*-uh: Climbing-dahlia.

Hieracium (*plant-hawk*) — Hye-er-*ray*-see-um: Hawkweed.

Hippeastrum (*horse-star, of uncertain significance, probably fanciful*) — Hip-pee-*ast*-rum: (Generally known as Amaryllis).

Hippocrepis (*horse-shoe, as to shape of pod*) — Hip-poh-*kreep*-iss.

Hippophaë — Hip-*poff*-uh-ee: Sea-buckthorn.

Hoffmannia (*for German botanist Georg Hoffmann*) — Hof-man-ee-uh.

Hoheria — Hoh-*heer*-ee-uh.

Holcus (*a kind of grain*) — *Hol*-kus.

Holmskioldia (*for Danish scientist Theodor Holmskiold*) — Holmskee-*old*-ee-uh.

Holodiscus (*entire-disk, as to flower character*) — Hol-oh-*disk*-us.

Homalanthus (*like-flowers*) — Hom-al-*lanth*-us.

Homalocephala (*like-headed*) — Hom-al-*seff*-al-uh.

Homalocladium (*like-branched, probably as to stems and canes of its single species*) — Hom-al-oh-*klay*-dee-um: Ribbon-bush, Centipede-plant.

Homalomena — Hom-al-oh-*mee*-nuh.

Hordeum (*classical name for Barley*) — Hord-ee-um.

Horminum (*classical name for Sage*) — Hor-*mye*-num.

Hosackia (*for American botanist David Hosack*) — Hoh-*sak*-ee-uh: See preferred generic name Lotus.

Hosta (*for German botanist N. T. Host*) *Hoss*-tuh: Plantain-lily.

Houstonia (*for English botanist William Houston*) — Hoos-*toh*-nee-uh.

Hovea — *Hoh*-vee-uh.

Hovenia (*for Dutch botanical patron David Hoven*) — Hoh-*veen*-ee-uh: Japanese Raisin-tree.

Howea (*for Lord Howe's Island in the South Pacific, its habitat*) — *How*-ee-uh.

Hoya (*for English gardener Thomas Hoy*) — *Hoy*-uh: Wax-plant.

Hudsonia (*for English botanist William Hudson*) — Hud-*soh*-nee-uh: Beach-heather.

Huernia (*for plant collector Justus Huernius*) — Hew-*ern*-ee-uh.

Humata (*of-the-earth, as to creeping rhizomes*) — Hew-*may*-tuh: Bears-foot-fern.

Humea (*for Lady Hume of Australia*) — *Hew*-mee-uh.

Humulus — *Hew*-mew-lus. Hop.

Hunnemannia (*for English botanical patron John Hunnemann*) — Hun-em-*man*-ee-uh: Mexican Tulip-poppy, Golden-cup.

Hura — *Hew*-ruh: Sandbox-tree.

Hutchinsia (*for a Miss Hutchins, Irish botanist*) — Hut-*chin*-zee-uh.

Hyacinthus (*for mythical character so named*) — Hye-uh-*sinth*-us: Hyacinth.

Hydrangea (*water-capsule, as to cup-shaped fruit*) — Hye-*drayn*-jee-uh.

Hydrastis (*water, perhaps as to its moisture nature*) — Hye-*drass*-tiss: Goldenseal, Orange-root.

Hydrocleys (*water-key, perhaps as to aquatic conditions it requires*) — *Hye*-droh-klyss: Water-poppy.

Hydrocotyle (*water-up, as to leaf shape of this aquatic plant*) — Hye-droh-*kot*-il-ee.

Hydrophyllum (*water-leaf*) — Hye-droh-*fill*-um: Water-leaf.

Hydrosme — Hye-*dross*-mee: Devilstongue.

Hylocereus (*wood-Cereus, as to tree-climbing habit*) — Hye-loh-*seer*-ee-us.

Hymenaea (*pertaining to marriage, for the night closing of the paired leaflets*) — Hye-men-*nee*-uh.

Hymenanthera (*membrane-flower, as to flower structure*) — Hye-men-*anth*-er-uh.

Hymenocallis (*membrane-beauty, as to the webbed filaments*) — Hye-men-oh-*kal*-liss: Spider-Lily.

Hyophorbe (*food-for-swine, as to its fleshy fruit*) — Hye-oh-*forb*-ee: Pignut Palm.

Hyoscyamus (*hog-bran, perhaps because it poisoned foraging hogs*) — Hye-oh-*sye*-am-us: Henbane.

Hypericum — Hye-*pehr*-ik-um: St. Johns-wort.

Hypochoeris — Hye-poh-*keer*-iss: Cats-ear.

Hypolepis (*underneath-scale, for position of spore-cases*) — Hye-*pol*-ep-iss.

Hypoxis (*underneath-sharp, as to leaf pod base*) — Hye-*pox*-iss: Stargrass.

Hyssopus — *Hiss*-op-us: Hyssop.

Hystrix (*porcupine, for barbed terminal spikelets*) — *Hiss*-trix: Bottle-brush-grass.

I

Iberis — Eye-*beer*-iss: Candytuft.

Iboza — Eye-*boh*-zuh.

Idesia (*for Dutch traveler Yobrantz Ides*) — Eye-*dee*-zee-uh.

Ilex — *Eye*-lex: Holly.

Illicium (*an allurement, as to its odor*) — Ill-*liss*-ee-um.

Impatiens (*impatient, probably as to the pods, which burst at a touch*) — Im-*pay*-shee-enz: Touch-me-not, Snapweed, or (*I. balsamina*) Garden Balsam.

Incarvillea (*after Jesuit missionary P. d'Incarville*) — In-kar-*vill*-ee-uh.

Indigofera (*indigo-bearing*) — In-dig-*goff*-er-uh: Indigo.

Inga — *In*-guh.

Inula — *In*-yew-luh.

Iochroma (*violet-color*) — Eye-oh-*kroh*-muh.

Ionidium (*violet-nest, vague except for violet color of flowers*) — Eye-oh-*nid*-ee-um.

Ionopsidium (*Violet-like*) — Eye-oh-nop-*sid*-ee-um: Diamond-flower.

Ipomoea (*worm-like, probably because of its twining habit*) — Eye-poh-*mee*-uh: Ipomea, Morning-glory.

Iresine (*wool-bound-wreath, as to woolly calyx*) — Eye-res-*sye*-nee: Blood-leaf.

Iris (*rainbow*) — *Eye*-riss.

Isatis — *Eye*-suh-tiss: Woad.

Isoloma (*equal-border, perhaps as to corolla*) — Eye-soh-*loh*-muh.

Isoplexis (*equal-cut, as to lips of corolla*) — Eye-soh-*plex*-iss.

Isopyrum — Eye-soh-*pye*-rum.

Isotoma (*equal-cut, perhaps as to corolla lips*) — Eye-*sot*-oh-muh.

Itea (*classical Willow*) — *It*-ee-uh: Sweet-spire, or Virginia-willow (*I. virginica*).

Ixia (*bird-lime, for viscid juice of some species*) — *Ix*-ee-uh.

Ixiolirion (*Ixia-like Lily*) — *Ix*-ee-oh-*lihr*-ee-on.

Ixora (*Hindu divinity*) — Ik-*soh*-ruh.

J

Jacaranda — Jak-ar-*rand*-uh.

Jacobinia — Jak-oh-*bin*-ee-uh.

Jamesia (*for its American discoverer Dr. Edwin James*) — Jay-*mee*-zee-uh.

Jasminum — *Jass*-min-um: Jasmine, Jessamine.

Jatropha (*physician-food, as to medicinal uses*) — *Jat*-roh-fuh.

Jeffersonia (*for President Thomas Jefferson*) — Jef-er-*soh*-nee-uh.

Juglans — *Joo*-glanz: Walnut.

Juniperus — Joo-*nip*-er-us: Juniper.

Jussiaea (*for French botanist Bernard de Jussieu*) — Juss-ih-*ee*-uh: Primrose-willow.

K

Kadsura — Kad-*soor*-uh.

Kalanchoe — Kal-an-*koh*-ee.

Kalmia (*for Swedish botanist Peter Kalm*) — *Kal*-mee-uh: (Mountain Laurel is *K. latifolia*).

Kennedia (*for English gardener Lewis Kennedy*) — Ken-*need*-ee-uh.

Kerria (*for English gardener William Kerr*) — *Kehr*-ree-uh.

Keteleeria (*for French nurseryman Jean Keteleer*) — Ket-el-*leer*-ee-uh.

Kickxia (*for Belgian botanist Jan Kickx*) — *Kik*-see-uh.

Kitaibelia — Kit-eye-*bee*-lee-uh.

Kleinia — *Klye*-nee-uh.

Kniphofia (*for German botanist Johann Kniphof*) — Nip-*hoh*-fee-uh: Torch-lily, Poker-plant.

Kochia (*for German botanist W. D. J. Koch*) — *Koh*-kee-uh: Summer Cypress (*K. scoparia*).

Koelreuteria (*for German naturalist J. G. Koelreuter*) — Kel-roo-*teer*-ee-uh: (*K. paniculata* is the Golden-rain-tree).

Kolkwitzia (*for German botanist Richard Kolkwitz*) — Kol-*kwits*-ee-uh: Beauty-bush.

Kosteletzkya (*for Bohemian botanist V. F. Kosteletzky*) — Kost-el-*lets*-kee-uh.

Krigia (*for David Krig, collector of Maryland plants*) — *Krig*-ee-uh.

L

Laburnum (*the classical name*) — Lab-*burn*-um: Golden-chain (*L. anagyroides*).

Lachenalia (*for Swiss botanist W. de Lachenal*) — Lak-en-*nay*-lee-uh: Cape-cowslip.

Lactuca — Lak-*tew*-kuh: Lettuce (*L. sativa*).

Laelia (*for Roman statesman Caius Laelius*) — *Lee*-lee-uh.

Laeliocattleya — Lee-lee-oh-*kat*-lee-uh: The name of a group of hybrids between the two Orchid genera Laelia (above) and Cattleya (see Cattleya).

Lagenaria (*flask*) — Lej-en-*nay*-ree-uh: White-flowered Gourd.

Lagerstroemia (*for Swedish merchant M. von Lagerstroem*) — Lay-gur-*streem*-ee-uh.

Lagunaria — Lag-yew-*nay*-ree-uh.

Lagurus (*hare-tail*) — Lag-*yew*-rus: Hares-tail-grass.

Lallemantia (*for botanist L. E. A. Lallemont*) — Lal-lem-*mont*-ee-uh.

Lamarckia (*for French naturalist Lamarck*) — Lah-*mark*-ee-uh: Golden-top.

Lamium — *Lay*-mee-um: Dead Nettle.

Lampranthus — Lamp-*ranth*-us.

Lantana — Lan-*tay*-nuh.

Lapageria (*for French botanist J. de la Pagerie*)—Lap-aj-*jeer*-ee-uh: Chilian Bellflower.

Lapeirousia (*for French naval officer*

Kuhnia (*for Philadelphia botanist Dr. Adam Kuhn*) — *Koon*-ee-uh.

Kunzea (*for German botanist Gustav Kunze*) — *Kunn*-zee-uh.

J. F. G. de la Peyrouse) — Lap-ay-*roo*-zee-uh.

Larix — *Lar*-ix. Larch.

Larrea — *Lar*-ree-uh: Creosote Bush.

Laserpitium — Lass-er-*pish*-ee-um.

Lasthenia — Las-*theen*-ee-uh.

Latania — Lat-*tay*-nee-uh.

Lathyrus — *Lath*-ihr-us: (The common Sweet Peas belong to the species *L. latifolius*).

Laurus (*the classical Laurel*) — *Law*-rus: Laurel, Sweet Bay.

Lavandula — Lav-*van*-dew-luh: Lavender.

Lavatera (*for Swiss physician Lavater*) — Lav-at-*teer*-uh: Treemallow.

Lawsonia (*for Scottish naturalist John Lawson*) — Law-*soh*-nee-uh: Henna, Mignonette-tree.

Layia (*for English botanist George T. Lay*) — *Lay*-ee-uh.

Ledum — *Leed*-um.

Leea (*for Scottish nurseryman James Lee*) — *Lee*-uh.

Leiophyllum (*smooth-leaf*) — Lye-oh-*fill*-um: Sand-myrtle.

Lemaireocereus (*for French horticulturist Charles Lemaire*) — Lem-may-ree-oh-*seer*-ee-us.

Lemna — *Lem*-nuh: Duckweed.

Lens — *Lenss*: Lentil.

Leonotis (*lion-ear, supposedly as to flower form*) — Lee-on-*noh*-tiss: Lions-ear.

Leontopodium (*lion's-foot, perhaps*

for furry nature) — Lee-on-toh-*poh*-dee-um.

Lepachys (*thick-scale, probably as to bracts*) — *Lepp*-ak-iss: Cone-flower.

Lepidium (*little-scale, as to small flat pods*) — Lep-*pid*-ee-um: Pepper-grass.

Leptodermis (*thin-skin*) — Lep-toh-*derm*-iss.

Leptopyrum (*thin-fruit*) — Lep-toh-*pye*-rum.

Leptospermum (*thin-seed*) — Lep-toh-*sperm*-um.

Leptosyne (*slenderness or delicacy*) — Lep-toh-*sye*-nee: (Often included in genus Coreopsis).

Lespedeza (*for a Spanish governor of Florida, D. Lespedez*) — Les-ped-*deez*-uh: Bush Clover.

Lesquerella (*for Swiss-American paleo-botanist Leo Lesquereux*) — Less-keh-*rell*-uh.

Leucadendron (*white-tree*) — Lew-kad-*den*-dron: Silver-tree (*L. argenteum*).

Leucaena (*to grow white, as to flowers*) — Lew-*seen*-uh: White Popinac.

Leucocrinum (*white-Lily*) — Lew-koh-*krye*-num.

Leucojum (*white-violet, as to flower colors*) — Lew-*koh*-jum: Snow-flake.

Leucophyllum (*white-leaf*) — Lew-koh-*fill*-um.

Leucothoë (*mythical princess of Babylon, supposed to have been changed by Apollo to a sweet-scented shrub*) — Lew-*koth*-oh-ee.

Leuzea (*for a man named De Leuze*) — *Lew*-zee-uh.

Levisticum — Lev-*vist*-ik-um: Lovage.

Lewisia (*after American explorer Capt. Meriwether Lewis*) — Lew-*iss*-ee-uh.

Leycesteria (*for William Leycester, a jurist in Bengal*) — Lye-sess-*teer*-ee-uh: Himalaya-honeysuckle.

Liatris — Lye-*ay*-triss: Blazing Star, Gayfeather, Button Snakeroot.

Libertia (*for Belgian writer Mary Libert*) — Lib-*bert*-ee-uh.

Libocedrus (*frankincense-Cedar*) — Lye-boh-*seed*-rus: Incense-Cedar.

Licuala — Lik-yew-*ay*-luh.

Ligularia (*little-strap, as to shape of flower rays*) — Lig-yew-*lay*-ree-uh.

Ligusticum — Lig-*gust*-ik-um.

Ligustrum — Lig-*gust*-rum: Privet.

Lilium (*classical name for Lily*) — *Lill*-ee-um: Lily.

Limnanthes (*marsh-flower*) — Lim-*nanth*-eez: Meadow-foam.

Limnocharis (*for marshy habitat*) — Lim-*nok*-uh-riss.

Limonium — Lim-*moh*-nee-um: Sea-lavender.

Linaria (*Linum-like*) — Lye-*nay*-ree-uh: Toadflax.

Lindelofia (*for German botanical patron F. von Lindelof*) — Lin-del-*loh*-fee-uh.

Lindera — Lin-*deer*-uh: Spice-bush (*L. benzoin*). This plant is often listed as *Benzoin aestivale*, a name now superseded.

Linnaea (*for Swedish Carolus Linnaeus, whose real name was Karl von Linné, and who ranks as one of the giants of botany for his Linnaean classification system*) — Lin-*nee*-uh.

Linosyris (*for its resemblance to Linum and Osyris*) — Lye-*noss*-er-iss: Goldilocks.

Linum — *Lye*-num: Flax.

Liparis (*oily, as to shining leaves*) — *Lip*-uh-riss: Twayblade.

Lippia (*for French physician Augustin Lippi*) — *Lip*-ee-uh.

Liquidambar—Lik-wid-*am*-ber: Sweet Gum (*L. styraciflua*).

Liriodendron (*Lily-tree, as to its flowers*) — Lihr-ee-oh-*den*-dron: Tulip-tree.

Liriope (*for mythical nymph*) — Lihr-*rye*-oh-pee: Lily-turf.

Listera (*for English physician Martin Lister*) — List-er-uh.

Lithocarpus (*stone-fruit*) — Lith-oh-*karp*-us: Tanbark-oak (*L. densiflora*).

Lithodora (*rock-dwelling*) — Lith-oh-*doh*-ruh: See Lithospermum.

Lithofragma (*rock-fence, for its habitat*) — Lith-oh-*frag*-muh.

Lithops (*stone-eyed*) — *Lith*-ops: Stoneface.

Lithospermum (*stone-seed*) — Lith-oh-*sperm*-um: Gromwell.

Lithraea — Lith-*ree*-uh.

Livistona (*for Scotsman Patrick M. Livistone*) — Liv-ist-*toh*-nuh.

Loasa — *Loh*-uh-suh.

Lobelia (*for Flemish botanist Matthias de Lobel*) — Loh-*beel*-ee-uh.

Lobivia — Loh-*biv*-ee-uh.

Lobularia — Lohb-yew-*lay*-ree-uh: Sweet-alyssum.

Loeselia (*for Prussian botanist John Loesel*) — Les-*seel*-ee-uh.

Logania (*for Irish botanist James Logan*) — Loh-*gay*-nee-uh.

Loiseleuria (*for French botanist J. C. A. Loiseleur-Deslongchamps*) — Loy-sel-*lew*-ree-uh: Alpine-azalea.

Lolium — *Loh*-lee-um: Rye-grass.

Lomatia (*edge, as to winged seeds*) — Loh-*may*-shee-uh.

Lomatium (*edge or small border, as to its fruit*) — Loh-*may*-shee-um.

Lonas — *Loh*-nass: African Daisy.

Lonicera (*for German botanist Adam Lonicer*) — Lon-*niss*-er-uh: Honeysuckle.

Lopezia (*for Spanish botanist J. Lopez*) — Loh-*peez*-ee-uh.

Lophophora (*crest-bearing*) — Loff-*off*-or-uh.

Loropetalum (*strap-petal*) — Lor-oh-*pet*-al-um.

Lotus (*classical plant which bears the "fruit of forgetfulness"*) — *Loh*-tus.

Luculia — Lew-*kew*-lee-uh.

Luetkea (*for Russian sea captain Luetke*) — Lew-*et*-kee-uh.

Luffa — *Luff*-uh.

Lunaria (*moon-like, as to silvery pods*) — Loo-*nay*-ree-uh: Moonwort, Satin-flower, Honesty.

Lupinus (*wolf, implying that the plant tends to impoverish the soil*) — Lew-*pye*-nus: Lupine.

Lycaste — Lye-*kast*-ee.

Lychnis (*lamp, perhaps, for brightness of flowers*) — *Lik*-niss.

Lycium (*for a kind of thorn*) — *Lish*-ee-um: Box-thorn, Matrimony-vine.

Lycopersicon — Lye-koh-*per*-sik-on: Tomato.

Lycopodium (*wolf-foot, for a rather fanciful resemblance*) — Lye-koh-*poh*-dee-um: Club-moss.

Lycopus (*wolf-foot, presumably as to leaf shape*) — *Lye*-koh-puss: Water Hoarhound.

Lycoris — *Lye*-kor-iss.

Lygodium (*flexible*) — Lye-*goh*-dee-um: Climbing-fern.

Lyonia (*for John Lyon, plant introducer*) — Lye-*oh*-nee-uh.

Lysichitum (*loose-cloak, as to its spathe*) — Lye-sik-*kye*-tum: Yellow Skunk-cabbage (*L. americanum*).

Lysimachia (*for King Lysimachus*)

— Lye-sim-*may*-kee-uh: Loose-strife.

Lythrum (*blood or gore, perhaps as to flower color*) — *Lith*-rum.

M

Maackia (*for Russian naturalist Richard Maack*) — Mahk-*ee*-uh.

Machaeranthera (*sword-flower*) — Mak-ee-*ranth-er-uh:* Tahoka Daisy.

Machaerocereus (*sword-Cereus, as to central spines*) — Mak-ee-roh-*seer*-ee-us.

Macleaya (*for Alexander Macleay*) — Mak-*lay*-uh: (Plume-poppy or Tree Celandine is *M. cordata*).

Maclura (*for American geologist William Maclure*) — Mak-*loor*-uh: Osage-orange.

Macradenia (*large-glands, as to pseudo-bulbs*) — Mak-rad-*deen*-ee-uh.

Macropiper (*large-Piper or Pepper, to which it is related*) — Mak-roh-*pye*-per.

Macrozamia (*large-Zamia*) — Mak-roh-*zay*-mee-uh.

Maddenia (*after Maj. E. Madden, botanical writer*) — Mad-*deen*-ee-uh.

Madia — *May*-dee-uh: Tarweed.

Magnolia (*for French botanist Pierre Magnol*) — Mag-*nohl*-ee-uh.

Mahernia — Mah-*hern*-ee-uh: Honey-bell.

Mahonia (*for American botanist Bernard McMahon*) — Mah-*hoh*-nee-uh.

Maianthemum (*May-flower*) — May-*anth*-em-um.

Majorana — Maj-or-*ray*-nuh: Sweet Marjoram (*M. hortensis*).

Malacocarpus (*soft-fruit*) — Mal-ak-oh-*karp*-us.

Malacothrix (*soft-hair, as to foliage of some species*) — Mal-ak-*koth*-rix.

Malcomia (*for English horticulturist William Malcolm*) — Mal-*koh*-mee-uh: Malcolm Stock.

Mallotus (*fleecy, as to seed capsule*) — Mal-*loh*-tus.

Malope (*classical name for Mallow*) — *Mal*-oh-pee.

Malpighia (*for Italian anatomist Marcello Malpighi*) — Mal-*pig*-ee-uh.

Malus (*a classical name*) — *May*-lus: Apple.

Malva — *Mal*-vuh: Mallow.

Malvastrum (*Mallow-like*) — Mal-*vast*-rum: False-mallow.

Mamillopsis — Mam-il-*lop*-siss.

Mammillaria (*for nipple-like protuberances*) — Mam-il-*lay*-ree-uh.

Mandevilla (*for English diplomat Henry J. Mandeville*) — Man-dev-*vill*-uh: Chilean-jasmine.

Manettia — Man-*net*-ee-uh.

Manfreda — Man-*freed*-uh.

Mangifera (*Mango-bearing*) — Man-*jiff*-er-uh: Mango.

Manihot — *Man*-ee-hot.

Maranta (*for medieval physician Bartolommeo Maranta*) — Mar-*rant*-uh: Arrow-root (*M. arundinacea*).

Marattia (*for Italian botanist J. L. Maratti*) — Mar-*rat*-tee-uh.

Margyricarpus (*pearly-fruit*) — Mar-gihr-ik-*karp*-us: Pearl-fruit.

Marrubium — Mar-*roo*-bee-um: Hoarhound, Horehound.

Marsdenia (*for English author W. Marsden*) — Marz-*deen*-ee-uh.

Marsilea (*for Italian naturalist Luigi Marsigli*) — Mar-*sill*-ee-uh: Pepperwort.

Masdevallia (*for Spanish botanist J. Masdeval*) — Mas-dev-*vall*-ee-uh.

Mathiola (*for Italian physician P. A. Mattioli*) — Math-*eye*-oh-luh: (The Stocks are included in this genus).

Matricaria (*mother, for supposed medicinal uses*) — Mat-rik-*kay*-ree-uh: Matricary.

Maurandia (*for Spanish botanist Maurandy*) — Maw-*ran*-dee-uh.

Maxillaria (*jaw-bone, as to mentum or projecting part of Orchids*) — Max-il-*lay*-ree-uh.

Maytenus — May-*teen*-us: Mayten.

Mazus — *May*-zus.

Meconopsis (*Poppy-like*) — Mee-kon-*nop*-siss.

Medeola — Med-*dee*-oh-luh: Indian Cucumber-root.

Medicago — Med-ik-*kay*-goh: Medick.

Medinilla (*for Spanish official D. J. de Medinilla y Pineda*) — Med-in-*nill*-uh.

Mediocactus (*intermediate-Cactus*) — Mee-dee-oh-*kak*-tus.

Melaleuca (*black-white, as to black trunk and white branches*) — Mel-al-*lew*-kuh: Bottle-brush.

Melampodium (*for mythical seer Melampus*) — Mel-am-*poh*-dee-um.

Melanthium (*black-flower, as to color of faded perianth*) — Mel-*anth*-ee-um: Bunch-flower.

Melastoma (*black-mouth, as to staining quality of its fruit*) — Mel-*last*-om-uh.

Melia — *Mee*-lee-uh: Bead-tree.

Melianthus (*honey-flower*) — Mel-ee-*anth*-us: Honey-bush.

Melica (*honey, for attractiveness to bees*) — *Mel*-ik-uh: Melic-grass.

Melilotus (*honey-Lotus, as to scent attractive to bees*) — Mel-il-*loh*-tus: Melilot, Sweet Clover.

Meliosma (*honey-odor, as to flowers*) — Mel-ee-*oss*-muh.

Melissa (*bee, which it attracts*) — Mel-*liss*-uh: Balm.

Melittis (*bee, which it attracts*) — Mel-*lit*-tiss.

Melocactus (*Melon-Cactus, as to shape of plants*) — Mel-oh-*kak*-tus.

Melothria (*from the classical word for a wild vine*) — Mel-*oth*-ree-uh.

Menispermum (*moon-seed*) — Men-iss-*sperm*-um: Moonseed.

Menodora — Men-oh-*doh*-ruh.

Mentha — *Menth*-uh: Mint.

Mentzelia (*for German physician and botanist Christian Mentzel*) — Ment-*zeel*-ee-uh.

Menyanthes (*month-flower, perhaps denoting period of bloom*) — Men-ee-*anth*-eez: Bogbean, Buckbean.

Menziesia (*for Scottish naturalist Archibald Menzies*) — Men-*zee*-zee-uh.

Meratia — Mer-*ray*-shee-uh: See preferred genus Chimonanthus.

Mercurialis (*for mythical Mercury*) — Mer-kew-ree-*ay*-liss: Herb-Mercury.

Mertensia (*for German botanist F. C. Mertens*) — Mer-*ten*-see-uh: Bluebells.

Mesembryanthemum (*midday-flower, as to flowers, which open in sun, close in shadow*) — Mes-em-bree-*anth*-em-um: Fig-marigold.

Mespilus — *Mess*-pil-us: Medlar.

Metrosideros (*tree-heart-iron*) — Mee-troh-sid-*deer*-os: (Sometimes called "Iron-tree").

Meum — *Mee*-um.

Michelia (*for Italian botanist Piero Micheli*) — Mye-*keel*-ee-uh.

Miconia (*for Spanish physician D. Micon*) — Mye-*koh*-nee-uh.

Microcitrus (*little-Citrus*) — Mye-kroh-*sit*-rus: Finger-lime (*M. australasica*).

Microcycas (*little-Cycas*) — Mye-kroh-*sye*-kas: Corcho.

Microglossa (*little-tongue, as to its short ray-petals*) — Mye-kroh-*gloss*-uh.

Microlepia (*little-scale, as to the covers of the spore cases*) — Mye-kroh-*leep*-ee-uh.

Micromeria (*small-part, as to flowers*) — Mye-kroh-*meer*-ee-uh.

Mikania (*for Bohemian botanist J. C. Mikan*) —Mik-*kay*-nee-uh: Climbing Hempweed.

Milla (*for Spanish gardener J. Milla*) — *Mill*-uh: Mexican Star.

Miltonia (*for Viscount Milton*) — Mil-*toh*-nee-uh.

Mimosa — Mim-*moh*-suh.

Mimulus (*little mime, as to its mask-like corolla*) — *Mim*-yew-lus: Monkey-flower.

Mirabilis (*wonderful*) — Mihr-*rab*-il-iss: (Four-o'clock or Marvel-of-Peru is *M. jalapa*).

Miscanthus (*stem-flower*) — Mis-*kanth*-os: Eulalia.

Mitchella (*for American botanist John Mitchell*) — Mit-*chell*-uh: Partridgeberry, Twin-berry, Squaw-berry.

Mitella (*little-cap, as to form of young pods*) — Mit-*tell*-uh: Bishops-cap.

Mitraria (*for cap-shaped pods*) — Mit-*ray*-ree-uh.

Molopospermum (*striped-seed*) — Mol-op-oh-*sperm*-um.

Moltkia (*for Danish Court Joachim Moltke*) — *Molt*-kee-uh.

Molucella (*for the Moluccas or Spice Is., where supposedly native*) — Mol-yew-*sell*-uh: (Shell-flower or Moluccabalm is *M. laevis*).

Momordica (*from word for bite, as to bitten-looking seeds*) — Mom-*mord*-ik-uh.

Monarda (*for Spanish physician-botanist N. Monardés*) — Mon-*nard*-uh: Horse-mint.

Monardella (*diminutive of Monarda, above*) — Mon-ar-*dell*-uh.

Moneses (*lone-delight, as to singly borne flowers*) — Mon-*nee*-seez: One-flowered Shinleaf.

Monotropa (*lone-turn, for solitary flower seeking the light—as in tropism*) — Mon-*not*-rop-uh: (*M. uniflora* is Indian Pipe).

Monstera — Mon-ster-uh.

Montanoa (*for Montano, Mexican statesman*) — Mon-tan-*noh*-uh.

Montia (*for Italian botanist Giuseppe Monti*) — *Mont*-ee-uh.

Monvillea — Mon-*vill*-ee-uh.

Moraea (*for Johannes Moraeus, father-in-law of Linnaeus*) — Moh-*ree*-uh.

Morinda (*contraction of Morus indica*) — Moh-*rind*-uh.

Moringa — Moh-*rin*-guh: Horse-radish-tree.

Morus — *Moh*-rus: Mulberry.

Moscharia (*musky-scented*) — Mos-*kay*-ree-uh.

Muehlenbeckia (*for Alsatian physician H. G. Muehlenbeck*) — Mew-len-*bek*-ee-uh: Wire-plant.

Murraea (*for Swedish botanist Johann Murray*) — *Muh*-ree-uh· Orange-jessamine (*M. exotica*).

Musa — *Mew*-zuh: Banana.

Myoporum (*close-pore, as to resinous leaf dots*) — Mye-*op*-or-um.

Myosotidium (*Myosotis-like*) — Mye-oh-soh-*tid*-ee-um.

Myosotis (*mouse-ear, as to leaf shape*) — Mye-oh-*soh*-tiss: Forget-me-not.

Myrica — *Mye*-rik-uh.

Myricaria (*Myrica-like*) — Mye-rik-*kay*-ree-uh: False-tamarisk.

Myriophyllum (*myriad-leaf*) —

Mihr-ee-oh-*fill*-um: Water-milfoil.

Myrrhis (*the classical name*) — Mihr-iss: Myrrh; (Sweet Cicely, M. odorata).

Myrsine — Mer-*sye*-nee.

Myrtillocactus (*Myrtle-like-Cactus, perhaps for fruit*) — Mer-til-oh-*kak*-tus.

Myrtus (*the classical name*) — *Mert*-us: Myrtle.

N

Naegelia (*for botanist Karl von Naegeli of Munich*) — Nee-*jeel*-ee-uh: See preferred genus Smithiantha.

Nananthus (*little-flower*) — Nan-*anth*-us.

Nandina — Nan-*dye*-nuh.

Narcissus (*name of mythical youth who was changed to a flower for love of his own reflection in a pool*) — Nar-*siss*-us: (Plural, Narcissi).

Nasturtium (*nose-twist, for its pungency*) — Nas-*tersh*-ee-um: (Water-cress is N. officinale. For common Nasturtium see genus Tropaeolum).

Neillia (*for Scotsman Patrick Neill*) — *Neel*-ee-uh.

Nelumbium — Nee-*lum*-bee-um: Lotus.

Nemastylis (*thread-like-styles*) — Nee-*mast*-il-iss.

Nemesia — Nem-*meesh*-ee-uh.

Nemopanthus (*thread-foot-flower, as to slender stalks*) — Nee-moh-*panth*-us: Mountain-holly.

Nemophila (*woods-loving, as to shade requirement*) — Nee-*moff*-il-uh.

Neolloydia (*new-Lloydia, as to classification*) — Nee-oh-*loy*-dee-uh.

Nepenthes (*an ancient drug, removing sorrow*) — Nep-*penth*-eez: Pitcher-plant.

Nepeta — *Nep*-et-uh.

Nephrolepis (*kidney-like-scale, as to spore-cases*) — Nef-*frol*-ep-iss: Sword-fern.

Nerine (*for the mythical nereid*) — Nee-*rye*-nee.

Nerium (*classical name for Oleander*) — *Neer*-ee-um: Oleander is N. oleander.

Nertera (*lowly, as to habit*) — *Nert*-er-uh: Bead-plant.

Neviusia (*for its discoverer, Rev. R. O. Nevius*) — Nev-ee-*yew*-see-uh: Snow-wreath.

Nicandra (*for Nicander, poet of ancient Colophon*) — Nye-*kand*-ruh.

Nicotiana (*for Jean Nicot, who introduced Tobacco in France*) — Nik-oh-shee-*ay*-nuh.

Nidularium (*little-nest, as to flower cluster*) — Nid-yew-*lay*-ree-um.

Nierembergia (*for Spanish Jesuit Juan Nieremberg*) — Nee-rem-*berg*-ee-uh: Cup-flower.

Nigella (*dark, as to black seeds*) — Nye-*jell*-uh: Fennel-flower.

Nolana (*little-bell, as to corolla shape*) — Nol-*lay*-nuh.

Nolina (*for French agriculturist C. P. Nolin*) — Nol-*lye*-nuh.
Noltea (*for German botanist E. F. Nolte*) — *Nolt*-ee-uh.
Nopalea — Noh-*pay*-lee-uh.
Nopalxochia — Noh-pal-*zok*-ee-uh.
Nothofagus (*false-Beech*) — Noth-oh-*fay*-gus.
Nothopanax (*false-Panax*) — Noth-oh-*pay*-nax.
Nothoscordum (*false-Garlic*) — Noth-os-*kord*-um.

Nyctocereus (*night-Cereus, as to bloom habit*) — Nik-toh-*seer*-ee-us.
Nymphaea (*for classical nymphs*) — Nim-*fee*-uh: Nymphea, Water-lily.
Nymphoides (*Nymphaea-like*) — Nim-*foy*-deez: Floating-heart.
Nyssa (*post, as to trunk; or for a mythical water nymph, as to its fondness for swampy places*) — *Niss*-uh: Tupelo.

O

Ochna (*classical name, no longer used, for Pear tree*) — *Ok*-nuh.
Ocimum (*classical name for Basil*) — *Oss*-im-um: (Several Basils are included in this genus, notably Basil, Bush Basil, Tree Basil).
Odontoglossum (*tooth-tongue, as to crested flower lip*) — Oh-don-toh-*gloss*-um.
Odontonema (*tooth-thread, as to toothed stamen filaments*) — Oh-don-toh-*neem*-uh.
Oenothera — Ee-noh-*theer*-uh.
Olea (*the classical name*) — *Oh*-lee-uh: Olive.
Olearia (*probably for Adam Olearius, German traveler*) — Oh-lee-*ay*-ree-uh: Tree-aster, Daisy-tree.
Omphalodes (*navel-like, as to seed shape*) — Om-fal-*loh*-deez: Navelwort.
Oncidium (*little-arrow-barb, as to shape of lip*) — On-*sid*-ee-um.
Oncoba — *On*-koh-buh.
Onobrychis (*classical name for a forage plant*) — On-oh-*brye*-kiss.
Onoclea — On-oh-*klee*-uh: Sensitive-fern.

Ononis (*the classical name*) — On-*noh*-niss: Rest-harrow.
Onopordum (*classical name for Cotton Thistle; literally, ass-fodder*) — On-oh-*pord*-um: (Scotch Thistle is *O. acanthium*).
Onosma (*ass-odor, presumably attractive to or reminiscent of the animal*) — On-*oss*-muh.
Onosmodium (*see Onosma above*) — On-os-*moh*-dee-um: False Gromwell.
Onyclium (*little-claw*) — Oh-*nik*-lee-um: Claw-fern.
Ophioglossum (*snake-tongue, as to fronds*) — Off-ee-oh-*gloss*-um: Adders-tongue-fern.
Ophiopogon (*snake-beard, presumably as to shape of flower cluster*) — Off-ee-oh-*poh*-gon: Lily-turf.
Ophrys (*brow, perhaps as to larger sepals than petals*) — *Off*-riss.
Opuntia — Op-*punt*-ee-uh: Prickly-pear.
Orchis (*testicle, as to tuber shape*) — *Ork*-iss.
Origanum (*mountain-beauty*) — Or-*rig*-an-um: Marjoram.

Orixa — Or-*rix*-uh.

Ornithochilus (*bird-lip, for beak-like flower*) — Or-nith-oh-*kye*-lus.

Ornithogalum (*bird-milk, perhaps for form and color of flowers of some species*) — Or-nith-*thog*-al-um.

Ornithopus (*bird-foot, as to pod form*) — Or-*nith*-op-us.

Orontium (*for the Orontes River, Syria*) — Oh-*ron*-tee-um: Golden-club.

Oroxylon (*mountain-tree, an inexact application*) — Or-*rox*-il-on.

Orthocarpus (*straight-fruit*) — Orth-oh-*karp*-us: Owls Clover.

Oscularia (*little-mouth, as to small flowers*) — Os-kew-*lay*-ree-uh.

Osmanthus (*scent-flower*) — Os-*manth*-us.

Osmaronia — Os-mar-*roh*-nee-uh: Osoberry.

Osmorhiza (*probably for scented root*) — Os-mor-*rye*-zuh.

Osmunda — Os-*mund*-uh: (Cinnamon-fern, *O. cinnamomea;* Interrupted-fern, *O. Claytoniana;* Royal-fern, *O. regalis*).

Osteomeles (*bone-fruit*) — Os-tee-oh-*mee*-leez.

Ostrowskia (*for Russian botanist N. Ostrowski*) — Os-*troh*-skee-uh: Giant Bellflower.

Ostrya — *Oss*-tree-uh: Hop-hornbeam.

Othonna — Oh-*thon*-nuh.

Ourisia (*for a Governor Ouris of the Falkland Is.*) — Oo-*riss*-ee-uh.

Oxalis (*sharp, pungent, as to leaf taste*) — *Ox*-al-iss: Wood-sorrel.

Oxera — *Ox*-er-uh.

Oxydendrum (*acrid-tree, as to bitter foliage*) — Ox-id-*den*-drum: Sourwood, Sorrel-tree.

Oxytropis (*sharp-keel, as to flower shape*) — Ox-*it*-rop-iss.

P

Pachistima (*thick-stigma*) — Pak-*kist*-im-uh.

Pachycereus (*thick-Cereus*) — Pak-iss-*seer*-ee-us.

Pachysandra (*thick-anther*) — Pak-iss-*sand*-ruh: Spurge.

Paeonia (*the classical name*) — Pee-*oh*-nee-uh: Peony.

Paliurus — Pal-ee-*yew*-rus: Christ-thorn or Jerusalem-thorn is *P. spina-Christi.*

Panax (*all-healing, panacea, as to the medicinal properties of its roots*) — *Pay*-nax: Ginseng.

Pancratium (*all-strength, as to supposed medical properties*) — Pan-*kray*-shee-um.

Pandanus — Pan-*day*-nus: Screw-pine.

Pandorea (*for mythical Pandora, whose name means all-gifted*) — Pan-*doh*-ree-uh.

Panicum (*the classical name for Millet*) — *Pan*-ik-um.

Papaver (*the classical name*) — Pap-*pay*-ver: Poppy.

Paphiopedilum (*Aphrodite's slipper, a slightly fanciful interpretation*) — Pap-ee-oh-*ped*-il-um: Lady-slipper.

Paradisea (*for paradise*) — Par-ad-*diss*-ee-uh: St.-Bruno-lily.

Paris (*equal, as to symmetrical parts*) — *Par*-iss.

Parkinsonia (*for English botanist John Parkinson*) — Park-in-*soh*-nee-uh.

Parmentiera (*for French horticultur-*

ist *Antoine Parmentier*) — Pahr-ment-*yeer*-uh.

Parnassia (*for Mt. Parnassus, sacred to mythical Apollo and the muses*) — Par-*nass*-ee-uh: Grass-of-Parnassus.

Parochetus (*beside-brook, as to habitat*) — Par-oh-*kee*-tus: Shamrock-pea, Blue-oxalis.

Paronychia (*like-a-nail, perhaps as to pointed bracts*) — Par-oh-*nik*-ee-uh: Whitlow-wort, Nail-wort.

Parrotia (*for German naturalist F. W. Parrot*) — Par-*roh*-tee-uh.

Parthenium (*virgin, for white flowers of some species*) — Pahr-*theen*-ee-um: Guayule (*P. argentatum*).

Parthenocissus (*virgin-ivy, of no known application*) — Parth-en-oh-*siss*-us: Virginia Creeper (*P. quinquefolia*); Boston Ivy (*P. tricuspidata*).

Passiflora (*passion-flower*) — Pass-if-*floh*-ruh: Passion-flower.

Pastinaca (*the classical name*) — Past-in-*nay*-kuh: Parsnip.

Paullinia (*for German botanist Christian Paullini*) — Pol-*lin*-ee-uh.

Paulownia (*for Russian Princess Anna Pavlovna*)—Pol-*loh*-nee-uh.

Pavonia (*for Spanish traveler Don José Pavon*) — Pav-*voh*-nee-uh.

Pedicularis (*pertaining to a louse, of unknown pertinence*) — Ped-ik-yew-*lay*-riss: Wood-betony, Louse-wort.

Pedilanthus (*shoe-flower, perhaps as to leaf shape*) — Ped-il-*anth*-us.

Pediocactus (*plain-Cactus, as to habitat*) — Ped-ee-oh-*kak*-tus: Snowball Cactus.

Pelargonium (*stork, for long, slender fruit*) — Pel-ahr-*goh*-nee-um: Geranium, Storksbill.

Pelecyphora (*hatchet-bearing, for a*

fancied resemblance to protuberant parts) — Pel-ee-*siff*-or-uh: Hatchet Cactus.

Pellaea (*dark-colored, as to frond stalks*) — Pel-*lee*-uh: Cliff-brake.

Pellionia (*for maritime officer J. A. Pellion*) — Pell-ee-*oh*-nee-ah.

Peltandra (*shield-anther, as to shape*) — Pel-*tand*-ruh: Arrow-arum.

Peltaria (*small-shield, as to pod shape*) — Pel-*tay*-ree-uh: Shield-wort.

Peltiphyllum (*shield-leaf*) — Pel-tif-*fill*-um: Umbrella-plant.

Peniocereus (*penis-Cereus, as to plant form*) — Pee-nee-oh-*seer*-ee-us.

Pennisetum (*feather-bristle, as to spikelets*) — Pen-nis-*seet*-um.

Penstemon (*five-stamens—though only four are fertile*) — Pen-*steem*-on: Beard-tongue.

Pentas (*five, as to most flower parts being in fives*) — *Pen*-tas.

Pentstemon — See preferred Penstemon above.

Peperomia (*pepper-like, not as to appearance but as to kinship*) — Pep-er-*roh*-mee-uh.

Pereskia (*for Provencal scientist N. C. F. de Peiresc*) — Peer-*resk*-ee-uh.

Pereskiopsis (*Pereskia-like*) — Per-esk-ee-*ops*-iss.

Perilla — Per-*rill*-uh.

Periploca (*a twining, as to habit*) — Per-*rip*-lok-uh: Silk-vine.

Peristeria (*dove, as to winged flower shape*) — Pehr-ist-*teer*-ee-uh.

Peristrophe (*around-belt or line, as to bract formation*) — Pehr-*rist*-rof-ee.

Pernettya (*for A. J. Pernetty, colleague of Bougainville*) — Per-*nett*-ee-uh.

Perovskia (*for Russian official B. A. Perovski*) — Pehr-*roff*-skee-uh.

Persea — *Purr*-see-uh.

Pescatoria (*for French Orchid collector M. Pescatore*) — Pes-kuh-*toh*-ree-uh.

Petalostemum (*petal-stamen, as to attachment*) — Pet-al-oh-*steem*-um: Prairie-clover.

Petasites — Pet-uh-*sye*-teez: Butterbur.

Petrea (*for English botanical patron Lord Petre*) — *Peet*-ree-uh: Purple-wreath.

Petrocallis (*rock-beauty, as to mountain habitat*) — Pet-roh-*kal*-liss.

Petrocoptis (*rock-cleft, as to habitat*) — Pet-roh-*kop*-tiss.

Petrophila (*rock-dwelling*) — Pet-*roff*-il-uh.

Petrophytum (*rock-plant, as to habitat*) — Pet-*roff*-it-um.

Petroselinum (*rock-Parsley*) — Pet-roh-sel-*lye*-num: Parsley.

Petteria (*for Dalmatian botanist Franz Petter*) — Pet-*teer*-ee-uh.

Petunia — Pet-*tew*-nee-uh.

Peucedanum — Pew-*sed*-an-um.

Phacelia (*bundle, as to crowded flower cluster*) — Fas-*seel*-ee-uh.

Phaedranthus (*splendid-flower*) — Feed-*ranth*-us.

Phaius (*dusty, as to flower colors*) — *Fay*-us.

Phalaenopsis (*moth-like, as to flower form*) — Fal-ee-*nops*-iss.

Phaseolus (*from the classical name for Bean*) — Fas-*see*-ol-us: Bean.

Phellodendron (*cork-tree*) — Fel-lon-*den*-dron: Cork-tree.

Phellosperma (*cork-seed, as to corky seed base*) — Fel-loh-*sperm*-uh.

Philadelphus (*sweet-flowering shrub*) — Fil-ad-*delf*-us: Mock orange.

Philesia (*lovely*) — Fil-*lee*-shee-uh.

Phillyrea — Fil-*lihr*-ee-uh.

Philodendron (*loving-tree, as to its tree-climbing propensities*) — Fil-oh-*den*-dron.

Phlomis — *Floh*-miss.

Phlox (*flame*) — *Flox:* Of the many species, Annual or Drummond Phlox is *P. Drummondi;* Summer Perennial Phlox is, for the most part, *P. paniculata.*

Phoenix (*classical name for Date Palm*) — *Fee*-nix.

Phormium (*a plaited mat, for which its fibres may have been used*) — *Form*-ee-um.

Photinia (*shining, as to foliage*) — Foh-*tin*-ee-uh.

Phygelius (*flight-from-sun, as to shade preference*) — Fye-*jeel*-ee-us.

Phylica — *Fill*-ik-uh.

Phyllanthus (*leaf-flower, for some species which seem to bear flowers on leaves*) — Fil-*lanth*-us.

Phyllitis (*for leaf; also a classical name for the plant*) — Fil-*lye*-tiss: Hearts-tongue-fern.

Phyllocactus (*leaf-Cactus*) — Fil-oh-*kak*-tus: See preferred names Epiphyllum and Disocactus.

Phyllocladus (*leaf-branch, referring to leaf-like stems*) — Fil-*lok*-lad-us.

Phyllodoce (*for mythical sea nymph*) — Fil-*lod*-oh-see.

Physalis (*bladder, for enlarged calyx containing its fruit*) — *Fye*-sal-iss: Husk-tomato, Ground-cherry.

Physocarpus (*bladder-fruit, as to inflated capsules*) — Fye-soh-*karp*-us: Ninebark.

Physostegia (*bladder-cover, as to*

fruiting calyx) — Fye-sos-*teej*-ee-uh: False Dragonhead.

Phyteuma (*plant*) — Fye-*tew*-muh: Horned-rampion.

Phytolacca (*a hybrid name, for plant and for lake, a crimson color— as to berries*) — Fye-toh-*lak*-uh: Pokeweed, Pokeberry.

Picea (*classical name for Pitch Pine*) — Pye-see-uh: Spruce.

Pieris (*for one of the mythical muses*) — Pye-er-iss.

Pilea (*cap, as to shape of part of flower*) — Pye-lee-uh.

Pilocereus (*cap-like-Cereus*) — Pye-loh-*seer*-ee-us: See preferred name Cephalocereus.

Pimelea (*fat, as to fleshy seeds*) — Pim-*meel*-ee-uh: Rice-flower.

Pimenta — Pim-*ment*-uh: Allspice (*P. officinalis*).

Pimpinella — Pim-pin-*nell*-uh: Anise (*P. anisum*).

Pinguicula (*rather fat, as to greasy leaves*) — Pin-*guik*-yew-luh: Butter-wort.

Pinus (*the classical name*) — Pye-nus: Pine.

Piper (*the classical name*) — Pye-per: Pepper.

Piptanthus — Pip-*tanth*-us.

Piqueria (*for Spanish physician A. Piquier*) — Pik-*weer*-ee-uh: Often called Stevia by florists.

Pistacia — Pis-*tay*-shee-uh: Pistache.

Pistia (*liquid, as to its free-floating aquatic habit*) — Pist-ee-uh: Water-lettuce.

Pisum (*the classical name*) — Pye-sum: Pea; Garden Pea (*P. sativum*).

Pitcairnia (*for Scottish physician Archibald Pitcairn*) — Pit-*karn*-ee-uh.

Pithecellobium (*monkey-lobe, for its odd pods*) — Pith-es-sel-*loh*-bee-um.

Pittosporum (*pitch-seed, as to resinous seed coating*) — Pit-*tosp*-or-um.

Pityrogramma (*bran-like, for powdery fronds*) — Pit-ihr-oh-*gram*-uh: Gold-fern; Silver-fern.

Planera (*for German physician J. J. Planer*) — Plan-er-uh: Water-elm.

Plantago (*the classical name*) — Plan-*tay*-goh: Plantain.

Platanus (*the classical name*) — Plat-an-us: Plane-tree.

Platycarya (*broad-nut, as to relative shape, not size*) — Plat-ik-*kay*-ree-uh.

Platycereum (*broad-honeycomb, for lace-like leaves*) — Plat-iss-*seer*-ee-um: Staghorn-fern.

Platycodon (*wide-bell, as to flower form*) — Plat-ik-*koh*-don: Balloon-flower.

Platystemon (*broad-stamen*) — Plat-iss-*steem*-on: Cream-ups.

Pleione (*perhaps for mythical mother of the Pleiades; or perhaps for literal meaning: greater-than-normal*) — Plye-*oh*-nee.

Pleiospilos (*more-spots, as to dotted leaves*) — Plye-oh-*spye*-los.

Pleurothallis (*side-branch, as to flowers borne in leaf axils*) — Ploor-oh-*thal*-liss.

Plumbago (*classical name*) — Plum-*bay*-goh: Leadwort.

Plumeria (*for French botanist Charles Plumier*) — Ploo-*meer*-ee-uh: Frangipani.

Poa (*a classical name for grass*) — Poh-uh: (Includes several important lawn grasses).

Podocarpus (*foot-fruit, as to prominent stem*) — Pod-oh-*karp*-us.

Podolepis (*foot-scale, as to claw-like base of bracts*) — Pod-*dol*-ep-iss.

Podophyllum (*foot-leaf, emphasizing the base of radiating leaf lobes*) — Pod-oh-*fill*-um: May-apple.

Pogonia (*beard, as to bearded flower lip*) — Poh-*goh*-nee-uh.

Poinciana (*for a French governor of West Indies, M. de Poinci*) — Poyn-see-*ay*-nuh.

Polanisia (*many-unequal, as to stamens*) — Pol-an-*niss*-ee-uh.

Polemonium (*the classical name*) — Pol-em-*moh*-nee-um: (*P. caeruleum* is Jacobs-ladder).

Polianthes (*gray-flower, though its flowers seem to be white*) — Pol-ee-*anth*-eez: Tuberose.

Polygala — Pol-*lig*-uh-luh: Milkwort.

Polygonatum (*many-knee, as to joints of rootstock*) — Pol-ig-on-*nay*-tum: Solomons-seal.

Polygonum (*many-joint, as to stems or pedicels*) — Pol-*lig*-on-um: Knot-weed, Fleece-flower.

Polypodium (*many-foot, as to rootstocks*) — Pol-ip-*poh*-dee-um: Polypody.

Polypteris (*many-feathered, as to bristly flower parts*) — Pol-*lip*-ter-iss.

Polyscias (*abundant-shade, as to heavy foliage*) — Pol-*liss*-ee-us.

Polystichum (*many-rows, as of spore cases*) — Pol-*list*-ik-um.

Pomaderris (*cover-skin, as to seed capsule*) — Poh-muh-*dehr*-riss.

Poncirus — Pon-*sye*-rus: Trifoliate-orange.

Pongamia — Pon-*gay*-mee-uh: Karum Oil Tree or Poonga Oil Tree.

Pontederia (*for Italian botanist Giulio Pontedera*) — Pon-ted-deer-ee-uh: Pickerel-weed.

Populus (*the classical name*) — *Pop*-yew-lus: Poplar, Aspen, Cotton-wood.

Portlandia (*for the Duchess of Portland*) — Port-*land*-ee-uh.

Portulaca — Port-yew-*lay*-kuh: Purslane.

Portulacaria — Port-yew-lak-*kay*-ree-uh.

Posoqueria — Pos-ok-*kweer*-ee-uh.

Potentilla (*somewhat-powerful, as to supposed medicinal properties*) — Poh-ten-*till*-uh: Cinquefoil.

Poterium — Poh-*teer*-ee-um.

Pothos — *Poh*-thoss: For more accurate generic designations, see Scindapsus and Anthurium.

Pratia (*for a Frenchman, Prat-Bernon*) — *Pray*-shee-uh.

Prenanthes (*drooping-flower*) — Pren-*anth*-eez: Rattlesnake Root.

Primula (*diminutive of word meaning first, as to spring blooming*) — *Prim*-yew-luh: Primrose.

Prinsepia (*for Swiss botanist Macaire-Prinsep*) — Prin-*seep*-ee-uh.

Pritchardia (*after civil official William T. Pritchard*) — Prit-*chard*-ee-uh: See preferred generic name Eupritchardia.

Proboscidiea (*snout, as to long-beaked fruit*) — Proh-bos-*sid*-ee-uh: Unicorn-plant.

Promenaea — Proh-men-*nee*-uh.

Prosopis (*classical name*) — Proh-*soh*-piss.

Prostanthera (*add-to-anther, as to connecting parts*) — Pross-*tanth*-er-uh.

Protea (*for Proteus, mythical sea god who assumed many forms, as to di-*

versity of its species) — *Proh*-tee-uh.

Prunella — Proo-*nell*-uh.

Prunus (*classical name for Plum*) — *Proon*-us: The stone-fruits, including Apricot, Cherry, Peach and Plum among the many species.

Pseuderanthemum (*false-Eranthemum*) — Soo-der-*anth*-em-um.

Pseudolarix (*false-Larch*) — Soo-doh-*lar*-ix: Golden-larch.

Pseudopanax (*false-Panax*) — Soo-doh-*pay*-nax.

Pseudotsuga (*false-Tsuga*) — Soo-doh-*tsoo*-guh: (Douglas-fir is *P. taxifolia*).

Psidium — *Sid*-ee-um: Guava.

Psoralea (*scabby, as to its glandular dots*) — Sor-*ray*-lee-uh: Scurfy-pea.

Ptelea (*classical name for Elm*) — *Teel*-ee-uh: Hop-tree.

Pteretis (*Pteris-like; see below*) — Tehr-*reet*-iss: Ostrich-fern.

Pteridium (*Pteris-form; see below*) — Tehr-*rid*-ee-um: Bracken, Brake.

Pteris (*wing, as to appearance of fronds*) — *Teer*-iss: Brake.

Pterocarya (*wing-nut*) — Tehr-oh-*cay*-ree-uh: Wing-nut.

Pterocephalus (*feather-head, as to appearance of faded flower head*) — Tehr-oh-*seff*-al-us.

Pterostyrax (*for winged fruit setting it apart from genus Styrax*) — Tehr-oh-*stye*-rax: Epaulette-tree.

Pueraria (*for Swiss botanist M. N.*

Puerari) — Pew-er-*ray*-ree-uh: Kud-zu-vine.

Pulmonaria (*lung, as to supposed curative power*) — Pull-mon-*nay*-ree-uh: Lungwort.

Pultenaea (*probably for Dr. Richard Pulteney*) — Pult-en-*nee*-uh.

Punica (*the classical name*) — Pew-nik-uh: Pomegranate.

Purshia (*for American botanist F. T. Pursh*) — *Pursh*-ee-uh: Antelope-brush.

Pushkinia (*for a Count M. Puschkin*) — Push-*kin*-ee-uh.

Puya — *Pew*-yuh.

Pycnanthemum (*compact-flower, as to flower heads*) — Pik-*nanth*-em-um: Mountain-mint.

Pycnostachys (*dense-spike, as to flower spike*) — Pik-*noss*-tak-iss.

Pyracantha (*fire-thorn, as to its bright red fruits and thorns*) — Pye-ruh-*kanth*-uh: Firethorn.

Pyrethrum (*much-fire, as to bitter roots*) — Pye-*reeth*-rum: This genus has now been superseded, largely by Chrysanthemum.

Pyrola — *Pihr*-ol-uh: Shinleaf.

Pyrostegia (*fire-roof, as to flowers and climbing habit*) — Pye-roh-*steej*-ee-uh.

Pyrus (*the classical name*) — *Pye*-rus: Pear.

Pyxidanthera (*Box-flowered*) — Pix-id-*danth*-er-uh: Pyxie, Flowering-moss.

Q

Quamoclit — *Kwam*-oh-klit: Star-glory.

Quassia (*for Graman Quassi of Surinam*) — *Kwosh*-ee-uh.

Quercus (*the classical name*) — *Kwurk*-us: Oak.

Quillaja — Kwil-*lay*-uh: Soap-bark Tree.

R

Ramonda (*for French botanist L. F. E. von Ramond de Carbonnieres*) — Ray-*mond*-uh.

Ranunculus (*little-frog, suggesting marshy habitat of many species*) — Ran-*nun*-kew-lus: Buttercup.

Raoulia (*for French surgeon Etienne F. L. Raoul*) — Rah-*ool*-ee-uh.

Raphanus (*the classical name*) — *Raff*-an-us: Radish.

Raphiolepis (*needle-scale, as to bract structure*) — Raf-ee-*ol*-ep-iss.

Ravenala — Rav-en-*nay*-luh: Travelers-tree.

Rebutia (*apparently named for one Rebut*) — Reb-*bew*-tee-uh.

Rehmannia (*for Russian physician Joseph Rehmann*) — Ray-*man*-nee-uh.

Reinwardtia (*for Dutch botanist K. G. K. Reinwardt*) — Ryn-*wahrt*-ee-uh.

Renanthera (*kidney-anther, as to shape, in one species*) — Ren-*nanth*-er-uh.

Reseda (*from word, to calm; for supposed sedative qualities*) — Res-*seed*-uh: Mignonette.

Retinospora; Retinispora (*resin-seed*) — Ret-in-*noss*(*niss*)-por-uh: Now the genus Chamaecyparis.

Rhabdothamnus (*rod-bush, as to form of branches*) — Rab-doh-*tham*-nus.

Rhamnus (*classical name for a prickly shrub*) — *Ram*-nus: Buckthorn.

Rhapidophyllum (*rod-leaf, as to narrow leaflets*) — Rap-id-oh-*fill*-um: Needle Palm.

Rhapis (*rod, as to leaf or corolla characters*) — *Ray*-piss: Lady Palm.

Rheum (*old name for the plant*) — *Ree*-um: Rhubarb.

Rhexia (*classical name*) — *Rex*-ee-uh: Meadow Beauty.

Rhinanthus (*nose-flower, as to shape*) — Rye-*nanth*-us: Rattlebox.

Rhipsalis (*wicker-work, for branch or stem masses*) — *Rip*-suh-liss.

Rhodochiton (*red-cloak, as to calyx*) — Roh-doh-*kye*-ton: Purple Bellvine.

Rhododendron (*Rose-tree, as to flower colors of many species*) — Roh-doh-*den*-dron: Rhododendron, Rose-bay, Azalea (as to various species).

Rhodomyrtus (*rose-Myrtle, as to flower colors*) — Roh-doh-*mert*-us: Downy-myrtle (*R. tomentosa*).

Rhodostachys (*rose-spike, as to flower color of some species*) — Roh-*doss*-tak-iss.

Rhodothamnus (*rose-shrub, as to flower colors*) — Roh-doh-*tham*-nus.

Rhodotypos (*Rose-type, as to form resembling that of a single Rose*) — Roh-doh-*tye*-pos: Jetbead.

Rhoeo — *Ree*-oh.

Rhombophyllum (*rhomboid-leaf, as to leaves of roughly diamond shape*) — Rom-boh-*fill*-um.

Rhopalostylis (*club-style, as to shape of flower styles*) — Roh-pal-*lost*-il-iss: Nikau Palm.

Rhus (*classical name*) — Russ: Sumac; (Poison-ivy and Poison-oak are now classified as *R. radicans*).

Ribes — *Rye*-beez: Currant, Gooseberry.

Ricinus — *Riss*-in-us: Castor-bean, Castor-oil-plant.

Ricotia (*for French botanist M. Ricot*) — Rik-*koh*-shee-uh.

Rivina (*for German botanist A. Q. Rivinus*) — Riv-*vye*-nuh: Rouge-plant.

Robinia (*for Vespasian Robin, who was introduced into Europe from North America*)—Roh-*bin*-ee-uh: Locust.

Rochea (*for Swiss botanist Francois de la Roche*) — *Roh*-kee-uh.

Rodgersia (*for U. S. Navy Commodore Rodgers*) — Rod-*jerz*-ee-uh.

Rohdea (*for German physician-botanist M. Rohde*) — *Roh*-dee-uh.

Romanzoffia (*for Russian Count Nicholas Romanzoff*) — Roh-man-*zoff*-ee-uh.

Romneya (*for astronomer A. Romney Robinson*) — *Rom*-nee-uh: Matilija-poppy.

Romulea — Rom-*yew*-lee-uh.

Rondeletia (*for French naturalist-physician Guillaume Rondelet*) — Ron-del-*leesh*-ee-uh.

Rosa (*ancient classical name for the genus*) — *Roh*-zuh: Rose.

Roseocactus (*rosy-Cactus, probably as to color in some species*) — Roh-zee-oh-*kak*-tus.

Rosmarinus (*sea-dew, as to its sea-shore habitat*) — Ross-muh-*rye*-nus: Rosemary.

Roystonea (*for American General Roy Stone*) — Roy-*stoh*-nee-uh: Royal Palm.

Rubus (*classical name for bramble plants*) — *Roo*-bus: This genus, the Brambles, includes Black-berries, Dewberries and Rasp-berries.

Rudbeckia (*for Swedish botanist Olans Rudbeck*) — Rud-*bek*-ee-uh: Coneflower.

Ruellia (*for French botanist Jean Ruel*) — Rew-*ell*-ee-uh.

Rumex (*classical name*) — *Roo*-mex: Dock, Sorrel.

Ruscus — *Russ*-kus: Butchers-broom (*R. aculeatus*).

Russelia (*for physician Alexander Russell*) — Russ-*seel*-ee-uh: Coral-blow.

Ruta (*classical name*) — *Root*-uh: Rue.

S

Sabal — *Say*-bal: Palmetto.

Sabatia (*for Italian botanist Liberatus Sabbati*) — Sab-*bay*-shee-uh.

Sagina (*fatness, as to presumed nutritive value*) — Saj-*jye*-nuh: Pearl-wort.

Sagittaria (*arrow-like, as to leaf shape*) Saj-it-*tay*-ree-uh: Arrow-head.

Saintpaulia (*for German discoverer Baron Walter von St. Paul*) — Saynt-Pawl-ee-uh: African-violet (*S. ionanthe*).

Salix (*the classical name*) — *Say*-lix: Willow.

Salpiglossis (*tube-tongue, as to form of corolla and style*) — Sal-pig-*gloss*-iss: Painted-tongue (*S. sinuata*).

Salvia (*the ancient classical name*) — *Sal*-vee-uh: Sage.

Salvinia (*for Italian scholar Antonio Salvini*) — Sal-*vin*-ee-uh.

Sambucus (*classical name*) — Sam-*bew*-kus: Elder.

Samuela (*for American botanist Sam*

F. Trelease) — Sam-yew-*ell*-uh: Date-yucca.

Sanchezia — San-*cheez*-ee-uh.

Sanguinaria (*bloody, as to color of root juice*) — San-gwin-*nay*-ree-uh: Blood-root.

Sanguisorba — San-gwis-*sorb*-uh: Burnet.

Sanseveria (*for Italian Prince of Sanseviero*) — San-sev-*veer*-ee-uh: Bowstring-hemp (known to florists and many gardeners as Snake-plant).

Santolina — San-toh-*lye*-nuh: Lavender-cotton (*S. chamaecyparissus*).

Sanvitalia (*for the Italian Sanvitali family*) — San-vit-*tay*-lee-uh.

Sapindus (*soap-India, as to use of berries for soap in India*) — Sap-*pind*-us: Soapberry.

Saponaria (*soap, for its juice which lathers in water*) — Sap-on-*nay*-ree-uh: Soapwort.

Sarchochilus (*fleshy-lip, as to flowers*) — Sar-koh-*kye*-lus.

Sarcococca (*fleshy-berry, as to fruit*) — Sar-koh-*kok*-uh.

Sarracenia (*for one D. Sarrazin*) — Sar-ras-*seen*-ee-uh: Pitcher-plant.

Sassafras (*probably named for Saxifraga, the Saxifrage, by Spanish discoverers because of similar medicinal properties*) — Sass-uh-frass.

Satureja (*the classical name*) — Sat-yew-*reej*-uh: Savory.

Sauromatum — Saw-*rom*-at-um.

Saururus (*lizard-tail, as to shape of flower spike*) — Saw-*roor*-us: Lizards-tail.

Saussurea (*for Swiss naturalists Benedict and Theodore Saussure*) — Soss-*yew*-ree-uh.

Saxifraga (*rock-break, variously thought to refer to the rock-cleft*

habitat of many species or to a supposed remedial value for gallstones) — Sax-*iff*-ruh-guh: Saxifrage, Rockfoil.

Scabiosa (*itching, as to possible therapeutic virtues of some species*) — Skay-bee-*oh*-suh: Scabious, Mourning Bride.

Schinus (*old name for Mastic-tree, as to its resinous quality*) — Skye-nus.

Schisandra (*cleavage-anther, as to cleft anthers*) — Skiss-*and*-ruh.

Schismatoglottis (*parting-tongue, as to the early falling of the spathe*) — Siz-mat-oh-*glott*-iss.

Schivereckia — Skiv-er-*rek*-ee-uh.

Schizaea (*split, as to fronds*) — Skye-zee-uh: Curly-grass-fern.

Schizanthus (*split-flower, as to the cleft corolla*) — Skye-*zanth*-us: Butterfly-flower.

Schizobasopsis (*Schizobasis-like, an unimportant similarity*) — Skye-zoh-bas-*ops*-iss.

Schizocentron (*split-thorn*) — Skye-zoh-*sent*-ron.

Schizopetalon (*cut-petals*) — Skye-zoh-*pet*-al-on.

Schizophragma (*cut-wall, as to splitting of capsules*) — Skye-zoh-*frag*-muh.

Schizostylis (*cut-style, as to threadlike style segments*) — Skye-*zoss*-til-iss: Crimson Flag, Kafir-lily.

Schlumbergera (*for one Friedrich Schlumberger*) — Schlum-ber-*jeer*-ee-uh.

Schomburgkia (*for naturalist Robert H. Schomburgk*) — Shom-*burg*-kee-uh.

Schotia (*for botanical traveler Richard Schot*) — Shot-ee-uh.

Schwantesia — Shwan-*tee*-shee-uh.

Sciadopitys (*shade-Pine, as to its*

foliage habit) — Sye-ad-*dop*-it-iss: Umbrella-pine.

Scilla (*the classical name*) — *Sill*-uh: Squill.

Scindapsus — Sin-*dap*-sus: Ivy-arum.

Sclerocactus (*hard-Cactus*) —Skleer-oh-*kak*-tus.

Scolymus (*a kind of Thistle*) — *Skoll*-im-us: Golden Thistle, Spanish Oyster-plant.

Scorzonera — Skor-zoh-*neer*-uh: Black Salsify (*S. hispanica*).

Scrophularia (*perhaps supposed in some form to have been a scrofula remedy*) — Skroff-yew-*lay*-ree-uh: Figwort.

Scutellaria (*tray or dish, as to calyx formation*) — Skew-tel-*lay*-ree-uh: Skullcap.

Scuticaria (*whip, as to its long whip-like, channeled leaves*) — Skew-tik-*kay*-ree-uh.

Sechium (*pen, perhaps for the fact that it was fed to hogs*) — *Seek*-ee-um: Chayote, Christophine.

Securigera (*hatchet-bearing, as to pod shape*) — Sek-yew-*rij*-er-uh.

Sedum (*classical name for House-leek*) — *Seed*-um: Stonecrop, Live-forever. (*Compare Semper-vivum.*)

Selaginella (*diminutive of irrelevant genus Selago*) — Sel-uh-jin-*nell*-uh.

Selenicereus (*Selene's Cactus: she was the mythical moon goddess*) — Sel-en-iss-*seer*-ee-us.

Selenipedium (*Selene's Orchid: see above*) — Sel-en-ip-*peed*-ee-um.

Semele (*mythical mother of Dionysus*) — *Sem*-el-ee: Climbing Butchers-broom.

Semmanthe — Sem-*manth*-ee.

Sempervivum (*live-forever*) — Sem-per-*vye*-vum: Houseleek. (*A va-gary of plant nomenclature will be illustrated by comparing with the genus Sedum, above.*)

Senecio (*the classical name*) — Sen-nee-see-oh: Groundsel.

Sequoia (*for Sequoya, actually George Guess, a Cherokee half-breed and originator of the Cherokee syllabary*) — See-*kwoy*-uh: Redwood (*S. sempervirens*).

Sequoiadendron (*Sequoia-tree*) — See-kwoy-ad-*den*-dron: Giant Sequoia.

Serenoa (*for American botanist Sereno Watson*) — Sehr-en-*noh*-uh: Saw-palmetto, Scrub-palmetto.

Serissa — Ser-*riss*-uh.

Serratula (*for serrate or roughish leaf margins*) — Sehr-*rat*-yew-luh.

Sesamum — *Sess*-uh-mum: Sesame (*S. orientale*).

Sesbania — Ses-*bay*-nee-uh.

Shepherdia (*for English botanist John Shepherd*) — Shep-*herd*-ee-uh: Buffalo-berry (*S. argentea*).

Shortia (*for American botanist Charles W. Short*) — *Short*-ee-uh.

Sibiraea (*for Siberia, its habitat*) — Sye-bir-*ree*-uh.

Sibthorpia (*for one John Sibthorp*) — Sib-*thorp*-ee-uh.

Sicana — Sik-*kay*-nuh: Curuba, Cassabanana.

Sidalcea — Sye-*dal*-see-uh.

Sideritis (*iron, perhaps as to tonic virtues*) — Sid-er-*rye*-tiss.

Sideroxylon (*iron-wood*) — Sid-er-*rox*-il-on.

Silene — Sye-*leen*-ee: Catchfly, Campion.

Silphium — *Sill*-fee-um: Rosinweed.

Silybum (*classical name for Thistle*) — *Sill*-ib-um.

Sinningia (*for German gardener Wilhelm Sinning*) — Sin-*nin*-jee-uh.

Sinomenium (*Chinese-moon, for moon-seed*) — Sye-noh-*meen*-ee-um.

Sisyrinchium (*classical name*) — Siss-ir-*rink*-ee-um: Blue-eyed-grass.

Skimmia — *Skim*-mee-uh.

Smilacina (*Smilax-like*) — Smye-las-*sye*-nuh: False Solomons-seal.

Smilax (*classical name for Bind-weed*) — *Smye*-lax: Greenbrier.

Smithiantha (*Smith's-flower, for botanical artist Matilda Smith*) — Smith-ee-*anth*-uh.

Sobralia (*for Spanish physician-botanist Francisco Sobral*) — Sob-*ray*-lee-uh.

Solandra (*for Swedish naturalist D. C. Solander*) — Sol-*land*-ruh: Chalicevine.

Solanum (*solace, the classical name*) — Sol-*lay*-num: Nightshade. (The genus includes Eggplant, Potato, and Tomato.)

Soldanella — Sol-dan-*nell*-uh.

Solidago (*to strengthen, as to supposed medicinal properties*) — Sol-id-*day*-goh: Goldenrod.

Sollya (*for English botanist Richard Solly*) — *Sol*-lee-uh: Australian Bluebell Creeper.

Sophora — Sof-*foh*-ruh.

Sophronites (*modest, at least as compared with many other Orchids*) — Sof-ron-*nye*-tiss.

Sorbaria (*for leaf resemblance to Sorbus*) — Sor-*bay*-ree-uh: False-spirea.

Sorbus (*the classical name*) — *Sor*-bus: Mountain-ash.

Sparaxis (*a tearing, as to torn-appearing spathe*) — Spuh-*rax*-iss: Wand-flower.

Sparmannia (*for Swedish naturalist A. Sparmann*) — Spahr-*mann*-ee-uh.

Spartium (*from the classical name*) — *Spahr*-tee-um: Spanish Broom, Weavers Broom.

Spathiphyllum (*spathe-leaf, for leaf-like spathe*) — Spath-if-*fill*-um.

Spathoglottis (*spathe-tongue, as to lip shape*) — Spath-oh-*glot*-iss.

Specularia (*for Venus' looking-glass*) — Spek-yew-*lay*-ree-uh: Venus Looking-glass (*S. speculum-Veneris*).

Sphaeralcea (*globe-Mallow*) —Sfeer-*ral*-see-uh: Globe-mallow.

Spigelia (*for Dutch botanist A. van der Spigel*) — Spye-*jeel*-ee-uh: Pink-root.

Spinacia (*spiny, as to fruit*) — Spin-*nay*-shee-uh: Spinach.

Spiraea (*wreath or garland, for which some species may have been used*) — Spye-*ree*-uh: Spirea.

Spiranthes (*coil-flower, as to twisted stalks*) — Spye-*ranth*-eez: Ladies-tresses.

Spironema (*spiral-thread, as to stamens*) — Spye-ron-*neem*-uh.

Spraguea (*for botanical artist Isaac Sprague*) — *Sprayg*-ee-uh.

Sprekelia (*for German botanist J. H. von Sprekelsen*) — Sprek-*keel*-ee-uh: Jacobean-lily, St. James-lily.

Stachys (*spike, not of apparent pertinence*) — *Stay*-kiss: Betony, Wound-wort.

Stachyurus (*spike-tail, for flowering character* — Stay-kee-*yew*-rus.

Stanhopea (*for the Earl of Stanhope*) — Stan-*hoh*-pee-uh.

Stapelia (*for Dutch physician-botanist J. B. van Stapel*) — Stap-*peel*-ee-uh: Carrion-flower.

Staphylea (*cluster-of-grapes, for fruiting habit*) — Staf-il-*lee*-uh: Bladder-nut.

Statice — *Stat*-iss-ee: This genus is now superseded by Armeria and Limonium.

Stauntonia (*for Sir G. L. Staunton*) — Ston-*toh*-nee-uh.

Steironema (*sterile-thread, as to staminodes*) — Style-roh-*neem*-uh: Loose-strife.

Stellaria (*star-like, as to flowers*) — Stel-*lay*-ree-uh.

Stenocactus (*slender-Cactus*) — Sten-oh-*kak*-tus.

Stenocarpus (*narrow-fruit, as to follicles*) — Sten-oh-*karp*-us.

Stenoglottis (*narrow-tongue, as to flower lip*) — Sten-oh-*glot*-iss.

Stenolobium (*narrow-lobe, as to fruit*) — Sten-oh-*loh*-bee-um: Yellow-bells.

Stenotaphrum (*narrow-trench, as to grooves bearing spikelets*) — Sten-oh-*taff*-rum: St. Augustine-grass.

Stephanandra (*crown-stamen, as to stamen arrangement*) — Steff-uh-*nand*-ruh.

Stephanotis (*crown-worthy, as to stamen arrangement*) — Steff-uh-*noh*-tiss: Madagascar-jasmine.

Sternbergia (*for Bohemian Count Kaspar Sternberg*) — Stern-*berj*-ee-uh.

Stewartia (*for plant patron John Stuart, Earl of Bute*) — Stew-*art*-ee-uh.

Stokesia (*for English botanist Jonathan Stokes*) — Stoh-*keez*-ee-uh: Stokes Aster.

Stranvaesia (*for English botanist William Fox-Strangeways*) — Stran-*veez*-ee-uh.

Strelitzia (*for Charlotte, Princess of Mecklenburg-Strelitz*) — Strel-*litt*-see-uh: Bird-of-paradise Flower.

Streptocarpus (*twisted-fruit*) — Strep-toh-*karp*-us: Cape-primrose.

Streptopus (*twisted-stalk, as to flower stalks*) — *Strep*-top-us: Twisted-stalk.

Streptosolen (*twisted-tube, as to corolla*) — Strep-toh-*soh*-len.

Stromanthe — Stroh-*manth*-ee.

Stylophorum (*style-bearing, as to long-lasting styles*) — Stye-*loff*-or-um: Celandine-poppy.

Styrax (*for a kind of resin or gum*) — *Stye*-rax: Storax.

Succisa (*cut off below, as to root appearance*) — Suk-*sye*-suh.

Sutherlandia (*for its cultivator James Sutherland*) — Suther*land*-ee-uh.

Swainsona (*for English horticulturist Isaac Swainson*) — Swain-*soh*-nuh.

Symphoricarpos (*accompanying-fruit, as to fruit in clusters*) — Sim-for-ik-*karp*-os.

Symphiandra (*for growing-together anthers*) — Sim-fee-*and*-ruh.

Symphytum (*grow-together, perhaps a reference to wound-healing properties*) — *Sim*-fit-um: Comfrey.

Symphlocarpus (*for growing-together-fruit*) — Sim-ploh-*karp*-us: Skunk-cabbage.

Symplocos (*interconnected, as to base of stamens*) — Sim-*ploh*-kos: Sweet-leaf.

Syntheris (*together-valve, as to a joining of the fruit capsules*) — *Sinth*-uh-riss.

Syringa — Sihr-*rin*-guh: Lilac.

T

Tabebuia — Tab-eb-*boo*-yuh.

Tabernaemontana (*for German botanist J. T. Tabernaemontanus*) — Tab-ern-ee-mon-*tay*-nuh.

Tacca — *Tak*-uh: Devil-flower (*T. Chantrieri*).

Taenidia (*a technical reference to the minute fruits*) — Tee-*nid*-ee-uh.

Tagetes (*an old but misapplied name*) — Taj-*jeet*-eez: Marigold.

Talinum — Tal-*lye*-num: Fame-flower.

Tamarix — *Tam*-uh-rix: Tamarisk (the classical name).

Tamus (*a classical vine name*) — *Tay*-mus: Black-bryony.

Tanacetum (*the classical name*) — Tan-uh-*seet*-um: Tansy.

Taraxacum — Tuh-*rax*-ak-um: Dandelion.

Taxodium (*Taxus-like, as to foliage*) —Tax-*oh*-dee-um: Bald Cypress (*T. distichum*).

Taxus (*the classical name*) — *Tax*-us: Yew.

Tecoma — Tek-*koh*-muh.

Tecomaria (*Tecoma-like*) — Tek-oh-*may*-ree-uh: Cape-honeysuckle.

Tellima (*anagram of Mitella, which it resembles*) — *Tel*-im-uh.

Templetonia (*for Irish botanist John Templeton*) — Temple-*toh*-nee-uh: Coral-bush.

Terminalia (*for leaves borne on terminal shoots*) — Ter-min-*nay*-lee-uh: Tropical- or Indian-almond, Myrobalan.

Testudinaria (*tortoise-like, as to aboveground root shape*) — Tes-tew-din-*nay*-ree-uh: Hottentots-bread, Elephants-foot.

Tetracentron (*four-spur, as to fruit parts*) — Tet-ruh-*sent*-ron.

Tetragonia (*four-angle, as to fruit shape*) — Tet-ruh-*goh*-nee-uh: New-Zealand-spinach (*T. expansa*).

Tetratheca (*four-cell, as to occasional anthers*) — Tet-ruh-*theek*-uh.

Teucrium (*the classical name*) — *Tewk*-ree-um: Germander.

Thalia (*luxuriant; or, perhaps, for one of the muses so named; or, also perhaps, for German naturalist Johann Thalius*) — *Thay*-lee-uh.

Thalictrum (*the classical name*) — Thal-*lik*-trum: Meadow Rue.

Thea — *Thee*-uh (*the "th" is soft, as in "thief"*): Tea (*T. sinensis*).

Thelesperma (*wart-seed, as to seed form*) — Thel-ess-sperm-uh.

Thelocactus (*wart-Cactus*) — Thel-oh-*kak*-tus.

Thermopsis (*Lupine-like*) — Therm-*mops*-iss.

Thespesia (*wonderful, divine*) — Thess-*peez*-ee-uh: Portia-tree.

Thevetia (*for French author André Thevet*) — Thev-*vee*-shee-uh: Yellow-oleander.

Thlaspi (*old name for a Cress*) — *Thlasp*-ee: Penny-cress.

Thomasia (*for the brothers Thomas, collectors of Swiss plants*) — Toh-*mass*-ee-uh.

Thrinax (*a three-pronged-fork or a fan, as to leaves*) — *Thrye*-nax: Peaberry Palm.

Thryallis — Thrye-*al*-liss.

Thuja — *Thew*-juh: Arbor-vitae.

Thujopsis (*Thuja-like*) — Thew-*jopp*-siss: False-arbor-vitae.

Thunbergia (*for Swedish botanist Karl Peter Thunberg*) — Thun-*berj*-ee-uh: Clock-vine.

Thunia (*for Orchid collector Count Thun-Tetschen*) — *Thew*-nee-uh.

Thuya — *Thew*-yuh: See preferred Thuja.

Thymophilla (*Thyme-leaf*) — Tye-moh-*fill*-uh: Dahlberg Daisy, Golden-fleece.

Thymus — *Tye*-mus: Thyme.

Tiarella (*coronet, as to pistil form*) — Tye-uh-*rell*-uh: False-mitre-wort.

Tibouchina — Tib-oo-*kye*-nuh: Glory-bush.

Tigridia (*tiger-like, as to flower markings*) — Tye-*grid*-ee-uh: Tiger-flower.

Tilia (*the classical name*) — *Till*-ee-uh; Linden, Lime, Basswood.

Tillandsia (*for Swedish botanist Elias Tillands*) —Til-*land*-zee-uh: Spanish moss (*T. usneoides*).

Tipularia (*named for likeness of its flowers to a kind of insect*) — Tip-yew-*lay*-ree-uh: Crane-fly Orchis.

Titanopsis — Tye-tan-*nopp*-siss.

Tithonia (*presumably for mythical Tithonus*) — Tith-*oh*-nee-uh.

Tococa — Tok-*koh*-kuh.

Tolmiea (*for a Hudson's Bay Co. surgeon, Dr. Tolmie*) — Tol-mee-*ee*-uh.

Tolpis — *Tolp*-iss.

Torenia (*for Swedish clergyman and botanist Olaf Toren*) — Tor-*reen*-ee-uh.

Torreya (*for American botanist John Torrey*) — *Torr*-ee-uh.

Tovara — Toh-*vay*-ruh.

Townsendia (*for Pennsylvania botanist David Townsend*) — Town-*send*-ee-uh.

Trachelium (*neck, for supposed remedial properties*) — Trak-*keel*-ee-um: Throatwort.

Trachelospermum (*neck-seed, as to seeds having necks*) — Trak-el-oh-*sperm*-um.

Trachycarpus (*rough-fruit*) — Trak-ik-*karp*-us: Windmill Palm (*T. Fortunei*).

Trachymene (*rough-membrane, as to fruits*) — Trak-*kim*-en-ee: Blue-lace-flower (*T. caerulea*).

Tradescantia (*for English gardener John Tradescant*) — Trad-es-*skant*-ee-uh: Spiderwort.

Tragopogon (*goat-beard*) — Trag-oh-*poh*-gon: Goats-beard.

Trapa — *Tray*-puh: Water-chestnut.

Trautvetteria (*for Russian botanist E. R. von Trautvetter*) — Trot-vet-*teer*-ee-uh.

Trichocaulon (*hair-stem*) — Trik-oh-*kawl*-on.

Trichocereus (*hair-Cereus*) — Trik-oh-*seer*-ee-us.

Trichopilia (*hair-cap, under which anthers hide*) — Trik-oh-*pill*-ee-uh.

Trichosanthes (*hair-flower, as to fringed petals*) — Trik-os-*anth*-eez.

Trichosporum (*hair-seed*) — Trik-*koss*-por-um.

Trichostema (*hair-stamen*) — Trik-oh-*steem*-uh: Blue-curls.

Tricyrtis (*three-arches, as to nectar-bearing perianth sacs*) — Trye-*surt*-iss: Toad-lily.

Trientalis (*one-third-of-a-foot, as to its height*) — Trye-en-*tay*-liss: Starflower.

Trifolium (*three-leaf, as to leaflets*) — Trye-*foh*-lee-um: Clover.

Trigonella (*three-cornered, as three-part leaves*) — Trye-gon-*nell*-uh.

Trilisa (*anagram of Liatris, which it*

resembles) — *Trye*-liss-uh: Carolina-vanilla (*T. odoratissima*).

Trillium (*for leaves and petals in threes*) — *Trill*-ee-um.

Tripterygium (*three-wing, as to winged fruit*) — Trip-ter-*rij*-ee-um.

Tritonia (*the name's author says it commemorates mythical Triton, in the sense of a weathervane, for its aimless stamens*) — Trye-*toh*-nee-uh.

Trochodendron (*wheel-tree, as to appearance of flowers with ring-form anthers*) — Trok-oh-*den*-dron.

Trollius — *Trol*-ee-us.

Tropaeolum (*diminutive of trophy*) — Trop-*pee*-ol-um: Nasturtium.

Tsuga — *Tsoo*-guh: Hemlock.

Tulipa (*from an ancient word for turban*) — *Tew*-lip-uh: Tulip.

Tunica (*tunic, as to close-fitting calyx*) — *Too*-nik-uh.

Turraea (*for Italian botanist Giorgio della Torre or Turra*) — Tur-*ree*-uh.

Typha (*ancient name*) — *Tye*-fuh.

U

Ulex (*ancient name for this or similar shrub*) — *Yew*-lex: Furze, Gorse.

Ulmus (*the classical name*) — *Ul*-mus: Elm.

Umbellularia (*bearing umbellules, a technical arrangement of grouped flowers*) — Um-bel-yew-*lay*-ree-uh: California-laurel.

Umbilicus (*navel, as to dimpled leaf centers*) — Um-bil-*lye*-kus.

Urginea — Ur-*jin*-ee-uh: Sea-onion.

Ursinea (*for German botanical author John Ursinus*) — Ur-*sin*-ee-uh.

Uvularia (*uvula- or palate-like, as to drooping flowers*) — Yew-vew-*lay*-ree-uh: Bellwort.

V

Vaccinium (*the classical name*) — Vak-*sin*-ee-um: Blueberry, Cranberry.

Valeriana (*the classical name*) — Val-eer-ee-*ay*-nuh: Valerinan.

Valerianella (*diminutive of Valeriana*) — Val-eer-ee-uh-*nell*-uh.

Vallaris — Val-*lay*-riss.

Vallota (*for French botanist Pierre Valot*) — Val-*loh*-tuh: Scarborough-lily.

Vancouveria (*for Capt. George Vancouver, explorer of the American northwest*) — Van-koo-*veer*-ee-uh.

Vanda — *Van*-duh.

Vandopsis (*Vanda-like*) — Van-*dops*-iss.

Vanilla (*little-sheath, as to pods of some species whose seeds yield vanilla extract*) — Van-*nill*-uh.

Veltheimia (*for a Count of Veltheim*) — Velth-*eye*-mee-uh.

Venidium — Ven-*nid*-ee-um.

Veratrum (*ancient name for Hellebore*) — Vehr-*ray*-trum: False-hellebore.

Verbascum (*the ancient name*) — Ver-*bask*-um: Mullein.

Verbena (*ancient name for Vervain*) — Ver-*bee*-nuh.

Verbesina (*probably suggested by the name Verbena*) — Ver-bes-*sye*-nuh: Crownbeard.

Vernonia (*for English botanist William Vernon*) — Ver-*noh*-nee-uh: Ironweed.

Veronica (*for St. Veronica*) — Ver-*ron*-ik-uh: Speedwell.

Veronicastrum (*Veronica-like*) — Ver-on-ik-*kast*-rum: Culvers-root.

Vesicaria (*bladder, as to pod shape*) — Vess-ik-*kay*-ree-uh.

Viburnum (*the classical name*) — Vye-*burn*-um.

Vinca (*from Pervinca, the classical name*) — *Vin*-kuh: Periwinkle.

Viola (*classical name*) — *Vye*-ol-uh: Violet.

Vitex (*the classical name for this or a similar shrub*) — *Vye*-tex: Chaste-tree (*V. agnus-castis*).

Vitis (*the classical name for the Vine*) — *Vye*-tiss: Grape.

Vriesia (*for Dutch doctor W. de Vriese*) — *Vree*-zee-uh.

W

Wahlenbergia (*for Swedish botanist Goran Wahlenberg*) — Wahl-en-*berj*-ee-uh.

Waldsteinia (*for Austrian botanist von Waldstein*) — Wold-*stye*-nee-uh.

Washingtonia (*for George Washington*) — Washing-*toh*-nee-uh.

Watsonia (*for English botanist Sir William Watson*) — Wot-*soh*-nee-uh.

Weigela (*for Swedish physician C. E. Weigel*) — Wye-*jeel*-uh.

Wigandia (*for Pomeranian Bishop Johannes Wigand*) — Wig-*gand*-ee-uh.

Wilcoxia (*for U. S. Brig.-Gen. Timothy E. Wilcox*) — Wil-*kox*-ee-uh.

Wisteria (*for Professor Caspar Wistar of Pennsylvania*) — Wiss-*teer*-ee-uh.

Woodsia (*for English botanist Joseph Woods*) — *Wood*-zee-uh.

Woodwardia (*for English botanist Thomas J. Woodward*) — Wood-*wahr*-dee-uh: Chain-fern.

Wulfenia (*for Austrian minerologist F. X. von Wulfen*) — Wool-*feen*-ee-uh.

X

Xanthisma (*that-which-is-dyed-yellow, as to flower color*) — Zanth-*iz*-muh.

Xanthoceras (*yellow-horn, as to blotch-like markings at base of disk-flowers*) — Zanth-oh-*seer*-as.

Xanthorhiza (*yellow-root*) — Zanth-or-*rye*-zuh: Shrub Yellow-root.

Xanthosoma (*yellow-body, as to its flower stigma*) — Zanth-oh-*soh*-muh: Malanga, Tanier, Yautia.

Xeranthemum (*dry-flower, as to "everlasting" quality*) — Zeer-*anth*-em-um: Common Immortelle (*X. annuum*).

Xerophyllum (*dry-leaf, as to tough, wiry leaves; or because it likes* *boggy conditions for its roots*) — Zeer-oh-*fill*-um: Turkey-beard.

Xylobium (*wood-life, as to its epiphy-* tic habit of living in, but not "on," trees) — Zye-*loh*-bee-um.

Xylophylla (*wood-leaf, as to its leaf-like branches*) — Zye-loh-*fill*-uh.

Y

Yucca — *Yukk*-uh: Includes Adams- needle, Spanish-bayonet, Joshua-tree.

Z

Zaluzianskya (*for Polish physician Adam Zaluziansky von Zaluzian*) — Zal-oo-zee-*an*-skee-uh: Night-phlox (*N. capensis*).

Zamia — *Zay*-mee-uh.

Zantedeschia (*for Italian botanist Francesco Zantedeschi*) — Zan-ted-*desh*-ee-uh: Calla.

Zanthorhiza (*yellow-root*) — Zanth-or-*rye*-zuh: See Xanthorhiza.

Zanthoxylum (*yellow-wood, as to color in some species*) — Zanth-ox-il-um.

Zauschneria (*for Bohemian botanist H. Zauschner*) — Zosh-*neer*-ee-uh: California-fuchsia (*Z. californica*).

Zea (*classical name for a cereal grain*) — *Zee*-uh: Maize or Indian Corn is *Z. mays,* the species of which Sweet or Sugar Corn is a variety.

Zebrina (*Zebra-like, as to striped leaves*) — Zeb-*rye*-nuh: Wandering Jew (*Z. pendula*).

Zelkova — Zel-*koh*-vuh.

Zenobia (*probably for Queen Zenobia of Palmyra*) — Zen-*noh*-bee-uh.

Zephyranthes (*West-wind-flower, a classical name compounded to indicate western origin*) — Zeff-er-*ranth*-eez: Zephyr-lily.

Zingiber (*the classical name*) — *Zin*-jib-er: Ginger.

Zinnia (*for German physician Johann Gottfried Zinn*) — *Zinn*-ee-uh.

Zygocactus (*Cactus with a technical joining of parts*) — Zye-goh-*kak*-tus: Christmas Cactus.

Zygopetalum (*joined-flowers, a technical aspect*) — Zye-goh-*pet*-al-um.

SPECIFIC PLANT NAMES
Species: both singular and plural

The specific name of a plant, denoting its species (pronounced *spee-sheez*) within a given genus, serves a plant much as a given name serves a person, while the plant's generic name (see page 433) is comparable to the surname of a person.

In the following pages are given, in alphabetical order, the accepted spelling for each of some 2400 species (**bold face type**); the phonetic spelling (ordinary type) with the stressed portion of the word in *italics*; the significant translation or meaning if available and of practical use.

The endings of most specific names may be varied according to the gender (masculine, feminine, or neuter) of whatever generic name they may accompany. Thus specific names ending in **-us** may also terminate with **-a** or **-um** (as albus, alba, album). Those ending in **-is** may also end in **-e** (gracilis, gracile). Certain **-er** endings may be replaced by **-ra** or **-rum** (niger, nigra, nigrum). In this list, masculine endings are given, where there is any choice.

Not included are specific names derived from proper names, as, for example, Wilsoni (or Wilsonii), Browni (or Brownii). Almost all such names end in -i (or -ii) and have little identification significance. (Variety names, which further modify horticultural species, are too many, too variable, and too confused for inclusion in this book.)

The phonetic spellings here given break the names into separate parts according to sound. When pronounced in normal speech, the resulting combination of sounds should add up to an accurate pronunciation of the whole word.

A

abbreviatus — ab-bree-vee-*ay*-tus: abbreviated, shortened.

abortivus — ab-or-*tye*-vus: aborted.

abruptus — ab-*rup*-tus: abrupt; suddenly changing.

acanthocomus — ak-anth-oh-*koh*-mus: with spine-like hairs.

acaulis — ak-*kaw*-liss: stemless.

acephalus — ass-*sef*-al-us: headless.

acerbus — ass-*serb*-us: harsh; sour tasting.

acerifolius — ay-ser-if-*foh*-lee-us: Maple-leaved.

aceroides — Ay-ser-*roy*-deez: Maple-like.

acerosus — ass-er-*roh*-sus: needle-shaped.

acicularis — ass-ik-yew-*lay*-riss: needle-like.

acidissimus — ass-id-*diss*-im-us: very sour.

acidosus — ass-id-*doh*-sus: acid; bitter.

acidus — *ass*-id-us: acid; sour.

acinaceus — ass-in-*nay*-see-us: saber-shaped.

acinacifolius — ass-in-ay-sif-*foh*-lee-us: with saber-shaped leaves.

aconitifolius — ak-oh-nye-tif-*foh*-lee-us: with leaves similar to Monks-hood (Aconitum).

acris — *ay*-kriss: acrid; sharp.

aculeatus — ak-kew-lee-*ay*-tus: prickly.

acuminatifolius — ak-yew-min-ay-tif-*foh*-lee-us: with narrowing, pointed leaves.

acuminatus — ak-kew-min-*nay*-tus: long-pointed; tapering.

acutangulus — ak-kew-*tan*-gew-lus: sharply angled.

acutifidus — ak-kew-*tif*-id-us: sharply cut.

acutifolius — ak-kew-tif-*foh*-lee-us: sharp-leaved.

acutilobus — ak-kew-til-*loh*-bus: sharp-lobed.

acutipetalus — ak-kew-tip-*pet*-al-us: sharp or pointed-petaled.

acutus — ak-*kew*-tus: sharp-pointed.

adenophyllus — ad-en-oh-*fill*-us: sticky-leaved.

admirabilis — ad-mir-*rab*-il-iss: noteworthy.

adnatus — ad-*nay*-tus: joined to.

adpressus — ad-*press*-us: pressed against.

adscendens — ad-*sen*-denz: ascending.

adsurgens — ad-*ser*-jenz: becoming erect.

aduncus — ad-*unk*-us: hooked.

advenus — ad-*veen*-us: newly arrived.

aeneus — *ee*-nee-us: bronze-colored.

aequinoctialis — eek-wee-nok-tee-*ay*-liss: pertaining to an equinox.

aequipetalus — eek-wee-*pet*-al-us: equal-petaled.

aequitrilobus — eek-wee-trye-*loh*-bus: with three equal lobes.

aeruginosus — eh-roo-jin-*noh*-sus: rust-colored.

aestivalis — ess-tiv-*vay*-liss: of summer.

aestivus — ess-*tye*-vus: of summer.

affinis — af-*fye*-niss: related (to another species).

africanus — af-rik-*kay*-nus: African.

agavoides — ag-av-*voy*-deez: Agave-like.

ageratoides — aj-er-at-*toy*-deez: Ageratum-like.

aggregatus — ag-reg-*gay*-tus: clustered.

agrarius — ag-*ray*-ree-us: of the fields.

agrestis — ag-*ress*-tiss: of the fields.

agrifolius — ag-rif-*foh*-lee-us: rough or scabby-leaved.

aizoides — ay-*zoy*-deez: Aizöon-like (evergreen or tenacious).

alatus — al-*lay*-tus: winged.

albescens — al-*bess*-senz: whitish, becoming white.

albicans — *al*-bik-kanz: whitish.

albicaulis — al-bik-*kaw*-liss: white-stemmed.

albidus — *al*-bid-us: white.

albiflorus — al-bif-*floh*-rus: white-flowered.

albifrons — *al*-bif-fronz: white-fronded, white-foliaged.

albi-plenus — al-bip-*pleen*-us: double white-flowered.

albispinus — al-bis-*spye*-nus: white-spined.

albocinctus — al-boh-*sink*-tus: white-girdled.

albomaculatus — al-boh-mak-yew-*lay*-tus: white-spotted.

albomarginatus — al-boh-mar-jin-*nay*-tus: white-margined.

albo-pleno — al-boh-*pleen*-oh: white and double-flowered.

albospicus — al-boh-*spye*-kus: white-spiked.

albo-variegatus — al-boh-vay-ree-eg-*gay*-tus: with white markings.

albulus — *al*-bew-lus: whitish.

albus — *al*-bus: white.

alexandrinus — al-ex-an-*drye*-nus: of Alexandria (Egypt).

alliaceus — al-lee-*ay*-see-us: Allium-like.

alnifolius — al-nif-*foh*-lee-us: with Alder (Alnus)-like leaves.

aloides — al-*loy*-deez: Aloe-like.

alpestris — al-*pest*-riss: Alpine (or nearly so).

alpinus — al-*pye*-nus: alpine (above timber-line).

altaicus — al-*tay*-ik-us: of the Altai mountains.

alternans — al-*tern*-anz: alternating.

alternifolius — al-ter-nif-*foh*-lee-us: with alternate leaves.

alternus — al-*tern*-us: alternate.

altifrons — *al*-tif-fronz: tall-fronded.

altissimus — al-*tiss*-im-us: very tall.

altus — *al*-tus: tall.

amabilis — am-*mab*-il-iss: lovely.

amaricaulis — am-ay-rik-*kaw*-liss: bitter-stemmed.

amarus — am-*may*-rus: bitter.

amazonicus — am-az-*zon*-ik-us: from or of the Amazon (region) River.

ambiguus — am-*big*-yew-us: doubtful (of type, origin, etc).

amelloides — am-el-*loy*-deez: Amellus-like.

americanus — am-eh-rik-*kay*-nus: American.

amethystinus — am-meth-*thist*-in-us: amethyst- or violet-colored.

amoenus — am-*meen*-us: charming, pleasing.

amphibius — am-*fib*-ee-us: amphibious (of both water and land).

amplexicaulis — am-plex-ik-*kaw*-liss: stem-clasping.

amplexifolius — am-plex-if-*foh*-lee-us: leaf-clasping.

amplissimus — am-*pliss*-im-us: very ample or full.

amplus — *am*-plus: large, full, extended.

amurensis — am-moor-*ren*-siss: of the Amur River region of Siberia.

amacanthus — am-ak-*kanth*-us: without spines.

anceps — *an*-seps: two-headed, two-edged.

andicolus — an-*dik*-ol-us: of the Andes mountains.

andinus — an-*dye*-nus: of the Andes.

androgynus — an-*drog*-in-us: with both staminate (male) and pistillate (female) flowers in one cluster: hence perfect-flowered.

anemoneflorus — an-nem-on-ee-*floh*-rus: with Anemone-like flowers.

anfractuosus — an-frak-tew-*oh*-sus: twisted.

anglicus — *an*-glik-us: English, or from England.

anguinus — an-*gwye*-nus: snaky, serpentine.

angularis — an-gew-*lay*-riss: angular.

angulatus — an-gew-*lay*-tus: angular angled.

angulosus—an-gew-*loh*-sus: angular.

angustifolius — an-gus-tif-*foh*-lee-us: narrow-leaved.

angustus — an-*gus*-tus: narrow.

anisatus — an-iss-*say*-tus: anise-scented.

annularis — an-yew-*lay*-riss: annular, ringed.

annulatus — an-yew-*lay*-tus: annular.

annuus — *an*-yew-us: annual (living but a year).

anomalus — an-*nom*-al-us: unusual; also of uncertain identity.

antarcticus — an-*tark*-tik-us: from (or near) the antarctic region.

antillaris — an-til-*lay*-riss: of the Antilles (West Indies).

antipodum — an-*tip*-od-um: of the Antipodes.

antiquorum — an-tik-*kwoh*-rum: of the ancients.

antiquus — an-*tik*-wuss: ancient.

antirrhinoides — an-tir-rin-*noy*-deez: Snapdragon-like.

apenninus — ap-pen-*nye*-nus: of the Apennines.

apertus — ap-*pert*-us: bare, uncovered.

apetalus — ap-*pet*-al-us: without petals.

aphyllus — af-*fill*-us: without leaves.

apiculatus — ap-pik-yew-*lay*-tus: with a pointed tip.

appendiculatus — ap-pen-dik-yew-*lay*-tus: with an appendage, extension, or added part.

applanatus — ap-plan-*nay*-tus: flattened.

applicatus — ap-plik-*kay*-tus: joined, attached.

apterus — *ap*-ter-us: wingless.

aquaticus — ak-*kwat*-ik-us: aquatic.

aquatilis — ak-*kwat*-il-iss: aquatic.

aqueus — *ak*-wee-us: watery.

aquilegifolius — ak-wil-ee-jif-*foh*-lee-us: Columbine-like.

aquilinus — ak-wil-*lye*-nus: aquiline (pertaining to the eagle).

arabicus — ar-*rab*-ik-us: of Arabia.

arachnoides — ar-rak-*noy*-deez: spider-like, cob-webby.

araucanus — ar-oh-*kay*-nus: from Arancana (So. Chile).

arborescens — ar-bor-*ress*-senz: becoming tree like, woody.

arboreus — ar-*boh*-ree-us: tree-like.

arbutifolius — ar-bew-tif-*foh*-lee-us: with Arbutus-like leaves.

arcticus — *ark*-tik-us: of the arctic.

arcuatus — ark-yew-*ay*-tus: bowed, bow-like.

arenarius — ar-en-*nay*-ree-us: of the sands, of sandy places.

areolatus — ar-ee-oh-*lay*-tus: pitted (areolate).

argentatus — arj-en-*tay*-tus: silvery, silvered.

argenteus — ar-*jen*-tee-us: silvery.

argophyllus — ar-goh-*fill*-us: silver-leaved.

argutus — ar-*gew*-tus: sharp-toothed.

argyraeus — ar-jee-*ree*-us: silvery.

aridus — *ar*-id-us: dry (arid).

arietinus — ar-ree-et-*tye*-nus: like a ram's head.

aristatus — ar-riss-*tay*-tus: bearded.

aristosus — ar-riss-*toh*-sus: bearded.

arizonicus — ar-iz-*zon*-ik-us: of or from Arizona.

armatus — arm-*may*-tus: armed (as with thorns).

aromaticus — ar-roh-*mat*-ik-us: aromatic.

arrectus — ar-*rek*-tus: raised, erect.

articulatus — art-ik-yew-*lay*-tus: jointed.

arundinaceus — ar-run-din-*nay*-see-us: reed-like.

arvensis — arv-*ven*-siss: of cultivated ground.

ascendens — ass-*send*-enz: ascending, turning upward.

asiaticus — ay-zee-*at*-ik-us: Asiatic.

asparagoides — ass-par-ag-*goy*-deez: Asparagus-like.

asper — *ass*-per: rough.

asperatus — ass-per-*ray*-tus: rough.

aspericaulis — ass-per-ik-*kaw*-liss: rough-stemmed.

asperrimus — ass-*pehr*-rim-us: very rough.

assimilis — ass-*sim*-il-iss: like, similar to (another plant or form).

assurgens — ass-*serj*-enz: clambering.

asteroides — ass-ter-*roy*-deez: Aster-like.

atlanticus — at-*lan*-tik-us: of Atlantic regions.

atratus — at-*ray*-tus: blackened.

atrocarpus — at-roh-*karp*-us: with blackish fruit.

atrocaulis — at-roh-*kaw*-liss: dark stemmed.

atropurpureus — at-roh-per-*pew*-ree-us: dark purple.

atrorubens — at-roh-*roo*-benz: dark red.

atrosanguineus — at-roh-san-*gwin*-ee-us: dark blood-red.

atrovirens — at-roh-*vye*-renz: dark green.

attenuatus — at-ten-yew-*ay*-tus: drawn to a point.

atticus — *at*-tik-us: of Athens or Greece.

augustissimus — aw-gus-*tiss*-im-us: most notable.

augustus — aw-*gus*-tus: notable, majestic.

aurantiacus — aw-ran-*tye*-ak-us: orange-red.

aureolus — aw-*ree*-ol-us: golden.

aureus — *aw*-ree-us: golden.

auriculatus — aw-rik-yew-*lay*-tus: with ears (auricled).

australiensis — os-tral-ee-*en*-siss: of Australia.

australis — os-*tray*-liss: southern.

austriacus — os-*try*-ak-us: Australian.

autumnalis — aw-tum-*nay*-liss: of autumn.

avicularis — av-ik-yew-*lay*-riss: relating to birds.

axillaris — ax-il-*lay*-riss: pertaining to the axils, of axillary significance.

azoricus — az-*zohr*-ik-us: from the Azores.

azureus — az-*yew*-ree-us: sky-blue, azure.

B

babylonicus — bab-il-*lon*-ik-us: from (ancient) Babylon.

baccatus — bak-*kay*-tus: berried.

bacciferus — bak-*siff*-er-us: berry-bearing.

balearicus — bal-ee-*ar*-ik-us: of the Balearic Islands.

balsameus — bal-*say*-mee-us: Balsam-like, balsam scented.

balsamiferus — bal-sam-*mif*-er-us: balsam bearing.

balticus — *bol*-tik-us: from or of the Baltic Sea region.

bambusoides — bam-boo-*soy*-deez: Bamboo-like.

barbadensis — bar-bad-*den*-siss: of Barbados.

barbarus — *bar*-bar-us: foreign, from a foreign place.

barbatus — bar-*bay*-tus: barbed, bearded.

barbigerus — bar-*bij*-er-us: bearing barbs, beards.

barbinodis — bar-bin-*noh*-diss: bearded at joints (nodes).

basilaris — bas-il-*lay*-riss: pertaining to the base or bottom.

belgicus — *bel*-jik-us: of Belgium.

bellus — *bell*-us: handsome.

benedictus — ben-ed-*dik*-tus: blessed.

bermudianus — ber-mew-dee-*ay*-nus: of Bermuda.

berolinensis — ber-ol-in-*en*-siss: of Berlin.

bessarabicus — bess-ar-*rab*-ik-us: of Bessarabia.

betaceus — bet-*tay*-see-us: beet-like.

betuloides — bet-yew-*loy*-deez: Birch-like.

bicarinatus — bye-kar-in-*nay*-tus: two-keeled.

bicolor — *bye*-kol-or: two-colored.

bicornis — bye-*korn*-iss: two-horned.

bicornutus — bye-kor-*new*-tus: two-horned.

bidentatus — bye-den-*tay*-tus: two-toothed.

biennis — bye-*en*-niss: biennial, living two years.

bifidus — *bye*-fid-us (*bif*-id-us): twice cut, two-parted.

biflorus — bye-*floh*-rus: two-flowered.

bifurcatus — bye-fur-*kay*-tus: two-forked, divided in two.

bigibbus — bye-*jib*-bus: with two swellings or protuberances.

biglumis — bye-*glew*-miss: two-glumed.

bijugus — bye-*jew*-gus (*bij*-ew-gus): yoked in pairs, joined.

bilobus — bye-*loh*-bus: two-lobed.

binatus — bye-*nay*-tus: twin, double.

binervis — bye-*nerv*-iss: two-nerved.

binocularis — bye-nok-yew-*lay*-riss: two-eyed, two-spotted.

bipartitus — bye-par-*tye*-tus: two parted.

bipetalus — bye-*pet*-al-us: two-petaled.

bipinnatifidus — bye-pin-at-*tif*-id-us: twice pinnately cut (bipinnatifid).

bipinnatus — bye-pin-*nay*-tus: twice pinnate (bipinnate).

bipunctatus — bye-punk-*tay*-tus: two-spotted.

bisectus — bye-*sek*-tus: cut in two.

bispinosus — bye-spin-*noh*-sus: two-spined.

biternatus — bye-ter-*nay*-tus: twice ternate (in double threes).

blandus — *bland*-us: mild.

boliviensis — bol-iv-ee-*en*-siss: of Bolivia.

bonus — *boh*-nus: good.

borbonicus — bor-*bon*-ik-us: of Bourbonne (France).

borealis — bor-ee-*ay*-liss: northern.

botryoides — bot-rye-*oy*-deez: in clusters, grape-like.

brachiatus — brak-ee-*ay*-tus: branched at right angles (brachiate).

brachypetallus — brak-ip-*pet*-al-us: short petalled.

brachypodus — brak-*kip*-pod-us: short-stalked.

bracteatus — brak-tee-*ay*-tus: with bracts (bracteate).

bracteosus — brak-tee-*oh*-sus: bract-bearing.

bractescens — brak-*tess*-enz: having bracts.

brasiliensis — braz-il-ee-*en*-siss: of or from Brazil.

brevicaulis — brev-ik-*kaw*-liss: short stemmed.

brevifrons — *brev*-if-fronz: short-fronded, short-leaved.

brevipedunculatus — brev-ip-ed-unk-yew-*lay*-tus: with short flower stalk.

brevipes — *brev*-ip-eez: short-footed (as: short-petioled).

brevis — *brev*-iss: short.

brevisetus — brev-iss-*see*-tus: short-bristled.

brevispathus — brev-iss-*payth*-us: short-spathed.

brevissimus — brev-*viss*-im-us: very short.

brilliantissimus — bril-lee-an-*tiss*-im-us: very brilliant.

brunneus — *brew*-nee-us: brown.

bucephalus — bew-*sef*-al-us: ox-headed.

bufonius — bew-*foh*-nee-us: pertaining to the toad.

bulbiferus — bulb-*iff*-er-us: bulb-bearing.

bulbosus — bulb-*oh*-sus: bulbous.

bulgaricus — bulg-*gay*-rik-us: of or from Bulgaria.

bullatus — bul-*lay*-tus: swelling, puckered (bullate).

buxifolius — bux-if-*foh*-lee-us: with leaves resembling Box.

C

caerulescens — see-rew-*less*-senz: turning or becoming dark blue.

caeruleus — see-*rew*-lee-us: dark blue.

caesius — *see*-see-us: blue-gray.

caespitosus—seess-pit-*toh*-sus: tufted, growing in low clumps (cespitose).

caffer — *kaf*-fer: pertaining to the Kafirs (South Africa).

calabricus — kal-*lab*-rik-us: of Calabria (in Italy).

calathinus — kal-ath-*eye*-nus: basket-like.

calcaratus — kal-kar-*ray*-tus: with spurs.

calcareus — kal-*kay*-ree-us: pertaining to lime.

calendulaceus — kal-en-dew-*lay*-see-us: brilliant yellow-orange (Calendula-like).

californicus — kal-if-*forn*-ik-us: of California.

callosus — kal-*loh*-sus: thick-skinned, having callosities.

calvus — *kal*-vus: hairless.

calycinus — kal-*liss*-in-us: calyx-like.

calyculatus — kal-ik-yew-*lay*-tus: having a calyx, stressing the calyx.

cambricus — *kam*-brik-us: Welsh (Cambrian).

campanulatus — kam-pan-yew-*lay*-tus: bell-shaped (campanulate).

campanuloides — kam-pan-yew-*loy*-deez: Bell-flower-like.

campestris — kam-*pest*-riss: of the fields or open country.

canadensis — kan-ad-*den*-siss: Canadian, of Canada.

canaliculatus — kan-al-ik-yew-*lay*-tus: grooved, channeled.

canariensis — kan-ar-ee-*en*-siss: of the Canary Islands.

candicans — *kand*-ik-anz: white, (or woolly-white).

candidissimus — kan-did-*diss*-im-us: very white (or woolly-white).

caninus — kan-*nye*-nus: referring to a dog.

candidus — *kan*-did-us: white.

canescens — kan-*ness*-senz: downy gray.

canus—*kay*-nus: ash-colored, hoary.

capensis — kap-*pen*-siss: of the Cape (Good Hope).

capillaris — kap-il-*lay*-riss: hair-like.

capillatus — kap-il-*lay*-tus: with fine hairs.

capreolatus — kap-ree-ol-*lay*-tus: winding, twining.

capsularis — kap-soo-*lay*-riss: capsule-bearing (capsular).

caribaeus — ka-rib-*bee*-us: from the Caribbean Sea region.

cardinalis — kard-in-*nay*-liss: cardinal (red).

carinatus — ka-rin-*nay*-tus: with a keel.

carneus — *karr*-nee-us: flesh-colored.

carnosus — kar-*noh*-sus: fleshy.

carolinianus — ka-rol-in-ee-*ay*-nus: of the Carolinas (states).

caroliniensis — ka-rol-in-ee-*en*-siss: pertaining to the Carolinas.

carolinus — ka-rol-*lye*-nus: from the Carolinas.

carpaticus — kar-*pat*-ik-us: from the Carpathians (in Europe).

carthaginensis — kar-taj-in-*en*-siss: from Cartagena (Spain or Colombia).

cartilagineus — kart-il-aj-*inn*-ee-us: cartilage-like.

caryophyllus — ka-ree-oh-*fill*-us: pertaining to the Pink family.

cashmerianus — kash-meer-ee-*ay*-nus: of Cashmere (in Asia).

catawbiensis — kat-aw-bee-*en*-siss: from the Catawba River region (N. Carolina).

catharticus — kath-*art*-ik-us: cathartic.

cathayensis — kath-ay-*en*-siss: of or from Cathay (China).

caucasicus — kaw-*kass*-ik-us: of or from the Caucasus (Eurasia).

caudatus — kaw-*day*-tus: with a tail (caudate).

caulescens — kaw-*less*-senz: having a stem (or stems).

cauliflorus — kaw-lif-*floh*-rus: with stemmed flowers.

cenisius — sen-*iss*-ee-us: from Mt. Cenis (Alps Mts.).

cephalatus — sef-al-*lay*-tus: with a head (or heads).

cerasiferus — see-ras-*sif*-er-us: bearing cherries or cherry-like fruits.

cerasiformis — see-ras-if-*form*-iss: cherry-shaped.

cerefolius—see-ref-*foh*-lee-us: waxy-leaved.

cerifera — see-*rif*-er-us: wax-bearing.

cernuus — *ser*-new-us: bent, nodding (cernuous).

ceylanicus—see-*lan*-ik-us: of Ceylon.

chalcedonicus — kal-sed-*don*-ik-us: of Chalcedon (Asia Minor).

chilensis — chil-*len*-siss: of Chile.

chinensis — chin-*nen*-siss: of China.

chloranthus — klor-*anth*-us: green-flowered.

chrysanthus — kriss-*anth*-us: golden-flowered.

chrysocarpus — kriss-oh-*karp*-us: golden fruited.

chrysophyllus — kriss-oh-*fill*-us: golden-leaved.

chrysostomus — kriss-*oss*-tom-us: golden-mouthed, golden-throated.

ciliaris — sil-ee-*ay*-riss: hairy-fringed or margined.

ciliatus — sil-ee-*ay*-tus: hairy fringed or margined (ciliate).

cinctus — *sink*-tus: girded, girdled.

cinereus — sin-*nee*-ree-us: ash-colored.

cinnabarinus — sin-ab-ar-*rye*-nus: cinnabar-red.

cinnamomeus — sin-am-*moh*-mee-us: cinnamon-brown.

circinalis — ser-sin-*nay*-liss: coiled (cercinate).

circinatus — ser-sin-*nay*-tus: coiled.

cirrhosus — sihr-*roh*-sus: with tendrils.

citratus — sit-*ray*-tus: Citrus like (in general).

citrifolius — sit-rif-*foh*-lee-us: Citrus-leaved.

citrinus — sit-*rye*-nus: Citrus-like, Lemon-colored.

citriodorus — sit-ree-oh-*doh*-rus: Lemon-scented.

citroides — sit-*roy*-deez: Citron-like.

citrosmus — sit-*roz*-mus: Lemon-scented.

clandestinus—klan-des-*tye*-nus: concealed.

clavatus — klav-*vay*-tus: club-shaped (clavate).

clematideus — klem-at-*tid*-ee-us: Clematis-like.

clypeatus — klye-pee-*ay*-tus: with a shield.

cocciferus — kok-*sif*-er-us: berry-bearing.

coccineus — kok-*sin*-ee-us: scarlet.

cochlearis — kok-lee-*ay*-riss: spoon-like.

cochleatus — kok-lee-*ay*-tus: spoon-like.

coelestinus — see-less-*tye*-nus: sky-blue.

coelestis — see-*less*-tiss: sky-blue.

coeruleus — see-*rew*-lee-us: dark blue.

coerulescens — see-rew-*less*-senz: darkish blue.

collinus — kol-*lye*-nus: of the hills.

coloratus — kol-or-*ray*-tus: colored (not applied to green).

colubrinus — kol-yew-*brye*-nus: snake-like.

columbianus — kol-lum-bee-*ay*-nus: from Colombia or British Columbia.

columnaris — kol-um-*nay*-riss: columnar.

comatus — kom-*may*-tus: with hair.

communis — kom-*mew*-niss: common, widespread.

commutatus — kom-mew-*tay*-tus: changed, changing, changeable.

comosus — kom-*moh*-sus: long-haired.

compactus — kom-*pak*-tus: compact, dense.

complanatus — kom-plan-*nay*-tus: flattened.

complexus — kom-*plex*-us: encircled.

complicatus — kom-plik-*kay*-tus: folded over or back (complicate).

compressus — kom-*press*-us: compressed, flattened.

comptus — *komp*-tus: ornamented.

concavus — *kon*-kav-us: hollowed, concave.

concinnus — kon-*sin*-us: neat, well-made.

concolor — *kon*-kol-or: all one color.

condensus — kon-*den*-sus: dense, crowded.

confertus — kon-*fer*-tus: crowded.

conformis — kon-*form*-iss: similar.

confusus — kon-*few*-sus: uncertain (characteristics).

congestus — kon-*jest*-us: congested, crowded.

conglomeratus — kon-glom-er-*ray*-tus: crowded, jumbled.

conicus — *kon*-ik-us: cone-shaped, conical.

coniferus — kon-*nif*-er-us: cone-bearing.

conjugatus — kon-jew-*gay*-tus: connected, joined.

conoides — kon-*noy*-deez: cone-like.

consolidus — kon-*sol*-id-us: solid, stable.

conspicuus — kon-*spik*-yew-us: showy.

constrictus — kon-*strik*-tus: constricted.

contiguus — kon-*tig*-yew-us: close (together).

contortus — kon-*tort*-us: twisted.

contractus — kon-*trak*-tus: contracted.

copallinus — kop-al-*lye*-nus: gummy, resinous.

corallinus — kor-*ral*-in-us: coral (-red).

cordatus — kor-*day*-tus: heart-shaped (cordate).

cordifolius—kor-dif-*foh*-lee-us: with heart-shaped leaves.

coreanus — kor-ee-*ay*-nus: of or from Korea.

coriaceus — kor-ee-*ay*-see-us: leathery, thick.

corniculatus — kor-nik-yew-*lay*-tus: horned.

cornigera — kor-*nij*-er-us: having horns.

cornutus — kor-*new*-tus: horned.

corrollatus — kor-oh-*lay*-tus: corolla-like.

coronarius — kor-oh-*nay*-ree-us: crowned.

cornatus — kor-oh-*nay*-tus: crowned.

corrugatus — kor-rew-*gay*-tus: corrugated.

corticosus — kor-tik-*koh*-sus: heavily-barked.

coruscans — kor-*rusk*-anz: glittering, vibrating.

corymbiferus — kor-im-*bif*-er-us: bearing flowers in corymbs.

corymbosus — kor-im-*boh*-sus: with corymbs.

costatus — kos-*tay*-tus: ribbed.

crassicaulis — krass-ik-*kaw*-liss: thick-stemmed.

crassifolius — krass-if-*foh*-lee-us: thick-leaved.

crassipes — *krass*-ip-peez: thick-footed or -stalked.

crassus — *krass*-us: thick.

crenatus — kren-*nay*-tus: scalloped (crenate).

crenatiflorus — kren-ay-tif-*floh*-rus: with scalloped-edge flowers.

crenulatus—kren-yew-*lay*-tus: somewhat scalloped (crenulate).

crepidatus — krep-id-*day*-tus: slippered.

crepitans—*krep*-it-anz: rattling, rustling.

cretaceus — kret-*tay*-see-us: chalky, pertaining to chalk.

crinitus — krin-*nye*-tus: hairy.

crispus — *kriss*-pus: crisped, curled.

cristatus — kris-*tay*-tus: crested.

crocatus — kroh-*kay*-tus: yellow (saffron).

croceus — *kroh*-see-us: saffron-yellow.

cruciatus — krew-see-*ay*-tus: cross-like (cruciate).

cruciferus — krew-*sif*-er-us: cross-bearing.

cruentus — krew-*en*-tus: blood-colored.

crystallinus — kriss-*tal*-in-us: crystalline, (crystal-clear).

cubensis — kew-*ben*-siss: of or from Cuba.

cucullatus — kuk-yew-*lay*-tus: hooded.

cultratus — kul-*tray*-tus: knife-shaped.

cultriformis — kul-trif-*form*-iss: knife-shaped.

cuneatus — kew-nee-*ay*-tus: wedge-shaped.

cuneifolius — kew-nee-if-*foh*-lee-us: wedge-leaved.

cuneiformis — kew-nee-if-*form*-iss: wedge-formed.

cupreatus — kew-pree-*ay*-tus: coppery.

cupreus — *kew*-pree-us: copper (-colored).

curvatus — ker-*vay*-tus: curved.

curvifolius — ker-vif-*foh*-lee-us: curving-leaved.

cuspidatus—kuss-pid-*day*-tus: sharply or stiffly pointed (cuspidate).

cyaneus — sye-*ay*-nee-us: blue.

cyanus — sye-*ay*-nus: blue.

cylindraceus — sil-in-*dray*-see-us: cylinder-like.

cylindricus — sil-*lin*-drik-us: cylindrical.

cymbiformis — sim-bif-*form*-iss: boat-shaped.

cymosus — sye-*moh*-sus: with flowers in cymes (cymose).

D

dactyliferus — dak-til-*lif*-er-us: finger bearing, finger-like.

dahuricus — da-*hew*-rik-us: of Dahuria (eastern Siberia).

dalmaticus — dal-*mat*-ik-us: of Dalmatia (the Adriatic).

damascenus — dam-ass-*see*-nus: of Damascus (Syria).

dasycarpus — das-ik-*karp*-us: thick-fruited.

dealbatus — dee-al-*bay*-tus: whitish, almost white.

debilis — *deb*-il-iss: weak, frail.

decapetalus — dek-ap-*pet*-al-us: ten petaled.

deciduus — des-*sid*-yew-us: with parts falling (as leaves), deciduous.

decipiens — des-*sip*-ee-enz: not obvious, deceptive.

declinatus — dek-lin-*nay*-tus: bent downward.

decolorans — dee-kol-*lohr*-anz: discoloring, staining.

decompositus — dee-kom-*poz*-it-us: more than once divided or compounded.

decorans — *dek*-or-anz: adorning.

decorus — *dek*-or-us: comely, becoming.

decumbens — dee-*kum*-benz: reclin-ing at base with tips upright; decumbent.

decurrens — dee-*ker*-renz: decurrent (as a leaf descending down a stem).

decussatus — dee-kuss-*say*-tus: arranged in pairs, with adjacent pairs at right angles (decussate).

deflexus — dee-*flex*-us: bent sharply downward, deflexed.

deformis — dee-*form*-iss: misshapen, deformed.

delectus — dee-*lek*-tus: chosen.

delicatissimus — del-ik-at-*tiss*-im-us: very delicate.

delicatus — del-ik-*kay*-tus: delicate, tender.

deliciosus — del-iss-ee-*oh*-sus: delicious.

deltoidius — del-*toy*-dee-us: deltoid (triangular).

deltoides — del-*toy*-deez: roughly triangular.

demersus — dee-*mer*-sus: submerged.

demissus — dee-*miss*-us: low, weak.

dendroideus — den-*droy*-dee-us: tree-like.

densiflorus — den-sif-*floh*-rus: densely flowered.

densus — *den*-sus: dense, compact.

dentatus — den-*tay*-tus: toothed, dentate.

denticulatus — den-tik-yew-*lay*-tus: somewhat toothed, denticulate.

dentosus — den-*toh*-sus: toothed.

denudatus — dee-new-*day*-tus:naked, bare.

dependens — dee-*pen*-denz: hanging down.

depressus — dee-*press*-us: flattened, depressed.

deustus — dee-*uss*-tus: burned.

diacanthus — dye-ak-*kanth*-us: two-spined, two-thorned.

diademus — dye-ad-*dee*-mus: two-crowned.

diandrus — dye-*and*-rus: two-stamened.

dianthiflorus — dye-anth-if-*floh*-rus: Dianthus-flowered.

diaphanus — dye-*aff*-an-us: thin, transparent.

dichotomus — dye-*kot*-om-us: forked, two-branched.

dicoccus — dye-*kok*-us: two-berried.

didymus — *did*-im-us: paired (as anthers).

difformis — dif-*form*-iss: differing.

diffusus — dif-*few*-sus: spreading (diffuse).

digitalis — dij-it-*tay*-liss: finger-form.

digitatus — dij-it-*tay*-tus: finger-form (digitate).

dilatatus — dye-lat-*tay*-tus: expanded.

dilatus — dye-*lay*-tus: expanded, spread-out.

dimidiatus — dye-mid-ee-*ay*-tus: halved, in two equal parts.

dimorphus — dye-*morf*-us: two-formed.

diodon — *dye*-od-on: two-toothed.

dioicus — dye-*oh*-ik-us: having male and female flowers on separate plants, dioecious (dye-*eesh*-us).

dipetalus — dye-*pet*-al-us: two-petaled.

diphyllus — dye-*fill*-us: two-leaved.

dipterus — *dip*-ter-us: two-winged.

dipterocarpus — dip-ter-oh-*karp*-us: with two-winged fruit.

disciformis — disk-if-*form*-iss: disc-formed.

discoideus — dis-*koy*-dee-us: rayless, discoid.

discolor — dis-*kol*-or: of two different colors.

dissectus — dis-*sek*-tus: deeply cut, dissected.

dissitiflorus — dis-sit-if-*floh*-rus: loose-flowered.

distachyus — dis-*tak*-ee-us: two spiked.

distans — *diss*-tanz: separate.

distichus — *diss*-tik-us: with leaves or flowers in two ranks on opposite sides of stem (distichous).

distylus — *diss*-til-us: two-styled.

diurnus — dye-*urn*-us: day-flowering.

divaricatus — div-ar-ik-*kay*-tus: widely divergent, spreading (divaricate).

divergens — div-*verj*-enz: wide-spreading.

diversiflorus — div-erss-if-*floh*-rus: variable-flowered.

diversifolius — div-erss-if-*foh*-lee-us: variable-leaved.

diversilobus — div-erss-il-*loh*-bus: diversely lobed.

divisus — div-*vye*-sus: divided, separated.

dolabratus — dol-ab-*ray*-tus: hatchet-shaped.

dolabriformis — dol-ab-rif-*form*-iss: hatchet-shaped.

dolosus — dol-*loh*-sus: deceptive.

domesticus — dom-*mess*-tik-us: domestic (or domesticated).

drupaceus — drew-*pay*-see-us: with drupe-like parts, having drupes.

drupiferus — drew-*pif*-er-us: bearing drupes.

dubius — *dew*-bee-us: doubtful (of origin or type).

dulcis — *dull*-siss: sweet.

dumetorum — dew-met-*toh*-rum: of bushes or hedges.

dumosus — dew-*moh*-sus: bushy.

duplex — *dew*-plex: double.

duplicatus — dew-plik-*kay*-tus: double, doubled (duplicate).

durabilis — dew-*rab*-il-iss: lasting, durable.

duracinus — dew-*rass*-in-us: hard berried.

durius — *dew*-ree-us: rather hard or tough.

E

ebenaceus — eb-en-*nay*-see-us: ebony-like.

ebracteatus — ee-brak-tee-*ay*-tus: bractless.

eburneus — ee-*burn*-ee-us: ivory-white.

echinatus — ek-in-*nay*-tus: bristly, prickly.

echinocarpus — ek-in-oh-*karp*-us: prickly-fruited.

echinosepalus — ek-in-oh-*sep*-al-us: prickly-sepaled.

ecornutus — ee-kor-*new*-tus: hornless.

edulis — *ed*-yew-liss: edible.

effusus — ef-*few*-sus: loose-spreading.

elasticus — el-*last*-ik-us: elastic (or rubber-producing).

elatior — ee-*lay*-tee-or: taller.

elatus — ee-*lay*-tus: tall.

elegans — *ell*-eg-anz: beautiful, elegant.

elegantissimus — el-eg-an-*tiss*-im-us: most beautiful or elegant.

elephantidens — el-ef-*fant*-id-enz: large-toothed.

ellipticus — el-*lip*-tik-us: elliptical (oval, tapering towards ends).

elongatus — ee-lon-*gay*-tus: lengthened, elongated.

emarginatus — ee-mar-jin-*nay*-tus: shallowly notched at tip (as of leaves), emarginate.

emeticus — em-*met*-ik-us: emetic.

emineus — *em*-in-enz: prominent.

enneaphyllus — en-nee-af-*fill*-us: nine-leaved.

ensatus — en-*say*-tus: sword-like.

ensifolius — en-sif-*foh*-lee-us: sword-leaved.

ensiformis — en-sif-*form*-iss: sword-shaped.

entomophilus — en-toh-*mof*-il-us: insect loving.

equestris — ek-*kwess*-triss: pertaining to horses.

equinus — ek-*kwye*-nus: of horses.

erectus — ee-*rek*-tus: upright, erect.

erianthus — ehr-ee-*anth*-us: woolly-flowered.

ericoides — ehr-ik-*koy*-deez: Heath-like, Erica-like.

eriocarpus — ehr-ee-oh-*karp*-us: woolly-fruited.

eriocephalus — ehr-ee-oh-*sef*-al-us: woolly-headed.

eriophorus — ehr-ee-*off*-or-us: woolly.

erosus — ee-*roh*-sus: jagged.

erraticus — ehr-*rat*-ik-us: unusual.

erubescens — ehr-rew-*bess*-senz: blushing.

erythrocarpus — ehr-ith-roh-*karp*-us: red-fruited.

erythrocephalus — ehr-ith-roh-*sef*-al-us: red-headed.

erythropodus — ehr-ith-*rop*-od-us: red-footed or -stalked.

erythropterus — ehr-ith-*rop*-ter-us: red-winged.

esculentus — es-kew-*lent*-us: edible.

estriatus — es-trye-*ay*-tus: without stripes.

etuberosus — ee-tew-ber-*roh*-sus: without tubers.

europaeus — yew-roh-*pee*-us: European.

exaltatus — ex-al-*tay*-tus: very tall.

excavatus — ex-kay-*vay*-tus: hollowed.

excellens — ex-*sel*-lenz: excelling, outstanding.

excelsus — ex-*sel*-sus: tall.

excisus — ex-*sye*-sus: cut away.

exiguus — ex-*ig*-yew-us: small, poor.

eximius — ex-*im*-ee-us: uncommon, distinguished.

exitiosus — ex-it-ee-*oh*-sus: pernicious, destructive.

exoticus — ex-*ot*-ik-us: foreign (not native).

expansus — ex-*pan*-sus: expansive.

exscapus — ex-*skay*-pus: stalkless, scapeless.

exsculptus — ex-*skulp*-tus: dug or carved out.

exsertus — ex-*sert*-us: protruding (exserted).

exsurgens — ex-*serj*-enz: rising or standing up.

extensus — ex-*ten*-sus: extended.

exudans — ex-*yew*-danz: exuding (something).

F

fabaceus — fab-*bay*-see-us: Bean-like.

falcatus — fal-*kay*-tus: sickle-shaped (falcate).

falcifolius — fal-sif-*foh*-lee-us: with sickle-shaped leaves.

falciformis — fal-sif-*form*-iss: sickle-formed.

farinaceus — fa-rin-*nay*-see-us: starchy or floury.

fariniferus — fa-rin-*nif*-er-us: having starch.

farinosus — fa-rin-*noh*-sus: mealy, powdery.

fasciatus — fas-see-*ay*-tus: flattened or broadened (fasciate).

fascicularis — fas-sik-yew-*lay*-riss: closely clustered (fascicled).

fasciculatus — fas-sik-yew-*lay*-tus: clustered.

fascinator — fas-sin-*nay*-tor: charming.

fastigiatus — fas-tij-ee-*ay*-tus: erect-branching (fastigiate).

fastuosus — fas-tew-*oh*-sus: proud.

fatuus — *fat*-yew-us: simple, insipid.

febrifugus — feb-*rif*-yew-gus: fever-dispelling.

fenestralis — fen-ess-*tray*-liss: with (window-like) openings.

ferox — *fee*-rox: very thorny.

ferreus — *fehr*-ee-us: pertaining to iron.

ferrugineus — fer-rew-*jin*-ee-us: rust-colored.

fertilis — *fer*-til-iss: fruitful (self-fruitful).

festivus — fes-*tye*-vus: gay, festive.

fibrosus — fye-*broh*-sus: markedly fibrous.

ficifolius — fye-sif-*foh*-lee-us: with fig-like leaves.

ficoideus — fye-*koy*-dee-us: fig-like.

filamentosus — fil-am-en-*toh*-sus: thread-like, having threads.

filicatus — fil-ik-*kay*-tus: fern-like.

filicaulis — fil-ik-*kaw*-liss: with thread-like stems.

filicifolius — fil-iss-if-*foh*-lee-us: fern-leaved.

filicinus — fil-iss-*sye*-nus: fern-like.

filicoides — fil-ik-*koy*-deez: fern-like.

filiferus — fye-*lif*-er-us: having threads or filaments.

filifolius — fil-if-*foh*-lee-us: thread-leaved.

filiformis — fil-if-*form*-iss: thread-like.

filipes — *fill*-ip-peez: with thread-like stalks.

fimbriatus — fim-bree-*ay*-tus: fringed (fimbriate).

firmatus — fir-*may*-tus: firm.

firmus — *firm*-us: firm, strong.

fissifolius — fiss-if-*foh*-lee-us: split-leaved.

fissilis — *fiss*-il-iss: cleft, split (fissile).

fissus — *fiss*-us: cleft, split.

fistulosus — fiss-tew-*loh*-sus: hollow-cylindrical.

flabellatus — flab-el-*lay*-tus: with fan-like parts (flabellate).

flabelliformis — flab-el-if-*form*-iss: fan-shaped.

flaccidus — *flak*-sid-us: soft, limp.

flagellaris — flaj-el-*lay*-riss: whip-like (flagellate).

flagellatus — flaj-el-*lay*-tus: whip-like

flagelliformis — flaj-el-if-*form*-iss: whip-formed.

flammeus — *flam*-ee-us: flame-colored.

flavescens — flav-*vess*-enz: yellowish, becoming yellow.

flavicomus — flay-*vik*-oh-mus: yellow-haired.

flavidus — *flay*-vid-us: yellow or yellowish.

flavirameus — flay-vihr-*ray*-mee-us: yellow-branched.

flavispinus — flay-viss-*pye*-nus: yellow-spined.

flavissimus — flay-*viss*-im-us: deep yellow.

flavus — *flay*-vus: yellow.

flavovirens — flay-voh-*vye*-renz: yellow-green.

flexilis — *flex*-il-iss: pliant, flexible.

flexuosus — flex-yew-*oh*-sus: tortuous, zig-zag.

floccosus — flok-*koh*-sus: woolly.

flore-albo — floh-ree-*al*-boh: white-flowered.

florentinus — flor-en-*tye*-nus: Florentine.

flore-pleno — floh-ree-*plee*-noh: double flowered.

floribundus — floh-rib-*bund*-us: flowering profusely.

floridus — *flor*-id-us: flowering freely.

floridanus — flor-id-*day*-nus: of Florida.

fluitans — *flew*-it-anz: floating.

fluviatilis — flew-vee-*at*-il-iss: of rivers.

foetidissimus — fet-id-*diss*-im-us: foul smelling.

foetidus — *fet*-id-us: ill-smelling.

foliatus — foh-lee-*ay*-tus: with leaves.

foliolatus — foh-lee-oh-*lay*-tus: with leaflets.

foliosus — foh-lee-*oh*-sus: leafy, full of leaves.

follicularis — fol-ik-yew-*lay*-riss: having follicles.

fontinalis — fon-tin-*nay*-liss: pertaining to spring.

forficatus — for-fik-*kay*-tus: shear-shaped.

formosissimus — for-moh-*siss*-im-us: very beautiful.

formosus — for-*moh*-sus: beautiful, handsome.

foveatus — foh-vee-*ay*-tus: pitted.

foveolatus — foh-vee-oh-*lay*-tus: somewhat pitted.

fragarioides — frag-ar-ee-*oy*-deez: Strawberry-like.

fragilis — *fraj*-il-iss: fragile, brittle.

fragrans — *fray*-granz: fragrant.

fragrantissimus — fray-gran-*tiss*-im-us: very fragrant.

frigidus — *frij*-id-us: from or of cold regions.

frondosus — fron-*doh*-sus: leafy.

fructescens — frook-*tess*-enz: fruitful.

fructiferus — frook-*tif*-er-us: bearing fruits.

fructigenus — frook-*tij*-en-us: fruitful.

frutescens — frew-*tess*-enz: shrubby, bushy.

fruticosus — frew-tik-*koh*-sus: shrubby, bushy (fruticose).

fruticulosus — frew-tik-yew-*loh*-sus: somewhat shrubby.

fucatus — few-*kay*-tus: painted, dyed.

fuchsioides — fook-see-*oy*-deez: Fuchsia-like.

fugax — *few*-gax: rapid.

fulgens — *full*-jenz: shining, glistening.

fulgidus — *full*-jid-us: shining.

fuliginosus — few-lij-in-*oh*-sus: sooty-black.

fulvescens — full-*vess*-enz: becoming tawny-orange.

fulvus — *full*-vuss: tawny-orange.

funebris — few-*nee*-briss: funereal.

fungosus — fun-*goh*-sus: spongy, pertaining to a fungus.

funiculatus — few-nik-yew-*lay*-tus: pertaining to rope or cord; with an ovule stalk (funicle).

furcans — *fur*-kanz: forked.

furcatus — fur-*kay*-tus: forked (furcate).

fuscatus — fuss-*kay*-tus: brownish.

fusco-rubra — fuss-koh-*roo*-brah: brownish red.

fuscus — *fuss*-cus: brown, dusky (fuscous).

fusiformis — few-sif-*form*-iss: spindle-shaped.

G

galacifolius — gay-las-if-*foh*-lee-us: Galax-leaved.

galericulatus — gal-er-ik-yew-*lay*-tus: helmet-like.

gallicus — *gal*-lik-us: French, of or from France.

garganicus — gar-*gan*-ik-us: of Gargano (Italy).

gelidus — *jel*-id-us: frigid (regions).

geminatus — jem-in-*nay*-tus: twin.

geminiflorus — jem-in-if-*floh*-rus: twin-flowered.

geminispinus — jem-in-iss-*pye*-nus: twin-spined.

gemmatus — jem-*may*-tus: jeweled (bud-bearing).

gemmiferus — jem-*mif*-er-us: having buds.

genevensis — jen-ev-*ven*-siss: of Geneva (Switzerland).

geniculatus — jen-ik-yew-*lay*-tus: jointed, kneed.

gentianoides — jen-shan-*noy*-deez: Gentian-like.

geoides — jee-*oy*-deez: of the earth.

geometricus — jee-om-*met*-rik-us: distinctly patterned.

germanicus — jer-*man*-ik-us: German, of Germany.

gibberosus — jib-er-*roh*-sus: humped, misshapen.

gibbiflorus — jib-if-*floh*-rus: with irregularly swollen flowers.

gibbus — *jib*-us: swollen on one side (gibbous).

giganteus — jye-*gan*-tee-us: large, huge.

giganticus — jye-*gan*-tik-us: large, gigantic.

glabellus — glab-*bell*-us: smoothish.

glaber (see glabrus) — *glay*-ber: smooth.

glaberrimus — glab-*behr*-im-us: very smooth.

glabratus — glab-*ray*-tus: rather smooth.

glabrescens — glab-*ress*-enz: becoming smooth.

glabrus — *glay*-brus: smooth (glabrous).

glacialis — glay-see-*ay*-liss: of glacial regions.

gladiatus — glad-ee-*ay*-tus: swordlike.

glanduliferus — glan-dew-*lif*-er-us: having glands.

glanduliflorus — glan-dew-lif-*floh*-rus: with gland-like (glandular) flowers.

glandulosus — glan-dew-*loh*-sus: glandular.

glaucescens — glaw-*sess*-senz: acquiring a "bloom" (fuzz), grayish.

glaucifolius — glaw-sif-*foh*-lee-us: bloomy- or grayish-leaved.

glaucophyllus — glaw-koh-*fill*-us: bloomy or grayish leaved.

glaucus — *glaw*-kus: "bloomy," grayish (glaucous).

globosus — gloh-*boh*-sus: almost spherical or globular (globose).

globularis — gloh-bew-*lay*-riss: like a little ball.

globuliferus — gloh-bew-*lif*-er-us: bearing small balls or globules.

globulosus — gloh-bew-*loh*-sus: globular but small.

glomeratus — glom-er-*ray*-tus: clustered (glomerate).

glomuliferus — glom-yew-*lif*-er-us: bearing small clusters (of flowers).

gloriosus — gloh-ree-*oh*-sus: superb.

glumaceus — glew-*may*-see-us: with chaffy bracts or scales (glumes).

glutinosus — glew-tin-*noh*-sus: gluey, sticky (glutinous).

gracilentus — gras-il-*len*-tus: slender.

gracilis — *grass*-il-iss: slender (graceful).

gracillimus — gras-*sil*-im-us: very slender.

graecus — *gree*-kus: Greek, of Greece.

gramineus — gram-*min*-ee-us: grassy, grass-like.

graminifolius — gram-in-if-*foh*-lee-us: grass-leaved.

grandiceps — *gran*-dis-seps: large-headed.

grandicuspis — gran-dik-*kusp*-iss: with large points.

grandidentatus — gran-did-en-*tay*-tus: big-toothed.

grandiflorus — gran-dif-*floh*-rus: large-flowered.

grandifolius — gran-dif-*foh*-lee-us: large-leaved.

grandiformis — gran-dif-*form*-iss: of a large sort.

grandipunctatus — gran-dip-unk-*tay*-tus: large-spotted.

grandis — *gran*-diss: large.

graniticus — gran-*nit*-ik-us: of granite soils or crevices.

granulatus — gran-yew-*lay*-tus: of grain-texture, granular.

granulosus — gran-yew-*loh*-sus: grainy, granulose.

gratissimus — grat-*tiss*-im-us: very pleasing.

gratus — *gray*-tus: pleasing.

graveolens — grav-*vee*-ol-enz: heavy-scented.

grossus — *grohss*-us: great, large.

guatemalensis — gwat-em-al-*len*-siss: of Guatemala.

guianensis — gwee-an-*nen*-siss: of Guiana.

guineensis — gwin-ee-*en*-siss: of Guinea (Africa).

gummiferus — gum-*mif*-er-us: gum-bearing.

gummosus — gum-*moh*-sus: gummy.

guttatus — gut-*tay*-tus: spotted, speckled.

gymnocarpus — jim-no-*karp*-us: naked-fruited.

gyrans — *jye*-ranz: gyrating, revolving (in a circle).

H

haemanthus — hee-*manth*-us: blood-red-flowered.

hamatus — ham-*may*-tus: hooked.

hamosus — ham-*moh*-sus: hooked, hook-like.

harpophyllus — harp-oh-*fill*-us: sickle-leaved.

hastatus — hass-*tay*-tus: spear-shaped (hastate).

hastiferus — hass-*tif*-er-us: spear-bearing.

hastilis — hass-*tye*-liss: referring to a spear.

hebecarpus—hee-bee-*karp*-us: hairy-fruited.

hederaceus — hed-er-*ray*-see-us: Ivy-like.

helveticus — hel-*vet*-ik-us: Swiss, of Switzerland.

helvolus — *hel*-vol-us: pale yellow.

hemisphaericus — hem-iss-*feer*-ik-us: like half a sphere.

heptaphyllus — hep-taf-*fill*-us: seven-leaved.

herbaceus — her-*bay*-see-us: fleshy stemmed, not woody (herbaceous).

heteracanthus — het-er-ak-*kanth*-us: variously spined.

heteranthus — het-er-*ranth*-us: variable-flowered, variously flowered.

heterocarpus — het-er-oh-*karp*-us: various-fruited.

heterodon — het-*tehr*-od-on: various toothed.

heteroglossus — het-er-oh-*gloss*-us: various-tongued.

heteromorphus — het-er-oh-*morf*-us: varying in form.

heterophyllus — het-er-oh-*fill*-us: various-leaved.

hexagonus — hex-*ag*-on-us: six-angled, six-sided.

hexandrus — hex-*and*-rus: six-stamened.

hexapetalus — hex-ap-*pet*-al-us: six-petaled.

hexaphyllus — hex-af-*fill*-us: six-leaved.

hians — *hye*-anz: open, gaping.

hibernalis — hye-ber-*nay*-liss: pertaining to winter.

hibernicus — hye-*bern*-ik-us: of or from Ireland.

hibiscifolius — hye-bis-sif-*foh*-lee-us: Hibiscus-leaved.

himalaicus — him-al-*lay*-ik-us: of the Himalayas.

hirsutissimus — herss-yew-*tiss*-im-us: very hairy.

hirsutulus — herss-*yew*-tul-us: somewhat hairy.

hirsutus — herss-*yew*-tus: hairy (hirsute).

hirtellus — her-*tel*-us: somewhat hairy.

hirtiflorus — her-tif-*floh*-rus: hairy-flowered.

hirtipes — *her*-tip-eez: hairy-stemmed.

hirtus — *hert*-us: hairy.

hispanicus — hiss-*pan*-ik-us: of or from Spain.

hispidissimus — hiss-pid-*diss*-im-us: very bristly.

hispidus — *hiss*-pid-us: bristly (hispid).

histrionicus — hiss-tree-*on*-ik-us: pertaining to actors or the drama.

hollandicus — hol-*land*-ik-us: of or from Holland.

holosericeus — hol-oh-ser-*riss*-ee-us: woolly, silky.

horizontalis — hor-iz-on-*tay*-liss: horizontal.

horridus — *horr*-id-us: horrid (as with spines).

hortensius — hor-*ten*-see-us: of gardeners.

hortensis — hor-*ten*-siss: belonging to the garden.

hortorum — hor-*toh*-rum: belonging to gardens.

hortulanus — hor-tew-*lay*-nus: of gardens.

humifusus — hew-mif-*few*-sus: sprawling on the ground.

humilis — *hew*-mil-iss: low-growing, dwarf.

hupehensis — hoo-pay-*en*-siss: from Hupei (China).

hyacinthinus — hye-ass-*sinth*-in-us: sapphire-colored.

hyacinthoides — hye-ass-inth-*oy*-deez: Hyacinth-like.

hyalinus — hye-*al*-in-us: translucent, transparent.

hybridus — *hib*-rid-us: mixed, hybrid.

hyemalis — hye-em-*may*-liss: pertaining to winter.

hymenanthus — hye-men-*nanth*-us: membranous-flowered.

hymenoides — hye-men-*noy*-deez: membrane-like.

hymenosepalus — hye-men-oh-*see*-pal-us: membrane-sepaled.

hyperboreus — hye-per-*boh*-ree-us: far-northern.

hypocrateriformis — hye-poh-kray-ter-if-*form*-iss: salver-shaped (flower).

hypogaeus — hye-poh-*jee*-us: underground (of growth).

hypoglaucus — hye-poh-*glaw*-kus: grayish or "bloomy" beneath.

hypoleucus — hye-poh-*lew*-kus: whitish, pale.

hypophyllus — hye-poh-*fill*-us: referring to underside of leaf.

hystrix — *hiss*-trix: bristly.

I

ianthinus — eye-*anth*-in-us: violet, violet-blue.

ibericus — eye-*behr*-ik-us: of Spain or Portugal.

ignescens — ig-*ness*-senz: fiery (colored).

igneus — *ig*-nee-us: fiery.

ilicifolius — il-iss-if-*foh*-lee-us: Holly-leaved.

illecebrosus — il-less-see-*broh*-sus: shade-growing.

illustris — il-*luss*-triss: brilliant, lustrous.

illyricus — il-*lihr*-ik-us: of Greece (Illyria).

imberbis — im-*berb*-iss: beardless, spineless.

imbricans — *im*-brik-anz: overlapping.

imbricarius — im-brik-*kay*-ree-us: overlapping.

imbricatus — im-brik-*kay*-tus: overlapping (imbricated).

immaculatus — im-mak-yew-*lay*-tus: spotless.

immersus — im-*mer*-sus: underwater.

imperialis — im-pee-ree-*ay*-liss: showy, regal.

implexus — im-*plex*-us: interwoven.

impressus — im-*press*-us: sunken.

inaequalifolius — in-ee-kwal-if-*foh*-lee-us: unequal-leaved.

inaequalis—in-ee-*kway*-liss: unequal, not uniform.

inaequilaterus — in-ee-kwil-*lat*-er-us: unequaled-sided.

incanus — in-*kay*-nus: grayish-white, hoary.

incarnatus — in-kar-*nay*-tus: flesh-colored.

incertus — in-*sert*-us: uncertain (origin or type).

incisifolius — in-sye-sif-*foh*-lee-us: cut-leaved.

incisus — in-*sye*-sus: cut (incised).

inclinatus — in-klin-*nay*-tus: bent downward.

incomparabilis — in-kom-par-*rab*-il-iss: excelling.

incomptus — in-*komp*-tus: unattractive.

inconspicuus — in-kon-*spik*-yew-us: not notable, inconspicuous.

incurvatus — in-kurv-*vay*-tus: bent inward (in curved).

indentatus — in-den-*tay*-tus: indented or toothed.

indicus — *inn*-dik-us: of India (the East Indies).

indivisus — in-div-*vye*-sus: undivided.

induratus — in-dew-*ray*-tus: hardened.

inermis — in-*erm*-iss: without thorns or spines (unarmed).

infectorius — in-fek-*toh*-ree-us: used for dyes.

infestus — in-*fess*-tus: dangerous.

inflatus — in-*flay*-tus: swollen.

infractus — in-*frak*-tus: broken.

infundibuliformis — in-fun-dib-yew-lif-*form*-iss: funnel shaped (flowers).

inodorus — in-oh-*doh*-rus: without fragrance.

inornatus—in-or-*nay*-tus: not showy.

inquinans — *inn*-kwin-anz: discoloring.

insignis — in-*sig*-niss: remarkable, outstanding.

intactus — in-*tak*-tus: intact.

integer — *inn*-tej-er: unbroken (entire).

integrifolius — in-teg-rif-*foh*-lee-us: "entire"-leaved (smooth-edged).

interjectus — in-ter-*jek*-tus: put between.

intermedius — in-ter-*meed*-ee-us: intermediate (in color, form, etc.).

interruptus — in-ter-*rup*-tus: not continuous, scattered.

intertextus — in-ter-*text*-us: interwoven, intertwined.

intortus — in-*tort*-us: twisted.

intricatus — in-trik-*kay*-tus: entangled (branches).

introrsus — in-*tror*-sus: turned inward (introrse).

intumescens — in-tew-*mess*-senz: swollen, puffy.

inversus — in-*verr*-sus: turned over (inverse).

invisus — in-*vye*-sus: unseen, overlooked.

involucratus — in-vol-yew-*kray*-tus: with a group or whorl of small leaves or bracts (involucres).

involutus — in-vol-*yew*-tus: rolled inward (involute).

ioensis — eye-oh-*en*-siss: from Iowa.

ionanthus — eye-oh-*nanth*-us: Violet-flowered.

ionopterus — eye-oh-*nop*-ter-us: winged like a Violet.

iridescens — ir-id-*dess*-senz: shimmering, changeable color.

iridifolius — eye-rid-if-*foh*-lee-us: Iris-leaved.

iridioides — eye-rid-ee-*oy*-deez: Iris-like.

irregularis — ihr-reg-yew-*lay*-riss: irregular, unsymmetrical.

isandrus — eye-*sand*-rus: equal-stamened.

isopetalus—eye-soh-*pet*-al-us: equal-petaled.

isophyllus — eye-soh-*fill*-us: equal-leaved.

italicus — it-*tal*-ik-us: of or from Italy.

ixocarpus — ix-oh-*karp*-us: sticky-fruited.

J

japonicus — jap-*pon*-ik-us: of or from Japan.

jasmineus — jas-*min*-ee-us: Jasmine-like.

jasminiflorus — jas-min-if-*floh*-rus: Jasmine-flowered.

jasminoides — jas-min-*noy*-deez: Jasmine-like.

javanicus — jav-*van*-ik-us: of or from Java.

jubatus — jew-*bay*-tus: crested, maned.

jucundus — jew-*koon*-dus: pleasing, amiable.

jugosus — jew-*goh*-sus: yoked.

juliflorus — jew-lif-*floh*-rus: with walnut-like flowers.

junceus — *joon*-see-us: rush-like.

juniperinus — jew-nip-er-*rye*-nus: Juniper-like.

K

kalmiaeflorus — kal-mih-ee-*floh*-rus: Laurel (Kalmia)-flowered.

kamtschatikus — kam-*chat*-ik-us: of Kamchatka (Siberia).

kashmirianus — kash-meer-ee-*ay*-nus: of Kashmere.

kewensis — kew-*en*-siss: of Kew Gardens (England).

korianus — koh-ree-*ay*-nus: of or from Korea.

L

labiatus — lay-bee-*ay*-tus: lipped (labiate).

labiosus — lay-bee-*oh*-sus: lipped.

laciniatus — las-in-ee-*ay*-tus: cut into narrow holes (laciniate).

laciniosus — las-in-ee-*oh*-sus: narrowly cut.

lactatus — lak-*tay*-tus: milky.

lacteus — *lak*-tee-us: milk-white.

lacticolor — lak-*tik*-ol-or: milk-colored.

lactiferus — lak-*tif*-er-us: milky-juiced.

lactiflorus — lak-tif-*floh*-rus: milk-white-flowered.

lacunosus — lak-yew-*noh*-sus: pitted.

laetevirens — lee-tev-*vye*-renz: vivid green.

laetus — *lee*-tus: bright, vivid.

laevicaulis — lee-vik-*kaw*-liss: smooth-stemmed.

laevigatus — lee-vig-*gay*-tus: smooth.

laevipes — *lee*-vip-peez: smooth-stalked.

laevis — *lee*-viss: smooth.

laeviusculus — lee-vee-*uss*-kew-lus: smoothish.

lanatus — lan-*nay*-tus: woolly, wool-like.

lanceolatus — lan-see-oh-*lay*-tus: slender-pointed (lanceolate).

lanceus — *lan*-see-us: lance-like, pointed.

lancifolius — lan-sif-*foh*-lee-us: pointed-leaved.

lanigerus — lan-*nij*-er-us: wool-bearing, woolly.

lanosus — lan-*noh*-sus: woolly.

lanuginosus — lan-yew-jin-*noh*-sus: woolly, downy.

laricifolius — lar-iss-sif-*foh*-lee-us: Larch-leaved.

laricinus — lar-iss-*sye*-nus: Larch (Larix)-like.

lasiacanthus — lay-see-ak-*kanth*-us: woolly-spined.

lasianthus — lay-see-*anth*-us: woolly-flowered.

lasiocarpus — lay-see-oh-*karp*-us: rough- or hairy-fruited.

lasiopetalus — lay-see-oh-*pet*-al-us: hairy-petaled.

lateriflorus — lat-er-if-*floh*-rus: with flowers on the side, lateral-flowered.

lateritius — lat-er-*rit*-ee-us: bright red.

latiflorus — lat-if-*floh*-rus: broad-flowered.

latifolius — lat-if-*foh*-lee-us: broad-leaved.

latifrons — *lat*-if-ronz: broad-foliaged or -fronded.

latimaculatus — lat-im-ak-yew-*lay*-tus: broad-spotted.

latipes — *lat*-ip-peez: broad-footed or -stalked.

latisquamus — lat-iss-*kway*-mus: with broad scale-like leaves or bracts.

latissimus — lat-*tiss*-im-us: very broad.

latus — *lay*-tus: broad.

laurifolius — law-rif-*foh*-lee-us: Laurel (Laurus)-leaved.

laurinus — law-*rye*-nus: Laurel (Laurus)-like.

lavandulaceus — lav-an-dew-*lay*-see-us: Lavender-like.

laxiflorus — lax-if-*floh*-rus: loose-flowered.

laxifolius — lax-if-*foh*-lee-us: loose-leaved.

laxus — *lax*-us.

leianthus — lye-*anth*-us: smooth-flowered.

leiocarpus — lye-oh-*karp*-us: smooth-fruited.

leiophyllus — lye-oh-*fill*-us: smooth-leaved.

lenticularis — len-tik-yew-*lay*-riss: lens-shaped (lenticular).

lentus — *lent*-us: pliant but tough.

leontoglossus — lee-on-toh-*gloss*-us: lion-tongued.

leopardinus — lee-op-ar-*dye*-nus: leopard-spotted.

lepidophyllus — lep-id-oh-*fill*-us: scaly-leaved.

leprosus — lep-*roh*-sus: scurfy.

leptocaulis — lep-toh-*kaw*-liss: thin-stemmed.

leptocladus — lep-*tok*-lad-us: thin-branched.

leptolepis — lep-*tol*-ep-iss: thin-scaled.

leptophyllus — lep-toh-*fill*-us: thin-leaved.

leptopus — *lep*-toh-pus: thin-stalked.

leptosepalus — lep-toh-*see*-pal-us: thin-sepaled.

leucanthus — lew-*kanth*-us: white-flowered.

leucobotrys — lew-koh-*boh*-triss: white-clustered.

leucocephalus — lew-koh-*sef*-al-us: white-headed.

leuconeurus — lew-koh-*new*-rus: white-veined.

leucophyllus — lew-koh-*fill*-us: white-leaved.

leucorhizus — lew-koh-*rye*-zus: white-rooted.

lignosus — lig-*noh*-sus: woody.

ligularis — lig-yew-*lay*-riss: strap-shaped.

ligulatus — lig-yew-*lay*-tus: strap-shaped.

ligustrinus — lye-gus-*trye*-nus: Privet (Ligustrum)-like.

lilacinus — lye-las-*sye*-nus: lilac-like or -colored.

liliiflorus — lil-ee-if-*floh*-rus: Lily-flowered.

liliifolius — lil-ee-if-*foh*-lee-us: with Lily-like leaves.

limbatus — lim-*bay*-tus: bordered.

limosus — lim-*moh*-sus: of marshy places.

linariifolius — lin-ay-ree-if-*foh*-lee-us: Linaria leaved.

linearifolius — lin-ee-ay-rif-*foh*-lee-us: narrow-leaved.

linearilobus — lin-ee-ay-ril-*loh*-bus: narrow-lobed.

linearis — lin-ee-*ay*-riss: narrow (linear).

lineatus — lin-ee-*ay*-tus: striped, lined.

linguus — *lin*-gwus: tongue-like.

lingulatus — lin-gew-*lay*-tus: tongue-shaped.

linifolius — lye-nif-*foh*-lee-us: with Flax (Linum)-like leaves.

linophyllus — lye-no-*fill*-us: Flax-leaved.

linoides — lin-*noy*-deez: Flax-like.

lithophilus — lith-*off*-il-us: rock-dwelling.

lithospermus — lith-oh-*sperm*-us: with stone-like seeds.

littoralis — lit-tor-*ray*-liss: of the seashore.

littoreus — lit-*tor*-ee-us: of the shore or coast.

lividus — *liv*-id-us: bluish, livid.

lobatus — loh-*bay*-tus: lobed.

lobularis — loh-bew-*lay*-riss: lobed.

longebracteatus — lon-jeb-brak-tee-*ay*-tus: long-bracted.

longepedunculatus — lon-jep-ped-unk-ew-*lay*-tus: with a long flower stalk.

longicaudatus — lon-jik-kaw-*day*-tus: long-tailed.

longiflorus — lon-jif-*floh*-rus: long-flowered.

longifolius — lon-jif-*foh*-lee-us: long-leaved.

longihamatus — lon-jih-ham-*may*-tus: long-hooked

longilaminatus — lon-jil-lam-in-*nay*-tus: with long plates (laminae).

longilobus — lon-*jil*-oh-bus: long-lobed.

longipes — *lon*-jip-eez: long-stalked.

longipetalus — lon-jip-*pet*-alus: long-petaled.

longipinnatus — lon-jip-pin-*nay*-tus: long-pinnate.

longiracemosus — lon-jih-ray-sem-*moh*-sus: long-racemed.

longiscapus — lon-jis-*skay*-pus: long-scaped.

longisepalus — lon-jis-*see*-pal-us: long-sepaled.

longispathus — lon-jis-*spayth*-us: long-spathed.

longispinus — lon-jis-*spye*-nus: long-spined.

longissimus — lon-*jiss*-im-us: very long.

longistylus — lon-jis-*stye*-lus: long styled.

longus — *lon*-gus: long.

lophanthus — loh-*fanth*-us: with crested flowers.

lorifolius — lor-if-*foh*-lee-us: strap-leaved.

lotifolius — loh-tif-*foh*-lee-us: Lotus-leaved.

lucidus — *lew*-sid-us: bright, shining.

ludovicianus — lew-doh-viss-ee-*ay*-nus: of Louisiana.

lunatus — lew-*nay*-tus: moon-shaped, crescent-shaped (lunate).

lunulatus — lew-new-*lay*-tus: somewhat moon-shaped.

luridus — *lew*-rid-us: pale yellow; also fiery, lurid.

lusitanicus — lew-sit-*tan*-ik-us: of Portugal (Lusitania).

luteolus — lew-*tee*-oh-lus: yellowish.

lutescens — lew-*tess*-senz: becoming yellowish.

luteus — *lew*-tee-us: yellow.

luxurians — lux-*yew*-ree-anz: luxuriant, thrifty.

lyratus — lye-*ray*-tus: deeply cut, with large terminal lobe (lyrate).

M

macilentus — mas-il-*lent*-us: lean, meagre.

macradenus — mak-rad-*deen*-us: with large glands.

macranthus — mak-*ranth*-us: large-flowered.

macrobotrys — mak-roh-*boh*-triss: large-clustered.

macrocanthus — mak-roh-*kanth*-us: large-thorned.

macrocarpus — mak-roh-*karp*-us: large-fruited.

macrocephalus — mak-roh-*sef*-al-us: large-headed.

macrodactylus — mak-roh-*dak*-til-us: large-fingered.

macrodontus — mak-roh-*don*-tus: large-toothed.

macromeris — mak-*krom*-er-iss: with large or many parts.

macropetalus — mak-roh-*pet*-al-us: large-petaled.

macrophyllus — mak-roh-*fill*-us: large-leaved.

macropodus — mak-*krop*-od-us: large-stalked.

macropterus — mak-*krop*-ter-us: large-winged.

macrorhizus — mak-roh-*rye*-zus: with a large rootstock.

macrospadix — mak-roh-*spay*-dix: with large spadix.

macrospermus — mak-roh-*sperm*-us: large-seeded.

macrostachyus — mak-roh-*stak*-ee-us: large-spiked.

macrostemus — mak-roh-*stee*-mus: with large filaments.

macrostylus — mak-roh-*stye*-lus: large-styled.

macrourus — mak-roh-*yew*-rus: large-tailed.

maculatus — mak-yew-*lay*-tus: spotted.

maculosus — mak-yew-*loh*-sus: spotted.

magellanicus — maj-el-*lan*-ik-us: of region of Straits of Magellan (So. America).

magnificus — mag-*niff*-ik-us: showy, magnificent.

majalis — maj-*ay*-liss: of May (May-blooming).

major (majus) — *may*-jor (*may*-jus): greater, larger.

malacoides — mal-ak-*koy*-deez: mucilajinous.

maliformis — may-lif-*form*-iss: Apple-formed.

malvacius — mal-*vay*-see-us: Mallow (Malva)-like.

malvaeflorus — mal-vee-*floh*-rus: Mallow-flowered.

mammosus — mam-*moh*-sus: with nipple- or breast-like parts.

mandshuricus — mand-*shoor*-ik-us: of Manchuria.

manicatus — man-ik-*kay*-tus: long-sleeved (often referring to tube-like calyx).

marcescens — mar-*sess*-senz: withering.

marcidus — *mar*-sid-us: withering (not falling).

margaritaceus — mar-gar-it-*tay*-see-us: pearly.

margaritiferus — mar-gar-it-*tif*-er-us: pearl-bearing (of flowers or fruit).

margaritus — mar-gar-*rye*-tus: pearly.

marginalis — mar-jin-*nay*-liss: mar-gined, with distinct or different margins.

marginatus — mar-jin-*nay*-tus: margined.

marginellus — mar-jin-*nell*-us: somewhat margined.

marianus — mar-ee-*ay*-nus: referring to Virgin Mary.

marilandicus — mar-il-*land*-ik-us: of or from Maryland.

maritimus — mar-*rit*-im-us: of the sea or shore.

marmoratus — mar-moh-*ray*-tus: mottled, marbled.

marmoreus — mar-*moh*-ree-us: marbled.

marmorophyllus — mar-mor-oh-*fill*-us: leaves marbled.

maroccanus — mar-rok-*kay*-nus: of Morocco.

martagon — *mar*-tag-on: from Italian word for turban.

mas — *mass:* male.

masculatus — mas-kew-*lay*-tus: masculine.

masculus — *mass*-kew-lus: male, masculine.

matronalis — mat-roh-*nay*-liss: sedate (sometimes hoary).

mauritianus — maw-rit-ee-*ay*-nus: Is. of Mauritius.

maxillaris — max-il-*lay*-riss: pertaining to jaw.

maximus — *max*-im-us: very large.

mediterraneus — med-it-er-*ray*-nee-us: of the Mediterranean region.

medius — *mee*-dee-us: intermediate.

medullaris — med-ul-*lay*-riss: pertaining to the center (also marrow or pith).

megacanthus — meg-ak-*kanth*-us: large-thorned.

megalanthus — meg-al-*lanth*-us: large-flowered.

megaphyllus — meg-af-*fill*-us: large-leaved.

megapotamicus — meg-ap-poh-*tam*-ik-us: referring to (a) large river.

megarrhizus — meg-ar-*rye*-zus: large-rooted.

megaspermus — meg-ass-*sperm*-us: large-seeded.

megastachyus — meg-ass-*stay*-kee-us: large-spiked.

megastigmus — meg-ass-*stig*-mus: with large stigma.

melananthus — mel-an-*nanth*-us: black-flowered (or black-marked flowers).

melancholicus — mel-an-*kol*-ik-us: hanging, drooping.

melanocarpus — mel-an-oh-*karp*-us: blacked-fruited.

melanocaulon — mel-an-oh-*kaw*-lon: black-stemmed.

melanococcus — mel-an-oh-*kaw*-kus: black-berried.

melanoleucus — mel-an-oh-*lew*-kus: black-and-white.

melanoxylon — mel-an-oh-*zye*-lon: black-wooded.

melantherus — mel-*lanth*-er-us: black-anthered.

meleagris — mel-ee-*ay*-griss: speckled.

melleus — *mell*-ee-us: pertaining to honey.

melliferus — mel-*lif*-er-us: honey-bearing.

meloformis — mel-oh-*form*-iss: melon-shaped.

membranceus — mem-bran-*nay*-see-us: thin, somewhat translucent, membranous.

meniscifolius — men-iss-sif-*foh*-lee-us: crescent-leaved.

mesoleucus — mess-ol-*lew*-kus: mixed with white.

metallicus — met-*tal*-ik-us: metallic (sheen).

mexicanus — mex-ik-*kay*-nus: of or from Mexico.

micans — *mye*-kanz: glittering, sparkling.

micranthus — mye-*kranth*-us: small-flowered.

microcarpus — mye-kroh-*karp*-us: small-fruited.

microcephalus — mye-kroh-*seff*-al-us: small-headed.

microdon — *mye*-kroh-don: small-toothed.

microglossus — mye-kroh-*gloss*-us: small-tongued.

microlepis — mye-*krol*-ep-iss: small-scaled.

micromeris — mye-*krom*-er-iss: with few or small parts.

micropetalus — mye-kroh-*pet*-al-us: small-petaled.

microphyllus — mye-kroh-*fill*-us: small-leaved.

micropterus — mye-*krop*-ter-us: small-winged.

microsepalus — mye-kroh-*sep*-al-us: large-sepaled.

microstemus — mye-kroh-*steem*-us: with small filaments or stemlets.

millefoliatus — mil-ef-foh-lee-*ay*-tus: thousand-leaved.

millefolius — mil-ef-*foh*-lee-us: many (thousand)-leaved.

minax — *mye*-nax: forbidding, repellent.

miniatus — min-ee-*ay*-tus: Vermilion.

minimus — *min*-im-us: very small.

minor — *mye*-nor: rather small.

minitissimus — mye-new-*tiss*-im-us: very tiny, infinitesimal.

minus — *mye*-nus: rather small.

minutus — *mye-new*-tus: tiny, minute.

mirabilis — mir-*rab*-il-iss: unusual, extraordinary.

mitis — *mye*-tiss: mild, tender (gentle).

mitratus — mye-*tray*-tus: turbaned.

mixtus — *mix*-tus: mixed.

modestus — mod-*dest*-us: shy, inconspicuous.

moldavicus — mol-*dav*-ik-us: of Moldavia (Rumania).

molleoides — mol-lee-*oy*-deez: seemingly soft-hairy.

mollis — *moll*-iss: soft (soft-hairy).

mollissimus — mol-*liss*-im-us: very soft-hairy.

monacanthus — mon-ak-*kanth*-us: single-thorned.

monadelphus — mon-ad-*delf*-us: in one group (as with stamens).

monandrus — mon-*nand*-rus: with one stamen.

mongolicus — mon-*goll*-ik-us: of Mongolia.

moniliferus — mon-il-*liff*-er-us: bearing a "necklace."

monocephalus — mon-oh-*sef*-al-us: single-headed.

monogynus — mon-*noj*-in-us: with one pistil.

monoicus — mon-oh-*eye*-kus: monoeceus (male and female flowers separate but on same plant).

monopetalus — mon-oh-*pet*-al-us: one-petaled.

monophyllus — mon-oh-*fill*-us: one-leaved.

monopterus — mon-*opt*-er-us: one-winged.

monosepalus — mon-oh-*sep*-al-us: one-sepaled.

monospermus — mon-oh-*sperm*-us: one-seeded.

monostachyus — mon-oh-*stak*-ee-us: one-spiked.

monstrosus — mon-*stroh*-sus: huge, abnormal or deformed.

montanus — mon-*tay*-nus: of mountainous regions.

monticolus — mon-*tik*-ol-us: native to mountains.

morifolius — moh-rif-*foh*-lee-us: Mulberry-leaved.

mosaicus — moh-*zay*-ik-us: with definite color pattern.

moschatus — mos-*kay*-tus: musky (odor).

mucosus — mew-*koh*-sus: mucilaginous, slimy.

mucronatus — mew-kron-*nay*-tus: sharp-tipped (mucronate).

mucronulatus — mew-kron-yew-*lay*-tus: with a small point.

multibracteatus — mul-tib-rak-tee-*ay*-tus: many-bracted.

multicaulis — mul-tik-*kaw*-liss: many-stemmed.

multicavus — mull-tik-*kay*-vus: very concave or hollowed out.

multiceps — *mull*-tiss-seps: many-leaved (-branched).

multicolor — mull-tik-*kol*-or: many colored.

multifidus — mull-*tif*-id-us: much-divided (multifid).

multiflorus—mull-tif-*floh*-rus: many-flowered.

multifurcatus — mull-tif-fur-*kay*-tus: much-forked.

multijugus — mull-tij-*yew*-gus: yoked in many pairs (leaflets).

multinervis — mull-tin-*nerv*-iss: many-veined.

multiplex — *mull*-tip-lex: multiple.

multiradiatus — mull-tihr-ray-dee-*ay*-tus: many-rayed (as with Daisy flower).

multisectus — mull-tiss-*sek*-tus: much cut (leaves).

multiscapoideus — mull-tiss-kap-*poy*-dee-us: many scapes.

mundulus — *mun*-dew-lus: trim, neat.

munitus — mew-*nye*-tus: armed (as with thorns).

muralis — mew-*ray*-liss: wall-growing.

muricatus — mew-rik-*kay*-tus: rough with hard points (muricate).

musaicus — mew-*zay*-ik-us: banana-like.

muscosus — muss-*koh*-sus: moss-like.

mutabilis — mew-*tab*-il-iss: changeable (color).

mutatus — mew-*tay*-tus: changed, changeable.

muticus — *mew*-tik-us: blunt, without points.

mutilatus — mew-til-*lay*-tus: malformed.

myriacanthus — mihr-ee-ak-*kanth*-us: with a great many thorns or spines.

myriocarpus — mihr-ee-oh-*karp*-us: very many-fruited.

myriostygmus — mihr-ee-oh-*stig*-mus: with a great many stygmas.

myrtifolius — mer-tif-*foh*-lee-us: Myrtle-leaved.

N

nankinensis — nan-kin-*nen*-siss: of Nankin (China).

nanus — *nay*-nus: small, dwarf.

napellus — nap-*pell*-us: Turnip-rooted.

napiformis — nap-if-*form*-iss: Turnip-shaped.

narbonensis — nar-bon-*nen*-siss: of Narbonne (So. France).

natans — *nay*-tanz: floating.

navicularis — nav-ik-yew-*lay*-riss: of (like) a ship.

neopolitanus — nee-ap-ol-it-*tay*-nus: of Naples.

nebulosus — neb-yew-*loh*-sus: cloudlike (of flower mass); obscure (of classification).

neglectus — neg-*lek*-tus: overlooked (of little value).

nemoralis — nem-or-*ray*-liss: of grooves or woods.

nemorosus — nem-or-*roh*-sus: of grooves (or shady places).

nepalensis — nep-al-*len*-siss: of Nepal.

neriifolius — neer-ee-if-*foh*-lee-us: Oleander (Nerium) -flowered.

nervosus — ner-*voh*-sus: veined.

nevadensis — nev-ad-*den*-siss: of the Sierra Nevadas (Spain or No. America).

nidus — *nye*-dus: Latin for nest.

niger — *nye*-jer: black.

nigratus — nye-*gray*-tus: blackish.

nigrescens — nye-*gress*-senz: becoming black.

nigricans — *nye*-grik-anz: black.

nigricornis — nye-grik-*korn*-iss: black-horned.

nigripes — *nye*-grip-eez: black-stalked or -footed.

nigrofructus — nye-groh-*frook*-tus: black-fruited.

niloticus — nye-*lot*-ik-us: of the Nile (region).

nipponicus — nip-*pon*-ik-us: of or from Japan.

nitidus — *nit*-id-us: shining.

nivalis — niv-*vay*-liss: ref. to snow (snowy white).

niveus — *niv*-ee-us: snow-white.

nivosus — niv-*voh*-sus: snowy white.

nobilior — noh-*bill*-ee-or: rather noble, impressive.

nobilis — *noh*-bil-iss: noble, outstanding.

nobilissimus — noh-bil-*liss*-im-us: very notable or impressive.

nocturnus — nok-*turn*-us: night-blooming.

nodiflorus — nod-if-*floh*-rus: flowers at nodes.

nodosus — nod-*doh*-sus: with nodes or joints.

nodulosus — nod-yew-*loh*-sus: having nodules or small protuberances (tubercles).

nonscriptus — non-*skrip*-tus: undescribed (unclassified).

notatus — noh-*tay*-tus: marked.

novae-angliae — noh-vee-*an*-glih-ee: of or pertaining to New England.

novae-caesareae — noh-vee-see-zar-*ree*-ee: of or pertaining to New Jersey.

novae-zealandiae — noh-vee-zee-*land*-ih-ee: of or from New Zealand.

noveboracensis — noh-vee-bor-ass-*sen*-siss: of or pertaining to New York.

novi-belgi — noh-vye-*bell*-jye: of New York.

nubicolus — new-*bik*-ol-us: living among clouds.

nuciferus — new-*sif*-er-us: nut-bearing.

nudatus — new-*day*-tus: bare, stripped.

nudicaulis — new-dik-*kaw*-liss: bare-stemmed.

nudiflorus — new-dif-*floh*-rus: naked-flowered.

nudus — *new*-dus: bare, naked.

numismatus — new-miss-*may*-tus: coin-like.

nummularius — num-mew-*lay*-ree-us: coin-like (round and thin).

nutans — *new*-tanz: nodding.

nycticalus — nik-*tik*-al-us: night-blooming.

O

obconicus — ob-*kon*-ik-us: inverted-cone-shaped.

obcordatus — ob-kor-*day*-tus: inverted-heart-shaped (obcordate).

obesus — ob-*bee*-sus: fat, large.

obfuscatus — ob-fus-*kay*-tus: confused, indeterminate.

oblatus — ob-*lay*-tus: flattened at ends (oblate).

obliquus — ob-*lye*-kwus: lopsided, slanting.

obliteratus — ob-lit-er-*ray*-tus: hidden, not apparent.

oblongatus — ob-lon-*gay*-tus: oblong.

oblongifolius — ob-lon-jif-*foh*-lee-us: oblong-leaved.

oblongus — ob-*lon*-gus: oblong.

obovatus — ob-oh-*vay*-tus: invertedly ovate (obovate: broad part upward).

obscurus — ob-*skew*-rus: hidden (or partly).

obsoletus — ob-soh-*lee*-tus: rudimentary (of a part).

obtusatus — ob-tew-*say*-tus: blunt (obtuse).

obtusifolius — ob-tew-sif-*foh*-lee-us: blunt-leaved.

obtusilobus — ob-tew-sil-*loh*-bus: blunt-lobed.

obtusus — ob-*tew*-sus: bluntly rounded (obtuse).

occidentalis — ok-sid-en-*tay*-liss: western, of the western world.

oceanicus — oh-see-*an*-ik-us: of the ocean or ocean regions.

ocellatus — os-el-*lay*-tus: with eyelets, small eyes.

ochroleucus — ok-roh-*lew*-kus: yellowish white.

octandrus — ok-*tand*-rus: eight-anthered.

octopetalus — ok-toh-*pet*-al-us: eight-petaled.

octophyllus — ok-toh-*fill*-us: eight-leaved.

oculatus — ok-yew-*lay*-tus: with eyes or eye-like marks.

oculiroseus — ok-yew-lye-*roh*-see-us: crimson-eyed.

odontites — od-on-*tye*-teez: tooth (-like).

odontochilus — od-on-tok-*kye*-lus: with toothed lip or edge.

odoratissimus — oh-dor-at-*tiss*-im-us: very fragrant.

odoriferus — oh-dor-*rif*-er-us: having fragrance.

odoratus — oh-dor-*ray*-tus: odorous, scent or fragrance.

odorus — oh-*doh*-rus: fragrant.

Officinalis — off-iss-in-*nay*-liss: medicinal (or supposedly medicinal).

officinarum — off-iss-in-*nay*-rum: pertaining to apothecary uses.

oleaefolius — oh-lee-ee-*foh*-lee-us: Olive-leaved.

oleiferus — oh-lee-*iff*-er-us: oil-bearing.

oleraceus — oh-ler-*ray*-see-us: of the vegetable garden or the kitchen.

oliganthus — ol-ig-*ganth*-us: few-flowered.

oligocarpus — ol-ig-oh-*karp*-us: few-fruited.

oligospermus — ol-ig-oh-*sperm*-us: few-seeded.

olitorius — ol-it-*toh*-ree-us: pertaining to vegetable gardens or gardeners.

olivaceus — ol-iv-*vay*-see-us: Olive-like or -colored.

olivaeformis — ol-iv-ee-*form*-iss: Olive-shaped.

olympicus — ol-*limp*-ik-us: of (Mt.) Olympus (Greece).

opacus — op-*pay*-kus: pale (clouded, shaded).

oppositiflorus — op-pos-it-if-*floh*-rus: opposite-flowered.

oppositifolius — op-pos-it-if-*foh*-lee-us: opposite-leaved.

opuloides — op-yew-*loy*-deez: Opulus-like: see opulus.

opulus — *op*-yew-lus: old name for Poplar misapplied to a species of Viburnum.

orbicularis — or-bik-yew-*lay*-riss: round.

orbiculatus — or-bik-yew-*lay*-tus: round.

orchideus — or-*kid*-ee-us: Orchid-like.

orchioides — or-kee-*oy*-deez: Orchid-like.

oreganus — or-eg-*gay*-nus: of Oregon.

orgyalis — or-jee-*ay*-liss: about 6 ft. long.

orientalis — or-ee-en-*tay*-liss: of the Orient (eastern world).

origanifolius — or-ig-an-if-*foh*-lee-us: with Marjoram-like leaves.

origanoides — or-ig-an-*noy*-deez: Marjoram-like.

ornatissimus — or-nat-*tiss*-im-us: very showy.

ornatus — or-*nay*-tus: showy, ornamental.

ornithocephalus — or-nith-oh-*sef*-al-us: like a bird's head.

ornithopodus — or-nith-*opp*-od-us: like a bird's foot.

ornithorhynchus — or-nith-or-*rink*-us: beak-like.

orthocarpus — orth-oh-*karp*-us: straight-fruited (see genus of same name).

orthochilus — orth-oh-*kye*-lus: straight-lipped.

orthopterus — orth-*opp*-ter-us: straight-winged.

ovalifolius — oh-val-if-*foh*-lee-us: oval-leaved.

ovalis — oh-*vay*-liss: oval.

ovatifolius — oh-vat-if-*foh*-lee-us: ovate-leaved.

ovatus — oh-*vay*-tus: of egg shape or egg-shaped pattern, with broad end downward or inward (ovate).

oviferus — oh-*vif*-er-us: bearing ovules (unfertilized seed).

ovigerus — oh-*vij*-er-us: ovule-bearing.

ovinus — oh-*vye*-nus: pertaining to sheep, woolly, used as sheep fodder.

oxyacanthus — ox-ee-ak-*kanth*-us: sharp-thorned or -spined.

oxygonus — ox-ig-*goh*-nus: sharp-angled.

oxyphyllus — ox-if-*fill*-us: sharp-leaved.

oxysepalus — ox-iss-*sep*-al-us: with sharp sepals.

P

pabularis — pab-yew-*lay*-riss: suitable for fodder.

pachyanthus — pak-ee-*anth*-us: thick-veined.

pachyneurus — pak-in-*new*-rus: thick-veined.

pachypterus — pak-*kip*-ter-us: thick-winged.

pacificus — pas-*sif*-ik-us: of the Pacific Ocean (regions).

palaestinus — pal-ee-*stye*-nus: of Palestine.

paleaceus — pal-ee-*ay*-see-us: chaffy.

pallens — *pal*-enz: pale.

pallescens — pal-*less*-senz: fading, becoming pale.

palliatus — pal-lee-*ay*-tus: cloaked.

pallidiflorus — pal-lid-if-*floh*-rus: pale-flowered.

pallidifolius — pal-lid-if-*foh*-lee-us: pale-flowered.

pallidispinus — pal-lid-iss-*spye*-nus: pale-spined.

pallidus — *pal*-id-us: pale.

palliflavens — pal-lif-*flay*-venz: pale-yellow.

palmatifidus — pal-mat-*tif*-id-us: palmately cut (like fingers).

palmatus — pal-*may*-tus: divided or lobed (like hand and fingers: palmate).

palmifolius — pal-mif-*foh*-lee-us: with handlike leaves.

paludosus — pal-yew-*doh*-sus: marsh-loving.

palustris — pal-*lust*-riss: marsh-loving.

panduratus — pan-dew-*ray*-tus: fiddle-shaped.

paniculatus — pan-ik-yew-*lay*-tus: having a type of flower cluster classified as a panicle.

paniculigerus — pan-ik-yew-*lij*-er-us: having panicles.

pannosus — pan-*noh*-sus: ragged, tattered-looking.

papaveraceus — pap-av-er-*ray*-see-us: Poppy (Papaver) -like.

papilionaceus — pap-il-ee-on-*nay*-see-us: with butterfly-like flowers.

papillosus — pap-il-*loh*-sus: with tiny nipple-like protuberances.

papyraceus — pap-ihr-*ray*-see-us: papery.

papyriferus — pap-ihr-*rif*-er-us: having paper-like part or parts.

paradisiacus — par-ad-iss-*sye*-ak-us: of parks or gardens (type or use).

paradoxus — par-ad-*dox*-us: strange, contrary to type.

parasiticus — par-ass-*sit*-ik-us: parasitical.

pardalinus — par-dal-*lye*-nus: leopard-spotted.

pardinus — par-*dye*-nus: leopard-spotted.

partitus — par-*tye*-tus: divided, separated.

parviflorus — par-vif-*floh*-rus: small-flowered.

parvifolius — par-vif-*foh*-lee-us: small-leaved.

parvissimus — par-*viss*-im-us: very small.

parvulus — *par*-vew-lus: very small or slight.

parvus — *par*-vus: small.

patellaris — pat-el-*lay*-riss: disk-like.

patens — *pay*-tenz: spreading.

patulus — *pat*-yew-lus: spreading.

pauciflorus — paw-sif-*floh*-rus: scanty-flowered.

paucifolius — paw-sif-*foh*-lee-us: scanty-leaved.

pauperculus — paw-*perk*-yew-lus: poor, meager.

pavoninus — pav-on-*nye*-nus: peacock-like.

pectinaceus — pek-tin-*nay*-see-us: comb-like.

pectinatus — pek-tin-*nay*-tus: comb-like (pectinate).

pectiniferus — pek-tin-*nif*-er-us: comb-bearing.

pectoralis — pek-tor-*ray*-liss: with a breastbone-shaped part.

pedatus — ped-*day*-tus: footed, of

significance for the foot or base; also with bird-like foot; also hand-like (palmate).

pedemontanus — ped-em-on-*tay*-nus: of Piedmont (Italy).

peduncularis — ped-unk-yew-*lay*-riss: with a stalk (peduncle).

pedunculatus — ped-unk-yew-*lay*-tus: stalked (pedunculate).

pedunculosus — ped-unk-yew-*loh*-sus: with many stalks or peduncles.

pekinensis — pee-kin-*nen*-siss: of Pekin (Peiping, China).

pellucidus — pel-*lew*-sid-sus: with translucent tissues or spots.

peltatus — pel-*tay*-tus: with leaf-stalk attached toward center of leaf (peltate), not at edge.

peltifolius — pel-tif-*foh*-lee-us: with peltate leaves.

pelviformis — pel-vif-*form*-iss: pelvis-shaped.

penduliflorus — pen-dew-lif-*floh*-rus: pendulous-flowered.

pendulinus—pen-dew-*lye*-nus: somewhat drooping.

pendulus — *pen*-dew-lus: drooping, hanging.

penicillatus — pen-iss-sil-*lay*-tus: like a little brush; very finely divided (pinnate).

pennatus — pen-*nay*-tus: feathered, with feathery veins or lobes; also pinnate.

penninervis — pen-nin-*nerv*-iss: feather-veined.

pennsylvanicus — pen-sil-*van*-ik-us: of Pennsylvania.

pentagonus — pen-tag-*goh*-nus: five-angled.

pentagynus — pen-taj-*eye*-nus: with five pistils.

pentandrus — pen-*tand*-rus: five-stamened.

Specific Plant Names 515

pentanthus—pen-*tanth*-us: five-flowered.

pentaphyllus — pen-taf-*fill*-us: five-leaved.

perbellus — per-*bell*-us: very beautiful.

peregrinus — per-eg-*grye*-nus: foreign (exotic).

perennans—per-*ren*-nanz: perennial.

perennis — per-*ren*-niss: perennial (living more than 2 years).

perfoliatus — per-foh-lee-*ay*-tus: with leaf surrounding stem (perfoliate).

perforatus — per-for-*ray*-tus: with holes.

pergracilis — per-*grass*-il-iss: very slender.

permixtus — per-*mix*-tus: much confused (as to type, origin, etc.).

persicaefolius — per-siss-ee-*foh*-lee-us: *see below.*

persicifolius — per-siss-if-*foh*-lee-us: Peach-leaved.

persicus — *per*-sik-us: of Persia (Iran); also pertaining to the Peach.

perspicuus — per-*spik*-yew-us: clear, transparent.

pertusus — per-*tew*-sus: perforated.

perulatus — per-oo-*lay*-tus: pocket-like.

peruvianus — per-oo-vee-*ay*-nus: of Peru.

petaloideus — pet-al-*loy*-dee-us: petal-like.

petiolaris — pet-ee-ol-*lay*-riss: with a leaf-stalk (petiole).

petiolatus — pet-ee-ol-*lay*-tus: with a leaf-stalk, petioled.

petraeus — pet-*ree*-us: rock-inhabiting.

phaeacanthus — fee-ak-*kanth*-us: dark-thorned.

philadelphicus — fil-ad-*delf*-ik-us: of Philadelphia.

philippinensis — fil-ip-in-*nen*-siss: of the Philippine Is.

phlogiflorus — floj-if-*floh*-rus: flame-flowered.

phoeniceus — fee-*niss*-ee-us: purple-red.

phoenicolasius — fee-nik-ol-*lay*-see-us: purple-haired.

phyllomaniacus — fil-om-an-*nye*-ak-us: abnormally leafy.

picturatus — pik-tew-*ray*-tus: variegated, painted on variegated leaves.

pictus — *pik*-tus: painted, variegated.

pileatus — pye-lee-*ay*-tus: with a cap.

piliferus — pye-*lif*-er-us: having soft hairs.

pilosiusculus — pye-loh-see-*usk*-yew-lus: somewhat shaggy or hairy.

pilosus — pye-*loh*-sus: hair, softly shaggy (pilose).

pilularis — pil-yew-*lay*-riss: globular, with globules.

pululiferus — pul-yew-*lif*-er-us: having globules.

pineus — *pye*-nee-us: of or pertaining to Pines.

pinifolius — pye-nif-*foh*-lee-us: Pine-leaved.

pinnatifidus — pin-nat-*tiff*-id-us: leaves cut or divided (pinnatifid) but not separate about a common axis (pinnate) or compound (leaves in groups).

pinnatifrons — pin-*nat*-if-fronz: with finely divided fronds or foliage.

pinnatinervis — pin-nat-in-*nerv*-iss: with finely divided veins.

pinnatus — pin-*nay*-tus: with leaflets on the sides of the main leaf axis (pinnate).

pisiferus — pye-*siff*-er-us: bearing Pea-like seed or fruit.

pisocarpus — pye-soh-*karp*-us: Pea-fruited.

placatus — plak-*kay*-tus: quiet, serene.

planiflorus — plan-if-*floh*-rus: flat-flowered.

planifolius — plan-if-*foh*-lee-us: flat-leaved.

plantaginaus — plan-taj-*inn*-ee-us: Plantain-like.

planus — *play*-nus: flat.

platanoides — plat-an-*noy*-deez: like the Plane-tree (Platanus).

platanthus — plat-*tanth*-us: broad-flowered.

platycanthus — plat-ik-*kanth*-us: broad-thorned.

platycarpus — plat-ik-*karp*-us: broad-fruited.

platycentrus — plat-iss-*sent*-rus: broad-centered.

platyceras — plat-iss-*see*-rass: having broadhorns.

platycladus — plat-ik-*klay*-dus: broad-branched.

platyglossus — plat-ig-*gloss*-us: broad-tongued.

platypetalus — plat-ip-*pet*-al-us: broad-petaled.

platyphyllus — plat-if-*fill*-us: broad-leaved.

pleioneurus — plye-oh-*new*-rus: many-veined.

pleniflorus — plen-if-*floh*-rus: with "double" or many-petaled flowers.

plenissimus — plen-*niss*-im-us: very "double" or full.

plenus — *pleen*-us: full, "double" (denoting many petaled flowers).

plicatus — plye-*kay*-tus: plaited or folded lengthwise (plicate).

plumarius — plew-*may*-ree-us: plumed.

plumatus — plew-*may*-tus: plumed.

plumosus — plew-*moh*-sus: feathery.

pluriflorus — plew-rif-*floh*-rus: many-flowered.

poculiformis — pok-yew-lif-*form*-iss: deep-cup-shaped.

podocarpus — pod-oh-*karp*-us: with stalked fruit.

poeticus — poh-*et*-ik-us: specific name usually recalling Poet's Narcissus (*N. poeticus*).

polifolius — pol-if-*foh*-lee-us: whitish-leaved (of irrelevant origin).

politus — pol-*lye*-tus: shining, polished.

polyacanthus — pol-ee-ak-*kanth*-us: many-thorned.

polyandrus — pol-ee-*and*-rus: with many stamens.

polyanthus — pol-ee-*anth*-us: many-flowered.

polycephalus — pol-iss-*sef*-al-us: many-headed.

polydactylus — pol-id-*dak*-til-us: many-fingered.

polygamus — pol-*lig*-am-us: having perfect (with both male and female parts) and imperfect (one-sexed) flowers on the same plant.

polylophus — pol-il-*loh*-fus: much-crested or -tufted.

polymorphus — pol-im-*morf*-us: variable, of many forms.

polypetalus — pol-ip-*pet*-al-us: many-petaled.

polyphyllus — pol-if-*fill*-us: many-seeded.

polyspermus — pol-iss-*sperm*-us: many-seeded.

polystachyus — pol-iss-*stak*-ee-us: many-spiked.

polystictus — pol-iss-*stik*-tus: many-dotted.

pomaceus — poh-*may*-see-us: resembling Apples or Pears.

pomeridianus — pom-er-id-ee-*ay*-nus: afternoon (blooming).

ponderosus — pon-der-*roh*-sus: heavy, massive.

ponticus — *pont*-ik-us: of Pontus (Asia Minor).

populifolius — pop-yew-lif-*foh*-lee-us: leaves like Poplar (Populus).

populneus — pop-*ull*-nee-us: pertaining to the Poplar, Poplar-like.

portoricensis — por-toh-riss-*sen*-siss: of Porto Rico.

praealtus — pree-*al*-tus: very tall.

portulaceus — por-tew-*lay*-see-us: thick-leaved (after genus Portulaca).

praecox — *pree*-cox: very early.

praestans — *preess*-tanz: distinguished, outstanding.

praetextus — pree-*text*-us: bordered.

prasinatus — prass-in-*nay*-tus: greenish.

prasinus — prass-*sye*-nus: grassgreen.

pratensis — prat-*ten*-siss: of the meadows.

pravissimus — prav-*viss*-im-us: very crooked.

primulinus — prim-yew-*lye*-nus: Primrose-like.

primuloides — prim-yew-*loy*-deez: Primrose-like.

princeps — *prin*-seps: of first quality.

prismaticus — pris-*mat*-ik-us: prism-shaped (parts).

proboscideus — proh-bos-*sid*-ee-us: nose-shaped.

procerus — proh-*see*-rus: tall.

procumbens — proh-*kumm*-benz: trailing (procumbent) but not rooting.

procurrens — proh-*kur*-renz: extended (parts).

productus — proh-*dukk*-tus: lengthened (parts).

profusus — proh-*few*-sus: profuse (flowering).

proliferus — proh-*lif*-er-us: producing offshoots; having abnormally numerous parts.

prolificus — proh-*lif*-ik-us: flowering or fruiting abundantly, prolific.

propendens — proh-*pen*-denz: hanging down.

propinquus — proh-*pin*-kwus: closely related.

prostratus — pross-*tray*-tus: lying flat.

protrusus — proh-*trew*-sus: protruding (parts).

provincialis — prov-in-see-*ay*-liss: provincial; of Provence (So. France).

pruinatus — prew-in-*nay*-tus: with a whitish "bloom" (pruinose).

pruinosus — prew-in-*noh*-sus: with whitish "bloom" (of fruit).

prunifolius — prew-nif-*foh*-lee-us: Plum- or Cherry-leaved.

pruritus — *prew*-rit-us: causing itching.

pseud- — *sood*-, **pseuda-**, **pseudo-**: when prefixed to (usually) generic name and used as a specific name, indicates a lack of trueness to type or classification despite implied similarity.

psycodes — sye-*koh*-deez: fragrant.

ptarmicus — *tar*-mik-us: sneeze-producing.

pteranthus — ter-*ranth*-us: wing-flowered.

pubens — *pew*-benz: downy.

puberulus — pew-*behr*-yew-lus: somewhat hairy.

pubescens — pew-*bess*-senz: downy (pubescent).

pudicus — *pew*-dik-us: bashful, retiring.

pugioniformis — pew-jee-on-if-*form*-iss: dagger-shaped.

pulchellus — pull-*kell*-us: pretty.

pulcher — *pull*-ker: handsome.

pulcherrimus — pull-*kehr*-im-us: very handsome, beautiful.

pullus — *pull*-us: dusky, almost black.

pulverulentus — pull-ver-oo-*lent*-us: dusty, powdery.

pulvinatus — pull-vin-*nay*-tus: cushion-like.

pumilus — *pew*-mil-us: small, dwarf.

punctatissimus — punk-tat-*tiss*-im-us: much-spotted.

punctatus — punk-*tay*-tus: with spots or dots, as on leaves or petals (punctate).

punctilobulus — punk-til-*loh*-bew-lus: with dotted or spotted lobes.

pungens — *pun*-jenz: sharp-pointed; pungent.

puniceus — pew-*niss*-ee-us: red-purple.

purpuraceus — pur-pew-*ray*-see-us: purple.

purpurascens — pur-pew-*rass*-senz: purplish.

purpuratus — pur-pew-*ray*-tus: purple.

purpureus — pur-*pew*-ree-us: purple.

pusillus — pew-*sill*-us: very dwarf; insignificant.

pycnacanthus — pik-nak-*kanth*-us: densely spined.

pycnanthus — pik-*nanth*-us: densely flowering.

pycnocarpon — pik-noh-*karp*-on: densely fruiting.

pycnostachyus — pik-noh-*stak*-ee-us: densely spiked.

pygmaeus — pig-*mee*-us: very small.

pyramidalis — pihr-am-id-*day*-liss: of pyramidal form.

pyrenaicus — pye-ren-*nay*-ik-us: of the Pyrenees.

pyrifolius — pye-rif-*foh*-lee-us: with Pear (Pyrus)-like leaves.

pyriformis — pye-rif-*form*-iss: Pear-shaped.

Q

quadrangularis — kwad-ran-gew-*lay*-riss: four-angled.

quadrangulatus — kwad-ran-gew-*lay*-tus: four-angled.

quadratus — kwad-*ray*-tus: in quadruplicate, in fours, four-sided (squared).

quadricolor — kwad-rik-*kol*-or: of four colors.

quadridentatus — kwad-rid-en-*tay*-tus: four-toothed.

quadrifidus — kwad-*rif*-id-us: divided into four segments.

quadrifolius — kwad-rif-*foh*-lee-us: four-leaved.

quadripartitus — kwad-rip-art-*tye*-tus: four-parted.

quercifolius — kwer-sif-*foh*-lee-us: with leaves like an Oak (Quercus).

quercinus — kwer-*sye*-nus: relating to the Oak.

quinatus — kwin-*nay*-tus: five-fold (parts), in fives.

quinquecolor — kwin-kwek-*kol*-or: five-colored.

quinqueflorus — kwin-kwef-*floh*-rus: five-flowered.

quinquefolius — kwin-kwef-*foh*-lee-us: five-leaved.

quinquelocularis — kwin-kwel-lok-yew-*lay*-riss: with five cells or compartments (locules).

quinquenervis — kwin-kwen-*nerv*-iss: five-veined.

quinquepunctatus — kwin-kwep-unk-*tay*-tus: five-spotted.

R

racemiflorus — ras-em-if-*floh*-rus: with flowers borne in racemes (types of elongated flower clusters).

racemosus — ras-em-*moh*-sus: with flowers in a type of elongated cluster (racemose) as compared to panicles, spikes, umbels, etc.

radiatus — ray-dee-*ay*-tus: with petals in rays, radiate (as with Daisies).

radicans — *rad*-ik-anz: rooting (along stem).

radicatus — rad-ik-*kay*-tus: rooted (strongly).

radicosus — rad-ik-*koh*-sus: many rooted.

radicum — *rad*-ik-um: referring to roots.

radiosus — ray-dee-*oh*-sus: with many rays.

ramentosus — ram-en-*tay*-see-us: with a hairy covering.

ramiflorus — ram-if-*floh*-rus: with branching inflorescence (flowering parts).

ramosissimus — ram-oh-*siss*-im-us: much branched.

ramosus — ram-*moh*-sus: branched.

rapaceus — rap-*pay*-see-us: Turnip-like.

rapunculoides — rap-unk-yew-*loy*-deez: with bell-like flowers.

rariflorus — rayr-if-*floh*-rus: loose-or scanty-flowered.

rarus — *rayr*-us: uncommon.

raucus — *raw*-kus: raw (looking).

reclinatus — rek-lin-*nay*-tus: bent backward.

rectus — *rek*-tus: straight, upright.

recurvatus — rek-kur-*vay*-tus: curved back (recurved).

recurvifolius — rek-kur-vif-*foh*-lee-us: backcurving leaves.

recurvus — rek-*kurv*-us: curved back.

redivivus — red-iv-*vye*-vus: literally, restored to life.

reduplicatus — red-dew-plik-*kay*-tus: redoubled (of multiple flowers or parts).

reflexus — ref-*flex*-us: bent back (reflex).

refractus — ref-*frak*-tus: broken.

refulgens — ref-*fulj*-enz: shining brightly.

regalis — reg-*gay*-liss: majestic, regal.

reginae — rej-*jye*-nee: referring to a queen (royal).

reginus — *ree*-jin-nus: kingly (royal), regal.

religiosus — rel-lij-ee-*oh*-sus: venerable; also referring to religious uses, sacred.

remotus — rem-*moh*-tus: with widely separated parts.

reniformis — ren-if-*form*-iss: kidney-shaped (reniform).

repandens — rep-*pan*-denz: wavy-margined.

repens — *ree*-penz: creeping.

reptans — *repp*-tanz: creeping.

resectus — ress-*sekk*-tus: cut-off (or seemingly so).

resiniferus — rez-in-*niff*-er-us: producing resin.

resinosus — rez-in-*noh*-sus: having resin (resinous).

reticulatus — ret-ik-yew-*lay*-tus: netted, net-veined (reticulate).

retortus — ret-*tort*-us: twisted back.

retroflexus — ret-roh-*flex*-us: bent backward.

retusus — ret-*tew*-sus: notched (at apex).

reversus — rev-*verss*-us: reversed.
revolutus rev-ol-*lew*-tus: rolled back (revolute).
rex: the King.
rhamnifolius — ram-nif-*foh*-lee-us: with leaves like the Buckthorn (Rhamnus).
rhizophyllus — rye-zoh-*fill*-us: root-leaved (stemless).
rhamnoides — ram-*noy*-deez: Buckthorn-like.
rhodanthus — roh-*danth*-us: Rose-flowered.
rhodochilus—roh-dok-*kye*-lus: Rose-lipped.
rhodocinctus — roh-doh-*sink*-tus: red-girdled.
rhodoneurus — roh-doh-*new*-rus: red-veined.
rhombifolius — rom-bif-*foh*-lee-us: with rhomboid leaves.
rhomboideus — rom-*boy*-dee-us: rhomboidal (quadrilateral with only opposite sides and angles equal).
ricinifolius — riss-in-if-*foh*-lee-us: with leaves like Castor-oil plant Ricinus.
rigens — *rye*-jenz: stiff, rigid.
rigidulus — rij-*jid*-yew-lus: somewhat stiff.
rigidus — *rij*-id-us: stiff.
ringens — *rin*-jenz: gaping (ringent).
riparius — rip-*pay*-ree-us: of river banks.
rivalis — riv-*vay*-liss: of brooks.
rivularis — riv-yew-*lay*-riss: growing by brooks.
robustus—roh-*bust*-us: sturdy, stout.
rosaceus—roh-*zay*-see-us: Rose-like.
robustispinus — roh-bus-tiss-*spye*-nus: stout-spined.
rosaeflorus — roh-zee-*floh*-rus: Rose-flowered.
roseus — *roh*-zee-us: rosy (color).

rostratus — ross-*tray*-tus: beaked (rostrate).
rosularis — roh-zew-*lay*-riss: in rosettes.
rotatus — roh-*tay*-tus: disc-like flower limb or corolla (rotate).
rotundifolius — roh-tun-dif-*foh*-lee-us: round leaved.
rotundus — roh-*tund*-us: round.
rubellus — roo-*bell*-us: reddish.
rubens — *roo*-benz: red or ruddy.
ruber — *roo*-ber: red.
ruberrimus — roo-*behr*-im-us: very red.
rubescens — roo-*bess*-senz: reddish, becoming red.
rubicundus — roo-bik-*kund*-us: red, ruddy.
rubiginosus — roo-bij-in-*noh*-sus: rusty (color).
rubricaulis — roo-brik-*kaw*-liss: red-stemmed.
rubrifolius — roo-brif-*foh*-lee-us: red-leaved.
rubrofructus — roo-broh-*frook*-tus: red-fruited.
rubronervis — roo-broh-*nerv*-iss: red-veined.
rubrus — *roob*-rus: red.
rudis—*roo*-diss: wild, not cultivated.
rufescens — roo-*fess*-senz: reddish.
rufinervis — roo-fin-*nerv*-iss: reddish-veined.
rufus — *roof*-us: reddish, red.
rugosus — roo-*goh*-sus: wrinkled (rugose).
runcinatus — run-sin-*nay*-tus: backwardly-toothed.
rupestris — roo-*pest*-riss: rock-growing.
rupicolus — roo-*pikk*-ol-us: growing on cliffs or ledges.
rusticanus — rust-ik-*kay*-nus: pertaining to the country.

rusticus — *rust*-ik-us: belonging to the country.

ruthennicus — rooth-*enn*-ik-us: Russian (Ruthenian).

rutilans — *root*-il-anz: red, reddening.

S

saccatus — sak-*kay*-tus: bag-like (saccate).

saccharatus — sak-ar-*ray*-tus: sugary (containing sugar).

sacchariferus — sak-ar-*riff*-er-us: sugar-bearing.

saccharinus — sak-ar-*rye*-nus: sugary.

saccharum — *sak*-ar-um: sugar.

sagittalis — saj-it-*tay*-lis: arrow-like.

saggittatus — saj-it-*tay*-tus: arrow-like (sagittate).

sagittifolius — saj-it-if-*foh*-lee-us: arrow-leaved.

salicarius — sal-ik-*kay*-ree-us: like the Willow (Salix).

salicifolius — sal-iss-if-*foh*-lee-us: Willow-leaved.

salicinus — sal-*liss*-in-us: Willow-like.

salinus — sal-*lye*-nus: salty.

sambucinus — sam-bew-*sye*-nus: like the Elder (Sambucus).

sanctus — *sank*-tus: holy (of sacred tradition).

sandwicensis — sand-wis-*sen*-siss: of the Sandwich or Hawaiian Islands.

sanguinalis — san-gwin-*nay*-liss: blood-red.

sanguineus — san-*gwin*-ee-us: blood-red.

sapidus — *sap*-id-us: savory.

sapientus — sap-ee-*ent*-us: pertaining to the wise.

saponaceus — sap-on-*nay*-see-us: soapy.

sarcodes — sar-*koh*-deez: fleshy, flesh-like.

sarmentosus — sar-men-*toh*-sus: having runners.

sarniensis — sar-nee-*en*-siss: of the Islands of Guernsey.

sativus — sat-*tye*-vus: cultivated.

saurocephalus — saw-roh-*sef*-al-us: lizard-headed.

saxatilis — sak-*sat*-il-iss: growing among rocks.

saxicolus — sak-*sik*-ol-us: growing among rocks.

saxosus — sak-*soh*-sus: pertaining to rocks.

scaber — *skay*-ber: rough (scabrous).

scabrellus — skay-*brell*-us: somewhat rough.

scaberrimus — skay-*behr*-im-us: very rough.

scandens — *skand*-enz: climbing (scandent).

scaposus — skay-*poh*-sus: with (distinctive) scapes.

scariosus — skay-ree-*oh*-sus: with leaf-like bracts or parts.

sceptrum—*sept*-rum: scepter (-like).

schistosus — shiss-*toh*-sus: readily divided.

schizopetalus — skye-zoh-*pet*-al-us: cut-petaled.

schizophyllus — skye-zoh-*fill*-us: cut-leaved.

schoenanthus — skee-*nanth*-us: reed-flowered.

schoenoprasus — skee-noh-*pray*-sus: reed-like.

scholaris — skol-*lay*-riss: pertaining to a school.

scilloides — sil-*loy*-deez: Squill (Scilla)-like.

sclerocarpus — sklehr-oh-*karp*-us: hard-fruited.

sclerophyllus — sklehr-oh-*fill*-us: hard-leaved.

scoparius — skop-*pay*-ree-us: Broom-like.

scopulorum — skop-yew-*loh*-rum: of rocky places.

scoticus — *skot*-ik-us: of Scotland.

sculptus — *skulp*-tus: cut, carved.

scutellaris — skew-tel-*lay*-riss: dish-shaped.

scutum — *skew*-tum: (like a) shield.

sebiferus — seb-*bif*-er-us: tallow-bearing.

sebosus — seb-*boh*-sus: full of tallow or grease.

secundus — sek-*kund*-us: side-flowering (secund).

secundiflorus — sek-kun-dif-*floh*-rus: with one-sided flower cluster.

securigerus — sek-yew-*rij*-er-us: with axe-like parts.

segetus — sej-*eet*-us: of cornfields.

semialatus — sem-ee-al-*lay*-tus: semi- or somewhat singed.

semicaudatus — sem-ik-kaw-*day*-tus: partially tailed.

semicylindricus — sem-iss-sil-*lind*-rik-us: somewhat cylindrical.

semipinnatus — sem-ip-pin-*nay*-tus: partly or imperfectly pinnate.

semperaurescens — sem-per-aw-*ress*-senz: ever-golden.

semperflorens — sem-per-*floh*-renz: ever-blooming.

sempervirens — sem-per-*vye*-rens: ever-green.

senilis — *sen*-il-iss: old, hoary.

sensibilis — sen-*sib*-il-iss: sensitive.

sensitivus — sen-sit-*tye*-vus: sensitive.

sepium — *seep*-ee-um: of hedges.

septangularis — sep-tan-gew-*lay*-riss: seven-angled.

septemfidus — sep-tem-*fye*-dus: seven-parted.

septemlobus — sep-tem-*loh*-bus: seven-lobed.

septempunctatus — sep-tem-punk-*tay*-tus: seven-spotted.

septentrionalis — sep-tent-ree-on-*nay*-liss: of the north.

septiceps — *sep*-tiss-seps: seven-headed.

sepultus — sep-*pull*-tus: buried.

sericeus — ser-*riss*-ee-us: silky.

sericoferus — ser-ik-*koh*-fer-us: having silk, silky.

serotinus — ser-*rot*-in-us: late-flowering or -fruiting.

serpens — *ser*-penz: creeping.

serpentinus — ser-pen-*tye*-nus: looping, waving; snake-like.

serratifolius — ser-at-if-*foh*-lee-us: tooth-leaved.

serratus — ser-*ray*-tus: saw-toothed (serrate).

serrulatus — ser-rew-*lay*-tus: somewhat toothed.

sesquipedalis — ses-kwip-ed-*day*-liss: one and a half foot lengths (roughly 18 inches).

sessiflorus — sess-if-*floh*-rus: stalkless-flowered.

sessifolius — sess-if-*foh*-lee-us: stalkless-leaved.

sessilifolius — sess-il-if-*foh*-lee-us: stalkless-leaved.

sessilis — *sess*-il-iss: stalkless sessile.

setaceus — set-*tay*-see-us: bristle-like (setaceous).

setigerus — set-*tij*-er-us: bristly.

setispinus — set-iss-*spye*-nus: bristly spined.

setosus — set-*toh*-sus: bristly.

setulosus — set-tew-*loh*-sus: with many small bristles (setose).

sexangularis — sex-an-gew-*lay*-riss: six-angled.

sibiricus — sye-*bihr*-ik-us: of Siberia.

siculus — *sik*-yew-lus: with or like a little dagger.

signatus — sig-*nay*-tus: marked, notable.

siliceus — sil-*liss*-ee-us: growing in sandy places.

silvaticus — sil-*vat*-ik-us: of the woods.

silvestris — sil-*vest*-riss: pertaining to woods.

simplex — *sim*-plex: unbranched.

simplicicaulis — sim-pliss-ik-*kaw*-liss: with unbranched stems.

simplicifolius — sim-pliss-if-*foh*-lee-us: with simple (single, not compound) leaves.

simulans — *sim*-yew-lanz: similar (type).

sinensis — sin-*nen*-siss: of China.

sinicus — *sin*-ik-us: Chinese.

sinuatus — sin-yew-*ay*-tus: wavy-margined (sinuate).

sinuosus — sin-yew-*oh*-sus: wavy edged (sinuate).

sitchensis — sit-*chen*-siss: of Sitka (Alaska).

soboliferus — sob-ol-*lif*-er-us: bearing creeping rooting stems or shoots.

socialis — soh-see-*ay*-liss: companionable.

solaninus — sol-on-*nye*-nus: Potato-like.

solaris — soh-*lay*-riss: of the sun.

solidus — *sol*-id-us: solid (not hollow).

somniferus — som-*nif*-er-us: sleep inducing.

sorbifolius — sorb-if-*foh*-lee-us: with Ash (Sorbus)-like leaves.

sordidus — *sord*-id-us: foul (appearance, odor).

spadiceus — spay-*diss*-ee-us: with a spadix.

sparsiflorus — spar-sif-*foh*-lee-us: few-leaved.

sparsus — *spar*-sus: scanty, few (parts).

sparteus — *spart*-ee-us: pertaining to Broom.

spathaceus — spath-*ay*-see-us: with a spathe.

spathulatus — spath-yew-*lay*-tus: spoon-shaped (spatulate).

speciosissimus — spee-see-oh-*siss*-im-us: very showy.

speciosus — spee-see-*oh*-sus: showy, handsome.

spectabilis — spek-*tab*-il-iss: exceptionally showy.

sphacelatus — sfass-el-*lay*-tus: withered.

sphaericus — *sfeer*-ik-us: spherical.

sphaerocarpus — sfeer-ok-*karp*-us: round-fruited.

sphaerocephalus — sfeer-oh-*sef*-al-us: round-headed.

sphaeroideus — sfeer-*royd*-ee-us: sphere-like.

sphaerostachyus — sfeer-oh-*stak*-ee-us: round-spiked.

spicatus — spye-*kay*-tus: spiked; or with flower spikes, raceme-like clusters of stalkless flowers (spicate); spike-like.

spicigerus — spye-*sij*-er-us: having spikes.

spiculifolius — spik-yew-lif-*foh*-lee-us: sharp pointed-leaved.

spinosissimus — spye-noh-*siss*-im-us: very spiny.

spinifex — *spin*-if-fex: spiny, prickly.

spinosus — spye-*noh*-sus: with many spines.

spinuliferus — spin-yew-*lif*-er-us: having small spines.

spinulosus—spin-yew-*loh*-sus: small- or soft-spined.

spiralis — spye-*ray*-liss: spiral (arrangement).

spirellus — spye-*rell*-us: (parts in) small spirals.

splendens — *splen*-denz: showy.

splendidissimus — splen-did-*diss*-im-us: most showy.

splendidus — *splend*-id-us: handsome, showy.

spumarius — spew-*may*-ree-us: frothy, with froth.

spurius — *spew*-ree-us: false.

squalens — *skway*-lenz: daubed, filthy-looking.

squalidus — *skwal*-id-us: filthy-looking or smelling.

squamatus — skwam-*may*-tus: with scale-like leaves or bracts (squamate).

squamigerus — skwam-*mij*-er-us: scaly.

squamosus — skwam-*moh*-sus: with many scales.

squarrosus — skwar-*roh*-sus: with spread or recurved parts.

stamineus — stam-*min*-ee-us: with prominent stamens.

stans — *stanz:* upright, erect.

stellaris — stel-*lay*-riss: starry, star-like.

stellatus — stel-*lay*-tus: star-like (stellate).

stellulatus — stel-yew-*lay*-tus: somewhat star-like.

stenocephalus — sten-oh-*sef*-al-us: narrow-headed.

stenogynus — sten-*noj*-in-us: with narrow stigma.

stenopetalus — sten-oh-*pet*-al-us: narrow-petaled.

stenophyllus — sten-oh-*fill*-us: narrow-leaved.

stenopterus — sten-*nop*-ter-us: narrow-winged.

sterilis — *stehr*-il-iss: infertile (sterile).

stigmaticus — stig-*mat*-ik-us: referring to markings; also stigmas.

stigmosus — stig-*moh*-sus: much marked; also refers to stigmas.

stipulaceus — stip-yew-*lay*-see-us: with stipules (small organs at leaf bases).

stipularis — stip-yew-*lay*-riss: with small organs (stipules) at leaf bases.

stipulatus — stip-yew-*lay*-tus: with stipules at leaf bases, often prominent.

stoloniferus — stoh-lon-*nif*-er-us: producing runners that take root (stolons).

stramineus—stram-*min*-ee-us: straw-colored.

strangulatus — stran-gew-*lay*-tus: constricted.

streptocarpus — strep-toh-*karp*-us: twisted-fruited.

streptopetalus — strep-toh-*pet*-al-us: twisted petaled.

streptophyllus — strep-toh-*fill*-us: twisted-leaved.

streptosepalus — strep-toh-*sep*-al-us: twisted-sepaled.

striatulus — strye-*at*-yew-lus: faintly striped.

striatus — strye-*ay*-tus: striped (striated).

strictiflorus—strik-tif-*floh*-rus: erect-flowered.

strictus — *strikt*-us: upright, erect.

strigillosus — strye-jil-*loh*-sus: with sharp hairs.

strigosus — strye-*goh*-sus: covered

with sharp, flat-pressed hairs (strigose).

striolatus — strye-ol-*lay*-tus: somewhat striped.

strobiliferus — stroh-bil-*lif*-er-us: bearing small cones (strobiles).

strobus — *stroh*-bus: specific name of White Pine.

strumarius — strew-*may*-ree-us: referring to tumors or ulcers.

strumatus — strew-*may*-tus: with tumors (or swellings).

strumosus — strew-*moh*-sus: with tumor-like swellings.

stylosus — stye-*loh*-sus: with prominent styles (the connection between flower stigma and ovary).

styracifluus — stye-rass-*sif*-lew-us: flowing with gum (storax).

suaveolens — swav-*vee*-ol-enz: pleasant (fragrance).

suavis — *sway*-viss: pleasant, sweet.

suavissimus — swav-*viss*-im-us: very sweet (fragrance).

subacaulis — sub-ak-*kaw*-liss: nearly stemless.

subalpinus — sub-al-*pye*-nus: nearly a true alpine.

subauriculatus — sub-aw-rik-yew-*lay*-tus: inconspicuously "eared".

subcarnosus — sub-kar-*noh*-sus: somewhat fleshy.

subcordatus — sub-kor-*day*-tus: nearly heart-shaped.

subdivaricatus — sub-div-ar-ik-*kay*-tus: slighty divergent.

subedentatus — sub-ee-den-*tay*-tus: nearly toothless.

suberectus — sub-ee-*rek*-tus: nearly straight; rather erect.

suberosus — soo-ber-*roh*-sus: cork-barked, corky.

subfalcatus — sub-fal-*kay*-tus: somewhat sickle-shaped.

subglaucus — sub-*glaw*-kus: somewhat downy; bluish.

subhirtellus — sub-her-*tell*-us: somewhat hairy.

sublunatus — sub-lew-*nay*-tus: somewhat crescent-shaped.

submersus — sub-*mer*-sus: (growing) under water.

subperennis — sub-per-*renn*-iss: almost perennial.

subpetiolatus — sub-pet-ee-ol-*lay*-tus: partially with petioles (leaf stalks).

subsessilis — sub-*sess*-il-iss: nearly stalkless.

subsinuatus — sub-sin-yew-*ay*-tus: somewhat wavey-margined.

subterraneus — sub-ter-*ray*-nee-us: underground.

subtomentosus — sub-toh-men-*toh*-sus: almost covered with hairs.

subulatus — sub-yew-*lay*-tus: awl-shaped.

subvolubilis — sub-vol-*lew*-bil-iss: rather twining.

succulentus — suk-kew-*lent*-us: fleshy, succulent.

suecicus — *swess*-ik-us: of Sweden.

suffrutescens — suf-frew-*tess*-senz: becoming shrubby, shrub-like.

suffruticosus — suf-frew-tik-*koh*-sus: rather shrubby.

sulcatus — sul-*kay*-tus: furrowed.

sulphureus — sul-*few*-ree-us: yellow.

sumatranus — soo-mat-*tray*-nus: of Sumatra.

superbus — soo-*perb*-us: very showy.

superciliaris — soo-per-sil-ee-*ay*-riss: eyebrow-like.

surculosus — sur-kew-*loh*-sus: producing suckers.

surinamensis — sur-in-am-*men*-siss: of Surinam (Dutch Guiana).

suspensus — sus-*pen*-sus: hanging suspended.

sylvaticus — sil-*vat*-ik-us: of the forests.

sylvestris — sil-*vess*-triss: of woods and forests.

sylvicolus — sil-*vik*-ol-us: growing in woods.

syphiliticus — sif-il-*lit*-ik-us: presum-ably once supposed to be a remedy for syphilis.

syriacus — sihr-*rye*-ak-us: of Syria.

syringanthus — sihr-in-*ganth*-us: Lilac (Syringa)-flowered.

systylus — siss-*stye*-lus: with joined styles.

T

tabularis — tab-yew-*lay*-riss: flattened (parts).

tabuliformis — tab-yew-lif-*form*-iss: table-like.

taedigerus — tee-*dij*-er-us: torch-bearing, resin-bearing.

taitensis — tye-*ten*-siss: from Tahiti.

tamariscifolius — tam-ar-iss-sif-*foh*-lee-us: Tamarisk-leaved.

taraxicifolius — tar-ax-iss-sif-*foh*-lee-us: with leaves like the Dandelion (Taraxicum).

tardiflorus — tar-dif-*floh*-rus: late flowering.

tardivus — tar-*dye*-vus: late.

tataricus — tat-*tar*-ik-us: from old Tartary (Central Asia).

taureus — *taw*-ree-us: referring to a bull or ox.

taurinus — taw-*rye*-nus: bull-like.

taxifolius — tax-if-*foh*-lee-us: Yew (Taxus)-leaved.

technicus — *tek*-nik-us: specialized.

tectorus — tek-*tohr*-us: pertaining to a roof (house).

tectus — *tek*-tus: concealed.

temulentus — tem-yew-*lent*-us: unsteady (drunken).

tenacissimus — ten-ass-*siss*-im-us: very strong or tenacious.

tenax — *ten*-ax: strong, tenacious.

tenebrosus — ten-eb-*roh*-sus: of dark, shady places.

tenellus — ten-*nell*-us: slender, tender, soft.

tentaculatus — ten-tak-yew-*lay*-tus: with short, projecting parts.

tenuicaulis — ten-yew-ik-*kaw*-liss: slender-stemmed.

tenuiflorus — ten-yew-if-*floh*-rus: slender-flowered.

tenuifolius — ten-yew-if-*foh*-lee-us: slender-leaved.

tenuilobus — ten-yew-il-*loh*-bus: slender-lobed.

tenuior — ten-*yew*-ee-or: rather slender.

tenuis — *ten*-yew-iss: slender, thin.

tenuissimus — ten-yew-*iss*-im-us: very slender or thin.

teres — *teer*-eez: circular in cross-section, cylindrical (terete).

teretifolius — ter-et-if-*foh*-lee-us: with leaves round or roundish in cross-section.

terminalis — ter-min-*nay*-liss: terminal (at end of stem, as with flowers, or branch).

ternatus — ter-*nay*-tus: in threes (ternate).

ternifolius — ter-nif-*foh*-lee-us: with leaves in threes.

terrestris — ter-*rest*-riss: of the earth.

tessellatus — tess-el-*lay*-tus: in a pattern of squares (tessellate).

testaceus — tess-*tay*-see-us: light brown, brick-toned; also (testaceous) having a prominent outer seed coat.

testiculatus — tess-tik-yew-*lay*-tus: with testicle-like parts.

testudinarius — tess-tew-din-*nay*-ree-us: tortoise- or tortoise shell-like.

tetracanthus — tet-rak-*kanth*-us: quadruple-thorned.

tetragonus — tet-*rag*-on-us: four-angled.

tetrandrus — tet-*rand*-rus: four-an-thered.

tetranthus — tet-*ranth*-us: four-flow-ered.

tetraphyllus — tet-raf-*fill*-us: four-leaved.

tetrapterus — tet-*rap*-ter-us: four-winged.

tetraquetrus — tet-rak-*kwet*-rus: four-cornered.

tetragonolobus — tet-rag-on-noh-*lob*-us: with a four-angled pod.

texanus — tex-*ay* nus: from Texas.

textilis — *tex*-til-iss: used in weaving.

theiferus — tee-*iff*-er-us: tea-bearing or Tea-like.

thermalis — therm-*may*-liss: of warm places.

thibeticus — tib-*bet*-ik-us: from or of Tibet.

thuyoides — thew-*yoy*-deez: Arbor-vitae (Thuja)-like.

thyrsiflorus — thir-sif-*floh*-rus: with flowers borne in a thyrse (a form of dense flower cluster).

thyrsoides — thir-*soy*-deez: like a thyrse (form of dense flower cluster).

tibeticus — tib-*bet*-ik-us: from Tibet.

tigrinus — tig-*rye*-nus: tiger-striped or -colored.

tinctorius — tink-*toh*-ree-us: notably colored (suggesting dyes).

tinctus — *tink*-tus: notably colored, colorful.

tipuliformis — tip-yew-lif-*form*-iss: shaped like a daddy-long-legs.

tomentosus—toh-men-*toh*-sus: dense-ly covered with matted hairs.

torosus — tor-*roh*-sus: unevenly cylindrical (torose).

tortilis — *tort*-il-iss: twisted.

tortuosus — tor-tew-*oh*-sus: twisting or zigzag (tortuose).

tortus — *tort*-us: twisted.

torulosus — tor-oo-*loh*-sus: some-what twisted.

toxicarius — tox-ik-*kay*-ree-us: poi-sonous.

toxicus — *tox*-ik-us: poisonous.

toxiferus — tox-*iff*-er-us: poison-pro-ducing.

trachypleurus — trak-ip-*ploor*-us: rough-ribbed or -veined.

transparens — trans-*pay*-renz: trans-parent.

trapeziformis — trap-ee-zif-*form*-iss: with four unequal sides.

trapezioides — trap-ee-zee-*oy*-deez: trapezoid-like (with four unequal sides).

tremuloides — trem-yew-*loy*-deez: resembling the Quaking Aspen.

tremulus — *trem*-yew-lus: quivering, trembling.

triacanthophorus — trye-ak-anth-*off*-or-us: bearing three spines.

triacanthos—trye-ak-*kanth*-us: three-spined.

triandrus — trye-*and*-rus: three-an-thered.

triangularis — trye-an-gew-*lay*-riss: three-angled.

triangulatus — trye-an-gew-*lay*-tus: three-angled.

triangulus — trye-*ann*-gew-lus: three-angled.

tricaudatus — trye-kaw-*day*-tus: three-tailed.

trichocalyx — trik-oh-*kay*-lix: with a hairy calyx.

trichocarpus—trik-oh-*karp*-us: hairy-fruited.

trichophyllus — trik-oh-*fill*-us: hairy-leaved.

trichosanthus — trik-oh-*santh*-us: hairy-flowered.

trichospermus — trik-oh-*sperm*-us: hairy-seeded.

trichotomus — trye-*kot*-om-us: three-branched or -forked.

tricolor — *trye*-kol-or: three-colored.

tricornis — *trye*-korn-iss: three-horned.

tricostatus — trye-kos-*tay*-tus: three-ribbed.

tricuspidatus — trye-kusp-id-*day*-tus: with three stiff, sharp points (cusps).

tridactylus — trye-*dak*-til-us: three-fingered.

tridens — *trye*-denz: with three teeth.

tridentatus — trye-den-*tay*-tus: three-toothed.

trifidus — *triff*-id-us: three-parted or thrice-cut.

triflorus — trye-*floh*-rus: three-flowered.

trifoliatus — trye-foh-lee-*ay*-tus: three-leaved (or with three leaflets).

trifoliolatus — trye-foh-lee-oh-*lay*-tus: with three leaflets.

trifolius — trye *foh*-lee-us: three-leaved.

trifurcatus—trye-fur-*kay*-tus: thrice-forked.

trigynus — trye-*jye*-nus: with three pistils.

trilineatus — trye-lin-ee-*ay*-tus: three-lined.

trilobus — trye-*loh*-bus: three-lobed.

trimestris — trye-*mest*-riss: pertaining to a three-month period.

trinervis—trye-*nerv*-iss: three-veined.

trinotatus — trye-noh-*tay*-tus: three-marked or -spotted.

tripartitus — trye-par-*tye*-tus: three-parted.

tripetalus — trye-*pet*-al-us: three-petaled.

triphyllus — trye-*fill*-us: three-leaved.

tripteris — *trip*-ter-iss: three-winged.

tripunctatus — trye-punk-*tay*-tus: three-spotted.

triquetrus — trye-*kwet*-rus: three-cornered.

tristachyus — trye-*stak*-ee-us: three-spiked.

tristis — *triss*-tiss: bitter, dull.

triternatus — trye-ter-*nay*-tus: thrice in threes (triternate).

triumphans — trye-*umff*-anz: excelling (triumphant).

trivialis — triv-ee-*ay*-liss: common, widespread.

tropicus — *trop*-ik-us: of tropical regions.

truncatus—trunk-*kay*-tus: cut square off (truncate).

tsus-simensis — suss-sim-*men*-siss: named after Japanese Island of Tsus-sima.

tuberculatus — too-ber-kew-*lay*-tus: with small tubers (tubercles); hence tuberculate.

tuberculosus — too-ber-kew-*loh*-sus: with small tubers; knotted (roots).

tuberosus — too-ber-*roh*-sus: having swollen underground stems (tubers).

tubiflorus — too-bif-*floh*-rus: tubular-flowered.

tubulosus — too-bew-*loh*-sus: with tubes or tube-like parts (tubulose).

tulipiferus — too-lip-*piff*-er-us: with Tulip-like flowers.

tumidus — *too*-mid-us: swollen.

turbaniformis — tur-ban-if-*form*-iss: turban-shaped.

turbinatus — tur-bin-*nay*-tus: top-shaped.

turgidus — *tur*-jid-us: full (turgid).

typhinus — tif-*fye*-nus: smoky; also, perhaps, relating to fever.

typicus — *tip*-ik-us: according to standard; normal or typical form.

U

ukranikus — yew-*kran*-ik-us: from the Ukraine.

uliginosus — yew-lij-in-*noh*-sus: of wet or marshy places.

ulmifolius — ulm-if-*foh*-lee-us: Elm (Ulmus)-leaved.

ulmoides — ulm-*moy*-deez: Elm (Ulmus)-like.

umbellatus — um-bel-*lay*-tus: with clusters of flowers whose stems rise from a common point (umbels).

umbellulatus — um-bel-yew-*lay*-tus: with small umbel-like flower clusters.

umbraculiferus — um-brak-yew-*liff*-er-us: umbrella-like.

umbraculiformis — um-brak-yew-lif-*form*-iss: umbrella-shaped.

umbrosus — um-*broh*-sus: growing in shade.

udatus — un-*day*-tus: wavy, waving.

undulatifolius — un-dew-lat-if-*foh*-lee-us: wavy leaved.

undulatus — un-dew-*lay*-tus: wavy, wavy edged (undulate).

unguiculatus — un-gwik-yew-*lay*-tus: clawed, narrow-shanked (unguiculate).

unguipetalus — un-gwip-*pet*-al-us: with clawed petals.

unicolor — yew-*nik*-kol-or: one-colored.

unicornis — yew-nik-*korn*-iss: one-horned.

uidentatus — yew-nid-den-*tay*-tus: one-toothed.

uniflorus — yew-nif-*floh*-rus: one-flowered.

unilateralis — yew-nil-lat-er-*ray*-liss: one-sided.

univittatus — yew-niv-it-*tay*-tus: one-striped.

urceolatus — ur-see-ol-*lay*-tus: urn-shaped.

urens — *yew*-renz: stinging, burning (to touch).

urentissimus — yew-ren-*tiss*-im-us: sharply stinging.

urophyllus — yew-roh-*fill*-us: tail-leaved.

urostachyuss — yew-roh-*stak*-ee-us: with tail-like spikes.

ursinus — ur-*sye*-nus: referring to the bear.

usitatissimus — yew-sit-at-*tiss*-im-us: very useful.

ustalatus — yus-tal-*lay*-tus: burned (looking), sere.

utilis — *yew*-til-iss: useful.

utriculatus — yew-trik-yew-*lay*-tus: having a small, one-seeded fruit (utriculate).

utriculosus — yew-trik-yew-*loh*-sus: having a small, one-seeded fruit.

uvarius — yew-*vay*-ree-us: (parts) resembling bunches of Grapes.

uva-ursi—yew-vuh-*oor*-sye: (Grape-bear) specific name under genus Arctostaphylos.

uviferus — yew-*vif*-er-us: having Grape-like fruit clusters.

V

vagans — *vay*-ganz: wandering.

vaginalis — vaj-in-*nay*-liss: sheathed.

vaginatus — vaj-in-*nay*-tus: sheathed (vaginate).

validus — *val*-id-us: strong.

variabilis — vay-ree-*ab*-il-is: of many forms.

varians — *vay*-ree-anz: variable.

variatus — vay-ree-*ay*-tus: variable.

varicosus — vay-rik-*koh*-sus: irregularly swollen.

variegatus — vay-ree-eg-*gay*-tus: variegated.

varifolius — vay-rif-*foh*-lee-us:

variiformis — vay-ree-if-*form*-iss: of diverse forms.

varius — *vay*-ree-us: varying.

vegetatus — vej-et-*tay*-tus: vigorous-growing

vegetus — *vej*-et-us: vigorous.

velaris — vel-*lay*-riss: veiled, with veil-like parts.

velutinus — vel-yew-*tye*-nus: velvety.

venenatus — ven-en-*nay*-tus: poisonous.

venosus — ven-*noh*-sus: notably-veined.

ventricosus — ven-trik-*koh*-sus: unevenly-swollen (as flowers and fruits), ventricose.

venustus — ven-*nuss*-tus: charming, handsome.

verecundus — vehr-ek-*kund*-us: modest.

veris — *vehr*-iss: true, true-to-type.

vermiculatus — ver-mik-yew-*lay*-tus: worm-like.

vernalis — ver-*nay*-liss: pertaining to spring, spring-blooming.

vernus — *vern*-us: associated with spring-time.

verrucosus — vehr-roo-*koh*-sus: with warty protuberances (verrucose).

verruculosus — vehr-rook-yew-*loh*-sus: somewhat warty.

versicolor — ver-sik-*kol*-or: variously colored.

verticillaris — ver-tiss-sil-*lay*-riss: (leaves) in whorls around stem (verticillate).

verticillatus — ver-tiss-sil-*lay*-tus: whorled, circling about a stem (as verticillate leaves.)

verus — *vehr*-us: true (to type, standard or classification).

vescus — *vesk*-us: weak.

vespertinus — vess-per-*tye*-nus: evening-flowering; pertaining to evening.

vestitus — vess-*tye*-tus: covered, clothed (with down, hairs, etc.).

villosus — vil-*loh*-sus: soft-hairy (villose).

vimineus — vim-*min*-ee-us: twiggy, interlaced in appearance.

viniferus — vye-*nif*-er-us: wine Grape (wine)-bearing.

vinosus — vye-*noh*-sus: full of wine.

violaceus — vye-ol-*lay*-see-us: violet (color).

violescens — vye-ol-*less*-senz: becoming violet-toned.

virens — *vye*-renz: green.

virescens — vye-*ress*-senz: becoming green, greenish.

virgatus — vir-*gay*-tus: wand-like, twiggy.

virginalis — vir-jin-*nay*-liss: white.

virgineus — vir-*jin*-ee-us: white.

virginianus — vir-jin-ee-*ay*-nus: from Virginia.

virginicus — vir-*jin*-ik-us: from Virginia.

virginiensis — vir-jin-ee-*en*-siss: from Virginia.

viridiflorus — vihr-id-if-*floh*-rus: green-flowered.

viridifolius — vihr-id-if-*foh*-lee-us: green-leaved.

viridis — *vihr*-id-iss: green.

viridissimus — vihr-id-*diss*-im-us: intensely green.

viridulus — vihr-*rid*-yew-lus: greenish.

viscidulus — viss-*sid*-yew-lus: somewhat sticky.

viscidus — *viss*-sid-us: sticky.

viscosus — viss-*koh*-sus: sticky.

vitaceus — vye-*tay*-see-us: Grape (Vitis)-like.

vitalbus — vye-*tal*-bus: denoting a white-flowered vine.

vitellinus — vye-tel-*lye*-nus: dull yellowish-red.

vitifolius — vye-tif-*foh*-lee-us: Grape (Vitis)-leaved.

vitis-idaea — vye-tiss-eye-*dee*-ah: a specific name, denoting Grape of Mt. Ida (Greece) applied to a member of the genus Vaccineum.

vittatus — vit-*tay*-tus: striped.

vittigerus — vit-*tij*-er-us: having stripes.

viviparus — vye-*vip*-ar-us: having organs which reproduce while still growing on the parent plant.

volgaricus — vol-*gar*-ik-us: from the Volga R. region.

volubilis — vol-*yew*-bil-iss: twining.

volutus — vol-*yew*-tus: roll-leaved.

vomitorius — vom-it-*toh*-ree-us: emetic.

vulcanicus — vul-*kay*-nik-us: pertaining to volcanoes or their regions.

vulgaris — vul-*gay*-riss: common.

vulgatus — vul-*gay*-tus: common.

W

washingtonianus — wash-ing-ton-ee-*ay*-nus: from Washington (state).

wolgaricus — wol-*gay*-rik-us: see volgaricus.

X

xanthacanthus — zanth-ak-*kanth*-us: with yellow thorns or spines.

xanthinus — *zanth*-in-us: yellow.

xanthocarpus — zanth-oh-*karp*-us: yellow-fruited.

xantholeucus — zanth-oh-*lew*-kus: yellowish-white.

xanthophyllus — zanth-oh-*fill*-us: yellow-leaved.

xanthorrhizus — zanth-or-*rye*-zus: yellow-rooted.

Y

yedoensis — yed-oh-*en*-siss: from Yeddo (Japan).

yunnanensis — yew-nan-*nen*-siss: from Yunnan (China).

yodogavus — yod-og-*gay*-vus: from Yodogowa (Japan).

Z

zebrinus — zeb-*rye*-nus: zebra-striped.

zinniaeflorus — zin-nih-ee-*floh*-rus: Zinnia-flowered.

zonalis — zoh-*nay*-liss: zoned or banded.

zonatus — zoh-*nay*-tus: zoned, banded.